March 16–17, 2013
Houston, Texas, USA

I0041880

Association for Computing Machinery

Advancing Computing as a Science & Profession

VEE '13

Proceedings of the ACM SIGPLAN/SIGOPS International Conference on

Virtual Execution Environments

Sponsored by:
ACM SIGOPS and ACM SIGPLAN

Supported by:
VMware, Bromium, Facebook, IBM and Microsoft

Association for Computing Machinery

Advancing Computing as a Science & Profession

The Association for Computing Machinery
2 Penn Plaza, Suite 701
New York, New York 10121-0701

Notice to Past Authors of ACM-Published Articles
ACM intends to create a complete electronic archive of all articles and/or other material previously published by ACM. If you have written a work that has been previously published by ACM in any journal or conference proceedings prior to 1978, or any SIG Newsletter at any time, and you do NOT want this work to appear in the ACM Digital Library, please inform permissions@acm.org, stating the title of the work, the author(s), and where and when published.

ISBN: 978-1-4503-1266-0 (Digital)

ISBN: 978-1-4503-2092-4 (Print)

Additional copies may be ordered prepaid from:

ACM Order Department
PO Box 30777
New York, NY 10087-0777, USA

Phone: 1-800-342-6626 (USA and Canada)
+1-212-626-0500 (Global)
Fax: +1-212-944-1318
E-mail: acmhelp@acm.org
Hours of Operation: 8:30 am – 4:30 pm ET

Printed in the USA

VEE 2013 Foreword

It is our great pleasure to welcome you to the 9th *ACM Conference on Virtual Execution Environments – VEE 2013*. The Conference brings together researchers across the many applications of virtualization in today's systems.

Virtualization has a central role in modern systems, being a key aspect of system development, operation, and management in a wide range of environments, from mobile computing devices to large-scale data centers. Virtualization techniques are applied at many interfaces, from hardware, to OS system calls, to high-level language run times, to cloud management stacks. While these approaches differ dramatically in implementation, they target similar benefits and often must tackle related challenges.

The eighteen papers selected for *VEE 2013* cover diverse and interesting topics related to virtual execution environments. Each paper received between 3 and 5 PC reviews, and authors were given the opportunity to comment on the reviews before the PC meeting. The discussion leader for each paper summarized the author response during each discussion. The authors' response directly impacted the outcome for a number of papers. A shepherd was assigned to some of the papers, which generally led to significantly improved papers.

Putting together *VEE 2013* was a team effort. Without the contributions of all the authors, the conference would not continue to be relevant and interesting. The program committee worked hard in reviewing papers, shepherding accepted submissions into their final forms, and acting as session chairs at the conference itself. Our colleagues on the organizing committee of ASPLOS 2013 were extremely helpful in coordinating the local arrangements, registration and logistics for the conference itself, while Rema Zogabe worked hard to ensure that the PC meeting, generously hosted by NICTA, ran smoothly. Finally, we would like to thank our sponsors, ACM SIGPLAN and SIGOPS, and corporate supporters – VMware, Bromium, Facebook, IBM and Microsoft – for their continued support of these successful meetings.

We hope that you find the conference interesting and stimulating, and that it provides the opportunity to meet and engage with colleagues from around the world, both new and old.

Steve Muir
VEE 2013 General Chair
VMware, USA

Steve Blackburn
VEE 2013 Program Chair
Australian National University, Australia

Gernot Heiser
VEE 2013 Program Chair
NICTA & University of New South Wales, Australia

Table of Contents

Session 5: VM Optimisation

Session 6: VMM Optimisation

VEE 2013 Conference Organization

General Chair: Steve Muir *(VMware, USA)*

Program Chairs: Gernot Heiser *(NICTA and University of New South Wales, Australia)*
Steve Blackburn *(Australian National University, Australia)*

Steering Committee Chair: Antony Hosking *(Purdue University, USA)*

Steering Committee: David F. Bacon *(IBM Research, USA)*
Dilma da Silva *(Qualcomm Research Silicon Valley, USA)*
Marc Fiuczynski *(Akamai, USA)*
Steve Hand *(University of Cambridge, UK)*
Orran Krieger *(Boston University, USA)*
Doug Lea *(SUNY Oswego, USA)*
Brian Noble *(University of Michigan, USA)*
Erez Petrank *(Technion, Israel)*
Andrew Warfield *(University of British Columbia, Canada)*

Program Committee: Keith Adams *(Facebook, USA)*
Jonathan Appavoo *(Boston University, USA)*
Muli Ben-Yehuda *(Technion and IBM Research, Israel)*
Marina Bilberstein *(Google, USA)*
Ada Gavrilovksa *(Georgia Institute of Technology, USA)*
David Grove *(IBM T. J. Watson Research Center, USA)*
Kiyokuni Kawachiya *(IBM Research – Tokyo, Japan)*
Anil Madhavapeddy *(University of Cambridge, UK)*
Matthias Meyer *(University of Stuttgart, Germany)*
Todd Mytkowicz *(Microsoft Research, USA)*
Erez Petrank *(Technion, Israel)*
Filip Pizlo *(Apple, USA)*
Doug Simon *(Oracle Labs, USA)*
Harvey Tuch *(VMware, USA)*
Leendert van Doorn *(AMD, USA)*
Dongyan Xu *(Purdue University, USA)*

VEE 2013 Sponsors & Supporters

Sponsors:

In association with:

Supporters:

IBM Research

facebook

SPIRE: Improving Dynamic Binary Translation through SPC-Indexed Indirect Branch Redirecting

Ning Jia   Chun Yang   Jing Wang   Dong Tong   Keyi Wang

Department of Computer Science and Technology, Peking University, Beijing, China

{jianing, yangchun, wangjing, tongdong, wangkeyi}@mprc.pku.edu.cn

Abstract

Dynamic binary translation system must perform an address translation for every execution of indirect branch instructions. The procedure to convert Source binary Program Counter (SPC) address to Translated Program Counter (TPC) address always takes more than 10 instructions, becoming a major source of performance overhead. This paper proposes a novel mechanism called SPc-Indexed REdirecting (SPIRE), which can significantly reduce the indirect branch handling overhead.

SPIRE doesn't rely on hash lookup and address mapping table to perform address translation. It reuses the source binary code space to build a SPC-indexed redirecting table. This table can be indexed directly by SPC address without hashing. With SPIRE, the indirect branch can jump to the originally SPC address without address translation. The trampoline residing in the SPC address will redirect the control flow to related code cache. Only 2–6 instructions are needed to handle an indirect branch execution. As part of the source binary would be overwritten, a shadow page mechanism is explored to keep transparency of the corrupt source binary code page. Online profiling is adopted to reduce the memory overhead.

We have implemented SPIRE on an x86 to x86 DBT system, and discussed the implementation issues on different guest and host architectures. The experiments show that, compared with hash lookup mechanism, SPIRE can reduce the performance overhead by 36.2% on average, up to 51.4%, while only 5.6% extra memory is needed.

SPIRE can cooperate with other indirect branch handling mechanisms easily, and we believe the idea of SPIRE can also be applied on other occasions that need address translation.

Categories and Subject Descriptors   D.3.4 [*Programming Languages*]: Processors – *Code generation, Optimization, Run-time environments*.

General Terms   Algorithms, Design, Performance

Keywords   Dynamic Binary Translation, Indirect Branch, Redirecting

1.   Introduction

Dynamic Binary Translation (DBT) is a technology that translates the source binary code to target binary code at run-time. DBT is widely used in many fields, such as ISA translator [1], dynamic instrumentation [2, 3], dynamic optimizing [4], program analysis [5], debugging [6], and system simulator [7].

In many cases, for a DBT system to be viable, its performance overhead must be low enough. How to handle control-transfer instructions is a key aspect to the performance. For conditional branch and direct jump instructions, whose branch targets are fixed, code block chaining [7] technique can significantly eliminate the overhead of transferring between code blocks. However, for Indirect Branch (IB) instructions, whose branch target cannot be determined until run-time, DBT system must perform an address translation from Source binary Program Counter (SPC) address to Translated Program Counter (TPC) address at every execution. Previous research [8, 9, 10] indicates that handling indirect branch instructions is a major source of performance overhead in DBT system.

DBT systems maintain an address mapping table to record the relationship between SPC and TPC, and a hash lookup routine is always used to perform the address translation. The SPC address is hashed to a key to select TPC from a hash table. However, even a carefully hand-coded hash lookup routine would cost more than 10 instructions [8], resulting in a non-trivial performance overhead.

This paper proposes a novel mechanism called SPc-Indexed REdirecting (SPIRE), which can significantly reduce the on-the-fly indirect branch handling overhead. SPIRE doesn't rely on hash lookup and the mapping table to perform address translation. It reuses the source binary code space to build a SPC-indexed redirecting table, which can be indexed directly by SPC address without hashing. The memory at SPC address originally contains source binary instructions, and would be overwritten by a redirecting trampoline before first used. With SPIRE, the indirect branch can jump to the originally SPC address without address translation. The trampoline residing in the SPC address will redirect the control flow to related code cache. Only 2–6 instructions is needed to handle an indirect branch execution.

As some source binary code is corrupted by SPIRE table entries, a shadow page mechanism is explored to keep transparency for other code that may access source binary, such as self-modifying code. To decrease the memory overhead, an online profiling mechanism is developed to classify indirect branches, and only hot indirect branches will be optimized by SPIRE.

We implemented SPIRE mechanism on an x86 to x86 DBT system. The experiment shows that, compared with hash lookup mechanisms, SPIRE can reduce the performance overhead by 36.2% on average, up to 51.4%, while only 5.6% extra memory is consumed by shadow code pages. Although x86 isn't the most suitable platform for SPIRE, we still gain a considerable performance improvement. We also discuss the implementation issues on different guest and host platforms in detail.

The rest of the paper is organized as follows. Section 2 provides an overview of indirect branch handling mechanisms and discusses related work. Section 3 shows the principle and main challenges of SPIRE. Section 4 implements SPIRE mechanism on x86 platform and discusses the implementation issues on different platforms. Section 5 describes our experimental results. Section 6 summarizes this work and discusses future directions.

2. Overview of Indirect Branch Handling

Figure 1 describes the general workflow of indirect branch handling in DBT systems. When the branch target is obtained, it's a SPC address, and the PC dispatcher is used to convert SPC to related code cache address (TPC). A mapping table is probably needed during address translation. The dispatcher will jump to the TPC after address translation. Because indirect branch always has multiple targets, so the PC dispatcher is a single-entry/multi-exits routine.

There are many methods to implement PC dispatcher. Classified by address translation method, the PC dispatcher can be prediction-based or table-lookup based. The prediction-based method can achieve a better performance while prediction hits, but have to perform a full table lookup while prediction fails.

Classified by code placement, the PC dispatcher can be private or shared. The private dispatch is always inlined in the code cache to eliminate the overhead of context switch. The shared PC dispatcher is used by more than one indirect branch, which can reduce the total code size.

Classified by implementation, the PC dispatcher can be pure-software or SW/HW co-designed. The co-designed mechanisms always achieve a considerable performance improvement, but poor versatility.

2.1. Related Work

In this section, we will discuss the previous indirect branch handling mechanisms of DBT systems. For clarity, we classified these mechanisms by whether special hardware or instruction is needed.

2.1.1. Pure-Software Mechanisms

DBT systems without special hardware always use hash table or software prediction to reduce the overhead of handling indirect branch.

There are many design options for hash table. The hash lookup routine can be inlined or be shared. The address mapping data can be stored in several small private tables or a large public table [8]. Typical hash table implementations include Indirect Branch Translation Cache (IBTC) in Strata system [11], and SIEVE in HDTrans system [12]. Hash table is easy to implemented, but even a carefully hand-coded hash lookup routine still need more than 10 instructions. For example, the IBTC lookup routine take approximately 17 instructions [8].

Based on the locality of indirect branch's targets, researchers propose another efficient technique called software prediction [13], also called indirect branch inlining [8], which is similar with de-virtualization [14] techniques in object oriented language. Software prediction uses a compare-jump chain to predict the branch target. When the compare instruction reports equal, the following jump instruction will lead the control-flow to related code cache. This technique is used in many well-known DBT systems, such as Pin [15] and DynamoRIO [10].

Software prediction mechanism performs well while prediction hits, but suffers extra hash lookup overhead while prediction fails. Its performance is highly related to prediction accuracy. Unfortunately, since the entire prediction routine should be completed by software instructions, complex mechanisms like correlated prediction and target replacing are hard to be applied on software prediction. Thus the prediction hit-hate is always not satisfied. Increasing the number of prediction slot can improve hit-rate, but also introduces extra overhead.

Balaji et al. propose a target replacing algorithm for software prediction [16], it dramatically improves the hit-rate from 46.5% to 73%, but gains a little speedup because of the expensive target replacing overhead. Their evaluations also point out short prediction chain can achieve better performance.

Compared with software prediction, SPIRE doesn't rely on the predictability of indirect branches, and can always gain a satisfied performance.

2.1.2. Co-Designed Mechanisms

Despite the pure-software techniques, researchers also propose a number of SW/HW co-designed techniques. Kim et al. design a Jump Target-address Lookup Table (JTLT)[13], which collaborates with the traditional Branch Target Buffer (BTB). JTLT is a hardware cache of the address mapping table. When an indirect branch is encountered, the CPU continues to execute with the prediction result of BTB, and queries the JTLT concurrently. The JTLT result is used to verify the prediction, if BTB prediction fails, the control-flow would jump to the JTLT result.

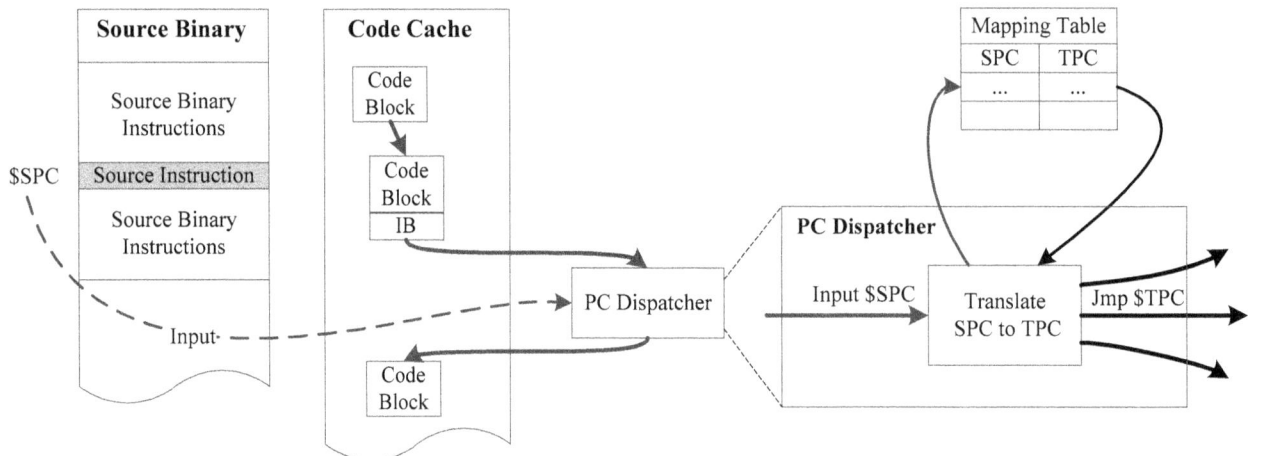

Figure 1. General workflow of indirect branch handling.

Hu et al. add a Content-Associated Memory (CAM) [17] to accelerate the address translation. Each CAM entry contains three fields: process ID, SPC, and TPC. When the branch target is determined, the system uses a special CAM lookup instruction to translate SPC to TPC. Li et al. propose a new CAM partition and replacing mechanism called PCBPC [18], which can reduce the CAM miss rate from 3.7% to 1.6%.

Guan et al. analyze the performance bottleneck of DBT systems, and design a SW/HW collaborative translation system called CoDBT [19]. CoDBT uses a specific hardware accelerator to deal with time-consuming operations, such as address translation. Mihocka et al. evaluate several systems, and point out that a major overhead of address translation is caused by context save/restore [20]. They believe that adding light-weighted eflags save/restore instructions will be helpful.

Compared with our SPIRE, co-designed mechanisms need to modify the hardware or ISA, thus cannot be widely used on existing platforms.

There are many other mechanisms to improve the performance of DBT system, such as translation path selection scheme [21], specialization for target system [22], process-shared and persistent code cache [23, 24], individual optimizing thread on multi-core platform [25]. As they don't focus on indirect branch handling, we won't discuss them here.

3. How SPIRE works

Previous indirect branch handling mechanisms primarily contain two steps: 1) Translate the SPC to TPC. 2) Jump to the TPC. The address translation process results in the major overhead.

What would happen if the control-flow jumps to the original SPC address without address translation? As most of the DBT systems load source binary into the same memory address as native execution, the memory on SPC address always contains an un-translated source binary instruction. Thus the system would fail if control-flow jumps here directly. However, if this source instruction was overwritten by a trampoline jumping to the related TPC in advance, the control flow would be redirected to the expected code cache address.

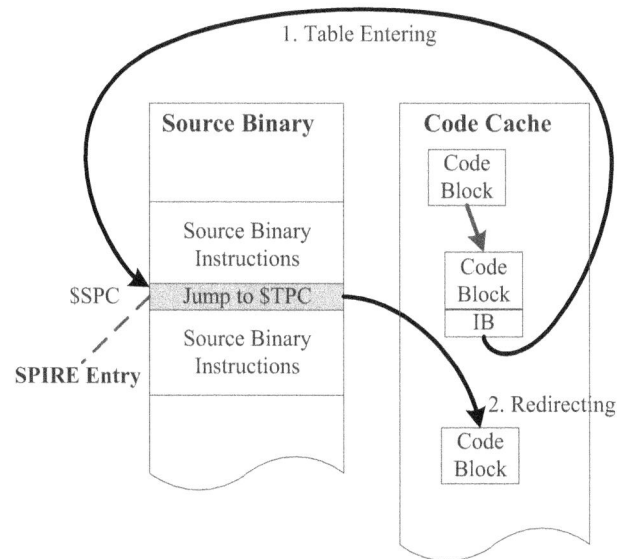

Figure 2. Workflow of SPIRE mechanism.

Therefore, we propose a novel indirect branch handling mechanism called SPC-Indexed Redirecting. SPIRE reuses virtual address space of source binary code to build a redirecting table. This table can be indexed by the SPC address directly. The table entries reside in the source binary code space sparsely, and each entry only contains one filed: a redirecting trampoline to TPC.

Since the source binary code may be accessed by translator and self-modifying code, it should always be kept in the memory. So SPIRE doesn't introduce too much extra memory overhead. For correctness, we develop a shadow page scheme to keep the corrupted source binary code transparency when being accessed.

3.1. Prototype of SPIRE

With SPIRE mechanism, each SPC address of branch target is regarded as a table entry of SPIRE. These entries initially contain source binary instructions, and would be filled with a redirecting trampoline before used.

Figure 2 presents the stable state of SPIRE mechanism. After the table entry is filled, only two steps are needed to handle an indirect branch execution: 1) Table-entering: jumps to SPC address directly. 2) Redirecting: jumps to code cache. The latter step only needs 1 instruction. If the source binary is loaded into the same address space as native execution, which is the most common case, the table-entering routine only needs 1 instruction too.

It should be noted that the prototype shown in Figure 2 is just a common implementation of SPIRE. Based on the core idea, several variants can be derived when necessary. For example, some DBT systems may load the source binary into different memory address with native execution, so the table-entering routine should add an offset to the SPC address, and about 4 more instructions are needed. Meanwhile, the "instruction-based" redirecting table can be converted to "data-based". Under the "date-based" variant, the redirecting instruction will be replaced with the TPC address, which can shorten the table entry. These variants will be discussed in the following section.

SPIRE leverages the relationship of memory address and its value to represent the mapping between SPC and TPC. SPC address of branch target is used to distinguish different branch occasions. Be different from the traditional translation-and-jump mechanisms, SPIRE can jump to the SPC address without address translation, and the trampoline will lead control-flow to expected code cache.

3.2. Main Challenges

The workflow of SPIRE seems simple and neat, but in order to keep the correctness and transparency while achieving a satisfied performance, there are several obstacles to overcome.

Table Filling. Since the branch target of indirect branch cannot be determined until executed, so SPIRE table is totally unfilled when system starts. The table entries will be filled after first used. Meanwhile, to ensure the correctness, there must be a scheme to distinguish whether the table entry is filled or not. An unfilled table entry should never be executed.

Table Entry Overlapping. SPIRE reuses the memory address of branch targets to build table entries, and the redirecting trampoline would take several bytes. If two branch targets are too close, a table entry may be overlapped with others. Such case becomes more complicated if the ISA of source binary is variable-length. The table entry overlapping must be avoided, or the system may fail.

Transparency. Due to the workflow of SPIRE, the source binary code may be corrupted by SPIRE table. However, even after being translated, source binary code still may be accessed by self-modifying code or re-translated routine. To make the program run correctly in all cases, SPIRE should keep the corrupted source binary code totally transparency to other code.

Architecture-Specific Issues. There are also some implemented issues related to the features of source/host architectures. For example, SPIRE may leverage page protection scheme to keep correctness, which relies on the support of memory management unit; the redirecting trampoline should contain a jump instruction, which may be limited by the addressing mode of ISA.

Next, we will discuss the general solutions to these challenges, and explore more details of SPIRE implementations on several typical platforms.

3.3. On-Demand Table Filling

Since the SPIRE table is unfilled when system starts, an on-the-fly entry filling method should be provided to fill the table entries at an appropriate moment, while ensuring the unfilled entries wouldn't be executed. Checking the status of entry at run-time is too time-consuming. So we propose a two-level exception-based entry filling scheme: page grained and instruction grained.

Inspired by the on-demand paging mechanism in memory management scheme of operating system, we develop a page-protection mechanism to distinguish whether the entry is filled. After the source binary is loaded, SPIRE will unset the EXEC permission of all the code pages. When the control-flow jumps to an unfilled table entry, a page fault exception would be triggered. Then the handler can fill the related table entry and set this page executable. However, this mechanism only works at page-grained, and cannot deal with the case that several entries belong to a same page. So we still need an instruction-grained mechanism to classify table entries.

After the first table entry of a page is filled, the other space of this page will be filled with software trap instructions of host platform, for example, the INT3 instruction on x86 platform. When the control-flow jumps to an unfilled table entry of this page, a software exception will be triggered. The exception handler will fill the related table entry.

3.4. Transparency

A shadow code page mechanism is developed to achieve the transparency goal. When a code page is overwritten by SPIRE entry, it will be copied to shadow page space, and the translator would disable the READ and WRITE permissions of this corrupted page. The shadow page space is managed by the translator. If some other code tries to access the corrupted code pages, a read/write page fault exception will be raised, and the handler will redirect the access to related shadow code page.

On Linux operating system, SPIRE uses the signal mechanism to handle the exceptions. Some guest applications may register their own signal handler, thus SPIRE must keep signal transparency to guest application. SPIRE registers its own handlers to operating system, and intercepts the guest application's signal registration. When a signal is raised, SPIRE's handler will check whether it is sent to SPIRE or to guest application, and then select the correlated handler.

When application has bugs, the control flow may jump to a wrong address which doesn't contain valid code. Then the behavior will be un-predicted and the program may fail. If such an application runs on a DBT system with SPIRE, when this type of bug exists, SPIRE cannot exactly reproduce same error states as native execution. It is hard for DBT systems to achieve 100% error transparency[3]. Current SPIRE implementation cannot keep transparency to such an illegal program counter bug, but SPIRE works well with stable applications.

Algorithm 1 describes the process of SPIRE entry filling. When all the table entries are filled, the control-flow will jump between code blocks without raising exceptions, achieving a satisfied performance.

Algorithm 1: SPIRE table entry filling

---

1   Unset the EXEC permission of all the pages of source binary code segment.
2   When an Execution page fault is raised.
    2.1   Copy the page to shadow page area.
    2.2   Fill the related table entry.
    2.3   Enable the EXEC permission of this page, and unset the READ and WRITE permissions.
3   When a software exception is raised
    3.1   If raised by SPIRE, then fill the related table entry. Else call the guest application's handler.
4   When a Read/Write page fault is raised.
    4.1   If raised by SPIRE, redirect the access request to related shadow page. Else call the guest application's handler.

3.5. Optimization

A profiling scheme is adopted by SPIRE to selectively optimize the indirect branch, and an invalidation routine will be called when SPIRE may do harm to the performance.

Online Profiling. As noted by many researchers, most of execution time costs on a small part of hot code, so do the indirect branches. Most of the dynamic executions of indirect branch happen on several hot branch sites, and some cold indirect branches only execute several times. As shown in Figure 3, on our benchmarks, about 40% indirect branch instructions execute less than 1000 times, and contribute less than 1% of the total executions.

SPIRE relies on the page fault and software exception to trigger the table filling routine, which may cost more than 1000 cycles. Thus using SPIRE to handle the cold indirect branches isn't worthy. Furthermore, more shadow pages will take more extra memory.

To minimalize the overhead of SPIRE, we explore an online profiling mechanism to identify hot instructions. When the execution count of an indirect branch exceeds the pre-defined threshold, it will be marked as hot instruction. Only hot instructions will be optimized by SPIRE, and cold indirect branches are still handled by other mechanism like hash lookup.

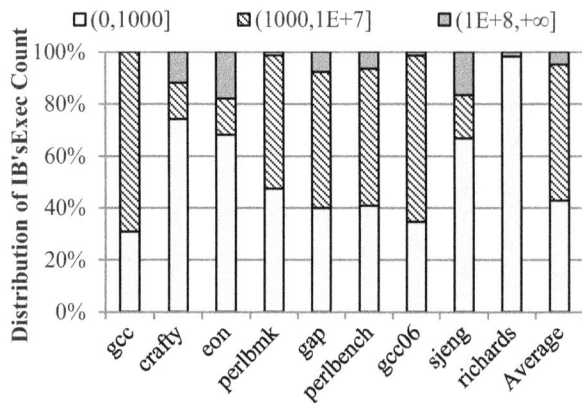

Figure 3. Distribution of IB's execution count.

Invalidation Scheme. SPIRE can be seen as a cache of the mapping table between SPC and TPC. When the mapping is changed by some events, e.g. self-modifying code, code cache flush, SPIRE needs to update the related table entries to maintain the consistency. A two-level invalidation scheme is proposed to ensure the correctness and performance.

1) Invalidate table entries. When the mapping of SPC and TPC is modified, the related SPIRE table entries would be invalidated.

2) Invalidate indirect branch sites. When some source code is modified frequently, the exceptions caused by table entry refilling would result in non-trivial overhead. To avoid performance decreasing, indirect branches related to this target would fall back to hash lookup mechanism.

4. Implementation of SPIRE

As discussed in section 3, to overcome the obstacles, SPIRE prefers some features of guest and host architecture. First, the permission of host architecture's memory page can be set to NO_READ | NO_WRITE | EXEC. So that the corrupted source code pages can be protected from being accessed. Second, the source binary instructions should be long enough, so that the trampoline can reside in the instruction slot.

The RISC architectures like ARM always can fulfill these requirements, but some architecture like x86 can't. However, SPIRE can still be applied on these architectures. In this section, we will implement our SPIRE mechanism on an x86 to x86 binary translator to illustrate the versatility of SPIRE.

4.1. Keep Transparency of Corrupted Code Page

The READ|WRITE permission of x86's page table is controlled by one bit, thus the READ and WRITE permission cannot be disabled simultaneously. As a result, the previous page protection scheme cannot prevent the corrupted code page from being accessed by self-reference or self-modifying code.

We modified the shadow page scheme to keep transparency of the corrupted source binary code page. After the source binary is loaded into memory, SPIRE allocates a continuous shadow code space with the same size of source binary code space. As shown in Figure 4, instead of reusing the source binary space, the SPIRE table is placed into the shadow page space, which has a fixed offset with the source binary space. So that the original code pages won't be corrupted. With this mechanism, the table-entering routine should jump to the address at SPC + Offset, instead of the original SPC.

In this case, instead of the original 1-instruction table entering route, SPIRE needs to cost about 5 instructions to add the offset to SPC, but still much better than hash lookup. The following code sequence is an example of SPIRE table entering routine.

```
push %ecx;    // spill register
mov %ecx, *dest;
lea %ecx, $offset;
jmp %ecx;     // jump to ($SPC + OFFSET)
pop %ecx;     // executed later
```

The shadow code space is a direct-mapping space of source binary code space. It needn't be initialized as a copy of source binary. Only the pages containing SPIRE table entries will be modified, and the unused pages can be left untouched. Due to the on-demand page allocating mechanism in operating system, only the page being accessed would be allocated a physical page frame. So the shadow page space won't take too much physical memory.

Some applications like virtual machine may generate/load binary code at runtime, SPIRE may not always be able allocate a shadow space with the fixed offset to the new generated code. When SPIRE finds that it cannot maintain a shadow code space which can map all the source binary code, it will invalidate all the optimized indirect branches, and totally fall back to hash lookup mechanism for safety.

4.2. Avoid Overlapping of Table Entries

As x86 is a variable-length ISA, its instruction length varies from 1-byte to 15-bytes. Meanwhile, the trampoline of SPIRE needs a 5-bytes long direct jump instruction on x86 host architecture. Therefore, the source instruction slot may be shorter than SPIRE table entry. If the table entry exceeds the instructions slot, it may be overlapped with another table entry. This situation happens when two branch targets are very close, and it will make the program failed.

To solve this problem, we propose an entry chain scheme. When the target source instruction slot is shorter than table entry, the "jmp TPC" trampoline cannot be filled directly. In this case, SPIRE fills the slot with a 2-bytes short jump, which can jumps to a

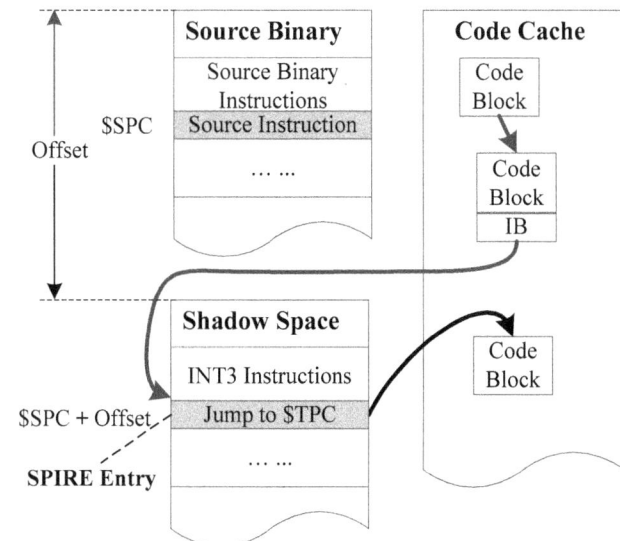

Figure 4. Workflow of SPIRE on x86 to x86 DBT

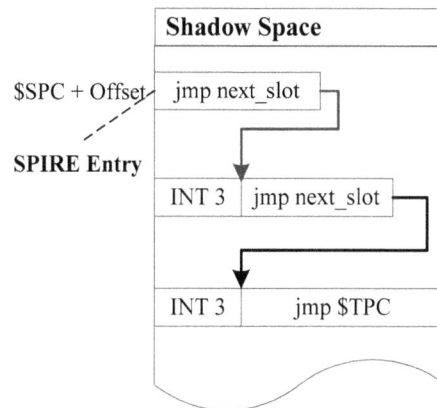

Figure 5. Structure of entry chain

following instruction slot long enough. If a long slot cannot be found inside the range of the short jump (0–127 bytes), the furthest appropriate slot is selected as an intermediate slot, which also be filled with a short jump. Then we can continue to search long slot by taking this new instruction as start point. This process can be recurred until the long slot is found or the number of intermediate slots exceeds the threshold. Figure 5 demonstrates the structure of entry chain.

To prevent the intermediate slot from conflicting with another table entry, we add a software exception instruction (INT3 on x86) in the front of the slot. So the intermediate instruction slot should be at least 3-bytes long. The ending slot should be no less than 6-bytes. If the intermediate slot is just a target of another indirect branch, when the control-flow jumps to this slot, the INT3 instruction will be executed, and a software exception will be raised. The exception handler will try to adjust the conflict entry chain to free this slot.

If it is failed to find an entry chain, the related indirect branch will be handled by hash lookup mechanism. The entry chain scheme costs extra instructions, but these direct jump instructions can be easily predicted by the branch predictor, so they won't introduce too much overhead.

4.3. Instruction Boundary Issue

On x86 platform, the control flow may jump to the middle of an instruction. To our knowledge, this technique is only used to across a prefix, such as LOCK. The following code sequence is excerpted from the benchmark 254.gap, showing an example that a branch instruction jumps across a LOCK prefix.

```
0x80a9807:    je    0x80a980a
0x80a9809:    lock cmpxchg %ecx, 0x817a160
```

Our implementation has considered this across-prefix case. The source binary instruction at branch target address is checked for prefix, an instruction with prefix wouldn't be selected as SPIRE table entry.

Many long x86 instructions can contain a shorter valid instruction, e.g. "mov %ch, 0" resides in "movl %esi, 0x08030000(%ebp)"[26]. Theoretically, a branch instruction can jump to the middle of an arbitrary instruction and continue executing correctly. Although this case may be impractical in real application, we also propose a heuristic scheme to deal with it. For example, when a 5-bytes long instruction at 0x8001000 will be selected as a table entry, the byte streams starting from 0x8001001 0x8001002, 0x8001003, 0x8001004 are decoded to instruction sequences. If all of these "middle instruction sequence" is illegal or much different from the original instruction sequence starting from 0x8001000, this table entry is considered as safe. Because we believe overlapping two totally different instruction sequences into one byte stream is unrealistic. This scheme isn't perfect, but can reduce the possibility that jumping to middle of instruction makes SPIRE failed. Actually, we checked lots of applications, including productive software like office and web browser, and never found such case.

4.4. Implementation on Other Platforms

In this section, we will discuss how to implement SPIRE on other popular platforms.

As we mentioned before, there are two architecture related features impacting the implementation of SPIRE: 1) Page permission control is needed to prevent corrupt code pages from being accessed by other code. 2) Source binary instruction should be

long enough to avoid entry overlapping. The former issue can be solved by shadow code space scheme described in section 4.1, so the instruction length becomes the main concern.

We classify the popular platform into two categories: variable-length ISA platform, represented by x86, and the fixed-length ISA platform, represented by ARM and MIPS. We will take x86 and ARM as examples to illustrate how to implement SPIRE on different DBT systems.

ARM to ARM DBT. Both guest and host instructions are fixed length, so the table overlapping issue wouldn't exist. However, there is another issue in such RISC platforms: the offset of direct jump instruction is limited. In ARM platform, the jump offset is a 26-bit signed integer, thus the jump range is limited to 32MB. This range limit may be enough for embedded applications, but not enough for desktop or server applications. If the source binary code size is larger than 32MB, the trampoline cannot reach the code cache.

We modify our SPIRE mechanism to solve this problem. Figure 6 shows the structure of this variant. Instead of storing a redirecting trampoline to TPC, we directly put the TPC address in the SPIRE entry. Thus the workflow of SPIRE becomes: 1) Load the TPC from the memory address SPC + OFF. 2) Jump to this TPC. With this variant, we cannot leverage the software trap instruction to identify the unfilled entry. Instead, we fill the corrupted memory page with a specific handler address. When an unfilled table entry is loaded, the control flow will jump to the pre-defined handler. The source binary code space is omitted in the figure. To keep the transparency to self-reference code, the SPIRE table should also reside in the shadow space.

ARM to x86 DBT. On ARM to x86 DBT systems, the source instruction slot is always 4-bytes. A trampoline of host x86 platform needs 5-bytes, which is too long. To solve this problem, it can adopt the same mechanism with ARM to ARM DBT.

x86 to ARM DBT. The source instruction slot is variable length which may be shorter than SPIRE table entry, and ARM doesn't own a short jump instruction to build entry chain as described in section 4.2. Storing the TPC in the entry cannot deal with the entry overlapping problem. So far, we haven't found an effective way to implement SPIRE mechanism on such a DBT system.

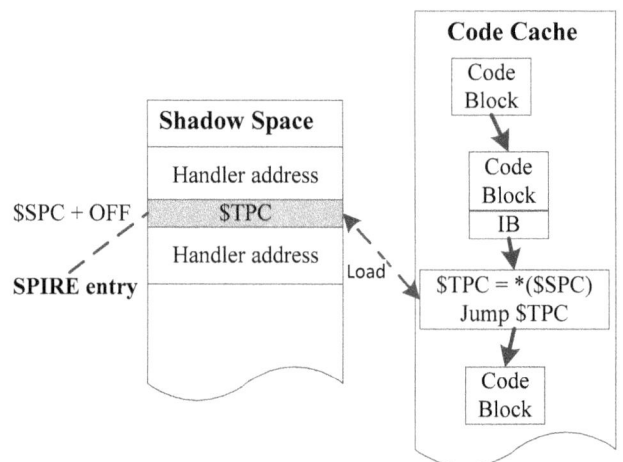

Figure 6. Workflow of SPIRE on ARM to ARM DBT.

Table 1. Details of benchmarks

Benchmarks	gcc	crafty	eon	perlbmk	gap	perlbench	sjeng	richard
Test Suite	SPEC CPU 2000					SPEC CPU 2006		
Language	C	C	C++	C	C	C	C	C++
Static Indirect Branch	250	50	100	131	419	167	48	50
Dynamic Indirect Branch ($1*10^8$)	1.37	4.14	6.24	12.0	28.3	82.3	40.1	6.58
Dynamic Instruction Count ($1*10^{10}$)	4.19	23.1	11.3	11.9	24.1	79.1	59.2	5.52
Dynamic ratio of Indirect Branch	0.3%	0.2%	0.5%	1.0%	1.2%	1.0%	0.7%	1.2%

5. Evaluation

Normalized execution time is the ratio of the execution time running on DBT system and on native machine, which is widely used to measure the performance of DBT system. We use "overhead reduction" to measure the performance improvement of our mechanism, the definition is as follows:

$$Overhead = Normalized\ Execution\ Time - 1$$

$$Overhead\ \mathrm{Re}\,duction =$$

$$\frac{Overhead_{before\ opt} - Overhead_{after\ opt}}{Overhead_{before\ opt}} *100\%$$

5.1. Experimental Setup

To get a convicting result, all of our experiments are running on the real machine. The experimental platform is shown in Table 2.

We implement our SPIRE technique in a high performance DBT system HDTrans[12]. HDTrans is a light-weight x86 to x86 binary translation and instrumentation system with a table-driven translator. It uses an very efficient hash lookup routine called SIEVE[27] to handle indirect branch, thus we selected the original HDTrans as the performance baseline.

The benchmarks are selected from SPEC CPU2000, SPEC CPU2006[28] and an individual C++ benchmark. All these benchmarks are indirect branch intensive, and widely used to measure the effect of indirect branch optimizing [29]. The details of benchmarks are shown in Table 1. We also evaluate all the SPEC CPU2000 benchmarks to show the side effect of SPIRE.

Due to the "Ret" instructions is highly predictable, there are a variety of efficient schemes to handle ret, such as "shadow stack" or "function cloning"[15]. Thus handling other indirect branches is a key factor to performance. Hiser et al. and Kim et al.'s evaluations [8, 13] show that indirect branch (excluding ret) handling mechanisms impact the performance significantly. The "Return Cache" mechanism of HDTrans also can handle "Ret" instructions efficiently, so our evaluation doesn't apply SPIRE on "Ret" Instructions.

Table 2. Experimental platform

Hardware	I3-550@3.20GHz, 2GB DRAM
Operation System	RHEL-5.4, Linux-2.6.18
Compiler	gcc-4.1.2 with –O2 flag
DBT system	HTrans-0.4(x86 to x86)

5.2. Performance Improvement

Execution Time Improvement. Figure 7 shows the performance comparison of several well-known DBT systems. Pin is a widely used dynamic binary instrumentation platform. It supplies a rich set of interface, which can be used to develop various pin-tools, such as memory checker, cache simulator. DynamoRIO is a dynamic optimization platform on x86 platform[10].

HDTrans-0.4 refers to the original HDTrans system, which use hash lookup to deal with indirect branch. HDTrans-SPIRE refers to the HDTrans system with our SPIRE mechanism. The original HDTrans doesn't have a software prediction mechanism, for comparison, we implement software prediction technique in

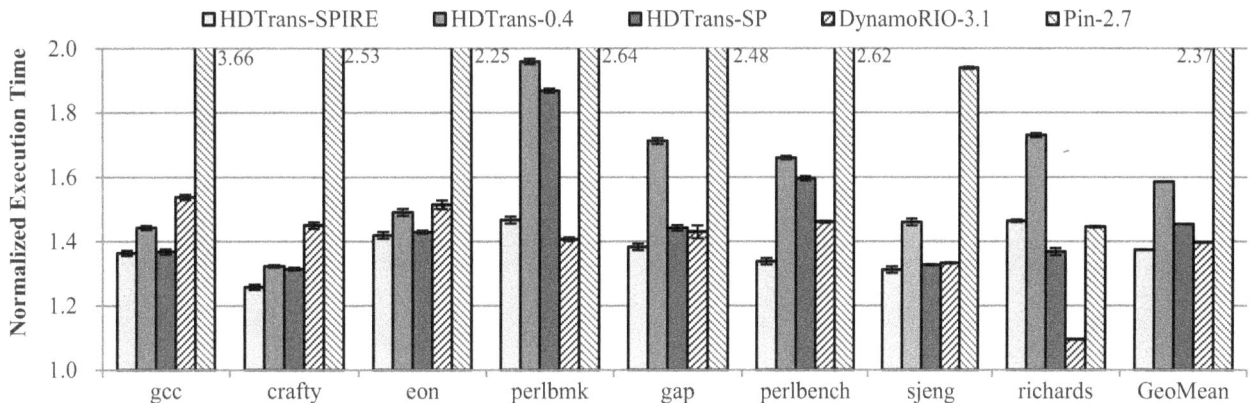

Figure 7. Performance comparison of DBT systems.

HDTrans, called HDTrans-SP. The length of its prediction chain is 3, which can achieve the best performance among different configurations. The GeoMean in the figure refers to the geometric mean of benchmarks. The error bars indicate the 95% confidence intervals.

The performance results show that HDTrans-SPIRE achieves the best performance. Compared with original HDTrans using hash lookup mechanism (HDTrans-0.4), SPIRE achieves a significant performance improvement, speedups the average normalized execution time from 1.58 to 1.37, reduces the performance overhead by 36.2% on average, up to 51.4% on perlbmk benchmark. The average execution time is improved by 15.4%.

Compared with the software prediction technique (HDTrans-SP), the SPIRE performs better at most benchmarks, and gets a 17.7% performance overhead reduction on average. Software prediction mechanism runs faster on "richards" benchmark, because the indirect branches in "richards" are highly predictable, which can achieve a 92.9% hit-rate in our evaluation.

DynamoRIO is designed as a dynamic optimization system with various optimizing techniques like trace generation. It runs much faster than original HDTrans. But HDTrans with SPIRE mechanism performs better than DynamoRIO, which proves the effectiveness of SPIRE. Pin mainly focuses on dynamic instrumentation for program analysis, so it runs relatively slower than others.

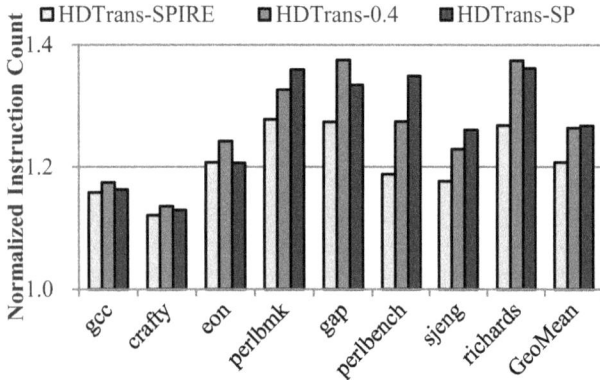

Figure 8. Dynamic instruction count comparison.

Dynamic Instruction Count Improvement. Because of the translation overhead and control transfer instruction handling overhead, DBT systems always suffer more dynamic instruction count than native execution. Our SPIRE mechanism can reduce the instruction count for handling indirect branch, which further improves the total dynamic instruction count. For example, a hash lookup takes more than 11 instructions on our implementation, while SPIRE only needs 6 instructions

Figure 8 shows the dynamic instruction count normalized to native execution. Compared with hash lookup, SPIRE can reduce the total instruction count by 4.9%. The software prediction mechanism executes a bit more instructions than hash lookup, but achieves a better performance. Probably because the compare and conditional branch instructions used in software prediction take less CPU cycles than the instruction sequence of hash lookup. More micro-architecture issues will be discussed in the later section.

Entry Chain Scheme. The case that two branch targets are quite close is very rare, which mostly exists in the indirect branches related with "Switch-Case" statement. According to our evaluation, the rate of closed-targets is less than 0.01% in dynamic (with execution count weighted).

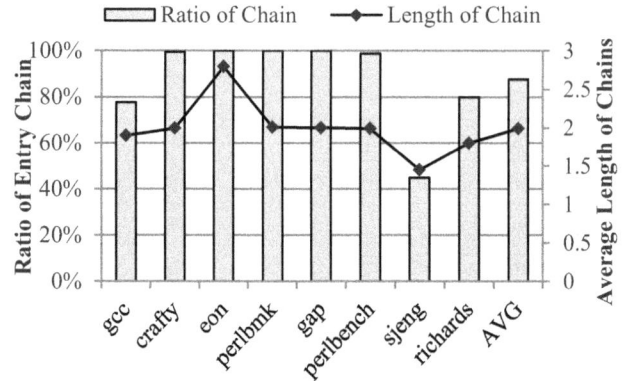

Figure 9. Raito and length of entry chain.

However, it's hard to detect this case before it happens. For safety, SPIRE entry chain scheme is used to avoid the possibility of table entries overlapping. Figure 9 shows the ratio of the chained table entries and the average length of chains. According to our evaluation, 87.6% of table entries must be chained. The average length of chains is 1.99. Fortunately, predictable direct jump instructions wouldn't introduce too much overhead.

Performance on Other Benchmarks. We also evaluate SPIRE mechanism on all other benchmarks of SPEC CPU 2000 INT. All these benchmarks are not indirect branch intensive. For example, the dynamic rate of indirect branch of 164.gzip is 0.04%, 175.vpr is 0.03%. With online profiling scheme, SPRIE mechanism would rarely be triggered on these benchmarks. The results presented in Figure 10 illustrate that SPIRE mechanism has no performance side effect on benchmarks that are not indirect branch intensive. The results also show that indirect branch un-intensive benchmarks suffer less overhead than indirect branch intensive benchmarks, which proves the importance of indirect branch handling.

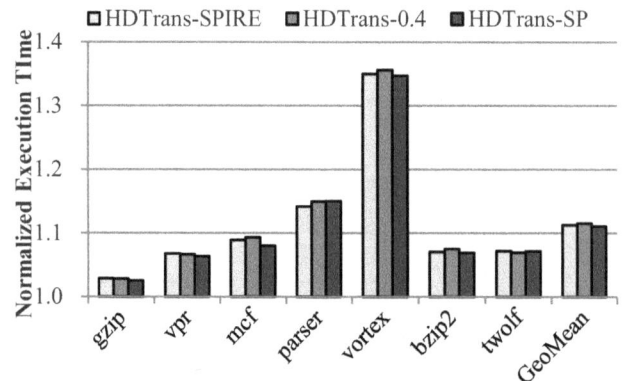

Figure 10. Performance on other benchmarks.

5.3. Memory Overhead

The shadow page mechanism introduces extra memory to store corrupted code pages or SPIRE table entries. On our x86 implementation, the shadow page space need a continuous virtual address space as large as source binary code space, but only the page containing SPIRE table entries will take the physical memory. The online profiling mechanism further reduces the number of shadow pages. As shown in Figure 11, SPIRE consumes 5.6% more physical memory than before on average, which is acceptable.

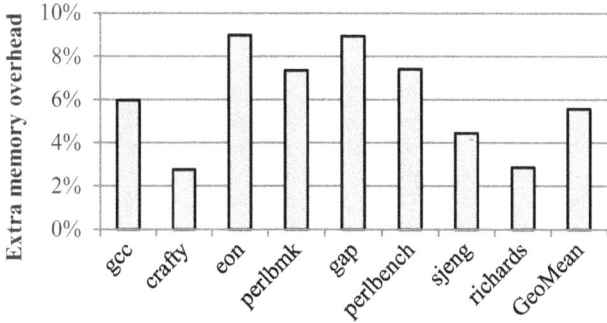

Figure 11. Memory overhead of SPIRE.

5.4. Impact on Micro-architecture features

The performance of DBT system is closely related to pipeline events, such as cache miss and branch prediction miss [30], especially on a super-scalar architecture like x86. In this section, several important micro-architecture features are evaluated to show the effectiveness of SPIRE.

Because DynamoRIO and Pin doesn't own the same code base with HDTrans, the behavior between them and HDTrans may be quite different. So we didn't include DynamoRIO and Pin into micro-architecture evaluation.

Branch Prediction Miss. SPIRE routine contains one indirect jump and one or several direct jump instructions. The target distribution of the indirect branch is the same as it in source program. A typical hash lookup routine contains at least one compare-jump pair and always ends with one indirect branch. If the hash lookup routine is shared by all branches, the ending indirect branch will be hard to predict. With software prediction mechanism, when prediction hits, only one or several compare-jump pairs are needed, but when predictions fails, a full hash lookup would be called.

Figure 12 describes the result of branch prediction miss, including indirect branch and conditional branch. SPIRE achieves the best result.

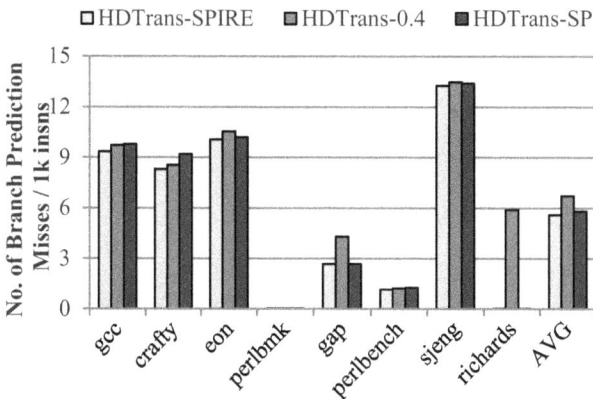

Figure 12. Branch prediction misses results.

I-Cache & I-TLB Miss. SPIRE mechanism jumps from code cache to source binary code space, and jumps back to code cache, which may pollute the I-Cache and I-TLB. Because branch instructions has strong locality, most of indirect branch executions occur on hot targets of hot branches, so that the extra pressure for I-Cache and I-TLB won't be too much, even in large code footprint applications. Meanwhile, SPIRE can reduce the code size of IB handling routines, which facilitates I-Cache and I-TLB hitting.

Figure 13 shows the results of L1 I-Cache miss. Software prediction has the lowest miss count, because the prediction routine is inlined in the code cache. SPIRE performs better than hash lookup mechanism. The I-TLB miss rate is too low to compare (less than 0.01 misses / 1k insns).

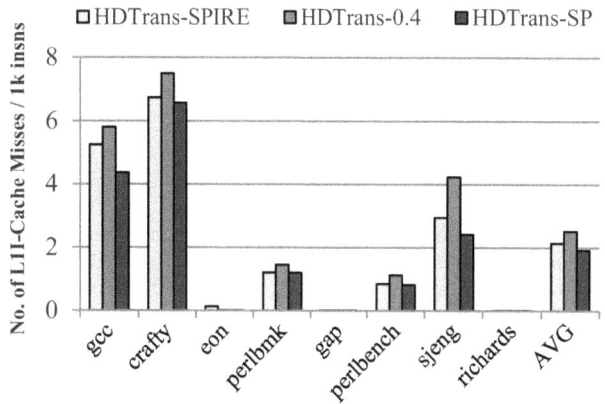

Figure 13. L1I-Cache misses results.

D-Cache & D-TLB Miss. SPIRE is an instruction-driven mechanism, and doesn't contain memory access instructions. The original HDTrans also uses an instruction-driven hash lookup routine. Software prediction routine embedded the data into instructions too. All of them won't impact the D-Cache and D-TLB significantly. As presented in Figure 14 and Figure 15, all three mechanisms have similar D-Cache and D-TLB misses results. It should be noted that the total instruction count of SPIRE is fewer than others, so the number of misses per instruction is relatively higher.

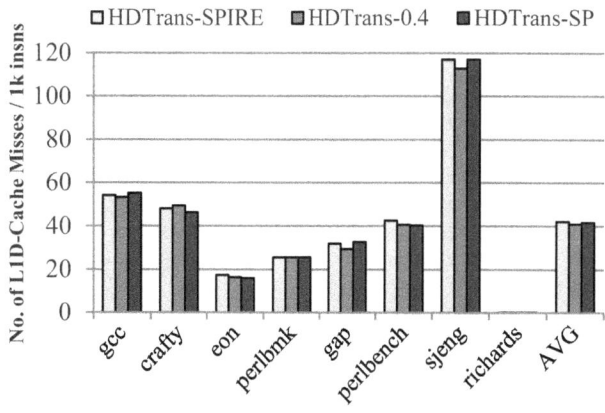

Figure 14. L1D-Cache misses results.

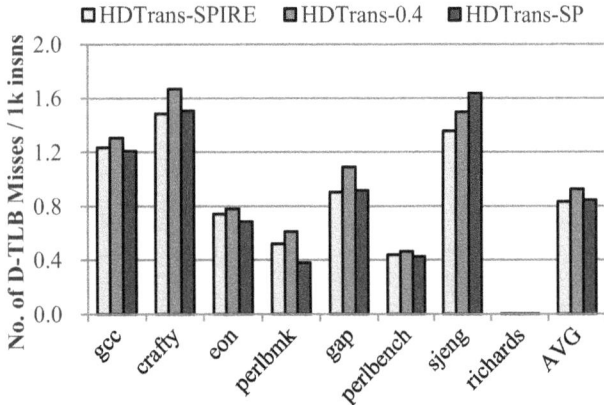

Figure 15. D-TLB misses results.

5.5. Performance on different CPU

The experimental results of Hiser et al. indicated that, the performance of IB handling mechanism is highly dependent on the implementation of underlying architecture[8], because different micro-architectures perform different on a same code sequence.

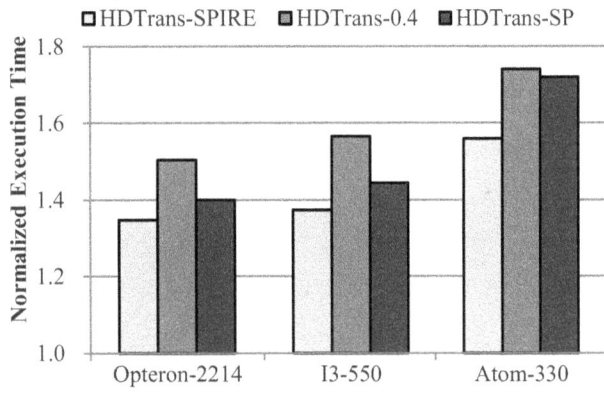

Figure 16. Performance on different CPUs.

To illustrate the effectiveness of our technique, we evaluate SPIRE on several different CPUs, including AMD Opteron processor for server, and Intel ATOM processor for netbook. The results shown by Figure 16 illustrate that SPIRE mechanism performs well on all of the experimental platforms.

The DBT overhead are highest on ATOM processor. That's probably because DBT introduces extra control transfer instructions, and increases footprint of the application, which may result in more cache misses or branch prediction misses. ATOM has a relatively simple micro-architecture, which has a low tolerance to these pipeline stall events.

6. Conclusion

In this paper, we propose a novel mechanism called SPIRE, which can significantly reduce the indirect branch handling overhead.

SPIRE mechanism reuses the virtual address space of source binary code to build a dispatching structure for indirect branches. With SPIRE, The indirect branch can jump to the originally SPC address without address translation. The trampoline residing in the table entry will redirect the control flow to related TPC. Only 2–6 instructions are needed to handle an indirect branch execution.

We implemented our SPIRE mechanism on x86 platform. The experiments prove that compared with the previous techniques, SIPRE can significantly improve the performance, while introducing an acceptable memory overhead. The evaluation of micro-architecture features and the evaluation on different CPUs also illustrate the effectiveness of SPIRE. Furthermore, we discuss the implementing issues of SPIRE on different architectures.

SPIRE doesn't need special hardware or instructions, so it can be widely used in DBT systems. It also can cooperate with other optimization mechanism. For example, it can be combined with software prediction. With this adaptive mechanism, the highly predictable IBs will be handled by software prediction, and the hard-to-predict IBs will be handled by SPIRE. We believe that the idea of SPIRE can also be applied on other occasions that need address translation.

References

[1] S. Bansal and A. Aiken. Binary translation using peephole superoptimizers. in *Proceedings of the 8th USENIX conference on Operating systems design and implementation*, San Diego, California, pages 177-192, 2008.

[2] N. Nethercote and J. Seward. Valgrind: a framework for heavyweight dynamic binary instrumentation. in *Proceedings of the 2007 ACM SIGPLAN conference on Programming language design and implementation*, San Diego, California, USA, pages 89-100, 2007.

[3] D. Bruening, Q. Zhao, and S. Amarasinghe. Transparent dynamic instrumentation. in *Proceedings of the 8th ACM SIGPLAN/SIGOPS conference on Virtual Execution Environments*, London, England, UK, pages 133-144, 2012.

[4] D. Pavlou, E. Gibert, F. Latorre, and A. Gonzalez. DDGacc: boosting dynamic DDG-based binary optimizations through specialized hardware support. in *Proceedings of the 8th ACM SIGPLAN/SIGOPS conference on Virtual Execution Environments*, London, England, UK, pages 159-168, 2012.

[5] Q. Zhao, D. Koh, S. Raza, D. Bruening, W.-F. Wong, and S. Amarasinghe. Dynamic cache contention detection in multi-threaded applications. in *Proceedings of the 7th ACM SIGPLAN/SIGOPS international conference on Virtual execution environments*, Newport Beach, California, USA, pages 27-38, 2011.

[6] G. Lueck, H. Patil, and C. Pereira. PinADX: an interface for customizable debugging with dynamic instrumentation. in *Proceedings of the Tenth International Symposium on Code Generation and Optimization*, San Jose, California, USA, pages 114-123, 2012.

[7] F. Bellard. QEMU, a fast and portable dynamic translator. in *Proceedings of the annual conference on USENIX Annual Technical Conference*, Anaheim, CA, pages 41-41, 2005.

[8] J. D. Hiser, D. W. Williams, W. Hu, J. W. Davidson, J. Mars, and B. R. Childers. Evaluating indirect branch handling mechanisms in software dynamic translation systems. *ACM Trans. Archit. Code Optim.*, vol. 8, pages 1-28, 2011.

[9] E. Borin and Y. Wu. Characterization of DBT overhead. in *Proceedings of the 2009 IEEE International Symposium on Workload Characterization (IISWC)*, pages 178-187, 2009.

[10] D. Bruening, T. Garnett, and S. Amarasinghe. An infrastructure for adaptive dynamic optimization. in *Proceedings of the international symposium on Code generation and optimization: feedback-directed and runtime optimization*, San Francisco, California, USA, pages 265-275, 2003.

[11] K. Scott and J. Davidson. Strata: A Software Dynamic Translation Infrastructure. in *IEEE Workshop on Binary Translation*, 2001.

[12] S. Sridhar, J. S. Shapiro, E. Northup, and P. P. Bungale. HDTrans: an open source, low-level dynamic instrumentation system. in

Proceedings of the 2nd international conference on Virtual execution environments, Ottawa, Ontario, Canada, pages 175-185, 2006.

[13] H.-S. Kim and J. E. Smith. Hardware Support for Control Transfers in Code Caches. in *Proceedings of the 36th annual IEEE/ACM International Symposium on Microarchitecture*, pages 253-264, 2003.

[14] K. Ishizaki, M. Kawahito, T. Yasue, H. Komatsu, and T. Nakatani. A study of devirtualization techniques for a Java Just-In-Time compiler. in *Proceedings of the 15th ACM SIGPLAN conference on Object-oriented programming, systems, languages, and applications*, Minneapolis, Minnesota, USA, pages 294-310, 2000.

[15] C.-K. Luk, R. Cohn, R. Muth, H. Patil, A. Klauser, G. Lowney, S. Wallace, V. J. Reddi, and K. Hazelwood. Pin: building customized program analysis tools with dynamic instrumentation. in *Proceedings of the 2005 ACM SIGPLAN conference on Programming language design and implementation*, Chicago, IL, USA, pages 190-200, 2005.

[16] B. Dhanasekaran and K. Hazelwood. Improving indirect branch translation in dynamic binary translators. in *Proceedings of the ASPLOS Workshop on Runtime Environments, Systems, Layering, and Virtualized Environments*, Newport Beach, CA, pages 11-18, 2011.

[17] W. Hu, J. Wang, X. Gao, Y. Chen, Q. Liu, and G. Li. Godson-3: A Scalable Multicore RISC Processor with x86 Emulation. *IEEE Micro*, vol. 29, pages 17-29, 2009.

[18] J. Li and C. Wu. A New Replacement Algorithm on Content Associative Memory for Binary Translation System. in *Proceedings of the Workshop on Architectural and Microarchitectural Support for Binary Translation*, pages 45-54, 2008.

[19] H. Guan, B. Liu, Z. Qi, Y. Yang, H. Yang, and A. Liang. CoDBT: A multi-source dynamic binary translator using hardware-software collaborative techniques. *J. Syst. Archit.*, vol. 56, pages 500-508, 2010.

[20] D. Mihocka and S. Shwartsman. Virtualization Without Direct Execution or Jitting: Designing a Portable Virtual Machine Infrastructure. in *Proceedings of the Workshop on Architectural and Microarchitectural Support for Binary Translation*, pages 55-70, 2008.

[21] A. Guha, K. hazelwood, and M. L. Soffa. DBT path selection for holistic memory efficiency and performance. in *Proceedings of the 6th ACM SIGPLAN/SIGOPS international conference on Virtual execution environments*, Pittsburgh, Pennsylvania, USA, pages 145-156, 2010.

[22] G. Kondoh and H. Komatsu. Dynamic binary translation specialized for embedded systems. in *Proceedings of the 6th ACM SIGPLAN/SIGOPS international conference on Virtual execution environments*, Pittsburgh, Pennsylvania, USA, pages 157-166, 2010.

[23] D. Bruening and V. Kiriansky. Process-shared and persistent code caches. in *Proceedings of the fourth ACM SIGPLAN/SIGOPS international conference on Virtual execution environments*, Seattle, WA, USA, pages 61-70, 2008.

[24] V. J. Reddi, D. Connors, R. Cohn, and M. D. Smith. Persistent Code Caching: Exploiting Code Reuse Across Executions and Applications. in *Proceedings of the International Symposium on Code Generation and Optimization*, pages 74-88, 2007.

[25] D.-Y. Hong, C.-C. Hsu, P.-C. Yew, J.-J. Wu, W.-C. Hsu, P. Liu, C.-M. Wang, and Y.-C. Chung. HQEMU: a multi-threaded and retargetable dynamic binary translator on multicores. in *Proceedings of the Tenth International Symposium on Code Generation and Optimization*, San Jose, California, USA, pages 104-113, 2012.

[26] J. Smith and R. Nair, *Virtual Machines: Versatile Platforms for Systems and Processes (The Morgan Kaufmann Series in Computer Architecture and Design)*: Morgan Kaufmann Publishers Inc., 2005.

[27] J. D. Hiser, D. Williams, W. Hu, J. W. Davidson, J. Mars, and B. R. Childers. Evaluating Indirect Branch Handling Mechanisms in Software Dynamic Translation Systems. in *Proceedings of the International Symposium on Code Generation and Optimization*, pages 61-73, 2007.

[28] Standard Performance Evaluation Corporation. *SPEC CPU*. http://www.spec.org

[29] H. Kim, J. A. Joao, O. Mutlu, C. J. Lee, Y. N. Patt, and R. Cohn. VPC prediction: reducing the cost of indirect branches via hardware-based dynamic devirtualization. in *Proceedings of the 34th annual international symposium on Computer architecture*, San Diego, California, USA, pages 424-435, 2007.

[30] J. D. Hiser, D. Williams, A. Filipi, J. W. Davidson, and B. R. Childers. Evaluating fragment construction policies for SDT systems. in *Proceedings of the 2nd international conference on Virtual execution environments*, Ottawa, Ontario, Canada, pages 122-132, 2006.

11

Limits of Region-Based Dynamic Binary Parallelization

Tobias J.K. Edler von Koch   Björn Franke

Institute for Computing Systems Architecture
School of Informatics, University of Edinburgh
10 Crichton Street, Edinburgh, EH8 9AB, U.K.
{t.v.koch,bfranke}@ed.ac.uk

Abstract

Efficiently executing sequential legacy binaries on chip multi-processors (CMPs) composed of many, small cores is one of today's most pressing problems. Single-threaded execution is a suboptimal option due to CMPs' lower single-core performance, while multi-threaded execution relies on prior parallelization, which is severely hampered by the low-level binary representation of applications compiled and optimized for a single-core target. A recent technology to address this problem is *Dynamic Binary Parallelization* (DBP), which creates a *Virtual Execution Environment* (VEE) taking advantage of the underlying multicore host to transparently parallelize the sequential binary executable. While still in its infancy, DBP has received broad interest within the research community. The combined use of DBP and thread-level speculation (TLS) has been proposed as a technique to accelerate legacy uniprocessor code on modern CMPs. In this paper, we investigate the limits of DBP and seek to gain an understanding of the factors contributing to these limits and the costs and overheads of its implementation. We have performed an extensive evaluation using a parameterizable DBP system targeting a CMP with light-weight architectural TLS support. We demonstrate that there is room for a significant reduction of up to 54% in the number of instructions on the critical paths of legacy SPEC CPU2006 benchmarks. However, we show that it is much harder to translate these savings into actual performance improvements, with a *realistic* hardware-supported implementation achieving a speedup of 1.09 on average.

Categories and Subject Descriptors C.1.4 [*Processor Architectures*]: Parallel Architectures; D.3.4 [*Programming Languages*]: Processors—Run-time environments

General Terms Performance, Experimentation

Keywords Dynamic Binary Parallelization, Automatic Parallelization, Runtime Systems, Thread-level speculation, Transactional Memory

1. Introduction

Multi-core processors have become the norm in computing systems as diverse as smartphones, games consoles, tablets, notebook and desktop computers, servers and data centers. While the current generation of multi-core processors still comprises relatively few, but powerful cores [3] it is anticipated that in the foreseeable future processor manufacturers will provide us with chip multi-processors (CMPs) containing more, but possibly less powerful cores [21]. A current example of such an architecture is the Intel Single-Chip Cloud Computer [12], where each SCC chip contains 48 P54C Pentium cores. How to run sequential legacy applications on such many-core architectures without incurring an unacceptable performance penalty is a key research challenge.

One obvious solution to this problem would be to include one or more ILP-rich cores specifically dedicated to the execution of sequential workloads in an *Asymmetric Multicore Processor* (AMP). While this is an entirely feasible approach [10], it creates a number of new problems related to the design and software control of such a heterogeneous processor [8]. An alternative approach to executing legacy code on CMPs is to employ *Dynamic Binary Parallelization* (DBP) [6, 9, 27, 28] to dynamically remap a sequential application to a *Symmetric Multicore Processor* (SMP) in a *Virtual Execution Environment* (VEE).

Despite the flexibility DBP offers, its main drawback is that the extraction of parallelism from a binary executable compiled and optimized for a particular single-core machine is a hard problem. This is not only due to the idiosyncrasies of the *Instruction Set Architecture* (ISA) the application has been compiled for, but also due to the low-level nature of the binary representation which obfuscates much of the higher-level code structure so vital to traditional control and data flow dependence analyses supporting parallelization. Recently proposed DBP approaches, e.g. [6, 9], seek to overcome these difficulties by incorporating *Thread-level Speculation* (TLS), *Dynamic Binary Rewriting* (DBR) and a wealth of behavioral information collected during the execution of a program. Such proposals often narrowly concentrate on a specific design point, though, and thus give only a limited insight into the constrains on the design space for DBP implementations.

In this paper, we attempt to remedy some of the shortcomings of previous DBP studies. Our work is the first to pursue a characterization approach that is, as much as possible, independent of specific DBP systems and architecture configurations. In particular, we explicitly make no assumptions on whether TLS is implemented in software or hardware. High-level DBP with minimal, light-weight TLS architectural support is explored in *one common, parameterizable framework*. In this way, a more accurate upper bound on the performance potential of DBP is obtained (as opposed to some particular implementation) and, moreover, relative performance sensitivity can be related to specific high-level system parameters.

We show that although the number of critical path instructions can be reduced by up to 54% using DBP for SPEC CPU2006 benchmarks, the introduction of realistic cycle penalties for parallelization ultimately translates this into an average speedup of 1.09x. However, we conclude that DBP opens up interesting new possi-

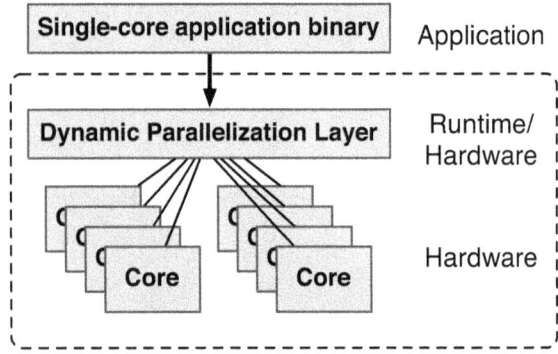

Figure 1. Overview of the general architecture of a dynamic binary parallelization system.

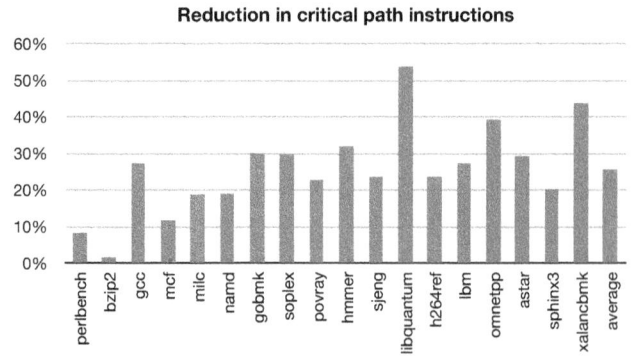

Figure 2. Reduction in critical path instructions when using dynamic binary parallelization on an 8-core speculative CMP architecture.

bilities which could achieve much greater potential, for instance, if used as part of a hybrid system incorporating prior information.

1.1 Contributions

Among the contributions of this paper are:

- a generic cost-adjustable dynamic binary parallelization scheme that allows the modeling of a variety of implementations;

- the use of *lightweight tracing* and *register value speculation* to aid dynamic binary parallelization; and

- an in-depth evaluation of the sensitivity of our model to varying costs using SPEC CPU2006 benchmarks.

1.2 Motivation

Consider the generic dynamic parallelization system in Figure 1. An unmodified single-core application binary is run on top of a multi-core architecture which parallelizes the application at runtime to improve its performance while remaining entirely transparent to the original application. DBP can be realized in a number of different ways ranging from runtime systems fully implemented in software, low-level firmwares relying on a limited degree of hardware support, to entirely hardware-based solutions.

The key idea behind such systems is to reduce the number of *critical path instructions* by overlapping the execution of subsequent segments of the instruction stream. The parallel execution has to respect true dependences between code segments. While this may seem similar to the exploitation of instruction level parallelism (ILP) in superscalar processors, the goal is usually to parallelize much larger sections of binary code.

To motivate the study presented in this paper, we have implemented a speculative DBP system based on an 8-core CMP RISC architecture and write-back caches to support memory transactions. The system overlaps sections of the instruction stream at runtime where there are no dependencies or where these can be trivially speculated (see section 2 for more architectural details). We run a number of SPEC CPU2006 benchmarks and identify the percentage of total instructions that can be taken off the critical path using this technique in functional simulation without regard for the overhead of speculation. In this sense, the results illustrate the scope for any concrete implementation of a DBP.

The results, shown in Figure 2, are encouraging. For all benchmarks, DBP reduces the number of instructions on the critical path. In the case of highly data-parallel benchmarks, such as `libquantum`, we achieve a reduction of up to 54%. Even a more task-parallel application, such as `gcc`, shows a 27% decrease. On the other hand, in the case of `bzip2`, the high degree of dependen-

cies due to the use of shared data structures leads to a rather poor overlap of only 2%.

These results show that there is significant scope for a dynamic binary parallelization system for a wide range of applications. The difficult question, however, is how to translate this into actual performance gains when considering the overheads incurred by a DBP system. Many of these overheads are adjustable – they depend on the particular implementation of the system and especially the amount of hardware support required. Feasibility and design considerations have to be guided by a thorough understanding of these factors. In the remainder of this paper, we will address precisely this question by analyzing the sensitivity of a DBP architecture to changes in various parameters.

1.3 Overview

The rest of the paper is structured as follows. We begin with a description of the architecture of our dynamic binary parallelization model in section 2. We then evaluate the sensitivity of this model to changes in various parameters. Our experimental setup is described in section 3, followed by the results of our evaluation in section 4. We discuss the limitations of our study in section 5 and provide an overview of the body of related work in section 6. Finally, we summarize and conclude in section 7.

2. Architecture for DBP

A dynamic binary parallelization system extracts parallelism from single-core applications at runtime to improve performance while remaining entirely transparent to the application. It operates directly on the level of binary code and therefore requires no access to the application source code. As an on-line method, DBP has the advantage of being able to exploit information about the actual runtime behavior of the application which may be difficult to obtain by static analysis of the source code. This allows it to target frequently executed code portions specifically.

On the other hand, DBP poses a number of challenges. The units of parallelism detected at runtime may be fairly small so low overheads become critical to achieving performance gains. Modern compilers produce dense and highly optimized code so the degree of dependencies between code sections can be high and it is often impossible to determine such dependencies ahead of execution

The consensus in existing research [6, 9, 27] in the area of DBP is therefore:

- Parallelization needs to be speculative, i.e. there must be a mechanism to recover from attempted parallelizations which turn out to violate dependencies or prove incorrect due to the execution taking a different path in the application code.

14

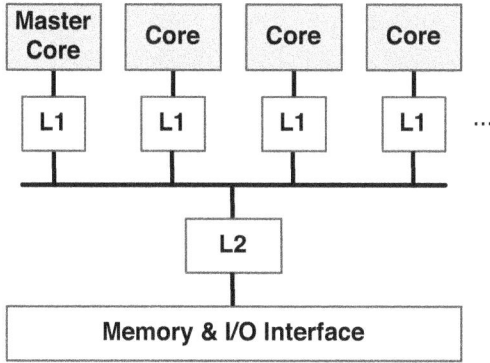

Figure 3. Architecture Overview

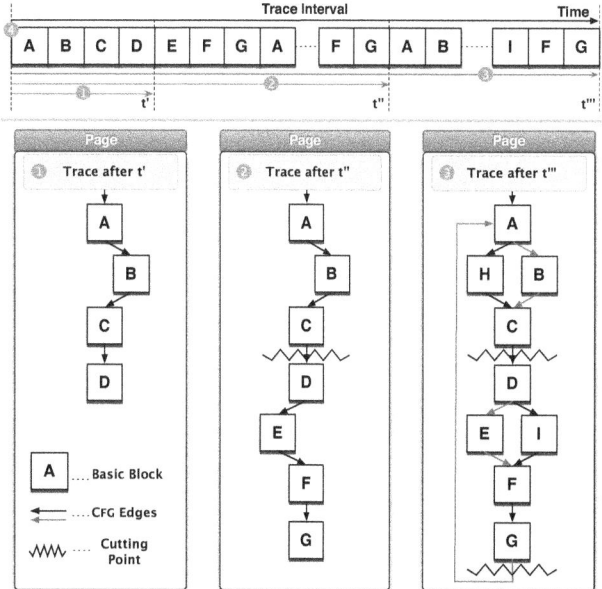

Figure 4. Incremental construction (①, ②, ③) of region traces from the sequence of basic blocks ④ executed during one trace interval. Cutting points separate segments of the trace whose execution is speculatively overlapped.

- A degree of hardware support, such as transactional memory buffers, is required to achieve a performance benefit from DBP.

Based on this experience, we have designed a cost-adjustable dynamic binary parallelization scheme. Our design is relatively conservative and provides the ability to vary the costs of various operations. This will allow us to gain insights on a wide variety of possible hard- and software-based DBP implementations.

2.1 Overview

We assume a CMP architecture with a number of cores with private L1 caches and a shared L2 cache connected to a shared bus (Figure 3). This ensures fast and low-latency communication between cores which is critical for efficient parallelization. Transactional memory support is implemented on top of write-back L1 caches which allow speculative data to be stored locally.

The available cores are divided into a *master core* and several *speculative cores*. Any application begins executing on the master core. At appropriate points, the master core launches speculative threads on the remaining cores. The code executed on the master core is always non-speculative and never reverted, while code running on speculative cores may turn out to violate dependencies or not be on the execution path of the program at all.

In Figure 5, we show examples of (a) successful and (b) unsuccessful speculation phases. The system launches two threads which speculatively execute code blocks further ahead in the predicted flow of execution, while the master core continues at the current program counter. Once its share of the code has finished executing, the master core waits for the speculative cores to either complete successfully or to abort execution if the speculation proves to be incorrect.

This epoch-based implementation of speculation is rather conservative, since idle cores could continue to speculate ahead as soon as they finish executing a section of code instead of waiting for the current parallelization phase to end. This would, however, make the speculation layer significantly more complex without leading to performance gains for the most common case of speculative execution – the overlapping of data parallel loop iterations – when most threads will be comparable in length.

2.2 Trace-based Thread Identification

A key feature of any DBP system is the manner in which it identifies sections of the instruction stream that can be run as parallel threads. In contrast to most TLS schemes, where compiler-based analysis identifies threads ahead of execution, a DBP system can only rely on information obtained from execution counters and analysis of the binary code of the application. In line with traditional off-line automatic parallelization, most systems target elementary loops as

the basic unit of parallelism [6, 9, 16, 28]. However, the use of more general structures such as *traces* [27] or *program slices* [25] has also been proposed.

We implement a lightweight region trace-based approach, a technique successfully employed in high-performance dynamic binary translation (DBP) systems [4]. At runtime, we construct control-flow graphs of the application on a per-page basis. Tracing is lightweight because we only record basic block entry points (i.e. memory addresses) as nodes, and pairs of source and target entry points as edges in the CFG traces. Edges are annotated with execution frequencies.

Execution time is partitioned into *trace intervals* (see Figure 4) whose *length* is determined by a user-defined number of executed instructions. The maximum length of a region trace is bounded by the page size. After each trace interval, the DBP system enters an analysis phase – which can be decoupled from execution and performed on an idle or dedicated core – to identify *cutting points* in the CFG traces. Based on this information, we can predict likely future control flow and speculatively overlap execution of segments of the predicted control path at cutting points when control reaches the same region again. We employ a number of heuristics (loop boundaries, backward branches, and a threshold on the maximum number of instructions) to identify such points in traces. Once speculation has been attempted for a given region, the outcome can be used to vary the location of cutting points as well as the likelihood of further attempts at speculation (*dynamic adaptation*).

Our region trace-based approach is sufficiently generic to subsume other, more fine-grained, thread identification algorithms proposed in related work (see section 6). We can express loop, task, and data parallelism at various granularities and hence derive results indicative of the upper bound performance that more targeted algorithms would exhibit. We discuss some of the limitations of our approach in section 5.

Regardless of their shape, the identification of suitable code sections for parallelization incurs an initial overhead and potentially ongoing costs. Unlike other parallelization costs, these overheads

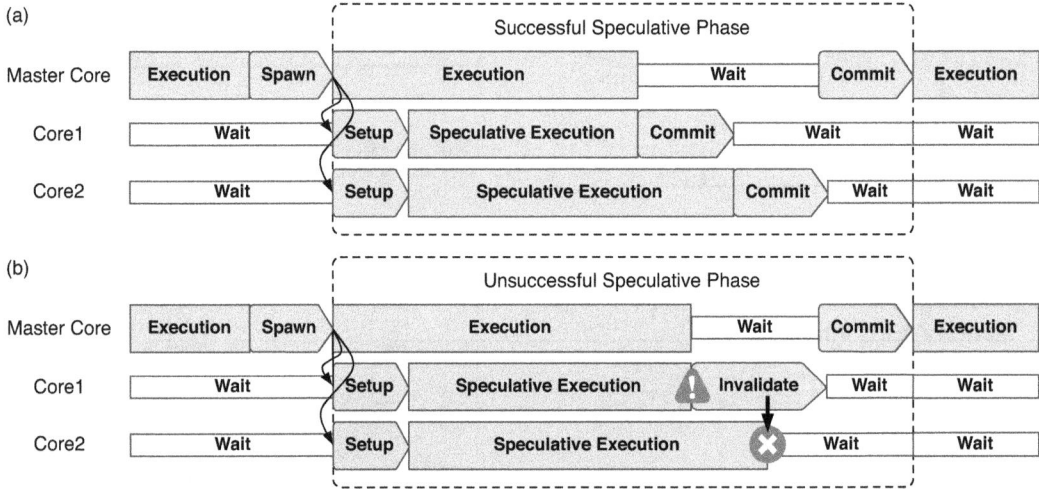

Figure 5. Example of two speculative parallel execution epochs on a 3-core system. In both cases, the *master* core spawns two speculative threads. In (a), the parallel execution completes successfully. In (b), core 1 detects a violation and enters the invalidation phase, rolling back memory transactions and canceling subsequent threads.

manifest themselves in delays until parallelization can be attempted but do not cause a potential slowdown compared to single-core execution. This is because any such overheads can be offloaded into a free hardware context (e.g. an idle core) where thread identification can take place concurrently with the execution of the binary.

2.3 Speculative Execution Costs

Once threads have been identified, speculative parallel execution involves a number of different steps. Figure 5 shows the four stages of thread spawning, setup, commit, and invalidation, all of which incur costs that are dictated by the particular implementation of the DBP system. We will now discuss them in more detail.

Thread spawning. After the identification of suitable sections for parallel execution and when execution has reached a point where such a section begins, the DBP system needs to *spawn* threads to begin parallel execution. This requires at least the sending of the current program counter (PC) to the various cores participating in parallel execution. It may also involve the transfer of *live-in* registers either through memory or dedicated communication lines. Costs for this stage can range from very few cycles (e.g. in the Multiscalar architecture [22]) to several hundreds in software-based solutions.

Thread setup. Before a newly spawned thread can begin execution, some setup work may be required. This can happen simultaneously on all cores running parallel threads and may involve value prediction for registers or memory locations, or the copying of state from the spawning core. Both [6] and [9] implement these features in software although the respective costs are not explained in detail.

Thread commit. At the end of a successful parallel execution, each core needs to commit its state. If execution was speculative, this includes checking whether there were violations of dependencies or mis-speculated values and making memory or register updates non-speculative. It may also involve waiting for predecessor threads to complete and the forwarding of data to successor threads. In RASP [9], for instance, speculative stores are marked non-speculative in constant time and become architecturally visible immediately, while value speculation is verified in software after waiting for predecessor threads to complete.

Thread invalidate. Speculative execution may fail for two reasons: (a) we may mispredict future control flow and hence execute code that is not on the actual execution path; or (b) we may dis-

cover a violation of dependences or an incorrect value speculation upon reaching the commit phase. In both cases, the speculative parallel execution has to be aborted and its possible effects reverted ('squashed'). The costs resulting from mis-speculation are twofold. Firstly, execution cycles are 'wasted' on code which later has to be squashed. This element of the cost is determined by the length of the speculative threads. In our model, it is represented by cycle-accurate simulation of the 'wasted' execution. Secondly, additional overheads may be incurred in invalidating the speculative execution phase, such as canceling a memory transaction and stopping successor threads. We allow these additional overheads to be modeled separately by a parameterizable cost.

2.4 Data dependency speculation

We have so far described a basic model for DBP. A number of optimizations are commonly employed in order to improve performance. Of particular importance are those which aim to reduce data dependencies between threads.

A data dependency between two threads can be classified as either a *flow*, an *anti*, or an *output* dependency. Anti and output dependencies can be eliminated using memory and register *renaming*. This is easily achieved through small modifications to the memory hierarchy which carry little overhead [9]. Flow dependencies, on the other hand, actually prevent parallelization.

Value prediction is one way of alleviating this problem. DBP implementations, such as [9], use it to predict values of memory locations and registers based on historic observations or typical code patterns, like spilling and reloading across calls, and thus speculatively break flow dependencies between threads. This is especially important for loop induction variables where future values need to be predicted in order to execute several loop iterations in parallel.

In our study, we use a less complex approach. We resolve anti and output dependencies using renaming. Flow dependencies on memory locations are always treated as violations; those on registers are speculated using a *last value* predictor. Whenever a read-after-write violation on a register occurs, we save the last value written to that register by the 'writer' thread in the metadata for the 'reader' thread. Every time the 'reader' thread is executed in the future, the register is speculatively set to this value on thread entry. Loop induction variables are detected and handled separately.

CMP	8-core RISC
Pipeline	3-Stage
Execution Order	In-Order
Branch Prediction	Static (BTFN)
ISA	ARCompact
Floating-Point	Hardware
Memory System	
L1 I-Cache	32k/4-way
L1 D-Cache	32k/4-way
L2 Unified Cache (shared)	1M/4-way
L2 Latency	10 cycles
Cache Replacement Policy	Pseudo-random
Bus Width/Latency/Clock Divisor	32-bit/16 cycles/2
Simulation	
Simulator	Full-system, cycle-accurate
I/O & System Calls	Emulated
Speculative parallelization costs	
Spawning, Setup, Commit, Invalidate	0 ... 1000 cycles

Table 1. ISS Configuration and Setup.

3. Experimental Setup

Before discussing the results of our DBP study, we briefly describe our experimental setup. All experiments were conducted using a fast, cycle-accurate, full-system instruction set simulator (ISS) of the target architecture. Its micro-architectural processor model has been verified against a synthesizable RTL implementation. We faithfully model the actual hardware execution of parallel threads, including waiting times for thread completion, wasted execution cycles on invalidation, and cache/memory effects of speculative execution. Thread management overheads (spawning, setup, commit, and invalidation) are represented using parameterized unit costs that are added to the cycle count whenever a given event occurs in simulation.

The speedups reported in the results section are based on *cycle count* measurements obtained from this simulation environment.

3.1 Processor Model

We simulate an 8-core CMP architecture of RISC processors. Our simulator faithfully models each core's 3-stage pipeline, mixed-mode 16/32-bit ARCompact instruction set, zero overhead loops, static branch prediction, branch delay slots, and four-way set associative data and instruction caches. The cores share a unified L2 cache. Cycle penalties for memory transactions and thread management are reflected in the parameterizable costs for the various DBP stages discussed in previous sections.

3.2 Benchmarks

Our evaluation focuses on the SPEC CPU2006 benchmark suite. We use all of the benchmarks implemented in C/C++, which include both integer and floating point codes[1]. These benchmarks are widely used and regarded as typical for a broad range of application domains. They are sequential applications and have been described as difficult to parallelize using existing automated compiler-based methods [18]. The benchmarks were compiled using arc-gcc-4.2.1 with -O2 optimization level.

We simulate complete runs of the benchmarks. In order to reduce simulation times, we use smaller data sets provided with the SPEC benchmark suite. The benchmarks execute an average of 10 billion RISC instructions each per run.

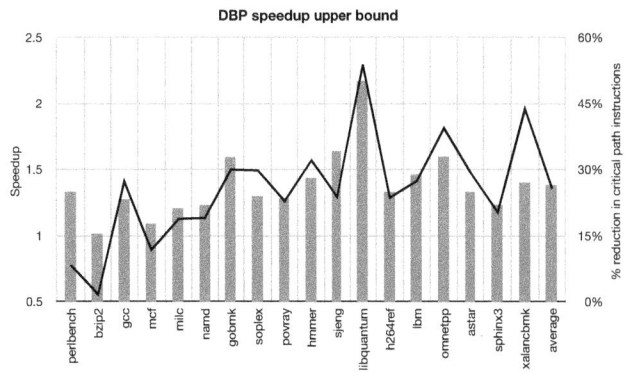

Figure 6. Upper bound to speedup if all DBP costs are set to zero (bars); and reduction in critical path instructions from Figure 2 (line).

4. Results

We begin our evaluation by establishing the theoretical maximum speedup achievable using our DBP technique in the absence of costs for speculative parallel execution. We then analyze the impact of the thread spawn, setup, and commit costs. Initially, we do this under the assumption that traces which our system would try to parallelize but fails to achieve a speedup with have already been identified and rejected prior to the measurement interval. In this way, we can illustrate the actual impact of successful parallel execution irrespective of the particular predictor used to decide whether parallelization should be attempted, and thus determine an upper bound for the performance under the given parameters.

Following on from these experiments, we continue with a more realistic model that does allow for the occurrence of mis-speculation. We investigate the impact of varying mis-speculation penalties and finally show the performance achieved with a realistic set of parameters determined in the course of our experiments.

4.1 Upper bounds

Before investigating the impact of individual DBP parameters, it is important to understand the theoretical maximum speedup achievable using the technique. This upper bound is reached if all costs are set to zero, i.e. if speculative parallelization does not incur any cycle penalties. Figure 6 shows the results.

We achieve an average speedup of 1.43x over single-core execution. The libquantum benchmark performs particularly well with a speedup of 2.17x. Only one benchmark, bzip2, fails to show any significant improvement from DBP.

Our work was motivated by the insight that a speculative DBP system can overlap sizable portions of the instruction stream for parallel execution. In Figure 6, we again show the possible reduction in critical path instructions, which we discussed earlier in section 1.2. A comparison with the DBP speedup figures indicates broadly similar trends, namely that a reduction in critical path instructions also translates into a corresponding reduction in the number of cycles executed.

However, the perlbench and xalancbmk benchmarks diverge significantly[2]. In the case of xalancbmk, we would expect a higher speedup given that there is significant parallelism on the instruction level. Conversely, for perlbench, a relatively low degree of instruction overlap should lead to similarly moderate performance gains. Further analysis of the two benchmarks reveals that in both

---

[1] 447.dealII was excluded due to issues in adjusting the data set size.

[2] bzip2 has little instruction overlap and consequently does not show any speedup.

Impact of variation of thread spawn cost

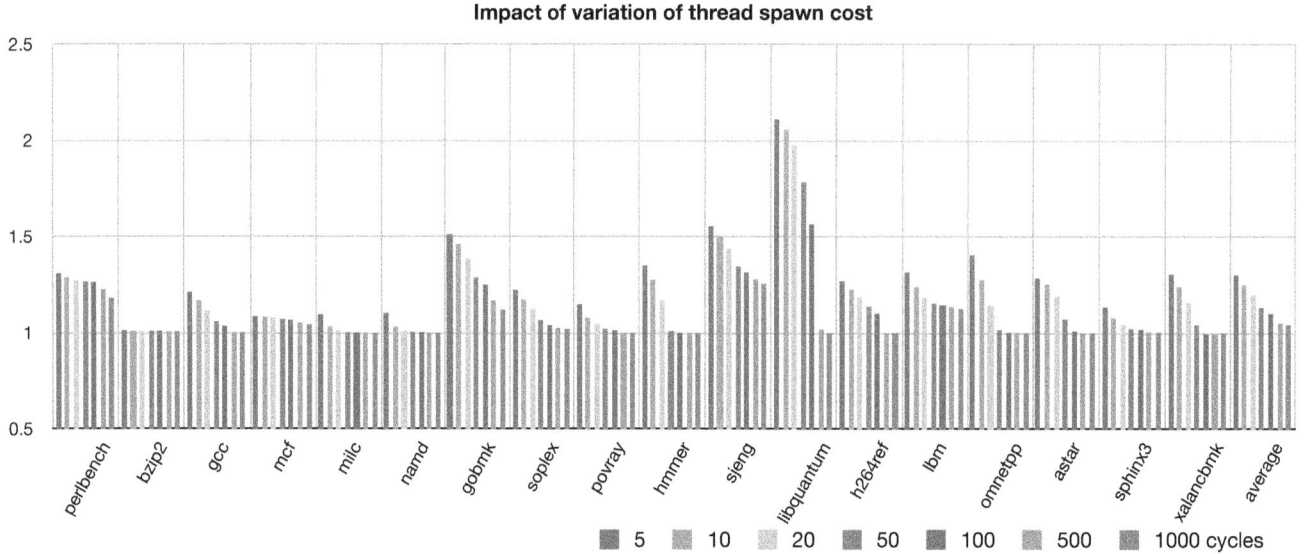

Figure 7. DBP speedup achieved with varying costs for thread spawning; all other costs are set to zero.

Impact of thread setup and commit costs

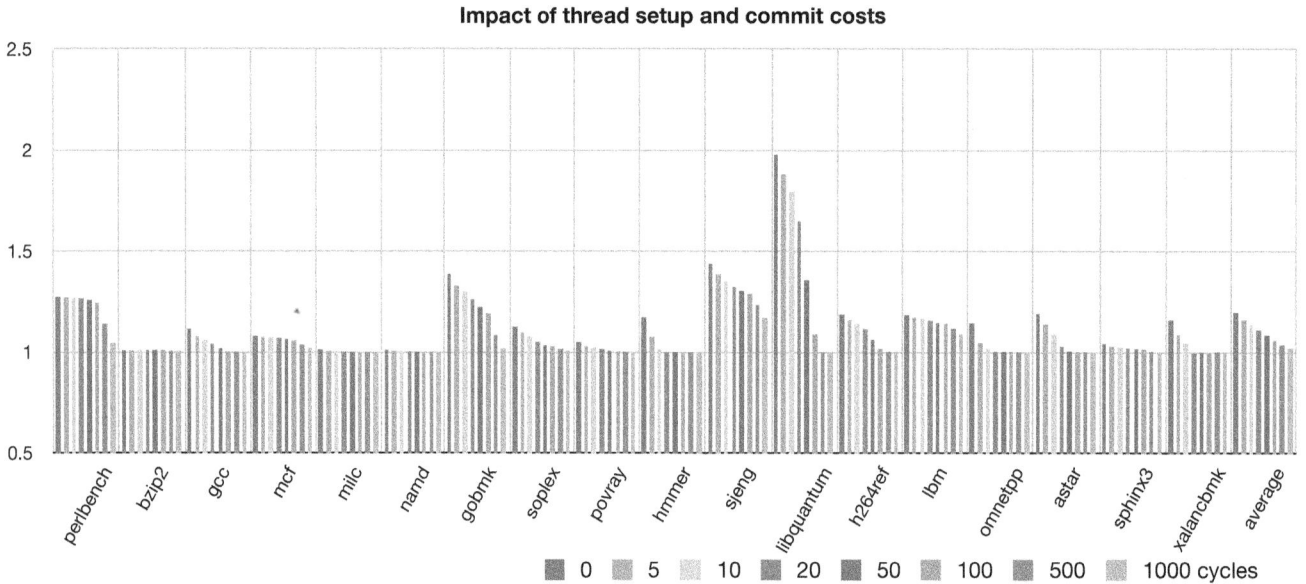

Figure 8. DBP speedup achieved with varying setup and commit costs and a fixed thread spawning cost of 20 cycles.

cases the behavior is caused by cache effects resulting from the execution of code sections on separate cores.

4.2 Thread spawn cost

The cost of spawning threads is seen as a key parameter in TLS systems and consequently much effort has been spent on optimizing this step in previous work, e.g. [17]. We thus begin by exploring the impact of the thread spawn cost parameter in a range from 5 to 1000 cycles, with all other costs (setup, commit, and invalidate) initially set to zero. This covers the spectrum from very aggressive hardware implementations to mostly software-based schemes. The results are shown in Figure 7.

The average speedup over single-core execution ranges from 1.30x with a spawn cost of 5 cycles to 1.04x for 1000 cycles. In

the more realistic range for optimized hardware implementations, we achieve 1.20x (20 cycles) and 1.13x (50 cycles).

The libquantum benchmark performs exceptionally well up to a cost of 100 cycles where we still observe a speedup of 1.57x. The most consistent performance is obtained with perlbench which shows a speedup of 1.18x even with 1000 cycles thread spawn cost. Among the remaining benchmarks there are some that gain little benefit from DBP at any cost level while the rest generally exhibit speedups at least up to a 50 cycle thread spawn cost.

4.3 Thread setup and commit costs

In the next step, we fix the thread spawn cost at 20 cycles and analyze the impact of varying thread setup and commit costs. A cost of 20 cycles for thread spawning achieved speedups for 15 out

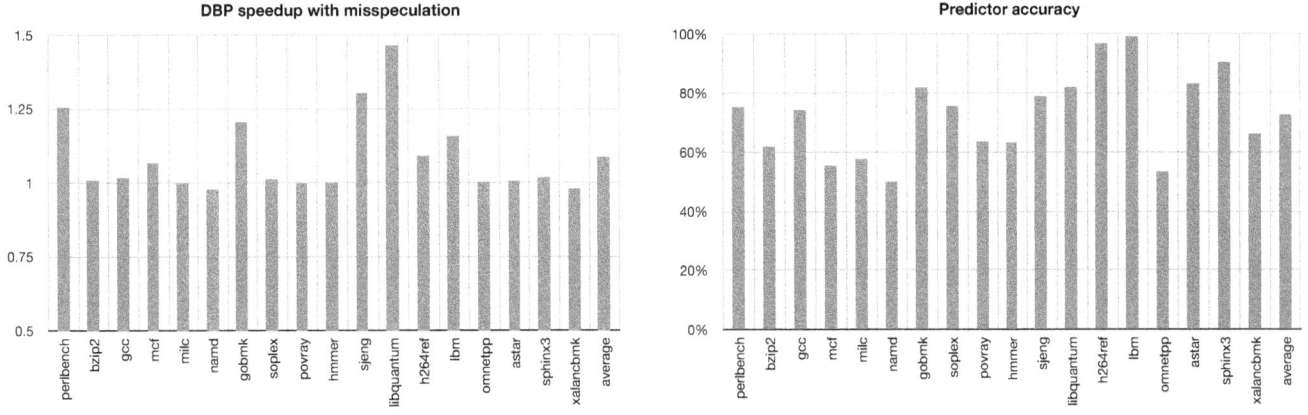

Figure 9. Results for realistic DBP model with mis-speculation and history-based predictor (all costs set to 20 cycles).

of 18 benchmarks in the experiments in the previous section and could be realized in an aggressive hardware implementation.

The thread setup and commit costs are set to values between 5 and 1000 cycles each. This again covers a relatively wide spectrum between aggressive hardware- and slower software-based DBP implementations. We also include the result for a thread setup and commit cost of zero from the previous section. The results are shown in Figure 8.

With the addition of these costs, the average speedup now ranges from `1.16x` for 5 cycles setup and commit costs to `1.02x` for 1000 cycles. This is a decrease of `3.1%` to `14.8%` in comparison to the speedup achieved with a thread spawn cost of 20 cycles and no other costs.

As the costs are increased, the average speedup decreases at a lower rate than it did when the thread spawn cost was increased in the previous section. This indicates that the introduction of a thread spawn cost mainly resulted in filtering out parallel sections that are too small to lead to any benefit on a realistic system where dynamic parallel execution incurs a penalty. The remaining parallel sections exhibit enough parallelism to absorb additional costs more readily. Nevertheless, some benchmarks, such as `omnetpp` and `hmmer` which exhibited speedups in our previous experiment, do not tolerate the introduction of increased setup and commit costs very well since their parallel sections are still too small or lack a sufficient degree of parallelism.

4.4 Mis-speculation

We have thus far assumed the availability of a perfect predictor to decide whether a section of code should be parallelized. While such a model is useful to show the impact of individual parameters, a realistic scheme has to account for the possibility of mis-speculation and cancellation of threads.

We now introduce a history-based predictor into our model to determine whether a section of the instruction stream should be parallelized and which traces to execute speculatively. We implement a *path-based next trace* predictor [14]. Thread spawn, setup, and commit costs are set to 20 cycles each (in line with previous TLS studies such as [7]) and the cycle penalty for thread invalidation is varied between 5 and 1000 cycles.

It is important to note that, as explained in section 2.3, the thread invalidation penalty represents the cost of operations that need to be carried out when mis-speculation is identified, such as rolling back memory transaction and stopping successor threads. These costs are a feature of the particular implementation of the DBP system and they are what we model by the thread invalidation cost parameter. In addition, mis-speculation incurs a different type of 'cost',

namely the wasteful execution of code until mis-speculation is detected. That cost is determined by the length of the erroneously executed threads and consequently varies in each speculative execution episode. Since we simulate actual parallel execution of the code, our system inherently models this overhead.

The experiments using this configuration show that the amount of the thread invalidation penalty is relatively insignificant compared to other parameters. The change in speedup resulting from varying this cost between 5 and 1000 cycles is `<0.01x` on average. We show the speedup results for a penalty of 20 cycles in Figure 9.

The reason for this low impact of mis-speculation is twofold: the history-based predictor performs surprisingly well with an average accuracy of `72.7%` across benchmarks (see Figure 9); and the amount of cycles gained due to successful speculation is several orders of magnitude larger than those lost due to mis-speculation. Mis-speculation is hence a comparatively rare and low-impact event, the cost of which is easily absorbed by successful speculative parallel executions. This suggests that a DBP scheme can be implemented in a way that permits mis-speculation penalties to be relatively high in relation to other parameters.

The model presented in this section represents a realistic DBP scheme since it includes actual costs for all the events related to parallel execution. The assumption of a penalty of 20 cycles for each of these, in line with previous studies such as [7], implies the need for hardware support for DBP. In this light, the execution speedup results in Figure 9 paint a rather somber picture of the benefit of DBP under realistic assumptions. On one hand, we do achieve a speedup of `1.09x` on average. Three benchmarks exhibit speedups of above `1.25x`. Only two of the benchmarks, `namd` and `xalancbmk`, suffer a minimal slowdown of `0.98x`. On the other hand, the die area likely to be taken up by a hardware DBP implementation and the associated increase in power consumption limit the benefits of using this configuration.

4.5 Benchmark sensitivity

Our results above show that there are large differences across benchmarks in terms of their response to dynamic binary parallelization. To gain a better understanding of this behavior, we investigate four benchmarks in more detail using the realistic DBP model from section 4.4. The two key indicators for the success of DBP are a) *how often* we can speculatively execute code sections in parallel, and b) *what benefit*, or loss, in terms of cycles taken off the critical path can be derived from such parallel executions.

In Figure 10, we show the development of these two factors over time during a complete run of four of the benchmarks. Time is quantized into 2.5s intervals. For each interval, we show the

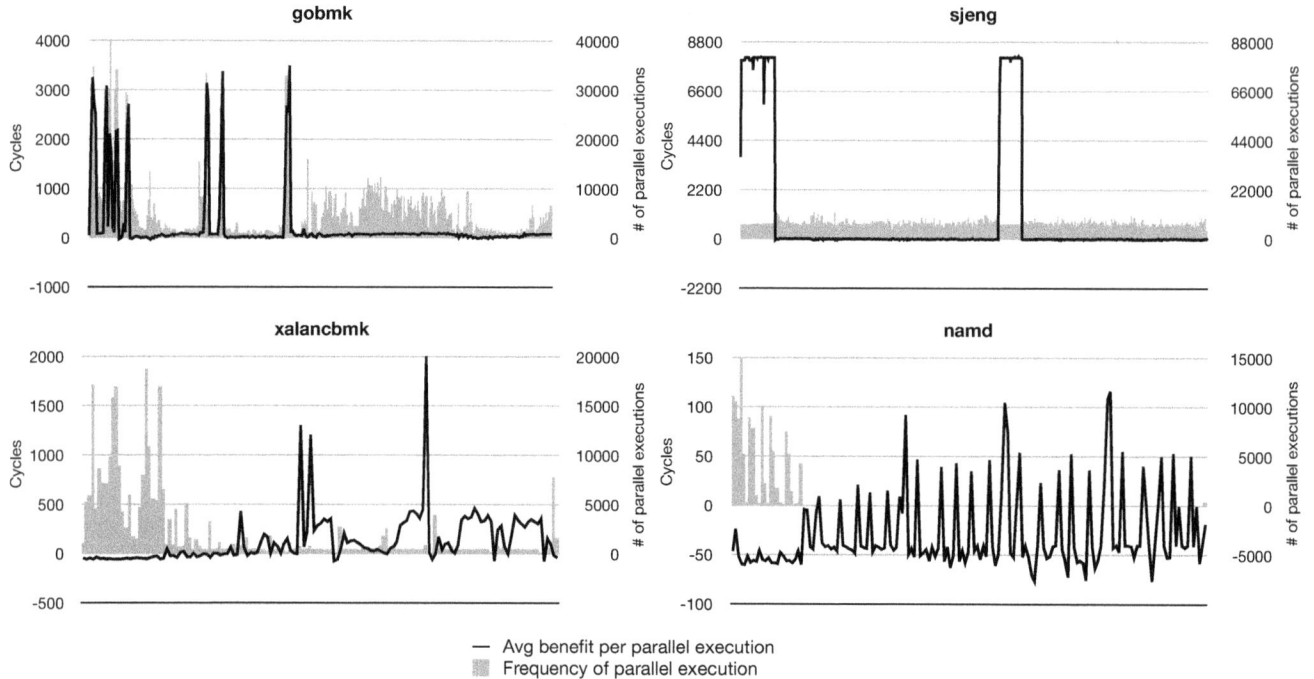

Figure 10. DBP behavior over time, showing both the frequency of speculative parallel execution and the average number of cycles taken off the critical path per parallel execution epoch. Time is quantized into 2.5s intervals.

Benchmark	Speedup	Reason
gobmk	1.21	Moderate, steady gains with high frequency of parallel execution
sjeng	1.30	Brief periods of very high gains
xalancbmk	0.98	High losses due to mis-speculation at beginning of execution
namd	0.98	Overall lack of opportunities for parallelization

Table 2. Sources of speedup or slowdown for benchmarks shown in Figure 10.

number of parallel executions and the average amount of cycles that were offloaded to the speculative cores per parallel execution epoch. This cycle count can be negative for two reasons: firstly, in the case of mis-speculation; and secondly, when speculative execution was successful but the parallel section is not large enough to recoup the costs associated with parallelization.

The first two benchmarks shown, gobmk and sjeng, both achieved significant speedups of above 1.20x in the previous section and were chosen as typical examples for the class of benchmarks that benefit from DBP. On the other hand, xalancbmk and namd are characteristic of the group of benchmarks that do not respond well to DBP, showing slight slowdowns of 0.98x.

The first half of gobmk's execution time is characterized by several brief episodes of high gains from parallel execution. The second half shows a long period of moderate but steady gains. The average number of cycles gained per parallel execution during this period is relatively low, but the high frequency of parallelization means that it becomes one of the main sources of speedup for this benchmark.

Sjeng derives most of its speedup from periods of very high parallelization gains both at the start of its execution and at the beginning of its second half, which result from hot loops that can

be parallelized in their entirety. The remainder of the execution time exhibits only moderate gains.

The xalancbmk benchmark incurs significant losses in the first quarter of its execution due to the high frequency of mis-speculated parallel executions. There are some gains later on, but much less opportunities for parallel execution. The gains cannot fully compensate for earlier losses, so we observe an overall slowdown.

Finally, namd presents much less opportunity for parallel execution than other benchmarks. A period of increased attempts at parallelization at the beginning of its execution incurs losses. During the remainder of the running time, DBP oscillates between gains and losses with even fewer attempts at parallelization. This again results in an overall slowdown.

A summary of these findings is provided in Table 2.

4.6 Comparison with RASP

Hertzberg and Olukotun [9] recently proposed an implementation of a DBP system of the type characterized by our study. RASP is a runtime system based on a dynamic binary translator from X86 to RISC. It leverages idle cores in a CMP to analyze, optimize, and speculatively parallelize sequential programs at runtime and thus enables a collection of simpler cores to achieve sequential performance on par with a significantly more complex core without any need for recompilation or hardware support beyond transactional memory.

RASP relies on aggressive runtime optimizations, such as global value numbering and feedback-guided dynamic loop unrolling, which are not exclusive to DBP and would also benefit sequential runtime systems. If any one of these optimizations is disabled, RASP achieves very similar results to those our study predicted for a realistic system in section 4.4. We measured an average speedup of 1.12x for the integer benchmarks in SPEC CPU2006, while RASP achieves 1.16x for the same benchmarks if dynamic loop unrolling is disabled. With all optimizations turned on, their speedup reaches 1.46x on average.

Comparison with RASP

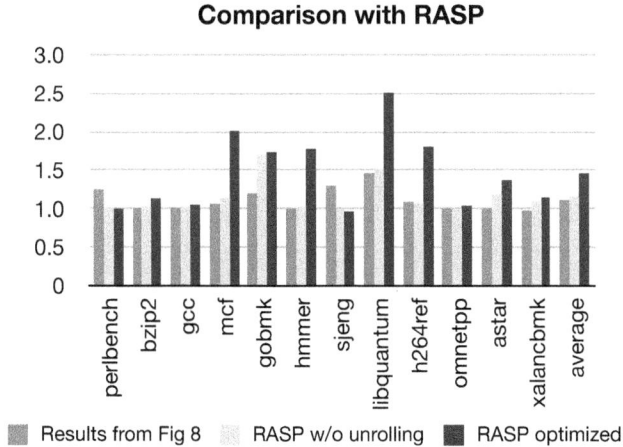

Figure 11. Comparison with [9] showing SPECINT2006 results for realistic DBP system predicted in section 4.4, RASP without dynamic loop unrolling, and RASP with all optimizations enabled.

This indicates that the main benefit of RASP arises from dynamically applied sequential code optimizations – similar to a system like DYNAMO [2] – rather than DBP. We chose not to implement such optimizations in our model as they obscure the innate benefits and drawbacks of DBP.

A detailed comparison of these results and those predicted by our model is shown in Figure 11. The minor variations between our predictions and the raw RASP results are mainly due to differences in the underlying parallelization approach (loops vs. generic *traces*).

5. Limitations

In this section, we briefly discuss some of the limitations of the approach chosen for our study.

Choice of thread identification method. We use region tracing as opposed to other thread identification methods previously described in the literature (see section 6). This choice of tracing was motivated by the large body of work on JIT compilation, where region-based tracing has emerged as a sweet spot between the two extremes of method- and instruction-based JIT compilation [4, 11, 23], balancing the cost of JIT compilation and scope for optimization. Such a region trace-based approach is sufficiently generic to subsume other, more fine-grained, thread identification algorithms since it can express loop, task, and data parallelism at various granularities.

Granularity of region traces. Nonetheless, region traces might be too fine-grained to capture all parallel regions. In our approach, regions are bounded by the page size and can thus reach up to 8k. This should capture most parallel loops. In fact, our experiments have shown that larger traces provide limited benefit due to the increasing number of memory and register dependences.

Overhead of tracing. Our approach is lightweight because we only record basic block entry points (i.e. memory addresses) as nodes, and pairs of source and target entry points as edges in the CFG region traces. In our experiments, we simulate the incremental construction of region traces in trace intervals and thus the delayed availability of opportunities for parallelization (see section 2.2) but we do not model the specific overheads of recording the region traces in the course of execution. It would be possible to implement this lightweight trace recording efficiently in hardware. Compared to the overheads of speculative execution, the analysis of which is the goal of our study, these overheads are significantly smaller.

Level of abstraction. We operate on the level of machine instructions. No attempt was made to raise the level of abstraction, e.g. to reconstruct polyhedral loop representations [19]. A higher level of abstraction would almost certainly create a larger scope for the discovery of parallelism in loops, but the costs would be prohibitive for an on-line method like DBP.

6. Related Work

Unlike its more mature siblings *Dynamic Binary Instrumentation* (DBI) [20] and *Dynamic Binary Translation* (DBT) [1], *Dynamic Binary Parallelization* is an emerging field and has only recently found attention [6, 9, 26–28] within the academic community.

The theoretical availability of significant amounts of parallelism in single-threaded binaries is known from studies like [24], which shows that up to 200% speedup may be obtained from binary parallelization but CMPs with 8-16 cores will be needed to unlock this potential.

Current DBP approaches span the entire range covered by our study, from solutions implemented in hardware [16] to those relying entirely on software runtime systems [26, 28]. All of these approaches are specific to a particular target system and usually focus on improvements resulting from the application of an isolated technique within the context of a distinct implementation. In this paper we instead seek to gain an understanding of the general limits of DBP, independent of any particular implementation.

Thread-level speculation (TLS) has been proposed as a way of extracting parallelism speculatively from legacy applications, but generally relies on complex additional hardware and the availability of source code for recompilation using a TLS-aware compiler. Its limits are evaluated in [13]. The Multiscalar architecture [22] represents an early implementation. Marcuello and González [16] propose a hardware-only TLS implementation, but this comes at the expense of increasing the complexity of the required hardware even further. Jrpm [5] implements TLS-based dynamic parallelization for the JVM.

A study involving manual parallelization of the SPEC2006 benchmarks for a TLS platform has been conducted in [18]. This study confirms the "conventional wisdom" that these benchmarks are 'difficult to parallelize' using traditional parallelizing compilers (Intel's ICC compiler in this case).

Krishnan et al. [15] use an initial offline stage to identify and annotate parallel work units and dependencies between them. The modified binaries are executed on a CMP with hardware speculation support implementing a complex register communication scheme based on synchronizing scoreboards. Pradelle et al. [19] rely entirely on off-line preprocessing of binaries to extract parallel loops using a polyhedral model. Our study differs in that it does not rely on a static preprocessing stage which would be limited in its ability to extract control and data flow information.

A DBP approach based on program slicing is presented in [25]. The speculative slicing algorithm and various other program transformations to expose parallelism are implemented in a runtime system. However, additional hardware for parallel slice execution is required on top of the already complex extensions for speculation support.

RASP [9] was discussed in section 4.6. DeVuyst et al. [6] propose a similar runtime system, but their study does not account for the possibility of mis-speculation and the technique is limited to loop parallelization. A recent paper [27] re-evaluates the feasibility of DBP using a trace parallelization process. This work remains on a proof-of-concept level and neither does it develop a realistic implementation nor a sound limit study.

Yardımcı and Franz [28] dynamically recompile binaries to generate parallelized code for frequently executed code regions. The system is entirely software-based and relies on a prior static analysis stage. It remains open whether there are limits to this approach and how it scales beyond dual-core configurations. In [26], a DBT-based simulator capable of emulating a superscalar X86 processor on the tile-based RAW architecture is presented. Parallelization is achieved by implementing the superscalar pipeline stages on distinct parallel processing elements of the tiled architecture.

7. Summary and Conclusions

In this paper we have experimentally evaluated the limits of dynamic binary parallelization. We target a CMP platform with hardware support for speculation and employ a region trace-based just-in-time parallelization scheme to extract threads for parallel execution. Using a parameterizable cost model for speculation based transactions and cycle-accurate simulation of pipeline and memory behavior we demonstrate that for a small number of relevant benchmarks DBP shows good performance gains, whereas for other benchmarks the improvements are rather small. This is despite a seemingly larger scope for overlapping execution threads. Our study confirms that for realistic speculative execution costs DBP suffers from diminishing returns. Cores in a many-core CMP cannot be made arbitrarily small without impeding single-thread performance, since DBP in its current form can only compensate for a relatively small loss of single-core performance through parallel execution.

We envisage a much greater potential for the technology if prior information – such as profiling data from previous runs of the application or static analysis of the source code – is available in a hybrid system and can be exploited during dynamic parallelization. We plan to investigate this further evolution of DBP in future work. In the near future, it seems likely that the next generation of CMPs will still rely on at least one ILP-rich CPU core to provide sufficient single-thread performance for workloads that contain significant portions of sequential code.

References

[1] E. R. Altman, D. R. Kaeli, and Y. Sheffer. Welcome to the opportunities of binary translation. *Computer*, 33(3):40–45, Mar. 2000.

[2] V. Bala, E. Duesterwald, and S. Banerjia. Dynamo: a transparent dynamic optimization system. In *Proceedings of the ACM SIGPLAN 2000 Conference on Programming Language Design and Implementation*, pages 1–12, New York, NY, USA, 2000. ACM.

[3] G. Blake, R. G. Dreslinski, and T. Mudge. A survey of multicore processors. *IEEE Signal Processing Magazine*, 26(6):26–37, Oct. 2009.

[4] I. Böhm, T. J. Edler von Koch, S. C. Kyle, B. Franke, and N. Topham. Generalized just-in-time trace compilation using a parallel task farm in a dynamic binary translator. *ACM SIGPLAN Conference on Programming Language Design and Implementation*, 2011.

[5] M. Chen and K. Olukotun. The Jrpm system for dynamically parallelizing java programs. *ACM/IEEE International Symposium on Computer Architecture*, 2003.

[6] M. DeVuyst, D. M. Tullsen, and S. W. Kim. Runtime parallelization of legacy code on a transactional memory system. *International Conference on High Performance Embedded Architectures and Compilers*, 2011.

[7] L. Gao, L. Li, J. Xue, and T.-F. Ngai. Loop recreation for thread-level speculation. In *International Conference on Parallel and Distributed Systems*, 2007.

[8] M. Gillespie. Preparing for the second stage of multi-core hardware: Asymmetric (heterogeneous) cores. Technical report, Intel, 2009. URL http://software.intel.com/file/1639.

[9] B. Hertzberg and K. Olukotun. Runtime automatic speculative parallelization. *International Symposium on Code Generation and Optimization*, 2011.

[10] M. D. Hill and M. R. Marty. Amdahl's law in the multicore era. *Computer*, 41:33–38, July 2008.

[11] H. Inoue, H. Hayashizaki, P. Wu, and T. Nakatani. A trace-based java jit compiler retrofitted from a method-based compiler. In *Proceedings of the 9th Annual IEEE/ACM International Symposium on Code Generation and Optimization*, pages 246–256, Washington, DC, USA, 2011. IEEE Computer Society.

[12] Intel. Single-chip cloud computer: Project. http://www.intel.co.uk/content/www/us/en/research/intel-labs-single-chip-cloud-computer.html, 2012.

[13] N. Ioannou, J. Singer, S. Khan, P. Xekalakis, P. Yiapanis, A. Pocock, G. Brown, M. Lujan, I. Watson, and M. Cintra. Toward a more accurate understanding of the limits of the TLS execution paradigm. *IEEE International Symposium on Workload Characterization*, 2010.

[14] Q. Jacobson, E. Rotenberg, and J. Smith. Path-based next trace prediction. *30th Annual International Symposium on Microarchitecture*, 1997.

[15] V. Krishnan and J. Torrellas. Hardware and software support for speculative execution of sequential binaries on a chip-multiprocessor. In *Proceedings of the 12th International Conference on Supercomputing*, International Conference on Supercomputing, pages 85–92, New York, NY, USA, 1998. ACM.

[16] P. Marcuello and A. González. Clustered speculative multithreaded processors. *International Conference on Supercomputing*, 1999.

[17] P. Marcuello and A. González. Thread-spawning schemes for speculative multithreading. *International Symposium on High Performance Computer Architecture*, 2002.

[18] V. Packirisamy, A. Zhai, W.-C. Hsu, P.-C. Yew, and T.-F. Ngai. Exploring speculative parallelism in SPEC2006. *IEEE International Symposium on Performance Analysis of Systems and Software*, 2009.

[19] B. Pradelle, A. Ketterlin, and P. Clauss. Polyhedral parallelization of binary code. *ACM Trans. Archit. Code Optim.*, 8(4):39:1–39:21, Jan. 2012.

[20] V. J. Reddi, A. Settle, D. A. Connors, and R. S. Cohn. PIN: a binary instrumentation tool for computer architecture research and education. *Workshop on Computer Architecture Education*, 2004.

[21] M. Reilly. When multicore isn't enough: Trends and the future for multi-multicore systems. *High Performance Embedded Computing Workshop*, 2008.

[22] G. S. Sohi, S. E. Breach, and T. N. Vijaykumar. Multiscalar processors. *ACM/IEEE International Symposium on Computer Architecture*, 1995.

[23] T. Suganuma, T. Yasue, and T. Nakatani. A region-based compilation technique for a java just-in-time compiler. In *Proceedings of the ACM SIGPLAN 2003 Conference on Programming Language Design and Implementation*, pages 312–323, New York, NY, USA, 2003. ACM.

[24] N. Vachharajani, M. Iyer, C. Ashok, M. Vachharajani, D. I. August, and D. Connors. Chip multi-processor scalability for single-threaded applications. *SIGARCH Comput. Archit. News*, 33:44–53, Nov 2005.

[25] C. Wang, Y. Wu, E. Borin, S. Hu, W. Liu, D. Sager, T. F. Ngai, and J. Fang. Dynamic parallelization of single-threaded binary programs using speculative slicing. *International Conference on Supercomputing*, 2009.

[26] D. Wentzlaff and A. Agarwal. Constructing virtual architectures on a tiled processor. *International Symposium on Code Generation and Optimization*, 2006.

[27] J. Yang, K. Skadron, M. Soffa, and K. Whitehouse. Feasibility of dynamic binary parallelization. *3rd USENIX Workshop on Hot Topics in Parallelism*, 2011.

[28] E. Yardımcı and M. Franz. Dynamic parallelization and mapping of binary executables on hierarchical platforms. *ACM International Conference on Computing Frontiers*, 2006.

Improving Dynamic Binary Optimization Through Early-Exit Guided Code Region Formation

Chun-Chen Hsu   Pangfeng Liu

National Taiwan University
{d95006,pangfeng}@csie.ntu.edu.tw

Jan-Jan Wu

Institute of Information Science,
Academia Sinica
wuj@iis.sinica.edu.tw

Pen-Chung Yew

University of Minnesota
yew@cs.umn.edu

Ding-Yong Hong

Institute of Information Science,
Academia Sinica
dyhong@iis.sinica.edu.tw

Wei-Chung Hsu

National Chiao Tung University
hsu@cs.nctu.edu.tw

Chien-Min Wang

Institute of Information Science,
Academia Sinica
cmwang@iis.sinica.edu.tw

Abstract

Most dynamic binary translators (DBT) and optimizers (DBO) target *binary traces*, i.e. frequently executed paths, as code regions to be translated and optimized. *Code region formation* is the most important first step in all DBTs and DBOs. The quality of the dynamically formed code regions determines the extent and the types of optimization opportunities that can be exposed to DBTs and DBOs, and thus, determines the ultimate quality of the final optimized code. The *Next-Executing-Tail (NET)* trace formation method used in HP Dynamo is an early example of such techniques. Many existing trace formation schemes are variants of NET. They work very well for most binary traces, but they also suffer a major problem: the formed traces may contain a large number of early exits that could be branched out during the execution. If this happens frequently, the program execution will spend more time in the slow binary interpreter or in the unoptimized code regions than in the optimized traces in code cache. The benefit of the trace optimization is thus lost. Traces/regions with frequently taken early-exits are called delinquent traces/regions. Our empirical study shows that at least 8 of the 12 SPEC CPU2006 integer benchmarks have delinquent traces.

In this paper, we propose a light-weight region formation technique called *Early-Exit Guided Region Formation (EEG)* to improve the quality of the formed traces/regions. It iteratively identifies and merges delinquent regions into larger code regions. We have implemented our EEG algorithm in two LLVM-based multithreaded DBTs targeting ARM and IA32 instruction set architecture (ISA), respectively. Using SPEC CPU2006 benchmark suite with reference inputs, our results show that compared to an NET-variant currently used in QEMU, a state-of-the-art retargetable DBT, EEG can achieve a significant performance improvement of

up to 72% (27% on average), and to 49% (23% on average) for IA32 and ARM, respectively.

Categories and Subject Descriptors C.4 [*Performance of Systems*]: Modeling techniques; D.3.4 [*Processors*]: Incremental Compilers; D.3.4 [*Processors*]: Optimization; D.3.4 [*Processors*]: Run-time environments

General Terms Design, Performance

Keywords Dynamic Binary Translation, Trace-Based JIT Compilation, Virtual Machine, Hardware-based Performance Monitoring, Hot Region Formation

1. Introduction

Dynamic binary translation and optimization are core technologies in system virtualization [22]. Most dynamic binary translators (DBTs) and optimizers (DBOs) target *binary traces*, i.e. frequently executed paths, as code regions to be translated and optimized. *Code region formation* is the most important first step in all DBTs and DBOs. The quality of the dynamically formed code regions determines the extent and the types of optimization opportunities that can be exposed to DBTs and DBOs, and thus, determines the ultimate quality of the final optimized code. As code regions are formed by traces, we will use the terms *trace* and *region* interchangeably for the rest of the paper.

Many DBT and DBO systems [6, 7] follow the well-known runtime trace formation algorithm, called Next-Executing-Tail (NET), developed in HP Dynamo [3].

Instead of profiling all execution traces at runtime to select the hottest trace, NET forms a trace by selecting the basic blocks[1] that are most recently executed. The idea is that when a basic block becomes hot, it is likely that the following basic blocks are also hot.

As a hot trace is formed by cascading a sequence of hot basic blocks, there will be a conditional branch at the end of each member basic block, referred to as the *early exit* of the trace. DBTs needs to generate *compensation code* at each of such early exits to handle the case when the conditional branch is taken [22]. If early exits are frequent, then not only will such extra compensation code need

---

[1] A basic block is a sequence of instructions terminated by a control transfer instruction

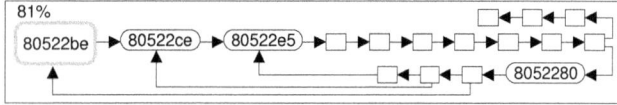

(a) CFG of the for-loop in 456.hmmer.

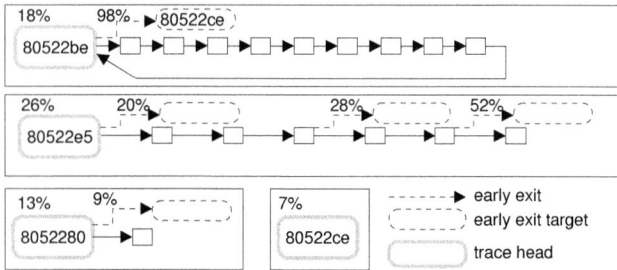

(b) Traces generated by NET

Figure 1. An example of delinquent traces of NET in 456.hmmer.

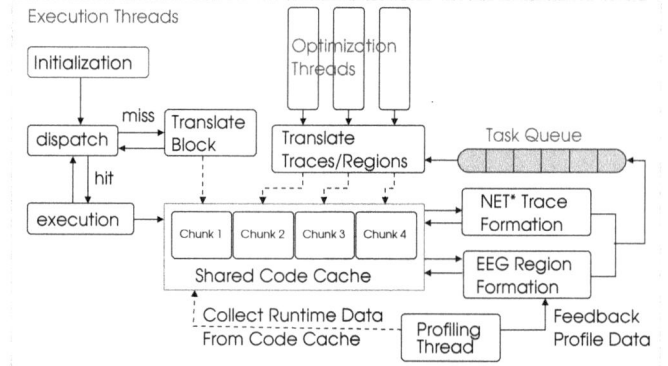

Figure 2. Control flow of execution threads and optimization threads

to be executed, but also program execution will spend more time in the slow binary interpreter or in unoptimized code regions. The benefit of trace optimization by the DBT is thus lost. Traces with frequently taken early-exits are called *delinquent* traces.

Since NET does not use edge profiling [3] information to select next basic blocks, early exits may occur when program behavior changes in different execution phases. For example, the function P7Viterbi in 456.hmmer (a SPEC 2006 CPU benchmark) contributes most of its execution time. P7Viterbi updates global variables according to different conditions in a performance critical for-loop as shown in Figure 1(a).

NET splits the for-loop into four traces as shown in Figure 1(b). Each large rectangle represents a trace. The execution time of each trace, shown as the percentage of total execution time, is noted on the left top corner of the trace. The probability of an early exit being taken is also noted on each exit edge. Figure 1(b) shows a trace for a loop starting at 0x80522be. The probability of taking an early exit during the loop execution is 98%. Such a high probability for an early exit will certainly diminish the performance benefit expected from the loop trace. Our proposed region formation technique (see Section 3) will merge those four traces into a large code region shown in Figure 1(a), which can improve its performance by 68%.

To accomplish this, we propose a light-weight technique called *Early-Exit Guided (EEG) region formation* to detect and merge delinquent regions. There are two key issues in EEG: (1) which regions should be merged, and (2) when to merge those regions. A simple approach for the first issue is to instrument counters into all traces. However, this approach is prohibitively expensive. Instead, we employ hardware-assisted dynamic profiling to select hot regions and to avoid monitoring and merging unimportant regions. To address the second issue, we monitor regions by instrumenting counters to detect early exits. When the counter exceeds a threshold, we merge this region with the region that begins at the branch target of the early exit. We also employ a heuristic to decide whether it is beneficial to merge the selected regions or not. We will not merge regions if it will cause too much register pressure; i.e. too many store/load operations to spill and fill values between registers and the stack (see Section 3.4).

We summarize the main contributions of this work as follows:

1. Our experimental results show that there is a substantial amount of delinquent traces, and that more than 100 early exits are taken for every million executed instructions in 65% of SPEC CPU2006 integer benchmarks. We proposed an *Early-Exit-Guided region formation* algorithm (EEG) that uses hardware-

assisted dynamic profiling and instrumented software counters to detect and merge delinquent traces/regions into larger regions.

2. We implement the EEG scheme in two LLVM-based [1] multi-threaded DBTs targeting ARM and IA32 instruction set architecture (ISAs), respectively. They off-load DBTs to other cores and allow more aggressive and sophisticated optimizations to be done on the larger code regions formed by EEG.

3. Using SPEC CPU2006 benchmark suite with reference inputs, our results show that compared to NET, EEG can achieve a significant performance improvement of up to 72% (27% on average) for IA32, and to 49% (23% on average) for ARM.

The rest of the paper is organized as follows. Section 2 presents our region-based multi-threaded DBT. Section 3 describes our early exit detection technique and early-exit guided region formation scheme. Section 4 presents our experimental results. Section 5 describes related work, and Section 6 gives some concluding remarks.

2. Region-Based Multi-threaded Dynamic Binary Translator

In this section, we describe the design of our region-based multi-threaded dynamic binary translator, called LnQ [14]. We have implemented the EEG scheme in LnQ. LnQ uses QEMU [2] as the front-end emulation engine, and uses LLVM [1] compilation infrastructure to handle its back-end code optimization and target code generation. We implement our EEG scheme using this framework. Figure 2 shows the major components and the control flow of our region-based multi-threaded dynamic binary translator.

We use *code segments* to refer *basic blocks* and *traces/regions*, and use *code fragment* to refer a *translated* code segment by DBT. Therefore, there are *basic block fragments* and *trace/region fragments*. Each code fragment has a *prologue* to load the guest architecture states, such as the content of the guest registers, from the memory to the host registers before execution. Also, each code fragment has an epilogue to store modified machine states back to memory before leaving the code fragment. Each code fragment has its own register mapping decided by the LLVM register allocator.

LnQ uses *execution threads* and *optimization threads*. *Execution threads* are responsible for translating basic blocks and executing translated code fragments. That is, if an *execution thread* reaches a new guest basic block during execution, the execution thread generates a *basic block fragment* using LLVM. *Optimization threads* generate optimized traces and regions fragments also using LLVM. Execution threads compile blocks with "O0" optimization level to minimize compilation overhead. On the other hand, optimization threads compile traces and regions with "O2" to generate optimized code. All execution threads share one software code cache. As shown in Figure 2, we partition the code cache into *sections*, and each thread has its own section to store the translated code fragments so that threads can generate code concurrently.

The DBT system separates trace compilation from program execution. By running optimization threads concurrently on other cores, the execution threads are not disrupted. Execution threads may create region compilation tasks and send them to a *Task Queue* (see Figure 2) when traces or regions are formed as described in Section 3. We use a lock-free concurrent FIFO queue [19] to implement the *task queue* so that execution threads can insert trace/region compilation tasks into the queue while the optimization threads take those tasks from the queue without locks.

When an optimization thread generates a new trace or region, it dispatch execution threads to the newly generated code fragment by *atomically* patching jump instructions in the code cache. To do this in IA32, we need to align the patched instructions to 4-byte alignment, and use the self-branch technique mentioned in [24] to patch jumps atomically.

3. Early Exit Index and Early-Exit Guided Region Selection

In this section, we first describe the NET algorithm used in our system. We then define an *early exit index* to quantify how often early exits are taken in a trace. Finally we describe our early exit guided region selection technique.

3.1 Trace Selection Algorithm

We adopt a modified NET algorithm called *NET**, which is similar to [6], to builds traces. The difference is that NET* considers *all* basic blocks as *potential* trace head candidates, while NET only considers blocks which are targets of backward branches as *trace head* candidates in that they may form potential loops.

The NET* algorithm has two advantages. First, the NET algorithm [3] was designed for DBT systems in which a *single* DBT thread is responsible for both execution and trace building. To reduce the overhead of building traces, NET needs to be very selective in potential traces. In contrast, NET* can take advantage of modern multi-core platforms to offload the overhead of building traces. Hence, it can afford to try all basic blocks as potential trace heads.

Second, NET may not identify all loops by only considering targets of backward branches. By considering all basic blocks as possible trace heads, NET* can discover more hot traces than NET can. As reported in Section 4.1.1, NET* achieves 12% and 5% performance improvement on average over NET for SPEC CINT2006 and CFP2006 benchmarks, respectively.

Our NET* algorithm works as follows. We instrument software counters to record the number of times each block is executed. A block becomes a *trace head* when the number of times the block has been executed exceeds a threshold value. NET* forms a trace by appending blocks along the execution path until one of the following terminal conditions is met: (1) A branch to the trace head is taken, (2) The number of blocks exceeds a threshold, (3) The next block is the head of another trace, or (4) A guest system call instruction is encountered.

3.2 Early Exit Index

We first define an *early exit* of a trace. A trace can be a straight-line execution path or a cycle. If a trace is a straight-line path, then all exit edges along the path are early exits except the exit edge of the

last basic block in the trace. If a trace is a cycle, all exit edges are early exit.

We define an *Early-Exit Index* (EEI) to measure the frequency of early exits taken in traces. More specifically, EEI is the number of early exits being taken for every million instructions executed in traces. It can be formally defined as in the following equation.

$$EEI = \frac{\sum_{i \in \Gamma} n_i \times \rho_i}{N}$$

where Γ is the set of traces, n_i is the number of times early exits being taken in trace i, ρ_i is the percentage of instructions executed in trace i, and N is the number of million instructions executed.

3.3 Early-Exit Guided Region Selection

In this section, we describe our proposed Early-Exit Guided (EEG) region selection scheme. It detects and merges regions that have frequently taken early exits. The key issues in EEG are (1) how to efficiently detect delinquent regions; and (2) when to merge them at runtime. We address them as follows.

The simplest approach to address the first issue is to instrument counters in all traces and regions. However, this approach is inefficient and may merge too many regions that are not frequently executed. Instead, we use a dynamic profiling approach with the help of on-chip hardware performance monitor (HPM) to select hot regions.

We create a profiling thread called *profiler* at the beginning of execution to perform dynamic profiling. The profiler collects program counters periodically for every million instructions retired. When a threshold number of samples are collected, the profiler accumulates the sample counts for each trace to determine the degree of *hotness* of each trace. The hotness of a trace is measured by the following equation.

$$H_T = \max\{\alpha, \beta\}$$

Here, α is the percentage of instructions executed in the trace during the *last* sampling period, and β is the percentage of instructions executed in the trace during the *entire* execution. Intuitively, α represents the hotness of the trace during the last period, and β represents the accumulated *hotness* during the entire execution. We choose the maximum of α and β as its hotness measure.

When the hotness of a trace exceeds a threshold, we start monitoring the trace by instrumenting counters to its early exits. Currently, we only monitor the early exits of conditional branches. If a counter exceeds a pre-defined threshold, it means the control leaves the region through the corresponding early exit very frequently. Then, we merge the monitored region with the target region of the early exit. We translate and optimize the merged region with our LLVM-based DBT, and replace the monitored region with the merged region.

We argue that the overhead of the instrumentation is negligible because early exits should be rarely taken. A frequently taken early exit would have triggered region formation when the counter exceeded the threshold.

3.4 Spill Index of a Region

The benefits of EEG region formation come from eliminating the overhead caused by frequently taken early exits, and potential optimization opportunities from a larger code region. Despite the fact that we can mostly eliminate the overhead of frequently taken early exits via region merging, we may not always have potential optimization opportunities from the merged region. In particular, if the quality of the translated code of a region is not good enough, it is not beneficial to merge such a region.

We define an index, called *Spill Index*, to assess the quality of the code generated by the LLVM compiler for a region formed

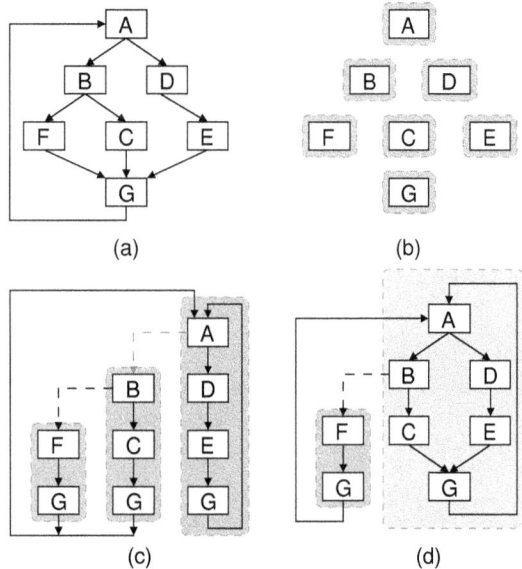

Figure 3. Illustration of region selection.

by the EEG technique. A *spill instruction* is an instruction for load/store operations between registers and stack. The *Spill Index* is the percentage of spill instructions in the translated code fragment. When the Spill Index of a code fragment exceeds a threshold, that region should not be further merged because a high percentage of spill instructions often forestalls good performance due to improper register allocation of the LLVM compiler.

3.5 Region Versus Trace

By creating larger regions, we reduce the amount of specialization that the compiler can do for traces. As we know, the benefit of traces comes from the instruction scheduling within traces [15].

However, we need to limit the instruction scheduling optimizations when we compile traces in dynamic binary translation, because we have to rematerialize full guest state in case a hardware exception or a signal was raised.

The main advantage of EEG region formation is that it can improve DBT performance by removing transition overhead among traces, such as removing redundant loads/stores of guest state among traces.

We use Figure 3 as an example to illustrate our region formation strategy. Figure 3(a) is the control flow graph (CFG) of a hot region in a guest application. During execution, each block is first translated as shown in Figure 3(b). Then NET* forms three traces as in Figure 3(c). Trace A would be the first selected for early exit detection (see Figure 3(c)) since a loop is likely to become hot. Thus the early exit of A, marked by a dashed arrow from the trace started with A (enclosed by the dotted rectangular) to the trace started with B, is monitored with an instrumented software counter.

We merge Trace A and Trace B to form a code region when the early exit is taken frequently. A code region, called Region A and is enclosed in the dotted rectangular in Figure 3(d), that consists of traces A and B is formed. After the code fragment of Region A is formed, we replace Trace A and Trace B with Region A so that Trace F now branches to Region A rather than to Trace A. Note that Region A will not be monitored because the spill index of Region A exceeds the threshold.

4. Experiments

In this section, we evaluate the performance of Early-Exit-Guided region selection algorithm in our LLVM-based parallel DBT systems. We start by describing our measurement methodology.

We evaluate the performance with SPEC CPU 2006 benchmarks on a 3.3GHz quad-core Intel Core i7 machine. The machine has 12 GB main memory and the operating system is 64-bit Gentoo Linux with kernel version 2.6.30. We use the *LnQ* [14] dynamic binary translation framework to build two translators which translate IA32 and ARM guest ISAs to x86_64 host ISA. For CFP2006 benchmarks, we only compile them into IA32 binaries because most CFP2006 benchmarks are written in Fortran and the ARM tool chain we use does not provide cross-compilation for Fortran. The result of ARM 464.h264ref is not reported because the SPEC runspec tool reports a mis-match error even when it runs 464.h264ref in a native ARM machine.

The benchmarks are compiled with GCC 4.3.4 for IA32 binaries and GCC 4.4.1 for ARM binaries. For all benchmarks, "-O2" flag is used. For IA32 benchmarks, we use "-m32" to generate IA32 binaries. For CFP2006, we use "-msse2 -mfpmath=sse" extra flags to generate SSE vector instructions. We use *runspec* script provided by SPEC to run benchmarks and report the median of 5 runs for all performance metrics.

We compare three region selection strategies in our experiments, which are *NET*, *NET** and *EEG* as described in Section 3. In EEG strategy, we first use NET* to select traces, and use EEG to merge traces into regions. We set block count threshold to 50 and allow at most 16 blocks in a trace. For EEG strategy, the threshold of spill index is set to 15%, i.e. regions cannot be further merged when the percentage of spill instructions in the translated fragment exceeds 15%.

We use Perfmon2 [21] for hardware-assisted dynamic profiling to collect runtime information for every one million retired instructions. The early exit threshold is set to 1000 and we use two optimization threads to compile traces and regions in all experiments.

4.1 Performance Results of SPEC CPU2006

The performance results of SPEC CPU2006 are shown in Figure 4 and Figure 5. For clearness of presentation, the benchmarks in both figures are sorted in decreasing order of speedup ratio so that it is easier to see the maximum, the minimum, and the geometric average of the results. We explain the results in the following sections.

4.1.1 Performance of NET*

The performance of NET* algorithm compared to NET in SPEC CINT2006 benchmarks is shown as red bars in Figure 4. For CINT2006 benchmarks, NET* achieves an average improvement of 12% and 10% for the IA32 and ARM benchmarks, respectively, with up to 53% and 46% for IA32 456.hmmer and ARM 471.omnetpp. The results show that NET* discovers more hot traces than NET does by considering all blocks as possible trace heads, and our DBTs do not incur significant overhead because the compilation overhead is offloaded to optimization threads.

We notice that only ARM 462.libquantum has 8% slowdown. We compare traces generated by the two algorithms and show the difference, in Figure 6, among traces generated by NET and NET* for a hot loop in function quantum_toffoli of 462.libquantum.

As shown in Figure 6 (a) and 6 (b), both NET and NET* have the same trace T-d10c, but NET* splits trace T-d094 of NET into T-d094 and T-d0b4 because NET* generates T-d0b4 before T-d094. The transition between traces T-d094 and T-d0b4 in NET* results in 8% slowdown compared to NET.

However, both NET and NET* have the delinquent trace T-d10c with frequently taken early exit to T-d094 due to an unbi-

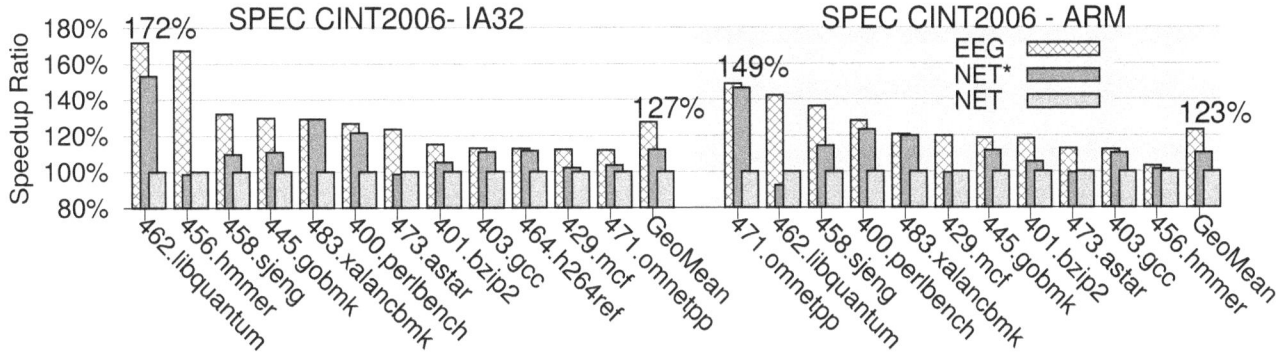

Figure 4. Performance results of NET* and EEG compared to NET in IA32 and ARM SPEC CINT2006.

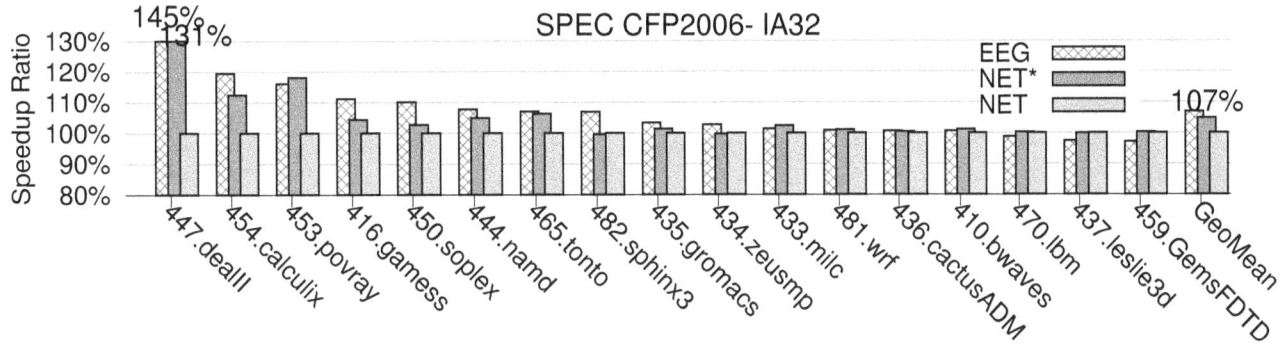

Figure 5. Performance results of NET* and EEG compared to NET in SPEC CFP2006.

ased branch in block d10c. In the next section, we show that EEG can merge the delinquent trace T-d10c into one region as shown in Figure 6(c) and improves the performance of NET* by 54%.

Figure 5 shows the speedup ratio of NET* algorithm with NET as baseline performance for the SPEC CFP 2006 benchmarks. NET* achieves significant improvement only in 447.dealII, 453.povray, and 454.calculix (31%, 18% and 12% respectively), and it gains 4.9% improvement on average in CFP2006 benchmarks. Most CFP2006 benchmarks spend their time in small number of hot loops, which can all be identified by NET and NET*. Thus, there is little difference between traces of NET and NET* in these benchmarks.

4.1.2 Performance of EEG Region Selection

The performance of EEG compared to NET in SPEC CINT2006 benchmarks is shown in Figure 4. For CINT 2006 benchmarks, EEG achieves an average improvement of 27.5% and 23% for the IA32 and ARM benchmarks, respectively, with up to 71.7% and 49% for IA32 456.hmmer and ARM 471.omnetpp. Merging traces can reduce the prologue and epilogue code executed hence the transition overhead among different traces/regions are reduced. As we will see in Section 4.3, the execution with EEG has less memory and branch operations compared to NET.

We now take a closer look at IA32 456.hmmer and ARM 462.libquantum to give more insight of the benefit of EEG. In 456.hmmer, the hottest function is P7Viterbi, which updates global variables according to different conditions in a performance critical for-loop. NET* splits this loop into four traces as shown in Figure 1(a).

Consequently, the transition among four traces results in significant overhead. Through early exit detection, EEG merges four traces into one region containing the loop as shown in Figure 1(b).

The merged region achieves 70% performance improvement because of the elimination of the transition overhead among traces.

For 462.libquantum, NET* splits a for-loop of function quantum_toffoli into three traces as shown in Figure 6(b). As described in the previous section, trace T-d10c is a delinquent trace with a frequently taken early exit to trace T-d094 due to an unbiased branch in block d10c. EEG improves performance by 54% by merging the two traces into one region as shown in Figure 6(c).

As shown in Figure 5, EEG improves NET* by 4.8% to 7% on CFP2006. The improvement is minor because there are few early exits in these floating point benchmarks. In the next section, we measure the early exit index and show the relation between the number of early exits and the performance improvement.

We also observe that EEG loses 2.7% and 2.9% performance compared to NET in 437.leslie3d, and 459.GemsFDTD respectively. In 437.leslie3d, the time is spent in a small number of nested loops in the procedure EXTRAPI of file tml.f. The regions generated by EEG contain nested loops while each trace generated by NET contains only the innermost loop. Therefore, in 437.leslie3d and 459.GemsFDTD, the translated code for traces is better than translated code for regions. As a result, EEG loses about 2.7% performance compared to NET.

4.2 Early Exit Index

In this section, we measure the Early Exit Index (EEI) of benchmarks with the NET* strategy. We insert counters at each side exit to collect the number of early exits taken in each trace, and we measure the execution frequency of traces by sampling program counters per one million retired instructions. We calculate EEI with the collected numbers as described in Section 3.2. The results are shown in Figure 7. The Y-axis on the left side shows the measured

27

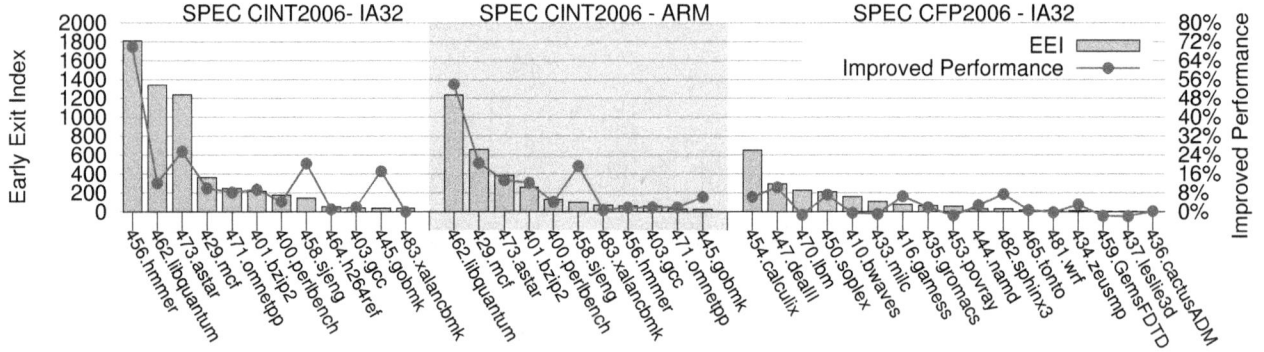

Figure 7. Measured Early Exit Index in NET* and the performance improvement of EEG.

IA32 CINT2006	Improved Ratio	Reduced Instructions or Misses			ARM CINT2006	Improved Ratio	Reduced Instructions or Misses		
		MemInst	BrInst	L1 ICache Misses			MemInst	BrInst	L1 ICache Misses
456.hmmer	69.9%	52.8%	36.9%	31.0%	462.libquantum	54.0%	69.0%	15.8%	-1.3%
473.astar	25.5%	35.4%	20.4%	3.3%	429.mcf	20.5%	45.5%	17.3%	59.4%
458.sjeng	20.4%	29.9%	17.0%	43.7%	458.sjeng	19.2%	17.9%	11.5%	35.5%
445.gobmk	17.1%	18.2%	7.6%	29.2%	473.astar	13.3%	21.1%	10.7%	3.7%
462.libquantum	12.1%	33.6%	9.3%	0.7%	401.bzip2	12.2%	26.8%	13.9%	20.4%
429.mcf	9.9%	33.9%	14.7%	18.2%	445.gobmk	6.1%	6.5%	5.3%	17.6%
401.bzip2	9.3%	18.8%	11.8%	19.0%	400.perlbench	4.1%	3.3%	6.3%	13.2%
471.omnetpp	8.2%	17.2%	7.1%	46.2%	471.omnetpp	1.8%	-0.8%	1.6%	7.8%
400.perlbench	4.2%	9.5%	4.1%	15.1%	456.hmmer	1.7%	0.2%	0.7%	59.7%
403.gcc	1.9%	5.6%	1.8%	9.8%	483.xalancbmk	0.7%	1.5%	7.2%	2.9%
464.h264ref	1.0%	1.3%	2.5%	18.6%	403.gcc	-0.6%	0.1%	2.4%	4.7%
483.xalancbmk	0.0%	6.8%	-3.5%	3.0%					

Table 1. Reduced memory/branch instructions and cache misses of EEG for CINT2006 benchmarks.

early exit indices; the Y-axis on the right side shows the performance improvement of EEG compared to NET*.

In Figure 7, we observe that integer benchmarks are likely to have high EEI values. For example, 65% of CINT2006 benchmarks have EEI values larger than 100, which means there are over 100 early exits per million instructions in those benchmarks in NET*. CINT 2006 benchmarks also show positive correlation between early exit index and performance improvement. The correlation coefficient of IA32 CINT2006 and ARM CINT2006 are 0.78 and 0.93.

For CFP2006 benchmarks, all the EEI values are relatively small compared to those in integer benchmarks. Only 35% of the benchmarks have EEI values larger than 100. The correlation coefficient of early exit index is 0.43 in CFP2006. Small EEI values are due to the fact that floating point benchmarks usually spend most of their time in simple loops with fewer early exits. We also notice that some benchmarks with small EEI values achieve good performance improvements, such as 445.sjeng and 445.gobmk, which improve 20% and 17%, with EEI values as low as 143 and 36 respectively. In the next section, we collect performance profiles to further analyze the sources of improvement.

4.3 Performance Profiles of EEG

In this section, we collect the number of *memory*, *branch* instructions and the *L1 instruction cache misses* of NET* and EEG through hardware performance monitoring. We calculate the percentage of reduced memory/branch operations and cache misses in EEG compared to NET*. We focus on the profiles of CINT2006, which are shown in Table 1.

As shown in Table 1, benchmarks with large improvement tend to have high percentage of reduced operations or L1 instruction cache misses. For example, IA32 456.hmmer reduces 52.8%, 36.9% and 31% of memory, branch instructions and L1 i-cache misses, and achieves 70% improvement over NET*. There are also significant percentage of reduced instructions and misses in 458.sjeng and 445.gobmk, which contributes to the improvement of these two benchmarks. The profiling data show that EEG can not only reduce the memory and branch instructions but also reduces L1 instruction cache misses by merging delinquent traces into regions.

4.4 Effect of The Threshold of Spill Index

In this section, we study the effect of the threshold of spill index, described in Section 3.4, on the performance of EEG. As shown in Figure 8(a), the performance of EEG is less sensitive to the threshold of spill index for IA32 benchmarks except 471.omnetpp. The results show that the register pressure is not a problem in the region fragments of IA32 benchmarks because the IA32 guest architecture has only 8 general purpose registers while there are 16 registers on x86_64 host architecture.

For 471.omnetpp, the performance degrades by 13.5% when the threshold changes from 15% to 20%. The reason is that when threshold changes from 15% to 20%, the spill index of the hottest fragment changes from 18% to 36% because that fragment merges one more region and its CFG becomes complex when threshold is set to 20%. As a result, the extra spill instructions degrade the performance of 471.omnetpp.

(a) Results of IA32 CINT2006.　　　　　　　　(b) Results of ARM CINT2006.

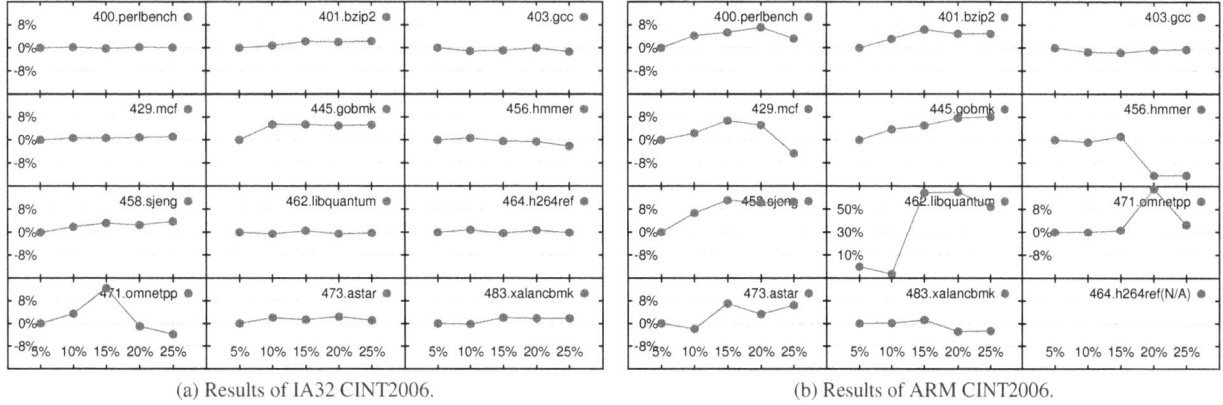

Figure 8. Effect of spill index. The X-axis of each plot is the improvement ratio using the performance of 5% threshold as the baseline, and the Y-axis is the threshold of spill indices ranged from 5% to 25%.

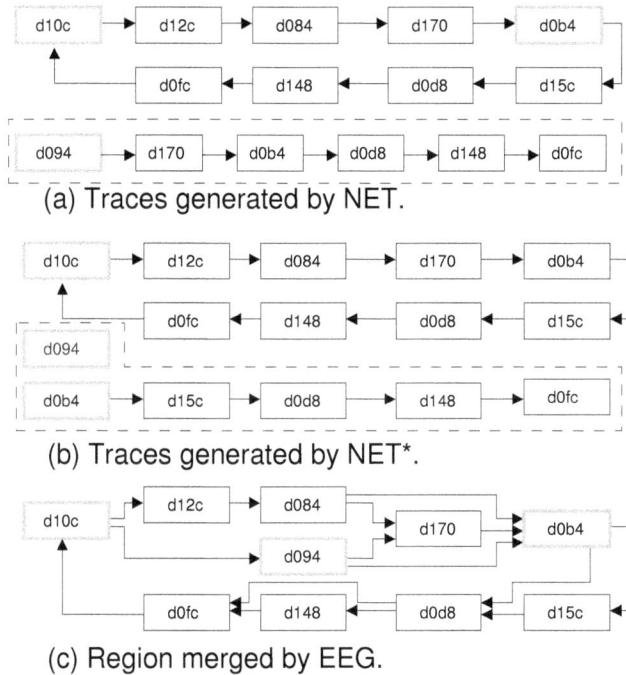

(a) Traces generated by NET.

(b) Traces generated by NET*.

(c) Region merged by EEG.

Figure 6. Traces/regions generated by NET, NET* and EEG for a loop in function `quantum_toffoli` of ARM `462.libquantum`.

For ARM benchmarks, the performance of EEG is more sensitive to the threshold of spill index as shown in Figure 8(b). This is because there are 16 general purpose registers in ARM guest architecture, and register pressure becomes a problem when translating ARM instructions to x86_64 instructions. Consequently, if we allow regions with high spill indices, i.e., high percentage of spill code in the translated code, to be merged, the performance tends to degrade. For example, in ARM `456.hmmer`, a 12% degradation is observed when the threshold of spill index increases from 15% to 20%.

4.5　Statistics of Selected Traces and Regions

Table 2 shows the statistics of selected regions in NET, NET* and EEG for CINT2006. First, the *number of traces* in NET* increase by 54% and 59% on average compared to NET for IA32 and ARM

benchmarks respectively. The *average numbers of blocks per trace* are similar in NET and NET*.

13.6% and 11.5% of traces in NET* are merged into regions by EEG for the IA32 and ARM benchmarks respectively, which indicates that our HPM-based region selection approach described in Section 3.3 can effectively select hot traces to be merged. The average numbers of blocks per region are 14.4 and 13.4 for the IA32 and ARM benchmarks respectively, which are 3.4X and 2.9X larger than the traces generated by NET*.

We also compute the number of merges in EEG. There are 2.1 and 1.7 merges per region on average in IA32 and ARM benchmarks, which indicates that most regions become stable after few number of merges. The last two columns of Table 2 are percentage of execution time spent in traces and regions. On average, our DBTs spend 72.3% and 58.4% execution time in regions for the IA32 and ARM benchmarks respectively.

5.　Related Works

The choice of optimization unit is critical to achieving good performance for Just-In-Time compilation systems. In this section, we categorize the related works of finding hot code region into dynamic binary translation systems, dynamic binary optimization systems, and language virtual machines.

5.1　Dynamic Binary Translation Systems

Dynamic binary translation (DBT) is widely used to support legacy binary code to run on a new architecture such as IA-32EL [4], DAISY [9], and Transmeta [8]. IA32-EL is a process virtual machine that enables IA32 applications to run on Intel Itanium. IA32-EL uses hyper-blocks as its unit of optimization in the hot code translation phase. A hyper block is a set of predicated basic blocks with a single entry and multiple exits. IA32-EL forms hyper blocks based on the execution counts of basic blocks and edge counters collected collected during the cold code execution.

DAISY and Transmeta are system virtual machines, where DAISY supports IBM PowerPC applications to run on VLIW processors and Transmeta supports IA-32 applications to run on a proprietary VLIW processor. Transmeta did not revealed details about how to find hot code regions. IBM DAISY uses *tree groups* as the translation unit. Tree groups have a single entry point and multiple exit points. No control flow joins are allowed within a tree group. Control flow joins can only occur on group transitions. Like IA32-EL, DAISY also uses profiling information collected during interpretation for tree group formation. Both hyper-blocks and tree groups have little advantage to non-VLIW machines, such as

IA32 CINT2006	NET		NET*		EEG		Merges		%Time Spent in	
	#Traces	Avg.Blks	#Traces	Avg.Blks	#Regions	Avg.Blks	Avg.	Max	Trace	Region
400.perlbench	6646	4.1	8966	5.9	1627	13.5	1.6	16	45.3%	51.6%
401.bzip2	583	3.8	894	5.0	206	14.4	1.8	6	19.2%	79.4%
403.gcc	23058	4.0	34019	3.9	2728	12.2	1.6	17	27.1%	37.0%
429.mcf	239	4.7	605	3.5	83	15.1	2.7	5	1.2%	95.3%
445.gobmk	9468	2.9	10961	3.9	2258	13.3	1.7	20	20.9%	71.6%
456.hmmer	424	3.8	687	3.6	61	25.5	4.5	6	1.5%	97.8%
458.sjeng	1216	3.3	1749	4.7	764	18.9	2.5	43	15.2%	84.5%
462.libquantum	200	2.5	326	2.2	20	8.4	1.8	4	17.6%	82.2%
464.h264ref	2434	3.3	3974	4.3	781	11.9	1.8	11	22.0%	73.3%
471.omnetpp	2918	5.0	4859	5.5	345	12.1	1.4	11	29.0%	69.6%
473.astar	613	5.2	942	4.5	185	24.3	5.3	7	2.3%	96.8%
483.xalancbmk	4453	5.9	8355	4.4	538	11.4	1.3	12	37.0%	59.1%
Geometric Mean		3.9		4.2		14.4	2.1		12.4%	72.3%

ARM CINT2006	NET		NET*		EEG		Merges		%Time Spent in	
	#Traces	Avg.Blks	#Traces	Avg.Blks	#Regions	Avg.Blks	Avg.	Max	Trace	Region
400.perlbench	7839	5.1	10438	5.1	1860	12.8	1.6	12	32.9%	62.2%
401.bzip2	672	4.7	1125	4.7	205	16.4	1.7	5	22.1%	75.0%
403.gcc	24703	3.7	36710	3.7	2595	12.1	1.5	10	13.1%	32.5%
429.mcf	362	3.6	726	3.6	125	22.3	2.9	6	1.2 %	96.8%
445.gobmk	14175	3.5	16587	3.5	3071	11.9	1.6	19	28.8%	60.9%
456.hmmer	847	4.8	1378	4.8	58	10.8	1.4	7	52.9%	46.7%
458.sjeng	1299	4.6	1811	4.6	760	14.7	2.5	35	19.8%	79.6%
462.libquantum	606	8.6	951	8.6	85	12.0	2.4	11	41.0%	58.4%
471.omnetpp	4584	3.5	7163	5.1	364	12.2	1.4	12	57.0%	41.6%
473.astar	959	3.9	1432	4.6	180	13.6	1.6	10	25.6%	72.8%
483.xalancbmk	4844	5.1	8690	3.9	559	11.9	1.3	8	49.1%	45.9%
Geometric Mean		4.1		4.6		13.4	1.7		23.0%	58.4%

Table 2. Statistics of Traces/Regions in NET* and EEG.

x86_64, since they are primarily designed to maximize instruction-level parallelism in VLIW architectures. Therefore we do not apply their approach in our system.

Moreover, DAISY, Transmeta, and IA32-EL handle early exits with chaining, i.e. the execution directly transfers to another code region. The transition overhead in those systems is not as high as in LnQ because most guest architecture states are mapped to the host architecture in these systems. For example, IA32-EL maps the state of IA-32 guest registers directly to Itanium registers. On the other hand LnQ, a retargetable dynamic binary translator, does not make any assumption about the guest and host ISAs. Consequently LnQ has to load guest states in the prologue of code fragments, and save them back to memory in the exit stubs, which incurs transition overheads.

5.2 Dynamic Optimization Systems

ADORE [18] and Dynamo [3] are same-ISA dynamic binary optimizers, which means the input and the output instructions are from the same instruction set architecture. Both ADORE and Dynamo use traces, i.e. super-blocks, as the unit of optimization.

ADORE uses Hardware Performance Monitor (HPM) sampling approach to collect path profiles from the Branch Target Buffer (BTB) hardware performance counters in Itanium. It forms traces based on the collected path profiles. Dynamo was the first trace-based dynamic optimizing compiler that used the Next-Executing-Tail (NET) algorithm. Dynamo pioneered many early concepts of trace formation and trace runtime management. Many DBT systems [6, 7, 13, 25] and just-in-time compilers [10, 16, 26] use NET or its variants to form traces.

StarDBT [25] uses MRET^2 [27], which improves NET by increasing the completion rate of traces. MRET^2 first uses NET to select a potential trace, then it clears block execution counters and restarts NET to select another potential trace. Both potential traces share the same starting address but may have different tails. MRET^2 then improves the completion rate by selecting the common path of both potential traces as a hot trace. Hiniker et al. [12] proposed Last-Executed Iteration (LEI) and a trace combination algorithm, which needs to interpret each taken branches to form traces.

The main difference between the proposed EEG and previous works is that EEG expands the existing regions and re-optimizes them during execution. The process of region expansion in EEG can be divided into three stages. The first stage is to decide how to form the initial region. The second stage is to decide when to expand the region. The third stage is to decide which blocks are to be merged. Previous trace formation algorithms, such as LEI and MRET^2, could be used in the first stage of EEG to build the initial regions. Therefore, the proposed EEG can be used effectively in most trace-based dynamic binary translators.

5.3 Language Virtual Machines

5.3.1 Method-Based Language Virtual Machines

Region expansion is widely used in method-based JIT systems, e.g., HotSpot Java VM [20]. These JIT systems compile methods as follows. When a method-based JIT system compiles a method for the first time, it only compiles those basic blocks whose execution counts exceed a threshold during interpretation. If the execution frequently leaves a region from side exits, the JIT system expands this region to include those basic blocks that are the destinations of these side exits.

Our EEG and method-based JIT systems use similar heuristics to decide when to expand regions during the second stage of region expansion, but they are very different in the first stage and the third stage of region expansion in terms of motivation and the type of blocks they merge.

The major difference between EEG and those systems in the first stage is the motivation in forming the initial regions. EEG uses traces as initial regions for two reasons. First, traces represent those frequently executed paths that may span across several methods. Second, it takes less time to optimize traces because of their simple control flow graph and small numbers of basic blocks. For example, we found only 4.2 blocks per trace in EEG. On the other hand, method-based JIT systems build initial regions by selecting blocks from hot methods, and excluding those blocks that are rarely executed. For example, HotSpot JVM excludes blocks that are never executed during interpretation.

The major difference between EEG and method-based JIT systems in the third stage is the type of blocks they merge. In the third stage EEG merges traces that contains frequently executed paths. However, in the third stage method-based JIT systems will only merge blocks that are rarely executed in the first stage, since those frequently executed blocks in the first stage have already been merged.

Suganuma et al. [23] investigate how to use region-based compilation to improve the performance of method-based Java Just-In-Time compilation. They use region-based compilation to partially inline procedures, instead of using traditional method inlining techniques. They collect execution counts of basic blocks in order to understand program runtime behavior, and they apply static code analysis on the Java bytecode to identify those rarely executed code blocks, such as those handle exception. They use these information to identify and optimize those often executed code blocks only, without optimizing the entire method.

In our case it is difficult to identify those rarely executed regions by a static code analysis, as they did for Java bytecode. Therefore we cannot apply their approach in our system.

5.3.2 Trace-Based Language Virtual Machines

Recently, trace-based compilation has gained popularity in dynamic scripting languages [5, 10] and high level language virtual machines [11, 16, 17, 26]. Wu et al. [26] and Inoue et al. [16, 17] investigate the performance of several variations of NET on trace-based Java virtual machines.

Gal et al. [10] propose merging loop traces into a *trace-tree*. Their approach requires adding annotation while compiling JavaScript into bytecode, and thus cannot be applied in our case.

In contrast, our EEG merges delinquent traces/regions, which are not necessarily loop traces. EEG uses hardware monitoring to identify often executed code traces, then determines whether they have many side exits, and finally merges those often executed code regions that have many side exits to avoid early exits from a region, EEG also uses spill index to prevent generating regions which may degrade performance.

6. Conclusion

We have identified and quantified the delinquent trace problem in the popular Next-Executing-Tail (NET) trace selection algorithm. Delinquent traces contain frequently taken early exits which cause significant overhead. Motivated by this problem, we develop a light-weight region formation strategy called Early-Exit Guided region selection (EEG) to improve the performance of NET by merging delinquent traces into larger code regions. The EEG algorithm

is implemented in two LLVM-based parallel dynamic binary translators (DBT), the IA32-to-x86_64 and ARM-to-x86_64 DBTs.

Experiment results show that EEG achieves performance improvement of up to 72% (27% on average), and up to 49% (23% on average) in IA32 and ARM SPEC CINT2006 benchmarks respectively. The profiling results show that EEG can reduce memory and branches instructions by up to 53% and 37% respectively because the transition overhead among traces is eliminated by merging delinquent traces. It also reduces the L1 instruction cache misses by up to 43.7% in CINT2006 benchmarks.

Acknowledgments

The authors would like to thank Dr. Filip Pizlo at Apple Inc. and the anonymous reviewers for their valuable comments and suggestions to improve the quality of this paper. This work is supported by the National Science Council of Taiwan under grant number NSC99-2221-E-001-003-MY3, NSC99-2221-E-001-004-MY3, and by NSF grant CNS-0834599.

References

[1] Low Level Virtual Machine (LLVM). http://llvm.org.

[2] QEMU. http://qemu.org.

[3] V. Bala, E. Duesterwald, and S. Banerjia. Dynamo: a transparent dynamic optimization system. In *PLDI '00*, pages 1–12. ACM, 2000.

[4] L. Baraz, T. Devor, O. Etzion, S. Goldenberg, A. Skaletsky, Y. Wang, and Y. Zemach. Ia-32 execution layer: a two-phase dynamic translator designed to support ia-32 applications on itanium-based systems. In *MICRO-36*, pages 191–201, Dec. 2003.

[5] M. Bebenita, F. Brandner, M. Fahndrich, F. Logozzo, W. Schulte, N. Tillmann, and H. Venter. Spur: a trace-based jit compiler for cil. *SIGPLAN Not.*, 45:708–725, October 2010.

[6] I. Bohm, T. E. von Koch, S. Kyle, B. Franke, and N. Topham. Generalized just-in-time trace compilation using a parallel task farm in a dynamic binary translator. In *Proc. PLDI*, 2011.

[7] D. Bruening. *Efficient, Transparent, and Comprehensive Runtime Code Manipulation*. Ph.d. thesis, Massachusetts Institute of Technology, Cambridge, MA, Sep 2004.

[8] J. C. Dehnert, B. K. Grant, J. P. Banning, R. Johnson, T. Kistler, A. Klaiber, and J. Mattson. The transmeta code morphing™software: using speculation, recovery, and adaptive retranslation to address real-life challenges. In *CGO '03: Proceedings of the international symposium on Code generation and optimization*, pages 15–24, Washington, DC, USA, 2003. IEEE Computer Society.

[9] K. Ebcioglu, E. Altman, M. Gschwind, and S. Sathaye. Dynamic binary translation and optimization. *IEEE Trans. Comput.*, 50(6):529–548, 2001.

[10] A. Gal, B. Eich, M. Shaver, D. Anderson, D. Mandelin, M. R. Haghighat, B. Kaplan, G. Hoare, B. Zbarsky, J. Orendorff, J. Ruderman, E. W. Smith, R. Reitmaier, M. Bebenita, M. Chang, and M. Franz. Trace-based just-in-time type specialization for dynamic languages. In *PLDI*, pages 465–478, 2009.

[11] H. Hayashizaki, P. Wu, H. Inoue, M. J. Serrano, and T. Nakatani. Improving the performance of trace-based systems by false loop filtering. In *ASPLOS*, pages 405–418, 2011.

[12] D. Hiniker, K. Hazelwood, and M. D. Smith. Improving region selection in dynamic optimization systems. In *MICRO 38*, pages 141–154, Washington, DC, USA, 2005. IEEE Computer Society.

[13] D.-Y. Hong, C.-C. Hsu, P. Liu, C.-M. Wang, J.-J. Wu, , P.-C. Yew, and W.-C. Hsu. Hqemu: A multi-threaded and retargetable dynamic binary translator on multicores. In *CGO '12: Proceedings of the 10th annual IEEE/ACM international symposium on Code generation and optimization*, 2012.

[14] C.-C. Hsu, P. Liu, C.-M. Wang, J.-J. Wu, D.-Y. Hong, P.-C. Yew, and W.-C. Hsu. Lnq: Building high performance dynamic binary

translators with existing compiler backends. In *ICPP*, pages 226–234, 2011.

[15] W.-M. W. Hwu, S. A. Mahlke, W. Y. Chen, P. P. Chang, N. J. Warter, R. A. Bringmann, R. G. Ouellette, R. E. Hank, T. Kiyohara, G. E. Haab, J. G. Holm, and D. M. Lavery. The superblock: an effective technique for vliw and superscalar compilation. *J. Supercomput.*, 7(1-2):229–248, May 1993.

[16] H. Inoue, H. Hayashizaki, P. Wu, and T. Nakatani. A trace-based java jit compiler retrofitted from a method-based compiler. In *CGO'11*, pages 246–256, 2011.

[17] H. Inoue, H. Hayashizaki, P. Wu, and T. Nakatani. Adaptive multi-level compilation in a trace-based java jit compiler. In *Proceedings of the ACM international conference on Object oriented programming systems languages and applications*, OOPSLA '12, pages 179–194, New York, NY, USA, 2012. ACM.

[18] J. Lu, H. Chen, P.-C. Yew, and W. chung Hsu. Design and implementation of a lightweight dynamic optimization system. *Journal of Instruction-Level Parallelism*, 6:2004, 2004.

[19] M. M. Michael and M. L. Scott. Simple, fast, and practical non-blocking and blocking concurrent queue algorithms. In *15th Annual ACM Symposium on Principles of Distributed Computing*, 1996.

[20] M. Paleczny, C. Vick, and C. Click. The java hotspot(tm) server compiler. In *In USENIX Java Virtual Machine Research and Technology Symposium*, pages 1–12, 2001.

[21] perfmon2. http://perfmon2.sourceforge.net.

[22] J. E. Smith and R. Nair. *Virtual Machines: Versatile Platforms for Systems and Processes*. Morgan Kaufman, 2005.

[23] T. Suganuma, T. Yasue, and T. Nakatani. A region-based compilation technique for a java just-in-time compiler. In *PLDI '03*, pages 312–323. ACM, 2003.

[24] V. Sundaresan, D. Maier, P. Ramarao, and M. Stoodley. Experiences with multi-threading and dynamic class loading in a java just-in-time compiler. In *CGO '06*, pages 87–97, Washington, DC, USA, 2006. IEEE Computer Society.

[25] C. Wang, S. Hu, H.-S. Kim, S. R. Nair, M. B. Jr., Z. Ying, and Y. Wu. Stardbt: An efficient multi-platform dynamic binary translation system. In *ACSAC'07*, pages 4–15, 2007.

[26] P. Wu, H. Hayashizaki, H. Inoue, and T. Nakatani. Reducing trace selection footprint for large-scale java applications without performance loss. In *OOPSLA '11*, pages 789–804, New York, NY, USA, 2011. ACM.

[27] C. Zhao, Y. Wu, J. G. Steffan, and C. Amza. Lengthening traces to improve opportunities for dynamic optimization. In *Proceedings of the Workshop on Interaction between Compilers and Computer Architectures*, 2008.

Superblock Compilation and other Optimization Techniques for a Java-Based DBT Machine Emulator

Marco Kaufmann   Rainer Spallek

Institut für Technische Informatik
Technische Universität Dresden
01062 Dresden, Germany
{marco.kaufmann, rainer.spallek}@tu-dresden.de

Abstract

Superblock compilation techniques such as control flow graph (CFG) or trace compilation have become a widely adopted approach to increase the performance of dynamically compiling virtual machines even further. While this was shown to be successful for many conventional virtual machines, it did not result in a higher performance for Java-based DBT[1] machine emulators so far. These emulators dynamically translate application binaries of a target machine into Java bytecode, which is then eventually compiled into the native code of the emulating host by the Java Virtual Machine (JVM). Successful superblock compilation techniques for this class of emulators must consider the special requirements that result from the two-stage translation as well as the characteristics of the JVM, such as the inability of most Java JIT compilers to handle large bytecode methods efficiently.

In this paper, we present a superblock compilation approach for a Java-based DBT machine emulator that generates a performance increase of up to 90 percent and of 32 percent on average. The key idea of our design is to provide a large scope over the control flow of target applications across basic block boundaries for the JVM, while still keeping small bytecode methods for the execution units.

In addition, we also present two further optimizations – interpreter context elimination and program counter elimination – which increase the emulation performance by 16 percent again. In total, the optimization techniques discussed in this paper provide an average performance gain of 48 percent for the surveyed emulator.

Categories and Subject Descriptors D.3.4 [*Programming Languages*]: Processors – Code generation, Run-time environments

Keywords Superblock, Optimization, Emulation, Virtualization, Java

[1] Dynamic Binary Translation

1. Introduction

Superblock compilation techniques have become a widely used approach for virtual machines that feature just-in-time compilation. While traditional DBT JIT compilers translate the target application at the unit of one basic block, superblock compilers use larger translation units and may increase the performance even further. Firstly, larger execution units mean less time is spent in the dispatch loop of a VM to select the next execution unit. Secondly, they also provide a larger scope for possible optimizations by the compiler during the JIT compilation.

While superblock compilation has been employed successfully in many conventional virtual machines, it did not result in a performance increase for Java-based DBT machine emulators so far. These emulators dynamically translate target machine application binaries into Java bytecode, which is then eventually compiled by the JVM into the native code of the emulating host. The advantage of this technique is that it is entirely platform-independent although it provides a high emulation performance due to dynamic compilation. In addition, it exploits the JVM as an external back end for native code generation that performs even optimizations specific to the host platform. However, a successful superblock compilation approach that actually results in a performance increase for this class of emulators must respect the special requirements that result from this two-stage translation as well as the characteristics of the JVM. Superblock compilation has already been researched for Java-based DBT machine emulators, but did not work very well due to the inability of many Java JIT compilers to efficiently translate large bytecode methods.

Our implementation pursuits the strategy of providing a large scope over the target application's control flow across basic block boundaries for the JVM while still keeping small bytecode methods for the execution units. This is achieved by a separation between the control flow logic of a CFG that implements the dispatch between the single CFG nodes and the actual behavior of these CFG nodes. While compiled superblocks actually only contain the control flow logic of the corresponding CFG, the behavior of the basic blocks is contained in separate Java classes that are statically invoked by the superblocks. Our experiments prove this approach to be successful with an average performance increase of 32 percent. Also, the separation between control flow and node behavior results in a very low code generation overhead for superblocks, which is smaller than 10 percent compared to the code generated in the plain basic block compilation mode.

In addition, we present two more optimizations that increase the speed of the emulation framework by further 16 percent. Sec. 2 presents the state of the art on superblock compilation and related work concerning Java-based DBT machine emulators. In Sec. 3, we give a short description of the underlying emulation framework before the optimizations that we applied to it are discussed in Sec. 4. Our experimental results are shown in Sec. 5. Sec. 6 concludes this paper and provides a summary of our results.

2. Related Work

As argued in Sec. 1, the usage of translation units which are larger than one basic block enables a higher emulation performance for virtual machines. In the remainder of this paper, we use the term *superblock compilation* for all these compilation techniques. Large translation and execution units that combine more than one basic block of the target application are called *superblocks*.

Different superblock compilation techniques vary in their profiling strategy and in their strategy to select a subgraph of the target application control flow graph to be compiled into a superblock. Basically, two main approaches can be distinguished: CFG compilation and trace compilation. For CFG compilation, the control flow graph (CFG) of a superblock may contain many execution paths. For trace compilation, a superblock contains only one execution path whose nodes are compiled in sequence.

Prominent examples for CFG compilation are implementations of the Java and the .NET runtime environments. Here, the translation unit typically is one method. However, in the case of Java, recent implementations also apply trace compilation [7, 8]. Another example for CFG compilation is EHS by Jones and Topham [10]. The authors implemented three different CFG compilation modes and compared them to each other in terms of simulation speed and average size of a superblock. In SCC mode, superblocks contain only strongly connected components (SCC), which means in fact that they contain exactly the CFG of a program loop. In CFG mode, superblocks are not restricted to loops, while in page mode, the CFG of a whole physical memory page is compiled into a superblock. While all these modes where superior to raw basic block compilation mode by the factor of 1.6 in terms of performance, none of them proved superior to the others in their experiments[2]. This might hint that superblocks that cross (outer) loop boundaries do hardly bear any benefit because most runtime is spend within loops anyway.

Trace compilation performs a sophisticated runtime profiling in order to determine the most frequently executed paths through an application CFG. One such a path, called a *trace*, is then compiled node by node into a sequential superblock. This sequential control flow inside the execution unit provides massive potential for optimizations by the JIT compiler. Also, branching is generally an expensive operation. However, there is still guarding code required for each CFG node that could possibly exit the trace. Therefore, superblocks are not free of branch instructions at all.

Because each superblock contains only one execution path, code duplication that occurs when two paths include the same CFG node is an even bigger problem for trace compilation than it is for CFG compilation. Anchor points for trace compilation must therefore be chosen more carefully. Bala et al. [5, 6] propose the targets of backward branches as anchors for trace compilation for their dynamic binary optimization system *Dynamo*, because they mark the entry point of a loop very likely. While this is a commonly accepted strategy, Hayashizaki et al. [9] argue that it also encounters *false loops*, which could degrade the performance of a virtual machine. False loops do actually not represent program loops but could instead occur when multiple callers invoke the same method. They propose a stack-based false loop filter to avoid them. This,

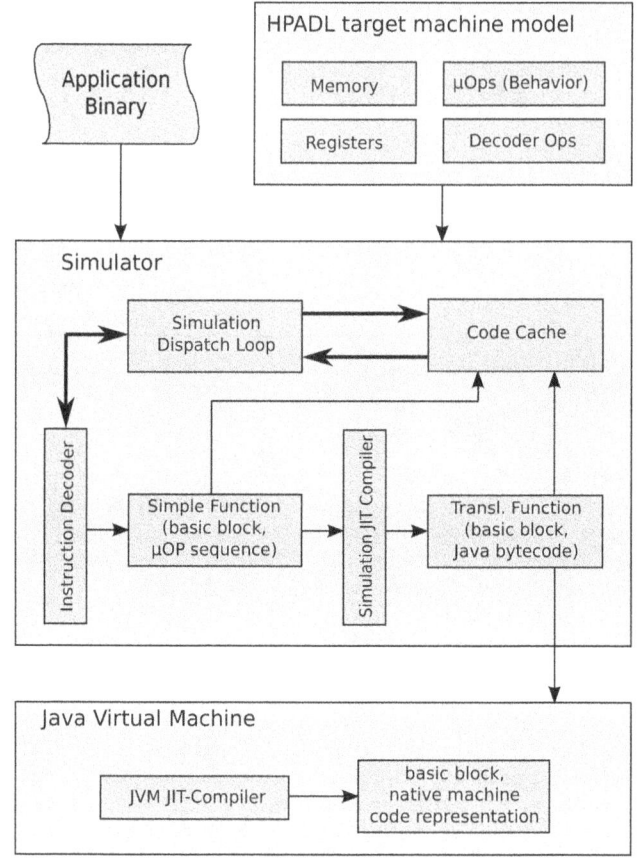

Figure 1. Underlying emulation framework

however, requires knowledge and makes assumptions about the target machine that are not fulfilled in the case of a generic machine emulator.

Meanwhile, Java-based machine emulators have emerged. These emulators translate target machine code dynamically into Java bytecode, which is then eventually compiled into the native code of the emulating host. Their benefits have been discussed in Sec. 1. Examples for this approach are Pearcolator/MRP [4, 12], JPC [3], JDosbox [2], as well as Jahris [11], the emulation framework that we built our superblock compilation upon. However, they feature the compilation of plain basic blocks only. While JxEmu/VEELS [15] also supports superblock compilation, the authors report poor performance when the size of a bytecode method for a superblock exceeds a certain threshold. They attribute this to the inability of many Java JIT compilers to translate large bytecode methods efficiently.

3. Underlying Emulation Framework

The Java-based DBT machine emulator that we built our optimizations upon is a generic emulation framework. Simulation models are constructed with an instruction set description language called *HPADL*. In this language, ISA models are split into three parts: the structural section describing the register set and the memory system of the target, the decoder description and the behavioral description. The decoder description models the instruction decoder of the target machine. For an input instruction word, it produces a sequence of micro operations that resembles the behavior of the decoded instruction. The behavioral description implements the behavior for the individual micro operations. The instruction control

---

[2] Jones and Topham report indeed a minor average performance gain of 1 percent for CFG over SCC and of 3 percent for page over CFG. This, however, can be regarded insignificant due to the heavy jitter. For many of their benchmarks, CFG is slower than SCC and page is slower than CFG.

flow is modeled within the behavioral part by assigning values to the program counter register.

Next to a model of the target machine, emulation requires an application binary compiled for the target machine. The binary is loaded into the memory system of the virtual target and decoded by the instruction decoder in units of basic blocks. The resulting micro operation sequences, called *simple functions*, reproduce the behavior of the basic blocks of the target application. They are stored in the simulation code cache for later reuse. Each basic block, as far as it is not removed from the cache in the meantime, is therefore decoded only once. Simple functions are interpreted by the simulation engine. As soon as the execution count for a simple function reaches a certain threshold, it is dynamically compiled into Java bytecode. The associated Java class, called a *translated function* (TF), is then dynamically loaded into the JVM and instantiated as a singleton via the Java Reflection API. It replaces the corresponding simple function in the simulation code cache. Further compilation and optimizations steps on the level of the TF, such as its translation into the native code of the emulating host platform, are then eventually performed by the JVM. The workflow of the framework is depicted in Fig. 1.

4. Optimization Techniques

4.1 Elimination of the Interpreter Context

When executing a basic block of the target application in interpreter mode (*Simple Function*), the machine context of the simulation target is mapped to a set of Variable objects, with each of these objects representing one machine register. This set is called the *interpreter context*. Variable objects provide a suitable form for the internal representation (IR) of HPADL statements, on which the simulation interpreter operates. They include a `get` and a `set` method in order to access the variable contents.

On the other hand, basic blocks compiled to Java bytecode (*Translated Function*) use another representation of registers. Here, the machine context of the simulation target is mapped to a Java class, in which each machine register is represented by a static field. This class is generated by the simulation compiler and is called the *compiled context*. The compiled context enables the more efficient execution of translated functions, in which each register read and write operation is implemented by a simple static field access (`getstatic`, `putstatic`).

This, however, implies that the machine context has to be copied from the interpreter to the compiled context whenever execution switches from a simple to a translated function, and vice versa when switching from a translated to a simple function. While this rarely happens for the mature stage of application execution when most of the simple functions have been compiled into translated functions, it causes a measurable impact during the *warm-up* phase.

In order to avoid this runtime overhead, we eliminate the interpreter context and use the compiled context also for the interpreter mode. Since field access via Java reflection might be orders of magnitude slower than direct field access [13], reflection is not feasible for this purpose and would slow down the interpreter up to impracticability. Instead, we let the simulation compiler generate a subclass of Variable for each static field in the compiled context, whose `get` and `set` methods contain a simple `getstatic` and `putstatic` bytecode to access the respective field. These classes are then instantiated as singletons that replace the original Variable objects of the interpreter context in the IR.

4.2 Program Counter Elimination

The control flow of target instructions is modeled by modifying the program counter register in HPADL architecture descriptions. It is incremented by sequential control flow instructions while branch

Listing 1. TF bytecode for an instruction sequence A, B, ... without program counter elimination

```
1   getstatic CTX0.r15  // increment PC
2   iconst 4
3   iadd
4   putstatic CTX0.r15
5   <A>                 // remainder bahavior of A
6   getstatic CTX0.r15  // increment PC
7   iconst 4
8   iadd
9   putstatic CTX0.r15
10  <B>                 // remainder bahavior of B
11  ...
12  ldc 0x40007F38
13  putstatic CTX0.r15  // PC = 0x40007F38 (branch)
14  getstatic CTX0.r15
15  ireturn             // return PC
```

instructions write the address of the branch target to it. From the view of the architecture description, it is just a regular machine register. It is handled as a regular register also by the emulation engine. Like for any other register, HPADL statements that address the program counter are translated one to one by the simulation compiler. For the emulation engine, its only speciality is that, between two execution units, the next instruction fetch address (IFA) is loaded from this register.

While providing an elegant way to model the control flow, this induces a huge overhead at emulation runtime because each instruction loads, modifies and writes the program counter. This is depicted in Listing 1 for the example of an ARMv4 Translated Function with R15 as the program counter. This overhead is, however, unnecessary as the program counter contents at the execution time of an instruction is already known to the instruction decoder when fetching the instruction word from a given address.

Therefore, we removed the program counter from the simulation while still keeping it in the architecture description. HPADL expressions that read from the program counter are replaced by constant load operations by the instruction decoder. Assign statements that write to it are simply ignored and do not produce any code in the case of sequential control flow and direct branch instructions (Listing 2). Only for indirect branch instructions, they are translated into a bytecode sequence that passes the value of the assign expression as the next IFA to the instruction decoder.

Direct and indirect branches can be distinguished by a data flow analysis on the micro operation sequence generated by the instruction decoder. In the case the branch target address is a constant expression in the context of the decoded instruction word, the branch is a direct branch and an indirect branch otherwise. If the assign statement occurs within a conditional statement, the branch is conditional. Finally, unconditional direct branches whose target is the address of the next instruction in the sequential control flow are no branches but sequential control flow instructions. Note, that this scheme is fully transparent for existing HPADL architecture models and does not require to modify them.

4.3 Superblock Compilation

A successful superblock compilation approach for Java-based DBT machine emulators must respect the special requirements that result from the two-stage compilation approach on the one hand (Sec. 3), and from the characteristics of Java Runtime Environments (JREs) on the other hand.

The optimization of translated functions on the bytecode level by the simulation compiler is largely irrelevant because code optimization is performed by the JVM anyway. Typical Java JIT com-

Listing 2. TF bytecode for instruction sequence A, B, ... with program counter elimination

```
1  <A>                // behavior of A
2  <B>                // behavior of B
3  ...
4  ldc 0x40007F38
5  ireturn            // return 0x40007F38 (next IFA)
```

pilers first transform Java bytecode into a high-level intermediate representation (HLIR), then into a low-level intermediate representation (LLIR) and apply optimizations to both of these representations. Finally, the LLIR is transformed into machine code for the host platform performing even platform specific optimizations in doing so. Modern JRE implementations may also apply sophisticated optimization techniques such as method inlining, loop unrolling and trace compilation using the runtime profile of an application. That is why most Java to bytecode compilers are non-optimizing, and even optimization tools such as Soot that operate merely on the bytecode level yield no significant performance gain for Java classes [14].

In order for these highly sophisticated runtime optimization techniques to score the best results, control and data flow analyses over a large portion of the target application are required. This is not a problem for conventional Java applications. For Java-based DBT machine emulators, however, the control flow between two execution units of the target application is masked by the emulator's code cache and its dispatch loop. Thus, it is not visible to the JVM so optimization cannot cross execution unit boundaries.

An obvious solution to this problem would be to combine more than one basic block into a translation unit. This would generate larger execution units and therefore provide a greater view of the target application control flow to the JVM. As discussed in Sec. 2, this, however, barely yields a performance increase due to the inability of many Java JIT compiler to handle big bytecode methods efficiently. We therefore conclude three design criteria for a successful superblock compilation in a Java-based DBT machine emulator:

1. Many small execution units – i.e., bytecode methods – are better than a few big ones.

2. The control flow between these units must be visible to the JVM.

3. The optimization of translated functions on the bytecode level is rather irrelevant. We leave optimizations up to the JVM.

Superblocks, CFGs and TFs   Our basic idea is to provide a large view to the JVM across basic block boundaries of the target application while still keeping small bytecode methods. Like in the original emulation framework without superblock compilation (Sec. 3), the target application is decoded basic block by basic block into Simple Functions (SF), which are then compiled into translated functions (TF) as soon as their execution count exceeds the compilation threshold. A TF therefore resembles only one basic block of the target application.

The execution of TFs is then further profiled in order to find appropriate starting points for the *control flow graph compilation*. We call these *CFG anchors*. Once such an anchor has been found, a static control flow analysis is performed based on it. The resulting control flow graph (CFG) contains all TFs that are statically reachable from the anchor – that is, by conditional or unconditional direct branch instructions from one TF to another – and that are, at the same time, contained in the simulation code cache. The nodes of the CFG are TFs while its edges resemble the control flow between TFs. We restrict the static control flow analysis to TFs that are con-

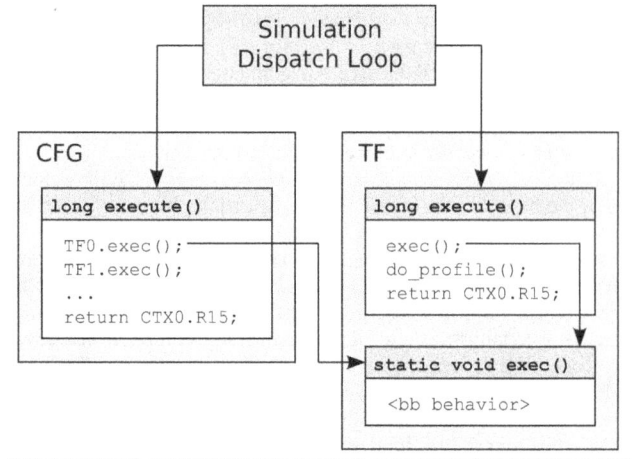

Figure 2. CFG and TF invocation

tained in the code cache because otherwise, they are obviously not executed frequently and therefore neither worth to be compiled into a TF nor worth to bloat the CFG. We only consider direct branches because otherwise the definite branch target is unknown, even when previous targets can be observed from the runtime profile. The resulting CFGs are compiled into Java classes and are put into the simulation code cache where they replace their corresponding CFG anchor. The code cache therefore contains three types of execution units: *simple functions* (SFs) that are interpreted, compiled basic blocks (TFs) that gradually replace SFs, and superblocks (CFGs) that gradually replace TFs.

When a CFG is compiled into a superblock, its nodes are not inlined, but instead, they are invoked statically from the superblock. Thus, the bytecode generated for a CFG contains only the dispatch logic between TFs but no behavior while the bytecode for a TF resembles the behavior of one basic block of the target application. This keeps bytecode methods small and yet provides large execution units. The control flow inside a superblock is visible to the JVM, which can then apply optimizations to it that go across basic block boundaries. Additionally, compared to conventional superblock compilation techniques, our approach reduces code duplication heavily because each TF exists only once, no matter how many superblocks contain it as a CFG node.

In the original emulation framework, TFs were invoked only by the dispatch loop. This invocation had to be non-static because otherwise the loop had to invoke them via reflection API. TFs contained a non-static `execute` method that implemented the behavior of the basic block and returned the IFA for the next look-up in the code cache. However, with superblock compilation TFs are also invoked by CFGs. This invocation is static and is not required to return an IFA, because the control flow logic is compiled into the superblock directly. For this purpose, a second, static method `exec` has been introduced that now implements the basic block behavior (Fig. 2). It is invoked by CFGs as well as the TFs own `execute` method. The `execute` method additionally returns an IFA, contains profiling code and is still invoked from the dispatch loop. While this means some overhead when a TF is invoked directly from the dispatch loop, most runtime is spent inside CFGs after the application warm-up phase anyway.

CFG Anchors: Execution Count vs. Loop Headers   In order to maximize the performance gain by superblock compilation, most runtime must be spent within superblocks (i.e., in CFGs or in TFs that are invoked by CFGs) rather than in basic blocks (i.e., TFs that are invoked directly by the dispatch loop). We implemented two

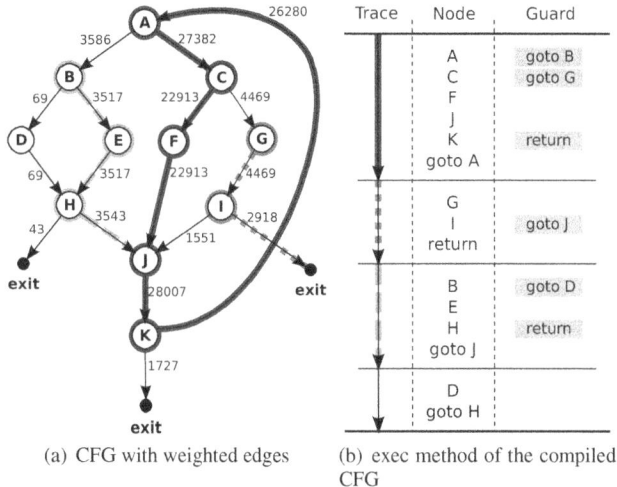

(a) CFG with weighted edges   (b) exec method of the compiled CFG

Figure 3. Hotpath Reordering: a control flow graph with 4 traces

strategies of profiling and anchor selection in our superblock compiler: counting the executions of a TF (*execution count*) and counting how often it has been the target of a backward branch (*back-branch count*). The latter is a strategy widely used to identify loop headers (Sec. 2). As soon as the respective count exceeds a certain threshold, a TF is used as an anchor for superblock compilation.

In general, loop headers are suitable anchor points for superblock compilation because most target application runtime is spent within loops. Also, the resulting superblocks for our compilation approach should comprise at least the complete CFG of a loop in this case. In our experiments, however, it turned out that even after a long warm-up phase when no more superblocks were added to the emulation code cache, most runtime was still spent in TFs that were invoked by the dispatch loop directly rather than from superblocks.

The explanation for this behavior is indirect branches. Because of the generic nature of the emulation framework, no assumptions but the given architecture description are made about the emulated target machine. Therefore, superblock compilation is unable to perform a control flow analysis across the subroutine boundaries of the target application. While the direct call instruction for a subroutine is handled as a direct branch, the corresponding return instruction is an indirect branch where the branch target address is not encoded within the instruction word but fetched from a link register or fetched from the stack. If a subroutine is called within a loop, this results in an incomplete CFG for the loop. If only loop headers are selected as superblock compilation anchors, the remainder of the loop, although executed as frequently as the loop header, will never get compiled into a superblock in such a case.

Thus, loop headers as the only CFG anchors is not a good design choice for our emulation framework. Instead, we use the execution count to trigger superblock compilation. Each TF that is executed frequently enough will be used as an anchor for superblock compilation whether or not it is a loop header. Note that this would result in massive code duplication for traditional superblock compilation approaches. Due to the separation between the control flow logic and node behavior of CFGs, this is not the case for our design however.

Path Profiling and Hotpath Reordering Our superblock compiler features a hybrid approach between traditional CFG compilation and trace compilation. CFG compilation in general compiles a part of the CFG of the target application into one execution unit at a time. The resulting execution unit may contain many execution paths. Trace compilation on the other hand is a special case of this. It uses a runtime profile to determine the most frequently executed paths through the CFG of the application. One such path, called a *trace*, is then selected for compilation and is compiled into a sequential instruction stream. Unlike for traditional CFG compilation, this provides a sequential control flow within execution units. Note, however, that there are still guarding code elements required after each CFG node that could possibly exit the trace. Thus, it is not free of branch instructions at all.

We do not compile single traces. Our superblocks may contain many execution paths. However, we also perform a runtime profiling on how often branches are taken. For each TF that exits with a conditional direct branch, there is a counter that indicates its branch count. For TFs that exit with an unconditional branch, there is no such counter required because their branch count always equals their execution count. Finally, for TFs that exit with a conditional indirect branch, the branch count is irrelevant because their branch target is not considered in the CFG analysis anyway. This results in a CFG whose edges are weighted by the branch count.

When a CFG is compiled into a superblock, its nodes are reordered so that the most frequently executed paths are compiled into a sequence. Starting with the compilation anchor, the node linked into the `execute` method at the offset behind the current node is always the one targeted by the heaviest-weighted edge. This is similar to trace compilation except that the guarding code elements may not only exit a superblock but may also transfer control to another execution path within the same superblock. This is illustrated in Fig. 3 with an example control flow graph including four traces and A as the compilation anchor.

5. Experimental Results

5.1 Emulation performance

We used the EEMBC AutoBench 1.1 Automotive/Industrial Benchmark Suite [1] in order to measure the simulation performance for the optimization techniques described in Sec. 4. The entire suite consists of 16 individual benchmarks that resemble a representative set of applications for embedded platforms in terms of their runtime profile and instruction mix. The suite was compiled with a GCC toolchain version 4.4.3 for ARM, floating point emulation enabled, optimization level O2 and with the default compiler settings otherwise. It was run with a HPADL ARMv4 machine model on our emulator. The host machine features an Intel® Core i7 with 6 GB memory and 64-Bit Ubuntu 11.04, kernel version 3.0.0-15-server. The emulator was executed with the Oracle JRE 7 HotSpot 64-Bit Server VM. The iteration number for the benchmarks was chosen so that a run took between 5 and 10 seconds. A benchmark was run 5 times for each mode with always the best score recorded.

In order to evaluate the performance increase achieved by superblock compilation and the other optimization techniques, we compared three operation modes of the emulator. In *TF-Only* mode, superblock compilation is disabled but program counter elimination and interpreter context elimination are still enabled. In *Exit-on-CFG* mode, superblock compilation is also enabled, but superblocks do not invoke each other. Instead, if a CFG node of a superblock during CFG analysis turns out to be another superblock rather than a TF, the compiled superblock will not invoke this node but return to the dispatch loop at this point. In contrast, superblocks do also invoke each other in *Invoke-CFG* mode. Note that this will never result in the recursive invocation of superblocks. This is because when a superblock B is being compiled and found to invoke another superblock A, A cannot invoke B in turn, because B did not exist at the time when A was compiled. A would instead statically invoke the TF that was selected as the compilation anchor for B at a later point in time.

Benchmark	Iterations per Second				Performance in % of Baseline		
	Invoke-CFG	Exit-on-CFG	TF-Only	Baseline	Invoke-CFG	Exit-on-CFG	TF-Only
a2time	205158	184631	112794	102329	200	180	110
basefp	46679	41722	29439	27001	173	155	109
bitmnp	9878	9778	7620	6654	148	147	115
cacheb	1324908	1334154	1388592	1161336	114	115	120
canrdr	1533481	1301330	1342482	1054975	145	123	127
aifftr	593	590	572	511	116	116	112
aifirf	115735	113884	103638	97490	119	117	106
idctrn	9864	9896	7865	5285	187	187	149
iirflt	79601	76849	72819	55788	143	138	131
aiifft	652	645	629	557	117	116	113
matrix	201	190	131	124	162	153	105
pntrch	22798	22759	5046	14164	161	161	106
puwmod	1991238	1934235	1643655	1488538	134	130	110
rspeed	2007528	1759014	1779755	1451115	138	121	123
tblook	65876	56361	46162	41814	158	135	110
ttsprk	48043	47195	36348	31873	151	148	114
Average					*148*	*140*	*116*
Geo. mean					*146*	*138*	*116*

Table 1. Emulation Performance by Optimizations

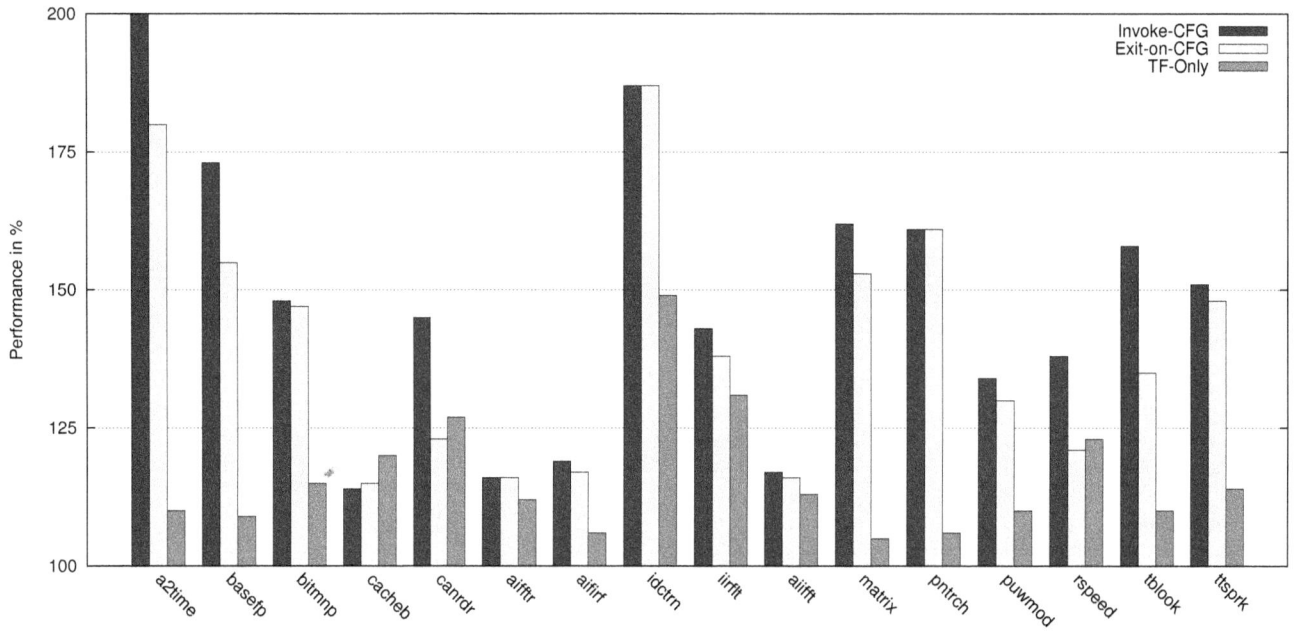

Figure 4. Emulation Performance by Optimizations Compared to Baseline

The results of our experiments are shown in Tab. 1 and Fig. 4. The baseline is the simulation performance of the same emulation framework without any of the optimizations applied as discussed in Sec. 4. Compared to the baseline, TF-Only increases simulation performance by up to 27 percent, and by 16 percent on average. Exit-on-CFG increases the performance by up to 87 percent and by 40 percent on average, while Invoke-CFG delivers the best performance with an increase of 100 percent for the *a2time* benchmark and of 48 percent on average. This means that program counter elimination and interpreter context elimination cause a significant performance gain of 16 percent for the emulator with the referred benchmark set. Invoke-CFG provides an average performance that is even 32 percentage points higher than this, which is attributed only to superblock compilation. Our superblock compilation ap-

proach described in Sec. 4.3 as well as our other optimization techniques discussed in Sec. 4 can therefore be considered successful.

5.2 Code Generation Overhead

Tab. 2 and Fig. 5 depict the total size of the classes generated for superblocks (CFG) and basic blocks (TF) for one run of each benchmark in Sec. 5.1. It turns out that the code generation overhead for superblock compilation is rather low. While the geometric mean of the total class size is 221800 bytes for generated TFs, the geometric mean of the total class size for CFGs is 20393 bytes. This means that on average only 8.4 percent of all class bytes dynamically generated are due to superblock compilation while the remaining 91.6 percent are attributed to basic block compilation.

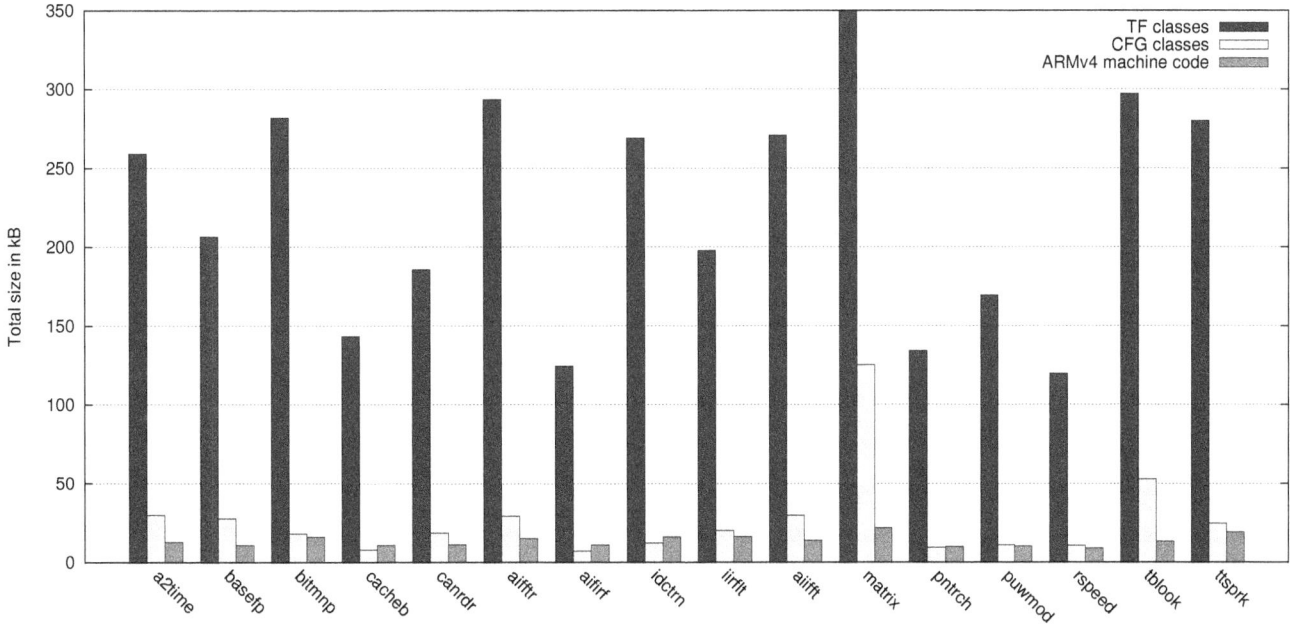

Figure 5. Superblock Code Generation Overhead

Benchmark	Total size in bytes		
	TF classes	CFG classes	ARMv4 machine code
a2time	265328	30578	13060
basefp	211512	28257	11132
bitmnp	288504	18507	16560
cacheb	146949	8188	11008
canrdr	190240	18926	11520
aifftr	300449	30084	15356
aifirf	127278	7411	11344
idctrn	275416	12556	16500
iirflt	202403	20622	16632
aiifft	277286	30343	14260
matrix	503186	128207	22400
pntrch	137438	9587	10152
puwmod	173472	11272	10334
rspeed	122519	10931	9144
tblook	304212	54105	13580
ttsprk	286786	25157	19612
Geo. mean	*221800*	*20393*	*13482*

Table 2. Superblock Code Generation Overhead

Class type	Class count	Class size in B	Bytecode size in B
TF	248.9	965	215 to 290
CFG	45.4	612	100 to 120

Table 3. Average Generated Class Count and Size

The reason for this is our separation between the control flow logic and the node behavior of CFGs in the execution units. While a CFG class contains only the control flow logic of a superblock, TF classes implement only the behavior of a basic block (Sec. 4.3). Each TF exists only once, no matter how many CFGs invoke it as a node. Code duplication due to overlapping parts of control flows,

which brings difficulties for traditional super block compilation approaches, is therefore no problem for our design.

Tab. 2 and Fig. 5 also show the size of the corresponding ARMv4 target machine code. This does not include the entire application binary but only the code regions that are actually executed during a run. It can be seen that, on average, the total size of the generated TFs is bigger than the total size of the executed target machine code by the factor of 16.5 and the total size of the generated CFGs is bigger by the factor of 1.5. Therefore, per 1 MB of ARMv4 machine code executed, one can expect an average total amount of 16.5 MB of Java classes to be generated when superblock compilation is disabled and an average total amount of 18 MB when superblock compilation is enabled. Note, however, that this involves the entire classes including their constant pools. If only the bytecode in the methods `exec` and `execute` is considered, this ratio is lower. While the average size of a TF is 965 bytes and that of a CFG is 612 bytes, a typical TF of that size contains only 215 to 290 bytes of Java bytecode in its `exec` method and a contains CFG only 100 to 120 bytes (Tab. 3).

6. Summary

This paper presented a superblock compilation approach for a Java-based DBT machine emulator, that, in contrast to earlier approaches, significantly increases the emulation performance by 32 percent on average compared to a plain basic block compilation. We achieved this due to a new strategy that generates small bytecode methods but still provides a large view on the control flow of the target application to the JVM. For this purpose, we separated the control flow logic for CFGs from the actual behavior of their nodes. While CFG classes (superblocks) contain only the control flow logic, TF classes, which are statically invoked by CFGs, implement only the behavior of a single basic block.

Our superblock compiler also features a hybrid technique between the traditional compilation of CFGs and trace compilation. While superblocks may contain many execution paths, branches between basic blocks are profiled at runtime. When a superblock is generated, the nodes of its CFG are reordered so that its most frequently executed paths are compiled to a sequence. Contrary to existing approaches that prefer loop headers as anchor points for superblock compilation, we use every basic block that is executed frequently enough as an anchor, whether or not it is the head of a loop.

While this would cause massive code duplication for traditional superblock compilers, our separation between the control flow logic and the node behavior ensures a low code generation overhead. In fact, our experiments show that not even 10 percent of the overall generated classes size is due to superblocks (CFG) while more than 90 percent are due to basic blocks (TF).

Additionally, we implemented two more optimizations. *Interpreter Context Elimination* removes the interpreter context and maps the registers of the simulation target onto a compiled machine context even in interpreter mode. *Program counter elimination* removes the program counter register from the simulation model and replaces it by constants, which are then compiled directly into Java bytecode by the simulation compiler. This is fully transparent for the HPADL machine descriptions, which still model the control flow between instructions by writing values to the program counter. These two optimizations increase the simulation performance by 16 percent on average again, which results in an average performance gain of 48 percent when also superblock compilation is applied.

Acknowledgments

This work has been supported by the *European Social Fund* (ESF) and by *pls Programmierbare Logik & Systeme GmbH*.

References

[1] EEMBC AutoBench 1.1 Benchmark Software. http://www.eembc.org/benchmark/automotive_sl.php, 2011.

[2] Java DOSBox. http://jdosbox.sourceforge.net, 2011.

[3] JPC – The Pure Java x86 PC Emulator. http://jpc.sourceforge.net, 2011.

[4] M. Baer. Emulating the ARM Architecture Using a Java Dynamic Binary Translator. Master's thesis, University of Manchester, School of Computer Science, 2007.

[5] V. Bala, E. Duesterwald, and S. Banerjia. Transparent dynamic optimization: The design and implementation of dynamo. Technical report, HP Laboratories Cambridge, June 1999.

[6] E. Duesterwald and V. Bala. Software profiling for hot path prediction: less is more. *SIGOPS Oper. Syst. Rev.*, 34(5):202–211, Nov. 2000. ISSN 0163-5980.

[7] A. Gal, C. W. Probst, and M. Franz. Hotpathvm: an effective jit compiler for resource-constrained devices. In *Proceedings of the 2nd international conference on Virtual execution environments*, VEE '06, pages 144–153, New York, NY, USA, 2006. ACM. ISBN 1-59593-332-8.

[8] C. Häubl and H. Mössenböck. Trace-based compilation for the java hotspot virtual machine. In *Proceedings of the 9th International Conference on Principles and Practice of Programming in Java*, PPPJ '11, pages 129–138, New York, NY, USA, 2011. ACM. ISBN 978-1-4503-0935-6.

[9] H. Hayashizaki, P. Wu, H. Inoue, M. J. Serrano, and T. Nakatani. Improving the performance of trace-based systems by false loop filtering. *SIGARCH Comput. Archit. News*, 39(1):405–418, Mar. 2011. ISSN 0163-5964.

[10] D. Jones and N. Topham. High speed cpu simulation using ltu dynamic binary translation. In *Proceedings of the 4th International Conference on High Performance Embedded Architectures and Compilers*, HiPEAC '09, pages 50–64, Berlin, Heidelberg, 2009. Springer-Verlag. ISBN 978-3-540-92989-5.

[11] M. Kaufmann, M. Häsing, T. Preußer, and R. Spallek. The java virtual machine in retargetable, high-performance instruction set simulation. In *Proceedings of the 9th International Conference on Principles and Practice of Programming in Java*, PPPJ '11, pages 21–30, New York, NY, USA, 2011. ACM. ISBN 978-1-4503-0935-6.

[12] I. Rogers and C. Kirkham. JikesNODE and PearColator: A Jikes RVM Operating System and Legacy Code Execution Environment. In *2nd ECOOP Workshop on Programm Languages and Operating Systems (ECOOP-PLOS'05)*, 2005.

[13] D. Sosniski. Java programming dynamics, part 2: Introducing reflection. http://www.ibm.com/developerworks/java/library/j-dyn0603, June 2003. [Online; accessed 2012/03].

[14] R. Vallée-Rai, E. Gagnon, L. J. Hendren, P. Lam, P. Pominville, and V. Sundaresan. Optimizing java bytecode using the soot framework: Is it feasible? In *Proceedings of the 9th International Conference on Compiler Construction*, CC '00, pages 18–34, London, UK, UK, 2000. Springer-Verlag. ISBN 3-540-67263-X. URL http://dl.acm.org/citation.cfm?id=647476.727758.

[15] A. Yermolovich, A. Gal, and M. Franz. Portable execution of legacy binaries on the java virtual machine. In *Proceedings of the 6th international symposium on Principles and practice of programming in Java*, PPPJ '08, pages 63–72, New York, NY, USA, 2008. ACM. ISBN 978-1-60558-223-8.

Efficient Live Migration of Virtual Machines Using Shared Storage

Changyeon Jo, Erik Gustafsson, Jeongseok Son, and Bernhard Egger

School of Computer Science and Engineering, Seoul National University

{changyeon, erik, jeongseok, bernhard}@csap.snu.ac.kr

Abstract

Live migration of virtual machines (VM) across distinct physical hosts is an important feature of virtualization technology for maintenance, load-balancing and energy reduction, especially so for data centers operators and cluster service providers. Several techniques have been proposed to reduce the downtime of the VM being transferred, often at the expense of the total migration time. In this work, we present a technique to reduce the total time required to migrate a running VM from one host to another while keeping the downtime to a minimum. Based on the observation that modern operating systems use the better part of the physical memory to cache data from secondary storage, our technique tracks the VM's I/O operations to the network-attached storage device and maintains an updated mapping of memory pages that currently reside in identical form on the storage device. During the iterative pre-copy live migration process, instead of transferring those pages from the source to the target host, the memory-to-disk mapping is sent to the target host which then fetches the contents directly from the network-attached storage device. We have implemented our approach into the Xen hypervisor and ran a series of experiments with Linux HVM guests. On average, the presented technique shows a reduction of up over 30% on average of the total transfer time for a series of benchmarks.

Categories and Subject Descriptors D.4.5 [*Operating Systems*]: Reliability—Checkpoint/restart; D.4.2 [*Operating Systems*]: Storage Management—Storage hierarchies; D.4.4 [*Operating Systems*]: Communications Management—Network communication

General Terms Design, Measurement, Performance, Reliability

Keywords Virtualization; Live migration; Storage; Xen

1. Introduction

Over the past few years, the availability of fast networks has lead to a shift from running services on privately owned and managed hardware to co-locating those services in data centers [1]. Along with the wide-spread availability of fast networks, the key technology that enables this shift is virtualization. In a virtualized environment, the software does not run directly on bare-metal hardware anymore but instead on virtualized hardware. The environment (such as the number of CPUs, the amount of RAM, the disk space, and so on) can be tailored to the customer's exact needs. From the perspective of the data center operator, virtualization provides the opportunity to co-locate several VMs on one physical server. This consolidation reduces the cost for hardware, space, and energy.

An important feature of virtualization technology is *live migration* [9]: a running VM is moved from one physical host to another. Live migration is attractive to data center providers because moving a VM across distinct physical hosts can be leveraged for a variety of tasks such as load balancing, maintenance, power management, or fault tolerance. The task of migrating a running VM from one host to another has thus attracted significant attention in recent years [6, 9, 12, 13, 15, 18, 20, 27]. Live migration is only useful if the service provided by the running VM is not interrupted, i.e., if it is transparent to the user. To migrate a running VM across distinct physical hosts, its complete state has to be transferred from the source to the target host. The state of a VM includes the permanent storage (i.e., the disks), volatile storage (the memory), the state of connected devices (such as network interface cards) and the internal state of the virtual CPUs (VCPU). In most setups the permanent storage is provided through network-attached storage (NAS) and does thus not need to be moved. The state of the VCPUs and the virtual devices comprise a few kilobytes of data and can be easily sent to the target host. The main caveat in migrating live VMs with several gigabytes of main memory is thus moving the volatile storage efficiently from one host to the other.

The prevalent approach for live VM migration is *pre-copy* [9]. The contents of the VM's memory are first sent to the target host and then the VM is restarted. To keep the *downtime*, i.e., the time during which the VM is not running, to a minimum, data is sent in several iterations while the VM keeps running on the source host. In each following iteration, only the pages that have been modified since the last round are sent. Another approach is *post-copy* [13]. Here, only the VM's VCPU and device state is sent to the target host and restarted there immediately. Memory pages accessed by the VM are then fetched in parallel and on-demand while the VM is running on the target host.

Both of these approaches minimize the downtime of the VM at the expense of the *total migration time*, i.e., the time from when the migration is started until the VM runs independently on the target and can be destroyed on the source host. Several techniques aim at reducing the total migration time through compression of memory pages [16] or trace-and-replay [18].

In this work, the goal is to reduce the total migration time by minimizing the data sent across the distinct physical hosts. Park *et al.* [22] have observed that in typical setups a considerable amount of data in the memory is duplicated on disk; they report up to 94% of duplication in extreme cases with lots of disk I/O. This duplication is caused by modern operating systems' disk caches with which the long latency to physical storage is to be hidden. Park *et al.* have used this observation to minimize the image size of VMs that are to be restarted on the same physical host at a later time. In our work, the same idea is applied to live migration for VMs using shared network-attached storage: instead of transferring the entire (possibly compressed) memory data, we only send the data of memory pages whose content is not available on the shared storage device. In order to restore the complete memory image on the target host, the source host sends a list of shared storage blocks along with the VM's memory locations. The target host then fetches these disk block directly from the attached network storage while the migration continues running. This approach is especially attractive in a setup where the maximum bandwidth between the hosts is limited but the NAS is connected through a high-speed network. Our approach aims to improve the total migration time of VMs within data centers with network-attached shared storage; the proposed method does not optimize live migration across data centers.

The presented method is independent of almost all other optimization techniques such as iterative pre-copying, post-copying, and data compression. Existing techniques can be augmented by integrating the approach presented here to (further) reduce the total migration time.

The contributions of this paper are as follows:

- we propose an efficient technique for live-migrating VMs from one host to another by transferring only unique memory pages directly from the source to the target. Pages that are duplicated on disk located on shared storage are fetched directly by the target host. To the best of our knowledge, this is the first approach that does not send duplicated data directly from the source to the target host.

- we show the feasibility of the proposed technique by providing an implementation of this technique in version 4.1 of the Xen hypervisor [8] for HVM guests.

- we demonstrate the effectiveness of the proposed technique by running a series of benchmarks. We achieve an average improvement in the total migration time of over 30% with up to 60% for certain scenarios at a minimal increase of the downtime. In addition, thanks to the shorter total migration time, the overhead caused by live migration is reduced which leads to an increased performance of the migrated VM.

The remainder of this paper is organized as follows: Section 2 gives an overview of related work on live migration of virtual machines. In Section 3, the technique to efficiently migrate a VM is described in more detail. Section 4 contains the design and implementation of the proposed live migration framework. Section 5 evaluates our technique, and Section 6 concludes the paper.

2. Related Work

Live migration is actively being researched and a number of techniques have been proposed to migrate a running VM from one host to another. The predominant approach for live VM migration is pre-copy. The bare-metal hypervisors VMware [28], KVM [12], and Xen [2], plus hosted hypervisors such as VirtualBox [21] employ a pre-copy approach. To reduce the downtime of the VM, the state of the VM is copied in several iterations [9]. While transferring the state of the last iteration, the VM continues to run on the source machine. Pages that are modified during this transfer are recorded and need to be re-transmitted in the following iterations to ensure consistency. The iterative push phase is followed by a very short stop-and-copy phase during which the remaining modified memory pages as well as the the state of the VCPUs and the devices are transferred to the target host. The pre-copy approach

achieves a very short downtime in the best case, but for memory-write-intensive workloads the stop-and-copy phase may increase to several seconds. Remote Direct Memory Access on top of modern high-speed interconnects can significantly reduce memory replication during migration [15].

Post-copy-based techniques take the opposite approach: first, the VM is stopped on the source host and the state of the VCPU and devices is transferred to the target host. The VM is immediately restarted on the target host. Memory pages are fetched on-demand from the source machine as the VM incurs page-faults when accessing them on the target machine. This approach achieves a very short down-time but incurs a rather large performance penalty due to the high number of lengthy page faults on the target machine. Hines *et al.* [13] combine post-copying with dynamic self-ballooning and adaptive pre-paging to reduce both the amount of memory transferred and the number of page faults. Hirofuchi *et al.* [14] employ a post-copy-based approach to quickly relocate VMs when the load of a physical host becomes too high.

Other techniques include live migration based on trace and replay [18], memory compression [16, 24], simultaneous migration of several VMs from one host to another [11], or partial VM migration [5]. Liu *et al.* [18] present a technique that first writes the state of the running VM to the local storage on the source machine. That state is then transferred once to the target machine. The VM continues to run on the source machine and all modifications to memory pages are logged in a trace file which is transferred iteratively to the target host. The target host then replays those modifications in the copy of the running VM. At the end of the iterative phase, a short stop-and-copy phase is used to transfer the final state to the target machine. Jin *et al.* [16] enhance the iterative pre-copy approach by compressing the data that is to be transferred in each round from the source to the target machine. Svärd *et al.* [24] extend this idea by delta-compressing changes in memory pages. Deshpande *et al.* [11] study the problem of simultaneous migration several VMs. Their idea is to detect memory pages of identical contents across different VMs and transfer duplicated pages only once. Our work in this paper is orthogonal to memory compression and simultaneous live-migration. Bila *et al.* [5] propose partial VM migration of idle VMs running on users' desktops to a consolidation server with the goal of reducing overall energy consumption. The authors use a post-copy approach where only the accessed memory pages and disk blocks are transferred to the server. The partially-migrated VMs continue running on the server while the desktops can be put into a low-power mode. As soon as the user continues to work on his desktop, the modified state of the partially migrated VM is transferred back to the desktop. The authors report significantly reduced transfer times to migrate the working set of the idle VM. Other than in our approach, however, the VM on the desktop can not be destroyed since it is never fully transferred.

The work most closely related to our technique was presented by Park *et al.* [22]. The amount of data saved during (iterative) checkpoints is significantly reduced by tracking memory pages residing in identical form on the attached storage device and not including such pages in the memory image. Instead, a mapping of memory pages to disk blocks is stored in the checkpoint image which is used to load the data directly from the storage device instead of the checkpoint image. We use the same technique as Park to transparently intercept I/O requests and maintain an up-to-date mapping of memory pages to disk blocks. Our work differs from Park's approach in that we apply the same idea to live migration: instead of transmitting memory data that exists in identical form on the network-attached storage device, we transfer a list of disk blocks along with the memory locations to the target host. The receiver on the target host then fetches these blocks directly from the attached network drive into the VM's memory.

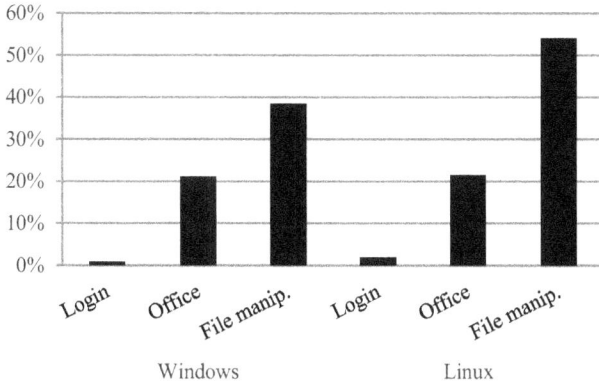

Figure 1. Amount of duplication between memory and external storage.

3. Efficiently migrating live VMs

Migrating a running VM from one physical host to another requires that the entire state of the VM is transferred. The state of a VM comprises the VCPUs, the configuration of the drivers, the VM's memory and the permanent storage. In data center setups, the permanent storage is typically a network storage device - an iSCSI partition or a drive mounted via NFS. Consequently, the contents of permanent storage do not need to be moved to the target host. With memory sizes of several gigabytes even for virtual machines, transferring the memory state to the target host thus becomes the bottleneck of live migration.

3.1 Motivation

Modern operating systems cache data from permanent storage in unused volatile memory to hide the long access latency. The longer the system is running, the bigger an amount of otherwise unused memory is dedicated to this cache. In data centers, the physical hosts are typically attached over a very fast network to a network storage device as well as to the external world. During live migration, a lot of data needs to be sent from one physical host to another. In order not to affect the quality of service of the whole data center, the maximum bandwidth with which data is sent between distinct physical hosts is usually limited. This can easily lead to migration times of tens of minutes for VMs that have several gigabytes of main memory. Our goal is thus to detect duplicated data and fetch this data directly from the attached storage device. This considerably reduces the amount of data sent between the two hosts involved in live migration and has the potential to significantly shorten the total migration time.

Duplication of data between memory and external storage. The operating system and the running applications often occupy only a small fraction of the total available memory, leaving most of the memory unused. Modern operating systems use this unused memory to cache recently accessed blocks of the attached storage device. The data of this cache is thus duplicated: one copy resides on the permanent storage device, another copy exists in the memory of the VM. In addition to cached data, application data such as code pages or read-only data pages also exist in external storage as well as in the memory. It is not uncommon that the amount of duplication between the permanent storage and the memory reaches more than 50%, and this trend is likely to continue with ever-increasing memory sizes. Park *et al.* [22] have measured the amount of duplication between disk and memory for Linux and Windows HVM guests running in Xen. Even for relatively small memories (1 GB), they have observed a duplication ratio of 93% for

the Linux HVM guest after heavy I/O. Figure 1 shows the results of our experiments with Linux and Windows HVM guests running on a VM with 4 GB of RAM. The first data point represents the amount of duplication after booting the system up and logging in. The second data point was taken after performing some editing in the LibreOffice application suite [25]. The third data point, finally, was taken after copying data from a USB stick to the local storage device. Both HVM guests, Windows and Linux, show that over time, more and more data is cached in memory. For the last data point in Figure 1, in the Windows HVM 40% or 1.5 GB of the total memory is duplicated on external storage. For Linux, the amount of duplication is even higher with 55% or 2.2 GB of data. These results demonstrate that there is a lot of potential for reducing the amount of data that needs to be sent from the source to the target host during live migration.

Transparent live migration. To make live migration as transparent as possible, the utmost concern is the *downtime*, that is, the time between the moment the VM is stopped on the source host and the moment when the VM is restarted on the target host. To achieve a short migration downtime, several techniques have been developed [9, 13, 18, 24] that have very short downtimes at the expense of the total amount of transferred data and/or the total migration time. The prevalent method is to send data in iterations to the target host while the VM keeps running on the source host [9]. Memory pages that get modified on the source host need to be retransmitted in one of the following iterations. With pre-copying approaches the total amount of data can thus be significantly bigger than the size of the VM's memory. Other techniques, such as postcopy [13] immediately restart the VM on the target host and fetch the accessed memory pages on-demand. Such approaches have a very short downtime and transmit each memory page exactly once; however, the VM on the target host can experience a significant performance degradation due to the frequent high-latency page fetch operations.

Network topology in data centers. A high-speed connection to the outside world as well as the network-attached storage device are indispensable for a data center setup. The interconnection network between the physical hosts, on the other hand, does not need to be as fast; furthermore, the available bandwidth is preferably used to provide access to the VMs from the outside world. To minimize the effects of live migration on the quality-of-service in a data center environment, the maximum bandwidth available during live migration is often limited. Unavoidably, a rate-limited connection increases the total migration time.

Based on the three observations above, we propose the following method to efficiently migrate a running VM: at runtime, we track all I/O operations to permanent storage and maintain an updated list of memory pages that are currently duplicated on the storage device. When migrating, instead of transferring those pages over the rate-limited connection from the source to the target host, the target machine reads them directly from the attached storage device. This technique is orthogonal to iterative pre-copying or postcopy approaches, and can also be combined with techniques that compress the data to be transferred. In the following section, the proposed method is described in more detail.

3.2 Design

The key idea of the proposed method is to fetch memory pages that also exist on the attached storage device directly from that device instead of transferring them directly from the source to the target host. Figure 2 illustrates the idea: memory pages that have been recently read from or written to external storage and are thus duplicated are shown in green. Such pages include pages from code and read-only data sections of running applications and cached disk

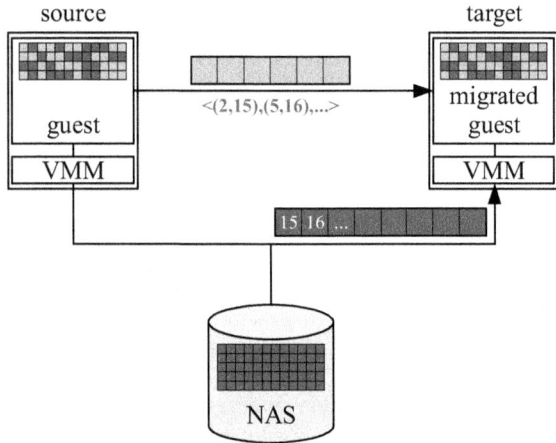

Figure 2. Duplicated memory pages are loaded directly from external storage.

blocks. Shown in blue are memory pages which contain data that is not duplicated. These pages include, for example, the stack.

Detecting duplication between memory pages and disk blocks immediately before transmission is infeasible due to the large computational overhead. One would have to keep a hash value for every disk block, then compute and compare the hash value of a memory page with those of all disk blocks. Instead, we transparently intercept all I/O requests issued by VMs and maintain an up-to-date list of memory pages to disk blocks.

Transparent I/O interception is possible because the VMM has to arbitrate accesses to shared devices such as NICs and attached storage devices in order to ensure correct operation and proper isolation between the different VMs. To detect changes to memory pages that contain disk block data, we re-map such pages *read-only*. Whenever a guest tries to modify such a page by writing to it, a memory page fault is raised. This page fault is intercepted by the VMM which then removes the page-to-block mapping, restores the write access permission of the page and restarts the operation. Transparently intercepting I/O operations and especially the extra page faults cause some overhead; however, as shown in Section 4.1, due to the long-latency nature of I/O operations and the fact that for each tracked memory page at most one extra page fault can occur, this overhead is not noticeable.

When a VM running on a source host is about to be migrated to a target host, the contents of the VM's memory are sent to the target host. We consider iterative pre-copying here, however, since the presented method is largely independent of existing techniques it can easily be integrated into those techniques as well. In an iterative pre-copy approach, the contents of the running VM's memory are sent to the target host over several iterations[9]. Since the VM continues to run while the data is being transferred, memory pages that have already been transferred can get modified. The VMM thus tracks changes to already transferred pages by marking the corresponding page table entry (PTE) in the memory management unit (MMU) *read-only*, much in the same way the I/O tracking process is operating. In the following iteration, only modified memory pages need to be sent to the target host. This iterative process stops if (a) only very few memory pages have been modified since the last iteration or (b) if a maximum number of iterations is reached. Which termination condition holds depends on what tasks the running VM is executing: tasks that generate only few modifications to memory pages (i.e., *dirty* pages at a low rate) tend to terminate the iterative process early, while VMs that dirty memory pages at a high rate will eventually hit the iteration threshold. Once the itera-

tive process has stopped, the VM is stopped on the source host, the remaining dirtied memory pages are sent to the target host along with the state of the VM's devices and VCPUs, and then restarted on the target host.

The proposed technique seamlessly integrates into the iterative pre-copy approach: instead of sending all dirtied memory pages to the target host, only pages whose contents are not duplicated on external storage are transferred. Dirtied pages whose contents are known - because they have been loaded from or written to external storage and have remained unmodified since - are assembled into a list containing pairs of the form (PFN, disk block) where PFN denotes the memory page in the guest and disk block contains the index of the disk block(s) containing the data.

The tracking of dirtied pages is identical to that in the unmodified iterative pre-copy approach, and happens in addition to the transparent interception of I/O. The list of duplicated pages is assembled by joining the bit vector containing the list of dirtied pages with the current mapping of memory pages to disk blocks. It is thus possible that in two subsequent iterations the identical element (PFN, disk block) appears in the list of pages to be loaded from external storage. This happens if, for example, block disk block is loaded into memory page PFN before the first iteration, then subsequently written to and flushed back to external storage between the first and the second iteration. The list of duplicated pages contains the same element (PFN, disk block), but the dirty bit for page PFN will trigger inclusion of the page in the current round.

On the target host, a receiver process fetches the list of duplicated pages and the contents of the dirty pages. Dirty pages are simply copied 1:1 into the memory space of the VM being migrated. The list of duplicated pages is sent to the *NAS fetch queue*, a background process that processes the items on the fetch queue by loading the contents from disk and copying them into the appropriate memory page. Since the NAS fetch queue operates in parallel to the migration process, it is possible that a data from disk arrives after a newer version of the same page has already been received in one of the successive iterations. To detect such cases, the target host maintains a version number for each memory page. For each memory page received in a successive iteration all outstanding requests to the same page in the NAS fetch queue are discarded. Similarly, if a fetch request is received for a page that is still in the NAS fetch queue, the old request is discarded as well. If the NAS fetch queue has just issued a load operation to the NAS device while the target memory page is being overwritten with newer data, then the data fetched from disk is discarded upon arrival at the host.

After the data in the final round has been sent to the target host, the VM cannot be restarted until all entries on the NAS fetch queue have been processed. This synchronization has the potential to adversely affect the downtime of live migration. A feedback mechanism ensures that this does not happen: the NAS fetch queue continuously measures the I/O bandwidth of the NAS device and reports it back to the source host along with the number of outstanding requests. The source host can estimate the time required to process all outstanding plus new requests and decide to send some duplicated pages over the direct link instead of including them in the list of duplicated pages. In the last round, all dirtied pages, duplicated or not, are send directly over the direct link.

Figure 3 illustrates the operation of the proposed technique with an example. When the live migration is started on the source host, initially all memory blocks are marked dirty. The list of duplicated pages shows that memory pages 2, 5, and 8 contain the contents of disk blocks 15, 16, and 3, respectively. During the first round, the source host thus first sends <(2,15), (5,16), (8,3)> to the target host, followed by the contents of memory pages 1, 3, 4, 6, and 7. The target host adds the list of duplicated pages to the (initially empty) NAS fetch queue and copies the memory pages

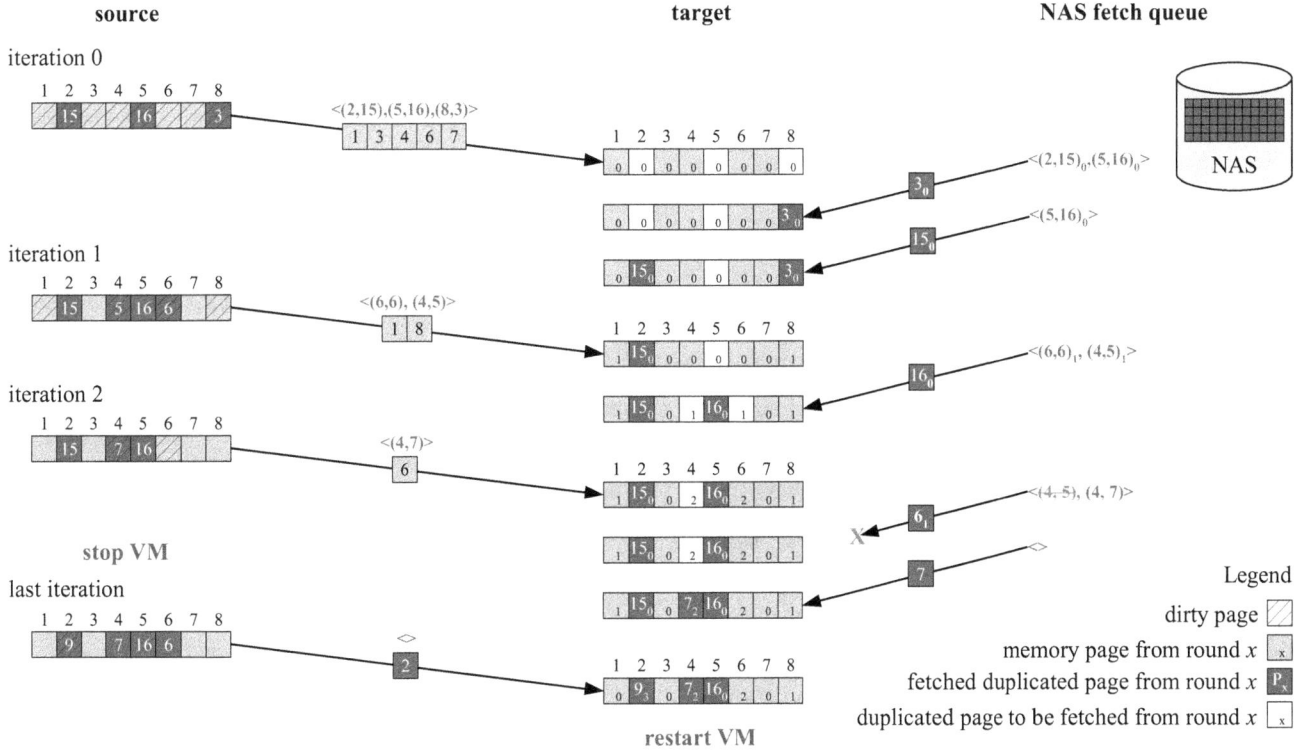

Figure 3. Memory pages whose contents are known to be duplicated on disk are fetched directly from the NAS device.

into the memory space of the VM being migrated. For each page and fetch request is recorded as well. The NAS fetch queue then proceeds to fetch disk blocks 3 and 15 from the NAS device while the VM continues to run on the source host. Each processed fetch request is removed from the queue. In iteration 1, the source host again sends the list of duplicated pages <(6,6), (4,5)> and the dirtied memory pages (1 and 8) to the target host. The list of duplicate pages is appended to the NAS fetch queue, and page data is directly written into the VM's memory. Between iteration 1 and 2, memory page 4 has been replaced by disk block 7 and is resent to the target host. The NAS fetch queue thus removes the old request for memory page 4, (4,5) from the queue and replaces it with the new one, (4, 7). Additionally, while the NAS fetch queue is processing the entry (6, 6), a new version for memory page 6 has also been received in iteration 2. Before writing the block data to memory page 6, the NAS fetch queue compares the versions of the data currently residing in page 6 (=2) and the version of the fetched block (=1). Since the memory page already contains a newer version, the data fetched from the NAS is discarded. In the final iteration, only one memory page has been modified. Its contents are duplicated on disk, however, since this is the last round the source sends the contents of the memory over the direct link to the target and does not include it in the list of duplicated pages. The target host waits until the NAS fetch queue has processed all outstanding entries and then restarts the VM.

4. Implementation

We have implemented the proposed technique in the open-source virtual machine monitor (VMM), Xen 4.1 [8]. This is section discusses the details and issues of our implementation. We focus on fully-virtualized guests (HVM guests) in our discussion; however, the implementation for para-virtualized guests is analogous.

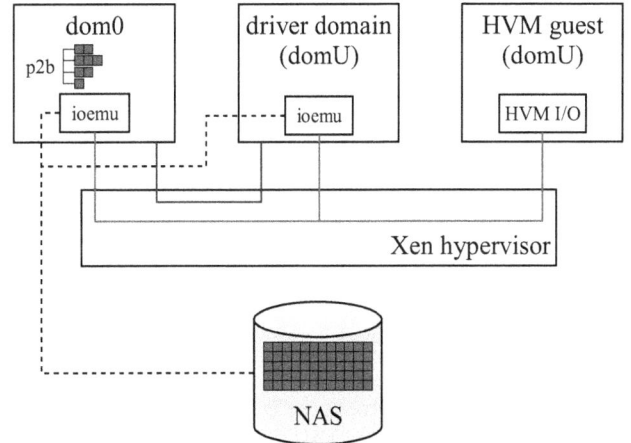

Figure 4. I/O operations in the Xen VMM

4.1 Transparent I/O Interception

In the Xen VMM, all I/O operations to secondary storage are under control of the VMM. The Xen hypervisor itself does not contain any device drivers; instead it delegates the task of dealing with a variety of hardware devices to the privileged dom0 or, more recently, unprivileged Xen driver (or *stub*) domains. In both cases, I/O requests of the HVM guest running in an unprivileged user domain (domU) go through ioemu, a modified version of the qemu processor emulator [3] (Figure 4).

Mapping page frames to disk blocks. We associate the VM's memory contents with physical storage blocks by transparently tracking all read and write requests from the HVM guest to external storage. The collected information is stored in a list of duplicated pages, the page-to-block map p2b. For each running VM, a separate p2b map is maintained. The map is indexed by the VM's memory page frame number (PFN), since the number of memory page frames is typically much smaller than the number of disk blocks. The data stored in the p2b map is the 8-byte storage block number.

Maintaining consistency. In order to maintain a consistent p2b map, the hypervisor needs to track memory writes to memory pages currently included in the p2b map. For HVM guests, the hypervisor either maintains shadow page tables [19] or hardware-assisted paging (HAP) provided by newer hardware [4]. We only support HAP at this moment; however, Park et al. [22] have shown that tracking modifications using shadow page tables is also possible. Whenever an entry is added to the p2b map, the corresponding memory page is marked *read-only* using the MMU's page tables. When the guest issues a store operation to such a page, the subsequent page fault is caught by the Xen hypervisor. If the affected memory page is currently included in the p2b map, the handler removes the entry, re-maps the page *read-write* and restarts the store operation.

Overhead. Both the space and runtime overhead of the p2b map are small: implemented as a hash map, the p2b map contains one entry per memory page that is currently duplicated on external storage. In terms of space requirements the worst case is when every memory block is duplicated on external storage. In that case, the number of entries is equal to the VM's memory size divided by the size of a memory page (typically 4KB). With 8 bytes per entry this translates to 2 MB of storage per one GB of virtual memory, a space overhead of 0.2%. The p2b map needs to be updated on each I/O operation to external storage. Such I/O operations have a long latency so that the p2b update operations are completely hidden. To track (memory) write operations to memory pages that are known duplicates of disk blocks, the Xen VMM maps such pages as *read-only*. A subsequent write operation thus incurs the overhead of an extra page fault during which the page table entry of the affected page is re-mapped *read-write* and the corresponding entry is removed from the p2b hash map. Since an entry is removed from the map on a write operation, each entry on the list can incur at most one additional page fault. To add an entry, a costly I/O operation is required; even in the worst-case where every page read from external storage is invalidated by performing one write operation to it, the time overhead caused by the extra page fault is hidden by the long-latency I/O operation.

4.2 Iterative Pre-Copy

When the live migration is started, all memory pages are initially marked dirty. In each iteration, the memory pages that are sent to the target host are marked clean. Similar to I/O tracking, Xen intercepts modifications to memory pages by mapping such pages *read-only* with the help of the MMU.

Integration of the proposed technique into the iterative pre-copy algorithm is easy: in each iteration, the pre-copy algorithm assembles the list of memory pages to be sent to the target host in this round. We do not modify this process; however, before the data is sent over the network, our implementation first inspects the list of assembled pages. Pages that are known to be duplicates of blocks residing on external storage are removed from the batch and added to the list of duplicated pages. This list is then sent first, followed by the data of memory pages that are not duplicated on external storage.

4.3 Assembling the Memory Image

On the target host, more changes are necessary. First, the receiver is modified to receive a list of duplicated pages before the actual page data. In each iteration, this list if given to a separate background process, the *NAS fetch queue*. This process maintains a queue of blocks that need to be fetched from external storage and loaded into memory. Consecutive blocks are coalesced whenever possible to improve the efficiency of the read requests to external storage. When adding a new batch of entries to the queue, older entries that refer to the same memory page are deleted from the queue. Additionally, all entries referring to memory pages whose contents are transferred in the current round are also removed from the queue.

The data fetched from external storage is not directly loaded into the VM's memory. Instead, it is first loaded in to a buffer. Before copying the buffer to the corresponding page in the VM's memory, the NAS fetch queue checks whether the page contains more recent data from a subsequent iteration. Such situations occur when a page that was known to be duplicated on external storage is added to the NAS fetch queue in iteration i, modified on the source host and then sent over the direct link by one of the following iterations j, where $j > i$. Page 6 in Figure 3 exhibits this situation: in iteration 1, the page is sent as part of the list of duplicated pages and added to the NAS fetch queue (element (6,6)). Between iteration 1 and 2, page 6 is modified on the source host and its content are sent and directly copied into the VM's memory in iteration 2. When the (now obsolete) contents of page 6 are finally fetched from external storage, the NAS fetch queue recognizes this situation by comparing the timestamp of both items and discards the old data.

Guaranteeing consistency. Since the proposed method accesses the same external storage device from distinct physical hosts data consistency is an issue. During migration, only the source host issues write requests to the external storage device while the target host only performs read operations. We can guarantee consistency by ensuring the following conditions hold:

- no *write-caching* occurs on any level (except for the guest VM itself) to external storage.

- the target host can issue *uncached reads* to external storage.

The first condition does not prevent the guest VM from performing write-caching; however, once the VM flushes the data to external storage there must be no more write-caching, for example in the source host or the NAS device itself. Similarly, the target host needs to read the most recent data. The attached storage device must provide either direct-I/O that bypasses all caches or not perform any read-caching on any level below the target host.

In order to prevent write-after-read (WAR) hazards - due to different network latencies the target host may read a block before the write command originating from the source host has completed - we ensure that entries on the p2b map are only considered committed when the write transaction to the external storage device has completed. Uncommitted entries are treated like ordinary memory pages, i.e., the contents are sent directly to the target host.

5. Evaluation

This section presents the performance characteristics of the proposed technique. We measure the total migration time, the total amount of transmitted data, and the downtime for a variety of benchmarks on a number of network setups. The results show that our approach has the potential to significantly improve the total migration time of live VM migration at an equal downtime.

5.1 Experimental Setup

All experiments are performed on two identical hosts equipped with an Intel Core i5-2500 processor running at 3.3 GHz and 16 GB of main memory. For external storage a QNAP NAS server is used. The two hosts and the NAS server are connected via Gigabit Ethernet. The hosts run the Xen hypervisor 4.1.2 [8] with our modifications. Dom0 runs Ubuntu Server 11.10 (kernel version 3.0.0) [7].

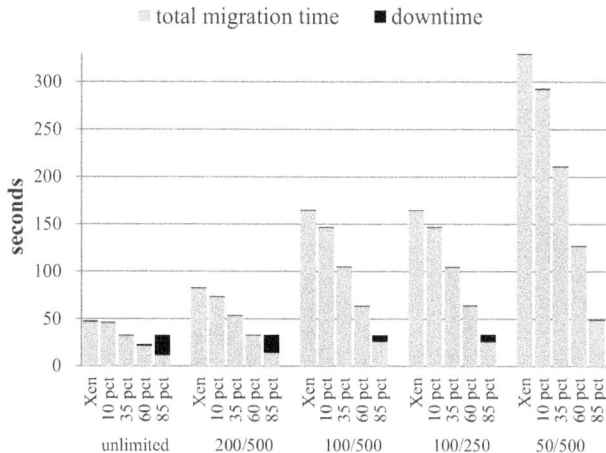

Figure 5. Performance in relation to duplication.

The experiments are performed on an HVM guest running Ubuntu Desktop 10.04 LTS with a 2.6.35 kernel. The VM is configured with two virtual CPUs and 2 GB of RAM. The guest's virtual disk is a file-backed image located on external storage mounted by dom0 using NFS.

5.2 Performance in Relation to Duplication

The proposed technique fetches memory pages whose contents are duplicated directly from external storage; the performance thus directly relates to the amount of duplication. In this first series of benchmarks, an idle VM is migrated. To trigger different ratios of duplication between memory and disk, the VM first copies a varying amount of data from disk to /dev/null. Figure 5 illustrates results. Unmodified represents the unmodified Xen. In 10 pct, the VM is booted up and then immediately migrated and thus represents a case with minimal duplication. 35 pct, 60 pct, and 85 pct show the results for duplication ratio of 10, 35, 60, and 85 percent, respectively. To illustrate the effect of the network bandwidth, we run each benchmark using Xen's rate-limiting algorithm with five different configurations: unlimited, 200/500, 100/500, 100/250, and 50/500. In unlimited the network bandwidth is not restricted; for the other configurations, the first number denotes the starting rate, and the second number the maximum network bandwidth available for migration in megabits per second.

The results show that the proposed technique successfully reduces the total migration time for all network configurations and amount of duplication. This is expected since if there is no duplication at all, then the proposed solution will perform exactly like unmodified Xen. As the amount of duplication increases, the benefits of the proposed solution become apparent. In the 100/500 configuration with about 50% of duplication (the bars labeled 512MB), the total migration time including the downtime is reduced from 165 to 64 seconds.

These benchmarks also reveal the main weakness of the proposed technique: the downtime of the VM can increase significantly if the VM is idle and almost all available memory is duplicated on disk. For unlimited and 1024MB, the worst case, we observe an increase of the downtime from 0.55 seconds to 20.8 seconds, almost a 40-fold increase. The reason for this extreme slowdown is as follows: with the proposed solution, live migration finishes within very few iterations. Most of the memory is duplicated on disk, hence only very few memory pages are sent directly to the destination host; the majority of the pages is given to the background fetch process on the destination host which then starts to

Table 1. Application Scenarios

Application	Description
RDesk I	web browsing, editing in an office suite
RDesk II	playing a movie
Admin I	compressing a large file
Admin II	compiling the Linux kernel
File I/O I	backing up data
File I/O II	Postmark benchmark

load these pages into the VM's memory. The adaptive iterative pre-copy algorithm notices that the amount of sent pages is sufficiently low to stop the VM on the source host, however, on the destination host the background process has not yet finished loading the pages from external storage. Since the current implementation waits for the background process to complete before resuming the VM, this delay can lead to a significant degradation in the downtime. For future work, we propose two strategies to eliminate this problem: (1) provide feedback about the progress of the background fetch process to the iterative pre-copy algorithm. The pre-copy algorithm can then, for example, send duplicated pages through the direct link if there is a long back-log of pages to be loaded on the target host. (2) resume the VM before the background fetch process has completed. This will require marking yet unloaded pages as invalid and interception of pagefaults caused by accesses to such pages.

5.3 Application Scenarios

Lacking a standard benchmark suite for live migration of virtual machines, we have selected several general application scenarios similar to what has been used in related work [10, 22] and that are representative for a Virtual Desktop Infrastructure (VDI) deployed in data centers. For all application scenarios the user is connected to the migrated VM by a VNC viewer using the RFB protocol [23].

Table 1 lists the application scenarios. RDesk I and II represent the standard usage scenario in VDI: a remote user connected to his virtual desktop. In RDesk I a Firefox [26] web browser is fetching a number of web pages and some scripted editing tasks are performed in the LibreOffice suite [25]. RDesk II plays a movie. These benchmarks exhibit moderate CPU and I/O activity and are expected to perform well both in unmodified Xen and our solution. Admin I and II represent administration tasks. In Admin I a 2 GB log file is compressed using gzip. Admin II compiles the Linux kernel. Both benchmarks exhibit a high CPU load, a large number of dirtied memory pages, as well as a high number of I/O requests (both read and write). We expect our solution to perform significantly better due to the high activity in the page cache and the rate of dirtied pages. The last group, File I/O I and II represents I/O-intensive benchmarks. In File I/O I a backup process backing up a large (2 GB) file. File I/O II runs Post-Mark [17] (500 files from 100 to 500 KB, 80'000 transactions, 4 KB read/write buffers). These benchmarks are expected to migrate quickly but exhibit performance degradation in the VM due to the simultaneous access to the shared storage caused by the background fetch process.

For each scenario, we measure the total migration time, the downtime of the VM, and the amount of data transferred in each round of the iterative pre-copy algorithm. For the Administration and File I/O scenario, we also measure the time to completion of the benchmarks running inside the migrated VM (the Remote Desktop scenarios have no well-defined completion point). The baseline is the unmodified Xen hypervisor 4.1.2.

All benchmarks are migrated using Xen's rate-limiting algorithm in three different configurations: 100/250, 200/500, and unlimited. As above, the first number represents the starting and the second number the maximal network bandwidth in megabits

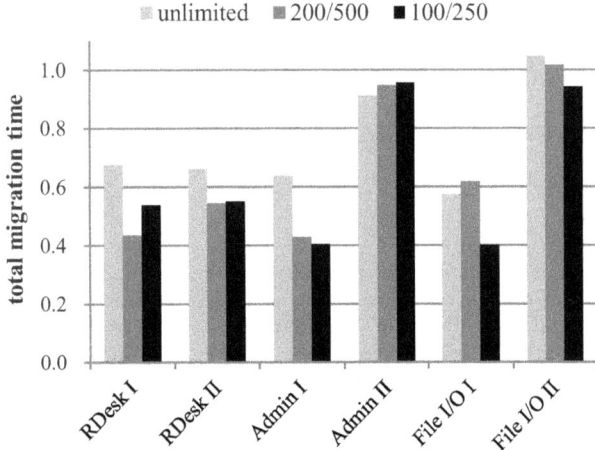

Figure 6. Normalized total migration time.

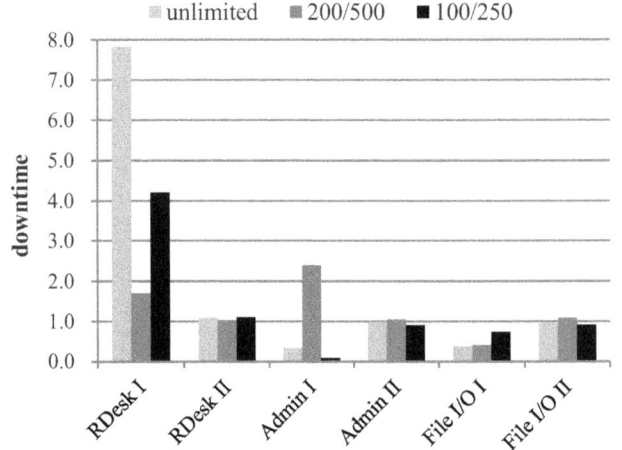

Figure 7. Normalized downtime.

per second, `unlimited` is allowed to use all of the available bandwidth. The rate-limiting algorithm is used as implemented in Xen. We expect that the proposed technique performs better in configurations with stricter rate-limiting, especially for benchmarks with lots of duplication, because the connection to the NAS device is always allowed to run at full speed.

5.4 Performance of Efficient Live Migration

Table 2 compares the performance of unmodified Xen with the proposed solution for the six application scenarios for three different network configurations. The first column lists the application scenario. Column two, denoted `dup`, shows the percentage of memory that is duplicated on disk when the live migration is started. The following columns show the performance for the three different network configurations, `unlimited`, `200/500`, and `100/250` for both `unmodified` Xen and the proposed solution (denoted `optimized`). For each network configuration, the total migration time (`mig`), the downtime (`down`), and the time to complete the benchmark inside the migrated VM (`bm`) is shown for unmodified Xen and the proposed solution. All time values are given in *seconds*.

Total Migration Time. Figure 6 shows the total migration time for the six application scenarios listed in Table 1. All results are normalized to unmodified Xen. Except for `File I/O II`, the PostMark benchmark, the proposed solution can improve the total migration time significantly. We observe that the proposed solution performs better if adaptive rate limiting (`200/500` and `100/250`) is used. This is not surprising; in the `unlimited` scenario, the source host can saturate the network connection to the destination host; parallel fetches from external storage thus have a smaller effect than in a constrained environment. In the case of `File I/O II` and sufficient memory bandwidth, the VM still running on the source host, the migration process, and the background fetch process are all competing for network resources which leads to a 5 and 2% increase of the total migration time for `unlimited` and `200/500`. On average, the proposed technique reduces the total migration time by 25, 34, and 37% for the different network configurations compared to unmodified Xen.

Downtime. Figure 7 displays the downtime of the application scenarios normalized to unmodified Xen. In most cases, the total migration time is similar to or even below unmodified Xen. `RDesk I` suffers from a severely increased downtime (up to 8-fold in the `unlimited` case). This scenario represents the worst-case for the proposed technique: an idle VM with lots of duplicated data. The synchronization with the background fetch process before the VM

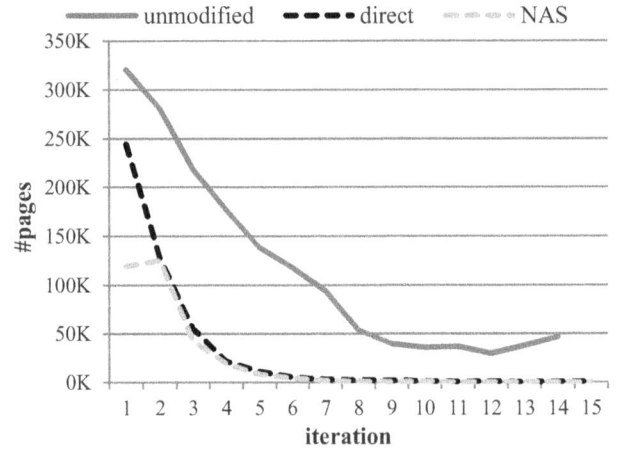

Figure 8. Pages per iteration for `File I/O I`.

is restarted on the target host is responsible for this increase; we have outlined two solutions to remedy this situation in Section 5.2. In many other cases, the downtime is actually *reduced*. This at first seemingly illogical result can be explained as follows: thanks to the reduced total migration time, the benchmarks running inside the VM are making less progress and therefore dirty fewer memory pages. In addition, the iterative pre-copy algorithm terminates the migration early because in each iteration less pages are sent directly to the destination host. This situation is illustrated in Figure 8 for the `File I/O I` scenario. The last iteration, during which the VM is stopped, comprises much fewer pages than in unmodified Xen. This leads to a reduced transfer time and in turn a shorter downtime of the VM.

Benchmark Performance The last important measure is performance degradation of the VM caused by live migration. Unmodified Xen itself causes a slight performance degradation due to the tracking of dirtied memory pages between iterations. A only source of performance degradation in the proposed solution is the additional load put on the NAS storage device. For I/O-intensive benchmarks that read or write a lot of data to the remote disk, the I/O requests generated by the background fetch process may hurt the running VM. Figure 9 shows the results for the application sce-

Table 2. Comparison of unmodified Xen with the proposed solution for the different application scenarios.

application	dup	unlimited						200/500						100/250					
		unmodified			optimized			unmodified			optimized			unmodified			optimized		
		mig	down	bm	mig	down	bm	mig	down	bm	mig	down	bm	mig	down	bm	mig	down	bm
RDesk I	45	61.0	1.02	-	41.2	7.95	-	94.6	0.59	-	51.0	2.50	-	175.8	0.57	-	76.3	0.97	-
RDesk II	46	53.2	1.04	-	35.2	1.13	-	83.3	1.05	-	45.9	1.16	-	165.4	1.01	-	90.2	1.05	-
Admin I	18	82.5	6.96	224	52.6	2.33	229	171.4	3.13	276	72.6	0.33	266	224.1	1.12	296	96.5	2.43	276
Admin II	10	62.4	5.37	215	56.8	5.31	237	88.8	7.13	217	84.8	6.47	234	155.7	8.57	229	147.5	9.06	242
File I/O I	24	92.6	19.49	222	53.2	7.31	226	176.6	4.52	266	69.3	1.02	223	127.7	22.81	249	79.1	9.41	205
File I/O II	12	51.8	8.49	240	54.3	8.09	262	85.0	7.35	252	79.5	7.75	270	147.1	9.04	274	149.5	9.81	290

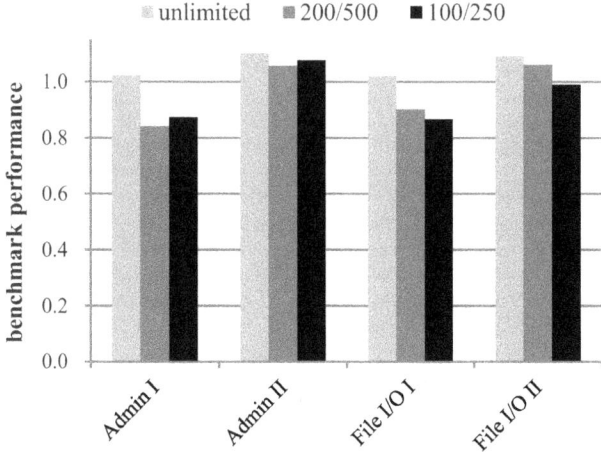

Figure 9. Normalized benchmark performance.

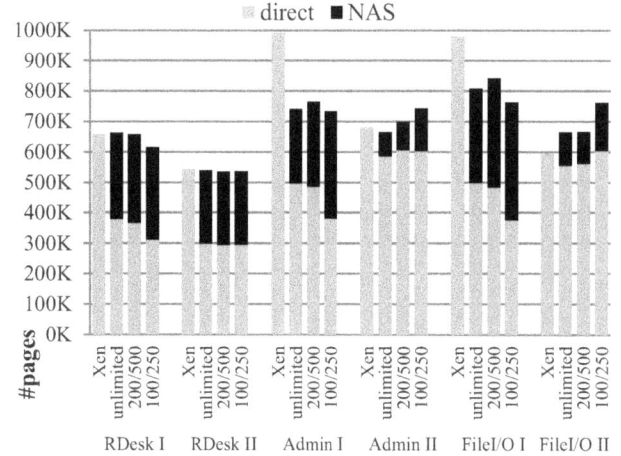

Figure 10. Number of pages transferred.

narios that run I/O-intensive benchmark with well-defined start and end points. We observe the expected behavior for `unlimited` in all benchmarks, and in the case of `Admin II` and `File I/O II` for rate-limited migrations. However, in the majority of cases the benchmark performance actually *improves*. The reason for this result is again the reduced total migration time: during migration, I/O-intensive benchmarks see a performance hit caused by the high network I/O activity of the migration and the overhead of tracking dirtied pages. Reducing the total migration time thus shortens the period during which the benchmark suffers from reduced performance which has a positive effect on the total benchmark time. On average, the benchmark time increased by 6% for `unmodified`, and is reduced by 4, resp. 5% in the case of `200/500` and `100/250`.

Pages transferred. Figure 10 shows the amount of pages transferred during the entire live migration. For each application scenario, unmodified Xen as well as the three network configurations are shown. In most cases, the total number of pages received by the target host is similar to unmodified Xen. `RDesk I and II` show the expected ratio of direct vs. pages fetched from NAS as listed in column two of Table 2. `Admin II` and `File I/O II`, on the other hand, show an increase in the total number of pages transferred. This is caused by two factors: first, the amount of duplication is low (10 and 12%, respectively) and both scenarios dirty many pages and generate a lot of I/O requests. Consequently, these two scenarios also perform worst when it comes to the total migration time (see Figure 6).

5.5 Limitations and Future Work

Overall, the proposed technique shows very promising results. The total migration time can be significantly reduced in almost all usage scenarios. The main weakness are idle VMs with a large amount of duplication which suffer from a significantly increased downtime. One might argue that an increased downtime does not matter that

much if the VM is idle; nevertheless, we are currently working on eliminating this problem by the approaches outlined in Section 5.2.

The proposed technique cannot be applied to live migration between hosts that do not share storage. Furthermore, there are a number of implementation issues that may prevent the use of this technique: first, we assume that the attached storage is mounted in dom0 and accessed as a file-backed disk in the VM. If the VM itself mounts the network-attached storage, then the current method of transparent I/O interception does not work anymore. A similar problem occurs with the newest PVH drivers where I/O requests cannot be intercepted transparently anymore. A possible solution to integrate the proposed technique in HVM guests using PVH drivers or VMs that mount the remote storage directly is providing a driver which communicates with `xentools` during live migration to inform the tools about the contents of the page cache. This is, in fact, the way we are implementing the proposed technique for PV guests. We are currently also working on a solution for PVH drivers.

Last but not least, the NAS fetch queue is required to synchronize with the receiver process before the VM can be restarted on the target machine. We plan to implement a post-copy approach in which the NAS fetch queue does not need to be empty before the VM can be restarted. Instead, all outstanding memory pages are marked *disabled*. The NAS fetch queue continues to fetch the pages in the background. If the VM traps on a yet unavailable page, that page is then fetched immediately via the page fault handler before the VM is restarted.

6. Conclusion

We have presented technique for efficient live migration of virtual machines. The key idea is that it is not necessary to send data of memory pages that are also duplicated on the attached storage device over the (often slow) network link between the distinct physical hosts; instead that data can be directly fetched from the NAS device.

To detect duplication between memory pages and storage blocks, we transparently track all I/O operation to the attached storage and maintain an up-to-date map of duplicated pages. When migrating a VM across distinct physical hosts, instead of sending the data of all dirty memory pages to the target host, only the data of ordinary (i.e., not duplicated) memory pages is sent. For pages that also exist on the attached storage device, the mapping memory pages to disk blocks is sent to the target host from where the data is fetched by a background process. We show that consistency can be guaranteed by keeping a version number for each transferred page. We have implemented and evaluated the proposed technique in the Xen hypervisor 4.1. For a number of benchmarks run on a Linux HVM guest we achieve an average reduction of the total migration time of over 30%; for certain benchmarks we observe a reduction of up to 60%.

While the implemented technique is effective in many cases, it still leaves room for improvement. For future work, we plan to implement a lazy-fetch algorithm on the target host. The VM can then be restarted even sooner and before all blocks have been fetched from the attached storage device. Minor improvements for the current implementation such as forwarding a list of skipped pages to the target host as well as support for para-virtualized guests are underway.

References

[1] Michael Armbrust, Armando Fox, Rean Griffith, Anthony D. Joseph, Randy Katz, Andy Konwinski, Gunho Lee, David Patterson, Ariel Rabkin, Ion Stoica, and Matei Zaharia. A view of cloud computing. *Communications of the ACM*, 53(4):50–58, April 2010.

[2] Paul Barham, Boris Dragovic, Keir Fraser, Steven Hand, Tim Harris, Alex Ho, Rolf Neugebauer, Ian Pratt, and Andrew Warfield. Xen and the art of virtualization. In *Proceedings of the nineteenth ACM symposium on Operating systems principles*, SOSP '03, pages 164–177, New York, NY, USA, 2003. ACM.

[3] Fabrice Bellard. QEMU. http://www.qemu.org, 2013. Online; accessed February 2013.

[4] Ravi Bhargava, Benjamin Serebrin, Francesco Spadini, and Srilatha Manne. Accelerating two-dimensional page walks for virtualized systems. In *Proceedings of the 13th international conference on Architectural support for programming languages and operating systems*, ASPLOS XIII, pages 26–35, New York, NY, USA, 2008. ACM.

[5] Nilton Bila, Eyal de Lara, Kaustubh Joshi, H. Andrés Lagar-Cavilla, Matti Hiltunen, and Mahadev Satyanarayanan. Jettison: efficient idle desktop consolidation with partial vm migration. In *Proceedings of the 7th ACM european conference on Computer Systems*, EuroSys '12, pages 211–224, New York, NY, USA, 2012. ACM.

[6] Robert Bradford, Evangelos Kotsovinos, Anja Feldmann, and Harald Schiöberg. Live wide-area migration of virtual machines including local persistent state. In *Proceedings of the 3rd international conference on Virtual execution environments*, VEE '07, pages 169–179, New York, NY, USA, 2007. ACM.

[7] Canonical Ltd. Ubuntu. http://www.ubuntu.com, 2013. Online; accessed February 2013.

[8] Citrix Systems, Inc. Xen Hypervisor. http://www.xen.org/products/xenhyp.html, 2012. Online; accessed February 2013.

[9] Christopher Clark, Keir Fraser, Steven Hand, Jacob Gorm Hansen, Eric Jul, Christian Limpach, Ian Pratt, and Andrew Warfield. Live migration of virtual machines. In *Proceedings of the 2nd conference on Symposium on Networked Systems Design & Implementation - Volume 2*, NSDI'05, pages 273–286, Berkeley, CA, USA, 2005. USENIX Association.

[10] Brendan Cully, Geoffrey Lefebvre, Dutch Meyer, Mike Feeley, Norm Hutchinson, and Andrew Warfield. Remus: high availability via asynchronous virtual machine replication. In *NSDI'08: Proceedings of the 5th USENIX Symposium on Networked Systems Design and Implementation*, pages 161–174, Berkeley, CA, USA, 2008. USENIX Association.

[11] Umesh Deshpande, Xiaoshuang Wang, and Kartik Gopalan. Live gang migration of virtual machines. In *Proceedings of the 20th international symposium on High performance distributed computing*, HPDC '11, pages 135–146, New York, NY, USA, 2011. ACM.

[12] Irfan Habib. Virtualization with KVM. *Linux Journal*, 2008(166), February 2008.

[13] Michael R. Hines and Kartik Gopalan. Post-copy based live virtual machine migration using adaptive pre-paging and dynamic self-ballooning. In *Proceedings of the 2009 ACM SIGPLAN/SIGOPS international conference on Virtual execution environments*, VEE '09, pages 51–60, New York, NY, USA, 2009. ACM.

[14] Takahiro Hirofuchi, Hidemoto Nakada, Satoshi Itoh, and Satoshi Sekiguchi. Reactive consolidation of virtual machines enabled by postcopy live migration. In *Proceedings of the 5th international workshop on Virtualization technologies in distributed computing*, VTDC '11, pages 11–18, New York, NY, USA, 2011. ACM.

[15] Wei Huang, Qi Gao, Jiuxing Liu, and Dhabaleswar K. Panda. High performance virtual machine migration with RDMA over modern interconnects. In *Proceedings of the 2007 IEEE International Conference on Cluster Computing*, CLUSTER '07, pages 11–20, Washington, DC, USA, 2007. IEEE Computer Society.

[16] Hai Jin, Li Deng, Song Wu, Xuanhua Shi, and Xiaodong Pan. Live virtual machine migration with adaptive, memory compression. In *Cluster Computing and Workshops, 2009. CLUSTER '09. IEEE International Conference on*, pages 1 –10, 31 2009-sept. 4 2009.

[17] Jeffrey Katcher. PostMark: A New File System Benchmark. Technical Report Technical Report TR3022, Network Appliance, October 1997.

[18] Haikun Liu, Hai Jin, Xiaofei Liao, Liting Hu, and Chen Yu. Live migration of virtual machine based on full system trace and replay. In *Proceedings of the 18th ACM international symposium on High performance distributed computing*, HPDC '09, pages 101–110, New York, NY, USA, 2009. ACM.

[19] Raymond A. Lorie. Physical integrity in a large segmented database. *ACM Transactions on Database Systems*, 2(1):91–104, March 1977.

[20] Michael Nelson, Beng-Hong Lim, and Greg Hutchins. Fast transparent migration for virtual machines. In *Proceedings of the annual conference on USENIX Annual Technical Conference*, ATEC '05, pages 25–25, Berkeley, CA, USA, 2005. USENIX Association.

[21] Oracle. VirtualBox. https://www.virtualbox.org, 2012. Online; accessed February 2013.

[22] Eunbyung Park, Bernhard Egger, and Jaejin Lee. Fast and space-efficient virtual machine checkpointing. In *Proceedings of the 7th ACM SIGPLAN/SIGOPS international conference on Virtual execution environments*, VEE '11, pages 75–86, New York, NY, USA, 2011. ACM.

[23] Tristan Richardson. The RFB protocol. http://www.realvnc.com/docs/rfbproto.pdf, 2010. Online; accessed February 2013.

[24] Petter Svärd, Benoit Hudzia, Johan Tordsson, and Erik Elmroth. Evaluation of delta compression techniques for efficient live migration of large virtual machines. In *Proceedings of the 7th ACM SIGPLAN/SIGOPS international conference on Virtual execution environments*, VEE '11, pages 111–120, New York, NY, USA, 2011. ACM.

[25] The Document Foundation. LibreOffice. http://www.libreoffice.org, 2013. Online; accessed February 2013.

[26] The Mozilla Foundation. Firefox. http://www.mozilla.org, 2013. Online; accessed February 2013.

[27] Franco Travostino. Seamless live migration of virtual machines over the MAN/WAN. In *Proceedings of the 2006 ACM/IEEE conference on Supercomputing*, SC '06, New York, NY, USA, 2006. ACM.

[28] VMware. VMware VMotion: Live migration of virtual machines without service interruption. http://www.vmware.com/files/pdf/VMware-VMotion-DS-EN.pdf, 2009. Online; accessed February 2013.

Introspection-based Memory De-duplication and Migration

Jui-Hao Chiang

Stony Brook University
Stony Brook, USA
juihaochiang@gmail.com

Han-Lin Li

Industrial Technology Research Institute
Hsinchu, Taiwan
astercase@gmail.com

Tzi-cker Chiueh

Industrial Technology Research Institute
Hsinchu, Taiwan
tcc@itri.org.tw

Abstract

Memory virtualization abstracts a physical machine's memory resource and presents to the virtual machines running on it a piece of physical memory that could be shared, compressed and moved. To optimize the memory resource utilization by fully leveraging the flexibility afforded by memory virtualization, it is essential that the hypervisor have some sense of how the guest VMs use their allocated physical memory. One way to do this is virtual machine introspection (VMI), which interprets byte values in a guest memory space into semantically meaningful data structures. However, identifying a guest VM's memory usage information such as free memory pool is non-trivial. This paper describes a bootstrapping VM introspection technique that could accurately extract free memory pool information from multiple versions of Windows and Linux without kernel version-specific hard-coding, how to apply this technique to improve the efficiency of memory de-duplication and memory state migration, and the resulting improvement in memory de-duplication speed, gain in additional memory pages de-duplicated, and reduction in traffic loads associated with memory state migration.

Categories and Subject Descriptors D.4.2 [*Storage Management*]: Main memory

General Terms Design, Management, Measurement

Keywords Memory de-duplication, VM Migration, Introspection

1. Introduction

Memory de-duplication [22] for virtualized servers identifies physical memory pages on a physical machine that are duplicates of each other, consolidates those with identical contents to a single page by pointing these *guest physical pages* to the same *machine physical page*, and marks the machine physical page as read-only. Once any of these guest physical pages is first written, a *copy-on-write* (COW) operation is triggered, which creates a new copy of the machine physical page so as to allow the write to go through. A common way to identify physical memory pages with identical contents is to hash each physical page's contents, compare the resulting hash values, and confirm the equivalence of two pages with the same hash value through a byte-by-byte comparison. Although the above approach has been shown to work empirically, it suffers

from the following drawback. Because the page equivalence check is based on hashed value, the above approach cannot establish the equivalence of memory pages whose contents are *don't-cares*, e.g., pages in the free memory pool of the guest OS or application processes. Because the contents of these pages are immaterial, they could have been treated as a zero page without affecting the system's correctness.

VM migration [11] is a powerful building block for improving the availability, power consumption and resource utilization efficiency of virtualized data centers. The bulk of work in moving a VM is the migration of its memory state. Although modern VM migration technology could effectively reduce the connection disruption time of a VM to a sub-second range, it is infrequently triggered in practice because the performance impact of a VM migration transaction on the network is non-negligible due to its bursty nature. One way to mitigate this network performance impact is to avoid migrating unnecessary memory pages, e.g., those that already exist on the target machine or those whose contents are immaterial and thus not worth transferring.

From the above analysis, it is clear that the hypervisor would be able to effectively optimize both memory de-duplication and memory state migration should it have full knowledge of the free memory pool information of every guest VM running on it. For memory de-duplication, the hypervisor could treat free memory pages as zero pages and de-duplicate them accordingly. Moreover, deduplicating these pages does not require page content hashing or byte-by-byte comparison. For memory state migration, the hypervisor could skip transferring free memory pages, and thus cut down the traffic load injected into the network.

One way for the hypervisor to obtain the free memory pool information in the guest kernel is to inject an agent into every guest VM, which at times could be cumbersome and error-prone. In this research, we explored an alternative approach, *virtual machine introspection (VMI)*, which converts memory byte values into semantically meaningful data structures. The accuracy requirement for our introspection technique is higher than those used in security forensics, because our target is a *live* VM and inaccuracy could lead to VM crash. Modern introspection techniques developed for forensics could modify the target VM, including running code inside the target VM where our technique does not have that latitude.

Among all existing VMI tools, most of them are developed based on manual reverse engineering efforts and include hard-coded parsers that are tailored to specific kernel versions. For example, although the base location of the free memory map is available from the debug symbol table for the guest OS and can be manually retrieved, as is done in Xenaccess [13, 17], the internal structures of the free memory map are undocumented and tend to vary from one kernel version to another. For example, the per-page descriptor size has been changed from 24 bytes in the 2006 version of Windows XP to 28 bytes in the 2009 version of Windows XP. We developed a *bootstrapping* VM introspection scheme that could programmatically identify the free memory pool information of multiple versions of Windows and Linux guests at run time. We believe this makes a novel contribution to the repertoire of techniques used in VMI tool development.

2. Related Work

Without directly hashing the page content, Linux's KSM (Kernel Same-Page Sharing) feature [9] uses the page contents as keys to construct a Red Black tree. Each time a new page is encountered, its content is used as a key to search the tree for a possible match. If a match is found, the new page may be de-duplicated. In addition to storing page contents, the Difference Engine [14] applies an additional *page patching* technique to store some pages as deltas with respect to pre-chosen reference pages.

Satori [16] considers the guest OS's page cache as a promising source for duplicated pages. To avoid periodically scanning the memory pages in guest VMs, it modifies the block device layer of the guest OS (Linux) so that it is *sharing-aware* and enables the Xen hypervisor to intercept all disk accesses. Upon each disk access that populates the page cache, Satori computes the hash values of those new pages that are pushed into the page cache and determines if they are duplicates. In addition, Satori also maintains a list of pages containing replaceable contents, similar to our *don't-care* pages, and provides them to the hypervisor as the new pages used in COW. However, maintaining this list requires modifications to the guest OS, which means that it is not applicable to closed-source OSs.

Besides *memory de-duplication*, there are other approaches to increasing the memory utilization efficiency. IBM's Collaborative Memory Management (CMM) system [21] modifies the guest OS to provide hints to the underlying IBM z/VM hypervisor, so that the hypervisor can page out memory pages of guests, called *host paging*, and use the reclaimed memory space for other purposes. In addition to guest OS modification, this host paging mechanism also requires pausing the guest whose memory is to be paged out, which incurs noticeable performance overhead.

Transcendent [15] modifies the *page cache* implementation of Linux such that the hypervisor provides a free memory pool, called *precache*, that serves as a second-level cache of the guests' page cache. Every time a guest needs to access the disk, it first queries the *precache* to avoid performing any disk I/O operation whenever possible. On the other hand, when a page is evicted out of a guest's page cache, the page is stored in the *precache* for future accesses. The hypervisor could dynamically shrink and expand this *precache* in an on-demand fashion. Because the *precache* is made visible to the guest OS, significant kernel modifications are required, which again limits its applicability.

Virtual machine introspection (VMI) was originally proposed to detect malware intrusion, e.g., kernel rootkits, in guests running on a virtualized server. To narrow the semantic gap between the byte values in a guest's memory pages and the high-level state information they contain, Dolan-Gavitt et al. [12] proposed to log an execution trace of a guest program, extract the instructions from the trace, create a *translated program* from the extracted instructions, and run the resulting program on *Dom0*[1] of Xen outside the monitored guest. This approach requires an OS version-specific step that identifies the instruction sequence to be recorded, extracted and translated, and is not fully automated.

Garfinkel et al. [13] leveraged the *crash* utility [3] to analyze memory pages in Linux guests and used the analysis results for intrusion detection. The *crash* utility was originally used to debug the Linux kernel, and has several hard-coded parts that are specific to each Linux kernel version. Xenaccess [17] was developed recently

to extract process and module information of both Windows and Linux guest OS in the Xen hypervisor. However, it could not parse free memory maps, and contains many hard-coded values specific to each guest OS version.

Bryant et al. [10] also proposed to use introspection to identify free memory pages in Linux guests and avoid copying them during VM state cloning. This research gave another example of memory virtualization optimization that benefits from VM introspection. However, this work did not address the issue of how to programmatically extract the free memory map information from different versions and configurations of Linux kernels. Our work does address this issue and the solution is discussed in Section 3.3.

3. Bootstrapping VM Introspection

3.1 Overview

Most existing VM introspection methods rely on manually constructed interpretation programs that extract high-level kernel data structure information from a guest VM's physical address space. The process of building these interpretation programs is usually time-consuming, error-prone, difficult to maintain, and sometimes next to impossible, especially for closed-source OS. One way to avoid these difficulties is to link an agent into the guest kernel when the kernel is built so that the agent could leverage the kernel's symbol and type information to make sense of the guest kernel's address space(e.g., Windows [4], Mac OS X [1]). However, the agent approach is not always possible for proprietary OSs, and entails its own problems for agent update and deployment.

As an alternative to the manual and agent approaches, we have developed two techniques that aim to *programmatically* exploit as much information about a given guest kernel as possible, so as to do away with hard-coded values and parsing logic. For the guest OSs throughout this paper, we focus **only** on the two prevalent ones in large data centers [2], the Windows and Linux OSs. As for other guest OSs, we have not explored and **do not claim** the applicability of VMI techniques to them.

The first technique identifies the type and version of a guest kernel, retrieves the kernel's debugging information either by fetching it from the original software publisher or dynamically building it from the corresponding kernel source code if available, and derives the type and base information of kernel variables and data structures of interest. The second technique takes one step further by incorporating code in the guest OS directly into the interpretation program so as to examine or even manipulate certain guest kernel data structures that are un-documented and even implementation-specific.

These two techniques form a new approach to VM introspection called *Bootstrapping VMI* or BVMI, which, instead of including kernel version-specific hard-coding, dynamically builds up its knowledge about a given guest kernel by fetching and exploiting all available compiler-generated and/or source code information associated with the kernel, and uses this knowledge to make sense of the bytes values in the guest memory space in a way that approximates the effectiveness of the agent approach. In the following two subsections, we describe how we applied these two techniques to successfully identifying the free memory pool of various versions of Windows and Linux OSs.

3.2 Free Memory Pool Identification for Windows

On Windows, executable files, dynamically linked libraries (DLLs), and kernel images are all in the Portable Executable or PE format [8]. When a PE file is loaded into memory, it is stored at a starting address known as the *base address*. The virtual address of every symbol in a PE file is represented as an offset with respect to the file's base address, also known as the Relative Virtual Address

---
[1] Dom0 is the privileged VM in Xen while other VMs are called DomU.

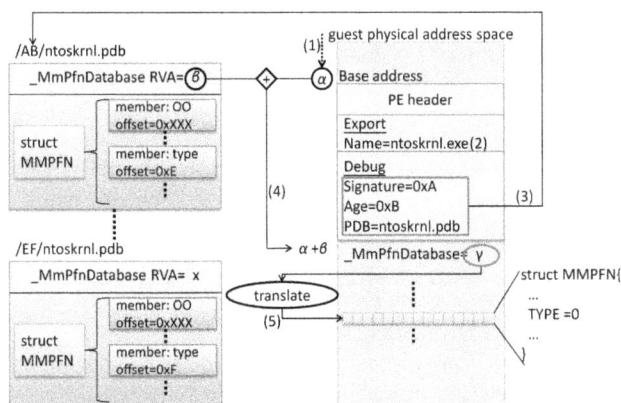

Figure 1. *Introspecting a Windows virtual machine requires matching a a Windows kernel PE file loaded into a guest VM (on the right) with its corresponding debugging PDB file fetched from Microsoft's Symbol Server (on the left).*

(RVA). Therefore, a symbol's absolute virtual address is equal to the sum of its RVA and the *base address* of where the associated PE file is loaded. As shown on the right side of Figure 1, when a PE file is loaded, its headers are also loaded. The two items in the PE header that are relevant here are *export data directory*, which contains the name of the current PE file, e.g., `ntoskrnl.exe` for the Windows kernel [20], and *debug data directory*, which contains a 128-bit *Signature* and a 32-bit *Age* to uniquely identify the PE file's associated debugging information.

For each PE file, the linker, e.g., Microsoft Visual C++, may optionally produce a PDB file that contains the associated debug information, such as the symbol table. For widely used PE files, Microsoft publishes their PDB files on its public web site. The PDB file by default contains the name, address, and type information for functions and variables, e.g., the RVA of a static variable declared in the program. To associate a PE file with its PDB file, both of them include a unique combination of *Signature* and *Age* values. In addition, Microsoft provides a Debug Interface Access (DIA) SDK [4] that allows developers to extract detailed debug information about a PE file, e.g., one can use a depth-first-search algorithm to query a specific member of a user-defined structure, because the latter is stored as a tree hierarchy inside its PDB file.

The *memory map* in a Windows kernel is called the PFN (Physical Frame Number) Database, which is a statically allocated array of page descriptors, each of type `struct _MMPFN`, and is located in a contiguous region of the guest physical address space [20]. The symbol name of the PFN Database is `_MmPfnDatabase`.

After a Windows OS boots up, all its free pages are in the *Zeroed* page list, which is the free memory pool every page in which is all-zero. When a free page is allocated to a process, it is taken out of the *Zeroed* page list. Upon the exit of a process, pages in its working set are returned to the *Free* page list. For security reasons, the Windows OS uses a *zero page thread* to zero out the pages in *Free* list and put them into the *Zeroed* page list for future reuse.

Based on the above information, we developed a BVMI program[2] to identify the free memory pool of multiple versions of the Windows OS. The BVMI program considers a guest page is free if it is located in the *Zeroed* list, i.e., when the *type* of the page descriptor is equal to `ZeroedPageList`, which is defined as a member of an enumeration type `_MMLISTS`. This rule applies to all Win-

dows OS versions ranging from Windows XP to the latest Windows 7 [18–20]. However, because the detailed layout of the enumeration type `_MMLISTS` may vary from kernel version to kernel version, we have to rely on kernel version-specific PDB files to help determine the exact layout of this data structure and use this knowledge to perform free memory page check.

To summarize, the BVMI program takes the following steps to programmatically traverse the PFN database and inspect each page descriptor, as outlined in Figure 1.

(1) Given a PE file, BVMI first scans its export data directory to confirm its name is indeed `ntoskrnl.exe` (a Windows kernel), and then scans the remaining file for a page containing the magic string "MZ", whose base address is the guest kernel's base address, $Base_{kernel}$.

(2) BVMI extracts the *Signature* and *Age* fields from the PE file's debug data directory, and uses them to construct an URL that can be used to access the PE file's PDB file from Microsoft's public symbol server.

After the kernel image's PDB file is downloaded, BVMI uses the DIA SDK to search for the relative virtual address of the PFN database, which is denoted as $Base_{PFN}$, and to traverse the `_MMPFN` structure to derive the data structure's size and the offset of its member *type*.

(3) BVMI computes the start physical address of the PFN database by adding $Base_{PFN}$ to $Base_{kernel}$, translates it to its corresponding machine physical address, maps the array into its own virtual address space, and examines the *type* field of every PFN database entry to determine if the corresponding physical page is free using the layout information extracted from the `_MMPFN` structure.

3.3 Free Memory Pool Identification for Linux

When a Linux kernel image is built, a special file called *System.map* is generated, which contains a mapping between the symbol names of all exported variables and functions in the kernel source and their absolute virtual addresses. A Linux kernel image contains a real-mode kernel image, whose header contains detailed Linux version information such as the kernel version, distribution, and build timestamp, which can be used to track down the corresponding distribution source package.

To avoid memory fragmentation, Linux uses a buddy system memory allocator, which organizes free memory pages into groups of physically contiguous pages, each with a size that is a power of two. The first page of every free memory page group is called a *Buddy page*, which represents the entire group and uses the *private* field of its page descriptor to record the number of physically contiguous pages in its group. For example, if the *private* field of a *Buddy page*'s descriptor is n, there are 2^n contiguous free pages in its group. Therefore, one can uncover free pages in a guest OS by first identifying Buddy pages and then all other pages in their groups. Linux supports two memory models: (1) a *flat* model using a one-dimensional memory map, and (2) a *sparse* model using a two-dimensional memory map. The exact memory model used in a kernel is selected at the kernel configuration step, and remains fixed after the kernel is built.

For the same kernel source, each Linux distribution, e.g., Ubuntu, maintains its installation package for kernel image, which is usually stripped off kernel debugging information. One could recreate the debug information associated with a kernel distribution, by downloading the distribution's corresponding kernel source and building a kernel image with the `CONFIG_DEBUG_INFO` option enabled from it.

The BVMI program for Linux is more difficult to develop than that for Windows, because the Linux kernel is highly configurable,

---

[2] For implementation, it runs in the Dom0 domain of Xen, which has the privilege to access all memory pages of guest VMs.

53

and the same kernel source could be compiled into kernel versions with very different structures and configurations. For example, configuration primitives such as `#ifdef` could conditionally trigger different compiler pre-processing and post the following issues. First, the memory model configuration option determines whether the memory map is represented as a one-dimensional or two-dimensional array. Second, size and layout of the page descriptor data structure may vary from one kernel version to another. Third, semantics associated with data structure values used to identify Buddy pages vary from one kernel version to another.

The first two issues could be resolved by using the GDB interface to query the debug information associated with the input kernel image. However, the last issue could not be easily resolved because which data structure field is used to identify Buddy pages changes from one kernel version to another. For example, in Linux versions older than 2.6.18, a page is said to be a Buddy page if the 19th bit of the `flags` field in the page's descriptor is set, but in version 2.6.38, it uses the `_mapcount` field.

Fortunately, across all Linux kernel versions, there is a standard inline function, `PageBuddy(struct page*)`, that takes a page descriptor structure as the input and returns true if the page is a Buddy page. However, the implementation of this function is different for different kernel versions. One way to solve the Buddy page identification problem is to incorporate the logic of the PageBuddy function for different Linux kernel versions into the BVMI program so as to identify free memory pages in guest OSs that run different versions of Linux. However, this approach is cumbersome and error-prone. Instead, we directly leverage the `PageBuddy` function's implementation in each Linux kernel version by calling it from the BVMI program. More concretely, we wrote a stub function, called `GFN_is_Buddy`, which determines whether a given GFN in a guest is a Buddy page or not by calling the guest's `PageBuddy` inline function. The input argument of this stub function is a GFN in a guest, and this interface is the same across all Linux kernel versions.

```
/* stub.c: guest kernel module */
int GFN_is_Buddy(unsigned long GFN)
{
    struct page *page;
#ifdef CONFIG_FLATMEM
    /* Flat model: use map as 1D array */
    page = (struct page*)mem_map[GFN];
    return PageBuddy(page);
#else
    ...
}
```

Given a guest VM using a specific Linux kernel version, we dynamically compiled this stub function against the kernel version's source code and configuration, and produced an ELF file, `stub.o`. Then we linked this `stub.o` file with the BVMI program so that the latter can call the `GFN_is_Buddy` function on every guest page descriptor it examines. We believe the above approach represents a new VM introspection technique in that it pioneers the use of kernel version-specific code to interpret kernel version-specific undocumented data structures. Although this technique needs access to the kernel source code and configuration file used by a Linux guest, it does not require any knowledge of the detailed layout or semantic information associated with any kernel data structures.

The following code snippet shows the independent free page check program (`FreePageCheck.c`) that includes the previous `GFN_is_Buddy` function and services requests from the BVMI program. The communications between the BVMI program and the free page check program is based on a shared memory mechanism.

```
/* FreePageCheck.c: kernel version-specific
 * code to check if a page is a Buddy page */
```

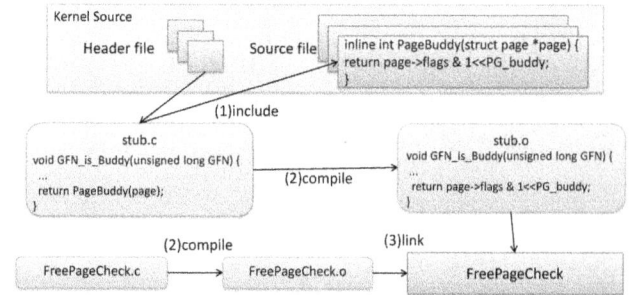

Figure 2. *Compiling the `GFN_is_Buddy` function against the source code and configuration file of a guest's Linux kernel version to generate a `stub.o` file, and linking it with `FreePageCheck.c` to form the independent free page check program.*

```
extern int GFN_is_Buddy(unsigned long);
void check_free_page(int *free_map)
{
    for (gfn = 0; gfn < guest_max_gfn; gfn++)
        if (GFN_is_Buddy(gfn)) free_map[gfn] = 1;
}

int main()
{
    check_free_page(free_map);
    /* Share free_map with BVMI program */
}
```

Figure 2 shows the steps taken to generate a kernel version-specific `stub.o` and link it with the compiled ELF object of `FreePageCheck.c` to form a kernel version-specific free page check program, which could answer queries from the BVMI program on whether certain pages are free. Note that the memory model is also determined in the stub.o after compiled with the guest kernel source. In summary, the steps to identify free memory pages in a Linux-based guest VM are

(1) Searches the header of Linux guest real-mode kernel image for the magic string "HdrS", then extracts the kernel version information, and uses the kernel version information to either retrieve the corresponding free page check program if it exists, or dynamically composes the corresponding free page check program based on the kernel version's source code and configuration file,

(2) Extracts from the `System.map` file associated with the guest kernel's version the location of the memory map, and

(3) Traverses every page descriptor in the memory map by calling the free page check program to determine if each traversed page is a Buddy page.

3.4 Discussions

The two techniques described in this section still require a prior knowledge of how to link high-level information being sought after (e.g. memory page status) with specific kernel data structures (e.g. memory map), and thus manual efforts to build the introspection mechanism. In addition, because a kernel image is a product of the kernel source code, the configuration file, and the compiler, these two techniques may fail to deliver correct introspection when any change is made to the source code, the configuration file, or the compiler used to build a guest kernel.

The second technique is an instance of exploiting a guest OS's own code to help the VMI program to make sense of its own byte sequences [12]. While conceptually simple, it has two potential issues. First, the guest OS functions used to interpret the guest physical address space must be self-contained and do not reference any other kernel variables or functions. Second, as the interpretation program inspects a guest's physical address space, the guest's state must not go through any modification; otherwise the interpretation program may break because of dangling pointers, e.g., a next pointer in a linked list item becomes invalid as a result of guest state modification. Based on our prototyping and test experiences, neither of these two issues becomes a real problem.

The principles underlying the proposed introspection technique are generic, and its applications to different versions of guest OS vary from one guest OS to another. With the help of these principles, it takes a much smaller amount of effort to custom-build a free-memory-pool introspection technique for a new version of guest OS than without such principles.

One may worry the applicability of such technique when VM uses highly customized guest OSs. However, the most common service scenario for IaaS (Infrastructure as a Service) is for the IaaS provider, e.g., Amazon [2], to supply a set of pre-prepared VM images for users to start their VMs, and users are discouraged from modifying their VMs' OSs. Therefore, the proposed introspection technique is a good fit with the prevailing IaaS service model, as well as PaaS (Platform as a Service) offerings, in which users do not get to choose VM images.

4. Generalized Memory de-duplication

We built a Generalized Memory de-duplication (GMD) engine that leverages the free memory pool information in guest VMs to de-duplicate pages that have identical or don't-care contents. This GMD prototype is based on the Xen hypervisor. In Xen, the *guest virtual* addresses in a VM are translated to their *guest physical* addresses, and then to *machine physical* addresses, i.e., which are the actual the physical addresses used to access the memory. Accordingly, the Machine Frame Number (**MFN**) is a page number in the machine physical address space whereas the Guest Frame Number (**GFN**) is a page frame number in the guest physical address space. Normally, each GFN of a guest OS is mapped to a unique MFN allocated by the hypervisor. To increase the memory utilization efficiency, Xen supports a *memory sharing* mechanism similar to that for sharing memory among processes in a conventional OS, the COW mechanism, i.e., all processes map a shared page as read-only; when a process Z first writes the shared page, a write-protection fault occurs and OS allocates and maps a new memory page for Z, which is marked as read-writable and initialized with the faulted page's content. In Xen, this is achieved by the *unshare* memory sharing API function.

Two other important API functions for memory sharing are *nominate* and *share*. The first function accepts a VM identifier and a GFN as input parameters, and marks the corresponding page as read-only with a returned *handle*, which uniquely identifies the page. Accesses to such a *handle* are protected by a global exclusive lock. The second function takes two *handles* as input parameters. If both *handles* are valid, Xen maps the two GFNs associated with these two *handles* to the MFN associated with the first *handle*, and thus frees the physical page corresponding to the MFN associated with the second *handle*. In addition to *nominate* and *share*, Xen also provides API calls that allow the *Dom0* kernel to *map* a GFN of a DomU VM into the virtual address space of a user-level program running on it, and to *translate* a given guest virtual address to its corresponding guest physical address.

The proposed GMD engine leverages the free memory pool information about guest VMs, treats the free memory pages as duplicates of an all-zero page, and de-duplicates them accordingly. The current GMD engine prototype is implemented as a user-level program that runs in *Dom0* and implements de-duplication using

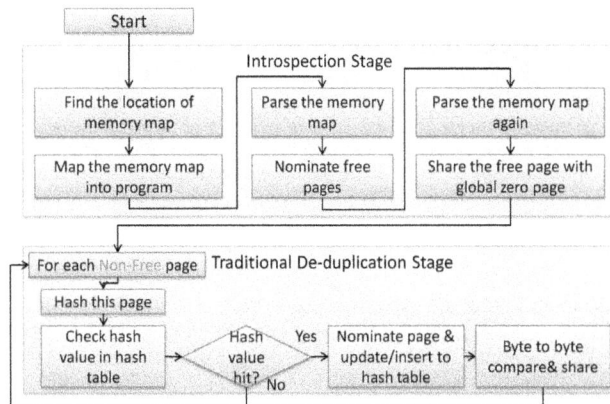

Figure 3. *The workflow of the proposed Generalized Memory de-duplication (GMD) engine, which comprises two stages: the* Introspection *stage to identify free memory page in guest VMs and the* de-duplication *stage that de-duplicates pages using hashing and byte-by-byte comparison.*

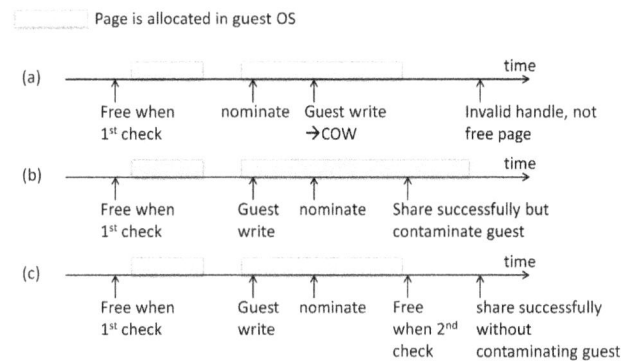

Figure 4. *The GMD engine checks if a guest page is free twice to avoid a race condition illustrated in (b), where a page is detected free, modified by the guest, and then nominated and shared by the GMD engine. Checking pages are free twice avoids the data corruption problem due to this race condition, as shown in (c).*

the Xen hypervisor's primitives mentioned above. As shown in Figure 3, the GMD engine consists of two stages: the *Introspection* stage and the *de-duplication* stage. In the *Introspection* stage, the GMD engine first calls the BVMI program to identify and record free guest pages into a bitmap, $free\_map1$, and nominates them, then walks the memory map again to check if those pages in $free\_map1$ are still free and marks those that are still free in another bitmap, $free\_map2$, and finally shares each page is that is in both $free\_map1$ and $free\_map2$ with the all-zero page without comparison.

In the *de-duplication* stage, for each non-free page P, the GMD engine computes a hash value using its page contents, looks up the resulting hash value in a global page content hash database, and if a hit is found, nominates P and shares P with the hit page. If the byte-by-byte comparison comes back with the match, the *share* function removes duplicate page and returns success.

The GMD engine checks *twice* if a memory page in a guest OS is free during the Introspection stage, because the GMD is implemented as a user-level program running in Dom0 and there is a potential race condition between when it detects a guest memory page is free and when it nominates the page for sharing. As shown in Figure 4(a), if a guest page that is identified as a free page is allocated and modified after it is nominated, the modification triggers the COW mechanism, which in turn destroys the page's *handle* returned by the *nominate* call, and the following *share* call will abort because the *handle* is invalid. If, however, the modification appears after the first free page check but before the *nominate* call, as shown in Figure 4(b), the page's *handle* continues to be valid when the GMD engine nominates and shares the page with the all-zero page, and eventually the modification is lost. Instead, we solve this problem by checking free memory pages twice. With a second free page check shown in Figure 4(c), a guest page can only be nominated and shared only if the second check also reports it is free. If a guest page is still free in the second check, it means the page could be safely de-duplicated with the all-zero page because its contents can be thrown away.

Proof For guest OS, we assume it performs the following two steps when allocating a memory page: (1) Mark the memory page as non-free (2) Give the page to the user or kernel component, which then stores information into it later. The dual-check mechanism includes three operations $C1$ (first check if the page is free), R (mark the page as read-only), and $C2$ (second check if the page is free). Only after $C2$ is successful will a page be mapped to a zero page. In the following, $X < Y$ means X happens before Y. Thus, it is true that $C1 < R < C2$ and $(1) < (2)$.

A race condition that could lead to data corruption must satisfy the following condition: $C1 < (1) < (2) < R$, i.e., the guest allocates the page after $C1$ and then modifies it before R. In this case, the COW mechanism does not have a chance to get triggered and the page may be corrupted if $C2$ is not included. However, after $C2$ is included, the proposed scheme could effectively detect this race condition and abort the attempt to reclaim the page, because $C2$ would find the page no longer free and thus won't map it to a zero page.

5. Free Memory Pages-Avoiding VM Migration

A major performance metric for VM migration is its impact on the network due to memory state transfer. Because the contents of the free memory pages of a VM are don't-cares, they do not need to be moved when the VM is migrated. Avoiding transferring free memory pages of a migrated VM is thus an effective way to reduce the network performance impact of a VM migration transaction.

Xen uses an iterative memory state transfer scheme by organizing each migrated VM's memory into chunks of 1024 pages. In the first iteration, for each chunk, Xen first sends to the target machine a map, *pfn_type*, each entry of which describes the type of each transferred memory page, e.g., *invalid* or *regular* data page, and then sends the contents of all valid pages in the current chunk. To avoid transferring free memory pages to the target machine, we introduced one more type, *free*, to denote pages that are valid but free. By consulting with the BVMI program, Xen on the source machine identifies the guest physical pages in a migrated VM that are free, marks the corresponding entries in the *pfn_type* map as *free*, and skips transferring them to the target machine. For all free pages of a migrated VM, as indicated in the received *pfn_type* map, Xen on the target machine de-duplicates them to an all-zero page. For the remaining iterations, Xen does not leverage introspection, but focuses only on the transfer of dirtied pages.

6. Performance Evaluation

The test machine used in this study contains an Intel Xeon E5640 quad-core processor with VT and EPT enabled, 24 GB physical memory, and a 500 GB hard disk. The host runs Xen-4.1 with CentOS-5.5 as the *Dom0* kernel. All our VMs are configured with 1 virtual CPU and 4 GB memory, which corresponds to something between the *Small Instance* and *Large Instance* classes of Amazon's Elastic Compute Cloud (EC2) service [2] and should be representative for normal server or desktop applications.

We tried guest VMs running 32-bit and 64-bit versions of Windows and Linux, including **Win7-64** (64-bit Windows 7), **WinXP-32** (32-bit Windows XP with Service Pack 2 installed), **Centos-64** (64-bit Centos 5.6 with the 2.6.18 Linux kernel and Sparse memory model configured), and **Debian-32** (32-bit Debian-6.0.2.1-i386 with the 2.6.32 Linux kernel and Flat memory model configured). As for input workloads, we ran the following three benchmarks inside the guest VMs:

- **Video-Creation**, **E-Learning**, and **Office**:
  Three workloads from SYSmark2007 [7] which simulates the three different classes of business user behaviors on Windows desktop machines.

- **Banking**, **Ecommerce**, and **Support**:
  Three workloads from Specweb2009 [6] which are designed to evaluate web server performance.

- **Specjbb**: Specjbb2005 [5]. A SPEC benchmark that emulates a three-tier client/server system and is designed to evaluate the performance of server-side Java applications.

While Sysmark is a stand-alone benchmark that runs on Windows guests, Specweb is used to generate workloads from simulated clients and require running a web server on a Linux-based guest VM. As for Specjbb, we apply it to both Windows and Linux guest OSs.

Table 1 show the percentage of free pages in the 4 test VMs running four different workloads when the free memory pool grows and shrinks during the test period. The results in these tables present the characteristics of the workloads running inside the test VMs. For memory de-duplication, we expect the average shared pages by introspection mechanism is proportional to the average percentage of free pages. As for VM migration, we also expect the percentage of skipped transferred pages by introspection to approximate the average percentage of free pages.

6.1 Memory de-duplication

We used three metrics to evaluate the effectiveness of a memory de-duplication scheme: (1) the number of pages it reclaims, (2) the performance overhead it incurs, and (3) the performance penalty it imposes on guest VMs. The performance overhead of conventional memory de-duplication schemes mainly comes from hash computation and byte-by-byte comparison, whereas that for the proposed introspection-based memory de-duplication approach arises from introspection, (2) and (3) are different for two reasons. First, one could minimize performance impacts on guest VMs by carefully scheduling memory de-duplication operations when the CPUs are less loaded. Second, guest VMs may encounter additional protection faults, context switches and hypercalls (*unshare* in the case of Xen) as a result of writes to pages that are protected by the copy-on-write mechanism. Therefore, a guest VM's run-time performance penalty depends on the number of *unshare* calls it triggers.

To isolate the performance benefit of memory de-duplication schemes based on hashing and introspection, we compare the following four configurations of the GMD engine, using the **Baseline** configuration as the basis of effectiveness calculation:

- **Baseline**: The GMD engine is totally turned off, no memory pages are de-duplicated and no memory de-duplication overhead is incurred.

	E-learning	Video-Creation	Office	Specjbb
Win7-64	77, 52, 2	75, 40, 4	69, 61, 57	84, 73, 69
WinXP-32	78, 58, 17	77, 43, 0	70, 65, 53	86, 72, 9
	Banking	Ecommerce	Support	Specjbb
Centos-64	93, 92, 90	93, 92, 91	92, 76, 69	91, 81, 77
Debian-32	92, 91, 90	92, 91, 90	93, 75, 68	92, 83, 79

Table 1. Percentage of free pages against the test VM's total memory size for four test VMs each under four different workloads where each grid shows the maximum, average, and minimum value.

- **Intro**: Only the *Introspection* stage of the GMD engine is turned on.

- **Dedup**: Only the *de-duplication* stage of the GMD engine is turned on.

- **IntroDedup**: Both stages of the GMD engine are enabled. Free pages are de-duplicated by the Introspection stage and non-free pages are de-duplicated by the de-duplication stage.

In this study, we mainly focused on the memory de-duplication within an individual VM, and ignore the inter-VM memory de-duplication, because traditional content-based de-duplication already does a credible job at removing inter-VM duplicates. As a result, in each experiment, we ran only one VM, on which a particular input application workload is run. Because the GMD engine takes less than one minute to complete one de-duplication round through a VM with 4GB of physical memory, we configured the GMD engine to run once every minute by default. We also varied the invocation frequency of the engine to explore the trade-off between the cost and gain of memory de-duplication.

6.1.1 Effectiveness of Introspection for Windows

Figure 5 shows the comparison of Win7-64 VM among the three GMD configurations, *Intro*, *Dedup* as well as *IntroDedup*, in terms of memory saved, de-duplication overhead, and performance impacts on guest VMs, under four different input workloads. Because the Windows OS zeros out a memory page before putting it in the free memory pool, *Dedup* can de-duplicate any free page that *Intro* can de-duplicate. So in theory, the amount of memory saved by *Dedup* should be larger than that by *Intro*, and is equal to that by *IntroDedup*, as shown in Figure 5(a), where the metric is the percentage of the test guest VM's physical memory that is de-duplicated and shared by the GMD engine at the end of each minute during the experiment run.

However, for the E-Learning workload, the amount of memory shared by *Dedup* is smaller rather than larger than that by *Intro*, and for the Video-Creation workload, the amount of memory shared by *Dedup* is smaller than rather than equal to that by *IntroDedup*. These anomalies arise mainly because the amount of time and work required to perform one memory de-duplication round through the test VM's physical memory space is different for these three configurations, as shown in Figure 5(b). As expected, *Dedup* is the most time-consuming because it needs to perform per-page content hashing and byte-by-byte comparison, *Intro* is the quickest because it only needs to examine specific guest kernel data structures, and *IntroDedup* is between the two extremes because it is a hybrid of *Intro* and *Dedup*.

Figure 5(c) shows the average percentage of total memory pages that are *unshared* each minute by the test VM under the four workloads, and mirrors the results in Figure 5(a), because the number of pages "unshared" is directly correlated with the number of pages that were previously shared by the GMD engine and later allocated and modified. Two factors affect the performance degradation of the test VM when memory de-duplication runs in the background: (1) the overhead of the GMD engine's own de-duplication operations, e.g., hashing computation and locking of

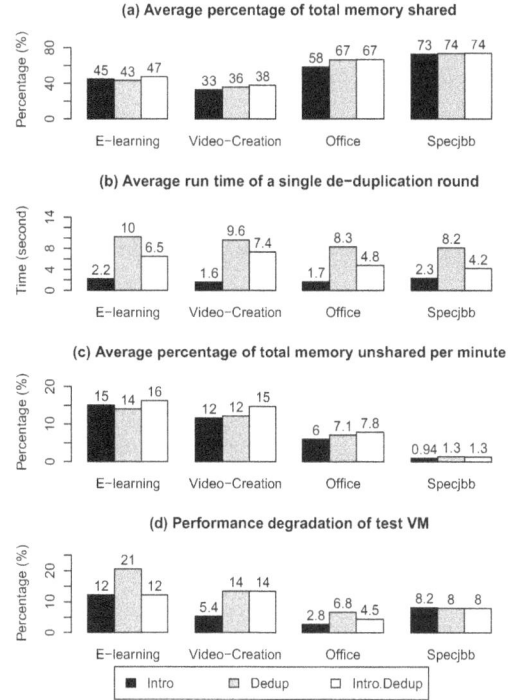

Figure 5. *Comparisons among Intro, Dedup and IntroDedup under four different workloads running on a Win7-64 test VM with 4GB physical memory in terms of (a) the average percentage of total memory shared by the GMD engine per minute, (b) the average time required to perform a single memory de-duplication round through the test VM's physical memory space, (c) the average percentage of total memory unshared by the test VM per minute, and (d) the performance penalty experienced by the test VM.*

memory pages, and (2) the number of copy-on-write exceptions because of the VM's writes to shared pages. Therefore, the test VM's performance degradations shown in Figure 5(d) reflect the combined effects in Figure 5(b) and Figure 5(c). Because the differences in the number of unshared pages among the three GMD configurations are small, the performance degradation is influenced more by the de-duplication overhead than by the amount of memory unsharing. Among the three configurations, *Intro* imposes the minimum performance penalty on the test VM. As for WinXP-32, the results are similar as Figure 6 shows. The overall performance degradation may be a little bit high at first sight. One major reason is that the current scanning frequency, e.g., every one minute, could be high comparing to other research work, e.g., the default scan frequency of VMware is once every 60 minutes, and we will look into this issue in Section 6.1.3.

The other way to evaluate the effectiveness of *Intro* is to analyze the relationship between the average percentage of free

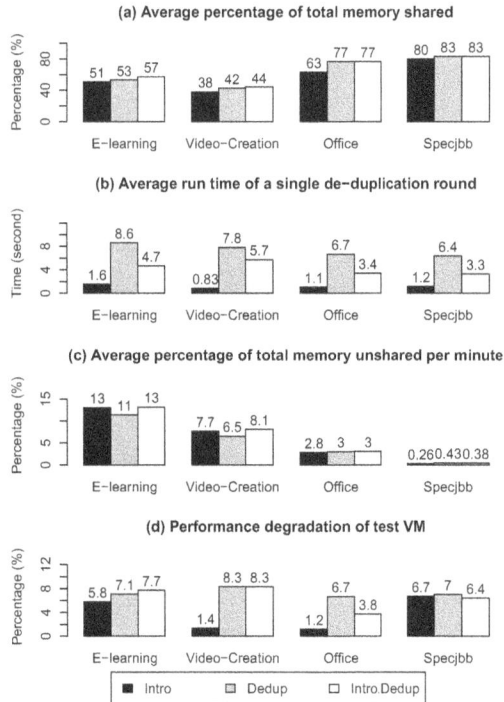

(a) Average percentage of total memory shared

(b) Average run time of a single de-duplication round

(c) Average percentage of total memory unshared per minute

(d) Performance degradation of test VM

■ Intro □ Dedup □ Intro.Dedup

Figure 6. *Comparisons among Intro, Dedup and IntroDedup under four different workloads running on a WinXP-32 test VM with 4GB physical memory in terms of the same set of metrics as in Figure 5.*

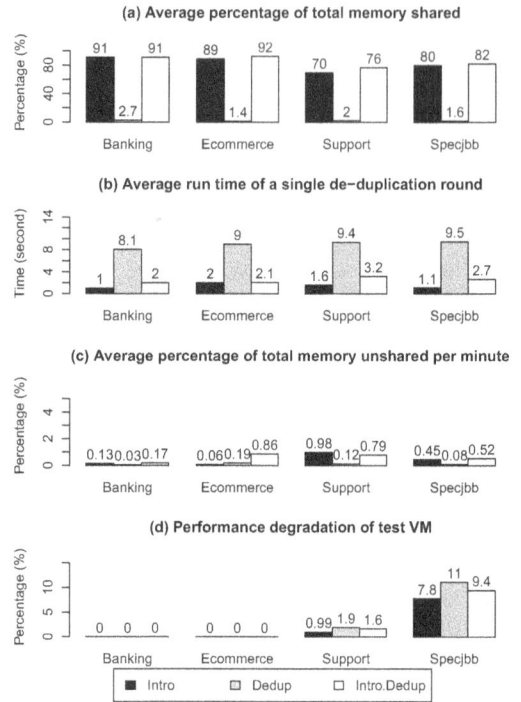

(a) Average percentage of total memory shared

(b) Average run time of a single de-duplication round

(c) Average percentage of total memory unshared per minute

(d) Performance degradation of test VM

■ Intro □ Dedup □ Intro.Dedup

Figure 7. *Comparisons among Intro, Dedup and IntroDedup under four different workloads running on a Centos-64 test VM with 4GB physical memory in terms of the same set of metrics as in Figure 5.*

pages and shared pages. If we subtract the average percentage of unshared pages from the average percentage of free pages, we expect the result to be proportional to the average percentage of shared pages. Taking Win7-64 VM as an example, the result of subtraction referring to Table 1 and Figure 5 is 36%, 28%, 54%, and 72% for the four workloads, which matches the trend of the average percentage of shared pages. The same kind of analysis can be applied to all other test VMs, which we will not repeat later due to redundancy.

In summary, on the Windows platform, most deduplicable pages within an individual VM are free memory pages that are zeroed; as a result, *Intro* is able to discover the majority of the deduplicable pages that *Dedup* can, and the marginal value provided by the vanilla de-duplication stage in *IntroDedup* is relatively minor. On the other hand, the de-duplication overhead of *Intro* is on average four times smaller than *Dedup*'s. In terms of performance impacts on the test VM, *Intro*'s is also significantly smaller than *Dedup*'s. Therefore, as far as intra-VM memory de-duplication for Windows guests is concerned, *Intro* is the clear choice.

6.1.2 Effectiveness of Introspection for Linux

Unlike Windows, the Linux kernel does not zero out a memory page to be freed before putting it in the free memory pool. Consequently, traditional memory de-duplication schemes cannot easily identify these pages and de-duplicate them, whereas the proposed GMD engine can. To ensure that free memory pages are not zero, we wrote a program to allocate as many free memory pages as possible, write random contents to them and then free all of them, before running any experiments. Without this tweak, our experiment results show what the *Intro* mechanism on Linux VMs still holds

the same advantage as the results from Windows VMs in terms of effectiveness of de-duplication and performance impact on guests.

As shown in Figures 7(a) and 8(a), *Dedup* can barely de-duplicate any memory page, whereas by leveraging free memory map information, *Intro* can de-duplicate most of the free memory pages. Moreover, the run time of *Intro* is significantly lower than that of *Dedup*, because the latter blindly computes hash values of all guest physical pages, as shown in Figures 7(b) and 8(b). For the same reason, the marginal value of the de-duplication stage of *IntroDedup* is also small when compared with *Intro*. Other than the above, the conclusions drawn from Figures 7 and 8 are similar to those drawn from Figure 5. One notable result is that the performance degradation when the test VM runs Specweb is close to zero, as shown in Figures 7(d) and 8(d). This is because the memory usage of Specweb is pretty static and hence not much memory unsharing takes place at run time.

6.1.3 Minimizing Performance Degradation

Ideally, the performance impact of a memory de-duplication scheme on the test VM should be minimal, preferably close to zero. Unfortunately, the performance degradations shown in Figures 5(d), 6(d), 7(d) and 8(d) are non-trivial. If the memory usage of a test VM is fluctuating dynamically, the free memory pages reclaimed by the GMD engine at one point are likely to be subsequently returned to the test VM when it allocates from the free memory pool. In such a case, the effort of sharing memory pages is a waste; worse yet, the test VM experiences additional performance penalty because of copy-on-write exceptions. Figure 9 shows the average amount of memory shared and the performance degradation of *Intro* when the test VM runs the four workloads on Win7-64 and when the invocation frequency is once per minute, per two minutes, per four

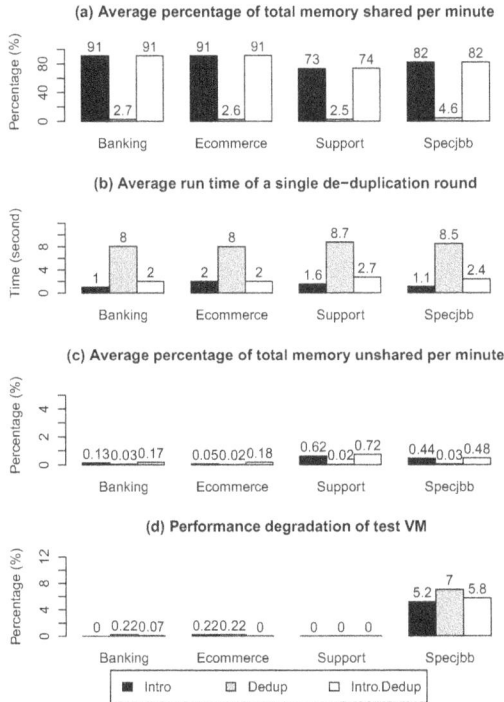

Figure 8. *Comparisons among Intro, Dedup and IntroDedup under four different workloads running on a Debian-32 test VM with 4GB physical memory in terms of the same set of metrics as in Figure 5.*

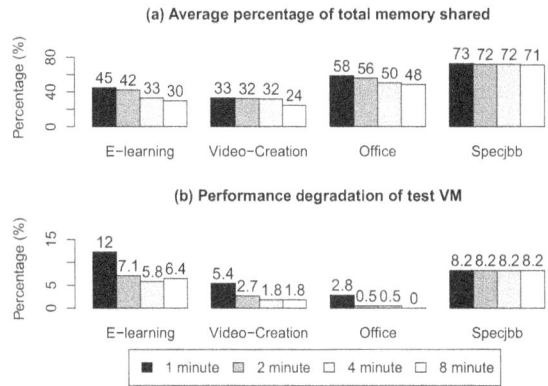

Figure 9. *Impacts of the invocation frequency of Intro (once every 1 minute, 2 minutes, 4 minutes and 8 minutes) on the average amount of memory shared and the performance degradation of the test VM when it runs the four test workloads on Win7-64.*

- **BaseMigrate**: The conventional VM migration scheme implemented in Xen.

- **IntroMigrate**: BaseMigrate with the optimization that avoids transferring free memory pages as identified via VM introspection.

In each run, we triggered a migration of the test VM at a randomly chosen time and measured the network traffic load and migration time, and reported the average of the measurements of multiple runs. Due to space constraint, we only present the results of two types of test VMs, Win7-64 and Debian-32, because WinXP-32 and Centos-64 have similar results.

Figure 10(a) compares the injected network traffic volumes of *BaseMigrate* and *IntroMigrate* for a Win7-64 VM under four different test workloads. Compared with *BaseMigrate*, *IntroMigrate* reduces the network traffic in the first iteration of memory state transfer, depicted as "1st-Iteration" in the figure, by 48%, 41%, 62%, and 81% for E-learning, Video-Creation, Office, and Specjbb, respectively. As expected, the percentage of network traffic reduction is roughly proportional to the average percentage of free pages shown in Table 1, because information extracted by introspection is used only in the first iteration.

For the remaining iterations of memory state transfer, depicted as "Remaining" in the figure[4], surprisingly *IntroMigrate* also cuts down the network traffic volume by 8%, 57%, 75%, and 9% for E-learning, Video-Creation, Office, and Specjbb, respectively, even though no introspection-derived information is used in these iterations. This reduction originates from the fact that when the first iteration is shortened, fewer memory pages are dirtied in the first iteration, the second iteration is also shortened, even fewer pages are dirtied in the second iteration, and so on. The introspection benefit to the remaining iterations is apparent for the Video-Creation and Office workload, but not so obvious for E-learning because the network traffic due to the remaining iterations is small to begin with, and for Specjbb because it is memory-intensive and introduces a large number of dirtied pages in the remaining iterations regardless of the length of the first iteration.

Figure 10(b) shows that *IntroMigrate* cuts down the total migration time from 40, 44, 52, and 56 seconds to 25, 29, 21, and 30 seconds, or by 38%, 34%, 60%, and 46% for E-learning,

minutes and per eight minutes. As expected, the more frequently the *Intro* GMD engine runs, the more memory pages it could de-duplicate, and the higher the performance degradation[3]. Unfortunately, while decreasing the de-duplication frequency decreases the amount of memory shared, it does not seem to be able to cut the performance degradation to 0%. This is because the current implementation of *Intro* shares *all* free pages, and the test VM is bound to encounter some copy-on-write exceptions when it allocates additional memory pages.

6.2 Memory State Migration

We used two metrics to evaluate the effectiveness of a VM migration scheme: (1) the amount network traffic injected by a VM migration transaction, and (2) the total VM migration time. Conventionally, the amount of network traffic injected by a VM migration transaction is directly proportional to the total memory size of the migrated VM, i.e., 4GB in our test setup. It takes roughly 40 seconds to transfer this VM's memory state on our Gigabit Ethernet-based testbed, whose TCP throughput is 819.2 Mbps. By leveraging BVMI to identify free memory pages in a VM that is to be migrated, the hypervisor could skip transferring these free memory pages during the VM migration transaction, and this significantly cuts down the migration-induced network traffic volume.

To assess the performance benefit of introspection-based VM migration, we compare the following two VM migration schemes using the above two metrics:

---

[3] Because Specjbb runs inside a JVM, its execution does not directly affect the memory footprint and the number of unshared pages in the underlying guest. Consequently, varying the invocation frequency of GMD has little impact on Specjbb's performance.

[4] The CPU and I/O states are only a few KBytes and thus ignored in this discussion.

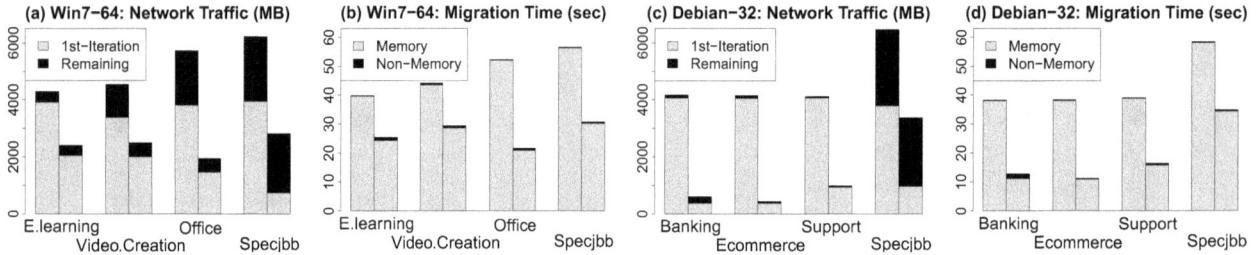

Figure 10. *Comparison of injected network traffic volume and total migration time between $BaseMigrate$ and $IntroMigrate$ for four different workloads running on a Win7-64 VM and a Debian-32 VM. For each workload, the left and right bar represent the result of $BaseMigrate$ and $IntroMigrate$ respectively. In subfigure (a) and (c), "1st-Iteration" and "Remaining" correspond to the injected network traffic volume in the first and remaining iterations during a VM migration transaction, respectively. In subfigure (b) and (d), "Memory" and "Non-memory" correspond to the memory state migration time and the migration time for other VM states, respectively.*

Video-Creation, Office, and Specjbb, respectively. The amount of migration time reduction is proportional to the amount of reduced network traffic or memory state transfer, which accounts for more than 96% of the total migration time. The non-memory portion of the migration time is too small to be noticeable.

Figure 10(c) and 10(d) show similar benefits for the Debian-32 test VM. When compared with $BaseMigrate$, $IntroMigrate$ reduces the network traffic load due to VM migration by 85%, 89%, 76%, and 48%, and the total migration time by 66%, 71%, 59% and 40%, for Banking, Ecommerce, Support, and Specjbb, respectively. Unlike the Win7-64 test VM, introspection does not benefit the remaining iterations much even when it produces a significant benefit in the first iteration for all four test workloads running on the Debian-32 VM. In addition, the reduction percentage in total migration time is not as significant as the reduction percentage in memory state transfer, and the ratio between these reduction percentages is smaller in the Debian-32 VM than in the Win7-64 VM. For example, for the Banking workload running on the Debian-32 VM, the network traffic reduction percentage due to introspection is 85% but the migration time reduction percentage due to introspection is only 66%; for the E-learning workload running on the Win7-64 VM, the network traffic reduction percentage due to introspection is 44% but the migration time reduction percentage due to introspection is only 38%. The reduction percentage ratio is 0.77 (66%/85%) for the Debian-32 VM and 0.86 (38%/44%) for the Win7-64 VM.

In the current implementation, the migration module first asks the hypervisor to map all pages in the migrated VM and then queries the hypervisor for each page's type information. This mapping and query step incurs a fixed overhead, which accounts for the discrepancy between the reduction in amount of memory state transfer and the reduction in total migration time. More specifically, this fixed overhead becomes relatively more significant when the total migration time becomes smaller. Consequently, when the performance benefit of $IntroMigrate$ increases, the reduction in the total migration time increases, the relative importance of this fixed overhead increases and finally the discrepancy also increases. Because the performance benefit of $IntroMigrate$ is more pronounced in the Debian-32 VM than in the Win7-64 VM, the discrepancy between network traffic volume reduction and total migration time reduction is therefore larger in the Debian-32 VM than in the Win7-64 VM.

7. Conclusion

Memory virtualization provides many opportunities for performance optimizations, and these optimizations are more effective when more memory usage knowledge about guest VMs is available. In this research, we propose using VM introspection to extract a key guest kernel data structure, free memory pool, and apply this free memory pool information to improve the efficiency of memory de-duplication and memory state migration. To make VMI possible for multiple types and versions of guest kernels, we develop a *bootstrapping VMI* technique that reduces kernel version-specific hardcoding by programmatically leveraging as much publicly available information about a guest kernel as possible, including its source code, and demonstrate its effectiveness by applying it to multiple versions of Linux and Windows OS to successfully extract their free memory pool information without manual intervention. By leveraging free memory pool information, we show that the amount of memory de-duplicated *and* the de-duplication speed in memory de-duplication are improved significantly, and the memory state migration time during VM migration is substantially reduced. In summary, this research makes the following three research contributions:

- Development of a novel bootstrapping VMI technique that could identify the free memory pool of multiple versions of Windows and Linux OS with minimal kernel version-specific hard-coding,

- Leveraging free memory pool information to improve the speed and effectiveness of memory de-duplication, and

- Leveraging free memory pool information in reducing the network traffic load associated with memory state migration.

References

[1] Mac developer library, technical note tn2118, kernel core dumps. http://developer.apple.com/library/mac/#technotes/tn2004/tn2118.html.

[2] Amazon ec2. amazon's web service for virtual machine privision. http://aws.amazon.com/ec2/.

[3] Crash, linux crash dump analysis tool. http://people.redhat.com/anderson/.

[4] Microsoft debug interface access sdk. http://msdn.microsoft.com/en-us/library/x93ctkx8.aspx.

[5] Specjbb2005. http://www.spec.org/jbb2005/, .

[6] Specweb2009. http://www.spec.org/web2009/, .

[7] Sysmark2007. http://www.bapco.com/products/sysmark2007preview/.

[8] Microsoft portable executable and common object file format specification. *ReVision*, page 97, 2010.

[9] A. Arcangeli, I. Eidus, and C. Wright. *Increasing memory density by using KSM*, pages 19–28. Linux Symposium, 2009.

[10] R. Bryant, A. Tumanov, O. Irzak, A. Scannell, K. Joshi, M. Hiltunen, A. Lagar-Cavilla, and E. de Lara. Kaleidoscope: cloud micro-elasticity via vm state coloring. EuroSys '11, 2011.

[11] C. Clark, K. Fraser, S. H, J. G. Hansen, E. Jul, C. Limpach, I. Pratt, and A. Warfield. Live Migration of Virtual Machines. In *NSDI*, 2005.

[12] B. Dolan-Gavitt, T. Leek, M. Zhivich, J. Giffin, and W. Lee. Virtuoso: Narrowing the semantic gap in virtual machine introspection. SP '11, pages 297–312, 2011.

[13] T. Garfinkel and M. Rosenblum. A virtual machine introspection based architecture for intrusion detection. In *NDSS*, 2003.

[14] D. Gupta, S. Lee, M. Vrable, S. Savage, A. C. Snoeren, G. Varghese, G. M. Voelker, and A. Vahdat. Difference engine: Harnessing memory redundancy in virtual machines. OSDI '08, 2008.

[15] D. Magenheimer. *Transcendent Memory on Xen*, page 3. XenSummit, February 2009.

[16] D. G. Murray, S. H, and M. A. Fetterman. Satori: Enlightened page sharing. ATEC '09, 2009.

[17] B. D. Payne, M. D. P. D. A. Carbone, and W. Lee. Secure and flexible monitoring of virtual machines. *ACSAC 2007*, 2007.

[18] M. Russinovich, D. A. Solomon, and A. Ionescu. *Microsoft Windows Internals: Including Windows Server 2008 and Windows Vista, 5th Edition*. Microsoft Press, Redmond, WA, USA, 2009. ISBN 0735625301.

[19] M. Russinovich, D. A. Solomon, and A. Ionescu. *Windows Internals: Covering Windows Server 2008 R2 and Windows 7*. Microsoft Press, Redmond, WA, USA, 2011. ISBN 0735648735.

[20] M. E. Russinovich and D. A. Solomon. *Microsoft Windows Internals, 4th Edition: Microsoft Windows Server 2003, Windows XP, and Windows 2000*. Microsoft Press, Redmond, WA, USA, 2004. ISBN 0735619174.

[21] M. Schwidefsky, R. Mansell, D. Osisek, H. Franke, H. Raj, and J. H. Choi. Collaborative memory management in hosted linux environments. In *OLS06*, pages 313–331, 2006.

[22] C. A. Waldspurger. Memory resource management in vmware esx server. *SIGOPS Oper. Syst. Rev.*, 36:181–194, 2002.

VMScatter: Migrate Virtual Machines to Many Hosts

Lei Cui   Jianxin Li   Bo Li
Jinpeng Huai   Chunming Hu   Tianyu Wo

Beihang University, Beijing, China
{cuilei, lijx, libo, hucm, woty}@act.buaa.edu.cn,
huaijp@buaa.edu.cn

Hussain Al-Aqrabi
Lu Liu

University of Derby, Derby, United Kingdom
{H.Al-Aqrabi, L.Liu}@derby.ac.uk

Abstract

Live virtual machine migration is a technique often used to migrate an entire OS with running applications in a non-disruptive fashion. Prior works concerned with one-to-one live migration with many techniques have been proposed such as pre-copy, post-copy and log/replay. In contrast, we propose VMScatter, a one-to-many migration method to migrate virtual machines from one to many other hosts simultaneously. First, by merging the identical pages within or across virtual machines, VMScatter multicasts only a single copy of these pages to associated target hosts for avoiding redundant transmission. This is impactful practically when the same OS and similar applications running in the virtual machines where there are plenty of identical pages. Second, we introduce a novel grouping algorithm to decide the placement of virtual machines, distinguished from the previous schedule algorithms which focus on the workload for load balance or power saving, we also focus on network traffic, which is a critical metric in data-intensive data centers. Third, we schedule the multicast sequence of packets to reduce the network overhead introduced by joining or quitting the multicast groups of target hosts. Compared to traditional live migration technique in QEMU/KVM, VMScatter reduces 74.2% of the total transferred data, 69.1% of the total migration time and achieves the network traffic reduction from 50.1% to 70.3%.

Categories and Subject Descriptors   D.4.7 [*Operating Systems*]: Organization and Design

General Terms   Design, Experimentation, Performance

Keywords   Live Migration, Virtualization, De-duplication, Multicast, Placement

1. Introduction

Live migration is a key point of the current virtualization technologies; it allows the administrator to migrate one virtual machine (VM) from one host to another without dropped network connection or perceived downtime. Live migration offers a flexible and powerful fashion to balance system load, save power and tolerant fault [19] in data centers. VMware proposes vMotion [25], a live migration technology that leverages the complete virtualization of servers, storage, and networking to move an entire running VM instantaneously. Xen proposes XenMotion [10], a similar technology to vMotion but implemented on Xen platform. Other virtualized technologies such as KVM, Hyper-V, VirtualBox also provide the live migration. Although the implementation details are different owing to heteromorphic virtualization technologies, the state of a VM reserved during live migration is analogous, involving CPU state, network state, memory state and disk state.

The existing live migration schemes focus on migrating VMs from one host to another (one-to-one). The methods, such as pre-copy [10], post-copy [27], memory compression [15], trace and replay [19] and live gang migration [11] have been proposed with the chief concern on reducing the amount of transferred memory data during live migration. It is remarkable that in practical scenarios such as online maintenance, power saving or fault tolerance, migrating multiple VMs to one host will overload the target host, and eventually crashing it. Therefore, a live migration technology that migrates VMs to many target hosts (one-to-many) is urgent.

We consider two important issues on one-to-many migration: live migration technology and placement of VMs. There has been many works [6, 23, 24, 29] sharing a similar philosophy but there still exists some unsolved issues which should be considered further. Firstly, no optimization has been proposed on live one-to-many migration technology. Prior works simply leverage the traditional ways to carry out migration; as discussed previously, these techniques are only concerned with one-to-one migration. Secondly, the de-duplication technology [11] may reduce the transferred data by merging identical pages that target one host, but it is unable to merge identical pages that target two or more hosts. Thirdly, the placement of VMs is derived from the scheduling algorithm that focus on the workload for the purpose of power saving [23], load balance [29] and SLA requirements [6]. However, considering network traffic, which is practically critical in today's data centers where a large scale of data exist for processing and transferring, frequent live migration caused by load balance or power saving will introduce additional heavy network traffic.

Note that in works [11, 14] where state there are plenty of identical pages across VMs, multicast may be a natural approach to transfer identical pages of VMs to associated hosts. In this paper, we propose a multicast based approach named VMScatter to implement live one-to-many migration. VMScatter employs multicast to deliver identical pages to a group of destinations simultaneously in a single transmission from the source host. This avoids transferring each page individually, thus it not only reduces the transferred data but also reduces the network traffic. During migration, others including the unique pages and dirtied pages will be unicasted to associated target hosts. Figure 1 presents the overview of one-to-many migration approach for migrating two VMs, each of which targets a respective host. The multicast-based live migration will

VEE'13,   March 16–17, 2013, Houston, Texas, USA.
Copyright © 2013 ACM 978-1-4503-1266-0/13/03...$15.00

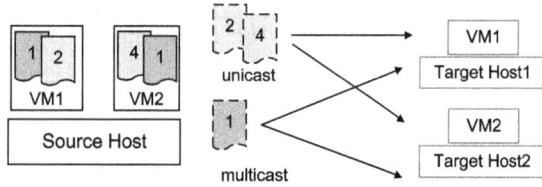

Figure 1. Overview of the live migration in VMScatter(Two pages with the same content 1 in VM1 and VM2 will be multicasted to Host1 and Host2 instead of individual transfer. Pages 2 and 4 that are unique will be unicasted to the associated host).

be valuable especially for the VMs having the same OS and applications, where result in plenty of identical pages.

Besides, two successive packets to be multicasted may target different hosts, thus some target hosts must join the multicast group for receiving expected packets while some quit to avoid receiving unneeded packets. This will introduce excessive network overhead owing to frequent *socket* related operations. We reduced this problem to be the Hamilton Cycle problem which is NP-complete, and leverage the existing algorithm to schedule an optimal permutation of packets for minimizing the overhead between multicast groups' switchovers.

Moreover, the network traffic of different placements are varied owing to the intricate association among pages, VMs and target hosts. To achieve better behavior, we introduce a grouping algorithm to specify the placement of VMs, with the aim of minimizing the network traffic while meeting the workload requirements meanwhile. We analyze the grouping impact on network traffic by a case study, give the problem formulation which is proved to be a bin-packing problem, and then present a greedy algorithm to find a preferable placement.

We implement VMScatter in QEMU/KVM, with User Datagram Protocol (UDP) to multicast the identical pages and Transmission Control Protocol (TCP) to unicast other pages. We design the protocol to guarantee consistency and integrity of the running state between the source and target hosts. Further, we implement various optimizations such as selective hashing for comparing pages, on-demand retransfer for transferring lost pages as well as compression and multithreading when sending packets. As we will see, the experiments conducted in a private data center under various workloads confirm the feasibility and efficiency of our multicast-based live one-to-many migration schema.

The remainder of this paper is organized as follows. Section II introduces the overview of live migration method via multicast, describes the phases of VMScatter, and proposes the greedy algorithm for finding a placement. Section III describes detailed implementation issues. Section IV presents the conducted experiments to evaluate the proposal. Section V surveys the related work to live migration, de-duplication, dynamic placement and multicast. Section VI concludes the paper and describes our future work.

2. Design of Live One-to-Many Migration

In this section, we present the overview of the VMScatter along with some design building blocks.

2.1 Design Objectives

The live migration process must be transparent to the operating system and applications running on top of VMs, and the overhead on the source host and network must be considered. We do not address the issue of migrating disk state within this paper, yet we suggest that as part of our future work.

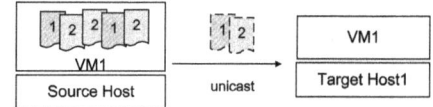

(a) ISVST

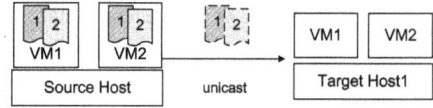

(b) IMVST

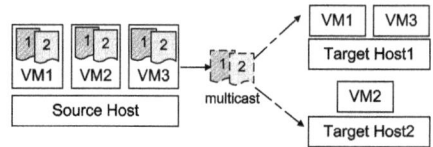

(c) IMVMT

Figure 2. Three situations of identical pages transfer.

Total migration time: The time duration from the preparation at the source host to the end of the last VM's migration at the target host.

Total transferred data: The amount of data send from the source host to the target hosts to synchronize the VMs' state.

Network traffic: The network traffic is network topology-specific actually; within the paper we refer this metric to the total amount of data received by all target hosts.

Performance degradation: The influence on the performance of the applications running in the migrating VMs.

2.2 Situations for Pages Transfer

The unique pages should be unicasted, yet for identical pages, the situation is much more complicated due to the association among pages, VMs and target hosts: the identical pages may be self-identical which means existing in only one VM or inter-identical implying across many VMs, and the VMs may target one or more hosts. Figure 2 demonstrates three situations for identical pages transfer and the details are described as follows:

ISVST (Identical pages, Single VM Single Target): The identical pages exist in only one VM (self-identical); in this situation shown in Figure 2(a), transferring only one copy of identical pages to the target host is sufficient. Apparently, this reduces both total transferred data and network traffic.

IMVST (Identical pages, Multiple VMs Single Target): The identical pages exist across multiple VMs (inter-identical), and these VMs are migrated to one target host. This is similar to ISVST where only one copy of the identical pages is required to be transferred. This situation illustrated in Figure 2(b), also reduces both the transferred data and network traffic.

IMVMT (Identical pages, Multiple VMs Multiple Targets): The identical pages exist across multiple VMs (inter-identical), and these VMs are migrated to different target hosts. In this scene, the multicast mechanism is carried out to transfer a single copy of these identical pages to the multicast group where associated target hosts join to receive expected pages. Figure 2(c) illustrates such a case where VM1 and VM3 are placed to Host1 while VM2 targets Host2. This reduces the total transferred data from two aspects: one is the inter-identical pages that target the single host which is the

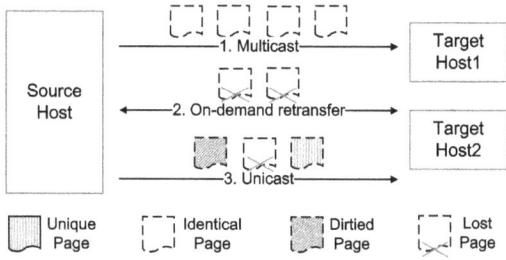

Figure 3. Three stages of page transfer.

same to IMVST, while another comes from multicasting the pages that target different target hosts. The network traffic reduction is due to the first aspect.

Since the identical pages will be transferred by single copy, the packet transferred via whether unicast or multicast must comprise three fields for referencing one page. The first is the *VM Id*, which tells the target host that which VM the page belongs to, and it can be the process id of VM, the MAC address or other unique marks. The second is the *Guest Physical Address (GPA)* of the page, which determines the memory position the page should be filled in. The last is the *Page Content*, which records the whole content of the page. The *VM Id* and *GPA* can be considered as a pair to reference one page exclusively. One packet would contain multiple *VM Id* and *GPA* pairs for the identical pages and a single copy of their *Page Content*.

2.3 Phases of Live One-to-Many Migration

VMScatter takes the similar approach to pre-copy[10], but the preparation phase contains collect stage and schedule stage, and page transfer phase consists of three stages: multicast, on-demand retransfer and unicast.

Preparation: The collect stage in preparation calculates the hash value of each page to distinguish pages having different content, and employs complete comparison to identify the identical pages. On the basis of these identical pages and their associated VMs, the schedule stage finds a preferable placement of VMs and specifies a permutation of packets to be multicasted.

Data transfer: The UDP transfers data without establishing a connection and consumes less resource, hence is suitable for multicast. Yet it is unreliable and can not guarantee successful transmission, and even results in the failure of running VM due to lost pages. As a result, TCP will be adopted as a supplementary of page transfer in a reliable manner.

As described in Figure 3, VMScatter transfers the identical pages first. For the IMVMT pages that target two or more target hosts, VMScatter packages them and multicasts the packets to associated targets via UDP. Because one lost packet may imply hundreds of lost pages(the packet loss rate is 0.3% in our private data center, and the same result can be seen in several work [8, 22]), which will bring the retransmission load for unicast, therefore we re-multicast the lost packets on-demand by the target host, which shares a similar philosophy to the post-copy method [27]. The packets in on-demand retransfer may be lost again, but the amount will be quite a few; for simplicity and robustness it is better to treat the twice lost pages as unique pages. These twice lost packets, with the unique pages among VMs, identical pages in ISVST and IMVST, and the dirtied pages during migration are unicasted to associated target host via reliable TCP.

2.4 Grouping Decision

Another key challenge in one-to-many migration is the placement of VMs, namely a grouping that describe the association between VMs and targets. In this section, we first illustrate the impact on network traffic of different groupings by a case study, then present the problem formulation which is proved to be an NP problem, and lastly propose a greedy algorithm to find a preferable grouping.

2.4.1 Grouping Impact Analysis

The grouping has few effects on the total transferred data, according to the three stages of page transfer: 1) The unique pages undoubtedly are unique regardless of the grouping, thus the amount is constant. 2) The identical pages whether multicast or unicast will be transferred by only one copy, thus the amount of transferred data is also constant. 3) The time cost is fixed in theory for transferring a constant amount of unique and identical pages, thus results in a constant amount of dirtied pages during live migration.

However for network traffic, different groupings result in significantly differences. This is because the network traffic reduction is mainly from the de-duplication of ISVST and IMVST pages that target the same host, and pages that should be transferred to the target is determined by the placement. For example, we assume the VM state is frozen and consider the state to be a set of pages; the assumption is reasonable because most pages would stay unchanged during live migration that last dozens of seconds. We suppose four VMs will be placed to two target hosts H_1 and H_2, the four VMs with their memory pages are: $V_1 = \{A, B, C\}$, $V_2 = \{A, B, D\}$, $V_3 = \{C, D, F\}$, $V_4 = \{A, C, E\}$. For one grouping in which V_1 and V_2 are placed on H_1, V_3 and V_4 target H_2, the memory pages transferred to H_1 are $\{A, B, C, D\}$, and are $\{A, C, D, E, F\}$ for H_2, the network traffic in this grouping is 9 pages. For another grouping that V_1 and V_3 target H_1 while V_2 and V_4 target H_2, the pages transferred to H_1 are $\{A, B, C, D, F\}$ and H_2 are $\{A, B, C, D, E\}$, this case generates 10 pages, which is one more page than the previous grouping. One thing to be noted is that the total transferred data of the two groupings are the same, i.e. $\{A, B, C, D, E, F\}$.

2.4.2 Problem Formulation

We consider a scenario where there are n VMs and m candidate target hosts, and we assume the VMs are frozen thus the memory pages in one VM are constant. We define the capacity of target host H_j is C_j, which refers to the maximum number of VMs that H_j can accept owing to the limited resource such as memory or workload specific factors. Each VM can be regarded as a set of memory pages and is denoted by V_i for VM i. We refer S_j to the set of VMs that are accepted by the target host H_j. The identical pages of VMs in S_j will be kept only one copy, therefore the network traffic related to target H_j can be regarded as the length of the union of memory pages owned by VMs in set S_j, we take L_j to denote the network traffic of the set S_j.

Problem definition. Given n VMs with their associated memory pages V, and m candidate target hosts with capacity C, we need to find a grouping that divides the n VMs to k target hosts $\{S_1, S_2, ..., S_k\}$, while minimizing the total network traffic L for these k target hosts.

$$L = \sum_{j=1}^{k} L_j = \sum_{j=1}^{k} |S_j| = \sum_{j=1}^{k} |\bigcup_{i=1}^{C_j} V_i|$$

This problem can be reduced from the bin-packing problem [20], and is proved to be NP-hard.

2.4.3 Greedy Algorithm

Because the global optimal solution is hardly acquired for NP-hard problem, we give the greedy algorithm for obtaining a preferable solution. Consider the purpose of grouping is placing the VMs to multiple target hosts, so the first key issue is to decide which target host should be selected prior. Note that the reduced network traffic is mainly from the de-duplication for ISVST and IMVST identical pages that target the same host (i.e., in one set S_j); intuitively, the network traffic may decrease greater if more VMs target one host in which more pages will become identical. So our greedy algorithm first fills the target host which has the maximum capacity, then fills the host with second largest capacity, and repeat until all the n VMs are filled into the targets. Moreover, this approximately minimizes the number of target hosts correspondingly.

Another key of the greedy algorithm is which VM should be selected prior to others. It is observed that for the set S_j with fixed number of VMs, the larger number of identical pages, the smaller length of the union of the set. Hence, we calculate the count of identical pages of every two VMs, and fill the target host with the VM which has the largest count. We use $N_{i,j}$ to denote the count between V_i and V_j, and define a V_i *relates* to a set if 1) the V_i has not been existed in any set, 2) there exits a V_j in the set, 3) the value of $N_{i,j}$ is nonzero. The VMs that *relate* to the set are candidates that can be added to the set. Similarly, we fill the set with the VM which has the largest $N_{i,j}$ among the candidates relate to the set.

The algorithm is described as follows: Firstly we select a target host with the maximum capacity, then we choose the two VMs which have the largest count in N, and place them into the host. Based on the two VMs, we select the VM that not only *relates* to the host but also has the largest $N_{i,j}$ among the rest N. This step will repeat until the capacity of this target host is reached. And the same procedure will be applied to other target hosts which have maximum capacity among the remaining hosts until all the n VMs are filled, thereafter we get the grouping. The algorithm 1 describes the procedure and some details are removed for clarity.

Algorithm 1 Greedy Algorithm

Require: $V = \{V_1, V_2, ..., V_n\}$; $S = \{S_1, S_2, ..., S_m\}$; $C = \{C_1, C_2, ..., C_m\}$;
1: Sort the hosts S in descending order by the capacity C;
2: Calculate $N_{p,q}$ between each two VMs V_p and V_q;
3: $N \leftarrow \{N_{1,2}, ..., N_{1,n}, N_{2,3}, ..., N_{p,q}, ..., N_{n-1,n}\}$;
4: Sort N in descending order;
5: $j = 0$;
6: **for** i from 1 to n **do**
7:    $S_j \leftarrow \{\}$;
8:    **while** $C_j \neq 0$ **do**
9:       **if** $S_j = \{\}$ **then**
10:          Get the maximum $N_{p,q}$;
11:          $S_j \leftarrow S_j \cup \{V_p\} \cup \{V_q\}$;
12:          $i \leftarrow i + 2, C_j \leftarrow C_j - 2$;
13:       **else**
14:          Get the maximum $N_{p,q}$ related to S_j;
15:          **if** $V_p \in S_j$ **then**
16:             $S_j \leftarrow S_j \cup \{V_q\}$;
17:          **else**
18:             $S_j \leftarrow S_j \cup \{V_p\}$;
19:          **end if**
20:          $i \leftarrow i + 1, C_j \leftarrow C_j - 1$;
21:       **end if**
22:    **end while**
23:    Seek to the next host by $j \leftarrow j + 1$;
24: **end for**

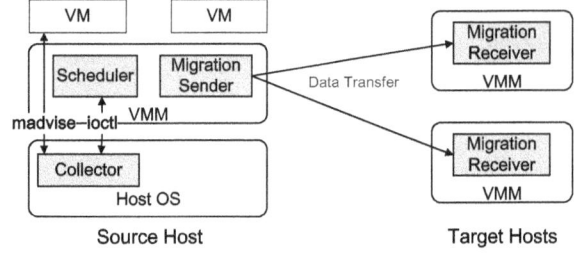

Figure 4. VMScatter architecture.

3. Implementation Issues

This section presents the implementation issues that we have made in VMScatter approach. We start by describing the overall architecture, then go on sub-level description of details and optimizations.

3.1 Architecture

We leverage the existing live migration mechanism in QEMU/KVM [16], and implement VMScatter using Linux 2.6.32 and qemu-kvm-0.12.5. We modify the QEMU code for support multicast in user mode, and implement a kernel module Collector to collect and organize the identical pages.

The VM, which is actually a process, uses a system call *madvise* to advise the Collector to handle the pages in the virtual memory address range, which represents the physical memory from the view of VM. Since the mapping from physical address of VM to virtual address of physical host is easily acquired, Collector only transfers the metadata including *Page Address* and *VM Id* of identical pages from kernel to QEMU via *ioctl*, and the Migration Sender accesses the page content in user space. According to the greedy algorithm, the Scheduler figures out a preferable grouping which determine the placement of VMs, and then the Migration Sender carries out the page transfer until all Migration Receivers in target hosts obtain the consistent state of associated VMs with that at the source host. Figure 4 illustrates the overall system architecture.

3.2 Collector Module and Selective Hash

We combine hash table and red-black tree to organize the identical pages in kernel: the pages in one hash bucket will be organized as a red-black tree, and the tree node represents a cluster of pages that have the same hash value. We adopt 32 bits hash value, the leftmost 20 bits are used to index the bucket in the hash table containing 1M (2^{20}) buckets, and the rightmost 12 bits are used to distinguish 4096 (2^{12}) tree nodes in each bucket. Therefore each node refers to unique hash value among all nodes in the hash table. For each page, we first calculate the hash value, then insert the page into the bucket indexed by the leftmost 20 bits of page hash value, and then organize the page into the red-black tree node indexed by the rightmost 12 bits of page hash value. Since hash collision may occur, resulting in the pages having the same hash value are still varied, the byte-by-byte content comparison of new inserted page to the pages have already in the node is carried out. Therefore, the different pages in the same tree node, which are hash value identical but have different content, will be distinguished.

Hashing the memory pages introduce time overhead, even the SuperFastHash [2] cost over 30s for twelve VMs with 1G memory in 2-way quad-core Xeon E6750 2GHz processors. To speedup the calculation, we just select disperse 200 bytes instead of the whole 4096 bytes to obtain the hash value of the page. Against the SuperFashHash method, the selective hash calculation for 12G memory can reduce the time cost from 37.3s to 1.8s, and the number of hash collisions increase from about 100 to only 1000, minor compared to millions of pages.

3.3 Page Classification: Identical or Unique

Some identical pages may be short-lived due to the dirtied content during the live migration, causing the page that is unique to become identical later and vice versa. Figure 5 shows such a case in which the identical page in collect stage turns to be unique during page transfer then becomes identical when the migration is over after cycles of updates. One common approach is dynamic tracking: by setting the pages to be write-protect, we can track the content change of each page, and reorganize the dirtied page in the hash table, then decide whether the page is identical or not in real-time. Afterwards we notify the Migration Sender to multicast or unicast the page correspondingly when transferring.

However in our implementation, we consider the pages to be identical or unique according to the memory state when collect stage finishes, without dynamic tracking during later migration. This is due to three reasons: 1) The write-protect skill will cause page fault for each memory write operation, which introduces a heavy burden for memory-intensive applications, hence seriously decrease the performance of VM; 2) Some part of memory pages may be dirtied frequently in a certain time, resulting in lots of notifications. Most notifications will be useless because the new arriving notification may cover the older one ahead of transfer; 3) The experimental result says that majority of identical pages will keep content constant and identical during dozens of seconds running, and these long-lived pages suggest us adopting the page type in one certain epoch is feasible and simple, with bringing about minor unnecessary multicast pages.

3.4 Successful Page Transfer

To guarantee the successful migration of VMs, VMScatter should fall in two ways of what is needed: integrity and consistency of transferred pages.

Integrity: Integrity means that we should construct a complete memory space for each VM at the target host. The lost packets owing to unreliable UDP may cause plenty of missing pages, leading to system runtime error or even crash. We keep the integrity via the on-demand retransfer and reliable unicast. Each target host maintains an array recording *Packet Id* which is associated with packet for indexing the lost ones, and then requests the lost packets from the source host by *Packet Id*. After receiving the request, the source host will re-multicast the packets to all associated targets. The unicast stage will employ reliable TCP to retransfer the pages lost in on-demand retransfer. Thus with the combination of UDP and reliable TCP, we achieve transferring the pages in an integral mode.

Consistency: Consistency of memory pages between the source and target hosts preserves the newest state for VMs after migration; the main cause of inconsistency is the new dirtied memory pages during migration. We leverage the method proposed by Clark et al. [10], use bitmap to index the dirtied pages during transfer, transfer the dirtied pages iteratively until the amount of dirtied pages converges to below the threshold, then we stop the VM, transfer the left pages via TCP, and lastly boot the VM at the target.

3.5 Join and Quit the Multicast Group

The multicast group reflects a group of target hosts intended to receive the packet. A target host must join the multicast group to receive the expected packet, and quit to avoid receiving unneeded packets for reducing both the network traffic and overhead. Since each packet is related to one certain multicast group which consists of hosts targeted by the packet, the various packets may be transferred to different multicast groups, therefore cause the tar-

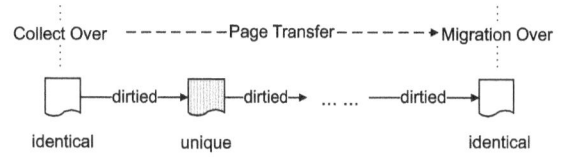

Figure 5. Page type change during migration.

get hosts to join and quit the multicast group frequently. Thus the network overhead rise heavily for thousands of multicast groups' switchovers for various packets. To avoid this unfortunate behavior, we need to specify a permutation of packets.

Note that the multicast group can remain unchanged for packets targeting the same hosts. In addition, the number of multicast groups is far fewer than the amount of packets, because there exists at most $2^k - 1 - k$ combinations for k target hosts (k is not more than the number of VMs) but has millions of packets, implying many packets target the same multicast group. The two reasons encourage us to firstly group the packets that have the same multicast group, and then design a sequence of these various multicast groups to minimize the overhead between the multicast groups' switchovers. And this sequence represents the permutation of packets.

We consider n multicast groups, and refer G_i to one multicast group i. Providing the cost for one target joining or quitting the group are equal and constant, says c; and $W_{i,j}$ denotes the overhead of switchover from G_i to G_j, thus $W_{i,j}$ is the product of the count of target hosts' joining and quitting in the switchover and the cost c. For example, G_i contains a set of hosts $\{H_1, H_3, H_4\}$ while G_j contains $\{H_2, H_3\}$; in the switchover from G_i to G_j, H_1 and H_4 will quit the multicast group, meanwhile H_2 joins in. Thus the value $W_{i,j}$ is $3*c$ for two quitting and one joining. Our purpose is to find a permutation of multicast groups with the aim of minimizing the total overhead W:

$$W = \sum_{i=0}^{n} W_{i,i+1} \qquad G_0 = G_{n+1} = \{\}$$

This can be reduced to be the classic Minimum Hamiltonian Cycle problem which is NP-complete, we simply adopt the algorithm proposed by Bollobas et al. [7], which approximates the optimal value in polynomial time.

The procedure of multicasting the packets to groups would be simple once the permutation is known. First of all, the Migration Sender selects the first multicast group in the permutation, notifies the associated target hosts to join the group, and then multicasts the packets target this multicast group. After the packets target this multicast group being send over, the Migration Sender will notify associated target hosts to join or quit this multicast group to switch to the next multicast group, and then transfer the packets to the new multicast group. This procedure will repeat until all packets are transferred to associated multicast groups.

3.6 Compression and Multithreading

Compression is an efficient approach to reduce the size of transferred packets; the algorithms such as LZ77 [30], LZW [17] can bring about as many as 50% or more data saving, which is significant in the live migration scene where large amount of data exists. We take *zlib* which is an effective compression library to compress the packets.

However, compression will introduce additional CPU overhead and cost more migration time. Multithreading is a valuable assisting technology to parallelize the tasks by overlapping the processing time of threads and distributing the tasks to multiprocessors, thus efficiently reduce the time for CPU intensive and IO intensive tasks running on multiple processors. In VMScatter, we exploit a thread pool containing six threads to reduce the thread creation and destruction overheads. Each thread will independently compose packets and then compresses the packets via *zlib*, lastly transfer the packets to targets during the thorough data transfer phase.

4. Experimental Evaluation

We test VMScatter on serval workloads, and give the detailed evaluation in this section. We begin by illustrating the results related to page content similarity of VMs acquired by Collector module, then compare the metrics including total migration time, total transferred data and network traffic between the QEMU/KVM live migration technology and VMScatter schema; furthermore, we present the results on network traffic of preferable grouping versus random groupings. Lastly we characterize the impacts on system performance both in a single VM and VM cluster.

4.1 Experimental Setup

We conduct our experiments on 14 physical servers, each with 2-way quad-core Xeon E6750 2GHz processors, 16GB DDR memory, and NetXtreme II BCM5708S Gigabit network interface card. The shared storage is configured with 1T disk, and connected to servers via switched Gigabit Ethernet. We configure 1GB memory for each VM unless specified otherwise; therefore the physical server can support as many as 16 VMs. The operating system on both physical and virtual machines is debian6.0, with Linux kernel version 2.6.32. All the servers share the storage so that the disk state does not need to be migrated. The workloads includes:

Idle workload means the VM does nothing except the tasks of OS self after boot-up.

Kernel Compilation represents a development workload involves memory used by the page cache. We compile the Linux 2.6.32 kernel along with all modules.

Sysbench [3] is a benchmark tool for evaluating OS parameters. We perform 5000 transactions on the database table containing 1 million entries.

TPC-W [4] is a transactional benchmark that simulates the activities of a business web server. We run TPC-W serving 600 simultaneous users accessing the site using the *shopping* workload that performs a mix of read/write operations.

4.2 Identical Rate Acquired by Collector

The identical rate, which is defined by the percentage of the identical pages on all the memory pages, is the key to this proposal because higher identical rate means more pages can be deduplicated and multicasted. The identical memory pages come from five sources: memory of kernel that loaded when booting up, the content of the loaded application data and code, some library codes related to the application, and content generated by application and zero pages. The zero pages will be dirtied after running a long time, in our experiment, the number of zero pages decreases from about 200,000 after boot-up to less than 5000 in one VM which has 262144 pages (1G memory). As a result we conduct the experiments after long time running to minimize the impact of zero pages. We illustrate the identical rate of the VMs with the same OS and applications, and then the identical rate of different VMs. Our experiment obtain similar results to many work [14, 21] which state about 50% to 90% of the pages have identical content with others for VMs having the same OS, providing a high degree of confidence that the VMScatter would be effective.

Same VMs. The same VMs have the same OS and the same applications. Figure 6 demonstrates the variation of identical rate with the increasing number of VMs. The rate is higher than 86%

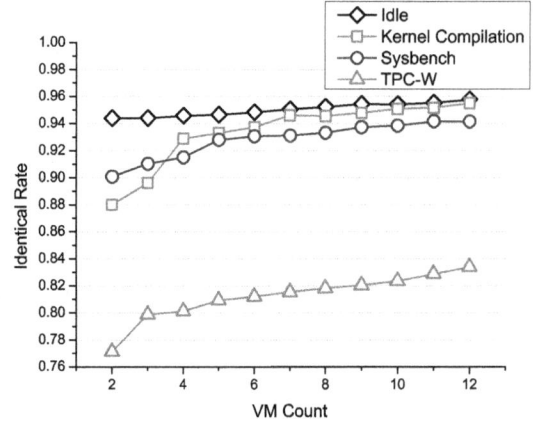

Figure 6. Identical rate of virtual machines.

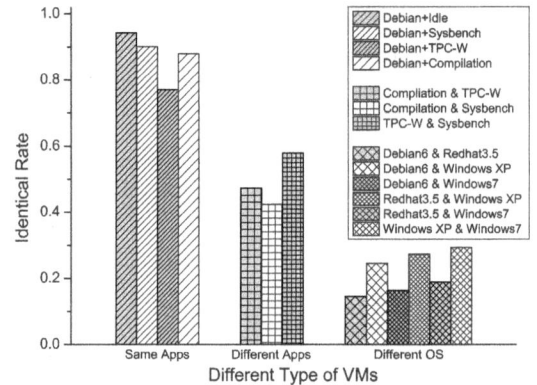

Figure 7. Identical rate of different VMs.

among the same VMs for Idle, Kernel Compilation and Sysbench workloads. Furthermore, we observe that the identical rate rises as the number of VMs increases, e.g. ranges from 88.03% to 95.3% with the Kernel Compilation as a test application. The rise is because the unique page may become identical to another page in the new added VM. This result is encouraging because more than 86% memory pages of 11 VMs may be eliminated via multicast, which will reduce the total transferred data by a lot.

Different VMs. We test two kinds of different VMs: 1) VMs with the same OS but different applications, in this case, we test on three VMs with debian6.0, and initiate Kernel Compilation, Sysbench, and TPC-W separately in each VM. 2) VMs with different OS, four VMs are equipped with Debian6.0, Redhat5.3, Windows XP, and Windows 7, with variety of applications running inside such as web browser, video player, office, etc.

As we can see from Figure 7, the identical rate between each two VMs with different applications varies, 47.34% for Kernel compilation and TPC-W workloads, 42.43% for Kernel Compilation and Sysbench, 57.85% for TPC-W and Sysbench (higher than the other two pairs because they are transactional benchmarks related to MySql), and the identical rate across all the three VMs is 51.84%. This result indicates that about half of the memory pages are identical for VMs with the same OS, and the reduced identical pages compared to the same VMs are due to the different applications and their content. However for different VMs with different

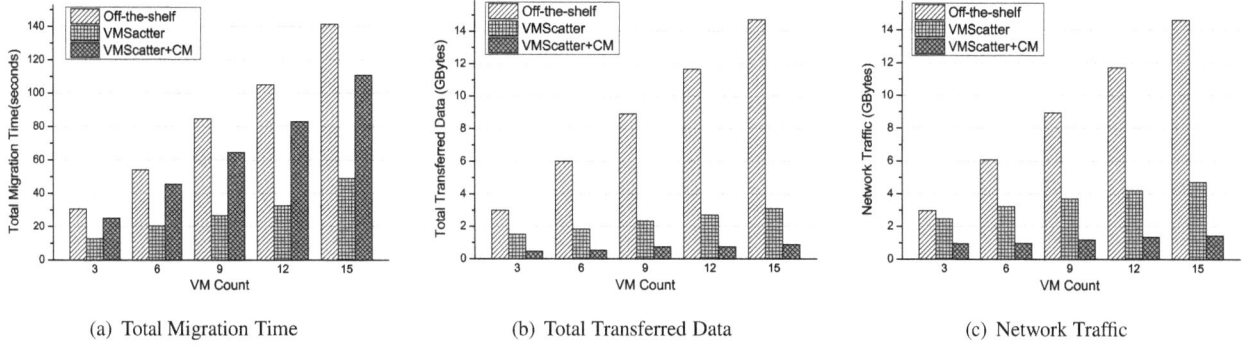

(a) Total Migration Time   (b) Total Transferred Data   (c) Network Traffic

Figure 8. Comparison of three metrics in different modes, for three target hosts and varied number of VMs.

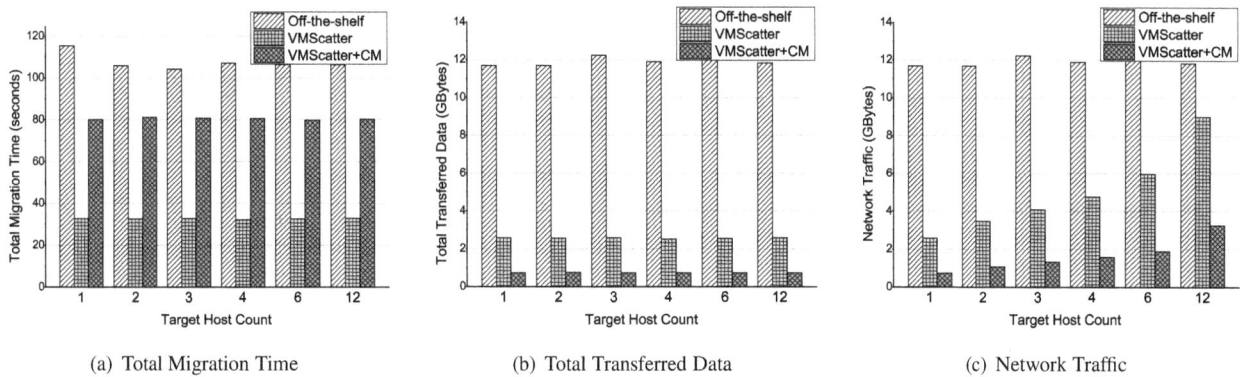

(a) Total Migration Time   (b) Total Transferred Data   (c) Network Traffic

Figure 9. Comparison of three metrics in different modes, for increasing number of target hosts and twelve VMs.

OS shown in the third set of bars, the identical rate is much lower, only at the average of 21.8% between two VMs. We suspect the identical pages mainly come from zero pages and universal libraries. These results imply VMScatter may still benefit for saving identical pages in transmission.

The above two results also suggest us that the identical rate is different in different number of VMs or various type of VMs. For fair comparison of all modes, we evaluate our method only on migrating equal numbers of VMs having the same OS and applications to each target host in the following experiments.

4.3 Live Migration via Multicast

We carry out the evaluation of live migration for the following three modes.

Off-the-shelf migration: This method is the simple live migration method used in QEMU/KVM without optimizations except the compression of the page whose bytes are the same such as zero page.

VMScatter: This is our live one-to-many migration method in that the identical pages will be merged into one page in the packet and multicasted to different hosts.

Compression and multithreading (VMScatter+CM): This mode extends the VMScatter work, with threads each of which composes, compresses and then sends the packets.

We first migrate 3, 6, 9, 12 and 15 VMs separately to three target hosts, then migrate twelve VMs simultaneously while varying the number of hosts to evaluate the live one-to-many approach on three metrics: total migration time, total transferred data and network traffic. The results illustrated are the average of 20 trials with Kernel Compilation running inside the VMs.

Total migration time. Figure 8(a) and Figure 9(a) compare the total migration time of the three modes of live migration. It can be seen that the VMScatter mode gives the lowest total migration time, migrating the 12 VMs in 32.7 seconds, achieving about 69.1% reduction against the off-the-shelf mode which costs about 105 seconds. This is due to the fact that the pages that have identical content are transferred by only a single copy with reference information such as *Page Address* and *VM Id*, which reduces large amount of transferred data and IO overhead. The performance of VMScatter+CM mode, however, reduces only 25% of migration time. The reason is straight: packets compression is CPU intensive so that consumes the additional time compared to VMScatter. Yet as observed in the graph, this mode still consumes less time than the off-the-shelf mode due to the benefit of multicast and page deduplication.

Total transferred data. Figure 8(b) and Figure 9(b) plot the total transferred data of the three modes. One small anomaly is in the off-the-shelf mode where the total transferred data is less than 12G which should be the sum of 1G memory size for 12 VMs. This is because the compression of zero pages implemented in QEMU/KVM, which involves representing one page by only one byte instead of the 4096 bytes during transmission. As expected, the VMScatter method transfers far fewer data than off-the-shelf mode, and brings about 74.2% reduction attributable to unimplemented transmission of duplicate pages. Note that total transferred data and the total migration time show a similar trend which both introduce about 70% reduction, this is due to the limited network band-

69

width between the physical hosts. Although the VMScatter+CM mode consumes more time, it enhances the VMScatter further by 70.6%, and achieves a total of 92.4% reduction over the off-the-shelf method.

As Figure 8(b) shows, the increase of total transferred data in VMScatter is not proportional to the number of VMs. This is because the inter-identical pages are only transferred by multicasting a single copy, so the identical pages in the new added VM will not need to be transferred any more except extra page references such as *Page Address* and *VM Id* pairs. The increased amount are mainly from the unique pages in the added virtual machines as well as the additional dirtied pages caused by longer migration time.

It should be observed in the Figures 9(a) and 9(b): both the total migration time and total transferred data remain unchanged regardless of the number of target hosts. The reasons are explained as follows. 1) The definitive identical rate of 12 VMs as shown in Figure 6 implies that the amount of packets is almost fixed for both identical and unique pages, which further indicates the transfer time for these two types of packets is definitive in limited network bandwidth. As a result, the amount of dirtied pages can be regarded as fixed. In addition, the lost packets increase the transferred data but only a small number (only about 0.3%). Consequently, the amount of total transferred data consists of the above three types of packets and can be considered to be constant. 2) For the total migration time, the time spent on the preparation phase including collecting identical pages and scheduling groups is almost constant for fixed page numbers, therefore the total migration time is in line with the page transfer time, thus it is also constant.

Network traffic. Although there is no exact method to quantify network traffic during the live migration, we provide an approximate measure by the sum of packets received by target hosts. Figures 8(c) and 9(c) compare the network traffic with the increasing number of VMs and target hosts respectively. The network traffic is equal to the total transferred data when the number of targets is one, this is easily understood by the way we measure the network traffic. Another result to be observed is that when three (12) VMs are migrated to three (12) target hosts as shown in Figure 8(c) (9(c)), i.e., each target host receives only one VM, the VMScatter method still reduces the network traffic by 17.8% attributable to the self-identical pages within the VM. For other scenarios, the network traffic in VMScatter mode decreases significantly with a range between 50.1% to 70.3%.

Different from Figure 9(b) where the total transferred data are constant over various number of hosts, the network traffic increases as the number of target hosts increase as illustrated in Figure 9(c). This is because one additional copy of the packets needs to be forwarded by the switcher to the new added target host during multicast over the network. The VMScatter+CM mode also gain performance, reducing the multicast traffic further by about 69.7%.

We also evaluate the three metrics under Sysbench and TPC-W workloads. For the TPC-W which has lower identical rate, the VMScatter live migration method still performs nicely by reducing 63.3% of the total migration time, 67.4% of the total transferred data and 55.8% of the network traffic.

Overall, these results confirm the effectiveness of VMScatter. Although the compression and multithreading method produces longer total migration time, it reduces numerous transferred data and network traffic further by about 70% on the basis of VMScatter mode.

4.4 Downtime

Downtime is another important metric of live migration. It consists of the time to suspend the VM at the source host, transfer the dirtied pages, and activate the migrated VM at the target host. The downtime is inevitable because the dirtied pages generated during

continuous data transfer will lead to the inconsistency of VM state between the source and target host.

Table 1 shows the comparison in terms of downtime for the three modes for migrating 12 VMs to three targets evenly. The variation in the downtime is due to the parallel migration. The VMScatter mode performs better than the off-the-shelf method, and this could because this mode generates less dirtied data in a shorter migration time, thus consumes less time in the final data transfer after suspending the VM. Consider the VMScatter+CM mode, the overhead of compression at the source and decompression at the target cause the minimum value to be larger than the other two modes, and the average is less than off-the-shelf due to lesser time to transfer the reduced packet size.

4.5 Grouping Benefit

The two most significant results we have seen so far are in Figures 8 and 9 where the total transferred data and network traffic are reduced. We then conduct experiments to evaluate our grouping method which aims to reduce the network traffic further by deciding a preferable placement.

Figure 9(c) demonstrates the variation of network traffic with different groupings when the number of target hosts varies. Furthermore, we fix the number of targets and construct a group that distributes twelve VMs evenly to each target, we distribute evenly for fair comparison since the difference in number may result in volatile identical rate which affects the results. For each fixed number of targets, we simulate 60 different groupings, migrate the 12 VMs to the associated target hosts decided by each grouping and then count the network traffic. Besides, we obtain the preferable grouping by the greedy algorithm. We set the capacity of target hosts as identical, which means the hosts will accept the same number of VMs.

Intuitively, there is only one grouping method when there is one host, where all the VMs would target one host; the same is true for 12 targets where each VM targets a respective host. Thus, the two scenarios are not our concern. Table 2 illustrates the results of the network traffic on different groupings under various workloads, including the maximum value, minimum value and average value of the network traffic on 60 groupings; along with the network traffic of our preferable grouping. As the table shows, the maximum traffic is 4.07G while the minimum value is 3.47G for targeting three hosts when Kernel Compilation running inside the VMs, and the difference between the two groupings is about 17.3%. Our preferable placement of VMs decreases the network traffic to 3.31G, a 13.4% reduction compared to the average value. Generally, the preferable grouping achieves 10% to 15% reduction of the network traffic against the average of random groupings, thus it proves the improvement of grouping algorithm. The 10% to 15% reduction of network traffic is particularly valuable in the data-intensive data centers.

4.6 Performance Impact

In this section, we quantify the side effects of migration on a couple of sample applications. We evaluate the performance impact on both single VM and VM cluster with migrating 12 VMs to

Modes	Max	Min	Avg.
Off-the-shelf	2351	192	1518
VMScatter	1573	184	863
VMScatter+CM	1483	576	1132

Table 1. Comparison of downtime (ms).

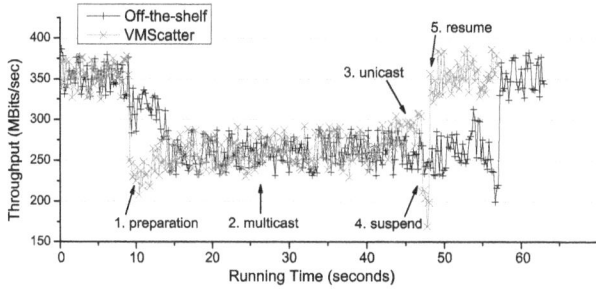

Figure 10. Throughput during live migration (result of off-the-shelf mode has been truncated to save space).

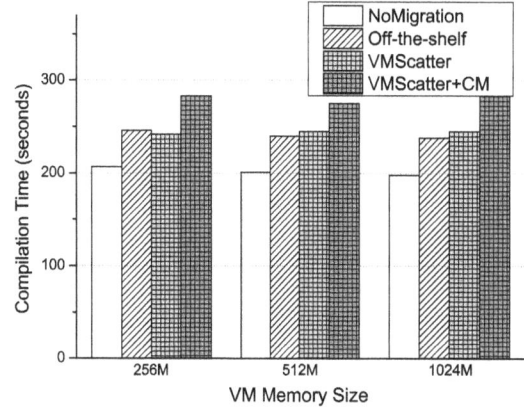

Figure 11. Compilation time on migration.

three targets, and illustrate the results of off-the-shelf mode versus VMScatter mode.

Impact on Single VM. We start first by measuring the performance on a single VM in terms of throughput per second by examining the live migration of a Apache web server serving static content at a high rate. The web server served 1000 files of 512 K-Bytes, all of which were cached on memory. In this experiment, 10 httperf processes in a remote client host sent requests to the server in parallel. Figure 10 illustrates the throughput achieved when continuously serving concurrent clients. At the start of the trace, the normal running of the VM can serve about 354Mbits/sec. After the live migration starts at the 9th second, the throughput of VMScatter decreases to about 214Mbits/sec which is lower than 309Mbits/sec of off-the-shelf. This is because the collecting and scheduling stages consume more CPU resource than off-the-shelf mode which only set flags. Then the page transfer phase serves 272Mbits/sec for about 24 seconds. There is no obvious decrease compared to off-the-shelf mode, thus implying the optimized permutation of packets takes effect. The throughput in transferring dirtied pages keeps about 305Mbits/sec which is higher than multicast. This may be because the amount of dirtied pages in unicast is less than the amount of pages during multicast, thus reserving more CPU and network resource for applications running inside VMs. One sudden decrease is the result of VM suspending. After the VM is resumed at the target host, the throughput returns to normal.

Impact on VM Cluster. We evaluate the performance of VM-Scatter on VM Cluster via *distcc* [1] to build a kernel compilation cluster to distribute the compilation tasks across the 12 VM-s, and migrate back and forth repeatedly between the source and three target hosts. Figure 11 compares the completion time for various memory size of VM under three live migration modes, the result without migration is also given for comparison. The VM-Scatter mode consumes almost the same compilation time as the off-the-shelf method, and both increase by less than 20% compared to NoMigration, owing to the similar CPU and network utilization. The VMScatter+VM mode cost more time because the CPU overhead of compression at the source host and decompression at the target hosts.

5. Related Work

Live Migration. Clark et al. [10] first propose the pre-copy live migration based on Xen platform, they transfer the page iteratively, and boot the VM when the consistent state are reserved in target host. However pre-copy migration may fail in harsh scenes such as low network bandwidth and memory-intensive workload where the amount of dirtied pages cannot converge. Hines et al. [27] propose post-copy method, they first boot the VM on target host and then copy the pages on demand, thus the memory pages will be transferred only once which both solves the problem of pre-copy and reduces the total transferred data. Liu et al. [19] adopt the methods of ReVirt [12], achieve live migration by transferring the log which records the execution of VM and replaying them at target host. Deshpande et al. [11] consider migrating multiple machines from one host to another, and propose live gang migration by page sharing and delta transfer to reduce the amount of transmission. In contrast, our concern is with the one-to-many migration and implementing VMScatter by multicasting a single copy of the identical pages instead of individual transfer.

Multicast. Multicast has been used to transfer images or snapshots for deploying multiple identical VMs in the IaaS platform [18, 26]. VMScatter employs the multicast method to transfer the identical pages by single copy, combined with unicast to transfer the unique pages and dirtied page. Besides, we specify a permutation of packets with the solution of Hamilton Cycle problem to reduce the network overhead occurred in multicast groups' switchovers.

Page Sharing and De-duplication. Page sharing saves memory consumption of VMs by merging the identical pages into one physical page. Bugnion et al. propose Disco [9], a tool that uses transparent page sharing to de-duplicate the redundant copies across VM-s. Waldspurger et al. [28] improve Disco further by content-based page sharing. Milos et al. [21] use sharing-aware block devices for detecting duplicate pages on Xen virtual machine monitor. Gupta et al. [14] improve the page sharing rate among VMs by dividing

Target Count	2				3				4				6			
Benchmarks	**Max**	**Min**	**Avg.**	**Prefer.**	**Max**	**Min**	**Avg.**	**Prefer.**	**Max**	**Min**	**Avg.**	**Prefer.**	**Max**	**Min**	**Avg.**	**Prefer.**
Compilation	3.56	3.12	3.37	3.05	4.07	3.47	3.82	3.31	4.86	4.11	4.65	4.03	5.97	5.12	5.73	5.18
Sysbench	3.82	3.33	3.67	3.32	4.22	3.69	4.07	3.52	5.08	4.33	4.86	4.30	6.23	5.34	6.02	5.45
TPC-W	4.84	4.37	4.60	4.34	5.33	4.71	5.15	4.89	6.17	5.41	5.98	5.49	7.29	6.86	7.15	6.89

Table 2. Comparison of network traffic(GBytes) for groupings, the target host count is 2, 3, 4, 6.

the page to sub-pages. Arcangeli et al. proposes KSM [5], a kernel module in Linux that uses an unstable red-black tree to improve the efficiency. We share a similar philosophy to page sharing, but against the motivation of page sharing that focus on less physical memory consumption, VMScatter is interested in de-duplicating the identical pages in the packet to be multicasted. Furthermore, our approach combines the selective hash with the red-black tree, and achieves an order of magnitude speedup over the original hash method on organizing millions of memory pages.

Placement of VMs. Many works have adopted live migration technology to achieve power saving [23], load balance [29], SLA [6], quality of service (QoS)[24], etc. In this paper, we consider the network traffic metric and propose a grouping algorithm with the aim of minimizing network traffic by selecting a preferable placement of VMs.

6. Conclusions

We implemented VMScatter to migrate VMs to multiple hosts. Our design and implementation addressed the issues involved in live one-to-many migration, placement of VMs and multicast specific options. By merging the identical pages into one page, VMScatter multicasts the single page to many targets instead of transferring these pages individually. The novel grouping method guides the VM's destination with respect to the network traffic over the network. And we explore a further benefit allowed by compression and multithreading. Through detailed evaluation, we show that the performance is sufficient to make VMScatter a practical tool in data centers even for VMs running interactive loads. In the future, we plan to investigate providing disk state migration, perhaps using existing techniques to improve VMScatter for hosts connected to independent storage, and evaluate VMScatter in complex network topologies such as BCube [13].

Acknowledgments

We acknowledge Yang Cao for his contributions to the algorithm of this work and Bin Shi, Kun Liu for the experimental setup. We also thank the anonymous reviewers for their valuable comments and help in improving this paper. This work is supported by the National Grand Fundamental Research 973 Program of China under Grant No. 2011CB302602, National High Technology Research 863 Program of China under Grant No. 2011AA01A202, National Nature Science Foundation of China under Grant No. 61272165, No. 60903149 and No. 91118008, and New Century Excellent Talents in University 2010 and Beijing New-Star R&D Program under Grant No. 2010B010.

References

[1] Distcc. http://code.google.com/p/distcc/.

[2] Superfasthash. http://www.azillionmonkeys.com/qed/hash.html.

[3] Sysbench. http://sysbench.sourceforge.net/.

[4] Tpc-w. http://www.tpc.org/tpcw/.

[5] A. Arcangeli, I. Eidus, and C. Wright. Increasing memory density by using ksm. In *Proceedings of the linux symposium*, pages 19–28, 2009.

[6] N. Boboroff, A. Kochut, and K. Beaty. Dynamic placement of virtual machines for managing sla violations. In *IFIP/IEEE International Symposium on Integrated Network Management*, pages 119–128, 2007.

[7] B. Bollobas, T. I. Fenner, and A. M. Frieze. An algorithm for finding hamilton paths and cycles in random graphs. *Combinatorica*, 7(4): 327–341, 1987.

[8] M. S. Borella, D. Swider, U. S, and B. G.B. Internet packet loss: Measurement and implications for end-to-end qos. In *Proceedings of ICPP Workshps*, pages 3–12, 1998.

[9] E. Bugnion, S. Devine, Kinshuk, Govil, and M. Rosenblum. Disco: running commodity operating systems on scalable multiprocessors. *ACM Transactions on Computer Systems*, 15(4):412–447, 1997.

[10] C. Clark, K. Fraser, S. Hand, J. G. Hansen, E. Jul, C. Limpach, I. Pratt, and A. Warfield. Live migration of virtual machines. In *Proceedings of NSDI*, pages 273–286, 2005.

[11] U. Deshpande, X. Wang, and K. Gopalan. Live gang migration of virtual machines. In *Proceedings of HPDC*, pages 135–146, 2011.

[12] G. W. Dunlap, S. T. Kin, S. Cinar, M. A. Basrai, and P. M. Chen. Revirt: Enabling intrusion analysis through virtual-machine logging and replay. In *Proceedings of OSDI*, pages 211–224, 2002.

[13] C. Guo, G. Lu, D. Li, H. Wu, X. Zhang, Y. Shi, C. Tian, Y. Zhang, and S. Lu. Bcube: A high performance, server-centric network architecture for modular data centers. In *SIGCOMM*, pages 63–74, 2009.

[14] D. Gupta, S. Lee, M. Vrable, S. Savage, A. C. Snoeren, G. Varghese, G. M. Voelker, and A. Vahdat. Difference engine: Harnessing memory redundancy in virtual machines. *Communications of the ACM*, 53(10): 85–93, 2010.

[15] H. Jin, L. Deng, and S. Wu. Live virtual machine migration with adaptive memory compression. In *Proceedings of CLUSTER*, pages 1–10, 2009.

[16] A. Kivity, Y. Kamay, D. Laor, U. Lublin, and A. Liguori. Kvm: the linux virtual machine monitor. In *Proceedings of the Linux Symposium*, pages 225–230, 2007.

[17] M. J. Knieser, F. G. Wolff, C. A. Papachristou, D. J. Weyer, and D. R. McIntyre. A technique for high ratio lzw compression. In *Design, Automation & Test in Europe*, pages 10–16, 2003.

[18] H. A. Lagar-Cavilla, J. A. Whitney, A. M. Scannel, P. Patchin, S. M. Rumble, E. de Lara, M. Brudno, and M. Satyanarayanan. Snowflock: Rapid virtual machine cloning for cloud computing. In *Proceedings of EuroSys*, pages 1–12, 2009.

[19] H. Liu, H. Jin, and X. Liao. Live migration of virtual machine based on full system trace and replay. In *Proceedings of HPDC*, pages 101–110, 2009.

[20] R. E. Miller and J. W. Thatcher, editors. *Complexity of Computer Computations*. Plenum Press., New York, 1972.

[21] G. Milos, D. Murray, S. Hand, and M. A. Fetterman. Satori: Enlightened page sharing. In *USENIX Annual Technical Conference*, pages 1–14, 2009.

[22] S. B. Moon, J. Kurose, P. Skelly, and D. Towsley. Correlation of packet delay and loss in the internet. Technical report, 1998.

[23] R. Nathuji and K. Schwan. Virtualpower: Coordinated power management in virtualized enterprise systems. In *ACM Symposium on Operating Systems Principles*, pages 265–278, 2007.

[24] R. Nathuji, A. Kansal, and A. Ghaffarkhah. Q-clouds: Managing performance interference effects for qos-aware clouds. In *Proceedings of EuroSys*, pages 237–250, 2010.

[25] M. Nelson, B.-H. Lim, and G. Hutchins. Fast transparent migration for virtual machines. In *USENIX '05 Technical Program*, 2005.

[26] B. Nicolae, J. Bresnahan, and K. Keahey. Going back and forth: Efficient multideployment and multisnapshotting on clouds. In *Proceedings of HPDC*, pages 147–158, 2011.

[27] M. R, Hines, and K. Gopalan. Post-copy based live virtual machine migration using adaptive pre-paging and dynamic self-ballooning. In *Proceedings of VEE*, pages 51–60, 2009.

[28] C. A. Waldspurger. Memory resource management in vmware esx server. In *Proceedings of OSDI*, pages 181–194, 2002.

[29] Y. Zhao and W. Huang. Adaptive distributed load balancing algorithm based on live migration of virtual machines in cloud. In *Fifth International Joint Conference on INC, IMS and IDC*, pages 170–175, 2009.

[30] J. Ziv and A. Lempel. A universal algorithm for sequential data compression. *IEEE Trans. on Information Theory*, 23(3):337–343, 1997.

Optimizing Virtual Machine Live Storage Migration in Heterogeneous Storage Environment

Ruijin Zhou
Intelligent Design of Efficient
Architectures Laboratory
University of Florida
USA
zhourj@ufl.edu

Fang Liu
State Key Laboratory of High
Performance Computing
National University of Defense
Technology
China
liufang@nudt.edu.cn

Chao Li
Intelligent Design of Efficient
Architectures Laboratory
University of Florida
USA
chaol@ufl.edu

Tao Li
Intelligent Design of Efficient
Architectures Laboratory
University of Florida
USA
taoli@ece.ufl.edu

Abstract

Virtual machine (VM) live storage migration techniques significantly increase the mobility and manageability of virtual machines in the era of cloud computing. On the other hand, as solid state drives (SSDs) become increasingly popular in data centers, VM live storage migration will inevitably encounter heterogeneous storage environments. Nevertheless, conventional migration mechanisms do not consider the speed discrepancy and SSD's wear-out issue, which not only causes significant performance degradation but also shortens SSD's lifetime. This paper, for the first time, addresses the efficiency of VM live storage migration in heterogeneous storage environments from a multi-dimensional perspective, i.e., user experience, device wearing, and manageability. We derive a flexible metric (migration cost), which captures various design preference. Based on that, we propose and prototype three new storage migration strategies, namely: 1) Low Redundancy (LR), which generates the least amount of redundant writes; 2) Source-based Low Redundancy (SLR), which keeps the balance between IO performance and write redundancy; and 3) Asynchronous IO Mirroring, which seeks the highest IO performance. The evaluation of our prototyped system shows that our techniques outperform existing live storage migration by a significant margin. Furthermore, by adaptively mixing our proposed schemes, the cost of massive VM live storage migration can be even lower than that of only using the best of individual mechanism.

Categories and Subject Descriptors D.4.8 [Operating Systems]: Performance; C.4 [Computer System Organization]: Performance of Systems

General Terms Management, Performance, Design

Keywords Live VM Storage Migration, Solid State Drive, Virtualization

1. Introduction

Nowadays, virtualization technology has been widely adopted as the base infrastructure for cloud computing. Major cloud providers, such as Amazon (EC2) [1] and Microsoft (Azure) [2], are selling their computing resources in the form of virtual machines (VMs). Load balancing has become essential for effectively managing large volumes of VMs in cloud computing environment. The cornerstone for moving virtual machines on the fly is the VM live migration, which only transfers CPU and memory states of VMs from one host to another. To allow the movement of persistent storage with VMs, several live storage migration techniques have been proposed, including Dirty Block Tracking (DBT) and IO Mirroring [10][11][12]. VM live storage migration significantly increases the mobility and manageability of virtual machines during disaster recovery, storage maintenance, and storage upgrade.

Meanwhile, Flash-based solid state drives (SSDs) have become one of the most popular storage media due to their high performance, silent operations and shock resistance [20, 21]. With the decrease in price, they become more affordable to be used in data centers. Currently, many leading Internet service provision companies, such as Facebook, Amazon and Dropbox, are starting to integrate SSDs into their cloud storage systems [3][4][5]. The storage media for data centers becomes more diverse as both SSDs and HDDs are being used to support cloud storage. Consequently, storage management, especially VM live storage migration, becomes more complex and challenging.

Although SSDs deliver higher IO performance, their limited lifetime is an inevitable issue. Our analysis shows that existing VM live storage migration schemes do not fully exploit the high performance characteristics of SSDs but aggravate the wear out problem. Even worse, during massive storage migrations, SSDs will be worn out significantly due to large volume of write operations. In this paper, we address the efficiency/cost of VM live storage migration (Migration Cost, MC) in heterogeneous storage environments from a multi-dimensional perspective, which incorporates user experience (IO penalty), cluster management (migration time) and device usage (degree of wear). The weights on IO penalty and SSD lifetime are also considered to reflect different design preferences. We propose and prototype three VM live storage migration mechanisms to minimize the migration cost, namely: 1) Low Redundancy (LR), which generates near zero redundant writes; 2) Source-based Low Redundancy (SLR), which aims to leverage faster source disk while still maintaining low redundancy merit; 3) Asynchronous IO Mirroring (AIO), which targets high IO performance. The empirical evaluation of our prototyped systems shows that they yield stable and short disk downtimes (around 200ms). Although the cost varies with different weights and storage media, on average, the migration costs for LR, SLR and AIO are 51%, 22% and 21% lower than those for traditional methods (i.e. DBT and IO Mirroring). Furthermore, by adaptively invoking our schemes during massive storage migration, the cost can be further reduced by 48% compared to using the best individual mechanism.

The rest of this paper is organized as follows: Sections 2 and 3 provide background and motivation for this work. Section 4 describes the evaluation metric. Section 5 discusses our proposed designs. Sections 6 and 7 present our prototypes and experimental results. Section 8 discusses related work and Section 9 concludes the paper.

2. Background

2.1. VM Live Storage Migration Techniques

Live storage migration for virtual machines is defined as the migration of VM disk images without service interruption to the running workload. The two mainstream techniques are dirty block tracking (DBT) and IO Mirroring. The DBT technique, which is widely adopted by many VM vendors (e.g. Xen and VMware ESX), is a well-known mechanism that uses bitmap to track write requests while the VM image is being copied. Once the entire image is copied to the destination, a merge process is initiated to patch all the dirty blocks (i.e. data blocks that are recorded in bitmap) from the original image to the new image. In order to prevent further write requests, the VM is paused until all the dirty blocks are patched to the new disk image. To mitigate downtime introduced by the merge process, incremental DBT, which keeps the VM running while iteratively patching dirty blocks to the new image, is proposed and used in several projects [11][12][13][14]. If the number of dirty blocks is stable for several iterations, the VM is suspended and the remaining dirty blocks are copied to the destination. Nevertheless, incremental DBT also has disadvantage: in case that the number of dirty blocks are not converged due to intensive write requests, the migration time and even the downtime can be significantly long. Note that in this paper, we refer incremental DBT as DBT.

To address the issue of long migration time and downtime, VMware proposed IO Mirroring technique [10] to eliminate the iteratively merge process. With IO Mirroring, all the write requests to the data blocks that have been copied will be duplicated and issued to both source and destination disks. The two write requests are synchronized and then the write completion acknowledgement is asserted (synchronous write). Write requests to the data blocks that have not yet been copied will only be issued to the source disk

while the writes to the data blocks that are currently being copied will be buffered and later issued to both source and destination when the being copied phase completes. By doing so, the data blocks will always be synchronized during the migration process. Note that once the process of copying VM disk image completes, merging is not needed, which leads to shorter migration time and lower downtime. However, IO Mirroring also raises some concerns: 1) workload IO performance is limited by the slower disk due to the synchronized write requests; 2) since the disk bandwidth is consumed by the duplicated IO requests, the progress of copying the VM image will be slowed down.

2.2. Storage Migration in Heterogeneous Storage Environments

Historically, mechanical hard disk drives (HDDs) are used as the primary storage media due to their large capacity and high stability in the long run. Recently, solid-state drives (SSDs), which have high IO performance [20], are emerging as promising storage media. The IOPS (IO per second) for VM running on SSDs in our experiments is 3.3X higher than that on HDDs. However, SSDs also have their limitations such as low capacity, high price tag, and limited lifetime. The more the writes and erases are performed, the shorter the remaining SSD lifetime will be [7, 22]. In the commercial market, cloud storage providers, such as Morphlabs, Storm on Demand, CloudSigma and CleverKite, are selling the SSD powered cloud [4]. On the other hand, device manufacturers, such as Intel and Samsung, are researching on reliable SSD for data centers [6, 27]. Thus, from the perspective of both seller and manufacturer, SSDs have been accredited as an indispensable component for cloud and data center storage. A data center will be equipped with several disk arrays. Some of the disk arrays are SSDs while the others are HDDs. Those disk arrays are connected to servers via Fibre Channel [8, 9, 26]. Our work focuses on the storage migration between different disk arrays.

VM live storage migration will be more sophisticated and challenging on heterogeneous storage environments. For instance, if a user requests more disk space, his/her VM image may need to be migrated from small capacity disk (SSD) to large capacity disk (HDD). On the other hand, if the user requests to upgrade IO performance, his/her VM image may need to be migrated from slow disk (HDD) to fast disk (SSD). Since VM live storage migration will inevitably be performed on various types of storage media, it should consider the characteristics of different storage devices, such as the high bandwidth, limited lifetime for SSD and the low access speed, large capacity for HDDs. Nevertheless, existing live storage migration schemes do not take the underlying storage media into consideration, which manifests several disadvantages, such as: 1) not fully exploiting the high performance of SSDs, 2) having longer migration time since the redundant write requests occupy a significant fraction of IO bandwidth, 3) quickly wearing down SSDs and reducing the remaining SSD lifetime. Even worse, large volume of redundant IO operations, which are generated during massive storage migration, will not only saturate the disk bandwidth but also severely affect the SSD's lifetime.

3. Performance Characterization

This section analyzes the behaviors of existing live storage migration schemes (e.g. DBT and IO Mirroring) in heterogeneous storage environments.

3.1. A Characterization of the Two Basic Processes for VM Live Storage Migration

In general, VM live storage migration involves two processes, namely 1) copy process that moves the VM image and 2) VM IO request handling process that ensures consistency between the two disk images. During storage migration, processes 1) and 2) compete for IO bandwidth, which largely affects the performance. Table 1 shows the performance of copying a 5GB image of an idle VM and Table 2 shows the measured IOPS of the same VM that is running but is not being migrated. As expected, the SSD effectively speeds up the copy process and the VM on SSDs achieves much higher IOPS than that on HDDs. Nevertheless, the resource competition between image copy and VM IO requests still exists even when SSDs are involved. Note that the VM IO requests can be issued to source or destination during the migration. The performance characteristics on copying VM image with running workloads are shown in Figures 1 (a) and (b). SSDs have faster access speed and better capability of handling intensive IO requests. In the case where both a SSD and a HDD are involved, the IOPS will be higher and the copy time will be shorter if the VM IO requests are directed to the SSD. In the case where both source and destination are SSDs, the copy time and IOPS will be similar no matter where the VM IO requests are issued. In the case where both source and destination are HDDs, higher IOPS can be achieved at the cost of longer migration time.

Table 1. The time to copy a 5GB idle VM image

SSD to SSD	SSD to HDD	HDD to SSD	HDD to HDD
30s	59s	55s	81s

Table 2. The IOPS of running VM

	75% Read	50% Read	25% Read
VM on SSD	5500	5900	6495
VM on HDD	2230	1744	1445

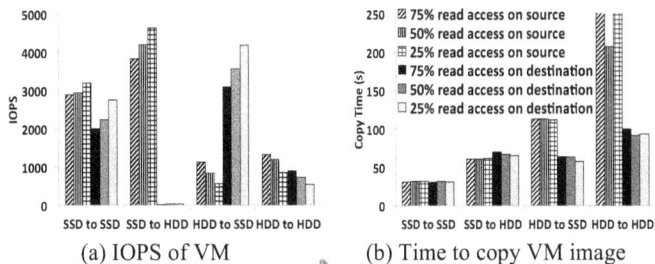

(a) IOPS of VM   (b) Time to copy VM image

Figure 1. Copying VM image while workloads are running inside

In the case that a VM is migrated from a HDD to a SSD and all the IO requests from VM are issued to the source disk (HDD) as in DBT, the performance for both copy process and IO requests will be significantly low, as shown in Figure 1. The reason is that the reads from the copy process and the IO requests from VM will saturate the bandwidth of the HDD. In the case that a VM is migrated from a SSD to a HDD, issuing all the VM IO requests to the source disk (SSD) will yield high IOPS and short copy time because the SSD has better capability for handling large volume of IO accesses. However, simply filtering all the IO requests to the SSD will exacerbate the degree of wearing for the SSD, which shortens the remaining SSD lifetime. Thus, blindly using SSD is also not a wise decision.

To summarize, when VM storage migration occurs in the storage environment that involves SSDs, redirecting the workload IO requests to SSDs will benefit the migration time and IOPS but the SSDs will be worn out quickly. When a VM is migrated between HDDs, there is trade off between migration time and IOPS.

3.2. A Characterization of Existing Live Storage Migration Schemes

We use Xen as our virtual machine monitor and implement the two existing storage migration techniques in Xen blktap2 modules (details in Section 6).

There are three well-known metrics to measure the performance of live storage migration: 1) downtime, 2) migration time, and 3) IO penalty. Downtime measures the time it takes to pause the VM and switchover between source and destination disks. Migration time represents the overall time it takes to accomplish the storage migration operation, which should be minimized to guarantee smooth and quick storage maintenance. IO penalty shows the performance degradation the user will experience during the VM live storage migration.

As can be seen in Table 3, DBT tends to have longer downtime than IO Mirroring because DBT needs to patch the last copy of dirty blocks during the downtime period while this is not necessary for IO Mirroring. Besides, when varying the underlying storage media, the downtime of DBT is less stable than that of IO Mirroring. Worse, when the destination is slower than the source (e.g. from SSD to HDD), DBT takes long time or even fails to complete since the last iteration of the merge process writes dirty data blocks to the slower disk.

Table 3. The Downtime of Migrating 30GB VM Image while Running IOmeter with 50% Reads / 50% Writes

	SSD to SSD	SSD to HDD	HDD to SSD	HDD to HDD
DBT	232ms	4000ms	266ms	900ms
IO Mirroring	198ms	249ms	298ms	199ms

Migration time for existing schemes is shown in Figure 2. We also use two emulated scenarios for comparison purposes. Copying disk image while VM IO requests are only issued to the source is denoted as Emulated_S and copying disk image while VM IO requests are only issued to the destination is referred as Emulated_D. In terms of migration time, the biggest difference between IO Mirroring and DBT is the iterative merge process. As

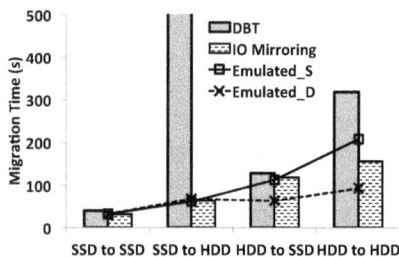

Figure 2. The migration time for a 5GB VM image under heterogeneous storage environment (Iometer is running inside the VM with 50% read, 50% write)

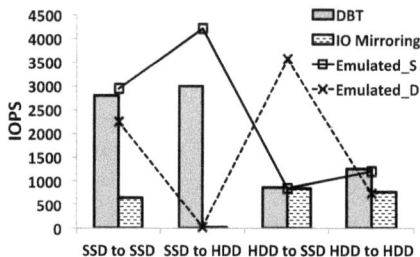

Figure 3. The IOPS for migrating VM images under heterogeneous storage environment (IOmeter is used to measure IOPS)

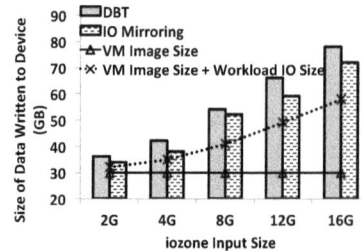

Figure 4. The total size of data that written to device when migrating 30GB VM from SSD to SSD (IOzone is set to perform write and rewrite operation)

can be seen in Figure 2, DBT exhibits longer migration time than IO Mirroring because it needs to iteratively merge dirty blocks to destination after copying the image. The slower the destination storage media are, the longer the merge process will be. Both migration schemes manifest longer migration time compared to the better of the two emulated scenarios.

When using IO Mirroring scheme, the IOPS inside the VM highly depends on the slowest disk due to synchronous write. On the other hand, the IOPS inside the VM when using DBT scheme only depends on the source disk. As can be seen from Figure 3, when the source disk is a SSD, DBT has advantage over IO Mirroring in terms of IO performance. If the source is a HDD, both DBT and IO Mirroring yield similar IOPS. However, neither of them reaches the performance of the two emulated scenarios (indicated by the dash-cross or solid-square lines, whichever is higher). In other words, conventional schemes do not fully exploit the high performance of SSDs.

Since introducing a large volume of write and erase cycles will unavoidably diminish the lifetime of SSDs [7], we add another measurement: the amount of data that is written to SSD, in our characterization. If only the copying of a VM disk image is considered (e.g. experiments shown in Figure 1), then the total amount of data written to SSD is determined by the workload IO traffic plus the VM image size. The live storage migration schemes introduce overhead and redundant data writes, further wearing off SSDs and shortening the SSD's lifetime.

Figure 4 shows the amount of data written to disk when migrating VM images from SSDs to SSDs. As can be seen, both mechanisms generate extra amount of data writes compared to simply copying the disk image of the running VM (dashed line). The heavier the workload's IO traffic is, the higher the extra volume of data write (the amount that exceeds the dashed line) will be. For DBT, the redundant data writes come from the merge process; for IO Mirroring, the redundant data writes come from the duplicated writes to data blocks that have been copied. DBT tends to have more redundant data writes than IO Mirroring.

To sum up, a good live storage migration technique in heterogeneous storage environments should have negligible downtime, short migration time, low IO penalty, and less

redundant writes to the SSD. The major issue with contemporary methods is that they do not take the underlying device characteristics into consideration. We believe that once the underlying storage becomes heterogeneous, new methods for live storage migration are needed and our analysis shows that there is still plenty of room for improvement in terms of migration time, IO penalty, and redundant writes. In this paper, we are motivated to explore better VM live storage migration schemes.

4. Metric for Live Storage Migration in Heterogeneous Environments

VM live storage migration behavior has impacts on three aspects: 1) VM user experience (IO penalty and downtime), 2) storage maintenance (migration time), and 3) SSD lifetime (extra amount of data writes). Thus, in this section, we propose a more comprehensive metric, which takes all three aspects into consideration.

For the VM user experience, the existing metric, IO penalty, can indicate the performance degradation the user will experience. Note that the value of traditional IO penalty may be negative when destination disk is faster than source disk. In order to avoid this (i.e. negative penalty), we define I/O penalty as:

$$\lambda_{IO} = \frac{Best\ IO\ Performance - IO\ Performance\ during\ migration}{Best\ IO\ Performance} \quad (1)$$

In equation (1), *Best IO Performance* means the best IO performance achieved from available storage media. For example, if VM is migrated from HDD to SSD, the *Best IO Performance* is the performance we can get from SSD. Ideally, when workloads always run on a faster disk, λ_{IO} will be close to 0. From the user perspective, the less the IO penalty is, the better the storage migration scheme will be. As a "live" storage migration, the disk downtime should be close to 0. Otherwise, workloads inside the VM may crash due to intolerably long interrupts. We believe that downtime should be used as a separate metric to quantify whether a storage migration design is "live" or not.

From the perspective of the data center administrator, migration time means how long he/she should wait until the next management can be performed. Longer migration time means higher possibility to fail the scheduled maintenance plan. Ideally, migration time should be close to the time it takes to simply copy the entire VM disk image without interference. We define the migration time factor $\lambda_{migration\ time}$ as:

$$\lambda_{migration\ time} = \frac{migration\ time}{image\ copy\ time} \qquad (2)$$

Since storage migration will inevitably introduce IO competition and runtime overhead, *migration time* will always be longer than *image copy time*. In other words, $\lambda_{migration\ time}$ is always greater than 1. The smaller the $\lambda_{migration\ time}$ is, the better the storage migration scheme is for the data center manager.

From the device point of view, the amount of data writes can indicate the degree of wear brought by live storage migration. Besides, the larger the amount of data writes is, the more quickly the SSD will be worn out, which leads to shorter remaining lifetime for the SSD. Thus, we define a wear-out factor $\lambda_{wear\ out}$ to indicate the SSD lifetime penalty per time unit during storage migration. There is one caveat: HDD does not have the wear out issue. Thus, $\lambda_{wear\ out}$ should equal to 0 when all the write requests are issued to HDD.

$$\lambda_{wear\ out} = \frac{data\ written\ to\ SSD\ per\ time\ unit}{Workload\ Data\ Writes\ per\ time\ unit} \qquad (3)$$

In equation (3), the denominator is the amount of data writes per time unit generated by the workloads while the nominator is the amount of data (generated by workload) written to SSD per time unit. For normal executing VMs, $\lambda_{wear\ out}$ equals to 1 if the VM is running on a SSD, 0 if the VM is running on a HDD. Any redundant writes, such as merge process in DBT and write request duplication in IO Mirroring, will make $\lambda_{wear\ out}$ greater. The smaller the $\lambda_{wear\ out}$ is, the less severely the SSD wears off during live storage migration.

Note that migration time indicates not only how long the user will suffer from the I/O penalty but also how long the device will be worn. In other words, the longer the migration time is, the higher overall penalty ($\lambda_{IO} * \lambda_{migration\ time}$) the user will observe and the higher overall degree of wearing ($\lambda_{wear\ out} * \lambda_{migration\ time}$) the SSD could receive. Therefore, we define the migration cost (MC) for VM live storage migration as:

$$
\begin{aligned}
MC &= \gamma * \lambda_{wear\ out} * \lambda_{migration\ time} \\
&\quad +(1 - \gamma) * \lambda_{IO} * \lambda_{migration\ time} \\
&= \lambda_{migration\ time} * (\gamma * \lambda_{wear\ out} + (1 - \gamma) * \lambda_{IO}) \qquad (4)
\end{aligned}
$$

where γ defines the weight on the lifetime of SSD while $(1 - \gamma)$ is the weight on the IO performance ($0 < \gamma < 1$). $\gamma > 50\%$ means wear out issue has higher priority while $\gamma < 50\%$ means IO performance is desired more.

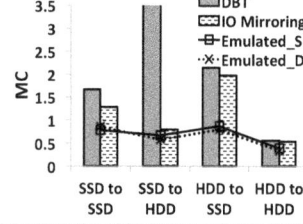

Figure 5. MC for current storage migration schemes when $\gamma = 0.5$

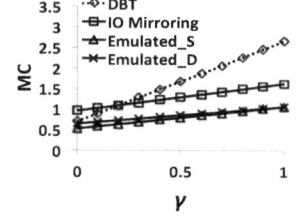

Figure 6 (a). MC when migrating a VM from SSD to SSD

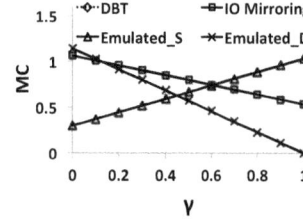

Figure 6 (b). MC when migrating a VM from SSD to HDD *(the value of DBT is too high to be shown)*

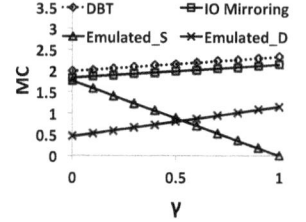

Figure 6 (c). MC when migrating a VM from HDD to SSD

Assuming neutral preference on wear-out issue and IO performance ($\gamma = 0.5$), Figure 5 shows the migration cost for existing storage migration schemes. As can be seen, no matter what type of underlying storage media are used, both DBT and IO Mirroring have extra migration cost compared to the two emulated scenarios (Emulated_S and Emulated_D). Further zooming in on each case, Figures 6 (a), (b) and (c) show how migration cost varies when the weight γ changes. In the case where both source and destination are SSDs, the larger the weight γ on $\lambda_{wear\ out}$ is, the higher the migration cost will be. In this situation, no matter where the VM IO requests are issued, the total writes to the SSD could not be reduced. When the source is SSD and the destination is HDD as shown in Figure 6 (b), the migration cost for DBT is way higher than that for IO Mirroring due to the long migration time (ranging from 11 to 21). Furthermore, since the source disk is SSD, running a VM on source (Emulated_S) will gain higher IO performance (lower λ_{IO}) than on the destination (Emulated_D), which leads to lower migration cost if the user cares more about the IO performance ($\gamma \to 0$). In contrast, if one prefers to extend the SSD lifetime ($\gamma \to 1$), Emulated_D will offer lower migration cost since $\lambda_{wear\ out}$ is 0 when all the IO requests are issued to the destination (HDD). In the case where a VM is migrated from HDD to SSD as shown in Figure 6 (c), although Emulated_D yields higher IO performance, Emulated_S will provide lower migration cost if longer SSD lifetime is preferred. Despite the value of γ, current storage migration schemes always yield higher migration cost than simply copying the running VM (Emulated_S or Emulated_D). Thus, we believe the migration cost can be reduced by adaptively balancing the three factors: $\lambda_{wear\ out}$, $\lambda_{migration\ time}$ and λ_{IO}.

5. VM Live Storage Migration Schemes under Heterogeneous Environments

5.1. Low Redundancy Live Storage Migration Mechanism (LR)

Since a VM will eventually run on the destination disk, we propose to issue all the write requests to the destination during the entire storage migration process, as shown in Figure 7. By doing so, the updated data will appear on the destination disk during the copy process and the read requests should be aware of which storage has the latest value. To implement this design, we leverage the bitmap from DBT and partition the disk image into 2 regions: copied region, whose data has already been copied to destination and to-be-copied region, whose data is going to be copied in the future. All the writes will be issued to the destination directly while the writes to the to-be-copied region also need to be recorded in the bitmap ("set" in the Figure 7). The reads to the copied area will fetch data from the destination while reads to the to-be-copied area need to check the bitmap first. If the data block is recorded in the bitmap, reads will be issued to the destination. However, if not recorded in the bitmap, data blocks will be read from the source. On the other hand, the copy process could skip the data blocks that are recorded in the bitmap. There is one caveat: requests to the data blocks, which are now being copied by copy process, will be deferred and put into a queue. They will be handled the same way as the requests to the copied area after the data blocks are released by the copy process.

The advantages of this design are: 1) there is zero redundant writes because it eliminates the merge process in DBT and duplicated writes in IO Mirroring; 2) copy process does not need to copy the entire disk image because the data blocks that have been written to the destination by VM write requests can be skipped; 3) the resource competition on disk is mitigated due to smaller volume of writes, which leads to higher IO performance and faster copy process. The benefits of this design become more evident when the destination disk (SSD) is faster than the source (HDD): when the storage migration begins, all the write requests are issued to faster disk (destination), which results in higher IO performance. In addition, the competition between copy process and VM IO requests is handled by SSD rather than HDD, which further improves the IO performance and migration time.

Note that implementing LR scheme introduces additional overhead (e.g. intercepting all IO requests, skipping data blocks in copy process, data recovery upon failure). With our implementation, the total cost of filtering IO requests and setting/checking the bitmap is less than 2us. In terms of the data recovery, our scheme forks a new process to compress and log the updates to the system hard drives (disk for OS). Upon a failure, the source disk image is recovered using the logged data. Since the logging process is parallel to the migration process and system hard drive is normally separated from data hard drives, the performance impact on our storage migration scheme is negligible.

5.2. Alternative Designs

LR scheme essentially runs the VM on the destination at the beginning of storage migration. If the destination has a slower hard drive (HDD) than the source (SSD), all the disk IO burden will be laid on the slow hard drives. Therefore, in this section, we propose two alternative designs to further exploit the IO performance from faster disk.

5.2.1. Source-based, Low Redundancy Storage Migration Mechanism (SLR)

In the situation where the destination disk is slower than the source, issuing the VM IO requests to the source can achieve better IO performance. Thus, based on LR design, we further propose source-based, low redundancy storage migration mechanism (SLR), as shown in Figure 8. We flip over the LR design by issuing as many requests as possible to the source disk. Similar to the LR design, all the IO requests are intercepted and the VM disk image is divided into 2 regions: copied and to-be-copied. The IO requests that are issued to the to-be-copied region will be issued to the source storage (faster disk). For those write requests that are issued to the copied area, SLR issues them to the destination and records them in the bitmap since doing so keeps the destination image up-to-date without invoking the merge process. All the reads falling in the copied area should first check the bitmap to find out whether the requested data has already been updated by writes or not. If so, the latest data is on the destination. Otherwise, the data will be fetched from the faster source disk (SSD). By doing so, most of the IO requests are now issued to the faster source disk.

Compared with traditional storage migration schemes, SLR has the edge on low redundant writes. Similar to LR, there is no merge process or duplicated write requests. Note that in SLR, most IO requests are issued to the source disk, which will yield better IO performance than LR. In addition, the copy process does not need to be interrupted every time to check the bitmap, which results in better migration time.

The implementation overhead of SLR is less than that of LR due to the simpler copy process. Also, the recovery process is both simpler and easier since we only need to log the write requests issued to the destination, which is significantly less than the LR. However, SLR has its limitation: not all the IO requests are issued to the (fast) source disk. Write requests and fraction of read requests to the copied region are issued to the (slow) destination. Thus, in the scenario that the workload keeps updating the data blocks in the copied area, the IO performance of SLR will become similar to running the VM on the slow disk.

5.2.2. Asynchronous IO Mirroring Storage Migration Mechanism (AIO)

In this section, we propose Asynchronous IO Mirroring (shown in Figure 9) as an alterative version of IO Mirroring design, to fully leverage the faster disk (SSD) and achieve higher IO performance.

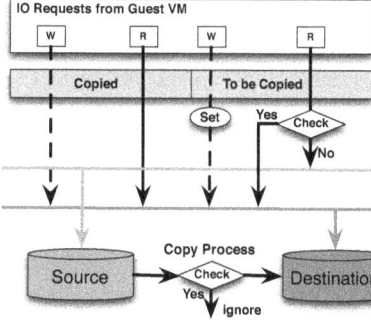

Figure 7. Low redundancy storage migration (LR)

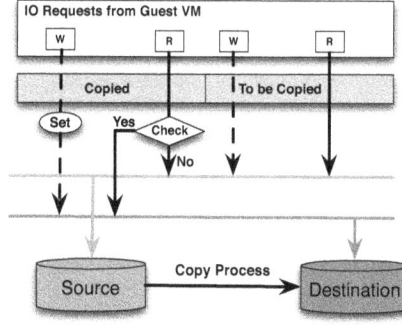

Figure 8. Source-based, low redundancy storage migration (SLR)

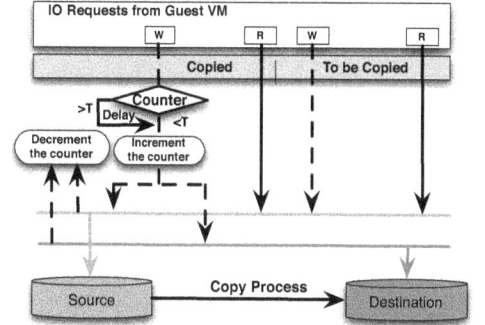

Figure 9. Asynchronous IO mirroring storage migration (AIO)

In the original IO Mirroring mechanism, the write requests are duplicated in the copied region and issued to both the source and the destination. Due to the synchronization requirement, the slower storage determines IO performance. With our AIO design, IO request is marked as completion and returned to the VM as soon as one of the duplicated IO operations is accomplished. A counter is used to track the number of unfinished IO operations. The counter will be incremented upon writes and decremented when both requests are completed. The requests to the faster disk will first check the counter to see how many requests are still pending. If the counter is larger than a threshold (T), the write request will be delayed by sleeping for a certain period. The pending write requests can be completed during that period so that the counter becomes smaller than the threshold (T). In real execution, delay will not occur frequently because the pending write requests can be completed during the CPU computation, memory access and disk reads. In the worst case (workload continuously perform writes), delay will keep occurring, which makes the overall performance as low as running on the slower disk.

The advantages of AIO are: 1) all the IO requests will be issued and handled by the faster disk (SSD) under regular IO access patterns, which yields high IO performance; and 2) Data recovery is not needed since the source disk always has up-to-date data upon failure.

Compared to LR and SLR, AIO duplicates IO requests and generates the same amount of redundant writes to the storage devices as IO Mirroring does. The disk resource competition between the copy process and IO requests becomes more intensive, which may lead to longer migration time.

5.3. An Analysis of Migration Cost of the Proposed Design and Further Extension to Massive Storage Migration

The migration cost (MC) is always expected to be as low as possible. But, which scheme should be used highly depends on the weight γ in equation (4). LR design with lowest redundant writes on device will benefit the lifetime of SSDs, which will result in lower migration cost (MC) for a user who cares more about the lifetime ($\gamma \rightarrow 1$). SLR design takes advantage of the higher IO performance of the source disk while still maintaining the low IO pressure on the device. Those who care about both the IO

performance and lifetime of SSDs will tend to use SLR when migrating from SSDs to HDDs. AIO, which maximally exploits high IO performance from the faster disk, is preferred when high IO performance has top priority ($\gamma \rightarrow 0$).

During the entire life cycle of data center, the weight γ could vary dramatically. When the user demands high IO performance for his/her VM, γ will be close to 0 to guarantee low IO penalty. On the other hand, when SSD is worn out after a period, the lifetime would be the most desired, which will cause $\gamma \rightarrow 1$. Once γ is set, a certain migration method (LR, SLR or AIO) could be chosen based on the MC in equation (4).

Upon storage upgrade or disaster recovery, massive storage migration will be triggered to move all VMs on the storage. The total migration cost for massive storage migration on heterogeneous storage can be further reduced by adaptively mixing our proposed three designs according to different weights (γ). For example, if the SSD's lifetime has top priority ($\gamma \rightarrow 1$), VMs that are migrated to or from the SSD will be migrated via LR, which has the least amount of writes to the SSD. Besides, by mixing our three designs in different ways, the overall IO penalty and migration time can be optimized accordingly.

6. Prototype and Experimental Setup

We implemented DBT, IO Mirroring, and prototyped our proposed designs in *blktap2* backend driver of Xen 4.1.2 [15], which intercepts every disk IO request coming from the VM. In order to track IO requests, we implemented a bitmap filter layer in *blktap2* driver module (/xen/tools/blktap2/drivers). The data sector is dirty if the corresponding bit is set to one. We also implemented the image copy function in *blktap2* control module (/xen/tools/blktap2/control), which can be executed in a separate process alongside with the *blktap2* driver module. Data structures, such as bitmap and copy address offset, are shared between both processes. We also integrated our command line interface into *tap-ctl* Linux command so that we can trigger the storage migration using generic Linux commands. The codes for the existing and the proposed schemes are integrated into *blktap* module, which will be enabled once the migration command is issued. When all the data is copied to the destination, we pause the disk driver and modify the file descriptor (*fd*) so that all the upcoming IO requests will be directed to the new disk image. We log the execution statistics for each scheme under the /var/log directory. We have also implemented additional design specific functions: 1) IO duplication is implemented by *memcpy*-ing the entire IO requests including address offset, size and data content. 2) Long writes are implemented by injecting constant delay into write requests. Besides, the delay is set to be 1ms and threshold is set to be 100 in our experiments. 3) IO requests to the destination disk are handled by a new IO ring structure so that the requests to the source and the destination do not compete for software resources (e.g. queue).

We evaluated the downtime, migration time, IO performance, and the migration cost by using disk or file system benchmarks: Iometer [16], Dbench [17], IOzone [18] and Linux kernel 2.6.32 compilation. Our workloads run in a VM with 1 vCPU and 2GB RAM. We also vary the input parameters of our benchmarks (e.g. outstanding IO (OIO) for Iometer, process number (proc) for Dbench, input size for IOzone) to simulate different I/O size and access patterns. Besides, kernel compilation, which is known as a comprehensive benchmark on CPU, memory and IO, is also used in our evaluation. Our virtual machines ran on self-customized servers with hardware specifications shown in Table 4. Two SSD disk arrays and Two HDD disk arrays are used as data drives while the local storage uses HDD to host Xen+OS and log files. Data Drives are connected to the server via 6Gb/s Data Link interface. Similar platform configurations were used in [10] from VMware. Our experimental VM has a 10GB system disk running Debian Squeeze 6.0 and a separate data disk (size ranging from 2GB to 30GB). To avoid the interference of OS behavior, our migration schemes and benchmarks are performed on the data disk. In order to ensure the significance of the results, we execute the workloads for at least five times. Then, we take the average of the five results and show it in this paper. Besides, we have tested our prototypes many times to guarantee its robustness.

Table 4. Hardware Specs for Our Experiment Platform

CPU	3.4GHz Intel core i7
Motherboard	ASUS Maximus V Extreme
Physical Memroy	8 GB
Hard Drives	Seagate 7200 rpm hard drives
	Avearge Data Rate:125MB/s
Solid State Drives	Intel 520 Series MLC Internal SSD
	4KB Random Reads 50,000 IOPS
	4KB Random Writes 60,000 IOPS
Disk Interconnect	6Gb/s Data Link

7. Evaluation Results and Analysis

7.1. Downtime

Table 5 shows the downtime when we migrate the VM with kernel compilation benchmark running inside. As can be seen, the downtime for DBT is worse when the destination is an HDD (rather than an SSD) because the final copy of dirty data block has to be written to the HDD. Besides, when workloads have intensive

IO requests and large IO working set, the merge process of DBT cannot even converge when the destination is a HDD. IO Mirroring and our proposed designs yield stable downtime. The reason is these designs do not have a merge process and the destination has the up-to-date data when the entire image is copied.

Table 5. The downtime of live storage migration

	DBT	IO Mirroring	LR-Design	SLR-Design	AIO-Design
SSD to SSD	232ms	198ms	197ms	120ms	124ms
HDD to SSD	266ms	249ms	197ms	140ms	200ms
SSD to HDD	4000ms	298ms	200ms	150ms	201ms
HDD to HDD	900ms	199ms	246ms	179ms	260ms

7.2. Impact on SSD Lifetime

Assume the model of write requests during the storage migration as: $\alpha\%$ of write requests are in the copied area while $(1-\alpha\%)$ of write requests are in the to-be-copied area. $\beta\%$ is the percentage of writes that are performed on different block addresses (a.k.a the write working set size of workloads). Table 6 summarizes the percentage of write requests that are issued to the SSD under different scenarios:

Table 6. Percentage of writes requests that are issued to SSD

	DBT	IO Mirroring	LR-Design	SLR-Design	AIO-Design
SSD to SSD	$1+\beta\%$	$1+\alpha\%$	$\alpha\%$	1	$1+\alpha\%$
HDD to SSD	$\beta\%$	$\alpha\%$	$\alpha\%$	$\alpha\%$	$\alpha\%$
SSD to HDD	1	1	0	$1-\alpha\%$	1
HDD to HDD	0	0	0	0	0

Note that $(1-\alpha\%)$ of the writes are skipped by the copy process for LR design. To be fair and to keep the amount of data writes in the copy process the same across all five schemes, those $(1-\alpha\%)$ writes are counted into the copy process for LR, which means only $\alpha\%$ of writes is issued to the destination. As shown in Table 6, LR has the lowest amount of data writes to the SSD. SLR also has smaller amount of data writes than DBT and IO Mirroring while AIO has the same amount of data writes as IO Mirroring. Thus, using LR design can mitigate the wear-out issue for SSDs.

To verify this, we run IOzone with different input parameters when migrating 30GB VM image on an SSD involved storage environment. In the case of migrating a VM disk image from an SSD to an HDD as shown in Figure 10 (a), LR has zero writes to the SSD because all writes are issued to the destination. When migrating from an HDD to an SSD as shown in Figure 10 (b), DBT will have more data writes to the SSD than the other four designs because $\beta\%$ is larger than $\alpha\%$ for this benchmark. When both source and destination are SSDs as shown in Figure 10 (c), LR produces the smallest amount of data writes while DBT yields the largest amount of data writes.

In general, DBT is the worst design while LR is the best in term of redundant data writes to SSDs. Since redundant data writes will affect the remaining lifetime of SSDs, LR can be awarded as SSD-preserved VM live storage migration design.

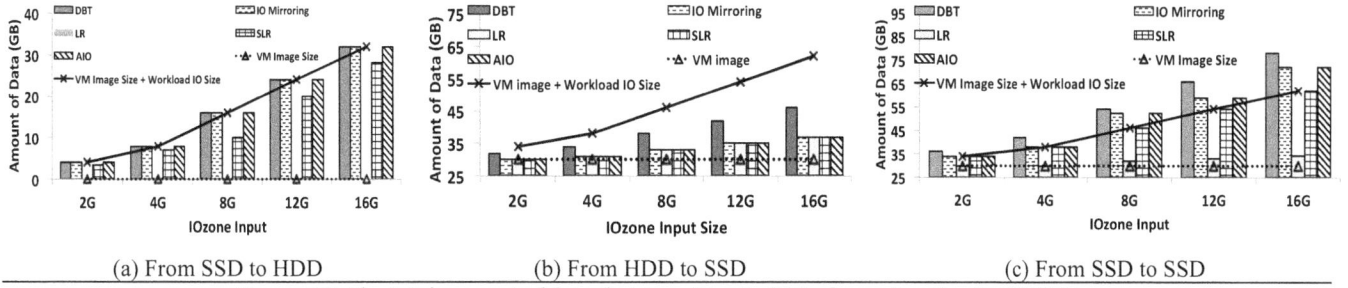

(a) From SSD to HDD   (b) From HDD to SSD   (c) From SSD to SSD

Figure 10. The total amount of data that is written to SSD when migrating 30 GB VM image

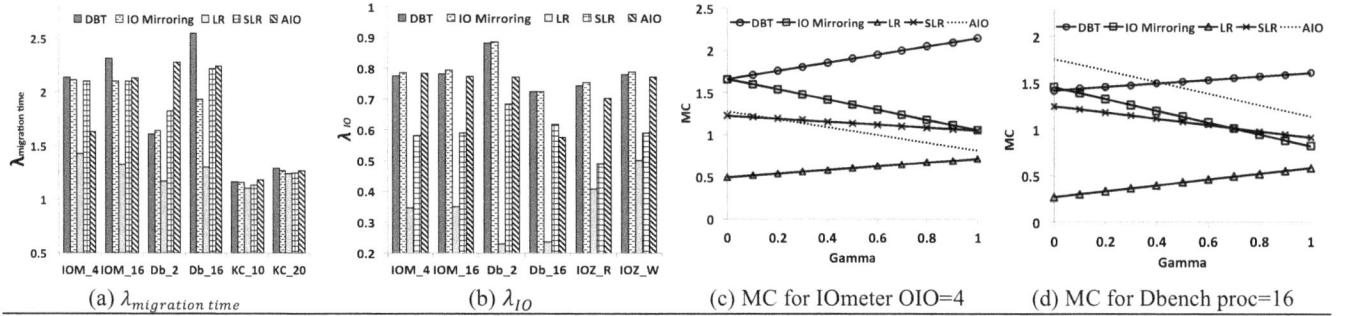

(a) $\lambda_{migration\ time}$ (b) λ_{IO} (c) MC for IOmeter OIO=4   (d) MC for Dbench proc=16

Figure 11. The case that VM is migrated from HDD to SSD

7.3. IO Penalty, Migration Time and Migration Cost

In this section, we compare DBT, IO Mirroring, LR, SLR and AIO in terms of migration time ($\lambda_{migration\ time}$), IO penalty ($\lambda_{IO}$) and Migration Cost (MC). The benchmarks with different input parameters are shown in Table 7.

Table 7. Benchmark list

Name	Benchmarks	Notes
IOM_4	IOmeter with OIO=4	IOmeter is configured as 75% reads and 25% writes
IOM_16	IOmeter with OIO=16	running in VM with 20GB disk image
Db_2	Dbench with proc=2	Dbench is configured to push the limits
Db_16	Dbench with proc =16	of throughput (-R 99999) running in VM with 20GB
IOZ_R	IOzone read file test	IOzone is used to test the IO Performance
IOZ_W	IOzone write file test	during the migration
KC_10	Kernel Compilation in 10GB image	Kernel Compilation is used to test our schemes
KC_20	Kernel Compilation in 20GB image	in comprehensive, real workloads

7.3.1. Migrating VMs from HDDs to SSDs

As shown in Figures 11 (a) and (b), LR exhibits advantages for both migration time (56% shorter than traditional design) and IO performance (at least 35% less IO penalty compared with traditional design). Issuing IO requests to the destination will not only benefits the IO performance but also decreases the migration time by skipping updated data blocks and mitigating IO contention. Although SLR and AIO are not designed specifically for this case, they both have better migration time and IO performance than the traditional design. By further considering the amount of redundant data writes ($\lambda_{wear\ out}$), we show the migration cost for two benchmarks in Figures 11 (c) and (d). As can be seen, LR has the lowest migration cost no matter what the weight γ is. Although LR does not exhibit advantages in terms of SSD data writes in this situation, it leverages the fast access speed from SSDs to the

greatest extent possible, which not only mitigates the IO penalty but also decreases the migration time.

By further digging into results shown in Figures 11(c) and (d), we observe that as the weight gets close to 1, the migration cost for DBT and LR are increased because $\lambda_{wear\ out}$ is larger than λ_{IO} for these two designs. On the other hand, the migration cost for IO Mirroring, SLR and AIO are reduced when γ ->1. That is because those three designs have smaller λ_{IO} than $\lambda_{wear\ out}$. In this situation, the benefits of having high IO performance and shorter migration time overwhelm the effect of $\lambda_{wear\ out}$ when using LR. Thus, LR always yields the least migration cost when a VM is migrated from an HDD to an SSD.

7.3.2. Migrating VMs from SSDs to HDDs

By analyzing Figures 12 (a) and (b), we found that in this situation, SLR has the shortest migration time on average while AIO has the least IO penalty. Since SLR uses the source (SSD) to handle IO requests and generates less redundant writes, the copy process can consume more disk bandwidth, which results in shorter migration time. On the other hand, AIO takes advantage of faster disk all the time, which would lead to lower IO penalty. Note that DBT is excluded from the comparison due to its frequent failure (merge process takes extremely long time). As discussed in section 7.2, LR has zero writes to the SSD in this situation, which means it has an edge in preserving SSD's lifetime.

Figures 12 (c) and (d) show migration cost as weight increases from 0 to 1. The area where γ is larger than 50% is defined as Lifetime Preference Zone, which includes users who consider SSD wear-out issue as top priority; the area where γ is less than 50% is defined as IO Performance Preference Zone, which includes those who prefer to have high IO performance. As can be seen in Figures

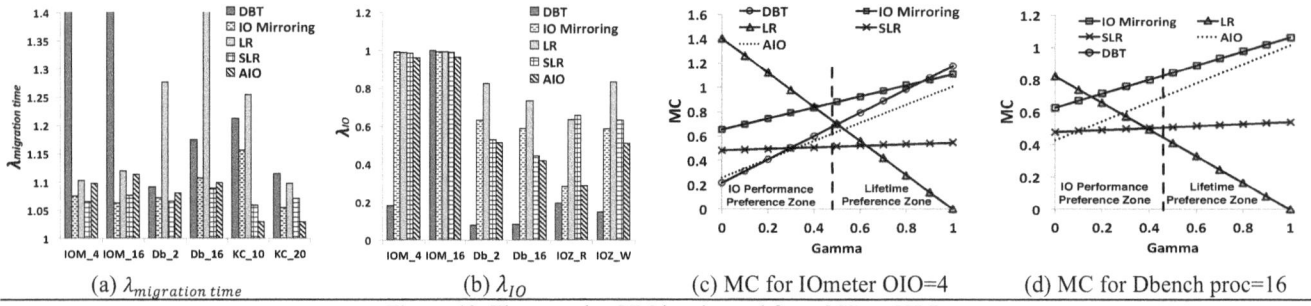

(a) $\lambda_{migration\ time}$ (b) λ_{IO} (c) MC for IOmeter OIO=4 (d) MC for Dbench proc=16

Figure 12. The case that VM is migrated from SSD to HDD

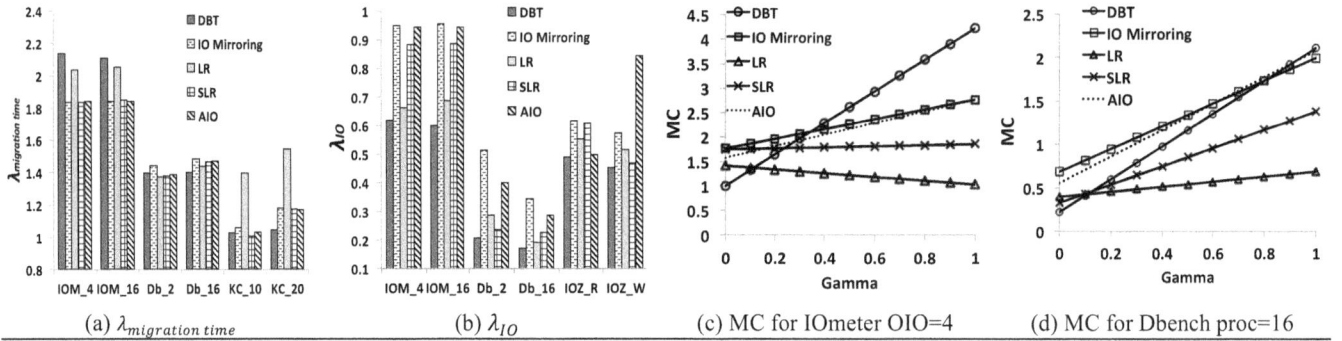

(a) $\lambda_{migration\ time}$ (b) λ_{IO} (c) MC for IOmeter OIO=4 (d) MC for Dbench proc=16

Figure 13. The case that VM is migrated from SSD to SSD

12 (c) and (d), LR has relatively low migration cost in Lifetime Preference Zone due to zero writes to SSDs. Besides, the more the γ is close to 1, the less the migration cost will be for LR. In IO Performance Preference Zone, AIO is more desired as γ becomes smaller. As SLR maintains the balance between migration time, IO penalty and the amount of SSD data writes, it has the lowest migration cost when γ is around 0.5.

Further investigating in the trend of migration cost, we found that the slope for LR is negative, which means that the migration cost for LR keeps decreasing as the weight moves towards 1. However, the migration cost will increase for the other four designs as γ increases. Thus, when migrating from SSDs to HDDs, the weight determines which design has the lowest migration cost. If IO performance is preferred, AIO is the most suitable decision; if SSD wear-out issue is the main concern, LR is the best policy; if the IO performance and SSD lifetime are equally important, SLR will yield the lowest migration cost.

7.3.3. Migrating VMs from SSDs to SSDs

When a VM is migrated from SSDs to SSDs, issuing requests to source or destination does not affect the migration time and IO performance significantly. In terms of migration time as shown in Figure 13 (a), on average, SLR and AIO take slightly shorter time. LR has slightly longer migration time because of the overhead to check bitmap in the copy process. In terms of IO penalty, DBT has the least IO penalty; LR ranks second as shown in Figure 13(b). However, DBT generates the largest amount of data writes to the SSD while LR has the least amount of data writes to the SSD as discussed in Section 7.2. When considering migration cost, which

is shown in Figures 13 (c) and (d), LR yields the least cost except when the weight (γ) is 0. Besides, the migration cost for DBT will increase faster than others as the weight increases because it has the largest slope rate. SLR, although yielding slightly more migration cost when γ =0, has a relatively low migration cost than DBT when γ lies between 0.1 and 1. In total, we believe that SLR will be the best choice when IO performance is desired. For the majority of cases (0.2<γ<1), LR is the best migration policy, which shows the lowest migration cost.

7.3.4. Migrating VMs from HDDs to HDDs

In the situation that no SSD is involved, the wear-out factor $\lambda_{wear\ out}$ will not affect migration cost at all. As shown in Figure 14 (a), LR takes the shortest time to migrate a VM while DBT takes the longest time and occasionally even fails to complete the migration. Besides, the downtime for DBT is longer than others as discussed in Section 7.1, which makes us exclude DBT from comparison. In terms of IO penalty, which is shown in Figure 14 (b), SLR is the best; AIO ranks second. There is a tradeoff between migration time and IO performance in this situation: lower IO penalty (λ_{IO}) can only be achieved by sacrificing the migration time $\lambda_{Migration\ time}$. Taking both factors into consideration, Figure 14(c) shows the migration cost (MC) for all the five designs. On average, SLR has the lowest migration cost; LR ranks the second.

7.4. Towards Lower Migration Cost in Massive Storage Migration by Mixing Different Designs

As mentioned before, each individual design has its own strength. In this section, we show an example to demonstrate how to further reduce the overall migration cost in massive storage migration by

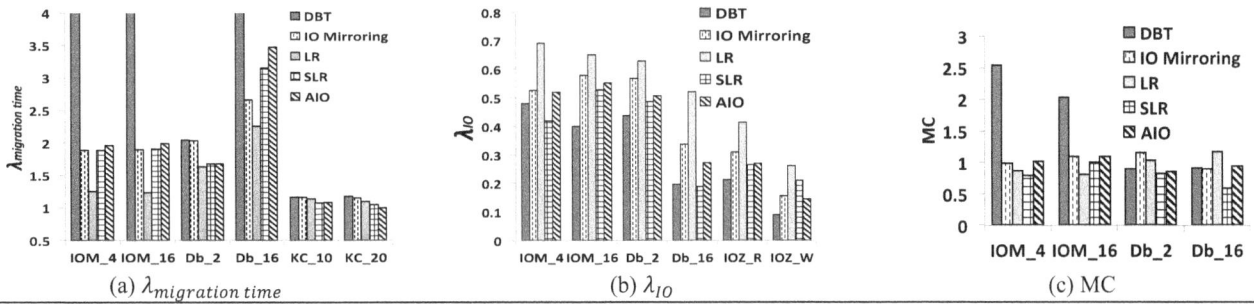

(a) $\lambda_{migration\ time}$ (b) λ_{IO} (c) MC

Figure 14. The case that VM is migrated from HDD to HDD

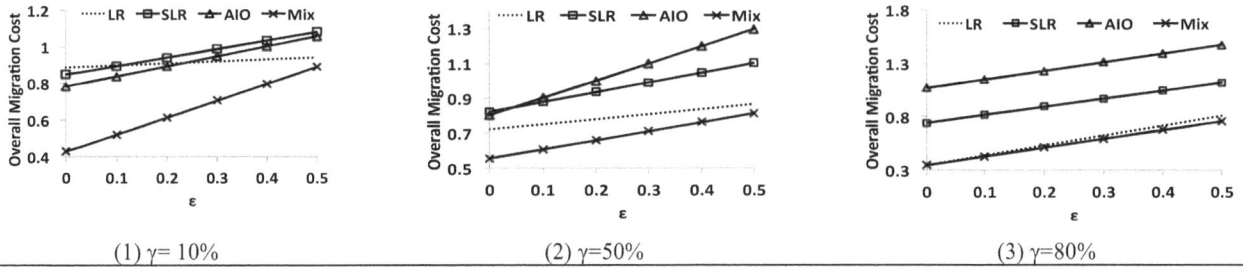

(1) $\gamma = 10\%$ (2) $\gamma = 50\%$ (3) $\gamma = 80\%$

Figure 15. Overall MC of the massive storage migration on heterogeneous storage environment

mixing all three designs. Consider that we want to move all the VMs from one storage pool to another for the purpose of storage maintenance. Assume the percentage of VMs that will be migrated from SSDs to SSDs is the same as the percentage of VMs that will be migrated from HDDs to HDDs (ε). And the number of VMs that are migrated from SSDs to HDDs is the same as the number of VMs that are migrated from HDDs to SSDs, which will be $(1-\varepsilon-\varepsilon)/2 = 0.5 - \varepsilon$. The migration cost of the massive storage migration will be the sum of cost for each individual storage migration. To simplify the discussion, we consider weight γ as 10%, 50% and 80%.

Figures 15 (1), (2) and (3) show the migration cost for the massive storage migration when we deploy each single storage migration design (LR, SLR and AIO) and mix them together (Mix). As can be seen, under different weights γ and percentage of migrating between heterogeneous storage media ($0.5 - \varepsilon$), mixing all the three designs (Mix) can always achieve lower migration cost. This is because Mix always chooses the migration scheme with the lowest migration cost for each single storage migration behavior. For instance, when the SSD lifetime is top priority ($\gamma > 50\%$), most of the VMs will be migrated using LR, which makes the migration cost of Mix close to that of LR (1% lower than LR but 69% lower than AIO). In the case that the IO performance is desired and most of the migration occurs on the same storage media ($\varepsilon \to 0$), Mix will be relatively close to AIO but still has the lowest migration cost (48% lower than AIO).

8. Related Work

To eliminate the merge process in DBT and achieve stable and low downtime and migration time across benchmarks, [10] proposed

IO Mirroring storage migration mechanism, which aims to maintain data consistency between the new and old images during migration by duplicating IO requests in the copied region. Our proposed techniques differ from IO Mirroring in that they fully exploit the performance characteristics of SSDs while taking SSD lifetime into consideration. [11, 14] implemented live VM migration in wide area network (WAN) equipped with persistent storage. The block-level disk pre-copy mechanism is employed to transfer the VM disk image. The write IO requests are throttled to reduce the dirty block rate and IP tunneling is used to make the network switching transparent to guest OS. [12] proposed to couple VM memory copy with disk copy to hide the downtime of VM live migration into that of storage migration and [13] takes workload behavior into consideration when performing storage migration. Our proposed techniques are orthogonal to these schemes and can be combined together to further improve the efficiency of virtual machine storage migration in light of heterogeneous storage media. [23] leverages the copy-on-write features in virtual storage and puts the read-only templates of VM disk images on SSDs. However, the storage migration behavior and the wear-out issue are not considered in their work. [24] focuses on file system level implementation of hybrid SSD storage systems, which intends to improve the IO performance via faster SSDs. However, their work does not consider the migration, wear-out issue, and virtual disk image. [25] implements a virtualized flash storage layer for Fusion-io device, which will yield shorter IO response. However, both wear-out issue and migration behavior are not considered.

9. Conclusion

As SSDs emerge as an indispensable media for cloud storage, their strength and weakness should be taken into account in storage management, such as VM storage migration. Nevertheless, existing mainstream storage migration schemes (e.g. DBT and IO Mirroring) do not fully exploit the features of SSDs. Even worse, they wear out SSD devices severely. In this paper, we propose a new metric, migration cost, which characterizes the cost for storage migration mechanisms from multiple aspects: migration time, IO penalty, SSD lifetime and preference (on IO performance and SSD lifetime). We propose three new storage migration mechanisms to achieve lower migration cost. Each of the proposed schemes has its own strength: 1) LR has the lowest possible redundant writes; 2) SLR leverages IO performance of the source disk while still maintaining the attribute of low redundancy and 3) AIO aims at achieving the highest possible IO performance. Our prototype-based evaluation shows that all three designs yield stable downtime (around 200ms) and lower migration cost than traditional mechanisms (DBT and IO Mirroring). By mixing them in massive storage migration, the overall migration cost can be further reduced by 48% at most compared with the best of each individual mechanism.

Acknowledgments

This work is supported in part by NSF grants 1117261, 0937869, 0916384, 0845721(CAREER), 0834288, 0811611, 0720476, by SRC grants 2008-HJ-1798, 2007-RJ-1651G, by Microsoft Research Trustworthy Computing, Safe and Scalable Multi-core Computing Awards, by NASA/Florida Space Grant Consortium FSREGP Award 16296041-Y4, and by three IBM Faculty Awards. Fang Liu is supported by the National High-Tech Research and Development Program of China (No. 2013AA013201), the National Natural Science Foundation of China (NO.61170288, NO.61025009, NO.61232003).

References

[1] "Amazon EC2", http://aws.amazon.com/ec2/
[2] "Microsoft Azure", http://www.windowsazure.com/en-us/
[3] "Flash Drives Replace Disks at Amazon, Facebook, Dropbox", http://www.wired.com/wiredenterprise/2012/06/flash-data-centers/
[4] "Morphlabs, Dell DCS Team on SSD-Powered Cloud", http://www.datacenterknowledge.com/archives/2012/03/28/morphlabs-dell-dcs-team-on-ssd-powered-cloud/
[5] "SolidFire Develops All-SSD System for Cloud Storage Providers", http://searchstoragechannel.techtarget.com/news/2240037093/SolidFire-develops-all-SSD-system-for-cloud-storage-providers
[6] "Intel Takes Their SSD Reliability to the Datacenter", http://www.zdnet.com/blog/datacenter/intel-takes-their-ssd-reliability-to-the-datacenter/1316
[7] Gokul Soundararajan, Vijayan Prabhakaran, et al., Extending SSD Lifetimes with Disk-Based Write Caches, FAST 2010
[8] EMC, http://www.us.emc.com/index.htm
[9] Winchester Systems, http://www.winsys.com
[10] Ali Mashtizadeh, et al., The Design and Evolution of Live Storage Migration in VMware ESX, ATC 2011
[11] Robert Bradford, Evangelos Kotsovinos, Anja Feldmann, Harald Schioberg, Live Wide-Area Migration of Virtual Machines Including Local Persistent State, VEE 2007
[12] Yingwei Luo, Binbin Zhang, et al., Live and Incremental Whole-System Migration of Virtual Machines Using Block-Bitmap, ICCC 2008
[13] Jie Zheng, T. S. Eugene Ng, Kunwadee Sripanidkulchai, Workload-Aware Live Storage Migration for Clouds, VEE 2011
[14] Takahiro Hirofuchi, et al., A Live Storage Migration Mechanism over WAN for Relocatable Virtual Machine Services on Clouds, CCGRID 2009
[15] XEN Project http://www.xen.org, January 2009
[16] Iometer Project, http://www.iometer.org
[17] Dbench, http://dbench.samba.org
[18] IOzone File System Benchmark, http://www.iozone.org
[19] Aameek Singh, Madhukar Korupolu, et al., Server-Storage Virtualization: Integration and Load Balancing in Data Centers, SC 2008
[20] Seonyeong Park, A Comprehensive Study of Energy Efficiency and Performance of Flash-based SSD, Journal of Systems Architecture, 2011
[21] Guanying Wu and Xubin He, ΔFTL: Improving SSD Lifetime via Exploiting Content Locality, EuroSys 2012
[22] Youngjae Kim, et al., HybridStore: A Cost-Efficient, High-Performance Storage System Combining SSDs and HDDs, MASCOTS 2011
[23] Heeseung Jo, Youngjin Kwon, Hwanju Kim, Euiseong Seo, Joonwon Lee, and Seungryoul Maeng, SSD-HDD-Hybrid Virtual Disk in Consolidated Environments, VHPC 2009
[24] Feng Chen, David Koufaty, Xiaodong Zhang, Hystor: Making the Best Use of Solid State Drives in High Performance Storage Systems, ICS 2011
[25] William K. Josephson, et al., DFS: A File System for Virtualized Flash Storage, ACM Transactions on Storage, Sept 2010
[26] Bob Laliberte, Delivering Greater Effectiveness and Efficiency for SANs in Virtualized Data Centers. White Paper, EMC
[27] "Intel Launches DC S3700 SSD for Data Centers", http://hothardware.com/News/Intel-Launches-New-Datacenter-SSDs-Emphasizes-Data-Protection-High-Performance/

Parallelizing Live Migration of Virtual Machines

Xiang Song †‡   Jicheng Shi†‡   Ran Liu †‡   Jian Yang†‡   Haibo Chen†

†Institute of Parallel and Distributed Systems, Shanghai Jiao Tong University   ‡Software School, Fudan University

classicxsong@gmail.com   rogershijicheng@gmail.com   naruilone@gmail.com   sheepx86@gmail.com
haibochen@sjtu.edu.cn

Abstract

Live VM migration is one of the major primitive operations to manage virtualized cloud platforms. Such operation is usually mission-critical and disruptive to the running services, and thus should be completed as fast as possible. Unfortunately, with the increasing amount of resources configured to a VM, such operations are becoming increasingly time-consuming. In this paper, we make a comprehensive analysis on the parallelization opportunities of live VM migration on two popular open-source VMMs (i.e., Xen and KVM). By leveraging abundant resources like CPU cores and NICs in contemporary server platforms, we design and implement a system called PMigrate that leverages data parallelism and pipeline parallelism to parallelize the operation. As the parallelization framework requires intensive mmap/munmap operations that tax the address space management system in an operating system, we further propose an abstraction called *range lock*, which improves scalability of concurrent mutation to the address space of an operating system (i.e., Linux) by selectively replacing the per-process address space lock inside kernel with dynamic and fine-grained *range locks* that exclude costly operations on the requesting address range from using the per-process lock. Evaluation with our working prototype on Xen and KVM shows that PMigrate accelerates the live VM migration ranging from 2.49X to 9.88X, and decreases the downtime ranging from 1.9X to 279.89X. Performance analysis shows that our integration of *range lock* to Linux significantly improves parallelism in mutating the address space in VM migration and thus boosts the performance ranging from 2.06X to 3.05X. We also show that PMigrate makes only small disruption to other co-hosted production VMs.

Categories and Subject Descriptors   D.4.7 [*Operating Systems*]: Organization and Design; D.4.8 [*Operating Systems*]: Performance

General Terms   Design, Performance

Keywords   Parallelized VM Migration, Parallelized VM Save/Restore, Range Lock

1. Introduction

Live VM migraion [13, 22] has been key enabling techniques in maintaining virtualized data-centers, including load balancing,

fault tolerance [20], and power management [21]. In many cases, such operation should be completed in a timely manner to avoid disruption and performance degradation of running services.

Usually, if the total downtime of live VM migration exceeds a certain number (usually several minutes in Giga-Ethernet), the clients will notice the unavailability of the service and the running service may be disrupted. Worse even, if a scheduled VM migration cannot be completed in time when proactively tolerating hardware/software faults, a possible server outage in the source machine might crash the VM and even a distributed service in a virtual cluster as a whole. Further, during live VM migration, the running service usually experiences a notably lower performance due to the overhead of tracking and processing the resources of the target VM.

On the other hand, the amount of resources allocated to a VM has been steadily increasing along with Moore's law. For example, the large and high-memory quadruple Extra Large VM instances in Amazon EC2 [4] are configured with 7.5 GByte and 68.4 GByte memory accordingly. It is also no surprise to see virtual machines with multiple dozens of Giga-bytes memory in some resource-intensive applications such as virtualized database servers (e.g., Oracle and Microsoft SQL Server). However, due to the necessity of touching a huge amount of resources, the execution time of live VM migration usually increases along with the amount of resources in a VM. For example, the total migration time and downtime for a modest-size Xen VM [9] with 16 GByte memory running a memcached server have increased to 1,586s and 251s accordingly (section 6). Such long migration time and downtime are apparently not satisfiable as the running service will be severely disrupted. Meanwhile, during the process of migration, the total throughput of the VM is only 74.5% of normal execution in our evaluation. Worse even, the migration may also degrade the performance of other co-located VMs.

In this paper, we conduct a comprehensive study on the parallelization opportunities of the live VM migration. Our analysis uncovers both data and pipeline parallelism underlying basic primitives of it, which motivates the design and implementation of PMigrate a system that aims at parallelizing live VM migation. PMigrate is inspired by that fact that the increasing amount of resources configured to a machine also opens opportunities to leverage such resources for parallelization. Actually, it is currently no surprise a server machine with several dozens of CPU cores, several hundreds of Giga-bytes memory and a dozen of NIC ports, which are not always being fully utilized.

The result of parallelization further uncovers a significant performance bottleneck to the parallelized live VM migration: concurrent mutation to an address space. This is because the migration operation requires frequent mapping/unmapping of memory pages owned by a guest VM to the address space of the management tool. However, our survey indicates that most commodity operating systems (e.g., Linux, Solaris and BSD) usually use a per-process lock to serialize mutation to an address space. To allow concurrent mutation to an address space, we further propose an abstraction called *range lock*, a dynamic fine-grained lock abstraction that allows fine-grained protection of some costly operations, instead of a complete serialization of mutation to the address space. By integrating *range lock* with existing address space management code in Linux, the parallelism with concurrent address space mutation for PMigrate is significantly increased.

We have extended Xen 4.1.2 to support the parallelization of live VM migration, which add 1,860 lines of code to Xen tools and domain0[1] kernel. We also integrate the support of *range lock* to Linux to improve the scalability of concurrent mutation to address spaces. To further demonstrate the applicability of parallelizing VM management operations, we implement live VM migration based on kvm-qemu 0.14.0, with the support of migrating both memory and disk data. The implementation adds 2,270 lines of code to the kvm-qemu tools.

To measure the effectiveness of the parallelized live VM migration operation and the performance benefits of devoting more resources, we have conducted several evaluations using several widely-used applications. Performance results show that parallelized migration operation significantly outperforms the vanilla one. It accelerates live VM migration ranging from 2.49X up to 9.88X, with the downtime decreased ranging from 1.9X to 279.89X. We further show that the performance impact of parallelized live VM migration on the target VM is also very small compared to the vanilla live migration: the average throughput is reduced by 12.5% (with the maximum be 16%). We also show that our integration of *range lock* to Linux significantly improves parallelism in mutating the address space in virtual memory management operations, which boosts the performance ranging from 2.06X to 3.05X. The performance impact on the co-located VMs is also quite small with the control of resources dedicated to VM operations. We further show that PMigrate can be integrated with other optimization by evaluating it with live VM migration using compression. Our evaluation results show that PMigrate improves the performance by 3.98X compared to the vallina one with compression.

In summary, the contributions of this paper are:

- A case for parallelizing live VM migration.

- The *range lock* abstraction and its integration in Linux that increases the parallelism of concurrent mutation to an address space.

- The design, implementation and evaluation of PMigrate on Xen and KVM that confirm the effectiveness of parallelization and *range lock*.

The rest of the paper is organized as follows. The next section provides an overview of live VM migration and the underlying parallelism, which motivates our design on parallelizing them in section 3. Section 4 illustrates the concurrent address space mutation problem and describes the *range lock* abstraction as well as how it is integrated to Linux. Section 5 describes our implementation on Xen and KVM. The experimental results are shown in Section 6. We relate our work with previous work in Section 7 and conclude our work in Section 8.

2. An Overview of VM Migration

In this section, we briefly illustrate live VM migration based on Xen [9, 13] and KVM [16], and present a quantitative analysis on the primitive operations and the source of parallelism accordingly. Though there are several variants in live VM migration, we mainly

describe the *Pre-copy* approach [24], which is the default strategy for most hypervisors such as Xen, KVM and VMWare. Parallelizing other migration strategies like *Post-copy* (which is rarely used due to its unreliability) is quite similar, which we omit here for brevity.

2.1 Basic Steps in Live VM Migration

For live VM migration, CPU states, memory, persistent storage and other device states are required to be migrated to the destination node on the fly. The *migrate_send* function in Figure 1 shows the send-side algorithm of the pre-copy live migration: the source node iteratively transfers the memory and disk data to the destination node while keeping the source VM alive through multiple iterations, which is called the pre-copy step. At the very beginning, the initial memory and disk data are considered to be dirty and will be transferred as a whole. In the following iterations, the hypervisor will track the newly dirtied data generated by VM execution and add the dirtied pages to a page pool, which will be sent out in the following iteration. The iteration stops only when 1) the dirty data left is small enough or 2) its size cannot be further reduced by introducing more iterations or 3) too many resources are wasted on the pre-copy iterations (e.g., the total memory sent exceeds a threshold). After that, the migration enters into a *stop-and-copy* phase that transfers the remaining memory and disk data as well as CPU and device states.

In each iteration, the memory and disk data are processed on the source node and the destination node. For memory data, a *dirty bitmap* is usually maintained to keep track of dirty pages. The dirty memory pages are divided into multiple batches and are processed in turn. When processing each batch of memory pages, the migration tool first maps the guest VM memory pages into its own address space, and then handles specifically on unused pages and page table pages. Finally, these memory pages will be grouped together and sent to the destination. In the destination node (the *migrate_receive* function in Figure 1), the memory pages are first received and copied to the address space mapped from the target VM. The disk data is handled similarly and a dirty bitmap is maintained to keep track of dirty data.

Typically, the downtime of migration is directly affected by the rate of sending VM's data and the dirty rate of memory and disk data. If the migration rate is close or even less than the page dirty rate, the migration will be either very hard to converge (indicating a long migration time) or result in a huge amount of data to be transferred in the stop-and-copy phase (indicating a lengthy downtime).

2.2 An Analysis of Parallelism

Table 1 provides an overview of the associated parallelism, the estimated cost for the most important basic operations in a live VM migration operation and where they locate in Figure 1. There are mainly two types of parallelism: data parallelism and pipeline parallelism.

Data Parallelism: During migration, as there is no dependency among different portions of memory and disk data in the same iteration, several steps in migration have very good data parallelism, including resetting disk data into readonly, mapping guest VM memory pages into the address space of the management tool, processing unused pages and page table pages, transferring memory and disk data and restoring memory data. There are several cases where data parallelism is not appropriate. For example, getting the dirty bitmap and resetting memory into readonly are mainly done through invoking hypercalls [2]. As the time spent on these operations is not significant, it is not worthwhile parallelizing them.

---

[1] Domain0 is the management VM in Xen.

[2] Hypercalls are calls from a guest VM to the hypervisor.

Primitives	Parallelism		Send	Receive	Cost
	Data	Pipeline			
Get memory dirty bitmap	no	no	line 6	N/A	small
Reset memory readonly	no	no	line 7	N/A	small
Get disk dirty bitmap	no	no	line 6	N/A	small
Reset disk readonly	yes	yes	line 15	N/A	small
Check dirty bitmap	no	yes	line 8	N/A	small
Map guest VM memory	yes	yes	line 11	line 4	heavy
Handle Unused/PT Page	yes	yes	line 12	line 5	modest
Transfer memory data	yes	yes	line 16	line 2	heavy
Restore memory data	yes	yes	N/A	line 6	modest
Load/Save disk data	no	yes	line 14	line 8	heavy
Transfer disk data	yes	yes	line 16	line 2	heavy
Migrate CPU/Device States	no	no	line 17	line 10	small

Table 1. A summary of parallelism in different steps of live VM migration.

```
1 migrate_send(...)
2    while (!iteration_end)
3       if (judge_iteration_end())
4          pause_VM();
5          iteration_end = 1;
6       get_dirty_bitmap();   //memory and disk
7       reset_memory_readonly();
8       check_dirty_bitmap();
9       for (num_of_batches) //memory and disk
10         if (memory_data)
11            map_guest_vm_memory();
12            handle_unused_page();
              handle_pagetable_page();
13         if (disk_data)
14            load_disk_data();
15            reset_disk_block_readonly();
16         transfer_data();
17      transfer_cpudev_state();
```

```
1 migrate_receive(...)
2    while (receive_data())
3       if (memory_data)
4          map_guest_vm_memory();
5          handle_unusedpg_ptpage();
6          restore_memory_data();
7       if (disk_data)
8          restore_disk_data();
9       if (cpudev_state())
10         restore_cpudev_state();
11   resume_vm();
```

Figure 1. An overview of basic steps in live VM migration.

	Send	Receive
Total migration time	1592.0s	
Downtime	257.0s	
Get/Reset memory dirty bitmap	0.59s	N/A
Map guest VM memory	381.0s	571.1s
Handle Unused/PT Page (send)	44.8s	N/A
Transfer memory data	1,200.5s	979.1s
Handle/restore memory data (receive)	N/A	31.7s
Migrate CPU/Device States	8.84ms	
# of iterations	10	
total memory sent	58.6 GByte	
Last iteration memory size	9.3 GByte	
Avg. Network Cost	37.7 MByte/s	
Avg. CPU usage	95.4%	

Table 2. Costs of primitives in live migrating a modest-sized VM.

Pipeline Parallelism: For some steps, if data parallelism is not appropriate, we can also leverage pipeline parallelism. For example, though it is not easy to apply data-parallelism to *check dirty bitmap*, we can partition it into a number of stages and feed the intermediate results to the next stage. Similarly, loading disk data can hardly be parallelized using data parallelism as the read from disk is constrained by the I/O system call. However, we can parallelize it with disk data transfer in a pipeline manner.

To give a sense on how to partition each operation into different threads and stages, we have conducted a quantitative evaluation to measure the cost in major primitive operations. The evaluation is done by migrating a modest-sized VM with 16 GByte memory, 4 virtual CPUs and 16 GByte disk. During migration, we run a memcached server on the guest VM with modest workload. Table 2 shows the primitive metrics of live VM migration. The migration takes about 1592s with a downtime of 257s. It takes about 10 iterations and then it is forced to be migrated. 58.8 GByte memory data was sent in total. In the example, about 29.9% of total time is spent on mapping memory of the guest VM, while the rest of time are spent mainly on data transferring through an SSH connection. The single thread migration process can only reach a network

throughput of 37.7 MByte/s with an average CPU utilization of more than 95%. The high CPU utilization is due to the high cost in mapping the guest VM memory, which includes acquiring a virtual address area for holding the guest memory, getting grants of accessing the guest pages and building up the page table through hypercalls as well as cleaning up the page table after processing the memory. It also includes high CPU consumption in encrypting and checksumming the data before transferring it. Thus, the key to parallelize live VM migration is to spawn multiple threads to leverage multiple cores to handle such tasks.

3. Parallelizing Live VM Migration

Based on our study on the sources of parallelism inside the live VM migration operation, this section describes how PMigrate leverages multiple cores and NICs to parallelize it.

3.1 Parallelizing Live VM Migration

Parallelizing live VM migration includes applying data parallelism and pipeline parallelism to most primitive operations shown in table 1. Figure 2 shows an overview of how live VM migration is parallelized. The stages inside the square are data parallelized and the connecting squares are pipeline parallized with each other. The squiggly lines shows how the data is moved. The migration data is divided and assigned to a number of tasks (the blue boxes mean the memory tasks and the pink boxes means the disk tasks) and the tasks are processed in parallel.

Source Node: The migration process spawns a memory task producer to process memory data, as well as a disk task producer to

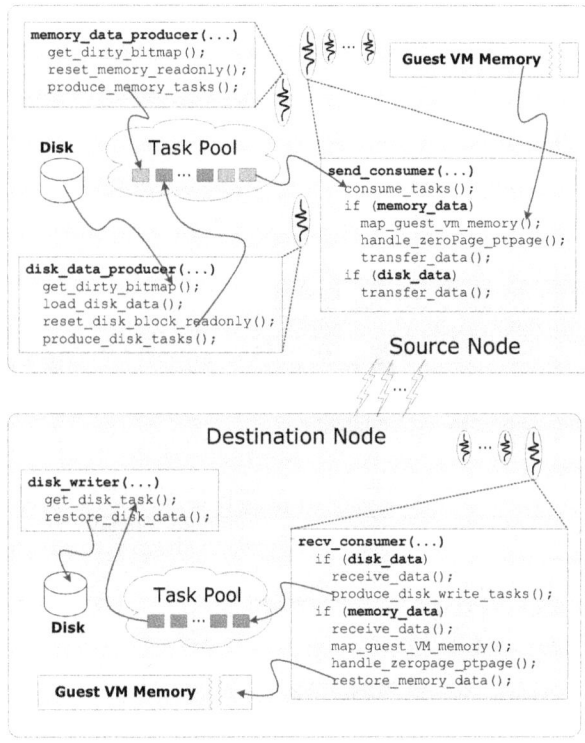

```
memory_data_producer(...)
  get_dirty_bitmap();
  reset_memory_readonly();
  produce_memory_tasks();
```

Guest VM Memory

Disk   **Task Pool**

```
send_consumer(...)
  consume_tasks();
  if (memory_data)
    map_guest_vm_memory();
    handle_zeroPage_ptpage();
    transfer_data();
  if (disk_data)
    transfer_data();
```

```
disk_data_producer(...)
  get_dirty_bitmap();
  load_disk_data();
  reset_disk_block_readonly();
  produce_disk_tasks();
```

Source Node

Destination Node

```
disk_writer(...)
  get_disk_task();
  restore_disk_data();
```

```
recv_consumer(...)
  if (disk_data)
    receive_data();
    produce_disk_write_tasks();
  if (memory_data)
    receive_data();
    map_guest_VM_memory();
    handle_zeropage_ptpage();
    restore_memory_data();
```

Disk   **Task Pool**

Guest VM Memory

Figure 2. An overview of Parallel VM Migration.

process disk data. Depending on the amount of available CPU cores and NICs, several consumer threads are spawned to handle the tasks using data parallelism for the most time-consuming primitive operations. Handling a memory task includes mapping guest VM memory into the address space of the migration tool, handling unused pages and page table pages and sending out memory data. By contrast, handling a disk task just needs to simply send out the disk data.

We currently do not parallelize the disk producer thread as the parallelization may not gain enough benefit unless there are multiple virtual disks, as the disk I/O itself is serialized. Fortunately, we still can pipeline it with disk data sending.

Further, checking the *dirty bitmap* is done by the producers due to performance concerns. Other than the first iteration, memory and disk data to be sent in each iteration may not be contiguous, as a lot of pages and blocks may not be dirtied during the previous iteration. If the producers do not check the *dirty bitmap* before creating tasks, a lot of tasks will be created unnecessarily, resulting in sending a large amount of redundant data. As the cost of checking *dirty bitmap* is quite small, we place it in the producer threads and pipeline it with the consumer threads that send the memory and disk data.

There are also several primitive operations that are not appropriate for data or pipeline parallelism:

- *Get Dirty Bitmap:* Generating a separate *dirty bitmap* for each task is rather time consuming, as a task producer will usually generate thousands of tasks in live VM migration. It is more appropriate to do this at the beginning of each iteration.

- *Reset Memory to Readonly:* Resetting the access right of dirty pages into readonly for each memory batch will cause not only performance problem but also correctness problem. This is because repeatedly invoking the corresponding hypercall for each memory batch is not only very time consuming, but also

may disturb the statistics in the *dirty bitmap*. This is because the access right for a memory page might have been changed before resetting its access right.

- *Handle CPU/Device States:* Loading and sending CPU and device states are done by a single thread as the basic cost is negligible. Parallelizing it may introduce cost instead of benefit.

Destination Node: The migration process spawns several consumer threads, each of which is responsible to handle the data batches sent from a corresponding consumer thread in the source node. Most of the work is done using data parallelism. Handling each memory data batch includes mapping guest VM memory pages; handling unused pages and page table pages; and restoring the data. By contrast, handling disk data only includes receiving disk data.

However, restoring data into disk image is not parallelized as it will ultimately be serialized by the disk itself. In this case, an additional disk thread is spawned to pipeline disk data restoring with disk data receiving. Finally, receiving and restoring CPU and device states and resuming the VM are done by the migration process itself.

3.2 Resource Usage Control

As the live VM migration tool needs to consume multiple resources that may also be needed by the production VMs, we try to control the amount of resources used by the tool to minimize disruption to other VMs, while use the spare resoures as much as possible.

Network Rate Control in Live Migration: In both the source node and the destination node, a network monitor daemon is spawned to collect the network usage of each NIC from the kernel. The destination daemon will periodically (1 second by default) negotiate with the source daemon to adjust the network bandwidth used by migration. In principle, the migration process will only consume the spare network bandwidth. The network bandwidth of each map consumer is adjusted by the daemon according to the network statistics of the corresponding NIC. To ensure a successful migration with certain requirement on migration time and downtime, a specific amount of bandwidth will be reserved by the migration process.

CPU Rate Control: There are lots of VMM scheduling strategies [12] to ensure the fairness and performance of VMs. The CPU usage of the migration process can be directly controlled by the VMM scheduler. By downgrading the execution priority of the migration process, we can limit its CPU consumption against the device backend daemons on a privileged VM. By upgrading its priority, we can devote more CPU resources into VM management tool. By default, its priority is set below the average.

Limiting Memory Consumption: As the time spent on different primitive operations varies and depends on the underlying execution environments (including software and hardware), there may be load imbalance between the producer and the consumer. Thus, the memory used to cache the data may become very large. To mitigate this problem, we maintain a memory pool for each pipeline stage. The memory buffers used to cache the "intermediate data" are directly allocated from this pool. The memory pool only contains a specific amount of memory (e.g., 128 MByte). If it is empty, the following allocation requests will be blocked. Thus, the total memory consumption can be limited.

4. Scaling Mutation to Kernel Address Space

After applying data and pipeline parallelism to the live VM migration, there is a serious kernel serialization: the frequent mmap/munmap operations from multiple threads require concurrent mutation to the address space of the management tool. This is unfortunately completely serialized by most existing OS kernel. For example, Linux and Solaris use a single read/write lock and FreeBSD uses a single write lock, which serializes the address space mutation. Windows prior Windows 7 similarly use a system-wide PFN lock. Though Windows 7 does not publish its implementation details, our evaluation with a concurrent mmap microbenchmark on a 4-core machine shows that it may have a similar scalability issue[3].

This section first illustrates and analyzes the problem and then describes the *range lock* abstraction to mitigate it.

4.1 Serialized Address Space Mutation

The live VM migration operation needs to frequent memory mapping operations that map the guest VM memory into the address space of the VM management tool and unmap the memory after reading or writing the corresponding data. Figure 3 shows the main body of the VM migration algorithms. When being parallelized, each thread will : 1) first use the *mmap* syscall to allocate a new virtual memory area (VMA) (line 5) ; 2) then use an *ioctl* syscall to map the guest VM memory into the address space of the management tool (line 7-9); and 3) finally *munmap* the area when the data has been processed (line 13).

Unfortunately, Linux, like other similar operating systems, protects the per-process address space using a single lock (called *mmap_sem* in Linux). All the three steps are treated as mutation to the address space by Linux, which should be mutually exclusive by acquiring the *mmap_sem* in write mode for all related operations. Worse even, mutating the process address space such as mapping the guest VM pages in *ioctl* and cleaning the mapping of the guest pages in *munmap* is pretty time-consuming, as it requires further calls to the hypervisor. Specifically, when mapping the guest VM pages using *ioctl*, the privileged VM has to build up the page table through hypercalls for each guest page. As the guest page does not belong to the privileged VM, such map operations (namely, the foreign page map) are rather costly. This significantly enlarges the critical section in the live VM migration operation.

To give a sense of how severe will the contention be, we profiled the execution time of the live VM migration operation and found that more than 8.91%, 22.94% and 16.08% of total execution time are spent within the *mmap_sem*. With a number of concurrent threads, the time spent on the critical section will be accumulated, which significantly degrade the performance.

One intuitive solution is to increase the memory chunk size processed in each thread, which may reduce the frequency of issuing the address space mutation operations. However, this will increase the size of the critical section for these operations, which, however, may even further exacerbate the contention on the critical section. Another approach to mitigating the contention would be using multiple processes instead of threads to parallelize the VM operations. Unfortunately, the relative complex task dispatching and synchronization make such an approach less appealing.

Read Protection of Guest VM Mapping: After a close inspection on the routine of mapping guest VM pages in the VM management tool, we find that holding the *mmap_sem* semaphore in write mode is too costly and largely unnecessary, as it only protects a private Xen-specific field in the VMA, which stores the grant mapping information. [4] Figure 4 shows how the guest VM memory is mapped. First, the *mmap_sem* is hold in write mode (line 3). Then the virtual memory area containing the requesting

```
1  map_consumer(...)
2    ...
3    while (task = get_task()) {
4      ...
5      addr = mmap(NULL, batch*PAGE_SIZE,
                      prot, MAP_SHARED, fd, 0);
6      ioctlx.num = batch;
7      ioctlx.addr = addr;
8      ioctl(fd,
           IOCTL_PRIVCMD_MMAPBATCH_V2, &ioctlx);
9      ...
10     memory_process()
11     ...
12     munmap(addr, batch*PAGE_SIZE);
```

Figure 3. The main body of a parallel live VM migration operation.

```
1  privcmd_ioctl_mmap_batch(...)
2    ...
3    down_write(&mm->mmap_sem);
4    vma = find_vma(mm, m.addr);
5    ...
6    ret = traverse_pages(m.num,
              sizeof(xen_pfn_t), &pagelist,
              mmap_batch_fn, &state);
7    up_write(&mm->mmap_sem);
8    ...
```

Figure 4. The main body of mapping the guest VM memory.

address is searched (line 4). After that, the required batch of guest VM memory is mapped by constructing the page table through the *mmap_batch_fn* call for each page (line 6). Finally, *mmap_sem* is released (line 7). As mapping guest VM memory (line 4 and 6) does not modify other virtual memory areas, the *mmap_sem* can be hold in read mode with a fine-grained lock to protect the field.

4.2 Range Lock

After changing the protection of mapping guest VM pages from write mode to read mode, there is still serious contention as the mutation to an address space is serialized. Actually, this is not a specific problem to PMigrate, but a general problem to most operating systems that use a per-process lock to serialize concurrent mutation to an address space. Though Clements et al. [14] have demonstrated the effectiveness in parallelizing the process of read accesses to address space (i.e., page faults) with write accesses (e.g., mmap) using a RCU balanced tree, the mutation to the address space like mmap/munmap still requires acquiring the *mmap_sem* in write mode. Hence, there is still only one mmap/munmap operation can proceed at a time.

To address this problem, an intuitive approach would be decomposing the per-process semaphore into a number of fine-grained locks that protect only the requesting ranges of an address space. However, the requesting range of a mmap/munmap system call is usually dynamic and unpredictable. Further, the requesting ranges from different requests may overlap. Hence, it is impossible to use a set of predefined fixed-size locks, which are also pretty costly in terms of space and execution time. To this end, we propose a dynamic lock-service to the address space, which is called *range lock*.

Range lock leverages a skip list [25] that dynamically maintains the address ranges that are currently locked. To acquire a range lock to a specific range, the *range_lock* function searches the skip list using the requesting address range ([start, start+len]). If there is already an existing/overlapping range in the skip list, another thread should be mutating the specific range and the requesting thread should wait and retry. Otherwise, a range will be added to the skip list, indicating that the range lock is granted. To release a range lock, the *range_unlock* function uses the requesting address to search the skip list and deletes the corresponding range in the list.

---

[3] In the microbenchmark, each thread mmaps a 4 MByte memory, touches the memory (thus causing page faults) and unmaps the memory. Our evaluation results in a 4-core machine with Windows 7 (x64_sp1) show that the execution time using 4 cores increases from 765ms in 1 core to 2,684ms in 4 core.

[4] Grant map is a mechanism used by Xen to share memory between VMs.

```
mmap(brk is similar):                    mremap:
  Down_write(mmap_sem)                     Down_write(mmap_sem)
    1. Obtain the address to map           Lock_range(addr, len)
  Lock_range(addr, len)                      1. Do remap
    2. Update VMAs/add new VMA             Unlock_range(addr, len)
  Unlock_range(addr, len)                  Up_write(mmap_sem)
  Up_write(mmap_sem)

munmap:                                   guest_map:
  Down_write(mmap_sem)                     Down_read(mmap_sem)
    1. Adjust first and last VMA             1. Find VMA
  Lock_range(addr, len)                    Lock_range(addr, len)
    2. Detach VMAs                         Up_read(mmap_sem)
  Up_write(mmap_sem)                         1. Buildup page table for
    3. Cleanup page table                       guest VM page
    4. Free pages                          2. Map guest page through
    5. TLB shoot down                           hypercalls
  Unlock_range(addr, len)                  Unlock_range(addr, len)
```

Figure 5. How range lock is integrated to Linux using hierarchical locking.

The reason why we use a skip list is because both *range_lock* and *range_unlock* requires intensive searching for existing/overlapping ranges and other data structures storing ranges such as *interval tree* and *segment tree* are a little bit too heavyweight for our purpose.

Ideally, it would be better to use a concurrent skip list to minimize the critical section. However, as typical concurrent skip list only supports either lookup or concurrent changes to one element in one operation, while *range lock* requires first looking up the range and then updates two elements (i.e., start, start + len) in the skip list. It would require non-trivial complexity and/or overhead to make the skip list concurrent. Hence, the skip list is currently protected by a spinlock. As the critical section of the range lock routines are very short, this spinlock does not become a new bottleneck in our evaluation.

Ideally, the entire address space can be protected in a fine-grained manner using *range lock*, where all accesses to different portions of the address space can be completely parallelized. In practice, there are a number of memory states that should be maintained consistently for an OS kernel. Further, current Linux kernel still uses a red/black tree like data structure to maintain both virtual memory areas and memory states, completely replacing it into a new data structure will be very resource-intensive due to a number of other correlated data structures such as *reverse map* and *mmap_cache* [14]. As a result, PMigrate currently only uses *range lock* to parallelize the time-consuming parts inside the mmap/munmap/foreign map calls by removing them from the critical sections protected by the *mmap_mem* and protecting them by the *Range Locks*, while still leaving the original data structure intact. This makes the related changes to Linux relatively small, yet still brings notable performance improvement. For example, the current *range lock* implementation comprises of 290 SLOCs and the related change to Linux is only with 120 SLOCs. The implementation is stable enough that it passed Linux Test Project [6].

Specifically, as shown in Figure 5, we still acquire the *mmap_sem* in *mmap* but additionally also acquires the corresponding *range lock*, as most operations in *mmap* just update the red/black tree for an address space, which is not time consuming. For *munmap*, we keep the *mmap_sem* in write mode for the portions of updating red/black tree. However, for the rest code in *munmap* such as clearing page table entries and free pages, freeing unused page table pages and shooting down local and remote TLBs, we release the *mmap_sem* but still keep the corresponding range lock. Similarly, in *guest_map*, we use both *mmap_sem* in read mode and the range lock to protect the VMA lookup (line 4 in Figure 4) but only use the range lock to protect the rest of execution. As the mutation and lookup of VMA tree usually only consists of a small portion of execution time, applying the range lock significantly increases the parallelism and boosts the performance of mutation-intensive workloads, as shown in section 6.

5. Implementation

To demonstrate the applicability of our parallelized scheme, we have implemented PMigrate based on Xen, a popular open-source VMM that has been used in many cloud platforms such as Amazon EC2, OpenNebula and OpenStack. To demonstrate the wide applicability of PMigrate, we further port PMigrate to KVM, a hosted-mode VMM that is also widely deployed in many cloud platforms.

Implementation on Xen: The current Xen VMM only supports live migration of memory and CPU states. We have parallelized live VM migration, namely PMigrate-Xen. The current PMigrate system is built by extending the vanilla Xen tools (version 4.1.2) by parallelizing most operations as shown in section 3 with the address space optimization mentioned in section 4. The overall implementation adds/changes 1,860 SLOCs to Xen tools and the privileged VM (i.e., Domain0) kernel.

Implementation on KVM: KVM supports live VM migration with both memory and persistent storage. The migration request is handled by the I/O thread which is also responsible to handle the I/O operations related to the guest VM. In vanilla KVM, the I/O thread uses an event-driven mode to handle both the migration process and guest I/O requests with time-slicing. In each migration time slice, namely one iteration, the I/O thread only processes a small chunk of data according to the rate limit. Then it will switch to handle the I/O requests from the guest VM and wait for the next migration time slice. Such iteration strategy spends too much time on generating *dirty bitmap* of memory and disk images and resetting the access right of dirty pages into readonly. It also results in notable performance disruption on the I/O intensive guest VMs as we will show in Section 6.2.2. Thus, we change the KVM's iteration strategy into image-oriented as the PMigrate-Xen, which sends the entire VM image in the first iteration and sends the dirtied data in the following iterations. Further, to keep the migration alive, in PMigrate-KVM, we let the I/O thread spawn a new migration thread to handle the migration task. Otherwise, I/O thread will be monopolized by the migration task as handling one image iteration is very time-consuming.

In the source node, the migration thread spawns a memory task producer and a disk task producer to prepare the memory and disk data. Several sender threads are spawned to handle the memory and disk tasks. One problem in preparing disk data is that the vanilla-KVM uses asynchronous I/O (AIO) operations to issue read request to disk data and let the I/O thread to handle the AIO completion notification. The I/O thread handles the notification when it is monitoring the guest VM I/O or when it is processing the disk data in migration. However, in PMigrate-KVM, the disk producer will process the disk data in migration and it executes with the I/O thread in parallel, resulting in a race condition in AIO processing. To handle this problem, we change the AIO operations into synchronized I/O operations. Using synchronized I/O will not block the migration process, as the disk task producer executes in parallel with the consumer threads.

In the destination node, the migration thread spawns several receiver threads to handle the memory data and receive the disk data. It also spawns a disk writer thread to restore disk data into the disk image.

The overall implementation takes about 2,270 SLOCs, which includes 830 SLOCs to change its iteration strategy into image-oriented.

6. Evaluation

This section evaluates the effectiveness of parallelizing live VM migration operation.

	Vanilla	PMigrate
Migration Time (sec)	422.8(3.6)	112.4(3.9)
Downtime (millisec)	310.0(11.5)	408.0(12.5)
# of Pre-copy Iterations	5.7(1.2)	4.3(0.6)
Total Memory Send (GByte)	16.2(0.0)	16.2 (0.0)
Downtime Send (MByte)	1.8(0.4)	1.7(0.2)
Avg. Network Cost (MByte/s)	39.3(0.3)	148.0(5.0)
Avg. CPU usage	89.6(0.5)%	364.9(14.0)%
Total CPU Cost (CPU-sec)	378.9(2.0)	409.9(1.9)

Table 3. Key metrics (with STDEV) of live migrating an idle VM on vanilla Xen and PMigrate-Xen.

	Vanilla	PMigrate
Migration Time (sec)	473.6(5.7)	115.8(10.8)
Downtime (millisec)	1,420.6(166.5)	746.6(74.2)
# of Pre-copy Iter.	29(0)	29(0)
Total Memory Send (GByte)	16.4(0.1)	16.8(0.03)
Downtime Send (MByte)	39.6(6.1)	28.4(9.0)
Avg. Network Cost (MByte/s)	35.4(0.31)	149.7(14.4)
Avg. CPU usage	82.8(2.1)%	359.7(46.5)%
Total CPU Cost (CPU-sec)	497.3	525.9
Avg. PostgreSQL Thr. (Trans/s)	497.3(3.6)	416.4(12.5)
Avg. Thr. Degrade	4.4%	20.31%

Table 4. Key metrics (with STDEV) of live migrating a PostgreSQL server VM on vanilla Xen and PMigrate-Xen.

6.1 Experimental Setup

All experiments were conducted on two Intel machines, each of which is with two 1.87 GHz Six-Core Intel Xeon E7 chips. Each core has a separate 32 KByte L1 data cache and 256 KByte L2 cache and each chip has a shared 18 MByte L3 cache. The size of physical memory is 32 GByte. Each machine is equipped with a quad-port Intel 82576 Gigabit Network Controller and a quad-port on-board Broadcom Gigabit Network Controller. We use another Intel machine as the NFS server to provide the shared global storage for guest VMs on Xen. We use an Intel machine as the client machine. It is with four 2.00 GHz Ten-Core Intel Xeon E7 chips and one quad-port Intel 82576 Gigabit NIC . All machines were connected to a subnet through a Gigabit switch. The maximum throughput of a single network connection is 117.6 MByte/s with the round trip time be 0.076ms, while the maximum throughput of an SSH connection is 48.6 MByte/s.

We evaluate the performance of PMigrate for both Xen and KVM. We use Debian GNU/Linux 6.0, Xen 4.1.2 and the management VM with Linux kernel version 3.2.6. The KVM version is kvm-qemu 0.14.0 with the host VM kernel version 3.2.6. The guest VM is launched using hardware-assisted virtualization technologies [1] with 16 GByte memory in total and a 16 GByte disk image running Debian GNU/Linux 6.0. All tests were conducted with five times and we report the average as well as the standard deviation.

6.2 Performance and Scalability of Parallelization

6.2.1 Parallelized Live VM migration in Xen

We use two widely-used applications, memcached [18] and PostgreSQL 9.1.2 [7], as well as an idle VM to evaluate the performance of memory-intensive, CPU-intensive and idle VMs for live VM migration. We spawn 8 consumer threads and set no limit on the maximum network bandwidth for each thread. The connections are with the SSH-style connection, which is the same as the vanilla Xen. The Intel NIC is used by migration, while the Broadcom NIC is used by the guest VM through an emulated network device. To minimize impact to the VM workloads, we separate the physical CPU set so that the migration process can be scheduled on a different core set from the production VMs. We let each two consumer threads share one port of the NIC.

Idle VM: Table 3 compares the basic metrics of live migrating an idle VM. It can be seen that the migration time is reduced by 3.76X, as the average data transferring throughput is increased by 3.76X. Although the average CPU utilization of PMigrate is increased by 4.07X, the total CPU cost is increased by only 8.2%.

PostgreSQL PostgreSQL [7] is a wide-used SQL server. In the evaluation, we use pgbench as the client to generate SQL requests using the workload from TPC-B [2]. The target database contains 5,000,000 accounts and the workload is generated using 32 concurrent connections through 8 threads. PostgreSQL is CPU-intensive and will generate moderate disk I/O workloads. However, the dirty rate of memory is low.

Table 4 compares the key metrics of live migrating a VM with PostgreSQL. It can be seen that the migration time is reduced by 4.09X and the total downtime is also reduced by 1.90X. The performance improvement is mainly due to the increased average migration network throughput (4.23X), as more CPU cores means more data will be available to be sent out. However, the accumulated CPU and network cost are not increased even if more resources are devoted into parallelized live migration. The performance degradation of PostgreSQL server on PMigrate-Xen is about 16% larger than that on vanilla Xen. It is mainly due to the side effect of the PMigrate threads on the NFS driver.

Memcached Memcached [18] caches multiple key/value pairs in memory. Each time the server receives a request containing a key, it will respond with the corresponding value. We use the memaslap testsuite from the libmemcached library [5] as the memcached client. The client first warms up the memcached server with multiple key/value pairs to fill the memory and then randomly issues get operations through 4 concurrent connections from 4 threads. The workload of memcached is both memory and network intensive.

Table 5 compares the key metrics of live migrating a memcached VM. It can be seen that the migration time is reduced by 9.88X. The tremendous performance improvement is due to two major reasons: 1) the average migration network throughput is increased by 3.8X; and 2) As the data processing and transferring speed is significantly increased, the execution time of each pre-copy iteration is also reduced, resulting in much less data being dirtied. As shown in the table, the total memory sent is reduced by 2.58X. Further, the total downtime is reduced by 279.89X. As the data migration speed on vanilla Xen is not faster than the memory dirty speed of the memcached server, the last migration iteration (which is offline) is mandated after several pre-copy iterations. As a result, a total of 9.2 GByte memory is transferred during the downtime. On the other side, as the data migration speed on PMigrate-Xen is much faster, the total amount of data to be sent during the downtime is greatly reduced to only 0.02 GByte after 29 pre-copy iterations. Thus, it is no surprise the total downtime on PMigrate-Xen is much shorter than that on vanilla Xen. Through PMigrate-Xen devotes more resources into parallelized live migration, the accumulated CPU and network cost is not increased, but instead reduced by 2.40X and 2.59X, respectively. The throughput of memcached on vanilla Xen is 17.4 MByte/s with a total of nonresponse time of 251.9s. While the throughput of it on PMigrate-Xen is 15.3 MByte/s with a total of non-responsive time less than 2.7s. Though the performance degradation of the server on PMigrate-Xen is about 9% larger than that on vanilla Xen, the overall negative performance impact is notably reduced as the migration time and downtime is significantly reduced.

	Vanilla	PMigrate
Migration Time (sec)	1,586.1(13.7)	160.5(2.2)
Downtime (sec)	251.9(12.1)	0.9(0.03)
Non-response Time (sec)	≈ 253.0(11.4)	<2.7(0.6)
# of Pre-copy Iterations	9.7(0.6)	29(0)
Total Memory Send (GByte)	58.6(0.03)	22.7(0.5)
Downtime Send (GByte)	9.2(0.3)	0.04(0.0)
Avg. Network thr. (MByte/s)	38.0(0.3)	145.0(4.3)
Avg. CPU usage	95.5(1.5)%	392.6(18.3)%
Total CPU Cost (CPU-sec)	1,514.1	629.9
Avg. Memcached Thr. (MByte/s)	17.4(0.9)	15.3(0.5)
Avg. Thr. Degradation	25.5%	34.6%

Table 5. Key metrics (with STDEV) of live migrating a memcached server VM on vanilla Xen and PMigrate-Xen.

	Vanilla	PMigrate
Migration Time (sec)	203.9(8.6)	57.4(6.1)
Downtime (millisec)	630.7(59.5)	15.8(1.7)
# of Pre-copy Iterations	9,735.7(314.6)	1(0)
Downtime send (MByte)	10.1(5.7)	2.1(0.4)
Total Memory Send (MByte)	396.8(7.2)	395.6(6.5)
Total Disk Send (GByte)	16(0.0)	16(0.0)
Avg. Network Thr. (MByte/s)	82.4(3.6)	294.7(32.0)

Table 6. Key metrics (with STDEV) of live migrating an idle VM on vanilla KVM and PMigrate-KVM.

6.2.2 Parallelized Live Migration of KVM

We also use an idle VM and a VM running memcached [18] to evaluate the performance of live migrating an idle and memory-intensive VM in KVM. As KVM further supports disk data migration, we further use DBench [3], a well-known file-system benchmark, to evaluate the performance of live migrating a I/O intensive VM. We spawn 4 consumer threads, and set no limit on the maximum network bandwidth for each thread. The connections are through the Intel NIC with each thread using one port, where the Broadcom NIC is used by the guest VM through an emulated network device. In both PMigrate-KVM and vanilla KVM, each zeropage is compressed into 1 byte. We do not show the CPU usage because a guest VM execute as a process in the host OS, which makes the CPU statistic inaccurate.

Idle VM: Table 6 compares the basic metrics of live migrating an idle VM. It can be seen that the migration time is reduced by 3.55X as the average data transferring throughput is increased by 3.58X. The total number of iterations are greatly reduced, as PMigrate-KVM changes the iteration strategy into image-oriented[5], which reduces the accumulated cost on preparing each iteration.

Memcached: Table 7 compares the key metrics of live migrating a memcached VM. The migration time is reduced by 2.49X and the downtime is reduced by 4.81X. The performance improvement is mainly from the increased migration network throughput due to parallelization. Further, as the vanilla KVM uses the I/O thread to process both the network requests of live migration a guest VM, the network I/O of the guest VM is significantly disrupted. The average throughput is reduced by 86.8% during migration on vanilla KVM. In contrast, the throughput is reduced by only 5.05% on PMigrate-KVM. Further, on vanilla KVM, the throughput of the

---

[5] For vanilla KVM, each pre-copy iteration only transfers a specific number memory or disk data (e.g., 2MByte), which results in a high pre-copy interation count.

	Vanilla	PMigrate
Migration Time (sec)	348.7(7.1)	140.2(6.5)
Downtime (millisec)	553.7(69.8)	115.1(65.2)
Non-response Time (sec)	≈ 163.0 (3.6)	<1.0 (0.0)
# of Pre-copy Iterations	16,776.7(3.6)	5.3(0.6)
Downtime Send (MByte)	37.8(12.9)	32.5(20.9)
Total Memory Send (GByte)	19.1(4.9)	23.5(1.5)
Total Disk Send (GByte)	16.2(0.3)	16.0(0.01)
Avg. Network Cost (MByte/s)	90.7(2.4)	289.1(13.5)
Avg. Memcached Thr. (MByte/s)	2.3(0.3)	15.9(2.1)
Avg. Thr. Degradation	86.8%	8.36%

Table 7. Key metrics (with STDEV) of live migrating a memcached VM on vanilla KVM and PMigrate-KVM.

	Vanilla	PMigrate
Migration Time (sec)	256.1(20.0)	77.1(13.6)
Downtime (millisec)	455.7(62.2)	102.9(12.1)
# of Pre-copy Iterations	12,159.0(677.2)	3.7(1.2)
Downtime Send (MByte)	33.3(5.9)	37.4(12.8)
Total Memory Send (MByte)	603.8(45.3)	690.9(164.4)
Total Disk Send (GByte)	19.8(1.0)	17.2(0.4)
Avg. Network Cost (MByte/s)	81.3(2.5)	242.1(7.0)
Avg. DBench Thr. (MByte/s)	963.9(11.8)	974.3(38.9)
Avg. Thr. Degradation	6.05%	4.72%

Table 8. Key metrics (with STDEV) of live migrating a DBench VM on vanilla KVM and PMigrate-KVM.

memcached server drops to only 0.22 MByte/s after the migration has been started for 185s and it lasts about 163.0s, which means that the server has nearly no response to the clients for a long period. As it takes nearly no workload during migration on vanilla KVM, it has less memory dirtied during memory precopy than that on PMigrate-KVM.

DBench: DBench is a file-system benchmark that will generate modest workload on the file system, which will result in data write into the disk. Table 8 compares the key metrics of live migrating a DBench VM. The migration time is reduced by 3.32X. The downtime is reduced by 4.43X. The performance improvement is mainly due to the increased migration network throughput and the reduced amount of disk data (about 2.6 GByte) being transferred as less data are dirtied within a shorter pre-copy time. PMigrate-KVM reaches a lower network throughput (compared to the Idle VM case and the memcached VM case) due to disk throttling in the source node as the migration process will contend with DBench VM on disk accesses.

6.2.3 Sources of Speedup and Scalability

Scalability and contribution of *range lock*: We spawns 1, 2, 4 and 8 consumer threads to do migration and restrict maximum network bandwidth for each thread to be 40 MByte/s as this is the maximum network throughput the vanilla Xen migration process can achieve. As PMigrate-KVM scales well on our 12-core Intel machines, we omit its scalability evaluation in this section.

Figure 6 and Figure 7 show the scalability of migrating the idle VM and the memcached VM respectively, by using PMigrate without optimization, PMigrate with the read-lock optimization and PMigrate with the range lock optimization. The range lock optimization significantly boosts the performance, as it significantly reduces the size of the critical sections of the address space management operations protected by the *mmap_sem*. Table 9 shows the average cost of each single memory management operation used in live VM migration, which confirms the performance benefit from read lock and range lock. After introducing the read lock, the time spent on mmap and munmap can be reduced. After introducing the range lock, the time spent on mmap and munmap are significantly reduced.

Performance of only Using Multiple Cores: To show whether PMigrate-Xen can work well with a single NIC port, we run PMigrate-Xen using an idle VM with 4 consumer threads sharing the same NIC port. The total migration time is 148.4s, which is quite close to that with four cores and four NIC ports (149.3s). this shows that PMigrate still performs reasonably well without an excessive number of NICs or bandwidth. Actually, the major benefit lies in using multiple cores to process and prepare the data to be sent. However, the average data transferring throughput of 112.1 MByte/s, which almost saturates the port. Here, adding additional NICs can further improve the performance if more cores are used for migration.

Performance of only using Multiple NICs: We also evaluate whether using multiple NICs along can provide reasonably good speedup. We assign four NIC ports to PMigrate-Xen and bind 4 threads to a single core. The total migration time is 377.28s, with an average throughput of 49.32 MB/s. The result indicates that using multiple NICs along can have very little performance benefit as there is not enough data prepared by CPUs to be sent through NICs.

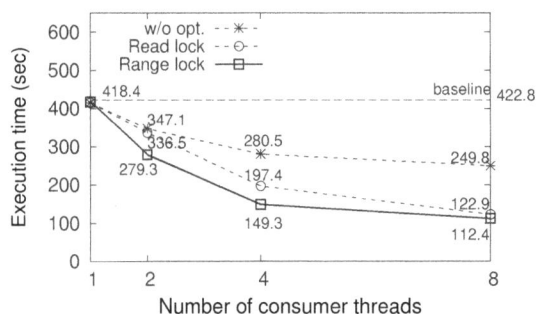

Figure 6. PMigrate Scalability of migrating idle VM on Xen using PMigrate without optimization, PMigrate with read lock and PMigrate with range lock.

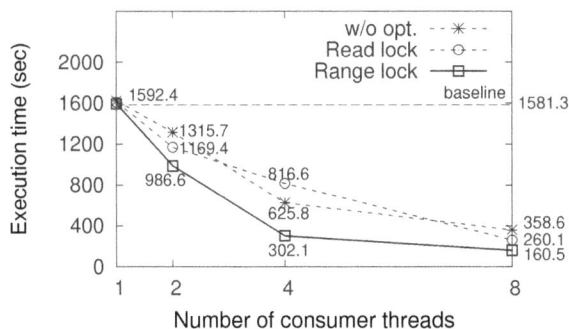

Figure 7. PMigrate Scalability of migrating memcached VM on Xen using PMigrate without optimization, PMigrate with read lock and PMigrate with range lock.

6.3 Impact on Other Co-located VMs

Ideally, if the resources of a virtual machine are abundant, the migration tool can be assigned with separated resources to the production VMs. In such cases, the performance impact of PMigrate

Time Cost	Idle			Memcached		
	no-opt	rd-lock	range	no-opt	rd-lock	range
mmap	1.39	1.80	0.05	1.10	1.26	0.18
guest map	18.1	16.3	14.8	16.8	15.5	15.2
munmap	7.27	6.22	0.75	5.57	5.30	0.85

Table 9. Average cost of a single memory management operation in live VM migration on Xen using PMigrate without optimization, PMigrate with read lock and PMigrate with range lock in microsecond.

on other VMs can be minimized. To evaluate the effectiveness of PMigrate in leveraging spare resources, we run a Xen VM with memcached serving requests from clients and measure its throughput during the parallel migration of an idle Xen VM.

Our evaluation found that during migration, the average throughput degraded from 42 MByte/s to 34.6 MByte/s. By contrast, the original Xen tools cause a performance degradation from 42 MByte/s to 38 MByte/s. This performance gap is due to the fact that we leverage multiple cores and NICs to do scheduling and these threads may inference with each other. However, the parallelized migration significantly shortens the overall migration time. This indicates that the parallelization may even help to reduce the impact on other VMs as a whole.

However, if the resources in a virtualized platform are limited, the migration tool may cause performance degradation on other co-located VMs. To evaluate the effectiveness of our resource rate control, we illustrate the effectiveness of our network rate control mechanism and our CPU rate control mechanism.

Network Rate Control To evaluate the effectiveness of network rate control mechanism of PMigrate, we run a VM with Apache web server serving requests from clients and measure its throughput during the parallel migration of an idle VM. The migration process uses two NICs, one of which is shared with the apache web server. Before the migration starts, the throughput of the web server is 101.7 MByte/s. While during the migration, its throughput only drops to 91.1 MByte/s. The average network bandwidth of the shared NIC consumed by the parallel migration process is 17.6 MByte/s, while the bandwidth of another NIC consumed by it is 57.2 MByte/s. The migration process does limit its network consumption of the busy NIC shared with other VMs.

CPU Rate Control To evaluate the effectiveness of CPU rate control of PMigrate, we run a VM with a memcached server serving requests from clients and measure its throughput during the parallel migration of an idle VM. The VM running memcached with four virtual CPUs (VCPU) scheduling on 4 physical CPUs. The throughput of the memcached server is 48.4 MByte/s before migratoin and the CPU usage is above 100%. During parallel migration, we spawns 4 consumer threads. We compare the throughput of the memcached server VM under two conditions: 1) The vanilla Xen migration process shares a physical CPU of the memcached server VM during migration (for example, CPU2); and 2) The PMigrate-Xen process shares only three physical CPUs of the memcached server VM (for example, CPU2, CPU3 and CPU4). As the result, the total migration time is reduced from 131s to 41s. While the throughput of memcached during migration drops to 48.1% from the origin on vanilla Xen and 34.9% on PMigrate-Xen. It can be seen that PMigrate-Xen does not introduce much further performance impact to VMs sharing CPU compared to vanilla Xen. However, the parallelized migration significantly shortens the overall migration time, which can help to reduce the overall impact on other VMs.

	Vanilla	PMigrate
Migration Time (sec)	114.7(0.1)	28.8(0.5)
Downtime (millisec)	45.3(0.6)	54.3(15.4)
# of Pre-copy Iterations	906.3(0.6)	1(0)
Total Memory Send (MByte)	122.8(1.2)	120.3(0.06)
Memory Compress Rate	28.0(0.0)%	28.1(0.0)%
Total Disk Send (MByte)	1692.0(2.9)	1693.8(0.6)
Disk Compress Rate	10.0(0.0)%	10.0(0.0)%
Total Compress Time (sec)	41.5(0.06)	10.8(0.06)

Table 10. Key metrics (with STDEV) of live migration with an idle VM on vanilla KVM and PMigrate-KVM with data compression.

6.4 Combining PMigrate with Compression

There have been several techniques [15, 23] on improving the performance of live VM migration, such as data compression. Here we show that techniques on improving the serial performance of live VM migration can also be applied to PMigrate by taking data compression as an example. We modify the vanilla KVM and PMigrate-KVM migration process to compress the memory data and disk data during migration using the quicklz [8] compression library. Figure 10 compares the basic metrics of live migrating an idle VM with 4 GByte memory and 16 GByte disk on vanilla KVM and PMigrate-KVM with 4 consumer threads. It can be seen that the migration time on both cases is reduced (compared to that shown in Table 6) due to the reduced amount of memory and disk data being transferred. The data compression rates on both cases are similar. The total compression time is significantly reduced on PMigrate-KVM as it takes more threads to process the data.

7. Related Work

Live VM Migration: Currently, most hypervisors have provided the support for live VM migration, such as VMWare [19, 22], Xen [13] and KVM [16]. Among these operations, VM migration has been extensively studied. Other than VM migration with only memory and within LAN, Bradford et al. [11] further extend Xen with the support of live VM migration with persistent states across wide-area network.

The increasing importance of live VM migration also stimulates interests in optimization. For example, though most VMMs uses pre-copy [26] VM migration by default for the sake of reliability, Hines et al. [15] propose a post-copy based migration methodology to reduce repetitive memory transfers under memory-intensive workloads. To save bandwidth, Svärd et al. [23] design and implement a memory delta compression technique to reduce memory copy during live VM migration. The storage VM migration solution in industry has also been evolved dramatically [19]. The SnowFlock [17] uses a set of technique to support fast application-aware VM clone, which leverages a post-copy clone policy. Using a post-copy policy may have the advantage of quickly creating a replicate VM and makes it alive. However, this suffers from lengthy post-copy migration time and a break in network collection may corrupt the target VM. Further, live VM clone usually requires specific OS support for state consistency.

However, none of the prior solutions have considered the parallelizing the process of VM migration. We believe the work of PMigrate can be integrated with most prior optimization, which may result in further performance improvements.

Scaling Operating Systems: There have been a number of studies on the scalability of commodity operating systems [10, 14]. Among them, the concurrent address space using RCU balanced tree [14] is the closest one. However, the RCU balance tree focuses on parallelizing the process of read accesses to an address space

(e.g., page faults) and mutation to the address space (e.g., mmaps), while the *Range Lock* abstraction parallelizes the mutation to an address space. We believe these two abstractions can be combined together to further improve the scalability of address space, which will be our future work. *Range lock* shares some similarity with byte-range locking in distributed file systems. However, *Range lock* targets at the address space management and is much simpler than file locking. Further, we are the first to demonstrate that *Range Lock* can be easily integrated into existing Linux kernel with very little programming effort.

8. Conclusion

The increasing amount of resources configured to both physical and virtual machines created both challenges and opportunities. This paper made an attempt to parallelize the live VM migration. Based on a comprehensive analysis on the underlying parallelism, this paper leveraged both data and pipeline parallelism to parallelize live VM migration. To mitigate intensive contention on concurrent mutation to an address space, this paper further proposed a new abstraction in operation system, called *Range Lock*, which provided more fine-grained protection to concurrent mutation of an address space. Performance evaluation with two popular open-source VMMs showed that the parallelized version significantly boosted the performance of the live VM migration, yet with small disruption to running services.

9. Acknowledgments

We thank the anonymous reviewers for their insightful comments. This work was supported by an NetApp Faculty Fellowship, China National Natural Science Foundation under grant numbered 61003002, a grant from Shanghai Science and Technology Development Funds (No. 12QA1401700), a Foundation for the Author of National Excellent Doctoral Dissertation of PR China and Fundamental Research Funds for the Central Universities in China.

References

[1] Intel virtualization technology. http://www.intel.com/technology/virtualization.

[2] TPC-B. http://www.tpc.org/tpcb/default.asp.

[3] Dbench. http://dbench.samba.org/.

[4] Instance Types of Amazon Elastic Compute Cloud (EC2). http://aws.amazon.com/ec2/#instance.

[5] LibMemcached. http://libmemcached.org/.

[6] Linux test project. http://ltp.sourceforge.net/.

[7] PostgreSQL. http://www.postgresql.org/.

[8] Quicklz. www.quicklz.com/.

[9] P. Barham, B. Dragovic, K. Fraser, S. Hand, T. Harris, A. Ho, R. Neugebauer, I. Pratt, and A. Warfield. Xen and the art of virtualization. In *Proc. SOSP*, 2003.

[10] S. Boyd-Wickizer, A. Clements, Y. Mao, A. Pesterev, M. Kaashoek, R. Morris, N. Zeldovich, et al. An analysis of linux scalability to many cores. In *Proceedings of the 9th USENIX conference on Operating systems design and implementation*, 2010.

[11] R. Bradford, E. Kotsovinos, A. Feldmann, and H. Schiöberg. Live wide-area migration of virtual machines including local persistent state. In *Proceedings of the 3rd international conference on Virtual Execution Environments*, pages 169–179, 2007.

[12] L. Cherkasova, D. Gupta, and A. Vahdat. Comparison of the three cpu schedulers in Xen. *Performance Evaluation Review*, 35(2):42, 2007.

[13] C. Clark, K. Fraser, S. Hand, J. Hansen, E. Jul, C. Limpach, I. Pratt, and A. Warfield. Live migration of virtual machines. In *Proceedings of the 2nd conference on Symposium on Networked Systems Design & Implementation*, pages 273–286, 2005.

[14] A. T. Clements, M. F. Kaashoek, and N. Zeldovich. Scalable address spaces using RCU balanced trees. In *Proceedings of the 17th international conference on Architectural Support for Programming Languages and Operating Systems*, pages 199–210, 2012.

[15] M. Hines and K. Gopalan. Post-copy based live virtual machine migration using adaptive pre-paging and dynamic self-ballooning. In *Proceedings of the ACM SIGPLAN/SIGOPS international conference on Virtual Execution Environments*, pages 51–60, 2009.

[16] A. Kivity, Y. Kamay, D. Laor, U. Lublin, and A. Liguori. KVM: the linux virtual machine monitor. In *Proceedings of the Linux Symposium*, pages 225–230, 2007.

[17] H. Lagar-Cavilla, J. Whitney, A. Scannell, P. Patchin, S. Rumble, E. De Lara, M. Brudno, and M. Satyanarayanan. Snowflock: rapid virtual machine cloning for cloud computing. In *Proceedings of the 4th ACM European conference on Computer systems*, pages 1–12, 2009.

[18] R. LERNER. Memcached integration in rails. *Linux Journal*, 2009.

[19] A. Mashtizadeh, E. Celebi, T. Garfinkel, and M. Cai. The design and evolution of live storage migration in VMware ESX. In *Proceedings of the USENIX Annual Technical Conference*, 2011.

[20] A. Nagarajan, F. Mueller, C. Engelmann, and S. Scott. Proactive fault tolerance for HPC with Xen virtualization. In *Proceedings of the 21st annual international conference on Supercomputing*, pages 23–32, 2007.

[21] R. Nathuji and K. Schwan. Virtualpower: coordinated power management in virtualized enterprise systems. In *Proceedings of 21st ACM SIGOPS Symposium on Operating Systems Principles*, pages 265–278, 2007.

[22] M. Nelson, B. Lim, and G. Hutchins. Fast transparent migration for virtual machines. In *Proceedings of the USENIX Annual Technical Conference*, 2005.

[23] J. T. Peter Svärd, Benoit Hudzia and E. Elmorth. Evaluation of delta compression techniques for efficient live migration of large virtual machines. In *Proceeding of the ACM SIGPLAN/SIGOPS International Conference on Virtual Execution Environments*, 2011.

[24] M. Powell and B. Miller. Process migration in DEMOS/MP. In *Proceedings of the 9th Symposium on Operating System Principles*, 1983.

[25] W. Pugh. Skip lists: a probabilistic alternative to balanced trees. *Communications of the ACM*, 33(6):668–676, 1990.

[26] M. Theimer, K. Lantz, and D. Cheriton. Preemptable remote execution facilities for the V-system. In *Proceedings of the tenth ACM Symposium on Operating Systems Principles*, 1985.

EXTERIOR: Using a Dual-VM Based External Shell for Guest-OS Introspection, Configuration, and Recovery

Yangchun Fu

Department of Computer Science
The University of Texas at Dallas
800 West Campbell RD
Richardson, TX 75080
yangchun.fu@utdallas.edu

Zhiqiang Lin

Department of Computer Science
The University of Texas at Dallas
800 West Campbell RD
Richardson, TX 75080
zhiqiang.lin@utdallas.edu

Abstract

This paper presents EXTERIOR, a dual-VM architecture based external shell that can be used for trusted, timely out-of-VM management of guest-OS such as introspection, configuration, and recovery. Inspired by recent advances in virtual machine introspection (VMI), EXTERIOR leverages an isolated, secure virtual machine (SVM) to introspect the kernel state of a guest virtual machine (GVM). However, it goes far beyond the *read-only* capability of the traditional VMI, and can perform automatic, fine-grained guest-OS writable operations. The key idea of EXTERIOR is to use a dual-VM architecture in which a SVM runs a kernel identical to that of the GVM to create the necessary environment for a running process (e.g., `rmmod`, `kill`), and dynamically and transparently redirect and update the memory state at the VMM layer from SVM to GVM, thereby achieving the same effect in terms of kernel state updates of running the same trusted in-VM program inside the shell of GVM. A proof-of-concept EXTERIOR has been implemented. The experimental results show that EXTERIOR can be used for a timely administration of guest-OS, including introspection and (re)configuration of the guest-OS state and timely response of kernel malware intrusions, without any user account in the guest-OS.

Categories and Subject Descriptors D.4.6 [*Operating Systems*]: Security and Protection; D.3.4 [*Software*]: Processors—Code generation; Translator writing systems and compiler generators

General Terms Security, Management

Keywords Virtual machine introspection, Semantic-gap, Binary code reuse

1. Introduction

Virtual machines (VMs) [18, 19] have significantly reshaped the landscape of our modern computer systems. They have provided a variety of new opportunities for operating system (OS) developers to deploy innovative, previously infeasible out-of-VM solutions, such as server consolidation [48], machine migration [10], strong isolation, better security [8, 15–17, 51], reliability and portability [7]. Un-doubtedly, system virtualization has pushed our computing paradigm from multi-tasking computing to multi-OS computing, and has already become ubiquitous in the realm of enterprise computing infrastructure (underpinning our cloud computing and data centers today).

In the physical world (without virtualization) all the application software runs on top of a particular OS that is installed on a particular physical machine. Both the application and OS kernel state is updated and stored in the system memory during their instruction execution. With the introduction of virtualization, all the hardware resources including physical memory and even CPU instructions are virtualized in a VM monitor (VMM) [18, 19], and today we still follow such a traditional program execution model. Namely, each of the program state (including kernel) in-VM is also stored in the system memory, and is updated through the execution of in-VM program code. For instance, to configure the host name, we have to execute `hostname` in-VM to update the kernel state; to remove a malicious kernel module (e.g., a detected installed rootkit), we have to execute `rmmod` in-VM to unload it from the OS kernel; and to stop a malicious process, we have to execute `kill` in-VM to remove it.

However, from a security perspective, the traditional program execution model has at least the following issues: (1) In-VM programs (e.g., `hostname`, `rmmod`, `ps`) and kernel states are directly faced by user level, as well as kernel level malware, and they can often be attacked. For instance, malicious processes and device drivers (or kernel modules) can hide from in-VM system enumeration tools (e.g., `ps`, `lsmod`) and can be immune to attempts of removal or disabling [24, 41, 42]. (2) End-users or administrators often have to be authenticated before running in-VM programs to update the kernel state, which may not be ideal for a timely response to intrusions (e.g., `kill` a rootkit hidden process), especially for cloud providers who in many cases do not have a user account in the guest-OS.

Therefore, in this paper we introduce EXTERIOR, a new program execution model in which we can run programs in an outer-shell for a guest-OS administration, with the same effect in terms of kernel state updates akin to running the programs inside the GVM. As such, unlike traditional in-VM program execution model, we update the in-VM kernel state entirely from the outside. We can thus ensure the trustworthiness of our out-of-VM programs because they are located out-of-VM and there is a world switch (far from reaching) with the in-VM programs such as the in-VM malware. Also, we do not have to be authenticated, and we execute the trusted out-of-VM programs in our outer-shell which is outside control of the in-VM software.

To realize EXTERIOR, we have to develop the out-of-VM programs that can precisely identify the memory locations that reflect the in-VM kernel state and update them correspondingly at the VMM layer. Unfortunately, this is challenging because of a semantic gap [7]. In particular, to the VMM, the view of the guest-OS is just the raw bits and bytes of the physical memory and register state. In contrast to the in-VM environment, where we have rich semantics (e.g., files, APIs, and system calls), at the VMM layer there is no OS-level abstraction. Consequently, we have to bridge the semantic gap and identify the in-VM kernel state variables at the VMM layer, which is typically a tedious, time-consuming, and error-prone process [13, 15, 24, 25, 39].

Fortunately, by tracing how the traditional in-VM program executes and updates the kernel state, we observe that OS kernel state is often inspected and updated at certain kernel system call (syscall for short in the rest of the paper) execution context. For instance, syscall `getpid` will return the `pid` of the running process, and syscall `sysctl` will update kernel parameters. If we are able to precisely identify these in-VM syscall execution contexts when the corresponding trusted utilities are executed at the VMM layer, and if we are able to maintain a secure duplicate of the running VM, through redirecting both their memory read and write operation from the secure VM to the running VM, then we can transparently update the in-VM kernel state of the running VM from the outside via the secure VM. In other words, the semantic-gap (e.g., the memory location of in-VM kernel state) is automatically bridged by the intrinsic instruction constraints encoded in the binary code in the duplicated VM.

As a result, it leads to a dual-VM architecture for EXTERIOR with a secure VM (SVM) and guest VM (GVM). Specifically, in EXTERIOR, we need a trusted, corresponding guest-OS kernel with the same version installed in a separate SVM, in which not only we have the full control and can ensure its integrity but also in which we can run the native administration utilities and perform the memory redirection. Through running the trusted binary code in the monitored SVM, EXTERIOR transparently redirects the memory read and write operations of kernel memory from SVM to GVM, thus modifying the state of the GVM. Therefore, the outer-shell for the GVM is actually located in our SVM, and now we can _execute_ trusted, native, widely tested administration utilities in SVM to _timely_ supervise the state of GVM, including _introspection_ and _(re)configuration_ of guest-OS kernel state as well as _recovery_ and response to intrusions (EXTERIOR is named based on these underscored characters).

In a nutshell, EXTERIOR has reshaped the traditional program execution model. Normally, a given program runs on top of a given OS within a shell. EXTERIOR changes this model and supports running programs completely outside of the OS with the same effect as running the program inside in terms of kernel state update, thanks to the powerful, programmable VMM. A direct outcome of EXTERIOR is that we can now run the trusted administration utilities to (re)configure the guest-OS and respond quickly to intrusions such as recovering the system from attacks (e.g., `kill` a rootkit created process, and `rmmod` a malicious kernel module) entirely from out-of-VM, without any user account inside the guest-OS. Therefore, EXTERIOR will significantly ease the administration of the guest-OS. When combined with the intrusion detection techniques from VM Introspection [13–15, 24, 25, 39], EXTERIOR can also provide a timely response to intrusions detected in the guest-OS.

In summary, this paper makes the following contributions:

- We present a dual-VM architecture based external shell, and demonstrate for the first time that using such a shell we can run a program completely out-of-VM to achieve the same effect of running it in-VM in terms of kernel state update, but with greater privilege depth.

- We systematically explore the principles behind such architecture, and devise a number of enabling techniques. In particular, unlike all of the existing VMI techniques, which only extract and distinguish coarse-grained process information, we are the first to present a new and binary code analysis technique to extract and isolate even the fine-grained thread information at VMM layer.

- We have built a prototype of EXTERIOR and performed an empirical evaluation with Linux kernels. Our experimental results show that EXTERIOR can be used in a timely, trusted manner for guest-OS administration, including but not limited to system _introspection_, _(re)configuration_ and _recovery_ of kernel intrusions.

The rest of the paper is organized as follows: §2 begins with a description of the further motivation and challenges we will be facing, and an overview of our approach. §3 elaborates by presenting a detailed design of EXTERIOR, including its kernel system call identification, kernel data identification and redirection, and GVM memory address mapping and updating. §4 shares the details on how we implement each component of EXTERIOR. §5 reports our evaluation results. §6 discusses known limitations of our system, and §7 provides direct comparisons to related work. Finally, §8 concludes.

2. Background and Overview

The central goal of EXTERIOR is to support the trusted, timely introspection (note that the term introspection means inspecting kernel state from outside, whereas inspection is still inside), (re)configuration, and recovery of guest-OS kernel state from out-of-VM. In this section, we first describe further why we need EXTERIOR in §2.1. Then we examine the challenges faced when realizing it as well as how we will address them in §2.2. Finally, we give an overview of our system in §2.3.

2.1 Further Motivation

There are a number of reasons why we need out-of-VM program execution to manage the guest-OS. Besides all the benefits such as isolation, portability, and reliability [7] while implementing the service out-of-VM, we could have the following additional benefits:

Trustworthiness Recent cyber attacks such as kernel rootkits have pushed our defense software into the hypervisor or even hardware layers (i.e., out-of-VM). It is generally believed to be much harder for attackers to tamper with the software running out-of-VM, because there is a world switch for the attacks from in-VM to out-of-VM (unless the VMM has vulnerabilities). Therefore, we can gain a higher trustworthiness of the out-of-VM software. For instance, we can guarantee that the administration utilities (e.g, `ps`) are not tampered before using them to manage a guest-OS in our SVM as our SVM is not directly faced by attackers.

Higher Privilege and Stealthiness Traditional security software (e.g., anti-virus, or host intrusion detection) runs inside the guest-OS, and in-VM malware can often disable the execution of these software. By moving the execution of security software out-of-VM, we can achieve higher privilege (same as hypervisor) and stealthiness, and make them invisible to attackers. For instance, malicious code (e.g., kernel rootkit) often disables the `ps` command from showing the running malicious process, and disables the `rmmod` command needed to remove a kernel module. Through enabling the execution of these commands out-of-VM, we can achieve higher privilege and stealthiness, and prevent the rootkits from tampering with the security software.

Automation When an intrusion is detected, it often requires an automated response. Current practice is often to notify the administrators or execute some automated responses inside the guest-OS. Unfortunately, again any in-VM responses can be disabled by attackers because they run at the same privilege level. However, with EXTERIOR we support running software out-of-VM, and we can quickly take actions to stop and prevent the attack without the help from any in-VM root privileges. Considering there are a great deal of VMI based intrusion detection systems (e.g., [13–15, 24, 25, 39]), EXTERIOR can be seamlessly integrated with them and provide a timely response to attacks, such as `kill` a rootkit created hidden process and `rmmod` a hidden malicious kernel module.

2.2 Challenges and Our Approach

Observation It is truly feasible to realize our out-of-VM guest-OS state introspection and update. The best example is to consider the operation we did for disk data inspection. Normally, a given OS usually has a mounted persistent disk storage; guest OS can use in-guest utilities to manage the disk data (e.g., `ls`, `rm`, `touch` a file). Meanwhile, we can also mount the disk into other OSes, and use the same utilities to manage these disks. From the state perspective, the disk data itself does not sense whether the management (e.g., inspection or editing) is performed in the guest OS or in other OSes, as long as we ensure the disk data remains in a consistent state.

For precision and clarity, we define a few formal notations for our following discussion. In general, a program $\mathcal{P}$ (including an OS kernel) is often composed of *code* $\mathcal{C}$ and *data* $\mathcal{D}$ (i.e., $\mathcal{P} = \mathcal{C}(\mathcal{D})$), where $\mathcal{C}$ determines how the software executes and $\mathcal{D}$ reflects the state of the execution. Normally, $\mathcal{C}$ and $\mathcal{D}$ reside in the same physical machine, and $\mathcal{D}$ gets updated when $\mathcal{C}$ gets executed.

We can further split $\mathcal{D}$ into user-level data $\mathcal{D}_{user}$ and kernel-level data $\mathcal{D}_{kernel}$, as illustrated in Fig. 1. At run-time, these data can be further classified into stack, heap, and global at both the user and kernel level. Thus, we denote $\mathcal{D}_{user} = \{\mathcal{D}_{user}^{stack}, \mathcal{D}_{user}^{heap}, \mathcal{D}_{user}^{global}\}$, and $\mathcal{D}_{kernel} = \{\mathcal{D}_{kernel}^{stack}, \mathcal{D}_{kernel}^{heap}, \mathcal{D}_{kernel}^{global}\}$, respectively. Also, note that $\mathcal{D}_{kernel}$ represents the run-time kernel state, is internally maintained by the kernel itself, and is indirectly accessed through OS system calls invoked by $\mathcal{P}$'s $\mathcal{C}$. Meanwhile, $\mathcal{D}_{kernel}$ can flow to $\mathcal{D}_{user}$ and get updated by $\mathcal{P}$'s $\mathcal{C}$. Therefore, we can have

$$\mathcal{P} = \mathcal{C}(\mathcal{D})$$
$$= \mathcal{C}(\mathcal{D}_{user}, \mathcal{D}_{kernel})$$
$$= \mathcal{C}(\{\mathcal{D}_{user}^{stack}, \mathcal{D}_{user}^{heap}, \mathcal{D}_{user}^{global}\}, \{\mathcal{D}_{kernel}^{stack}, \mathcal{D}_{kernel}^{heap}, \mathcal{D}_{kernel}^{global}\})$$

(1)

Meanwhile, a process always consumes data within its own physical machine, and has its own $\mathcal{D}_{user}^{stack}$, $\mathcal{D}_{user}^{heap}$ and $\mathcal{D}_{user}^{global}$. When a syscall is trapped from user space to kernel space, there will be a $\mathcal{D}_{kernel}^{stack}$ to maintain the kernel execution state for this particular syscall. During the execution of a syscall, many other kernel events can occur, such as interrupts, exceptions, and context switches, causing kernel control to jump to the execution of these events.

During the execution of one syscall, the other syscalls for this running process will not be executed until it returns (multi-thread process is discussed in §3.1). Also, there is an active kernel stack at kernel level for a running process (with limited size) that stores the return addresses of the called functions and the local variables when each syscall gets executed. When a syscall returns, the kernel stack for that specific process is empty, and the kernel stack frame is dynamically allocated from the kernel heap.

There exist a number of approaches that may be feasible to achieve our goal of timely out-of-VM kernel state introspection and update. In the following, we study these possible solutions and outline our approach.

Approach-I: Memory Diffing Given the dual-VM architecture, one intuitive approach is to take the snapshot of the GVM memory

```
1  execve("/sbin/sysctl",["sysctl", "-w","kernel..=1"],...) = 0
2  brk(0)                                    = 0x604000
3  access("/etc/ld.so.nohwcap",F_OK)         = -1 ENOENT
4  mmap(NULL, 8192, PROT_READ|.., -1,0) = 0x7f07b1749000
5  access("/etc/ld.so.preload",R_OK)         = -1 ENOENT
6  open("/etc/ld.so.cache", O_RDONLY)        = 3
...
47 open("/proc/sys/kernel/randomize_va_space",O_WRONLY|...) = 3
48 fstat(3, {st_mode=S_IFREG|0644, st_size=0, ...}) = 0
49 mmap(NULL, 4096, PROT_READ|.., -1, 0) = 0x7f07b1748000
50 write(3, "1\n", 2)                        = 2
51 close(3)                                  = 0
...
57 exit_group(0)                             = ?
```

Figure 2. Syscall trace of running `sysctl -w` to turn on the address space randomization in Linux kernel 2.6.32.

at state $\mathcal{M}_0$, and then resume the GVM execution with the state of $\mathcal{M}_1 = \mathcal{M}_0 + \mathcal{M}_\delta$. To acquire $\mathcal{M}_\delta$, we can run our SVM and take its memory snapshot before ($\mathcal{M}_{before}$) and after ($\mathcal{M}_{after}$) executing a configuration utility, and then we can get $\mathcal{M}_\delta = \mathcal{M}_{after} - \mathcal{M}_{before}$.

However, such an approach only works if and only if $\mathcal{M}_\delta$ is located in $\mathcal{D}_{kernel}^{global}$. If $\mathcal{M}_\delta$ includes any $\mathcal{D}_{kernel}^{heap}$ data, it will fail unless it also identifies heap data differences and resolves the mapping. Also, this intuitive approach might only work for kernel parameter reconfiguration (e.g., `hostname`,`chrt`,`sysctl`). If we want to kill a malicious process, we cannot use this memory diffing approach as our SVM does not contain the to-be-killed malicious process. We also cannot use this approach for state introspection (e.g., `ps`) as we do not know what will be the involved $\mathcal{M}_\delta$ in GVM.

Approach-II: Process Implanting Because of the semantic-gap from the outside world, the second approach is to implant a configuration and recovery process into the guest OS, as demonstrated in Process Implanting [21]. However, the biggest problem for this approach is it has to pick up a victim process from the guest-OS and replace its program execution context with the implanted one. Thus, to the victim process, its semantics has been completely disrupted. Meanwhile, it will also execute the in-guest user-library and kernel code which may have been altered by malware. As such, this approach cannot guarantee the trustworthiness from the out-of-VM injected process except with other code integrity protection techniques from GVM.

Approach-III: Our Approach Inspired by our recent VM space traveler (VMST [14]) work, our approach is to use a *dual-VM* execution architecture with a kernel syscall *context aware* scheme that monitors the instruction execution of the trusted utilities at SVM, and transparently redirects each individual piece of memory update $\mathcal{M}_\delta$, at *binary code* instruction level from SVM to GVM when the syscall of interest gets executed, to achieve our state introspection, (re)configuration and recovery for GVM.

For instance, considering running `sysctl(8)` to configure the kernel parameters, as shown in Fig. 2, there are in total 57 syscalls, and only 4 of them (highlighted in the figure) are of our interest because these syscalls are responsible to tune the kernel parameters. If we can redirect the kernel data access of these four syscalls, we can achieve the same effect of configuring the kernel from outside VM.

More specifically, suppose we want to implement a new out-of-VM program $\mathcal{P}_{out}$, which could be a state inspection program (e.g., `ps`, `lsmod`, `netstat`) , a configuration or attack recovery program (e.g., `kill`, `rmmod`). We can reuse the execution context of the original in-VM program $\mathcal{P}_{in} = \mathcal{C}_{in}(\mathcal{D}_{user}, \mathcal{D}_{kernel})$ with the same $\mathcal{D}_{user}$, but with different $\mathcal{D}'_{kernel}$. However, we cannot reuse the $\mathcal{D}'^{stack}_{kernel}$ because the data in the stack is transient and mostly related to kernel control flow. Therefore, in order to implement $\mathcal{P}_{out}$, we can have

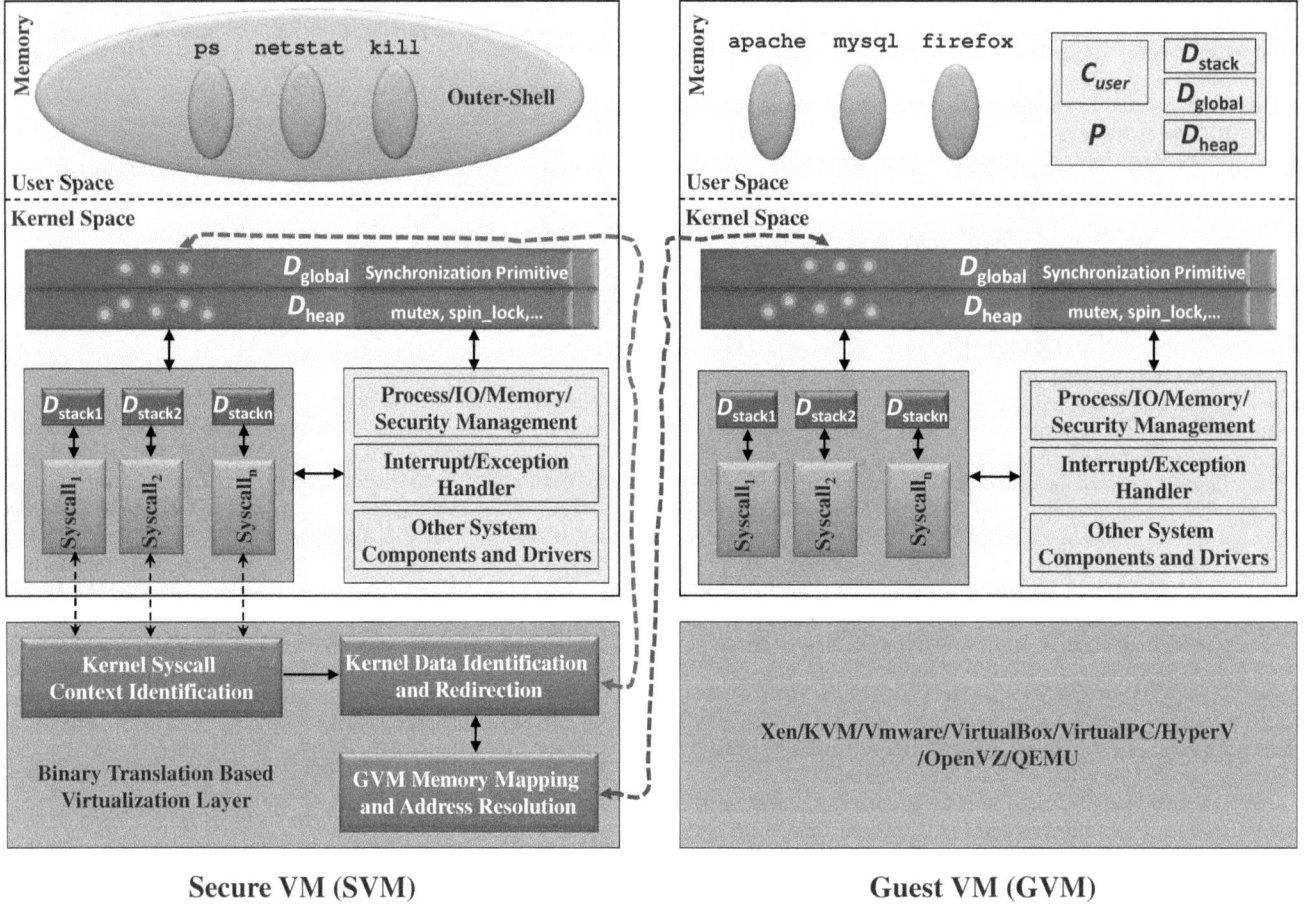

Figure 1. Overview of Our Dual-VM based EXTERIOR, which supports the execution of native administration utilities in the outer-shell of SVM to manage GVM. At a high level, suppose syscall$_2$ in SVM is of interest and executed in process `kill` context, then all the accessed $\mathcal{D}_{kernel}^{global}$ and $\mathcal{D}_{kernel}^{heap}$ (denoted as circle) under this process context will be redirected to GVM except those synchronization primitives such as `spin_lock` which often have unique instruction sequences.

$$
\begin{aligned}
\mathcal{P}_{out} &= \mathcal{C}_{out}(\mathcal{D}_{user}, \mathcal{D}_{kernel}) \\
&= \mathcal{C}_{in}(\mathcal{D}_{user}, \mathcal{D}'_{kernel}) \qquad (2) \\
&= \mathcal{C}_{in}(\mathcal{D}_{user}, \{\mathcal{D}_{kernel}^{stack}, \mathcal{D}'^{heap}_{kernel}, \mathcal{D}'^{global}_{kernel}\})
\end{aligned}
$$

where $\mathcal{P}_{out}$ is the new out-of-VM program; $\mathcal{C}_{out} = \mathcal{C}_{in}$, $\mathcal{D}'^{heap}_{kernel}$ and $\mathcal{D}'^{global}_{kernel}$ are from the GVM; and $\mathcal{C}_{in}$, $\mathcal{D}_{user}$ and $\mathcal{D}_{kernel}^{stack}$ are from the SVM.

Interestingly, from formula (2) we can see that the semantic gap is automatically bridged for the out-of-VM program $\mathcal{P}_{out}$ that is running in our SVM. This is because the new $\mathcal{P}_{out}$ satisfies $\mathcal{C}_{out}(\mathcal{D}_{user}, \mathcal{D}_{kernel}) = \mathcal{C}_{in}(\mathcal{D}_{user}, \mathcal{D}'_{kernel})$ by reusing the legacy binary code $\mathcal{C}_{in}$ of $\mathcal{P}_{out}$. In other words, $\mathcal{P}_{out}$ can use all the syscall, APIs invoked by itself in SVM, and it transparently updates the state of $\mathcal{D}'_{kernel}$ of GVM and achieves the same effect of running the corresponding $\mathcal{P}_{in}$ in GVM, but with higher trustworthiness.

Challenges While EXTERIOR is inspired by our own VMST, to realize it there are still many new challenges including: (**C1**) How to precisely isolate the target process execution context in SVM, given that OS can run multiple processes and threads. While our VMST is able to identify the process level context, it does not have techniques to identify thread-level context, which is crucial for memory update in GVM. (**C2**) What those syscalls of our interest are. In VMST, we only identified introspection related syscall, and we have not

extended it further to identify the configuration and recovery related syscalls. (**C3**) How to identify the corresponding $\mathcal{M}_\delta$ in $\mathcal{D}_{kernel}^{global}$ and $\mathcal{D}_{kernel}^{heap}$ while executing the program $\mathcal{P}$ in SVM. Note that in VMST we have developed techniques to solve this challenge, and EXTERIOR will directly leverage them. (**C4**) What would happen if there is any synchronization primitives (such as `mutex` and `spin_lock` in $\mathcal{D}'^{global}_{kernel}$ and $\mathcal{D}'^{heap}_{kernel}$. While VMST also faces this issue, it is less severe as many of these primitives are accessed in interrupt handlers. However, in EXTERIOR, we have to investigate this problem further as some memory write operations do involve synchronization primitives (e.g., when removing a kernel module, `delete_module` syscall needs to lock the `module list`. (**C5**) How to reflect the $\mathcal{M}_\delta$ from SVM to GVM, such that GVM feels that $\mathcal{P}$ is executed in its own VM. In VMST, we do not need to update the GVM memory as it is only used for *read-only* introspection.

2.3 Architecture Overview

An overview of EXTERIOR is presented in Fig. 1. Since we need to monitor the kernel instruction level memory access of $\mathcal{M}_\delta$, our SVM is based on the instruction translation based VMM. In our system design, we use the open source QEMU [1]. The GVM could be any VMM, such as Xen/KVM/vSphere/HyperV. Note that the design of EXTERIOR is only bounded with SVM, which will only be used for security and administration.

There are three key components designed in our SVM at its binary translation based VMM layer. Specifically, to precisely isolate the target process execution context in kernel space (addressing **C1**), we devise a *Kernel Syscall Context Identification* (§3.1) component, which identifies the target process and thread execution context in the kernel space at the syscall granularity in SVM. During the execution of $\mathcal{P}$, not all the syscall related data is of interest to our $\mathcal{M}_\delta$ (as discussed in the above sysctl example), our *Kernel Process-Context Identification* will also pinpoint which syscall context needs the $\mathcal{D}_{kernel}^{global}$ and $\mathcal{D}_{kernel}^{heap}$ redirection (addressing **C2**). In addition, it will identify those interrupt execution context to filter the redirection of synchronization primitives (addressing **C4**). After that, our second component *Kernel Data Identification and Redirection* (§3.2) intercepts the data access of in guest $\mathcal{D}_{kernel}^{global}$ and $\mathcal{D}_{kernel}^{heap}$ (addressing **C3**), when the particular syscall of interest gets executed. In the meantime, it sends the GVM data read-and-write request to our third component *GVM Memory Mapping and Address Resolution* (§3.3). Our third component is responsible for mapping the physical memory of GVM, resolving the corresponding kernel virtual address, and performing the read and write operations of the involved $\mathcal{M}_\delta$ to GVM (addressing **C5**).

Scope and Assumptions As a proof-of-concept, we focus on the x86 architecture and Linux kernel. Currently, we do not support *arbitrary* state updates from the outside, and we *only* focus on the state update related to our memory introspection, configuration and recovery utilities we tested in §5. Disk data introspection and update is out-of-scope of EXTERIOR.

Also, we assume we know the specific kernel version running in the GVM, and we have a corresponding trusted kernel copy in SVM. The specific kernel version could be either reported by the VM administrator, or through guest-OS fingerprinting if there is any potential cheating (or the administrator cannot report). For example, recently proposed techniques such as CPU context-based approaches (e.g., [44]) or memory-only approaches (e.g., [20]) could be leveraged.

In addition, we assume our SVM is trusted, and we are able to maintain a clean state. Note that our SVM only consumes data from GVM, and will not execute any code from GVM (we can achieve this because we control each instruction execution in SVM). Finally, we assume there is no ASLR [4] inside the guest-OS kernel. That is, the virtual address of the kernel global variables should be always identical across different machines for the same version of the OS. In fact, this is true for many OSes including all of the available Linux kernels, and pre-Windows 7 kernels from Microsoft.

3. Detailed Design

In this section, we present the detailed design of the three key components of our SVM. We first describe how we identify the specific process execution context at VMM layer in §3.1; then describe how we intercept the kernel instruction execution, and identify the global as well as heap data in §3.2; finally we present how we map and resolve the data access (including both read and write) of the physical memory from SVM to GVM in §3.3.

3.1 Kernel Syscall Context Identification

The goal of our *Kernel Syscall Context Identification* is to identify the target-process kernel-level execution context, and pinpoint the exact syscall context at the VMM layer. We present how we achieve this in greater detail below.

Identifying Process Kernel Execution Context All the modern OSes running in the x86 architecture grant each process a private page directory that is often pointed by a control register CR3, and the value of the CR3 can hence naturally be used to differentiate the process execution context. This observation has been widely used in many of the VM introspection systems (e.g., [14, 25, 26, 39, 40]).

In addition to using CR3 to differentiate the process execution context, we have to further retrieve process name to pin-point our targeted process (such as ps,kill,rmmod). While we could traverse kernel data structures (e.g., task_struct) to retrieve such information, our approach is to inspect the system call arguments (e.g., the argument of execve(2)) of process creation to make our system more OS-agnostic.

However, there is still a caveat. A process could run with multiple threads. Using CR3 and process name can only pin-point the process execution context, and it cannot precisely isolate the specific syscall context yet. This is because all of the threads for the same process can execute syscalls. As such, we have to differentiate the thread context for the same process at VMM layer. But the Linux kernel does not have any thread specific support (to Linux kernel, a thread is uniformly treated as a process) and multi-threading is implemented at user level (e.g., pthread library which takes care of creating unique stack address for each thread). In fact, when using pthread_create to create a new thread, this function will use syscall clone(2) that has a user specified virtual address for child stack, instead of the default process fork(2).

Fortunately, we have a new observation: while multi-threads for the same process share the same CR3 (threads share the same virtual address), each process at kernel level has a unique kernel stack (this is dynamically allocated) which can be used to isolate the thread execution context at kernel level. Therefore, we propose to use CR3, process name, and kernel esp register (with a lower 12bits cleared by mask) together, to uniquely differentiate and isolate the fine-grained thread execution context. To the best of our knowledge, none of the existing VMI techniques (e.g., [11, 13–15, 24–26, 35, 39, 40]) except vProbe [2] have reached this level of granularity. While vProbe is able to retrieve thread level information, it requires the access to kernel data structure information.

Identifying Specific Syscall Execution Context After having been able to identify the *fine-grained* process context, we need to further identify the specific syscall context under the target process execution. Note that syscalls are the exported OS services. As illustrated in Fig. 2, user level processes must invoke syscalls to request the OS services, such as file access.

Since our SVM monitors all the instructions executed inside the computer system, it is trivial to intercept the entry point and exit point of the syscall execution. Specifically, in the x86 architecture, syscall execution has unique instruction pairs. In the Linux kernel, they are int 0x80/iret and sysenter/sysexit (this pair is used since kernel-2.5). The specific syscall is indexed by register eax when invoking a syscall. Therefore, by monitoring these instructions, we can detect the entering (int 0x80/sysenter) and exiting (iret/sysexit) of a syscal.

Unfortunately, the kernel level execution between a syscall entry point and a syscall exit point is not entirely for the execution of this syscall as discussed in our VMST [14]. Besides the normal control flow such as call/ret/jump, as illustrated in Fig. 1, kernel control flow is also driven by the asynchronous event: interrupt (e.g., context switch timer) and exception (e.g., page fault). These events will be responsible for managing the system resources and executing device drivers. Certainly, we have to precisely identify these execution contexts and exclude their data access of $\mathcal{D}_{kernel}^{global}$ and $\mathcal{D}_{kernel}^{heap}$ (because our analysis with kernel source code reveals that many of the spin_locks and mutexes are accessed in these context). Otherwise, when reading these data from GVM, most likely our SVM kernel will lead to an inconsistent state (such as dead lock) and even crash during the execution of these execution contexts. For instance, if the page fault handler of SVM is about to allocate new pages for a process, but if it reads a different state from GVM, it will likely render the page fault handler unusable.

Whereas the kernel has such a very complicated, unpredictable control flow, we can precisely identify the syscall execution context. All of these asynchronous events are driven by interrupts and exceptions, and our SVM emulates all these hardware level resources. As such, we are able to identify the beginning execution of these events because the SVM controls the hardware. For the end of these events, they will have an `iret` instruction, which we can also capture precisely. Meanwhile, for the bottom up handlers of an interrupt and exception, they will be executed during context switch. Our SVM controls the interrupt and timer, and we hence control the context switch. Therefore, our SVM is able to precisely identify the syscall execution of the target process, and keep it running successfully in SVM. Note that this syscall context identification approach has been proposed in our VMST [14], and we directly leverage this technique when building our EXTERIOR.

Eventually, the output of our first component will precisely tell the exact execution context of the syscalls, excluding any other kernel execution such as context switch and interrupt (and exception) handler. Next, our second component will perform the identification of $\mathcal{D}_{kernel}^{global}$ and $\mathcal{D}_{kernel}^{heap}$ accessed during the syscall execution of our interest (recall only 4 out of 57 system calls are of our interest when executing `sysctl(8)`).

3.2 Kernel Data Identification and Redirection

The goal of this component is to intercept all the data access, pinpoint the precise $\mathcal{D}_{kernel}^{global}$ and $\mathcal{D}_{kernel}^{heap}$, and read data from or write data to the memory in GVM with the facilitation of our third component, while executing the monitored syscall of our interest.

Identifying $\mathcal{D}_{kernel}^{global}$ and $\mathcal{D}_{kernel}^{heap}$ during a Syscall Execution Similar to user level stack data, $\mathcal{D}_{kernel}^{stack}$ is also transient. While $\mathcal{D}_{kernel}^{stack}$ does contain some localized state variables, it actually does not contribute to the state of kernel introspection, configuration, and recovery. $\mathcal{D}_{kernel}^{global}$ and $\mathcal{D}_{kernel}^{heap}$ are the memory regions that store the persistent kernel state. Therefore, our primary focus is to precisely identify these $\mathcal{D}_{kernel}^{global}$ and $\mathcal{D}_{kernel}^{heap}$ when the syscall of our interest gets executed.

After a kernel is compiled, the addresses of $\mathcal{D}_{kernel}^{global}$ become literal values in kernel instructions. As such, it is trivial to identify $\mathcal{D}_{kernel}^{global}$ by simply looking at the address ranges of the literal values. Then the real challenge comes from how to identify $\mathcal{D}_{kernel}^{heap}$. Fortunately, based on the observation that it will have the same effect as precisely identifying all the $\mathcal{D}_{kernel}^{stack}$ and excluding them, since a kernel data x either belongs to $\mathcal{D}_{kernel}^{stack}$, $\mathcal{D}_{kernel}^{global}$, or $\mathcal{D}_{kernel}^{heap}$.

It may seem to be trivial to identify the $\mathcal{D}_{kernel}^{stack}$ as we monitor all the instruction, we can check whether $x \in \mathcal{D}_{kernel}^{stack}$ by looking at the address range. However, it turns out that such an approach will not work considering the fact that $\mathcal{D}_{kernel}^{stack}$ is also dynamically allocated from $\mathcal{D}_{kernel}^{heap}$. On the other hand, $\mathcal{D}_{kernel}^{stack}$ often has data dependencies with the kernel stack pointer (esp). Therefore, we leveraged a stack data dependence tracking algorithm from our VMST [14] to track the data directly and indirectly derived from kernel stack pointer esp. This algorithm is a variant of standard taint analysis, which has been widely investigated and used in many applications (e.g., [9, 32, 37]). In our scenario, any data derived from stack pointer esp as well as their propagations will be tainted by instrumenting data movement and data arithmetic instructions. Then for a given kernel address x, if its taint bit is set, then it belongs to $\mathcal{D}_{kernel}^{stack}$; otherwise, it is $\mathcal{D}_{kernel}^{global}$ or $\mathcal{D}_{kernel}^{heap}$.

```
<spin_lock> in 2.6.34
0xc0129950: 55                   push ebp
0xc0129951: ba 00 01 00 00       mov edx, 0x100
0xc0129956: 89 e5                mov ebp, esp
0xc0129958: 3e 66 0f c1 10       xadd word ptr ds[eax], dx
0xc012995d: 38 f2                cmp dl, dh
0xc012995f: 74 06                jz 0xc0129967
0xc0129961: f3 90                pause
0xc0129963: 8a 10                mov dl, byte ptr ds[eax]
0xc0129965: eb f6                jmp 0xc012995d
0xc0129967: 5d                   pop ebp
0xc0129968: c3                   ret
<spin_lock> in 3.0.4
0xc1026a70: 55                   push ebp
0xc1026a71: ba 00 01 00 00       mov edx, 0x100
0xc1026a76: 89 e5                mov ebp, esp
0xc1026a78: 3e 66 0f c1 10       xadd word ptr ds[eax], dx
0xc1026a7d: 38 f2                cmp dl, dh
0xc1026a7f: 74 06                jz 0xc1026a87
0xc1026a81: f3 90                pause
0xc1026a83: 8a 10                mov dl, byte ptr ds[eax]
0xc1026a85: eb f6                jmp 0xc1026a7d
0xc1026a87: 5d                   pop ebp
0xc1026a88: c3                   ret
```

Figure 3. Disassembled Instruction Sequence of `spin_lock` Primitive in different Linux Kernels.

Enumerating Syscall of Interest Recall as illustrated in Fig. 2, not all the syscall contributes to the kernel state inspection and update, and we have to systematically enumerate the syscalls of our interest. As discussed in VMST [14], this enumeration is often application-specific and has to be done by kernel experts, not the end users of our EXTERIOR. In particular, after manually examining all the syscalls, we classify those of our interest into the following three categories:

(1) **Inspection** In order to reconfigure the OS or recovery from an attack, we have to introspect the OS to get its current status and perform the response. Many user level utilities such as `ps(1)`, `lsmod(8)`, `lsof(8)`, `netstat(8)` are designed for this inspection purpose. Interestingly, all these utilities read `proc` files to inspect the kernel state. Therefore, file access related syscalls: `open(2)`, `read(2)`, `fstat(2)`, `stat(2)`, `lseek(2)`, `readv(2)`, `readdir(2)`, `close(2)` are of our particular interest. Note that Linux kernel leverages `proc` files to enable user-level program accessing kernel state.

(2) **Configuration** Similar to the inspection, many configuration utilities such as `sysctl(8)` use `write(2)` to change the kernel state through `proc` file system. Therefore, `write(2)` is of interest. In addition, there is also a `sysctl(2)` syscall for kernel to directly change its parameters. Meanwhile, we are interested in other syscalls such as `socket(2)`, `ioctl(2)` (for `route(8)`) and `nice(2)` because they can also dynamically change the kernel state.

(3) **Recovery** Once we have detected a kernel attack such as a hidden malicious process or a hidden device driver in GVM (using the inspection utility in SVM to introspect GVM for instance), we need to quickly remove them from the guest kernel. Therefore, syscalls `kill(2)` and `delete_module(2)` are also of our interest.

Identifying Synchronization Primitives in Syscalls While many synchronization primitives are executed in the interrupt context, we also find some syscalls do contain them. For instance, `delete_module(2)` will call `spin_lock`, `spin_unlock`, two functions widely used in kernel synchronization, to lock and unlock the `modlist_lock` that is a kernel global variable. As such, we have to filter the data redirection of `modlist_lock`. It might be viable by white-listing the program counters (PCs) of the involved instructions. However, this is tedious, challenging, and also kernel-specific (we have to perform such analysis for each kernel to filter these PCs).

After analyzing the instruction sequences of these synchronization primitives, we realize that we can still have a systematic solution to identify their execution contexts by looking for the particular instruction sequences of the synchronization primitives. Specifically, as illustrated in Fig. 3, when executing a function prologue in SVM (say `push ebp` or even at `xadd` instruction in Fig. 3), we forward scan these instruction sequences (the scanning window is determined by each specific primitive), and if they fall into the sequences of kernel synchronization primitives such as `spin_lock` (that has 25 bytes with byte sequence `55 ba 00 .. f6 5d c3`) and `spin_unlock`, or `__up` and `__down` (for a semaphore), we will filter the data redirection for these primitive functions. Our experiment with a number of Linux kernels confirms these instruction sequence patterns are also stable across different kernels.

3.3 Mapping the GVM Memory Address

Having identified a given kernel address x in the syscall of our interest belongs to $\mathcal{D}_{kernel}^{global}$, or $\mathcal{D}_{kernel}^{heap}$, we will dynamically instrument the executing instruction to make it fetch the data from and write the data to the physical memory (PM) of GVM. This is achieved by our third component *GVM Memory Mapping and Address Resolution*. Also, this component makes EXTERIOR substantially different compared to VMST [14] which has just read-only capability of guest-OS.

3.3.1 GVM Memory Mapping

We devise two approaches to map the PM of GVM to our SVM. One is the *online mapping* and we directly map the pages that belong to GVM to our SVM with the support from the VMM (i.e., hypervisor) . The other is the *offline mapping* and we directly take the memory snapshot of GVM and attach it to SVM; once we finish the update in SVM, we restore the updated memory to GVM. Since the second approach is very simple, we focus on the first approach in our following design.

As our SVM uses binary code translation based virtualization (or emulation), it has to run in a host OS. Depending on whether the underneath hypervisor of GVM is hardware-based or software-based, we have two different strategies.

Mapping Software Virtualization Based GVM When a GVM uses software virtualization (such as QEMU), we also have two situations. One is if the GVM also resides in the host OS with our SVM, then to our SVM, the GVM is just another process and we can use inter-process communication between the two VMMs to share the physical memory of GVM. The other is that the GVM resides in a different host OS, and we have to transfer the memory snapshot of GVM to the SVM, or just the references and updates to save the network bandwidth. For both situations, we develop a host or network stub in the VMMs of our SVM and GVM for the communication.

Mapping Hardware Virtualization Based GVM A GVM could also run on top of hardware virtualization such as Xen. In this case, the hypervisor underneath is able to identify the page frames which belong to the GVM. Also, if the host VM of the SVM running in the same hypervisor with GVM, then the hypervisor is able to map the memory of GVM to the SVM. Otherwise, we transfer the memory images of GVM to SVM through network communications.

3.3.2 GVM Memory Address Resolution

After having performed the mapping of the GVM physical memory (G-PM) to our SVM, the G-PM is just another piece of added

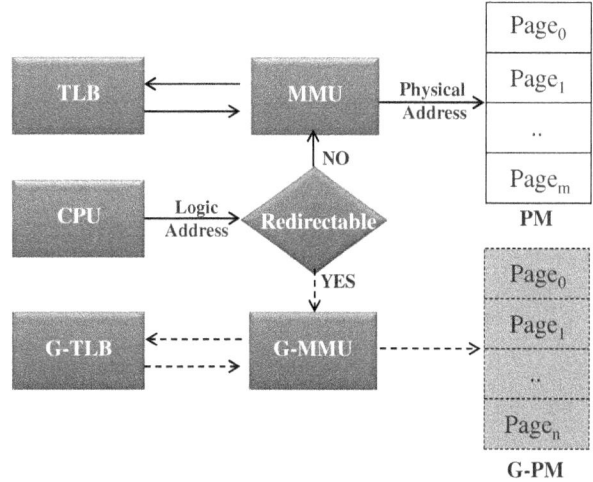

Figure 4. The VMM Extension of our SVM to Map and Resolve the Physical Memory Address of GVM.

physical memory (PM) no matter whether the GVM is software or hardware virtualization based. Note that PM and G-PM could have different sizes since they are in two different machines. Next, we have to instrument the hypervisor of our SVM to transparently access it.

More specifically, as illustrated in Fig. 4, CPU in x86 operates with virtual address (i.e., logic address), and MMU (a hardware component) together with a TLB is responsible for translating the virtual address to physical address (V2P). The TLB is used as a cache to avoid the expensive page table lookup while performing the V2P.

For a given redirectable kernel address x, we could just traverse the page tables to perform its V2P. However, this will be very expensive as each time there will be three memory references. Therefore, adopted from VMST [14], we extend the software-translation based VMM with a G-MMU (GVM's MMU) and G-TLB (GVM's TLB) component, which performs V2P translation in G-PM instead of the original PM, as shown in Fig. 4.

Also, while performing the V2P for a redirectable kernel address x, we need the address of the page directory (PGD) of GVM. In x86 architecture, the PGD is stored in the control register CR3. Therefore, we will retrieve the value of CR3 from GVM when we perform the mapping.

The GVM Status during the SVM Updating When SVM is updating the memory of GVM, there could be some concurrent issues if we keep GVM running as well. Therefore, during the update, our current design is to pause the GVM execution and resume it once the update finishes. Although the proper execution free of concurrency introduced by EXTERIOR is not guaranteed, we have tested with our utilities and confirmed that we can also run them without pausing the GVM.

4. Implementation

We have implemented a prototype of EXTERIOR to support the out-of-VM execution of trusted utilities. In the following, we share the implementation details of interest. As there are two VMs (SVM and GVM) in our dual-VM architecture, we present how we instrument and modify them below. All of our implementation is at the VMM layer, and we will not introduce any components to, or modify, the guest OS.

Category	Utility	Description	Effective? Syntactics	Effective? Semantics
Introspection	ps (1)	report a snapshot of the current processes	✗	✓
	pstree (1)	display a tree of processes	✗	✓
	lsmod (8)	show the status of modules in the Linux Kernel	✓	✓
	dmesg (1)	print or control the kernel ring buffer	✓	✓
	vmstat (8)	Report virtual memory statistics	✗	✓
	netstat (8)	show network connections, routing tables, interface statistics, etc.	✓	✓
	lsof (8)	list open files	✗	✓
	uptime (1)	tell how long the system has been running	✗	✓
	df (1)	report file system disk space usage	✗	✓
Configuration	sysctl (8)	configure kernel parameters at runtime	✓	✓
	route (8)	show / manipulate the IP routing table	✓	✓
	hostname (1)	show or set the system's host name	✓	✓
	chrt (1)	manipulate real-time attributes of a process	✓	✓
	renice (1)	alter priority of running processes	✓	✓
Recovery	kill (1)	send a signal to a process	✓	✓
	rmmod (8)	simple program to remove a module from the Linux Kernel	✓	✓

Table 1. Effectiveness evaluation of our EXTERIOR. The syntactics and semantics is compared with the result of running the corresponding utility inside and outside of the GVM.

SVM Our SVM is built on top of a most recent QEMU-1.0 [1], which is an emulation-based VMM. There are three key components designed in §3 to be added to QEMU. The code size of our own implementation is about 9,300 LOC.

In particular, for the first component, we instrumented the interrupt/exception handler (do_interrupt_all function) and sysenter/sysexit instructions in QEMU to identify the exact syscall execution context. Our second component *Kernel Data Identification and Redirection* needs to perform run-time taint analysis. To this end, we instrument the instruction translation of QEMU (disas_insn) such that we can intercept each instruction, and based on the instruction semantics (e.g., data movement or data arithmetic), we perform data dependence tracking. For our third component, we extended the i386-softmmu component in QEMU, and leveraged the original TLB and MMU translation code to implement our G-TLB and G-MMU. Also, for simplicity, we implemented a snapshot-based stub to map and update the GVM memory. That is, we will map the physical memory which is a snapshot of the GVM.

GVM There are a number of hardware virtualization or software virtualization based GVM. For proof-of-concept and simplicity, we took two typical VMs: a KVM based, and a QEMU based. Both VMs already support pausing the execution of the machine, taking the snapshot of the physical memory, and resuming the machine with a new snapshot. As such, we just extended KVM and QEMU with a CR3 value collection component (with less than 100 LOC).

5. Evaluation

This section presents the experimental result. We first evaluate what kind of introspection, (re)configuration and recovery EXTERIOR can do, and how much user input it requires in §5.1, then we evaluate the performance costs of EXTERIOR in §5.2, and finally we evaluate the generality of our approach regarding different guest-OS kernels in §5.3. Our host environment runs Ubuntu 11.04 with Linux kernel 3.1.0, on Intel Core i7 CPU with 8G memory.

5.1 Effectiveness

Our goal is to support the out-of-VM execution of a given utility, to achieve the same effect of running it in-VM. To this end, as presented in Table 1, we took 16 commonly used administration utilities as the benchmarks and classified them into three categories:

introspection, (re)configuration, and recovery. Our experiment is to verify whether we are able to run these utilities in our external shell and achieve the same effect while running these software inside the VM. The testing guest OS is debian 6.0 with Linux kernel 2.6.32 and 512M memory, and we tested our GVM with both KVM and QEMU.

5.1.1 Introspection

Native inspection utility allows users to examine the state of an OS, which includes the running processes and their relationship (ps, pstree), the opened files by the running processes (lsof), the network connections (netstat), the list of the device drivers (i.e., kernel modules) running in the system (lsmod), and how long the system has been running (uptime), etc.

Interestingly, these *inspection* utilities automatically become *introspections* for GVM kernel when running them in our SVM shell. As shown in the 4th-column of Table 1, some of them do not have the equivalent syntactic output with the result running inside GVM. More specifically, there will be one running process less while testing ps, pstree in SVM to introspect the state of GVM. This missing process is ps, pstree itself when we executing them inside GVM. Because of the different timings of the snapshots (we took the snapshot after we run ps, pstree), it is not in the snapshot. Similarly while running lsof to show all the opened files for all the processes, there are some syntactic differences as well because of this missing running lsof process. For the syntactics difference of uptime, vmstat, it is due to the time differences of executing them in SVM and GVM. For all other commands (i.e., lsmod, dmesg, netstat), we get equivalent syntactics results. For the semantics (i.e., the meanings), these commands achieve the same effect respect to the inspections as shown in the 5th-column of Table 1.

5.1.2 Configuration

We also tested seven configuration utilities to reconfigure kernel parameters (sysctl), routing table (route), host name (hostname), and process priority (chrt, renice). All of these five utilities successfully reconfigured the kernel state, and achieve the same effect while executing them inside.

5.1.3 Recovery

Removing the malicious processes/modules The OS kernel is often contaminated by kernel rootkit that hides malicious processes or kernel modules. When a hidden process is detected, an immediate step would be to remove the malicious process (`kill`). Similarly, when a malicious module is detected, we also need to immediately remove it from the kernel (`rmmod`). In the extreme case, we may have to reboot the system to stop the attack. We also evaluated these capabilities, and our experiments show that EXTERIOR directly supports run these utilities out-of-VM, and achieves the same effect of running in-VM. Note that for the `reboot`, since at the VMM layer we control everything, we can directly reset GVM without executing the `reboot` inside.

Recovering the contaminated function pointers However, it is just a first step to `kill` the malicious process or `rmmod` the malicious modules for the attack recovery. We also need to recover the kernel function pointers that have been modified by kernel rootkits. To this end, we developed a static memory mapping-based, kernel function pointer recovery tool (MAKEUP), which runs in the VMM of our SVM to recover the rootkit attacks (by updating the G-PM).

Most kernel rootkits (over 96% [43]) hijack the runtime OS kernel control flow by modifying such as the syscall table and other kernel function pointers. These syscall tables and other global kernel function pointers are usually static, having the same virtual addresses and values across different machines for the same kernel. Therefore, we can directly compare the values of these static function pointers guided by the `system.map` in the physical memory of SVM which is trusted, with the memory from GVM, to identify which kernel function pointer has been contaminated, and then recover it from the trusted value which is present in our SVM.

In particular, if the value of a function pointer does not match in PM and G-PM, and if this function pointer is not pointed to kernel modules (usually in kernel heap) in our trusted kernel, then our MAKEUP tool will recover this contaminated function pointer. The reason why we cannot compare the pointers which are pointing to heap is because kernel modules usually have different dynamic addresses across different machines including the SVM and GVM.

We took 12 open source rootkits from from *packetstormsecurity.org* and tested them with our MAKEUP tool. By verifying with source code, we can hence make sure we indeed identified all of the contaminated function pointers. Surprisingly, as presented in Table 2, MAKEUP performs incredibly well and it can recover all of the contaminated kernel pointers for 11 rootkits, leaving only one of the rootkits, adore-2.6, unrecovered. This is because adore-2.6 modifies the function pointers in both kernel global and kernel heap. However, MAKEUP cannot identify the kernel heap pointers statically. All other rootkits which modify either system call table, interrupt descriptor table (IDT), or some global kernel function pointer (e.g., `tcp4_seq_show`), MAKEUP successfully recovered the kernel from these attacks by comparing the static pointers in SVM and GVM.

5.1.4 Automation

As we have demonstrated in §5.1.2 and §5.1.3 that we can use EXTERIOR to perform the guest-OS introspection, reconfiguration and recovery, but we have not evaluated how much user input it requires. In fact, much like all the utilities can be automated using script in-VM, all of our tested utilities can also be automated (without any user input) out-of-VM.

To demonstrate this feature, we developed a component with scripts to enable our SVM to periodically introspect the GVM (using commands `ps` and `lsmod`), and then perform a cross-view comparison with the result from a signature scanning approach [12,

Rootkit	Targeted Function Pointer	Succeed?
adore-2.6	kernel global, heap object	✗
hookswrite	IDT table	✓
int3backdoor	IDT table	✓
kbdv3	syscall table	✓
kbeast-v1	syscall table, tcp4_seq_show	✓
mood-nt-2.3	syscall table	✓
override	syscall table	✓
phalanx-b6	syscall table, tcp4_seq_show	✓
rkit-1.01	syscall table	✓
rial	syscall table	✓
suckit-2	IDT table	✓
synapsys-0.4	syscall table	✓

Table 2. Rootkit Recovery with Our MAKEUP Tool.

Tested-Item	Original-Qemu	EXTERIOR	Slowdown
Context switch (ms)	18.3	18.8	2.7%
Mmap (ms)	23300	23600	1.3%
Sh proc (ms)	10000	10000	0.0%
10k file create (ms)	372.7	380.4	2.0%
Mem read (MB/s)	1629	1621	0.4%
Bcopy (libc) (MB/s)	901	883	2.0%

Table 3. Overhead of micro-benchmarks

34] (in this way we do not have to install anything inside GVM): if there is a hidden process or device driver, we `kill` or `rmmod` it and at the same time using our MAKEUP tool to recover from the attack. We tested this component with both a process hidden rootkit and a malicious driver, our EXTERIOR quickly identified the hidden object and removed it from the GVM kernel. Depending on the time window we set for the periodically checking, the quickest one takes less than a second.

Finally we emphasize again that to run the introspection, reconfiguration and recovery commands, there is no requirement of the `root` privilege (as well as the guest-OS root password) from the GVM. This is one of the unique benefits of our system, which can enable a timely response for attacks. One may wonder whether our SVM has broken the administrator trustworthiness of the GVM. However, we have to note that to all the in-VM programs including OS kernel, they often trust their underlying VMM. Our SVM is located in its VMM, and it should therefore be trusted.

5.2 Performance Costs

Next, we measure the performance overhead of EXTERIOR. From the system design in §3, we can notice that the major system overhead of EXTERIOR is only at SVM side, and the overhead comes from the instrumentation of our syscall context identification, data dependence tracking, and GVM mapping and update. In the following, we use two sets of benchmarks to evaluate the performance overhead introduced by our instrumentation.

Micro-benchmarks To evaluate the OS-primitive level performance slowdown of our SVM, we use the standard micro-benchmark LMBench suites to estimate our instrumentation impacts on various aspects of OS operations in SVM.

Interestingly, as shown in Table 3, we could see there is little impact on the regular kernel primitives, such as the latency of context switch and `mmap` syscall, the time spent to execute the C library function system (the `sh proc` row), the latency to create a 10KB file, the memory read bandwidth, and the time to copy 1MB data using the C library function. The explanation is that all of our instrumentation such as process context identification, data

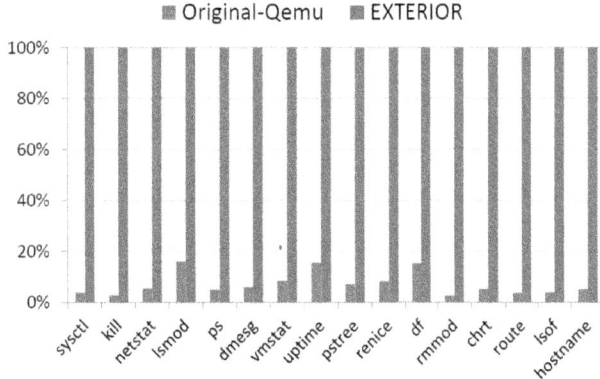

Figure 5. Overhead of macro-benchmarks.

Linux Distribution	Kernel Version	Release Date	Transparent?
Debian 4.0	2.6.26	2007-04-06	✓
Debian 5.0	2.6.28	2009-02-12	✓
Debian 6.0	2.6.32	2010-01-22	✓
Fedora-8	2.6.23	2007-11-08	✓
Fedora-10	2.6.27	2008-11-25	✓
Fedora-12	2.6.31	2009-11-17	✓
Fedora-14	2.6.35	2010-11-02	✓
Fedora-16	3.1.0	2011-11-08	✓
OpenSUSE-10.3	2.6.22	2007-10-04	✓
OpenSUSE-11.0	2.6.25	2008-06-19	✓
OpenSUSE-11.1	2.6.27	2008-12-18	✓
OpenSUSE-11.2	2.6.31	2009-11-12	✓
OpenSUSE-11.3	2.6.34	2010-07-15	✓
OpenSUSE-12.1	3.1.0	2011-11-16	✓
Ubuntu-8.04	2.6.24	2008-04-24	✓
Ubuntu-8.10	2.6.27	2008-10-30	✓
Ubuntu-9.04	2.6.28	2009-04-23	✓
Ubuntu-9.10	2.6.31	2009-10-29	✓
Ubuntu-10.04	2.6.32	2010-04-29	✓
Ubuntu-10.10	2.6.35	2010-10-10	✓
Ubuntu-11.04	2.6.38	2011-04-28	✓
Ubuntu-11.10	3.0.4	2011-10-13	✓

Table 4. OS-Agnostic Testing of EXTERIOR.

dependence tracking and memory redirection is only active for some particular process in its particular syscall of interest. The LM-Bench does not contain any syscall context of our interest (introspection, configuration, and recovery), and these little performance slowdown actually comes from the check of the need of process context identification, the data dependence tracking, and memory redirection.

Macro Benchmarks We use the same set of effectiveness benchmarks in §5.1 to quantify the performance slowdown of our instrumentation. More specifically, we measure the performance of these 16 utilities in Table 1 by running each of them 100 times, and calculate the running time with Linux `time` command and report the average time.

The experimental result is reported in Fig. 5. We could see that our instrumentation has introduced 23X overhead on average compared with the programs running inside the OS. The major overhead comes from our dynamic dependence tracking in which we have to instrument all the data movement, data arithmetic instructions when running at kernel mode for a particular syscall of interest. Therefore, if a utility is syscall intensive, it tends to have larger overhead. For instance, there is a 37.5X overhead when running `kill`. Note that `kill` is interesting as it has to traverse kernel running list to find the target process (data redirection intensive) and then modify the `pending` field in the `task_struct`. While we have such large overhead, we have to emphasize that the absolute running time is small, which is only 1.83 seconds on average. Also, our SVM will not be used for any production runs and solely for EXTERIOR, such as serving as a web server.

5.3 Generality

While we have evaluated EXTERIOR with 16 native, trusted utilities to manage the guest-OS out-of-VM, we have not answered the question of how general our techniques are with respect to different kernels. To this end, we took 22 Linux distributions from four major vendors, and installed them on top of our SVM and GVM.

From our technical design, we have already noticed that EXTERIOR does not require both kernels to have the same configuration. To validate this, we explicitly configure each GVM with different physical memory size, and different kernel modules. Then we execute these 16 utilities to manage the GVM from SVM. As described in Table 4, our SVM directly supports running these kernels without any modification (transparent). Our explanation is static computer configurations are often stored in $\mathcal{D}_{kernel}^{global}$ and dynamic kernel modules are often stored in $\mathcal{D}_{kernel}^{heap}$. Our SVM just creates the skeleton execution context with the necessary binary as well as kernel code to execute the administration utilities of our

interest, and these redirected $\mathcal{D}_{kernel}^{global}$ and $\mathcal{D}_{kernel}^{heap}$ from GVM will be reflected in our SVM, and thus they can fulfill our introspection, configuration, and recovery tasks.

6. Limitations and Future Work

As we have demonstrated in §5, our EXTERIOR can be used for out-of-VM guest-OS introspection, (re)configuration, and recovery. In this section, we describe what EXTERIOR cannot do as well as our future work.

6.1 Limitations

From the technical point of view, for our EXTERIOR to succeed, we must require (1) the two kernels to have identical $\mathcal{D}_{kernel}^{global}$, (2) the identical instructions of the monitored syscall, (3) the monitored syscall will not be blocked, and (4) the monitored syscall only operates on memory data. Therefore, we cannot run arbitrary administration utilities and support arbitrary kernels.

More specifically, if two kernels have different $\mathcal{D}_{kernel}^{global}$, when we redirect the data access from SVM to GVM we will read different data. Consequently, it will not only impact $\mathcal{D}_{kernel}^{global}$, but also impact $\mathcal{D}_{kernel}^{heap}$ as $\mathcal{D}_{kernel}^{heap}$ is often dereferenced from $\mathcal{D}_{kernel}^{global}$. Therefore, if there is any address space randomization (e.g., [4, 49]) or data structure layout randomization [33] for $\mathcal{D}_{kernel}^{global}$, our current EXTERIOR cannot support this.

Meanwhile, if the monitored syscall has different instructions such as calling some additional functions in GVM kernel modules to fulfill certain tasks, but our SVM does not contain these modules, certainly EXTERIOR cannot support such syscalls. In addition, if the monitored syscall can be blocked, EXTERIOR will fail as well, because our SVM disables the context switch during the execution of the syscall of interest, and the monitored process cannot be woken up. Fortunately, all the 16 utilities we tested do not involve the execution of the syscall context to these execution states.

Finally, if the monitored syscall accesses disk data, EXTERIOR will fail because we do not transfer disk image from GVM to SVM.

Therefore, currently we do not support running any disk related utilities (e.g., `ls,fsck`). Also, the GVM kernel state should not be swapped to disk. For the Linux kernels, we confirmed from kernel source code that Linux kernel state will not be swapped.

6.2 Future Work

Dealing with Kernel ASLR EXTERIOR assumes there is no ASLR for kernel global variables. In fact, this is true for many OSes including all the available Linux kernels, and pre-Windows 7 kernels from Microsoft. Fortunately, we have an observation that for Windows 7 the randomization of kernel global variables is through a sliding window. That is, the relative offset between two global variables are not randomized. Thus, as long as we can align one of the kernel global variables, we shall be able to align all others. One of our future efforts will address this issue and enable EXTERIOR to support Microsoft Windows systems including kernel ASLR-enabled Windows 7.

Introducing Primitives for Synchronization EXTERIOR only supports the kernel state introspection, (re)configuration and recovery utilities, and our simple design is to *pause* the GVM execution when we update its kernel state. Therefore, we would like to transparently introduce lock primitives at the VMM layer to the kernel such that we can keep executing the GVM without pausing its execution.

In fact, we believe this is an interesting research problem, as essentially we are working on *a new system architecture that has multiple-CPUs where each has its own OS with the same version with others and they share the same kernel global and heap data*. For security reasons, the OS code and private kernel stack data for each CPU are isolated. We are realizing this architecture using a dual-VM approach. One of our future efforts will investigate other alternative approaches.

Handling Other Attacks Obviously, current EXTERIOR cannot recover the direct kernel object manipulation (DKOM) attack, and our MAKEUP tool for kernel pointer recovery does not check any pointers in kernel heap. Thus, part of our future work will investigate how to fix the kernel heap pointers.

Finally, our design assumes there is no virtualization based attacks to target either our SVM or GVM (such as Bluepill [45], SubVert [29], or DKSM [3]). Defending these virtualization based attacks is another venue of our future work.

7. Related Work

Virtual machine introspection (VMI) Our EXTERIOR is closely related to the VMI [15] in the sense that we all monitor the guest OS state at the outside VMM layer. Some of the VMI techniques only perform purely monitoring (i.e., *read-only*), such as Liveware [15], Antfarm [25], XenAccess [39], VMwatcher [24], Ether [11], Virtuoso [13], and VMST [14]. Some of them will take active actions once an attack is detected. For instance, IntroVirt [27] will execute the vulnerability-related predicates at VMM level to detect and respond to an intrusion, Lycosid [26] will patch the executable code to disable the malicious code execution once a hidden process is detected, and Manitou [35] will make a corrupted instruction page non-executable when the instruction page mismatches are detected.

Compared to all of these VMI techniques including the recent VMST [14], the key difference is: EXTERIOR for the first time enables an out-of-VM shell with a guest-OS writable and executable capability. Moreover, the writable is at the fine-grained memory cell level, and guided by the intrinsic constraints of the kernel code itself.

Intrusion Recovery To recover from attacks, a common approach is through monitoring and logging the behavior of intrusions to replay and restore the infected data. Such an approach has been recently instantiated to recovery from host intrusion (e.g., [23,

28]) or web applications (e.g, [6]), and repair malware damages (e.g., [38]). Unlike these techniques that must perform the logging and replay, EXTERIOR introduces a new technique to remediate the intrusions out-of-VM.

In general, EXTERIOR is also related to the system failure recovering [5], and system self-healing [36, 46], in that we all allow the system to keep running and we all are able to recover from attacks. The difference is EXTERIOR complements all of these existing techniques and exploits new dimensions from an out-of-VM perspective to recover from attacks.

Kernel Rootkit Defense Kernel-level rootkits are one of the biggest threats to the integrity of the modern OS. To detect their presence, a large number of techniques have been proposed, such as using a specification-based approach [22, 41, 42]), or VMI-based (e.g., [15, 24, 40]), or binary analysis-based [30], or using the signatures (e.g., field value invariants [12], or structural-invariants [34]). Meanwhile, as kernel hooks are directly related to the intrusions of kernel rootkits, there are also many techniques focusing on kernel hook identification [50] and protection [47], and profiling [31].

The substantial difference compared with these techniques is EXTERIOR not only focuses on the kernel rootkit detection by exploring new techniques such as our out-of-VM MAKEUP, but also introduces a new technique towards the recovery from a kernel rootkit attack.

8. Conclusion

We have presented EXTERIOR, a novel dual-VM based external *shell* for trusted, native, out-of-VM program execution for guest-OS administration including introspection, configuration, and recovery. The key idea is to leverage an identical trusted kernel with the guest-OS to create the necessary environment for a running process in a SVM, and dynamically and transparently redirect and update the memory at the VMM level to a GVM, thereby achieving the same effect in terms of kernel state updates of running a program inside a guest-OS. We have implemented EXTERIOR and demonstrated that EXTERIOR can be used for (automatic) introspection, (re)configuration of the guest-OS state (in the cloud), and can perform a timely response such as recovery from a kernel malware intrusion. In addition to the trustworthiness, higher privilege and stealthiness gained from out-of-VM, another distinctive feature of EXTERIOR is that it does not require any user account in the guest-OS to perform these tasks. Finally, we believe EXTERIOR has demonstrated a new program execution model on top of virtualization, and it will open new opportunities for system administration and security.

Acknowledgments

We would like to thank the anonymous reviewers for their insightful comments and suggestions. We are also grateful to Haibo Chen, Yuan Ding, Kenneth Miller, Richard Wartell, and Junyan Zeng for their invaluable feedback on an early draft of this paper. This research was supported in part by a AFOSR grant FA9550-12-1-0077 and a research grant from VMware Inc. Any opinions, findings, conclusions, or recommendations expressed are those of the authors and not necessarily of the AFOSR and VMware.

References

[1] QEMU: an open source processor emulator. *http://www.qemu.org/*.

[2] Vprobe toolkit. https://github.com/vmware/vprobe-toolkit

[3] S. Bahram, X. Jiang, Z. Wang, M. Grace, J. Li, D. Srinivasan, J. Rhee, and D. Xu. Dksm: Subverting virtual machine introspection for fun and profit. In *The 29th IEEE Symposium on Reliable Distributed Systems*, 2010.

[4] E. Bhatkar, D. C. Duvarney, and R. Sekar. Address obfuscation: an efficient approach to combat a broad range of memory error exploits. In *Proceedings of the 12th USENIX Security Symposium*, pages 105–120, 2003.

[5] A. B. Brown and D. A. Patterson. Undo for operators: building an undoable e-mail store. In *Proceedings of the annual conference on USENIX Annual Technical Conference*, San Antonio, Texas, 2003.

[6] R. Chandra, T. Kim, M. Shah, N. Narula, and N. Zeldovich. Intrusion recovery for database-backed web applications. In *Proceedings of the Twenty-Third ACM Symposium on Operating Systems Principles*, SOSP '11, pages 101–114, Cascais, Portugal, 2011. ACM. ISBN 978-1-4503-0977-6.

[7] P. M. Chen and B. D. Noble. When virtual is better than real. In *Proceedings of the Eighth Workshop on Hot Topics in Operating Systems (HOTOS'01)*, page 133, Washington, DC, USA, 2001. IEEE Computer Society.

[8] X. Chen, T. Garfinkel, E. C. Lewis, P. Subrahmanyam, C. A. Waldspurger, D. Boneh, J. Dwoskin, and D. R. Ports. Overshadow: a virtualization-based approach to retrofitting protection in commodity operating systems. In *Proceedings of the 13th international conference on Architectural support for programming languages and operating systems*, ASPLOS XIII, pages 2–13, Seattle, WA, USA, 2008. ACM.

[9] J. Chow, B. Pfaff, K. Christopher, and M. Rosenblum. Understanding data lifetime via whole-system simulation. In *Proceedings of the 13th USENIX Security Symposium*, 2004.

[10] C. Clark, K. Fraser, S. Hand, J. G. Hansen, E. Jul, C. Limpach, I. Pratt, and A. Warfield. Live migration of virtual machines. In *Proceedings of the 2nd conference on Symposium on Networked Systems Design & Implementation - Volume 2*, NSDI'05, pages 273–286. USENIX Association, 2005.

[11] A. Dinaburg, P. Royal, M. Sharif, and W. Lee. Ether: malware analysis via hardware virtualization extensions. In *Proceedings of the 15th ACM conference on Computer and communications security (CCS'08)*, pages 51–62, Alexandria, Virginia, USA, 2008. ISBN 978-1-59593-810-7.

[12] B. Dolan-Gavitt, A. Srivastava, P. Traynor, and J. Giffin. Robust signatures for kernel data structures. In *Proceedings of the 16th ACM Conference on Computer and Communications Security (CCS'09)*, pages 566–577, Chicago, Illinois, USA, 2009. ACM. ISBN 978-1-60558-894-0.

[13] B. Dolan-Gavitt, T. Leek, M. Zhivich, J. Giffin, and W. Lee. Virtuoso: Narrowing the semantic gap in virtual machine introspection. In *Proceedings of the 32nd IEEE Symposium on Security and Privacy*, pages 297–312, Oakland, CA, USA, 2011.

[14] Y. Fu and Z. Lin. Space traveling across vm: Automatically bridging the semantic gap in virtual machine introspection via online kernel data redirection. In *Proceedings of 33rd IEEE Symposium on Security and Privacy*, May 2012.

[15] T. Garfinkel and M. Rosenblum. A virtual machine introspection based architecture for intrusion detection. In *Proceedings Network and Distributed Systems Security Symposium (NDSS'03)*, February 2003.

[16] T. Garfinkel, B. Pfaff, J. Chow, M. Rosenblum, and D. Boneh. Terra: a virtual machine-based platform for trusted computing. In *Proceedings of the nineteenth ACM symposium on Operating systems principles*, SOSP '03, pages 193–206, Bolton Landing, NY, USA, 2003. ACM. ISBN 1-58113-757-5.

[17] T. Garfinkel, K. Adams, A. Warfield, and J. Franklin. Compatibility is Not Transparency: VMM Detection Myths and Realities. In *Proceedings of the 11th Workshop on Hot Topics in Operating Systems (HotOS-XI)*, May 2007.

[18] R. P. Goldberg. Architectural principles of virtual machines. PhD thesis, Harvard University. 1972.

[19] R. P. Goldberg. Survey of Virtual Machine Research. *IEEE Computer Magazine*, pages 34–45, June 1974.

[20] Y. Gu, Y. Fu, A. Prakash, Z. Lin, and H. Yin. Os-sommelier: Memory-only operating system fingerprinting in the cloud. In *Proceedings of the 3rd ACM Symposium on Cloud Computing (SOCC'12)*, San Jose, CA, October 2012.

[21] Z. Gu, Z. Deng, D. Xu, and X. Jiang. Process implanting: A new active introspection framework for virtualization. In *Proceedings of the 30th IEEE Symposium on Reliable Distributed Systems (SRDS 2011)*, pages 147–156, Madrid, Spain, October 4-7, 2011.

[22] O. S. Hofmann, A. M. Dunn, S. Kim, I. Roy, and E. Witchel. Ensuring operating system kernel integrity with osck. In *Proceedings of the sixteenth international conference on Architectural support for programming languages and operating systems*, ASPLOS '11, pages 279–290, Newport Beach, California, USA, 2011. ISBN 978-1-4503-0266-1.

[23] F. Hsu, H. Chen, T. Ristenpart, J. Li, and Z. Su. Back to the future: A framework for automatic malware removal and system repair. In *Proceedings of the 22nd Annual Computer Security Applications Conference*, pages 257–268, 2006. ISBN 0-7695-2716-7.

[24] X. Jiang, X. Wang, and D. Xu. Stealthy malware detection through vmm-based out-of-the-box semantic view reconstruction. In *Proceedings of the 14th ACM Conference on Computer and Communications Security (CCS'07)*, pages 128–138, Alexandria, Virginia, USA, 2007. ACM. ISBN 978-1-59593-703-2.

[25] S. T. Jones, A. C. Arpaci-Dusseau, and R. H. Arpaci-Dusseau. Antfarm: tracking processes in a virtual machine environment. In *Proceedings of the annual conference on USENIX '06 Annual Technical Conference*, Boston, MA, 2006. USENIX Association.

[26] S. T. Jones, A. C. Arpaci-Dusseau, and R. H. Arpaci-Dusseau. Vmm-based hidden process detection and identification using lycosid. In *Proceedings of the fourth ACM SIGPLAN/SIGOPS international conference on Virtual execution environments*, VEE '08, pages 91–100, Seattle, WA, USA, 2008. ACM. ISBN 978-1-59593-796-4.

[27] A. Joshi, S. T. King, G. W. Dunlap, and P. M. Chen. Detecting past and present intrusions through vulnerability-specific predicates. In *Proceedings of the twentieth ACM symposium on Operating systems principles (SOSP'05)*, pages 91–104, Brighton, United Kingdom, 2005. ISBN 1-59593-079-5.

[28] T. Kim, X. Wang, N. Zeldovich, and M. F. Kaashoek. Intrusion recovery using selective re-execution. In *Proceedings of the 9th USENIX conference on Operating systems design and implementation*, OSDI'10, Vancouver, BC, Canada, 2010. USENIX Association.

[29] S. T. King, P. M. Chen, Y.-M. Wang, C. Verbowski, H. J. Wang, and J. R. Lorch. Subvirt: Implementing malware with virtual machines. In *Proceedings of the 2006 IEEE Symposium on Security and Privacy*, pages 314–327, 2006. ISBN 0-7695-2574-1.

[30] C. Kruegel, W. Robertson, and G. Vigna. Detecting kernel-level rootkits through binary analysis. In *Proceedings of the 20th Annual Computer Security Applications Conference(ACSAC'04)*, pages 91–100, 2004. ISBN 0-7695-2252-1.

[31] A. Lanzi, M. I. Sharif, and W. Lee. K-tracer: A system for extracting kernel malware behavior. In *Proceedings of the 2009 Network and Distributed System Security Symposium, San Diego, California, USA,*, 2009.

[32] Z. Lin, X. Jiang, D. Xu, and X. Zhang. Automatic protocol format reverse engineering through context-aware monitored execution. In *Proceedings of the 15th Annual Network and Distributed System Security Symposium (NDSS'08)*, San Diego, CA, February 2008.

[33] Z. Lin, R. D. Riley, and D. Xu. Polymorphing software by randomizing data structure layout. In *Proceedings of the 6th SIG SIDAR Conference on Detection of Intrusions and Malware and Vulnerability Assessment (DIMVA'09)*, Milan, Italy, July 2009.

[34] Z. Lin, J. Rhee, X. Zhang, D. Xu, and X. Jiang. Siggraph: Brute force scanning of kernel data structure instances using graph-based signatures. In *Proceedings of the 18th Annual Network and Distributed System Security Symposium (NDSS'11)*, San Diego, CA, February 2011.

[35] L. Litty and D. Lie. Manitou: a layer-below approach to fighting malware. In *Proceedings of the 1st workshop on Architectural and*

system support for improving software dependability, ASID '06, pages 6–11, San Jose, California, 2006. ISBN 1-59593-576-2.

[36] M. E. Locasto, S. Sidiroglou, and A. D. Keromytis. Software self-healing using collaborative application communities. In *In Proceedings of Network and Distributed Systems Security Symposium*, pages 95–106, 2006.

[37] J. Newsome and D. Song. Dynamic taint analysis for automatic detection, analysis, and signature generation of exploits on commodity software. In *Proceedings of the 14th Annual Network and Distributed System Security Symposium (NDSS'05)*, San Diego, CA, February 2005.

[38] R. Paleari, L. Martignoni, E. Passerini, D. Davidson, M. Fredrikson, J. Giffin, and S. Jha. Automatic generation of remediation procedures for malware infections. In *Proceedings of the 19th USENIX conference on Security*, USENIX Security'10, Washington, DC, 2010. ISBN 888-7-6666-5555-4.

[39] B. D. Payne, M. Carbone, and W. Lee. Secure and flexible monitoring of virtual machines. In *Proceedings of the 23rd Annual Computer Security Applications Conference (ACSAC 2007)*, December 2007.

[40] B. D. Payne, M. Carbone, M. I. Sharif, and W. Lee. Lares: An architecture for secure active monitoring using virtualization. In *Proceedings of 2008 IEEE Symposium on Security and Privacy*, pages 233–247, Oakland, CA, May 2008.

[41] N. L. Petroni, Jr., T. Fraser, J. Molina, and W. A. Arbaugh. Copilot - A coprocessor-based kernel runtime integrity monitor. In *Proceedings of the 13th USENIX Security Symposium*, pages 179–194, San Diego, CA, August 2004.

[42] N. L. Petroni, Jr., T. Fraser, A. Walters, and W. A. Arbaugh. An architecture for specification-based detection of semantic integrity violations in kernel dynamic data. In *Proceedings of the 15th USENIX Security Symposium*, Vancouver, B.C., Canada, August 2006. USENIX Association.

[43] N. L. Petroni, Jr. and M. Hicks. Automated detection of persistent kernel control-flow attacks. In *Proceedings of the 14th ACM Conference on Computer and Communications Security (CCS'07)*, pages 103–115,

Alexandria, Virginia, USA, October 2007. ACM. ISBN 978-1-59593-703-2.

[44] N. A. Quynh. Operating system fingerprinting for virtual machines, 2010. In DEFCON 18.

[45] J. Rutkowska. Introducing blue pill, June 2006. http://theinvisiblethings.blogspot.com/2006/06/introducing-blue-pill.html.

[46] S. Sidiroglou, O. Laadan, C. Perez, N. Viennot, J. Nieh, and A. D. Keromytis. Assure: automatic software self-healing using rescue points. In *Proceedings of the 14th international conference on Architectural support for programming languages and operating systems*, ASPLOS '09, pages 37–48, Washington, DC, USA, 2009. ISBN 978-1-60558-406-5.

[47] Z. Wang, X. Jiang, W. Cui, and P. Ning. Countering kernel rootkits with lightweight hook protection. In *Proceedings of the 16th ACM conference on Computer and communications security*, CCS '09, pages 545–554, Chicago, Illinois, USA, 2009. ISBN 978-1-60558-894-0.

[48] A. Whitaker, M. Shaw, and S. D. Gribble. Scale and performance in the denali isolation kernel. In *Proceedings of the 5th symposium on Operating systems design and implementation*, OSDI '02, pages 195–209, Boston, Massachusetts, 2002. ACM. ISBN 978-1-4503-0111-4.

[49] J. Xu, Z. Kalbarczyk, and R. K. Iyer. Transparent runtime randomization for security. In *Proceedings of the 22nd International Symposium on Reliable Distributed Systems (SRDS'03)*, pages 260–269. IEEE Computer Society, 2003.

[50] H. Yin, Z. Liang, and D. Song. Hookfinder: Identifying and understanding malware hooking behaviors. In *Proceedings of the Network and Distributed System Security Symposium*, 2008.

[51] F. Zhang, J. Chen, H. Chen, and B. Zang. Cloudvisor: retrofitting protection of virtual machines in multi-tenant cloud with nested virtualization. In *Proceedings of the Twenty-Third ACM Symposium on Operating Systems Principles*, SOSP '11, pages 203–216, Cascais, Portugal, 2011. ACM. ISBN 978-1-4503-0977-6.

A Lightweight VMM on Many Core
for High Performance Computing

Yuehua Dai   Yong Qi   Jianbao Ren   Yi Shi   Xiaoguang Wang   Xuan Yu

Xi'an Jiaotong University, China

xjtudso@gmail.com, {qiy, shiyi}@mail.xjtu.edu.cn

Abstract

Traditional Virtual Machine Monitor (VMM) virtualizes some devices and instructions, which induces performance overhead to guest operating systems. Furthermore, the virtualization contributes a large amount of codes to VMM, which makes a VMM prone to bugs and vulnerabilities.

On the other hand, in cloud computing, cloud service provider configures virtual machines based on requirements which are specified by customers in advance. As resources in a multi-core server increase to more than adequate in the future, virtualization is not necessary although it provides convenience for cloud computing. Based on the above observations, this paper presents an alternative way for constructing a VMM: configuring a booting interface instead of virtualization technology. A lightweight virtual machine monitor - OSV is proposed based on this idea. OSV can host multiple full functional Linux kernels with little performance overhead. There are only 6 hyper-calls in OSV. The Linux running on top of OSV is intercepted only for the inter-processor interrupts. The resource isolation is implemented with hardware-assist virtualization. The resource sharing is controlled by distributed protocols embedded in current operating systems.

We implement a prototype of OSV on AMD Opteron processor based 32-core servers with SVM and cache-coherent NUMA architectures. OSV can host up to 8 Linux kernels on the server with less than 10 lines of code modifications to Linux kernel. OSV has about 8000 lines of code which can be easily tuned and debugged. The experiment results show that OSV VMM has 23.7% performance improvement compared with Xen VMM.

Categories and Subject Descriptors   D.4.0 [*Operating System*]: General;   D.4.8 [*Operating System*]: Performance

General Terms   Design, Measurement, Performance

Keywords   Multi-core, Cloud Computing, Virtualization, Hardware Assist Virtualization

1. Introduction

Multi-core processors are default for nowadays servers. Modern servers are configured with more and more cores and RAM [5]. In the future, the cores in a die will double steadily [17]. Based on this

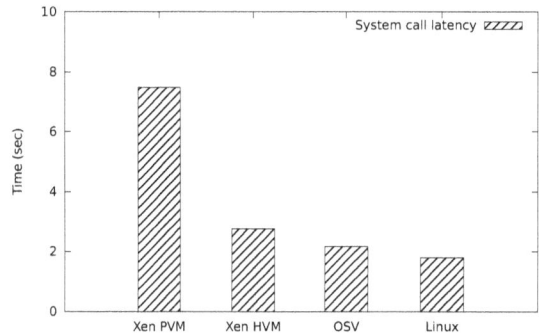

Figure 1. System call benchmark for native x86_64 Linux and Linux on Xen. The benchmark creates a socket by calling the socket system call, and then close the socket by calling system call of close on a AMD 32-core server. The time measured is the total time of calling the socket and close pair 1 million times. The para-virtualized Linux on Xen has the most significant latency. For x86_64 Linux, the system call is issued by *syscall* instruction, which is intercepted by Xen for para-virtualized Linux to prepare a faked system call frame for the guest Linux. The *syscall* instruction is not intercepted by HVM Xen which is based on AMD SVM technology, the performance overhead is mainly caused by the memory access overhead.

observation, in this paper, we introduce a new lightweight VMM architecture for future servers with redundant computing resources (CPU cores and RAM). The new architecture reduces performance overhead induced by traditional virtualization technology and also makes the VMM more reliable.

With the support of the virtualization, a server with limited resources can host multiple operating systems with good isolation. These operating systems can share same CPU core and RAM. The VMM dynamically schedules these operating systems based on their states, idle or active. However, the virtualization technology in traditional VMM also induces performance overhead to guest operating systems [8]. The virtualization of instructions, memory operations and emulation of devices are sources of the performance overhead. For different virtualization technologies, performance overhead is different. Figure 1 shows the total time of socket and close system calls. In this micro benchmark, a socket is created by *socket* system call and immediately closed by *close* system call. Total time of calling this system call pair 1 million times is measured. Para-virtualized Linux has the most significant latency. The interception operations for *syscall* instruction of Xen mainly contribute to the performance overhead. HVM Xen in this paper is based on AMD'SVM technology [6]. In HVM Xen, the *syscall* instruction

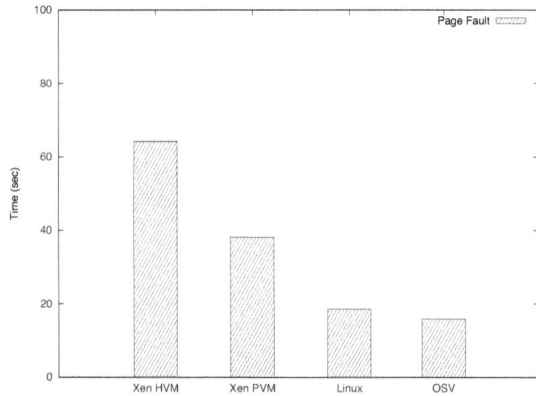

Figure 2. Memory management micro benchmark for native x86_64 Linux and Linux on Xen. Two threads allocate a 4KB page using *malloc*, then the page causing a page fault. The time measured is the total time of 1 million times. The HVM-Linux on Xen has the most significant latency. For x86_64 Linux, an extra nested page fault contributes to the latency. For para-virtualized Linux, the page is managed by the shadow page table, which is slower than native Linux. For OSV, the NUMA resource allocation makes it the low latency.

is not intercepted by Xen. The virtualization also contributes to the overhead of page fault handler of Linux. Figure 2 shows the total time of two threads touching 1GB memory in a 4KB page size fashion. The time for HVM Linux is larger than para-virtualized and native Linux. The extra time of HVM Linux is induced by nested page handler of Xen.

Virtualization layer is quite complex and makes whole VMM prone to bugs and security problems. For example, Xen has about 200K lines of code in the hypervisor itself, and over 1M in the host OS [19]. Some vulnerabilities and bugs in Xen have been reported [1–4]. Malicious users can attack Xen through these vulnerabilities, and take control over the whole system.

Nowadays, more and more companies are adopting VMM for their computing resource management. In a company, the employees are provided with thin computer clients which are connected to remote virtual machines allocated by VMM. The number of employees doesn't change so much in a period. The performance of virtual machines will affect efficience of employees. In this senario, virtualization provides convenience but is not necessary.

Besides, modern operating systems are capable of distributed services,for example, networked file system (NFS). Some devices can be exported as a service and shared by other operating system through standard distributed protocols. So, in a VMM, all devices can be managed by a privileged guest. The guest then exports these devices as a service to other guests through existing distributed protocols. In this way, devices can be shared between guest OS without virtualization. This can significantly simplify the VMM.

OSV is guided by the principle that guest operating systems should run directly on the server without the interceptions of VMM. This principle has two implications. First, the VMM should isolate operating systems from each other. Second, guest operating system manages its CPU core and RAM itself. The intended result is that CPU cores and RAM are not shared by guest operating systems. This limits the number of guest operating systems running on a server. However, as the number of CPU cores and RAM in a server increases, this is reasonable.

In this paper, we present an alternative approach - OSV, a light weight VMM, for constructing the VMM for these computers with

number of cores. Rather than virtualizing resources in the computer, OSV only virtualizes the multiprocessor and memory configuration interfaces. Operating systems access the resources allocated by OSV directly without the intervention of the VMM, and OSV just controls which part of the resources are accessible to an operating system. OSV VMM also allows the operating systems to cooperate and share resources with each other, which makes the many core servers become a distributed system and keeps compatible with current computing base.The resulting system contains most of the features of traditional VMM, but with only a fraction of their complexity and implementation cost. This is quite suitable for the cloud computing.

In section 2, we provide our motivation for the OSV. Section 3 describes the design principles of OSV, while section 4 details the implementation. Section 5 evaluates the OSV and shows the experimental results. Section 6 summarizes related work. Limitations of OSV are discussed in section 7 and conclusion is given in section 8.

2. Motivation

The main goal of OSV is to simplify the design and implementation effort for constructing a VMM on multi-core servers. This section details why the design for OSV is reasonable on multi-core servers.

Virtual Machine Monitor(VMM) is prevalent in Cloud-Computing. By running numbers of operating systems concurrently, a single computer can satisfy various needs of applications at the same time, which makes the hardware running more efficient and reduces the hardware cost. Despite the convenience mentioned above, the VMM also incurs performance overhead. Performance overhead is varied with the types of application [8, 27]. The performance overhead is mainly caused by the virtualization of hardware resources and dynamic resource schedule policy. Virtualization and dynamic resource schedule are needed by a traditional VMM. This is because there are limited hardware resources in a computer such as CPUs, DRAM, I/O devices, etc, while operating systems use these resources in an exclusive fashion. Traditional VMM uses a privileged operating system to manage all the hardware resources. Other operating systems access the hardware resources through the privileged OS. In order to manage the hardware resources more efficiently, the VMM is becoming more and more complex.

In order to run the operating systems concurrently, traditional VMM must schedules the operating systems to make each operating system have the chance to get the CPU and do not conflict with each other, when there are a limited number of CPUs in a computer. The scheduler and virtualization are harmful to the system's performance and contribute large number of codes to VMM. For example, for a null system call the para-virtualized Linux one Xen needs 1042 cycles for an entry to the kernel and 476 cycles for returning to user space, while it is 148 and 134 cycles for the native Linux. That's why system call in PV guest is slow. On the other hand, as the number of cores and the amount of DRAM in a computer increase, the requirements for virtualizing the CPU and dram are not necessary. The maximum resources used by an operating system in a virtual machine is specified in a configuration file and is fixed when been created. The virtualization layer dynamically allocates the actual amount of physical resources to a virtual machine. For future multi-core servers, the physical resources is sufficient to fulfill all the guest operating systems. So, each guest operating system can be statically allocated with the amount of CPU cores and RAM as the configuration file specified.

The main functions of the virtualization layer are arbitrating access to memory, CPU, and devices, providing important network functionality, and controlling the execution of virtual machines [19]. Based on the cloud computing model and the major functions of VMM, using the static resource allocation policy is reasonable [24].

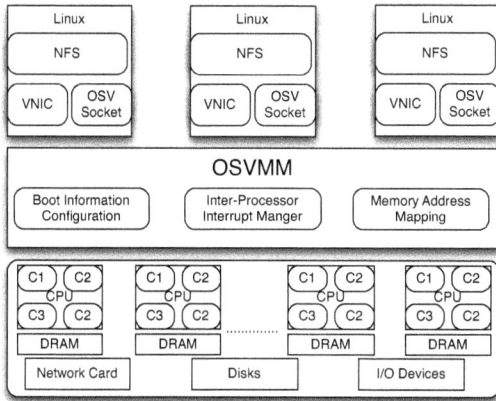

Figure 3. The architecture of OSV Kernel.

3. Design

The VMM poses several challenges for partitioning of a machine to support the concurrent execution of multiple operating systems. The most important one is that virtual machines must be isolated from each other. In a traditional VMM, VMM virtualizes or para-virtualizes the limited resources in a computer to isolate the virtual machines from affecting each other, but at the cost of increased complexity and reduced performance. This section details the design principle of OSV VMM. The intent is that the design principal will improve the guest operating systems' performance and simplify the VMM. The overall architecture of OSV kernel is shown in Figure 3.

3.1 CPU Cores

The architecture for future computers is far from clear, but the trend of increasing amounts for both cores and DRAM is evident. Commodity VMM virtualizes the CPUs and DRAM to run as many virtual machines as possible. This induces the performance overhead. We provide the virtual machines with physical CPU cores and DRAM without virtualization in OSV VMM. Each operating system running in a virtual machine manages the physical cores and DRAM itself without the intervention of the VMM. The operating system can only access the physical resources allocated to the virtual machine. The policy for CPU cores and DRAM allocated to a virtual machine is based on their NUMA node affinity. All of these approaches can promise the performance of the operating system.

The isolation for CPU cores between each virtual machine is guided by modifying the computers's processor information table such as ACPI or Multi-processor configuration table for Intel's Specification. OSV VMM masks processor entries in the table for the CPU cores not belonging to the virtual machine as unusable, which makes the operating system ignore these cores during booting period. The CPU cores allocated to the virtual machine are all in a NUMA node. By using the faked information, operating systems will only access the processors allocated to it. In the other hand, the VMM must guard all the procedure of SMP-booting, because the processors may be reset by the booting signal. The current implementation of OSV emulates the Intel's multi-processor specification [18] for SMP booting. The inter-processor interrupt(IPI) is widely used in the commodity operating system. When the IPI is issued by using the logical ID for a processor, the CPU cores in other virtual machines with the same logical ID will also get reaction to the IPI which will cause the virtual machine to break down. When the operating system initializes the CPU information and updates the APIC value, the VMM catches these updates and stores

the corresponding physical ID for the logical ID of the CPU core. When sending the IPI, the VMM gets the physical ID from previous stored information and replaces the logical ID for sending the IPI. These operations need some minor changes to the source code of the operating system, for Linux, this just five lines of c code with inlined asm code. As the OS manages the processors itself, there is no need for OSV to intercept some privileged instructions such as *syscall* which improves the system call performance of the OS. The implementation details will be discussed in section 4.1.

3.2 Main Memory

The amounts of physical maim memory allocated to a virtual machine are as many as it requires. In this way, VMM can promise the performance of operating system. This approach requires more memory which can be easily satisfied by current servers. Traditional VMM uses a shadow page table to maintain the memory ranges accessed by an operating system. Furthermore, a VMM page fault handler for processing a physical page frame request from operating system should be provided. All of the above increase the complexity of traditional VMM and decrease the performance of operating system. Allocating as many amounts of physical meoroy to an operating system as it declares can avoid page faults in the VMM. This can improve the performance of the operating system and reduces the code size of VMM. Also, the operating system can access the main memory with real physical address which is helpful for DMA operations. When a device submit a DMA operation, it will use the exact page physical address to exchange the data. This can reduce the overhead of VMM for guaranteeing the isolation of the device operation in each operating system.

3.3 Devices

VMM nowadays is used to provide multiple special services in a server by running multi customized operating system instances. In this scenario, disks and network cards are the most used devices. In OSV, all devices are allocated to a privileged operating system. The I/O interrupts are all processed by it. The timer interrupt is forwarded to other virtual machines by sending an IPI to a CPU core of the virtual machine. Operating systems running on other virtual machines can share these devices via services exported through standard distributed protocol. There is a NFS server in the privileged operating system. All other virtual machines access the file systems via a NFS client which is widely used in nowadays commodity operating systems. All the file accesses are synchronized by the NFS protocol. There is no need for the guarantees of the VMM, which reduces the complexity of the VMM and improves the performance.

3.4 Virtual Network Interface

In order to allow the virtual machines to communicate each other, virtual network interfaces are provided by the VMM. The virtual machines can communicate with each other using standard distributed protocols over the virtual network interface. For example, the virtual machines share file through NFS. By the virtual network interface, traditional distributed protocol based applications can run on OSV VMM without code modification. This can keep compatible with current computing base.

There is a virtual network interface card(VNIC) for each virtual domain. Each VNIC has a private memory queue for receiving data packets. When the network code of the operating system submits a packet to the VNIC, the packet will be forwarded to the corresponding memory queue of the VNIC whose hardware address matches the packet's destination. When receiving a packet, the VNIC passes the packet to the network stack code. These memory operations for processing the packet are all done by the operating system without the interception of the VMM, which can increase the performance of the network stack. VNIC is provided as a driver module which can be installed in Linux without modifying Linux's source code.

3.5 Inter-OS Communication Socket

The performance of inter-OS communication via virtual network interface is limited by Linux's TCP/IP network stack. In order to increase the performance, a UNIX IPC like socket has been provided by the OSV. The API is the same as UNIX IPC socket. When creating a socket, one just needs to specify the socket type to OSV type. Then traditional socket functions such as listen, accept, send and so on are used to send and receive data. The data transmission mechanism is similar to virtual network interface: there is a memory queue for each virtual machine, each data packet is placed into proper queue by the destination virtual machine ID and the port. The memory operations are like the virtual network interface all done by operating systems which need not trap into the VMM.

As VNIC mentioned in 3.4, OSV socket is also a driver module installed in guest OS. Extra head files for C programmes are also provided. Applications with source code can be easily ported to this socket. By changing the socket type to OSV and using OSV defined address spaces, applications can communicate across guests via OSV socket. This is helpful for applications which are sensitive to the communication bandwidth.

3.6 Hypervisor Call

The design principle for the OSV kernel is that VMM restricts resource ranges accessed by operating system and lets the operating system to make the decision of resource usage. This principle reduces the interface complexity between operating system and VMM. In OSV VMM, it has only two types of hyper-call: resource access restrict functions and communication channel construction functions.

The resource restrict functions are used to isolate the resources allocated to each virtual machine and synchronize the accesses to shared resources. The resources are such as I/O devices, Local APIC, I/O APIC and so on. The later type of functions are used by the communication between operating systems. When two operating systems need to communicate with other, one operating system calls the function with the arguments of physical address of allocated memory and the two virtual machines ID pair, then the other operating system traps into the virtual machine to get the memory address with the ID pair. The shared memory and ID pair compose the communication channel. The memory queues for virtual network interface and inter-OS communication socket are constructed using these functions. The trap into VMM is only needed when the construction of the communication which can improve the performance of the communication and also reduce the complexity of OSV VMM.

3.7 Virtual Machine Construction

A virtual machine instance contains physical processor cores and main memory. Each virtual machine has statically allocated amounts of processor cores and main memory which can not be changed when constructed. The resources are allocated based on their NUMA node affinity. The main memory allocated are in the same NUMA domain with the processor cores which can reduce the memory access time. The I/O devices are only allocated to the privileged domain. Other domains can access the services provided by these devices through standard distributed services exported by the privileged domain. The OS image and its drivers are loaded into main memory when the system is booting.

The resources needed by a domain are preallocated before they are booted. A domain is created when the system load is high. The virtual machine instance is created by issuing a hypervisor call in privileged domain. When the virtual machine is booted, the tasks can be submitted to it using standard distributed protocols.

3.8 Isolation Between Guests

CPU cores and memory are preallocated to a guest OS. Guest OS initialises its internal structures based on these resources. So resources out of this range will not be accessed by the guest OS. OSV should control devices and interrupts to avoid guest OS interfering with each other.

For devices as described in previous section 3.3, all devices are allocated to a privileged operating system. So, interrupts from devices are not intercepted by OSV. The only thing OSV to do is to control port operations to avoid error states, such as reboot or reset operations. If a guest OS attempts to write a port, it will trap into OSV. OSV analyzes this operation to detect abnormal states, such as reboot operation, etc. If a reboot operation is found, OSV only reboots the corresponding guest OS not the computer. Operations which cause the server crash are denied by OSV.

IPI is a special interrupt used by operating system. OSV intercepts IPI to avoid a guest OS sending IPI to other guests. A miss-sending IPI will corrupt other guests. Based on these mechanisms, although there is no virtualization layer in OSV, guest OS can be well isolated from each other in OSV.

3.9 Application Programme Framework

A many core server running with OSV VMM is more like a distributed system. A map-reduce programming framework is provided in OSV. Applications written with the programming framework provided by the OSV are distributed among the OSes. The applications are submitted in the manager OS, and the results are also resembled in it. The framework is implemented on top of the OSV socket which can provides good performance.

4. Implementation

OSV VMM is implemented as a multithreaded program running on multi-core processor based servers. OSV differs from existing systems in that it pays more attention to the resources isolation rather than virtualize these resources. For example, OSV does not contain any structure to virtual the processor cores and main memory. The code size for OSV is about 8,000 lines of code which make it easier for tuning. The current implementation is based on AMD Opteron processors with SVM technology support and can run multiple Linux operating systems concurrently. The table 1 lists the approaches used by OSV to host multiple operating systems.

4.1 Multi-Processor Support

In order to support commodity SMP operating systems, traditional VMM needs a virtual CPU struct to provide IPI and schedules the mapping for the virtual CPUs and physical cores. In OSV, operating systems use physical CPUs directly. There are two challenges:

Multi-Processor Boot x86 based multi-processor systems are booted using universal SMP boot protocol. This protocol is to send two init inter-processor interrupts to the processor core. The init IPI will cause the processor to reset and jump to a specified location to execute. The reset action will make the processor's all the states be cleared including the registers initialized by the OSV. This will make OSV lose the control of CPU cores.

Inter-Processor Interrupt Traditional operating systems need the IPI to synchronize the system state and specify jobs for a CPU. Some IPIs are sent in logical destination mode which causes the CPU cores with the same logical id in other operating system making reaction to the IPI. This will lead the system to a unstable state.

Main Memory	
NUMA nodes	Each operating system can access the DRAM belongs to a NUMA node. The DRAM in other nodes are invisible to the OS. This is initialized in the E820 ram map.
Paging	For the privileged operating system, it works the same as in a bare metal. Other operating systems are controlled by a ncr3 register in AMD processors. Page size used in nested page table is splited, for low address 4KB size is used while 1GB for high address
Processor cores	
Multi processor	The processor cores allocates to an OS is in a NUMA node fashion. The cores in a NUMA node are allocated to an OS, which can reduce the remote cache access. The multi processor boot interrupt is redirected to a SX exception.
Interrupt	All the I/O interrupts are delivered to the privileged OS. Other OSes access the I/O through distributed protocols.
Timer	The external timer interrupt is dispatched by the privileged OS through the IPI.
Disks and I/O Devices	
Network Interface card	All the network cards are controlled by the privileged OS. An virtual network card is provided to other OS.
Disks, etc	These devices are exported as services by the privileged OS to other OS, which can be accessed through standard distributed protocols.

Table 1. The approaches for OSV to control resources for operating system

For the first one, we redirect the init interrupt to a Security Exception which will be caught by OSV VMM. In this way, the processor core can avoid being reset. When OSV catches the init IPI, OSV initialises the guest CPU mode to 16bit mode and gets the start code ip address for CPUs to execute after the init interrupt and redirects the CPU to this instruction when it returns from the VMM. The CPU will do as the traditional multiboot protocol does except for the reset action. The start code ip address is stored by Linux kernel which is 0x467. This address is specified by multiboot specification. Current implementation of OSV is some tricky and hardly dependable for the AMD processors. Because init IPI redirection is based on the AMD's SVM technology. Modifying the source code of the OS is another way to support the multi-processor booting. The SMP-booting code is not so complex and irrelative for the performance of OS. For example, the SMP-booting code for Linux is all located in a C file. The modifications to the source code is less than 10 lines of c code, including init IPI sending functions and some port operations. This can make the VMM more portable.

For Inter-Processor Interrupts, some minor code modification should be made to operating systems as mentioned in section 3.1. OSV catches writes to some APIC registers. Normal APIC register operations are not intercepted by the OSV kernel except for IPI related registers. These registers are 0xD0 (Logical Destination Register) and 0x300 (Interrupt Command Register Low). OSV distinguishes logical and physical IPI destination mode through the APIC register 0x300. For physical mode, OSV lets it as the normal operating system does, while for logical mode, the kernel replaces the logical destination id with corresponding physical id and send the IPI with physical mode. The physical id for each CPU is unique which avoids CPUs in a domain making reaction to other domains IPI. This is lightweight compared with traditional VMM. The extra overhead for the APIC register interception is about 120-170 cycles for our servers. Compared to the latency of IPI interrupts, this is not critical to operating systems' performance.

4.2 OSV Socket

In cloud computing, operating systems running on a VMM communicate with each other frequently. They can communicate with each other through traditional network. In OSV, a socket is provided for improve the communication performance between operating systems running on OSV. The socket is UNIX IPC like. The data transfer between operating systems can be done without the intervention of the OSV kernel. This is about the implementation

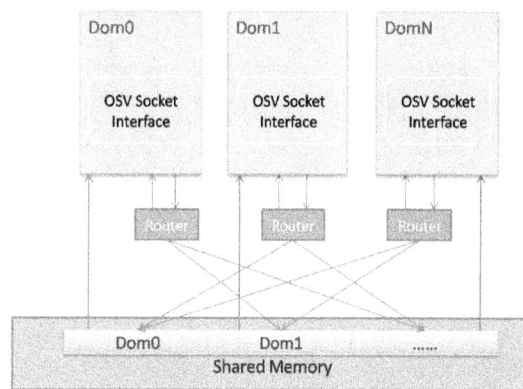

Figure 4. Structure for OSV socket.

of the osv-protocol. This protocol is based on shared memory and implements the Berkeley Sockets interface. Programmer could use this protocol as normal inet. Each domain in our OSV kernel is addressed by IP , and each program in a domain is distinguished by a access point, a port number. Figure 4 shows the overall structure of OSV socket.

There is only one receive buffer in each domain and one work queue is responsible for scanning the buffer periodically. In order to make domains be able to put message into each other's buffer, the kernel allocates the receive buffer in initialization and returns each buffer's physical address. For a socket, it has a buffer list to store the messages received but not handled. One socket is corresponding to one access point, distinguished by a unique integer.

There are two types of communication in osv protocol:

Inter-process communicate in a domain: The transfer procedure packages message into a osv message data structure which includes sender and receiver address, sender and receiver port number, message length, message data, message type. And then constructs a OSV skb, inserts it into the receiver's skb list. When receiver revokes a receive procedure, it will get this message form it's skb list.

Inter-process data transfer across domains: During the protocol initialization, each domain get the information about other domain's physical receive buffer address. So, they can put data in each other's receive buffer easily. Like IPC in a domain, the transfer packages the message firstly. After that, it puts the data into the corresponding domain's receive buffer according to the receive IP address. As each domain has a work queue scanning it's own receive buffer, the message can be discovered after being put into buffer immediately. And then, the message data is picked up from osv message data structure, packaged into a osv skb, inserted into the receiver's skb list. The remainder things will be done like IPC in a domain.

4.3 Linux Kernel

In order to host multiple Linux kernels concurrently, some modifications must be made to linux source code. Modifications to domain 0 and other domains are different:

Domain 0 The domain 0 needs to dispatch the external timer to other domains. So, in the domain 0 timer interrupt function should send IPI to other domains. This is done by issuing a hyper-call to *irq0_forward()*. The codes added to the linux kernel is just 5 line of inlined asm code.

Domain x The external timer interrupt for normal domains is received through IPI, so the timer interrupt should issue an EOI to the APIC of the CPU. So, the function of *ack_APIC_irq()* should be called in the timer interrupt function. Linux kernel assign each online CPU a logical id. When running multiple Linux, the logical id may be confused while sending IPIs. So assign of logical id to APIC should be intercepted by OSV kernel. And also, the action for sending IPI needs to be intercepted. The work is done by intercepting the writes to APIC registers. When the linux kernel writes the APIC register, it traps to the OSV kernel, the OSV translates the logical id to physical id and then send the IPI using the physical id.

All the modifications of Linux kernel is summarized in table 2. Total lines of code are less than 10, which is easily ported for linux.

5. Evaluation

This section demonstrates that the OSV's approach is beneficial to operating systems' performance. Performance of OSV is evaluated in this section.We first measure the overhead of virtualization using a set of operating system benchmarks. The performance is compared with Xen and native Linux kernel. Then the performance for the OSV's network system is measured. Finally, *memcached* is used to show the overall performance of OSV. The experiments were performed on two servers: Dell T605 two quad-core processors 2.0GHZ 2350 Opteron server with 16GB RAM, a Broadcom NetXtreme 5722 NIC and a 146GB 3.5-inch 15K RPM SAS Hard Drive, and Sun x4600M2 eight quad-core processors 2.8GHZ 8478 Opteron server with 256GB RAM and 1TB RAID0 Hard Drive. Linux version 2.6.31 was used, and compiled for architecture x86_64. The NFS version 4.1 was used. The opteron processors in both machines are with SVM and NPT support which are used by OSV. Both Xen and OSV guests are based on Linux kernel 2.6.31. The PV guest of Xen is configured without *superpage*.

5.1 Operating System Benchmarks

In order to measure the performance overhead of OSV VMM, we performed some experiments targeting particular subsystems. The lmbench [21] benchmark is used to measure the overhead. We compared the performance of Linux on bare metal, XEN HVM and PVM. The configuration for XEN guest OS is binded to a NUMA node: Guest OS can only access the drams and cpu cores on the specified node. This can reduce the schedule overhead of XEN and avoid cross NUMA node memory accesses. This expriment is carried on the 32-core server. For native Linux, lmbench is not configured to bind to a NUMA node. This is because for a 32-core

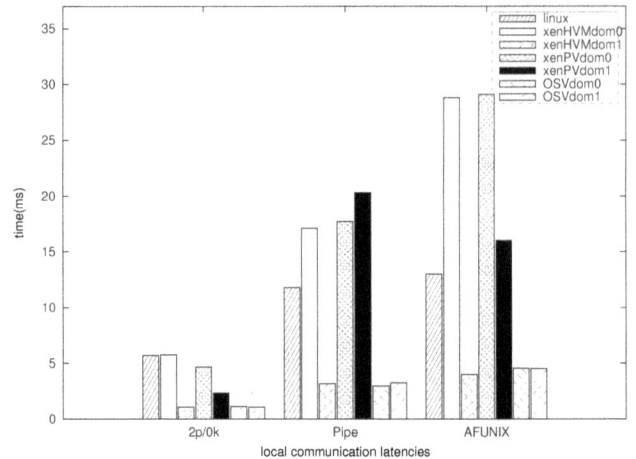

Figure 5. Local Communication Latency.

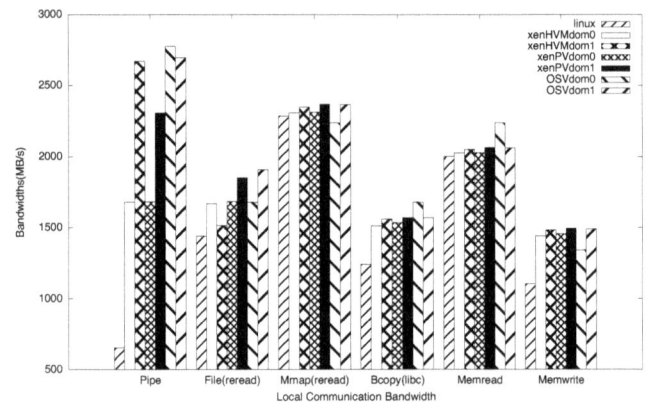

Figure 6. Local Communication Bandwidth.

server lmbench needs more memory than a NUMA node. Besides, lmbench also measures remote resource access latencies (including CPU cores and memory) which makes it should not be bound to a NUMA node. For OSV and Xen, guest OS kernels are configured with 4 cpu cores and 16GB drams.

The figure 5 shows the local communication latency. XEN HVM based guest OS gets the similar performance to OSV kernels and better than Linux and other PVM guests. This is mainly caused by the NUMA architecture of multi-core server: local access time is smaller than remote access. The resources used by the OSV kernel and XEN HVM is bound to a NUMA node so the cpu cores only have local dram accesses which make the performance better than Linux. The performance of XEN PVM guests is limited by the intervention of XEN when accessing the system resources.

Local communication bandwidth is shown in figure 6. The OSV kernel gets a high bandwidth compared to Linux and XEN HVM guest, especially in mem read test. The guest OS in OSV VMM accesses the resources allocated to it without the intervention of OSV VMM which makes it lower performance overhead. For the remote dram and cache coherent latencies, the Linux's bandwidth is the lowest with large number of cpu cores, 32-core in this experiment. In the File reread test, the OSV domain1 has the highest bandwidth. This is caused by the NFS based file system. When a file has already been accessed, it will remain in the NFS client cache, which

Domain 0	irq0_forward hyper-call is added to the timer interrupt function. 5 lines of inlined asm code.
Normal Domains	ack_APIC_irq() function call is added in the timer interrupt function; apic->write is replaced with osv_apic_write. 4 lines of c code.

Table 2. The modifications made to Linux kernel.

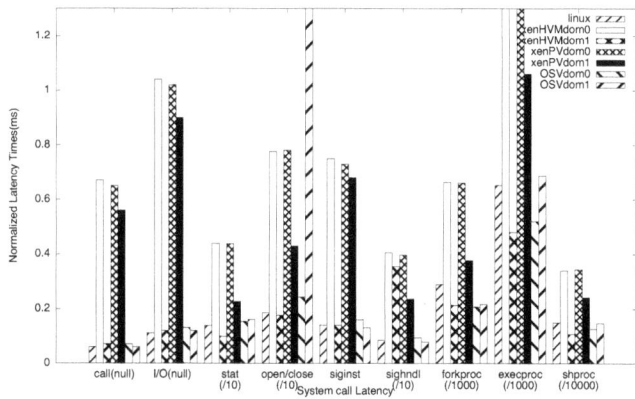

Figure 7. Processor and System call latency.

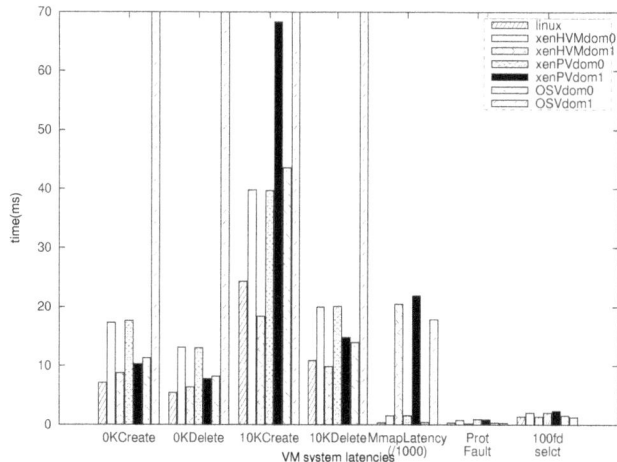

Figure 9. File and VM system latency.

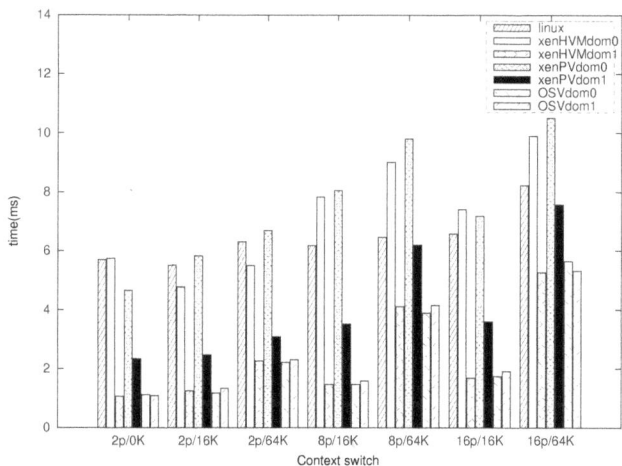

Figure 8. Context Switch Latency.

can accelerate the file read. The device of HVM guest on XEN is emulated, so the file reread bandwidth is lower then PVM guest.

In the context switch latency test shown in figure 8, the latency for OSV kernel is small which is similar to the HVM guest on XEN. The NUMA architecture and the TLB *shootdowns* contributes to the high latencies for Linux. The TLB *shootdowns* are expensive, when the number of cores is large. This contributes to the high latency. For PVM guest on XEN, each context switch needs the modification of shadow page table, so its latency is as high as the Linux. All the systems latency increases with the number of processes. The Xen domain 0 of both HVM and PVM have a high latency. This is because the domain 0 of XEN need to frequently be in service of the guest.

System call latency is critical to application's performance. The benchmark results are listed in figure 7. The Linux has the lowest latency for system calls, while OSV kernel and HVM guest on XEN get a similar result. The domain 0 for OSV kernel has the similar

performance compared to Linux. The domain 1 of OSV kernel in the open/close test get a super high latency. This is mainly caused by the NFS based File system. When opening and closing a file, the domain 1 needs two more network connection to finish the job which brings in the high latency. PVM guests on XEN have high latency in all the tests. These are all caused by the intervention of XEN when PVM performs some privileged operations.

The results for File and VM system tests which are shown in figure 9 are similar to the System call test. The domain 1 on OSV kernel has the biggest latency in tests except in prot fault and fd select. This also caused by the NFS filesystem. The network latency between domain 0 and domain 1 contributes the high latency. The domain 0 has a comparable performance to the Linux and XEN HVM guest. For mmap test, the domain 1 of XEN and OSV kernel all get a high latency, which is caused by the NFS file descriptor operations.

5.2 Socket Performance

In order to improve the communication performance of operating systems running on OSV, OSV socket is provided. We examine the bandwidth of the socket based on the TCP/IP over virtual network interface card and OSV socket protocol. The comparison is taken between Linux loopback and UNIX IPC which are widely used in the Linux system for SMP servers. We examine the time for transmitting 1GB data in different block size. The sender and receiver work in two different domains for OSV socket and VNIC. The VNIC is configured with 1500 MTU. For loopback test, the ip 127.0.0.1 is used. The UNIX IPC is measured between two processes. All the tests results are a median of 5 experiments.

The results are shown in table 3. When the block size is small the performance of OSV socket is comparable to UNIX IPC especially for the 256KB block size. This the same situation for the VNIC. For loopback card, when receiving a packet, it just passes the received sk_buffer to up layer by calling the function *netif_rx*. While works with VNIC, when receiving a packet from the packet buffer, the driver should make a call to *dev_alloc_skb* to get a sk_buffer for storing the received data, then passes it to

	OSV Socket	UNIX IPC	VNIC	lo
1K	1.82	1.59	4.73	2.32
8K	1.04	0.92	3.22	1.65
32K	0.93	0.77	2.75	1.3
128K	0.91	0.74	2.47	1.22
256K	0.87	0.74	2.51	1.16
1M	1.04	0.72	3.01	1.11

Table 3. Socket performance test, time in seconds. The test measures the time for transmitting 1GB data in different data block size.

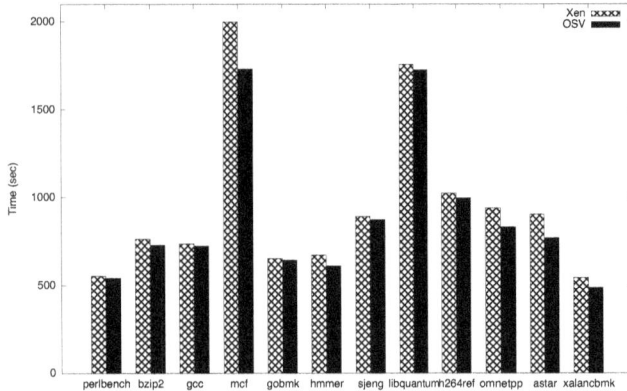

Figure 10. SPECint2006.

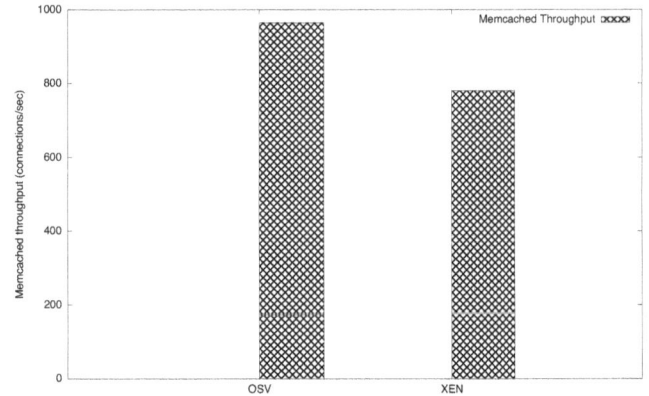

Figure 11. Memcached Throughput.

the up layer by calling the function *netif_rx*. This somewhat makes the performance for the VNIC worse than loopback. This is similar to the OSV socket and UNIX IPC. When the block size becomes large, the performance for VNIC and OSV socket decreases a little while the UNIX IPC and loopback card get good performance. This caused by the page frame management mechanism in Linux kernel. When the data block becomes large, it is difficult for the kernel to get continuous page frames to store these data from user space, this contributes mainly to the poor performance for the OSV socket and VNIC.

5.3 Application Performance

SPEC SPEC benchmarks are used to test the performance of the system under different workloads. We ran the benchmarks in both OSV and Xen with HVM Linux. Each VM was configured with four cores, 32GB of memory. The cores and memory allocated the a VM are in a NUMA node. There was only one VM running on the system. The device emulation was not used.

The results of our experiments are show in figure 10. We saw an approximately 2%-17% performance improvement across the board. The *astar* and *mcf* has the most significant performance improvement, which are 14% and 17%. *Mcf* and *astar* are memory heavy work, for example, *mcf* needs 1700 megabytes when running. The memory micro-benchmark results in figure 2 shows that OSV is efficient than Xen HVM. The performance improvement comes from the removal of the virtualization layer and the dedicated resource allocation policy.

Memcached Memcached is an in-memory key-value store for small chunks of arbitrary data (strings, objects) from results of database calls, API calls, or page rendering. Wikipedia, Youtube and Twitter all use memcached. We evaluated memcached in both OSV and Xen. The virtual machine configurations are the same as the SPEC experiments. Both Xen HVM and OSV are using

virtual network card. Physical network card in the privileged virtual machine is configured with port forwarding. Then, other computers can access memcached service provided by the virtual machine.

The connection throughput is measured. Results in figure 11 show that there is 23.7% performance improvement. For Xen HVM, the performance is limited by the frequently Nested Page Fault (NPT). HVM Linux needs frequently to trap into Xen. The context switch induces the performance overhead.

6. Related Work

Our work is inspired by many prior works. This section details the related work and summarizes them for differences between OSV VMM.

6.1 Virtual Machine Monitor

The VMM is used for hosting multiple operating system in a server for different application usage. OSV makes the many core system distributed which is similar to a VMM such as Xen [8], VMware [27]. But the OSV does not virtualize the resources and provides scalable performance while with little code base. No-hype [19] VMM is also focused on the removal of the virtualization layer from VMM. NoHype is focused on building a secure cloud VMM, while OSV is to improve the performance of VMM. In No-Hype, the hardware paging mechanisms are used to isolate each guest OS. For OSV, the hardware paging mechanisms only used in the boot time of guest OS, which is used to emulate some CMOS operations. After booted in OSV, the hardware paging mechanisms is turned off. So, OSV has lower performance overhead compared with Xen, while NoHype has a similar performance compared with Xen. OSV uses existing distributed services to share resources among guest OS. These services are based on a VNIC provided by OSV. NoHype is based on Xen and emulated devices are still needed.

6.2 Multicore OS

In order to make the operating system scalable on many core servers, researchers have done lots of work. K42 [7], Tornado [14] is developed in a object-oriented fashion. The kernel structures are controlled in distributed fashion, which makes the kernel scalable on many core platform. The multi-kernel [9] is similar to our work, it treats each core individually using message passing instead of shared memory to communication. Helios [22] is developed for heterogeneous architectures, it provides a seamless, single operating system abstraction across heterogeneous devices. These kernels scale well for multi-core servers, but the ABI(Application Binary Interface) is not compatible with current computing system. Disco [12, 16, 26] is a VMM developed to running multiple operating system concurrently to improve the scalability on multicore servers, which induces the virtualization overhead.

6.3 New Kernel

Exokernel [13] and Corey [10] are operating systems developed to provide the application more flexible resource management, which can reduce the overhead for resource contention and management overhead. Saha et al. have proposed the Multi-Core Run Time (McRT) for emerging desktop workloads [23] and explored configurations in which McRT runs on the bare metal, with an operating system running on separate cores. Salias et al have tuned the linux kernel for many core servers which can achieve the scalability for network applications [11], this needs the system specialized for an application. Libnuma [20] is proved by the linux kernel to improve the performance on NUMA based many core systems. Several studies with Linux on multicore processors [15, 25] have identified challenges in scaling existing operating systems to many core. All these work have inspired the work of OSV VMM.

7. Discussion

The motivation of implementing OSV is to build a neat and low performance overhead VMM. OSV tries to remove virtualization layer and uses a static resource allocation policy. Processor cores and memory ranges are pre-configured by OSV. So, OSV lacks the flexibility compared with traditional VMM. It is suitable for a cloud-computing model where users specify their resources demand in advance. Current implementation of OSV is based on AMD processors. It is easy to port OSV to other platforms with similar hardware assit virtualization technology. The only thing needs to pay attention to is the multi-processor boot trick used in OSV. However, this can be done by modifying the Linux source code which is described in section 4.1.

OSV demonstrates a way for constructing a lightweight VMM. The results above should be viewed as a case for the principle that VMM only controls the resources rather than a conclusive proof⁵. OSV lacks many features of commodity VMM, such as Xen, which influences experimental results both positively and negatively. Many of the ideas in OSV could be applied to existing VMM such as Xen. For example, booting guest OS with a predefined information table can be applied to Xen. Finally, it may be possible for Xen to provide a guest like the guest in OSV.

8. Conclusion

OSV is a lightweight VMM for many core servers. It provides the system scalability on many core servers, while keeps compatible with current computing base. It removes the virtualization layer in traditional VMM. Current distributed protocols are employed for resource sharing. TCP/IP and OSV socket are provided, by which the operating system can communicate with each other by standard distributed protocols, while by the OSV socket with high performance. The performance overhead for operating systems running in OSV is low compared with Xen VMM. The line of code for OSV kernel is about 8000, which make the system can be tuned for safety and reliability.

Acknowledgments

We would like to thank our shepherd, Leendert van Doorn, the anonymous reviewers, and Haibo Chen for their helpful suggestions for how to improve this paper. This research was supported in part by NSFC under Grant No.(60933003, 61272460), RFDP(20120201110010) and 863 Program (2012AA010904).

References

[1] CVE-2010-0633. http://cve.mitre.org/cgi-bin/cvename.cgi?name=CVE-2010-0633, 2010.

[2] CVE-2010-4255. http://cve.mitre.org/cgi-bin/cvename.cgi?name=CVE-2010-4255, 2010.

[3] CVE-2010-4247. http://cve.mitre.org/cgi-bin/cvename.cgi?name=CVE-2010-4247, 2010.

[4] CVE-2012-0217: SYSRET 64-bit operating system privilege escalation vulnerability on Intel CPU hardware. http://cve.mitre.org/cgi-bin/cvename.cgi?name=CVE-2012-0217, 2012.

[5] HP ProLiant DL980 G7 Server Data Sheet. http://h20195.www2.hp.com/V2/GetPDF.aspx/4AA1-5671ENW.pdf, 2012.

[6] AMD. Amd64 architecture programmer's manual volume 2: System programming. *Publication No. 24593*, September 2007.

[7] J. Appavoo, D. Silva, O. Krieger, M. Auslander, M. Ostrowski, B. Rosenburg, A. Waterland, R. Wisniewski, J. Xenidis, M. Stumm, et al. Experience distributing objects in an SMMP OS. *ACM Transactions on Computer Systems (TOCS)*, 25(3):6–es, 2007. ISSN 0734-2071.

[8] P. Barham, B. Dragovic, K. Fraser, S. Hand, T. Harris, A. Ho, R. Neugebauer, I. Pratt, and A. Warfield. Xen and the Art of Virtualization. *Proceedings of the 19th ACM symposium on Operating systems principles*, pages 164–177, 2003.

[9] A. Baumann, P. Barham, P. Dagand, T. Harris, R. Isaacs, S. Peter, T. Roscoe, A. Sch "upbach, and A. Singhania. The multikernel: a new OS architecture for scalable multicore systems. In *Proceedings of the ACM SIGOPS 22nd symposium on Operating Systems Principles*, pages 29–44. ACM, 2009.

[10] S. Boyd-Wickizer, H. Chen, R. Chen, Y. Mao, F. Kaashoek, R. Morris, A. Pesterev, L. Stein, M. Wu, Y. Dai, et al. Corey: An operating system for many cores. In *Proceedings of the 8th USENIX conference on Operating systems design and implementation*, pages 43–57. USENIX Association, 2008.

[11] S. Boyd-Wickizer, A. Clements, O. Mao, A. Pesterev, M. Kaashoek, R. Morris, and N. Zeldovich. An analysis of Linux scalability to many cores. In *Proceedings of the 9th USENIX conference on Operating systems design and implementation*. USENIX Association, 2010.

[12] E. Bugnion, S. Devine, and M. Rosenblum. Disco: running commodity operating systems on scalable multiprocessors. *ACM SIGOPS Operating Systems Review*, 31(5):143–156, 1997. ISSN 0163-5980.

[13] D. Engler, M. Kaashoek, et al. Exokernel: An operating system architecture for application-level resource management. *ACM SIGOPS Operating Systems Review*, 29(5):251–266, 1995.

[14] B. Gamsa, O. Krieger, J. Appavoo, and M. Stumm. Tornado: Maximizing locality and concurrency in a shared memory multiprocessor operating system. *Operating systems review*, 33:87–100, 1998. ISSN 0163-5980.

[15] C. Gough, S. Siddha, and K. Chen. Kernel scalability—expanding the horizon beyond fine grain locks. In *Proceedings of the Linux Symposium*, pages 153–165, 2007.

[16] K. Govil, D. Teodosiu, Y. Huang, and M. Rosenblum. Cellular Disco: Resource management using virtual clusters on shared-memory multiprocessors. In *Proceedings of the seventeenth ACM symposium on Operating systems principles*, pages 154–169. ACM, 1999. ISBN 1581131402.

[17] J. Held, J. Bautista, and S. Koehl. White paper from a few cores to many: A tera-scale computing research review.

[18] Intel. The MultiProcessor Specification Version 1.4. http://download.intel.com/design/archives/processors/pro/docs/24201606.pdf, 1997.

[19] E. Keller, J. Szefer, J. Rexford, and R. B. Lee. Nohype: virtualized cloud infrastructure without the virtualization. In *Proceedings of the 37th annual international symposium on Computer architecture*, ISCA '10, pages 350–361, New York, NY, USA, 2010. ACM. ISBN

978-1-4503-0053-7. doi: 10.1145/1815961.1816010. URL http://doi.acm.org/10.1145/1815961.1816010.

[20] A. Klein. An NUMA API for Linux. http://www.firstfloor.org/andi/numa.html, August 2004.

[21] L. McVoy and C. Staelin. lmbench: Portable tools for performance analysis. In *Proceedings of the 1996 annual conference on USENIX Annual Technical Conference*, page 23. Usenix Association, 1996.

[22] E. Nightingale, O. Hodson, R. McIlroy, C. Hawblitzel, and G. Hunt. Helios: heterogeneous multiprocessing with satellite kernels. In *Proceedings of the ACM SIGOPS 22nd symposium on Operating systems principles*, pages 221–234. ACM, 2009.

[23] B. Saha, A. Adl-Tabatabai, A. Ghuloum, M. Rajagopalan, R. Hudson, L. Petersen, V. Menon, B. Murphy, T. Shpeisman, E. Sprangle, et al. Enabling scalability and performance in a large scale CMP environment. In *ACM SIGOPS Operating Systems Review*, volume 41, pages 73–86. ACM, 2007.

[24] J. Szefer, E. Keller, R. B. Lee, and J. Rexford. Eliminating the hypervisor attack surface for a more secure cloud. In *Proceedings of the 18th ACM conference on Computer and communications security*, CCS '11, pages 401–412, New York, NY, USA, 2011. ACM. ISBN 978-1-4503-0948-6. doi: 10.1145/2046707.2046754. URL http://doi.acm.org/10.1145/2046707.2046754.

[25] B. Veal and A. Foong. Performance scalability of a multi-core web server. In *Proceedings of the 3rd ACM/IEEE Symposium on Architecture for networking and communications systems*, pages 57–66. ACM, 2007.

[26] B. Verghese, S. Devine, A. Gupta, and M. Rosenblum. *Operating system support for improving data locality on CC-NUMA compute servers*, volume 31. ACM, 1996. ISBN 0897917677.

[27] C. Waldspurger. Memory resource management in VMware ESX server. *ACM SIGOPS Operating Systems Review*, 36(SI):194, 2002.

Traveling Forward in Time to Newer Operating Systems using ShadowReboot

Hiroshi Yamada

Tokyo University and Agriculture and Technology,
JST CREST

hiroshiy@cc.tuat.ac.jp

Kenji Kono

Keio University, JST CREST

kono@ics.keio.ac.jp

Abstract

Operating system (OS) reboots are an essential part of updating kernels and applications on laptops and desktop PCs. Long downtime during OS reboots severely disrupts users' computational activities. This long disruption discourages the users from conducting OS reboots, failing to enforce them to conduct software updates. This paper presents *ShadowReboot*, a virtual machine monitor (VMM)-based approach that shortens downtime of OS reboots in software updates. ShadowReboot conceals OS reboot activities from user's applications by spawning a VM dedicated to an OS reboot and systematically producing the rebooted state where the updated kernel and applications are ready for use. ShadowReboot provides an illusion to the users that the guest OS travels *forward* in time to the rebooted state. ShadowReboot offers the following advantages. It can be used to apply patches to the kernels and even system configuration updates. Next, it does not require any special patch requiring detailed knowledge about the target kernels. Lastly, it does not require any target kernel modification. We implemented a prototype in VirtualBox 4.0.10 OSE. Our experimental results show that ShadowReboot successfully updated software on unmodified commodity OS kernels and shortened the downtime of commodity OS reboots on five Linux distributions (Fedora, Ubuntu, Gentoo, Cent, and SUSE) by 91 to 98%.

Categories and Subject Descriptors D.4.5 [*Operating Systems*]: Reliability

General Terms Reliability

Keywords Software Updates, Virtual Machines

1. Introduction

Operating system (OS) reboots are an essential part of updating contemporary kernels and applications on our laptops and desktop PCs. In updating a kernel, an OS reboot is typically invoked to terminate the older kernel and start the newer one after the update patches are applied. OS kernels are still being developed to improve their performance, add new functionality, and repair security vulnerabilities. The Linux Foundation reports that on average 3.83

VEE'13, March 16–17, 2013, Houston, Texas, USA.
Copyright © 2013 ACM 978-1-4503-1266-0/13/03... $15.00

patches are applied to the Linux kernel tree every hour between the 2.6.11 and 2.6.30 kernel [12].

An OS reboot is also required for updating applications. Application updates sometimes involve system configuration changes such as Windows Registry keys and shared component updates such as glibc and WebKit. To activate updates, we commonly conduct an OS reboot, which is the easiest way to restart all applications. For example, an OS reboot is often needed for updates of Internet Explorer and Safari because they involve changing Windows Registry keys and updating WebKit.

The downtime during OS reboots, however, severely disrupts users' computational activities. While an OS is rebooting, the user cannot perform his or her computational tasks. This disruptive downtime is becoming longer and more costly since there are more and more software updates. Although announced updates should be applied as soon as possible since they often fix critical vulnerabilities, the long disruption caused by the OS reboots discourages users from rebooting OSes, so they often fail to update software. As a result, users cannot benefit from new functionality or better performance, and even worse, unfixed vulnerabilities can be exploited by attackers. A research literature [2] notes that "many desktop machines are not rebooted to apply kernel patches because of the burden imposed by rebooting".

To eliminate the need for an OS reboot with software updates, dynamic updatable kernels are effective for applying patches to the kernels at runtime. However, making the systems "reboot-free" is still difficult even when using dynamic updatable kernels for the following reasons. First, some of these kernels are designed for fixing bugs in the kernel code region, such as condition misses [2]. Therefore, it is difficult to manage the semantic changes to memory objects, such as when adding a new field to a data structure. They also cannot manage system configuration updates because a restart of all the processes is not involved. In these cases, we have no choice but to conduct an OS reboot. Second, some dynamic updatable kernels require intimate knowledge about the target kernels [5, 16]. To use them, we have to develop special patches from the original ones. This task is non-trivial because it requires knowledge about the internal structures of the target kernels at the source code level. Lastly, we have to pay a high engineering cost for redesigning and modifying a large part of the target kernel [3, 11, 19]. This is difficult and often impossible because recent kernels are more complex and some are closed-source and/or proprietary. We believe that there is room for improvement in managing OS reboots in software updates.

Our goal is to mitigate the disruption to users' computational tasks caused by OS reboots to encourage users to conduct software updates as soon as possible. *ShadowReboot*, presented in this paper, is a virtual machine monitor (VMM)-based approach to shortening downtime of OS reboots in software updates. ShadowReboot conceals OS reboot activities by spawning a VM dedicated to an OS reboot and systematically producing a rebooted state. In ShadowReboot, users can run their applications while simultaneously rebooting the OS. ShadowReboot engenders an OS reboot effect by restoring the produced rebooted state where the updated kernel and applications are ready for use. It provides an illusion to users that an OS travels *forward* in time to the rebooted state.

The contributions of this paper are as follows:

- We present ShadowReboot, which offers the following advantages: (1) It shortens the downtime during software updates, thus mitigating the disruption to users' application activities. (2) ShadowReboot can be used to apply any patch to the kernels and even to update system configuration. (3) It does not require intimate knowledge about the target kernels at the source code level; we do not have to develop kernel modules or special patches. (4) ShadowReboot requires no modification of the target kernels. These features make ShadowReboot complementary to existing systems and dynamic updatable kernels.

- We introduce the ShadowReboot semantics and show it is applicable to five real Linux distributions (Fedora, Ubuntu, Gentoo, Cent, and SUSE). In Sec. 6, we describe how the Linux distributions have been configured to be suitable for ShadowReboot.

- We implement ShadowReboot and evaluate a prototype on VirtualBox 4.0.10 OSE with the five real Linux distributions. The experiments also show that ShadowReboot successfully updates software on unmodified Linux kernels and the downtime caused by ShadowReboot is 91 to 98% shorter than that of commodity OS reboots on the five Linux distributions.

Note that ShadowReboot does not keep the memory states of user's running applications through the restoration of the rebooted state. Although process migration approaches can be used to move the running applications to the rebooted state, selecting processes to be migrated is a challenge because the components linked to the migrated processes would conflict with the newer ones in the rebooted state. The challenge of keeping running applications' states across an OS reboot in software updates is out of the scope of this paper. Fortunately, we can quickly restore the applications' states after shadow-rebooting by taking advantage of the applications' support that saves their states to disks, such as a FireFox extension of restoring the contents in each tab.

The rest of this paper is organized as follows. Section 2 presents key observations and an overview of ShadowReboot. Sections 3 and 4 describe the design and implementation of ShadowReboot, respectively. Section 5 discusses limitations and a use case of ShadowReboot. Section 6 details our experimental results, and Section 7 describes work related to ours. Finally, Section 8 concludes this paper.

2. Key Observations and ShadowReboot

ShadowReboot allows users to perform their applications while the OS is rebooting. To produce an OS reboot effect successfully, ShadowReboot introduces a directory view and constraints based on file accesses patterns of users' applications and OS reboots. In this section, we describe key observations behind ShadowReboot, its overview, and its semantics.

2.1 Key Observations

In ShadowReboot, we exploit the file access patterns of commodity OSes during their reboots in software updates. We checked the directories and files accessed during the OS reboots after software updates. To obtain the names, we started monitoring the file accesses when an OS shutdown operation is triggered after a software update is completed. We continued to monitor the file accesses until the OS

displays a login prompt. We ran Windows XP professional edition (`winxp`) and five Linux distributions: Fedora Core 10 (`fedora`), Ubuntu 9.04 (`ubuntu`), Gentoo Linux 2007.0 (`gentoo`), CentOS 5.3 (`cent`), and OpenSUSE (`suse`). Their configurations are in default. The updates conducted on `winxp` include all the Windows updates for the service pack 3 that need reboots, which were announced before October 2010, and an Internet Explorer upgrade to version 8. For the five Linux distributions, we applied a kernel patch to each kernel and updated each `glibc` library.

The results on `winxp` show that it basically accesses the same files and directories during the reboots. It frequently accesses \WINDOWS\system32\ and \WINDOWS\ Fonts\ for restarting services. In the shutdown phases, `winxp` accesses \Program Files\ to stop applications. Since the Windows Updates request an OS reboot during logging on, the shutdown phases involve accessing the user setting files such as \Document and Settings\username\NT-LOGIN.DAT, and \Document and Settings\username\NTLOG-IN.LOG. `Winxp` also stores the volume states in \System Volume Information\ for recovery. In the boot phases, winlogon.exe accesses \Documents and Settings, \Documents and Settings-\NetworkService, and \Documents and Settings\LocalServices for a logon. `Winxp` also sometimes accesses \WINDOWS\SoftwareDistribution\ and \WINDOWS\LastGood.Tmp for unknown reasons.

The results from the five Linux distributions show that during each reboot they all access the administrative files but never the user files in /home. All the Linux distributions frequently access files in /lib in their boot phase because almost all the daemon processes are linked to the glibc shared library whose files are stored in /lib/. In addtion, the files in /etc are often accessed because the configuration files are conventionally in /etc. Each Linux distribution performs slightly different file accesses due to the configuration difference. For example, `fedora` accesses /lib/libselinux.so, while `gentoo` does not. This is because `gentoo` does not support the selinux service that `fedora` does.

These results indicate that files accessed during OS reboots tend to be in administrative directories that cannot be modified without an administrative privilege. In other words, almost no files in user directories, such as \Documents and Settings\username\My Documents and /home/users/Desktop, are accessed. The characteristics of the file access patterns give us the following points. Even if we heavily modify files in the user directories while the OS is simultaneously rebooting, the modification does not interfere with the reboot activity. Moreover, the modification of files in administrative directories by service processes such as Linux daemons and Windows services does not disturb common users' applications. This motivates us to execute the users' tasks and an OS reboot in parallel.

2.2 ShadowReboot

ShadowReboot leverages system virtualization. Virtual machine monitors (VMMs) are a software layer on which existing OS kernels can be executed without any modification. A new feature implemented inside a VMM becomes available to all the guest OSes running on it. System virtualization is commonplace in desktop PCs and laptops as well as data centers.

An overview of ShadowReboot is shown in Figure 1. ShadowReboot executes users' tasks in parallel with the OS reboot. To create the context of an OS reboot, ShadowReboot spawns a VM dedicated to an OS reboot, called a *reboot-dedicated VM*. It has a copy of the virtual disks of the original VM and identical resources such as memory and registers. In ShadowReboot, an OS is rebooted on the reboot-dedicated VM after software updates are applied, while the user is executing applications on the original VM. After the OS reboot is completed, ShadowReboot takes a snapshot

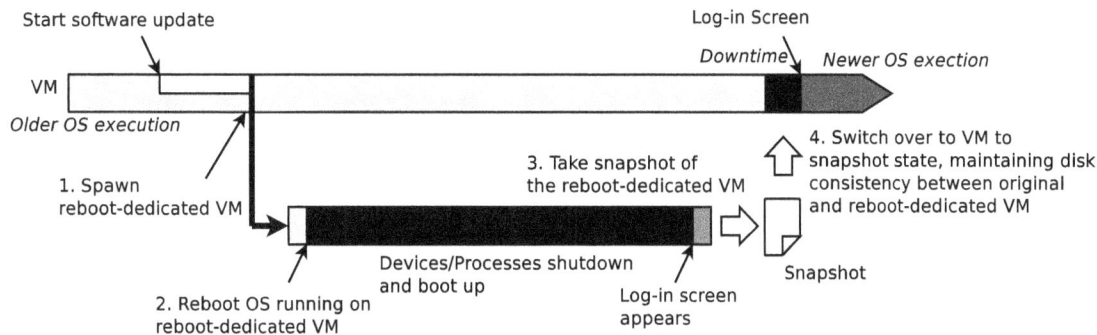

Figure 1. An Overview of ShadowReboot. *ShadowReboot consists of four operations: (1) spawning VM dedicated to OS reboot, (2) rebooting OS on reboot-dedicated VM, (3) taking snapshot of reboot dedicated VM when OS reboot is completed, and (4) switching over to the snapshot state.*

of the reboot-dedicated VM. ShadowReboot enables the user to restore the snapshot state at a convenient time, providing the directories in a manner described in Sec. 2.3. This design also allows us to treat a given update as a *blackbox* since the concealed OS reboot refreshes the software component in the same way as the normal OS reboot. Due to this advantage, ShadowReboot does not require analysis of the update patches and is applicable to existing updates such as Windows Updates.

2.3 ShadowReboot Semantics

2.3.1 Challenge

The parallel execution of the applications and OS reboot poses a challenge: how can we to maintain disk consistency in a rebooted state? Since files can be modified simultaneously by both activities of the applications and OS reboot, we may fail to produce a reboot state users expect. For example, when the service processes have been launched in the concealed OS reboot before the user's task modifies the configuration files on the original VM, their running states in the produced rebooted image are based on the files before modification. Another problem is that computational results saved by the applications are overwritten when the concealed OS reboot activity modifies the files. As a result, some data that the user does not expect would be saved in the application's files. Although we can solve this problem by carefully tracking service process and users' task behavior, semantically maintaining consistency is complicated and may require users' interaction like `fsck`, which would discourage users from employing ShadowReboot.

2.3.2 ShadowReboot Directory View

To cope with this problem, ShadowReboot builds directories in the restored VM by appropriately selecting directories from the original and reboot-dedicated VM. Specifically, ShadowReboot selects the user-specified working directories in the original VM to preserve the user's computational results during the OS reboot. The other directories including administrative directories come from the reboot-dedicated VM. This directory view is based on the fact that user's non-administrative applications tend to modify only their own working directories, which are typically stored in the user directory, while reading the shared libraries and system configuration files stored in administrative directories. Also, the view allows us to maintain the consistency between the service processes' states and the accessed files such as configuration files since the service processes access the administrative directories in the reboot-dedicated VM.

For example, suppose a user is executing a video player or a word processor during shadow-rebooting. He or she can use these

applications as usual even under the ShadowReboot constraints since they edit files in user's directories and typically read administrative files such as shared libraries. At this time, the user cannot conduct administrative tasks such as system configuration changes due to the constraint in order to maintain the consistency between the configuration and the service processes states saved in the rebooted image. In the context of the OS reboot, the kernel and service processes are ready for use. After the OS reboot, ShadowReboot returns the consistent rebooted state with user's expectations, providing its directory view; it preserves user's computational results in the working directories and administrative files whose contents are consistent with the running service processes.

2.3.3 Constraints

To successfully produce a consistent rebooted state with users' operations, ShadowReboot enforces constraints on the original and reboot-dedicated VM. One constraint forces applications running on the original VM to modify only the working directories specified in advance, which is used after the restoration of the produced snapshot. This means that the constraint prevents the applications from updating files in the other directories that are discarded after the restoration. Although the user cannot perform administrative tasks such as system configuration changes during this time, ShadowReboot allows them to execute non-administrative tasks such as web browsing and text editing. To avoid conflicting with the applications running on the original VM, ShadowReboot also imposes a constraint that forbids the concealed OS reboot to modify the files in the applications' working directories. When file operations performed in the original VM or reboot-dedicated VM violate the constraints, ShadowReboot notifies the user of the violation and destroys the reboot-dedicated VM. After that, he or she can try ShadowReboot again or perform a normal OS reboot.

We can mitigate the constraints with knowledge of the applications. Even if some files are modified simultaneously by both VMs, file contents are consistent with user's file operations and service processes' states in the restored VM. For example, service processes sometimes cache their data into a directory such as /var/cache and \Windows\Prefetch. Another example is that some processes temporally save their results in some directories such as /tmp and \Windows\Temp. Even if these files are updated in the original VM and are discarded through the restoration, the files are regenerated in the reboot-dedicated VM and thus are consistent with service processes in the restored VM.

Specifically, we found three types of files for which the constraints can be mitigated: temporary files, state files, and log files. Temporary files include cache files such as files in /var/cache and temporal results such as files in /tmp. Even if these files are updated in the original VM and discarded through the restoration of ShadowReboot, the restored VM can consistently start, as described above. State files include pid files such as /var/run/yum.pid and /var/run/anacron.pid, and lock files such as /var/lock/makewhatis.lock and /var/lock/subsys/vsftpd. Since these files depend on the states of running service processes, we do not track updates to them in the original VM since they are appropriately generated in the reboot-dedicated VM. Log files include application's logs such as /var/log/messages. The update of log files is a main cause of violations of constraints. To solve this problem, we reconfigure logger services to switch their log file to files in a working directory just after spawning a reboot-dedicated VM. By doing so, we can avoid the constraints violation and preserve logs containing events happened in the original VM. On the basis of these points, we can configure the five Linux distributions to be shadow-rebootable, as described in Sec. 6.

Note that configuration changes for end users to make their system shadow-rebootable can be avoided completely in some scenarios. One compelling use case of ShadowReboot is in a cloud computing platform. The cloud provider can provide a selection of operating system images with the ShadowReboot configuration changes already applied. Such a scenario completely eliminates the need for the user to do any OS configuration themselves. This means that the user can benefit from ShadowReboot even if he or she is a novice.

3. Design Details

Designing ShadowReboot poses several questions: (1) how can we efficiently spawn a reboot-dedicated VM? (2) how can we appropriately restore directories from the original and reboot-dedicated VM? (3) how does ShadowReboot check whether the applications and the concealed OS reboot follow the constraints? We answer these questions in this section.

3.1 VM Fork

We need an efficient approach to creating a reboot-dedicated VM. A naive approach is to run a new VM instance with the same configuration as the original VM. However, at every announcement of software updates, we have to create a new VM instance, copy the image of the VM, boot the OS, update the software, and conduct an OS reboot. However, this is tedious and may discourage users from updating software.

To create a reboot-dedicated VM efficiently, we introduce a *VM fork* that forks a running VM, borrowing an idea from previous research [13, 23]. The semantics of the VM fork are similar to those of the familiar process fork; users issue a fork call to the VMM that creates a child VM. The child VM inherits the runtime state of the parent VM such as memory and registers. It then proceeds with an identical view of the system. The child VM has its own independent copy of the OS, virtual disk, network interface card (NIC), and snapshot. The state updates of the child VM are not propagated to the parent.

Our VM fork is semantically different from the other ones [13, 23]. Flash cloning [23] swiftly clones the VM from the reference image using a copy-on-write technique. However, this cannot provide stateful runtime cloning; all new VMs are copies of a frozen template. SnowFlock [13] is designed to clone VMs to use them temporally to handle sudden and huge workloads. It discards the state changes of child VMs when they stop. Our VM fork preserves the disk changes conducted by a child VM to restore the directories of the reboot-dedicated VM.

We use a page reclaiming mechanism running inside the VMM. We run it if there is not enough memory space to execute a child VM, though the resources in desktop environments are basically idle [1, 8]. Our mechanism leverages a page sharing technique like memory ballooning [24]. It allows one physical page to be shared with several virtual pages whose contents are the same. If there are not enough memory pages to run a reboot-dedicated VM, we run a process on the original VM that fills its memory region with the same data. The page sharing mechanism reclaims the memory pages of the process, which means the number of free memory pages increases. Therefore, we can reclaim the memory pages for a child VM without needing kernel modules such as a balloon driver. If we need to share pages more aggressively, novel sharing techniques [10, 17] can be employed.

3.2 Use of Unrollback Virtual Disks

To build working directories in the restored VM, we leverage an unrollback virtual disk that is independent of snapshot restoration. Unlike normal virtual disks, unrollback virtual disks do not roll back even if the VM is restored to a snapshot. By saving files into an unrollback virtual disk in the original VM, the files are accessible in the VM restored from a snapshot of the reboot-dedicated VM. We prepare two policies for the use of unrollback virtual disks: *all-copy* and *partial-copy*. Users can choose the one more suitable for their environments.

- **All-copy policy:** The all-copy policy records update operations that occur in the working directories of the original VM during shadow-rebooting, and replays them on the restored VM. We start monitoring file update operations (including write, remove, and rename) to the working directories just after a reboot-dedicated VM is spawned. When the rebooted state is about to be restored, we mount an unrollback virtual disk on the original VM, shut down applications, and save the file update operations into the log in the mounted directory. After the logging completes and the rebooted snapshot has been restored, we mount the unrollback virtual disk again and replay the recorded operations in the restored VM. We can execute the all-copy policy without any modification in the existing directory layout. However, saving and replaying file update operations take longer as more files are updated.

- **Partial-copy policy:** The partial-copy policy *partially* saves and replays file update operations at the expense of the use of the existing directory layout. Under this policy, we assign some working directories to a partition of the unrollback virtual disk. Since an unrollback virtual disk keeps its contents through snapshot restoration, updated files and directories in the partition remain after the restoration of the rebooted state, thus accessing them without replaying any file operation. We monitor file update operations to the other working directories and log and replay them like the all-copy policy. A typical partial-copy configuration of Linux systems is that the mount point of the working directory (/home/users/work) is assigned to the unrollback virtual disk and the other directories' mount points are assigned to standard virtual disks. When we restore the snapshot of the reboot-dedicated VM, the /home/users/work directory is not restored because its mount point is assigned to the unrollback virtual disk.

Similar to unrollback virtual disks, some approaches can protect the files and directories from snapshot restoration. We can protect them by using an additional VM on which an NFS server is running. The files and directories that are stored in the NFS server are not affected by snapshot restoration. However, this approach requires setting up a VM and incurs network virtualization overhead that tends to cause a large performance penalty. We can also protect the files and directories by sharing them with the host OS. Although they are not rolled back by snapshot restoration, users sometimes want isolation between the VMs and the host to protect the host against VMs compromised by viruses or malicious attacks.

Note that we carefully configure a guest OS so that the OS does not mount the partitions of the unrollback virtual disks in its boot phase. Common file systems read their metadata, such as super blocks, from disks only once when the partitions are mounted. After a file system has been mounted, it manages its metadata in memory and only writes updates to the disks. When we take a snapshot of the reboot-dedicated VM after the unrollback virtual disks' partitions have been mounted, the restored file system states are inconsistent with the disk contents. Since the restored file system objects are not reflected on the disk updates conducted on the original VM after the OS mounts the partitions on the reboot-dedicated VM, the user cannot access the updated contents.

3.3 File Access Monitor

To notify a user of the violation of the ShadowReboot constraints, we have developed a mechanism that checks whether or not user's tasks and the OS reboot follow the constraints. The mechanism consists of two processes. One monitor runs on the reboot-dedicated VM and monitors file accesses to the working directories to detect file updates violating ShadowReboot constraints. The other monitor runs on the original VM. It monitors file operations to user-specified working directories to log them in order to realize the all-copy and partial-copy policies. It also monitors file accesses to the other directories to detect the violations of the constraints. When a violation is detected on a VM, the process notifies the user and requests the VMM to destroy the reboot-dedicated VM.

The file access monitor also helps us set up our system configuration to be shadow-rebootable. Since the file access monitor checks whether or not the system follows the constraints through shadow-rebooting, we can configure the service processes and our applications to be suitable for the constraints, based on the checks. We believe that the file access monitor makes it easier to configure the VM to be shadow-rebootable.

4. Implementation

We implemented a prototype of ShadowReboot on VirtualBox 4.0.10_OSE [18] and Linux. VirtualBox is an open-source VMM for x86 hardware, where we can execute OSes such as Windows and Linux without any modification to them. Our prototype consists of three modules: *vmm-module*, *guest-module* and *host-module*. The vmm-module is a part of VirtualBox. It provides and performs VM fork and unrollback virtual disks. The guest-module is a process running on the guest OS. It executes the file access monitor. The host-module runs on the host Linux executing the VirtualBox. The host-module requests the VMM to fork a VM and take/restore a snapshot. It exchanges network messages with the guest-module, which requests a VM fork. We describe implementation issues of the VMM-module and guest module in this section.

4.1 VMM Module

To implement the VM fork, we use online snapshot functionality. Online snapshot functionality enables us to take a snapshot without the downtime of the VM. When a snapshot of a VM is taken, VirtualBox produces two files. One contains the current memory image of the VM. The other is a delta disk file for preserving the current state of the virtual disk. When a VM fork is requested, the vmm-module first registers a new VM instance for a child VM and sets the same hardware configuration as the target VM such as memory size and virtual disks. Next, it takes a snapshot of the target VM and sets the child VM's memory state to the memory image and creates delta disk files for each virtual disk. After that, the new VM is launched as the child VM.

We also implemented a content-based page sharing mechanism [24]. The vmm-module performs two operations: sharing machine pages and handling copy-on-write faults. To detect sharable

pages, the vmm-module tracks machine pages with a data structure of the VirtualBox page manager and calculates an MD5 digest value, whose key is the contents of each page. Then it groups the physical pages on the basis of the value. After finishing grouping, it compares the contents of the pages in the same group. If the contents are the same, we share one machine page. After finishing the above instructions, we invalidate the shadow page tables related to the changed physical pages. To handle copy-on-write faults, we modify the existing physical page allocation handler in a way that the shared page is duplicated. After that, we invalidate the shadow page tables related to the page since the pointed machine address is changed.

To implement unrollback virtual disks, we extended a type of virtual disk named write-through. Write-through disks fully support read and write operations like normal disks. The difference from normal disks is that the state of write-through disks is not saved when a snapshot is taken and not restored when a VM's state is reverted. We extended the write-through disk so that multiple VMs can connect to them. When the VM fork is invoked, it creates two delta files to save the disk updates committed by each VM. When we take a snapshot of the reboot-dedicated VM and terminate it, the snapshot is connected to the delta file for the original VM and the other one is discarded.

4.2 Guest Module

We implemented a file access monitor on Linux with the i-notify function. The i-notify function allows us to monitor file operations for specified files and directories. When ShadowReboot is invoked, our file access monitor starts to record file writes, deletions, and creations to administrative directories on the original VM. It continues to run until we restore the snapshot of the reboot-dedicated VM. On the other hand, it monitors the user-specified working directories on the reboot-dedicated VM. After the shutdown phase, it does not monitor files since the the partitions containing working directories are not mounted. To lower the monitoring cost, we do not monitor pseudo file systems such as /proc and /sys, and device file directories such as /dev.

Also, the file access monitor logs file operations to user-specified directories on the original VM and memorizes the operated file names. The file access monitor mounts an unrollback virtual disk just before the produced snapshot is restored. For simplicity of the implementation, the current prototype copies the updated files to a partition in the unrollback virtual disk. It copies them to the restored VM by mounting the unrollback virtual disk in it just after the restoration. To enhance our implementation, the use of some tools such as versioning systems is attractive for effectively managing file update operations.

5. Discussion

Although the prototype is runnable only on Linux platforms, we believe that ShadowReboot can be applied to other OS platforms. Our vmm-module can be reused for other OSes running on the VirtualBox since it is a part of the VMM. The file access monitor can be implemented with file I/O monitoring mechanisms supported by the target OS. For example, Windows supports the filter driver mechanism that allows us to monitor file system events. One of our future directions is to implement a file access monitor on Windows, configure Windows to be shadow-rebootable, and confirm the effectiveness of ShadowReboot.

We note that ShadowReboot cannot handle all types of software updates: it fails to manage software updates that involve accessing the directories on unrollback virtual disks. This behavior violates the ShadowReboot constraints, which means that our file access monitor detects this violation and stops shadow-rebooting. In this case, the user needs to conduct a normal OS reboot.

Controlling the resource usage of a reboot-dedicated VM is another challenge. If the reboot-dedicated VM obtrusively utilizes computational resources, it interferes with the original VM so severely that we cannot adequately do our tasks. To minimize the interference of the reboot-dedicated VM, we schedule it as a background task and the original VM as a foreground task. Many schemes for properly scheduling foreground and background processes have been proposed [1, 8, 15]. We can employ these novel schemes to mitigate the interference of the reboot-dedicated VM.

We pay attention to a case where the user wants to assign a fixed IP address to the target VM. When the user does not use a fixed IP address, he or she can enjoy the network without any consideration since our VM fork provides the child VM virtual NICs whose mac addresses are different from the parent ones. When the user wants to assign the VM a fixed IP address through the OS configuration or a DHCP server, we need to extend the current ShadowReboot. To assign a fixed IP address after shadow-rebooting, ShadowReboot provides the child VM virtual NICs whose mac addresses are the same as those of the parent. When a reboot-dedicated VM is rebooted and the guest OS starts to boot, we take a snapshot before the guest OS turns on its NICs. Although it takes a longer time until we can perform our tasks since some services may not finish launching, the user can obtain a fixed IP address.

6. Experiments

We conducted experiments to examine the effectiveness of ShadowReboot. In this paper, we investigate the following fundamental questions. The first is how ShadowReboot shortens downtime of OS reboots. The second is whether our page sharing mechanism shares pages. The third is how much overhead the file access monitor incurs. The fourth is how long the disk managements of all-copy and partial-copy policies take. The fifth is whether ShadowReboot can successfully produce a rebooted state under real software updates. The last is how applications behave through ShadowReboot.

The experiments described in this section were conducted on a DELL OptiPlex 780DT with a 3.0 GHz Core 2 Duo processor, 4 GB of memory and a 160 GB SATA disk. Our prototype runs on this machine on which Linux 2.6.34 runs. To confirm the applicability of ShadowReboot, we used five Linux distributions, Fedora Core 10 (`fedora`), Ubuntu 9.04 (`ubuntu`), Gentoo Linux 2007.0 (`gentoo`), CentOS 5.3 (`cent`), and OpenSUSE (`suse`). These OSes were installed on VMs provided by VirtualBox. Each VM is assigned one VCPU and connected to a 20 GB normal virtual disk and a 10 GB unrollback virtual disk as a primary master and slave, respectively. Its memory size was changed in the experiments. We installed the OSes with their desktop configurations. The normal virtual disk was partitioned by the default install instruction, and the unrollback virtual disk was formatted manually. In the experiments, the default system configurations were used.

6.1 Experimental Setup

We configured the five Linux distributions to be shadow-rebootable with our file access monitor. In addition, we checked whether installed applications adhere to the ShadowReboot constraints. These configurations were carried out manually. Developing an automatic configuration scheme to set the system suitable for ShadowReboot is out of the scope of this paper.

The configuration details are as follows.

- `Fedora`: We change `rsyslog`, `auditd`, and `sendmail` configurations to switch their log files on the original VM just after a VM fork is invoked. To do so, when the file access monitor launches on the original VM, it modifies /etc/rsyslog.conf, /etc/audit/auditd.conf, and /etc/mail-/sendmain.cf so that their files can be stored into a file in the working directories to

preserve the contents through the restoration. We also configure the file access monitor to avoid monitoring temporary and state files. Specifically, it does not monitor directories including /tmp, /usr/tmp, /var/tmp, /var/lock, /var/cache, or /var/run.

- `Ubuntu`: Similarly to `fedora`, we modify the configuration file of a `syslog` daemon. Specifically, the file access monitor modifies /etc/syslog.conf to switch log files into files in the working directories on the original VM just after a VM fork is invoked. Moreover, the file access monitor running in the original VM does not monitor files in /tmp, /var/tmp, /var/lock, /var/cache, /usr/tmp, /var/run, or /run. In addition, the file access monitor ignores file updates to /var/lib/apt-xapian-index/update-lock and /var/lib/apt-xapian-index/update-socket, which are state files of the Ubuntu update system.

- `Gentoo`: We change a `syslog-ng` configuration to switch a log file on the original VM when the VM fork is invoked. The file access monitor modifies /etc/syslog-ng.conf for `syslog-ng` to store log events into a file in the working directories. Also, the file access monitor running in the original VM does not monitor files in /tmp, /var/tmp, /var/lock, /var/cache, /usr/tmp, or /var/run.

- `Cent`: We reconfigure `sendmail` and `syslog` to switch the directories where their produced files are stored. We modify /etc/syslog.conf and /etc/mail-/sendmail.cf on the original VM. The file access monitor does not log file operations to /tmp, /usr/tmp, /var/tmp, /var/lock, /var/cache, or /var/run.

- `Suse`: Similarly to the other four Linux distributions, we change `rsyslog` and `postfix` configuration to change log files. The file access monitor modifies /etc/rsyslog.conf and /etc/postfix/main.cf to write events in files in the unrollback virtual disk. The file access monitor does not log file operations to /tmp, /usr/tmp, /var/tmp, /var/lock, /var/cache, or /var/run.

Some applications log their states to files when they finish. For example, `firefox` saves its configurations into the user's directory. If such applications are running when a VM fork is invoked, the files are saved in the disks in the reboot-dedicated VM, which violates a ShadowReboot constraint. To avoid this problem, we configured the VM in such a way that these files on the original VM are used on the restored VM. Specifically, the file access monitor brings the files from the original VM with the unrollback virtual disk. This is because such state files are the latest in the original VM.

In our investigation, one application (`terminal`) violates ShadowReboot constraints by logging a login event to /var/log/wtmp when it launches. To use this applications through shadow-rebooting, we need to switch the log files to a file in the unrollback virtual disk.

6.2 Downtime

To demonstrate that ShadowReboot shortens downtime of OS reboots, we compared the downtime of ShadowReboot and normal OS reboots. Our prototype causes downtime when a snapshot of a rebooted state is restored. We measured downtime caused by the snapshot restores. We varied the VM memory size: 256 MB, 512 MB, 1024 MB, 2048 MB, and 2560 MB. The maximum memory size the VirtualBox can assign in our environment was 2560 MB.

Table 1 lists the downtimes of ShadowReboot and normal OS reboots. The results show that the downtime of ShadowReboot is shorter than that of normal OS reboots. For example, with 256 MB, the downtime of ShadowReboot is 98.3% shorter than that of the normal OS reboot in `cent`. Even in `ubuntu`, the downtime of ShadowReboot is 91% shorter than that of the normal OS reboot. When we assigned 2560 MB of memory, downtime of ShadowReboot is 1.42 seconds in `gentoo`, while that of the normal OS

Table 1. Downtime of ShadowReboot and Normal OS Reboot.

	fedora [sec]		ubuntu [sec]	
VM memory size	ShadowReboot	Normal Reboot	ShadowReboot	Normal Reboot
256 MB	2.49	42.23	2.43	27.47
512 MB	2.56	42.80	2.41	27.63
1024 MB	2.38	44.55	2.46	39.61
2048 MB	2.37	45.03	2.53	43.64
2560 MB	2.39	45.04	2.49	45.49

gentoo [sec]		cent [sec]		suse [sec]	
ShadowReboot	Normal Reboot	ShadowReboot	Normal Reboot	ShadowReboot	Normal Reboot
1.38	55.39	2.42	141.11	3.16	30.95
1.43	54.89	3.32	154.09	4.86	30.71
1.38	57.82	3.20	132.84	5.12	43.29
1.43	58.17	3.15	142.83	5.29	56.24
1.42	58.21	3.35	132.05	5.22	55.99

Table 2. Memory Pages Reclaimed by Page Sharing.

Process Memory Usage (MB)	Reclaimed Pages (MB)
64	931
128	853
256	723
512	453
1024	52

Table 3. Overhead of the File System Monitor.

	grep	make
W/o File System Monitor [sec]	24.37	174.35
W/- File System Monitor [sec]	24.52	176.18
Overhead [%]	0.61	1.05

reboot is 58.21 seconds. ShadowReboot downtime is 2.49 seconds in ubuntu, which means ShadowReboot is 94% shorter than the normal OS reboot.

Also, the downtime of restoring a rebooted state tends to be stable even if the memory size is varied, except for cent and suse. In VirtualBox, the downtime of restoring a snapshot depends on how much memory a guest OS utilized. In cent and suse, their daemons utilize the memory in their boot phase, depending on the memory size of the machine. For example, readahead_early warms the file cache by accessing files that are frequently used.

6.3 Reclaiming Memory Pages

To confirm that the page sharing mechanism can reclaim pages, we measured the number of pages reclaimed by our mechanism under different system conditions. We set up a process that fills different values in its allocated pages to avoid being page-shared. This process simulates the memory usage of applications. We set up a VM and ran Linux (fedora). We assigned it 1152 MB of memory. We first ran a process of our mechanism and ran the application-simulated process whose memory sizes are 64 MB, 128 MB, 256 MB, 512 MB, and 1024 MB.

Table 2 shows the reclaimed memory size under these various conditions. The results show that the number of reclaimed pages depends on application memory usage. When the application-simulated process is assigned 64 MB of memory, we reclaim 931 MB and 794 MB of memory on fedora. On the other hand, we reclaim only 53 MB and 13 MB of memory in the 1024 MB case. When we want to shadow-reboot a VM if the VMM does not have enough free pages to run a reboot-dedicated VM, we need to kill some applications on the running VM.

6.4 Overhead for File Monitoring

To measure overhead incurred by the file system monitor, we compared execution times of the applications with and without the file access monitor. We prepared two applications: grep and make.

Grep searches for lines containing 'shadowreboot' in the source code and documents of Linux 2.6.29. Make compiles Apache 2.0.64 [22]. We ran these applications on fedora with 1600 MB of memory, which is the size recommended by the VirtualBox.

The result is shown in Table 3. From the result, we can say that the overhead of the file system monitor is very small. The overhead in grep is 0.61%, while that in make is 1.05%. The reason make's overhead is larger than that of grep is that make reads more library object files in administrative directories that are monitored by the file access monitor.

6.5 Overhead for File Saving/Restoring

To measure overhead for file saving to and restoring from unroll-back virtual disks, we measured time for saving and restoring files under all-copy and partial-copy policies. We used fedora with 1600 MB of memory. We generated files of various sizes during an OS reboot in the reboot-dedicated VM. We generated the files in a partition in the unrollback virtual disk under the partial-copy policy.

The results are shown in Fig. 2. The results reveal that the all-copy policy takes longer as the file size becomes bigger. This is because the all-copy policy copies all the updated files in the working directories to a partition of the unrollback virtual disk. On the other hand, the partial-copy policy does not copy the files in the unrollback virtual disk. When we create 1 KB, 10KB, and 100KB of files, required times in the all-copy policy are about 200 msec, which are similar to ones of the partial-copy policy. When the file is more than 25MB, the required time is longer than one second. The time of the partial-copy policy is constant regardless of file sizes since the files are created in the unrollback virtual disk and thus need not be copied.

6.6 Software Updates

To confirm that ShadowReboot successfully performs given software updates, we conducted real software updates on the five distribution. We chose updates including kernel updates, library updates, and window system updates by using the package system each distribution employs. We conducted 43 updates on fedora, eight on ubuntu, four on gentoo, 19 on cent, and 24 on suse.

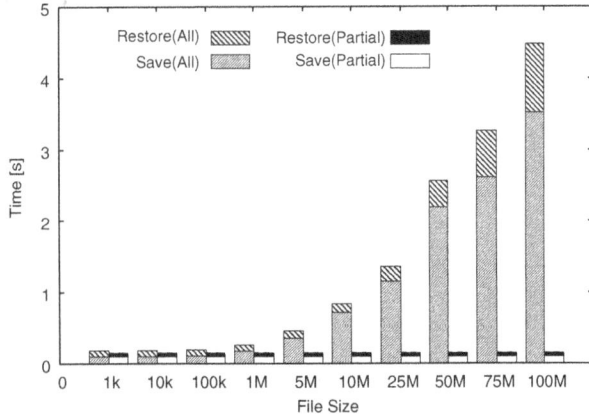

Figure 2. Time for Saving/Restoring Files under All- and Partial-copy Policies.

The result is that all of the software was successfully updated through ShadowReboot. During the OS reboots in the reboot-dedicated VM, our file system monitor does not warn of any violations in the updates. It detects a violation when we update software in `cent`. This is because `logrotate` is triggered by `cron` on the original VM and then starts compressing the log files in /var/log. We successfully performed the update by invoking ShadowReboot after the `logrotate`'s task completes.

6.7 Case Study

To demonstrate how a user's application behaves through ShadowReboot, we observed application behavior through the normal OS reboot and ShadowReboot. We ran a video player named `ffplay`, which is bundled in `ffmpeg` [9]. It plays a MPEG-4 format video at 24 frames per second (fps) with resolution 854 x 480 on `fedora` with 1600 MB of memory. We started `ffplay` and recorded its fps. After 30 seconds had been passed, we performed each reboot. When the log in prompt appears, we logged in `fedora` and restarted `ffplay`.

The results are shown in Figure 3. From Fig. 3, we can see that ShadowReboot downtime is shorter than that of the normal OS reboot. In the normal OS reboot (Fig. 3(a)), `ffplay` stopped its activity at 30 seconds when we conducted the OS reboot. It could not proceed until the OS reboot completed. After we logged in `fedora` and executed `ffplay`, it restarted playing the video. In ShadowReboot (Fig. 3(b)), `ffplay` could proceed when ShadowReboot was performed. We rebooted the OS on the reboot-dedicated VM at the 50 seconds when the VM fork finished and the reboot-dedicated VM started to run. During the OS reboot, `ffplay` continued to decode the video as usual. We took a snapshot on the reboot-dedicated VM at 99 seconds when a log in prompt appeared on the reboot-dedicated VM. When we restored the snapshot, `ffplay` stopped (at 105 seconds). It was executed again after we finished logging in. In both cases, `ffplay`'s performance was degraded just after we restarted it. This is because other processes were running to set up the user's desktop environment and thus resource contention occurred.

7. Related Work

Using dynamic updatable kernels is an effective way to apply patches to the kernels at runtime so that we do not need to conduct an OS reboot [2, 3, 5, 11, 16, 19]. Ksplice [2] dynamically translates the function code at a safe time when no thread's instruction pointer falls within that function's text and when no thread's kernel

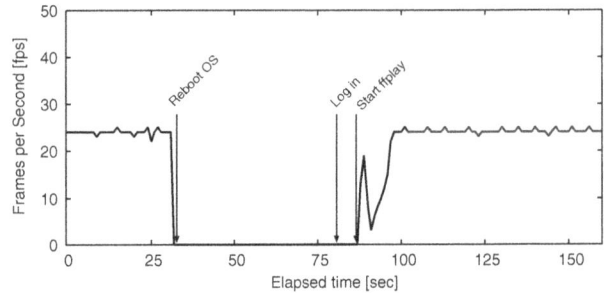

(a) OS Reboot

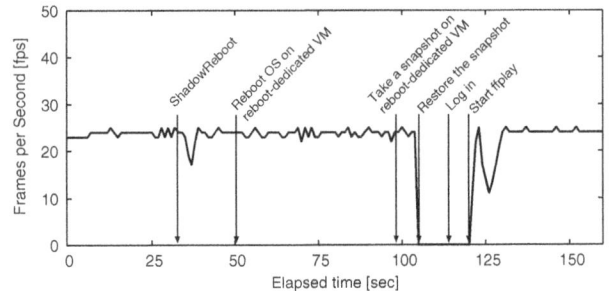

(b) ShadowReboot

Figure 3. Frames per seconds in `ffplay` during normal OS reboot and ShadowReboot.

stack contains a return address within that function's text. Ksplice is designed to manipulate the text region, not to handle the memory objects in the kernel heap region. Additionally, this approach cannot update the *non-quiescent* kernel functions that are always on the call stack of some kernel threads. These approaches also do not manage the system configuration changes or shared component updates because the running processes are not restarted. We can complementarily use ShadowReboot to handle such updates with shorter downtime.

Some approaches require the development of special patches from the original ones. LUCOS [5] forces users to implement new functions that can handle the kernel memory objects to keep them consistent before and after the translation. In DynAMOS [16], users have to investigate how the target functions are used by the kernel threads and implement a routine that consistently updates them. ShadowReboot does not need to perform such tasks.

Other approaches involve paying the high engineering cost of redesigning and modifying a large part of the kernels. To use K42's techniques [3, 11, 19] on commodity OS kernels, we have to redesign the target kernels in an object-oriented manner. Commodity OS kernels are often difficult to modify because recent kernels are complex and some are closed-source and/or proprietary. ShadowReboot does not require any modification of the OS kernels.

MicroVisor [14] conducts a process migration between two VMs connected to a shared network storage, such as an NFS server and a SAN. An administrator runs the applications in one VM and maintains the kernel in the other. When the maintenance has finished, the applications running on the older kernel in the first VM are migrated to the newer kernel in the second VM. Finally, the first VM is discarded. Although these approaches successfully hide the downtime of the kernel maintenance, the process migration is unsuitable for system configuration changes and shared components updates. Since migrated processes are running with the configuration of the older OS, their states remain older on the newer OS. An administrator has to carefully choose the processes that can be migrated to avoid a configuration mismatch of the processes between the older and newer OSes, on the basis of which the configuration or component is updated. ShadowReboot systematically provides users a consistent system state.

Some studies have explored ways to manage downtime of OS reboots. Phase-based Reboot [25] shortens the downtime of reboot-based recovery. It takes snapshots every boot phase such as OS kernel boot and service process boot phases, and reuses them if the next boot is the same execution as the previous boot. Since Phase-based Reboot focuses on reboot-based recovery and reuse of the previous states, it is not applicable to software updates. Otherworld [7] hides the kernel termination from the user-level applications. When a kernel failure occurs, Otherworld restarts only the OS kernel, keeping the user-level memory states of the processes. After the OS kernel has been rebooted, the processes are resumed. However, Otherworld still has a longer downtime than ShadowReboot. Furthermore, Otherworld is not applicable to software updates since an OS kernel, which is loaded when the main kernel is stopped, needs to be set up when it launches.

The shadow driver technique [20] conceals device driver crashes from user's applications. When a device driver crashes, the shadow driver hooks the communications between the kernel and devices, restarts the crashed driver, and queues the messages until its restart completes. The shadow driver transmits the messages to the restarted driver. This technique also allows us to efficiently update device drivers [21]. While the shadow driver technique focuses on device driver restarts, our focus is on OS restarts.

8. Conclusion

This paper presented ShadowReboot, a VMM-based approach that shortens downtime of OS reboots in software updates. ShadowReboot provides an illusion that a guest OS travels *forward* in time to the rebooted state where the updated kernel and applications are ready for use. Specifically, ShadowReboot conceals OS reboot activities from user's applications by spawning a VM dedicated to an OS reboot and systematically producing the rebooted state. Our experimental results show that ShadowReboot succeeded in software updates on unmodified commodity OSes and has 91 to 98% shorter downtime than commodity OS reboots on the five Linux distributions.

One future direction is to exploit cloud environments for rebooting an OS by combining cloud-aware clone techniques with ShadowReboot. Recent studies [4, 6] have shown techniques that clone the system states and send the cloned ones to the cloud platform. By spawning reboot-dedicated VMs in the cloud, we can perform ShadowReboot with less local resource contention with the original VM. In other words, we will build a "Reboot as a Service" platform that reboots an OS transparently for users and sends the rebooted image back to them, which will be able to encourage users to perform software updates more often.

Aknowledgements

We would like to thank the anonymous reviewers and our shepherd, Doug Simon, for their valuable comments on this paper.

References

[1] Y. Abe, H. Yamada, and K. Kono. Enforcing Appropriate Process Execution for Exploiting Idle Resources from Outside Operating Systems. In *Proceedings of the 3rd ACM European Conference on Computer Systems (EuroSys '08)*, pages 27–40, Apr. 2008.

[2] J. Arnold and M. F. Kaashoek. Ksplice: Automatic Rebootless Kernel Updates. In *Proceedings of the 4th ACM European Conference on Computer Systems (EuroSys '09)*, pages 187–198, Apr. 2009.

[3] A. Baumann, J. Appavoo, R. W. Wisniewski, D. D. Silva, O. Krieger, and G. Heiser. Reboots are for Hardware: Challenges and Solutions to Updating an Operating System on the Fly. In *Proceedings of the USENIX Annual Technical Conference (ATC '07)*, pages 337–350, Jun. 2007.

[4] N. Bila, E. de Lara, K. Joshi, H. A. Lagar-Cavilla, M. Hiltunen, and M. Satyanarayanan. Jettison: Efficient Idle Desktop Consolidation with Partial Migration. In *Proceedings of the 7th ACM European Conference on Computer Systems (EuroSys '12)*, pages 211–224, Apr. 2012.

[5] H. Chen, R. Chen, F. Zhang, B. Zang, and P.-C. Yew. Live Updating Operating Systems Using Virtualization. In *Proceedings of the 2nd ACM International Conference on Virtual Execution Environments (VEE '06)*, pages 35–44, Jun. 2006.

[6] B.-G. Chun, S. Ihm, P. Maniatis, M. Naik, and A. Patti. CloneCloud: Elastic Execution between Mobile Device and Cloud. In *Proc. of the 6th ACM European Conference on Computer Systems (EuroSys '11)*, pages 301–314, Apr. 2011.

[7] A. Depoutovitch and M. Stumm. Otherworld - Giving Applications a Change to Servive OS Kernel Crashes. In *Proceedings of the 5th ACM European Conference on Computer Systems (EuroSys '10)*, pages 181–194, Apr. 2010.

[8] L. Eggert and J. D. Touch. Idletime Scheduling with Preemption Intervals. In *Proceedings of the 20th ACM Symposium on Operating Systems Principles (SOSP '05)*, pages 249–262, Oct. 2005.

[9] FFmpeg Project. Ffmpeg. http://ffmpeg.org/.

[10] D. Gupta, S. Lee, M. Vrable, S. Savage, A. C. Snoeren, G. Varghese, G. M. Voelker, and A. Vahdat. Difference Engine: Harnessing Memory Redundancy in Virtual Machines. In *Proceedings of the 8th USENIX Symposium on Operating Systems Design and Implementation (OSDI '08)*, pages 309–322, Dec. 2008.

[11] O. Krieger, M. Auslander, B. Rosenburg, R. W. Wisniewski, J. Xenidis, D. D. Silva, M. Ostrowski, J. Appavoo, M. Butrico, M. Mergen, A. Waterland, and V. Uhlig. K42: Building a Complete Operating System. In *Proceedings of the 1st ACM European Conference on Computer Systems (EuroSys '06)*, pages 133–145, Apr. 2006.

[12] G. Kroah-Hartman, J. Corbet, and A. McPherson. Linux kernel development, 2009.

[13] H. A. Lagar-Cavilla, J. A. Whitney, A. M. Scannell, P. Patchin, S. M. Rumble, E. de Lara, M. Brudno, and M. Satyarayanan. SnowFlock: Rapid Virtual Machine Cloning for Could Computing. In *Proceedings of the 4th ACM European Conf. on Computer Systems (EuroSys '09)*, pages 1–12, Apr. 2009.

[14] D. E. Lowell, Y. Saito, and E. J. Samberg. Devirtualizable Virtual Machines Enabling General, Single-Node, Online Maintenance. In *Proceedings of the 11th ACM International Conference on Architectural Support for Programming Languages and Operating Systems (ASPLOS '04)*, pages 211–223, Oct. 2004.

[15] C. R. Lumb, J. Schindler, and G. R. Ganger. Freeblock Scheduling Outside of Disk Firmware. In *Proceedings of the 1st USENIX Symposium on File and Storage Technologies (FAST '02)*, pages 10–22, Jan. 2002.

[16] K. Makris and K. D. Ryu. Dynamic and Adaptive Updates of Non-Quiescent Subsystems in Commodity Operating System Kernels. In *Proceedings of the 2nd ACM European Conference on Computer Systems (EuroSys '07)*, pages 327–340, Mar. 2007.

[17] G. Milos, D. G. Murray, S. Hand, and M. A. Fetterman. Satori: Enlightened page sharing. In *Proceedings of the USENIX Annual Technical Conference (USENIX '09)*, pages 1–14, Jun. 2009.

[18] ORACLE. Virtualbox, 2007. http://www.virualbox.org.

[19] C. A. N. Soules, J. Appavoo, K. Hui, R. W. Wisniewski, D. D. Silva, G. R. Ganger, O. Krieger, M. Stumm, M. Auslander, M. Ostrowski, B. Rosenburg, and J. Xenidis. System Support for Online Reconfiguration. In *Proceedings of the USENIX Annual Technical Conference (ATC '03)*, pages 141–154, Jun. 2003.

[20] M. M. Swift, M. Annamalai, B. N. Bershad, and H. M. Levy. Recovering device drivers. In *Proceedings of the 6th USENIX Symposium*

on Operating Systems Design and Implementation (OSDI '04), pages 1–16, Dec. 2004.

[21] M. M. Swift, D. Martin-Guillerez, M. Annamalai, B. N. Bershad, and H. M. Levy. Live Update for Device Drivers. Technical Report CS-TR-2008-1634, University of Winsconsin Computer Sciences, Mar. 2008.

[22] The Apache Software Foundation. Apache HTTP server, 1995. `http://www.apache.org/`.

[23] M. Vrable, J. Ma, J. Chen, D. Moore, E. Vandekieft, A. Snoeren, G. Voelker, and S. Savage. Scalability, Fidelity, and Containment in the Potemkin Virtual Honeyfarm. In *Proceedings of the 20th ACM Symposium on Operating Systems Principles (SOSP '05)*, pages 148–162, Oct. 2005.

[24] C. A. Waldspurger. Memory Resource Management in VMware ESX Server. In *Proceedings of the 5th USENIX Symposium on Operating System Design and Implementation (OSDI '02)*, pages 181–194, Dec. 2002.

[25] K. Yamakita, H. Yamada, and K. Kono. Phase-based Reboot: Reusing Operating System Execution Phases for Cheap Reboot-based Recovery. In *Proc. of the 41st Annual IEEE/IFIP International Conference on Dependable Systems and Networks (DSN '11)*, pages 169–180, Jun. 2011.

Performance Potential of Optimization Phase Selection During Dynamic JIT Compilation

Michael R. Jantz   Prasad A. Kulkarni

Electrical Engineering and Computer Science, University of Kansas
{mjantz,kulkarni}@ittc.ku.edu

Abstract

Phase selection is the process of customizing the applied set of compiler optimization phases for individual functions or programs to improve performance of generated code. Researchers have recently developed novel feature-vector based heuristic techniques to perform phase selection during online JIT compilation. While these heuristics improve program *startup* speed, *steady-state* performance was not seen to benefit over the default fixed single sequence baseline. Unfortunately, *it is still not conclusively known whether this lack of steady-state performance gain is due to a failure of existing online phase selection heuristics, or because there is, indeed, little or no speedup to be gained by phase selection in online JIT environments*. The goal of this work is to resolve this question, while examining the phase selection related behavior of optimizations, and assessing and improving the effectiveness of existing heuristic solutions.

We conduct experiments to find and understand the potency of the factors that can cause the phase selection problem in JIT compilers. Next, using long-running genetic algorithms we determine that program-wide and method-specific phase selection in the HotSpot JIT compiler can produce *ideal* steady-state performance gains of up to 15% (4.3% average) and 44% (6.2% average) respectively. We also find that existing state-of-the-art heuristic solutions are unable to realize these performance gains (in our experimental setup), discuss possible causes, and show that exploiting knowledge of optimization phase behavior can help improve such heuristic solutions. Our work develops a robust open-source production-quality framework using the HotSpot JVM to further explore this problem in the future.

Categories and Subject Descriptors D.3 [*Software*]: Programming languages; D.3.4 [*Programming languages*]: Processors—Compilers, Optimizations; I.2.6 [*Artificial intelligence*]: Learning—Induction

General Terms Performance, Experimentation, Languages

Keywords Phase selection, Compiler optimizations, HotSpot

VEE'13, March 16–17, 2013, Houston, Texas, USA.
Copyright © 2013 ACM 978-1-4503-1266-0/13/03... $15.00

1. Introduction

An optimization phase in a compiler transforms the input program into a semantically equivalent version with the goal of improving the performance of generated code. Quality compilers implement many optimizations. Researchers have found that the set of optimizations producing the best quality code varies for each method/program and can result in substantial performance benefits over always applying any single optimization sequence [5, 12]. *Optimization phase selection* is the process of automatically finding the best set of optimizations for each method/program to maximize performance of generated code, and is an important, fundamental, but unresolved problem in compiler optimization.

We distinguish phase selection from the related issue of *phase ordering*, which explores the effect of different orderings of optimization phases on program performance. We find that although phase ordering is possible in some research compilers, such as VPO [17] and Jikes Research Virtual Machine (VM) [19], reordering optimization phases is extremely hard to support in most production systems, including GCC [8] and the HotSpot VM, due to their use of multiple intermediate formats and complex inherent dependencies between optimizations. Therefore, our work for this paper conducted using the HotSpot JVM only explores the problem of phase selection by selectively turning optimization phases ON and OFF.

The problem of optimization selection has been extensively investigated by the static compiler community [2, 8, 12, 25]. Unfortunately, techniques employed to successfully address this problem in static compilers (such as *iterative compilation*) are not always applicable to dynamic or JIT (Just-in-Time) compilers. Since compilation occurs at runtime, one over-riding constraint for dynamic compilers is the need to be fast so as to minimize interference with program execution and to make the optimized code available for execution sooner. To realize fast online phase selection, researchers have developed novel techniques that employ feature-vector based machine-learning heuristics to quickly customize the set of optimizations applied to each method [5, 23]. Such heuristic solutions perform the time-consuming task of *model learning* offline, and then use the models to quickly customize optimization sets for individual programs/methods online during JIT compilation.

It has been observed that while such existing online phase selection techniques improve program *startup* (application + compilation) speed, they do not benefit throughput or *steady-state* performance (program speed after all compilation activity is complete). Program throughput is very important to many longer-running applications. Additionally, with the near-universal availability of increasingly parallel computing resources in modern multi/many-core processors and the ability of modern VMs to spawn multiple asynchronous compiler threads, researchers expect the compilation overhead to become an even smaller component of the total program runtime [16]. Consequently, achieving steady-state or *code-quality* improvements is becoming increasingly important for modern systems. Unfortunately, while researchers are still investing in the development of new techniques to resolve phase selection, *we do not yet conclusively know whether the lack of steady-state performance gain provided by existing online phase selection techniques is a failure of these techniques, or because there is, indeed, little or no speedup to be gained by phase selection in online environments.* While addressing this primary question, we make the following contributions in this work.

1. We conduct a thorough analysis to understand the phase selection related behavior of JIT compiler optimization phases and identify the potency of factors that could produce the phase selection problem,

2. We conduct long-running (genetic algorithm based) iterative searches to determine the *ideal* benefits of phase selection in online JIT environments,

3. We evaluate the accuracy and effectiveness of existing state-of-the-art online heuristic techniques in achieving the benefit delivered by (the more expensive) iterative search techniques and discuss improvements, and

4. We construct a robust open-source framework for dynamic JIT compiler phase selection exploration in the standard Sun/Oracle HotSpot Java virtual machine (JVM) [21]. Our framework prepares 28 optimizations in the HotSpot compiler for individual fine-grain control by different phase selection algorithms.

The rest of the paper is organized as follows. We present related work in the next section. We describe our HotSpot based experimental framework and benchmark set in Section 3. We explore the behavior of HotSpot compiler optimizations and present our observations in Section 4. We present our results on the ideal case performance benefits of phase sequence customization at the whole-program and per-method levels in Section 5. We determine the effectiveness of existing feature-vector based heuristic techniques and provide feedback on improving them in Section 6. Finally, we present our planned future work and the conclusions of this study in Sections 7 and 8 respectively.

2. Background and Related Work

In this section we provide some overview and describe related works in the area of optimization phase selection research. Phase selection and ordering are long-standing problems in compiler optimization. Several studies have also discovered that there is no single optimization set that can produce optimal code for every method/program [2]. A common technique to address the phase selection problem in static compilers is to iteratively evaluate the performance of many/all different phase sequences to find the best one for individual methods or programs. Unfortunately, with the large number of optimizations present in modern compilers (say, n), the search space of all possible combinations of optimization settings (2^n) can be very large. Therefore, researchers have in the past employed various techniques to reduce the space of potential candidate solutions. Chow and Wu applied a technique called fractional factorial design to systematically design a series of experiments to select a good set of program-specific optimization phases by determining interactions between phases [6]. Haneda et al. employed statistical analysis of the effect of compiler options to prune the phase selection search space and find a single compiler setting for a collection of programs that performs better than the standard settings used in GCC [11]. Pan and Eigenmann developed three heuristic algorithms to quickly select good compiler optimization settings, and found that their combined approach that first identifies phases with negative performance effects and greedily eliminates them achieves the best result [22]. Also related is the work by

Fursin et al. who develop a GCC-based framework (MILEPOST GCC) to automatically extract program *features* and learn the best optimizations across programs. Given a new program to compile, this framework can correlate the program's features with the closest program seen earlier to apply a customized and potentially more effective optimization combination [8].

Machine-learning techniques, such as genetic algorithms and hill-climbing, have been commonly employed to search for the best set or ordering of optimizations for individual programs/methods. Cooper et al. were among the first to use machine-learning algorithms to quickly and effectively search the phase selection search space to find program-level optimization sequences to reduce code-size for embedded applications [2, 7]. Hoste and Eeckhout developed a system called *COLE* that uses genetic algorithm based multi-objective evolutionary search algorithm to automatically find pareto optimal optimization settings for GCC [12]. Kulkarni et al. compared the proficiency of several machine-learning algorithms to find the best phase sequence as obtained by their exhaustive search strategy [17]. They observed that search techniques such as genetic algorithms achieve benefit that is very close to that best performance. *We use this result in our current study to characterize the GA-delivered best performance as a good indicator of the performance limit of phase selection in dynamic compilers.*

Also related is their more recent work that compares the ability of GA-based program and function-level searches to find the best phase sequence, and finds the finer-granularity of function-level searches to achieve better overall results in their static C compiler, VPO [18]. All these above studies were conducted for static compilers. Instead, in this work, we use the GA searches to determine the performance limits of phase selection in dynamic compilers.

While program-specific GA and other iterative searches may be acceptable for static compilers, they are too time-consuming for use in dynamic compilers. Consequently, researchers have developed novel techniques to quickly customize phase sequences to individual methods in dynamic JIT compilers. Cavazos and O'Boyle employed the technique of logistic regression to learn a predictive model offline that can later be used in online compilation environments (like their Jikes Research VM) to derive customized optimization sequences for methods based on its features [5]. Another related work by Sanchez et al. used support vector machines to learn and discover method-specific compilation sequences in IBM's (closed-source) production JVM [23]. This work used a different learning algorithm and was conducted in a production JVM. While these techniques reduce program startup times due to savings in the compilation overhead, the feature-vector based online algorithm was not able to improve program steady-state performance over the default compiler configuration. Additionally, none of the existing works attempt to determine the potential benefit of phase selection to improve code-quality in a dynamic compiler. While resolving this important question, we also evaluate the success of existing heuristic schemes to achieve this best potential performance benefit in the HotSpot production JVM.

In this paper, we also investigate the behavior of optimizations to better understand the scope and extent of the optimization selection problem in dynamic compilers. Earlier researchers have attempted to measure the benefit of dynamic optimizations, for example, to overcome the overheads induced by the safety and flexibility constraints of Java [14], in cross-platform implementations [15], and to explore optimization synergies [20]. However, none of these works perform their studies in the context of understanding the optimization selection problem for JIT compilers.

3. Experimental Framework

In this section, we describe the compiler and benchmarks used, and the methodology employed for our experiments.

Optimization Phase	Description
aggressive copy coalescing	Perform aggressive copy coalescing after coming out of SSA form (before register allocation).
block layout by frequency	Use edge frequencies to drive block ordering.
block layout rotate loops	Allow back branches to be fall through when determining block layout.
conditional constant prop.	Perform optimistic sparse conditional constant propagation until a fixed point is reached.
conservative copy coalescing	Perform conservative copy coalescing during register allocation (RA). Requires RA is enabled.
do escape analysis	Identify and optimize objects that are accessible only within one method or thread.
eliminate allocations	Use escape analysis to eliminate allocations.
global code motion	Hoist instructions to block with least execution frequency.
inline	Replace (non accessor/mutator) method calls with the body of the method.
inline accessors	Replace accessor/mutator method calls with the body of the method.
instruction scheduling	Perform instruction scheduling after register allocation.
iterative global value numbering (GVN)	Iteratively replaces nodes with their values if the value has been previously recorded (applied in several places after parsing).
loop peeling	Peel out the first iteration of a loop.
loop unswitching	Clone loops with an invariant test and insert a clone of the test that selects which version to execute.
optimize null checks	Detect implicit null check opportunities (e.g. null checks with suitable memory operations nearby use the memory operation to perform the null check).
parse-time GVN	Replaces nodes with their values if the value has been previously recorded during parsing.
partial loop peeling	Partially peel the top portion of a loop by cloning and placing one copy just before the new loop head and the other copy at the bottom of the new loop (also known as loop rotation).
peephole remove copies	Apply peephole copy removal immediately following register allocation.
range check elimination	Split loop iterations to eliminate range checks.
reassociate invariants	Re-associates expressions with loop invariants.
register allocation	Employ a Briggs-Chaitin style graph coloring register allocator to assign registers to live ranges.
remove useless nodes	Identify and remove useless nodes in the ideal graph after parsing.
split if blocks	Folds some branches by cloning compares and control flow through merge points.
use loop predicate	Generate a predicate to select fast/slow loop versions.
use super word	Transform scalar operations into packed (super word) operations.
eliminate auto box*	Eliminate extra nodes in the ideal graph due to autoboxing.
optimize fills*	Convert fill/copy loops into an intrinsic method.
optimize strings*	Optimize strings constructed by StringBuilder.

Table 1. Configurable optimizations in our modified HotSpot compiler. Optimizations marked with ∗ are disabled in the default compiler.

3.1 Compiler and Benchmarks

We perform our study using the server compiler in Sun/Oracle's HotSpot Java virtual machine (build 1.6.0_25-b06) [21]. Similar to many production compilers, *HotSpot imposes a strict ordering on optimization phases* due to the use of multiple intermediate representations and documented or undocumented assumptions and dependencies between different phases. Additionally, the HotSpot compiler applies a fixed set of optimizations to every method it compiles. The compilation process parses the method's bytecodes into a static single assignment (SSA) representation known as the *ideal graph*. Several optimizations, including method inlining, are applied as the method's bytecodes are parsed. The compiler then performs a fixed set of optimizations on the resultant structure before converting to machine instructions, performing scheduling and register allocation, and finally generating machine code.

The HotSpot JVM provides command-line flags to optionally enable or disable several optimizations. However, many optimization phases do not have such flags, and some also generate/update analysis information used by later stages. We modified the HotSpot compiler to provide command-line flags for most optimization phases, and factored out the analysis calculation so that it is computed regardless of the optimization setting. Some transformations, such as *constant folding* and *instruction selection*, are required by later stages to produce correct code and are hard to effectively disable. We also do not include a flag for *dead code elimination*, which is performed continuously by the structure of the intermediate representation and would require much more invasive changes to disable. We perform innovative modifications to deactivate the compulsory phases of *register allocation* (RA) and *global code motion* (GCM). The disabled version of RA assumes every register conflicts with every live range, and thus, always spills live ranges to

memory. Likewise, the disabled version of GCM schedules all instructions to execute as late as possible and does not attempt to hoist instructions to blocks that may be executed much less frequently. Finally, we modified the HotSpot JVM to accept binary sequences describing the application status (ON/OFF) of each phase at the program or method-level. Thus, *while not altering any optimization algorithm or the baseline compiler configuration, we made several major updates to the HotSpot JIT compiler to facilitate its use during phase selection research.* Table 1 shows the complete set of optimization phases that we are now able to optionally enable or disable for our experiments.

Our experiments were conducted over applications from two suites of benchmarks. We use all SPECjvm98 benchmarks [24] with two input sizes (10 and 100), and 12 (of 14) applications from the DaCapo benchmark suite [4] with the small and default inputs. Two DaCapo benchmarks, *tradebeans* and *tradesoap*, are excluded from our study since they do not always run correctly with our *default* HotSpot VM.

3.2 Performance Measurement

One of the goals of this research is to quantify the performance benefit of optimization phase selection *with regards to generated code quality* in a production-grade dynamic compiler. Therefore, the experiments in this study discount compilation time and measure the *steady-state* performance. In the default mode, the VM employs *selective compilation* and only compiles methods with execution counts that exceed the selected threshold. Our experimental setup first determines this set of (hot) methods compiled during the *startup* mode for each benchmark. All our steady-state experiments only compile this hot method set for all its program runs. Both the SPECjvm98 and DaCapo harness allow each benchmark to be iterated multiple times in the same VM run. During our steady-state program runs we disable background compilation to force all these hot methods to be compiled in the first program iteration. We modify our VM to reset execution counts after each iteration to prevent methods from becoming hot (and getting compiled) in later iterations. We allow each benchmark to iterate five more times and record the median runtime of these iterations as the steady-state program run-time. To account for inherent timing variations during the benchmark runs, *all the performance results in this paper report the average and 95% confidence intervals over ten steady-state runs* using the setup described by Georges et al. [9].

All experiments were performed on a cluster of Dell PowerEdge 1850 server machines running Red Hat Enterprise Linux 5.1 as the operating system. Each machine has four 64-bit 2.8GHz Intel Xeon processors, 6GB of DDR2 SDRAM, and a 4MB L2 cache. Our HotSpot VM uses the stand-alone server compiler and the default garbage collector settings for "server-class" machines [13] ("parallel collector" GC, initial heap size is 96MB, maximum is 1GB). We make no attempt to restrict or control GC during our experiments. Finally, there are no hyperthreading or frequency scaling techniques of any kind enabled during our experiments.

4. Analyzing Behavior of Compiler Optimizations for Phase Selection

Compiler optimizations are designed to improve program performance. Therefore, it is often (naïvely) expected that always applying (turning ON) all available optimizations to all program regions should generate the best quality code. However, optimizations operating on the same program code and competing for finite machine resources (registers) may interact with each other. Such interactions may remove opportunities for later optimizations to generate even better code. Additionally, program performance is often very hard for the compiler to predict on the current generation of machines with complex architectural and micro-architectural features. Consequently, program transformations performed by an optimization may not always benefit program execution speed. The goal of effective phase selection is to find and disable optimizations with negative effects for each program region. In this section we conduct a series of experiments to explore important optimization selection issues, such as why and when is optimization selection effective for standard dynamic JIT compilers. We are also interested in finding indicators to suggest that customizing optimization selections for individual programs or methods is likely to benefit performance. We report several interesting observations that help explain both the prior as well as our current results in phase selection research for dynamic JIT compilers.

4.1 Experimental Setup

Our setup to analyze the behavior of optimization phases is inspired by Lee et al.'s framework to determine the benefits and costs of compiler optimizations [20]. Our experimental configuration (*defOpt*) uses the default HotSpot server compilation sequence as baseline. The execution time of each benchmark with this baseline ($T(OPT < defOpt >)$) is compared with its time obtained by a JIT compiler that disables one optimization (x) at a time ($T(OPT < defOpt - x >)$). We use the following fraction to quantify the effect of HotSpot optimizations in this configuration.

$$\frac{T(OPT < defOpt - x >) - T(OPT < defOpt >)}{T(OPT < defOpt >)} \quad (1)$$

Each experimental run disables only one optimization (out of 25) from the optimization set used in the default HotSpot compiler. Equation 1 computes a negative value if removing the corresponding optimization, x, from the baseline optimization set improves

performance (reduces program runtime) of the generated code. In other words, a negative value implies that including that optimization harms performance of the generated code. The HotSpot JIT compiler uses an individual method for its compilation unit. Therefore, in this section we evaluate the effect of compiler optimizations over distinct program methods.

Our experiments in this section are conducted over 53 *hot* focus methods over all the programs in our benchmark suite. These focus methods are selected because each comprises *at least* 10% of its respective benchmark run-time. More details on the rationale and selection of focus methods, as well as a complete list of these methods, are provided in Section 5.3.1.

4.2 Results and Observations

Figure 1 (left Y-axis, bar-plot) illustrates the *accumulated* negative and positive impact of each optimization calculated using Equation 1 over all our 53 individual program methods. For each HotSpot optimization, Figure 1 (right Y-axis, line-plot) also shows the number of program methods that witness a negative or positive impact. These results enable us to make several important observations regarding the behavior of optimizations in the HotSpot JIT compiler. **First**, the results validate the claims that optimizations are not always beneficial to program performance. This observation provides the motivation and justification for further developing and exploring effective phase selection algorithms to enable the JIT compiler to generate the best possible output code for each method/program. **Second**, we observe that *most* optimizations in the HotSpot JIT compiler produce, at least occasional, negative effects. This observation indicates that eliminating the optimization phase selection issue may require researchers to understand and update several different compiler optimizations, which makes a compiler design-time solution very hard. **Third**, most optimizations do not negatively impact a large number of program methods, and the typical negative impact is also not very high. However, we also find optimizations, including *AggressiveCoalesce*, *IterGVN*, and *SplitIf-Blocks*, that, rather than improving, show a degrading performance impact more often. This result is surprising since dynamic compilers generally only provide the more conservative compiler optimizations.[1] Thus, this study finds optimizations that need to be urgently analyzed to alleviate the optimization selection problem in HotSpot. **Fourth**, we unexpectedly find that most of the optimizations in the HotSpot JIT compiler only have a marginal individual influence on performance. We observe that *method inlining* is by far the most beneficial compiler optimization in HotSpot, followed by *register allocation*.[2]

Figure 2 plots the accumulated positive and negative optimization impact (on left Y-axis, bar-plot) and the number of optimizations that impact performance (on right Y-axis, line-plot) for each of our focus methods represented along the X-axis. These results allow us to make two other observations that are particularly enlightening. **First**, there are typically not many optimizations that

---

[1] Compare the 28 optimization flags in HotSpot with over 100 such flags provided by GCC.

[2] Method inlining is a difficult optimization to control. Our experimental setup, which uses a fixed list of methods to compile, may slightly exaggerate the performance impact of disabling method inlining because some methods that would normally be inlined may not be compiled at all if they are not in the hot method list. To avoid such exaggeration, one possibility is to detect and compile such methods when inlining is disabled. However, an inlined method (say, P) that is not otherwise compiled spends its X inlined invocations in compiled code, but other Y invocations in interpreted code. With inlining disabled for the focus method, if P is compiled then it will spend all 'X+Y' invocations in compiled code. We chose the exaggeration because we found that it was very uncommon for methods not in the fixed list to still be inlinable.

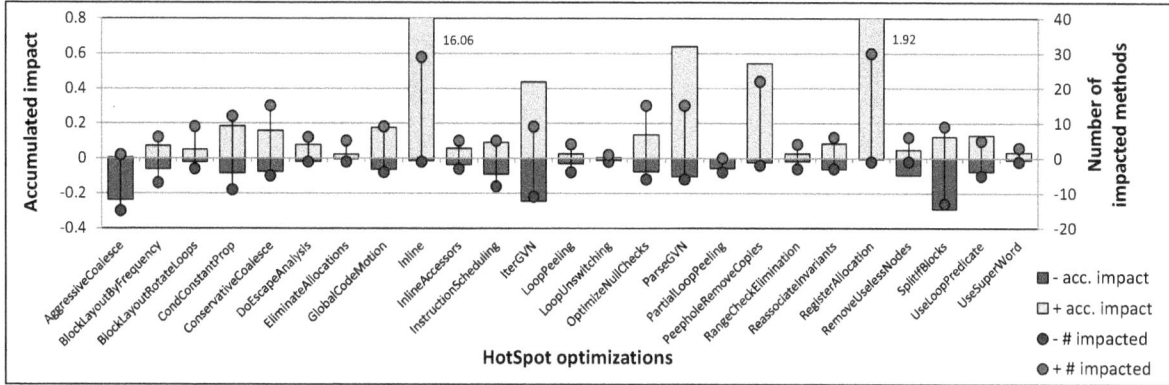

Figure 1. Left Y-axis: Accumulated positive and negative impact of each HotSpot optimization over our focus methods (non-scaled). **Right Y-axis:** Number of focus methods that are positively or negatively impacted by each HotSpot optimization.

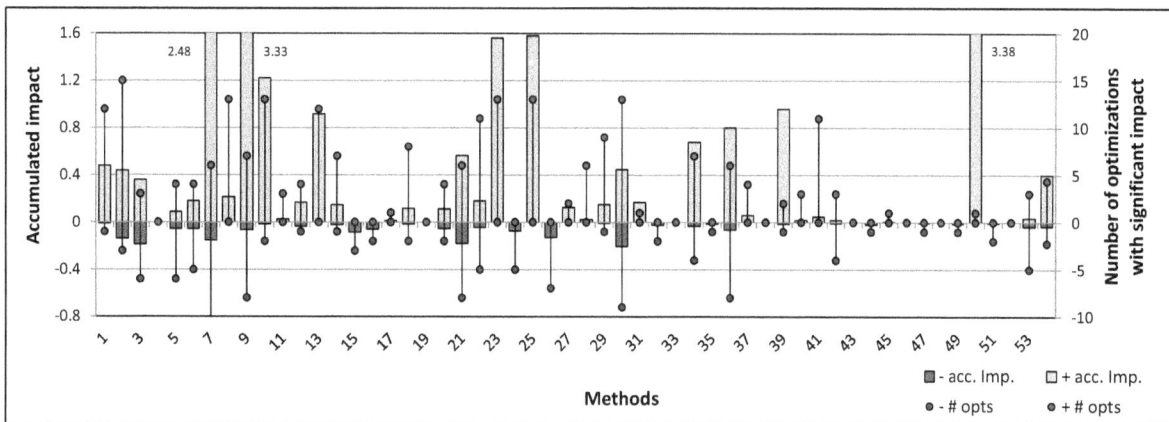

Figure 2. Left Y-axis: Accumulated positive and negative impact of the 25 HotSpot optimizations for each focus method (non-scaled). **Right Y-axis:** Number of optimizations that positively or negatively impact each focus method.

degrade performance for any single method (2.2 out of 25, on average). More importantly, even for methods with several individual degrading optimizations, the accumulated negative impact is never very high. This result, in a way, tempers the expectations of performance improvements from ideal phase selection in JIT compilers (particularly, HotSpot). In other words, we can only expect customized phase selections to provide modest performance benefits for individual methods/programs in most cases. **Second**, for most methods, there are only a few optimizations (4.36 out of 25, on average) that benefit performance. Thus, there is a huge potential for saving compilation overhead during program *startup* by disabling the *inactive* optimizations. It is this, hitherto unreported, attribute of JIT compilers that enables the online feature-vector based phase selection algorithms to improve program startup performance in earlier works [5, 23].

Finally, we note that although this simple study provides useful information regarding optimization behavior, it may not capture all possible optimization interactions that can be simultaneously active in a single optimization setting for a method. For example, phase interactions may cause compiler optimization phases that degrade performance when applied alone to improve performance when combined with other optimizations. However, these simple experiments provided us with both the motivation to further explore the potential of phase selection for dynamic compilers, while lowering our expectations for large performance benefits.

5. Limits of Optimization Selection

Most dynamic JIT compilers apply the same set of optimization phases to all methods and programs. Our results in the last section indicate the potential for performance gains by customizing optimization phase selection for individual (smaller) code regions. In this section we conduct experiments to quantify the steady-state speed benefits of customizing optimization sets for individual programs/methods in JIT compilers. The large number of optimizations in HotSpot makes it unfeasible to perform *exhaustive* optimization selection search space evaluation. Earlier research has demonstrated that genetic algorithms (GA) are highly effective at finding near-optimal phase sequences [17]. Therefore, we use a variant of a popular GA to find effective program-level and method-level optimization phase selection solutions [7]. Correspondingly, *we term the benefit in program run-time achieved by the GA derived phase sequence over the default HotSpot VM as the ideal performance benefit of phase selection for each program/method.*

We also emphasize that it is impractical to employ a GA-based solution to customize optimization sets in an online JIT compilation environment. Our program-wide and method-specific GA experiments are intended to only determine the performance limits of phase selection. We use these limits in the next section to evaluate the effectiveness of existing state-of-the-art heuristics to specialize optimization sets in online JIT compilers.

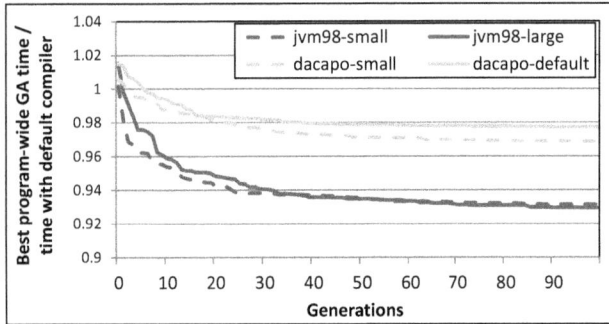

Figure 3. Average performance of best GA sequence in each generation compared to the default compiler.

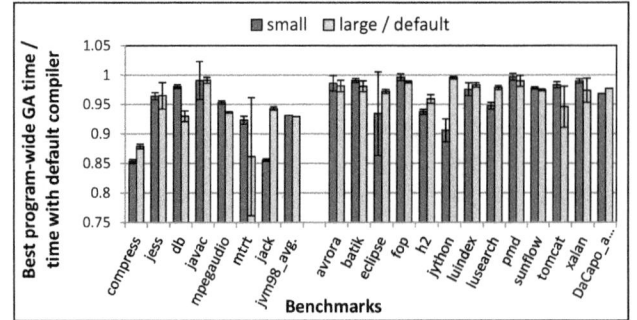

Figure 4. Performance of best program-wide optimization phase sequence after 100 generations of genetic algorithm.

5.1 Genetic Algorithm Description

In this section we describe the genetic algorithm we employ for our phase selection experiments. Genetic algorithms are heuristic search techniques that mimic the process of natural evolution [10]. *Genes* in the GA correspond to binary digits indicating the ON/OFF status of an optimization. *Chromosomes* correspond to optimization phase selections. The set of chromosomes currently under consideration constitutes a *population*. The evolution of a population occurs in *generations*. Each generation evaluates the *fitness* of every chromosome in the current population, and then uses the operations of *crossover* and *mutation* to create the next population. The number of *generations* specifies the number of population sets to evaluate. Chromosomes in the first GA generation are randomly initialized. After evaluating the performance of code generated by each chromosome in the *population*, they are sorted in decreasing order of performance. During *crossover*, 20% of chromosomes from the poorly performing half of the population are replaced by repeatedly selecting two chromosomes from the better half of the population and replacing the lower half of each chromosome with the lower half of the other to produce two new chromosomes each time. During *mutation* we flip the ON/OFF status of each gene with a small probability of 5% for chromosomes in the upper half of the population and 10% for the chromosomes in the lower half. The chromosomes replaced during crossover, as well as (up to five) chromosome(s) with performance(s) within one standard deviation of the best performance in the generation are not mutated. The *fitness criteria* used by our GA is the steady-state performance of the benchmark. For this study, we have 20 chromosomes in each population and run the GA for 100 generations. We have verified that 100 generations are sufficient for the GA to reach saturation in most cases. To speed-up the GA runs, we developed a parallel GA implementation that can simultaneously evaluate multiple chromosomes in a generation on a cluster of identically-configured machines.

5.2 Program-Wide GA Results

In this experiment we use our GA to find unique optimization selections for each of our benchmark-input pairs. Figure 3 plots the performance of code compiled with the best optimization set found by the GA in each generation as compared to the code generated by the default compiler sequence averaged over all programs for each benchmark suite. This figure shows that most (over 75%) of the average performance gains are realized in the first few (20) GA generations. Also, over 90% of the best average performance is obtained after 50 generations. Thus, 100 generations seem sufficient for our GA to converge on its near-best solution for most benchmarks. We also find that the SPECjvm98 benchmarks benefit more from optimization specialization than the DaCapo benchmarks. As

expected, different inputs do not seem to significantly affect the steady-state optimization selection gains for most benchmarks.

Figure 4 compares the performance of each program optimized with the best program-wide optimization phase set found by our genetic algorithm with the program performance achieved by the default HotSpot server compiler for both our benchmark suites. The error bars show the 95% confidence interval for the difference between the means over 10 runs of the best customized optimization selection and the default compiler sequence. We note that the default optimization sequence in the HotSpot compiler has been heavily tuned over several years to meet market expectations for Java performance, and thus presents a very aggressive baseline. In spite of this aggressively tuned baseline, we find that customizing optimization selections can significantly improve performance (up to 15%) for several of our benchmark programs.

On average, the SPECjvm98 benchmarks improve by about 7% with both their *small* and *large* inputs. However, for programs in the DaCapo benchmark suite, program-wide optimization set specialization achieves smaller average benefits of 3.2% and 2.3% for their *small* and *default* input sizes respectively. The DaCapo benchmarks typically contain many more *hot* and *total* program methods as compared to the SPECjvm98 benchmarks. Additionally, unlike several SPECjvm98 programs that have a single or few dominant hot methods, most DaCapo benchmarks have a relatively flat execution profile with many methods that are similarly hot, with only slightly varying degrees [4]. Therefore, program-wide optimization sets for DaCapo benchmarks are customized over much longer code regions (single optimization set over many more hot methods), which, we believe, results in lower average performance gains from program-wide optimization selection. Over all benchmarks, the average benefit of ideal program-wide phase selection is 4.3%.

5.3 Method-Specific Genetic Algorithm

The default HotSpot compiler optimizes individual methods at a time, and applies the same set of optimizations to each compiled method. Prior research has found that optimization phase sequences tuned to each method yield better program performance than a single program-wide phase sequence [1, 18]. In this section, we explore the performance potential of optimization selection at the method-level during dynamic JIT compilation.

5.3.1 Experimental Setup

There are two possible approaches for implementing GA searches to determine the performance potential of method-specific optimization phase settings: (a) running multiple simultaneous (and independent) GAs to gather optimization sequences for all program methods *concurrently* in the same run, and (b) executing the GA for each method *in isolation* (one method per program run). The first

#	Benchmark	Method	% Time
1	db-large	Database.shell_sort	86.67
2	compress-small	Compressor.compress	54.99
3	compress-large	Compressor.compress	53.42
4	avrora-default	LegacyInterpreter.fastLoop	50.85
5	db-small	Database.shell_sort	50.72
6	jess-small	Node2.findInMemory	48.57
7	jack-small	TokenEngine.getNextTokenFromStream	48.05
8	avrora-small	LegacyInterpreter.fastLoop	44.49
9	jack-large	TokenEngine.getNextTokenFromStream	44.23
10	sunflow-default	KDTree.intersect	40.52
11	luindex-default	DocInverterPerField.processFields	40.43
12	sunflow-default	TriangleMesh$WaldTriangle.intersect	39.20
13	sunflow-small	KDTree.intersect	37.92
14	sunflow-small	TriangleMesh$WaldTriangle.intersect	36.78
15	jess-large	Node2.runTestsVaryRight	34.31
16	jython-small	PyFrame.getlocal	32.73
17	luindex-small	DocInverterPerField.processFields	30.51
18	lusearch-small	SegmentTermEnum.scanTo	29.88
19	lusearch-default	SegmentTermEnum.scanTo	28.76
20	jess-large	Node2.runTests	27.41
21	compress-large	Decompressor.decompress	24.86
22	compress-small	Compressor.output	23.39
23	mpegaudio-small	q.l	23.12
24	batik-default	MorphologyOp.isBetter	22.26
25	mpegaudio-large	q.l	21.87
26	jython-small	PyFrame.setline	21.79
27	xalan-small	ToStream.characters	21.70
28	db-small	ValidityCheckOutputStream.strip1	21.52
29	compress-large	Compressor.output	21.40
30	compress-small	Decompressor.decompress	21.23
31	xalan-default	ToStream.characters	20.00
32	pmd-default	DacapoClassLoader.loadClass	19.26
33	batik-small	PNGImageEncoder.clamp	17.74
34	sunflow-small	BoundingIntervalHierarchy.intersect	15.22
35	h2-small	Query.query	13.84
36	sunflow-default	BoundingIntervalHierarchy.intersect	13.79
37	javac-large	ScannerInputStream.read	13.46
38	javac-large	ScannerInputStream.read	13.17
39	luindex-small	TermsHashPerField.add	13.01
40	mpegaudio-small	tb.u0114	12.88
41	jython-default	PyFrame.setline	12.68
42	mpegaudio-large	tb.u0114	12.61
43	jess-large	Funcall.Execute	12.25
44	luindex-small	StandardTokenizerImpl.getNextToken	12.23
45	lusearch-small	IndexInput.readVLong	11.82
46	lusearch-default	StandardAnalyzer.tokenStream	11.49
47	lusearch-default	IndexInput.readVLong	11.46
48	lusearch-small	StandardAnalyzer.tokenStream	11.44
49	h2-default	Command.executeQueryLocal	11.37
50	luindex-default	TermsHashPerField.add	10.65
51	jython-default	PyFrame.getlocal	10.62
52	eclipse-default	Parser.parse	10.52
53	luindex-default	StandardTokenizerImpl.getNextToken	10.49

Table 2. Focus methods and the % of runtime each comprises of their respective benchmark runs

approach requires instrumenting every program method to record the time spent in each method in a single program run. These individual method times can then be used to concurrently drive independent method-specific GAs for all methods in a program. The VM also needs the ability to use distinct optimization selections to be employed for different program methods. We implemented this experimental scheme for our HotSpot VM by updating the compiler to instrument each method with instructions that employ the x86 TSC (Time-Stamp Counter) to record individual method run-times. However, achieving accurate results with this scheme faces several challenges. The HotSpot JVM contains interprocedural optimizations, such as *method inlining*, due to which varying the optimization sequence of one method affects the performance behavior of other program methods. Additionally, we also found that the order in which methods are compiled can vary from one run of the program to the next, which affects optimization decisions and method run-times. Finally, the added instrumentation to record

method times also adds some noise and impacts optimization application and method performance.

Therefore, we decided to employ the more straight-forward and accurate, but also time-consuming, approach of applying the GA to only one program method at a time. In each program run, the VM uses the optimization set provided by the GA to optimize one *focus method* and the default baseline set of optimizations to compile the other hot program methods. Thus, any reduction in the final program run-time over the baseline program performance can be attributed to the improvement in the single focus method. In an earlier *offline* run, we use our TSC based instrumentations with the baseline compiler configuration to estimate the fraction of total time spent by the program in each focus method. Any improvement in the overall program run-time during the GA is scaled with the fraction of time spent in the focus method to determine the run-time improvement in that individual method. We conduct this experiment over the 53 *focus methods* over all benchmarks that each comprise at least 10% of the time spent in their respective default program run. These methods, along with the % of total runtime each comprises in their respective benchmarks, are listed in Table 2.

5.3.2 Method-Specific GA Results

Figure 5(a) shows the *scaled* benefit in the run-time of each focus method when compiled with the best optimization set returned by the GA as compared to the method time if compiled with the baseline HotSpot server compiler. Methods along the x-axis in this graph are ordered by the fraction that they contribute to their respective overall program run-times (the same order methods are listed in Table 2). The final bar shows the average improvement over the 53 focus methods. Thus, we can see that customizing the optimization set for individual program methods can achieve significant performance benefits in some cases. While the best performance improvement is about 44%, method-specific optimization selection achieves close to a 6.2% reduction in run-time, on average. Figure 5(b) provides a different view of these same results with methods on the x-axis grouped together according to their respective benchmarks.

The plot in Figure 6 verifies that the (*non-scaled*) improvements in individual method run-times add-up over the entire program in most cases. That is, if individually customizing two methods in a program improves the overall program run-time by x and y respectively, then does the program achieve an $(x + y)$ percent improvement if both customized methods are used in the same program run? As mentioned earlier, our focus methods are selected such that each constitutes at least 10% of the baseline program run-time. Thus, different benchmarks contribute different number (zero, one, or more than one) of focus methods to our set. The first bar in Figure 6 simply sums-up the individual method run-time benefits (from distinct program runs) for *benchmarks that provide two or more focus methods*. The second bar plots the run-time of code generated using the best customized optimization sets for all focus methods *in the same run*. We print the number of focus methods provided by each benchmark above each set of bars. Thus, we find that the individual method benefits add-up well in many cases, yielding performance benefit that is close to the sum of the individual benefit of all its customized component methods.

Please note that the experiments for Figure 6 only employ customized optimization selections for the focus methods. The remaining hot benchmark methods are compiled using the baseline sequence, which results in lower average improvements as compared to the average in Figure 5(a). Thus, customizing optimization sets over smaller program regions (methods (6.2%) vs. programs (4.3%)) realize better overall performance gains for JIT compilers.

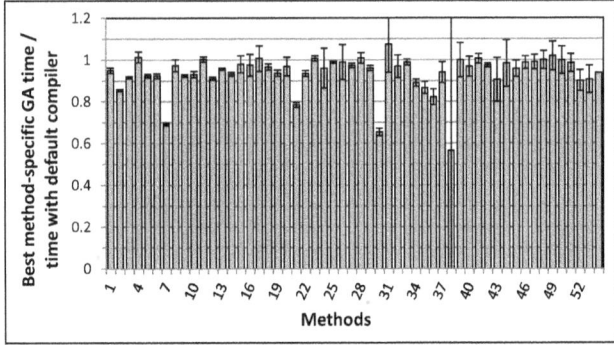

(a)

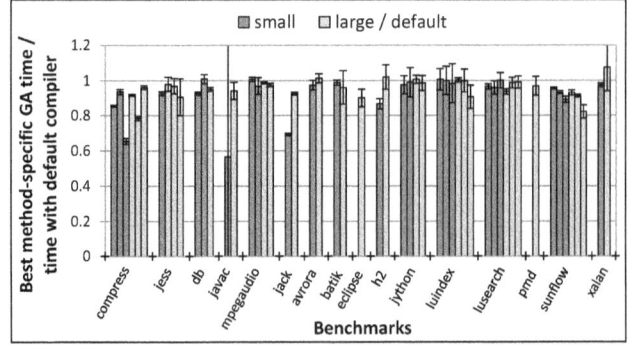

(b)

Figure 5. Performance of method-specific optimization selection after 100 GA generations. Methods in (a) are ordered by the % of run-time spent in their respective benchmarks. In (b), methods from the same benchmark are shown together. All results are are scaled by the fraction of total program time spent in the focus method and show the run-time improvement of that individual method.

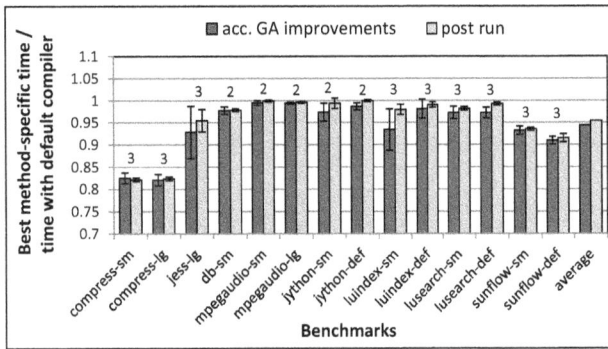

Figure 6. Accumulated improvement of method-specific optimization selection in benchmarks with multiple focus method.

It is important to note that we observe good correlation between the ideal method-specific improvements in Figure 5(a) and the per-method accumulated positive and negative impact of optimizations plotted in Figure 2. Thus, many methods with large accumulated negative effects (such as methods numbers #2, #3, #7, #21, #30, and #36) also show the greatest benefit from customized phase sequences found by our iterative (GA) search algorithm. Similarly, methods with small negative impacts in Figure 2 (including many methods numbered between #40 – #53) do not show significant benefits with ideal phase selection customization. While this correlation is encouraging, it may also imply that optimization interactions may not be very prominent in production-grade JVMs, such as HotSpot.

6. Effectiveness of Feature Vector Based Heuristic Techniques

Experiments in Sections 5.2 and 5.3 determine the potential gains due to effective phase selection in the HotSpot compiler. However, such iterative searches are extremely time-consuming, and are therefore not practical for dynamic compilers. Previous works have proposed using feature-vector based heuristic techniques to quickly derive customized optimization selections during online compilation [5, 23]. Such techniques use an expensive *offline* approach to construct their predictive models that are then employed by a fast *online* scheme to customize phase selections to individual methods. In this section we report results of the first evaluation (compared to

ideal) of the effectiveness of such feature-vector based heuristic techniques for finding good optimization solutions.

6.1 Overview of Approach

Feature-vector based heuristic algorithms operate in two stages, *training* and *deployment*. The training stage conducts a set of offline experiments that measure the program performance achieved by different phase selections for a certain set of programs. This stage then selects the best performing sets of phases for each method. The approach then uses a set of program *features* to characterize every compilation unit (method). The features should be selected such that they are representative of the program properties that are important and relevant to the optimization phases, and are easy and fast to extract at run-time. Finally, the training stage employs statistical techniques, such as logistic regression and support vector machines, to correlate good optimization phase settings with the method feature list.

The deployment stage installs the learned statistical model into the compiler. Now, for each new compilation, the algorithm first determines the method's feature set. This feature set is given to the model that returns a customized setting for each optimization that is expected to be effective for the method. Thus, with this technique, each method may be compiled with a different phase sequence.

6.2 Our Experimental Configuration

We use techniques that have been successfully employed in prior works to develop our experimental framework [5, 23]. Table 3 lists the features we use to characterize each method, which are a combination of the features employed in earlier works and those relevant to the HotSpot compiler. These features are organized into two sets: *scalar features* consist of counters and binary attributes for a given method without any special relationship; *distribution features* characterize the actual code of the method by aggregating similar operand types and operations that appear in the method. The *counters* count the number of bytecodes, arguments, and temporaries present in the method, as well as the number of nodes in the intermediate representation immediately after parsing. *Attributes* include properties denoted by keywords (*final, protected, static*, etc.), as well as implicit properties such as whether the method contains loops or uses exception handlers. We record distribution features by incrementing a counter for each feature during bytecode parsing. The *types* features include Java native types, addresses (i.e. arrays) and user-defined objects. The remaining features correspond to one or more Java bytecode instructions. We use these features during the technique of logistic regression [3] to learn our model for

Scalar Features	Distribution Features		
Counters	**Types**		**ALU Operations**
Bytecodes	byte char		add sub
Arguments	int double		mul div
Temporaries	short long		rem neg
Nodes	float object		shift or
	address		and xor
			inc compare
Attributes	**Casting**		**Memory Operations**
Constructor	to byte		load load const
Final	to char		store new
Protected	to short		new array / multiarray
Public	to int		
Static	to long		**Control Flow**
Synchronized	to float		branch call
Exceptions	to double		jsr switch
Loops	to address		
	to object		**Miscellaneous**
	cast check		instance of throw
			array ops field ops
			synchronization

Table 3. List of method features used in our experiments

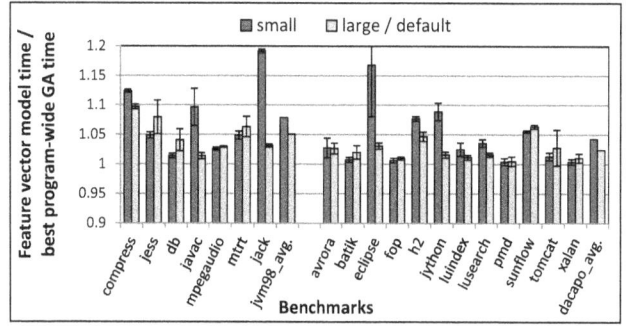

Figure 7. Effectiveness of benchmark-wide logistic regression. Training data for each benchmark consists of all the remaining programs from both benchmark suites.

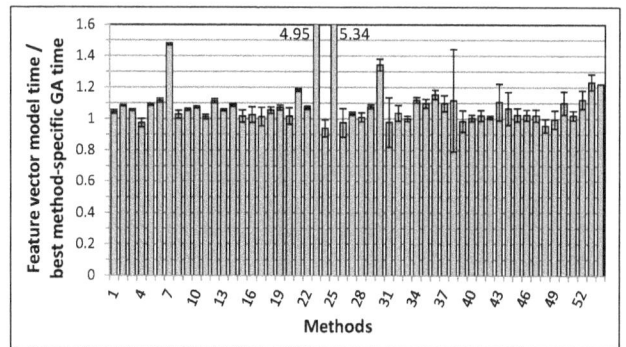

Figure 8. Effectiveness of method-specific logistic regression. Training data for each method consists of all the other focus methods used in Section 5.3.

these experiments. Logistic regression has the property that it can even output phase sequences not seen during the model-training. We have tuned our logistic regression model to make it as similar as possible to the one used previously by Cavazos and O'Boyle [5].

6.3 Feature-Vector Based Heuristic Algorithm Results

We perform two sets of experiments to evaluate the effectiveness of a feature-vector based logistic regression algorithm to learn and find good phase sequences for unseen methods during dynamic JIT compilation. As done in our other experiments, all numbers report the steady-state benchmark times. *All our experiments in this section employ cross-validation.* In other words, the evaluated benchmark or method (with both the small and large/default inputs) is never included in the training set for that benchmark or method.

Figure 7 plots the performance achieved by the optimization set delivered by the logistic regression algorithm when applied to each benchmark method as compared to the performance of the best benchmark-wide optimization sequence from Section 5.2. The training data for each program uses the top ten methods (based on their baseline run-times) from all the *other* (SPEC and Da-Capo) benchmarks. While distinct benchmarks may contain different number of methods, we always consider ten methods from each program to weigh the benchmarks equally in the training set. For every benchmark, each top ten method contributes a distinct feature vector but uses the single benchmark-wide best optimization sequence from Section 5.2. The logistic regression algorithm may find a different optimization selection for each method during its online application. In spite of this flexibility, the feature vector based technique is never able to reach or improve the ideal single benchmark-wide optimization solution provided by the GA. Thus, figure 7 shows that, on average, the feature-vector based solution produces code that is 7.8% and 5.0% worse for SPECjvm98 (small and large data sets respectively) and 4.3% and 2.4% worse for Da-Capo (small and default) as compared to the ideal GA phase selection. However, this technique is some times able to find optimization sequences that achieve performances that are close to or better than those realized by the default HotSpot server compiler. On average, the feature-vector based heuristic achieves performance that is 2.5% better for SPECjvm98-small benchmarks, and equal in all other cases (SPECjvm98-large and DaCapo small and default) as compared to the *baseline server compiler*.

Figure 8 compares the performance of the logistic regression technique for individual program methods to their best GA-based performance. Since we employ cross-validation, the training data for each method uses information from all the other focus methods. Similar to the experimental configuration used in Section 5.3, each program run uses the logistic regression technique only for one *focus* method, while the remaining program methods are compiled with the baseline optimization sequence. The difference in program performance between the feature-vector based heuristic and the focus-method GA is scaled with the fraction of overall program time spent in the relevant method. Thus, we can see from Figure 8 that the per-method performance results achieved by the feature-vector based heuristic are quite disappointing. We find that, on average, the heuristic solutions achieve performance that is over 22% worse than the GA-tuned solution, and 14.7% worse than the baseline HotSpot server compiler.

6.4 Discussion

Thus, we find that existing state-of-the-art online feature-vector based algorithms are not able to find optimization sequences that improve code quality over the default baseline. We note that this observation is similar to the findings in other previous works [5, 23]. However, these earlier works did not investigate whether this lack of performance gain is because optimization selection is not especially beneficial in online JIT compilers, or if existing feature-vector heuristics are not powerful enough to realize those gains. Our experiments conclusively reveal that, although modest on average, the benefits of optimization customization do exist for several methods in dynamic compilers. Thus, additional research in

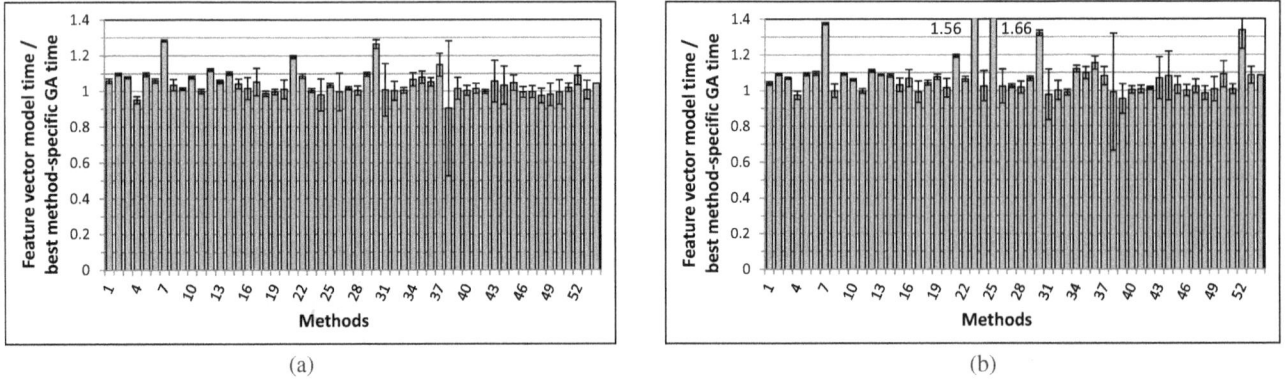

Figure 9. Experiments to analyze and improve the performance of feature-vector based heuristic algorithms for online phase selection. (a) Not using cross-validation and (b) Using observations for Section 4.

improving online phase selection heuristic algorithms is necessary to enable them to effectively specialize optimization settings for individual programs or methods. We conduct a few other experiments to analyze (and possibly, improve) the effectiveness of the logistic regression based feature-vector algorithm employed in this section.

In our first experiment we use the same per-method feature-vector based heuristic from the last section. However, instead of performing cross-validation, we allow the training data for each method to include that same method as well. Figure 9(a) plots the result of this experiment and compares the run-time of each method optimized with the phase selection delivered by the heuristic algorithm to the method's run-time when tuned using the ideal GA sequence. Thus, without cross-validation the heuristic algorithm achieves performance that is only 4.3% worse than ideal, and 2.5% *better* compared to the default HotSpot baseline. This result indicates that the logistic regression heuristic is not intrinsically poor, but may need a larger training set of methods, more subsets of methods in the training set with similar features that also have similar ideal phase sequences, and/or a better selection of method *features* to be more effective.

We have analyzed and observed several important properties of optimization phases in Section 4. In our next experiment, we employ the observation that most optimizations do not negatively impact a large number of methods to improve the performance of the feature-vector based heuristic (using cross-validation). With our new experiment we update the set of configurable optimizations (that we can set to ON/OFF) for each method to only those that show a negative effect on over 10% of the methods in the training set. The rest of the optimizations maintain their baseline ON/OFF configuration. Figure 9(b) shows the results of this experimental setup. Thus, we can see that the updated heuristic algorithm now achieves average performance that is 8.4% worse than ideal, and only 1.4% worse that the baseline.

There may be several other possible avenues to employ knowledge regarding the behavior and relationships of optimization phases to further improve the performance of online heuristic algorithms. However, both our experiments in this section show the potential and possible directions for improving the effectiveness of existing feature-vector based online algorithms for phase selection.

7. Future Work

There are multiple possible directions for future work. First, we will explore the effect of size and range of training data on the feature-vector based solution to the optimization selection problem for dynamic compilers. Second, we will attempt to improve existing heuristic techniques and develop new online approaches to better

exploit the potential of optimization selection. In particular, we intend to exploit the observations from Section 4 and focus more on optimizations (and methods) with the most accumulated negative effects to build new and more effective online models. It will also be interesting to explore if more expensive phase selection techniques become attractive for the most important methods in later stages of *tiered* JIT compilers on multi-core machines. Third, we observed that the manner in which some method is optimized can affect the code generated for other program methods. This is an interesting issue whose implications for program optimization are not entirely clear, and we will study this issue in the future. Finally, we plan to repeat this study with other VMs and processor architectures to validate our results and conclusions.

8. Conclusions

The objectives of this research were to: (a) analyze and understand the phase selection related behavior of optimization phases in a production-quality JVM, (b) determine the steady-state performance potential of optimization selection, and (c) evaluate the effectiveness of existing feature-vector based heuristic techniques in achieving this performance potential and suggest improvements. We perform our research with the industry-standard Oracle HotSpot JVM to make our results generally and broadly applicable.

We found that most optimization phases in a dynamic JIT compiler only have a small effect on performance, and most phases do not negatively impact program run-time. These experiments also hinted at modest improvements by phase selection in dynamic JIT environments. Correspondingly, the GA-based *ideal* benchmark-wide and per-method optimization phase selection improves performance significantly in a few instances, but the benefits are modest on average (6.2% and 4.3% for per-method and whole-program phase selection customization respectively). This result is not very surprising. To reduce compilation overhead, JIT compilers often only implement the more conservative optimization phases, which results in fewer optimizations and reduced, and possibly more predictable, phase interactions.

We also found that existing feature-vector based techniques used in dynamic compilers are not yet powerful enough to attain the ideal performance. We conducted experiments that demonstrate the directions for improving phase selection heuristics in the future. As part of this research, we have developed the first open-source framework for optimization selection research in a production-quality dynamic compilation environment. In the future, we expect this framework to enable further research to understand and resolve optimization application issues in JIT compilers.

References

[1] F. Agakov, E. Bonilla, J. Cavazos, B. Franke, G. Fursin, M. F. P. O'Boyle, J. Thomson, M. Toussaint, and C. K. I. Williams. Using machine learning to focus iterative optimization. In *CGO '06: Proceedings of the Symposium on Code Generation and Optimization*, pages 295–305, 2006.

[2] L. Almagor, K. D. Cooper, A. Grosul, T. J. Harvey, S. W. Reeves, D. Subramanian, L. Torczon, and T. Waterman. Finding effective compilation sequences. In *Proceedings of the 2004 Conference on Languages, Compilers, and Tools for Embedded Systems*, pages 231–239, 2004.

[3] C. M. Bishop. *Neural Networks for Pattern Recognition*. Oxford University Press, Inc., New York, NY, USA, 1995.

[4] S. M. Blackburn, R. Garner, C. Hoffmann, A. M. Khang, K. S. McKinley, R. Bentzur, A. Diwan, D. Feinberg, D. Frampton, S. Z. Guyer, M. Hirzel, A. Hosking, M. Jump, H. Lee, J. E. B. Moss, B. Moss, A. Phansalkar, D. Stefanović, T. VanDrunen, D. von Dincklage, and B. Wiedermann. The DaCapo benchmarks: Java benchmarking development and analysis. In *Proceedings of the 21st annual ACM SIGPLAN conference on Object-oriented programming systems, languages, and applications*, OOPSLA '06, pages 169–190, 2006.

[5] J. Cavazos and M. F. P. O'Boyle. Method-specific dynamic compilation using logistic regression. In *Proceedings of the conference on Object-oriented programming systems, languages, and applications*, pages 229–240, 2006.

[6] K. Chow and Y. Wu. Feedback-directed selection and characterization of compiler optimizatons. Proc. 2nd Workshop on Feedback Directed Optimization, 1999.

[7] K. D. Cooper, P. J. Schielke, and D. Subramanian. Optimizing for reduced code space using genetic algorithms. In *Proceedings of the ACM SIGPLAN 1999 workshop on Languages, compilers, and tools for embedded systems*, pages 1–9, 1999.

[8] G. Fursin, Y. Kashnikov, A. Memon, Z. Chamski, O. Temam, M. Namolaru, E. Yom-Tov, B. Mendelson, A. Zaks, E. Courtois, F. Bodin, P. Barnard, E. Ashton, E. Bonilla, J. Thomson, C. Williams, and M. OBoyle. Milepost gcc: Machine learning enabled self-tuning compiler. *International Journal of Parallel Programming*, 39:296–327, 2011.

[9] A. Georges, D. Buytaert, and L. Eeckhout. Statistically rigorous java performance evaluation. In *Proceedings of the conference on Object-oriented programming systems and applications*, OOPSLA '07, pages 57–76, 2007.

[10] D. E. Goldberg. *Genetic Algorithms in Search, Optimization and Machine Learning*. Addison-Wesley Longman Publishing Co., Inc., Boston, MA, USA, 1st edition, 1989.

[11] M. Haneda, P. M. W. Knijnenburg, and H. A. G. Wijshoff. Optimizing general purpose compiler optimization. In *Proceedings of the 2nd conference on Computing frontiers*, CF '05, pages 180–188, New York, NY, USA, 2005. ACM. ISBN 1-59593-019-1.

[12] K. Hoste and L. Eeckhout. Cole: compiler optimization level exploration. In *Proceedings of the 6th annual IEEE/ACM international symposium on Code generation and optimization*, CGO '08, pages 165–174, New York, NY, USA, 2008.

[13] http://www.oracle.com/technetwork/java/javase/memorymanagement-whitepaper 150215.pdf. Memory Management in the Java HotSpot Virtual Machine, April 2006.

[14] K. Ishizaki, M. Kawahito, T. Yasue, M. Takeuchi, T. Ogasawara, T. Suganuma, T. Onodera, H. Komatsu, and T. Nakatani. Design, implementation, and evaluation of optimizations in a just-in-time compiler. In *Proceedings of the ACM 1999 conference on Java Grande*, JAVA '99, pages 119–128, 1999.

[15] K. Ishizaki, M. Takeuchi, K. Kawachiya, T. Suganuma, O. Gohda, T. Inagaki, A. Koseki, K. Ogata, M. Kawahito, T. Yasue, T. Ogasawara, T. Onodera, H. Komatsu, and T. Nakatani. Effectiveness of cross-platform optimizations for a java just-in-time compiler. In *Proceedings of the 18th annual ACM SIGPLAN conference on Object-oriented programming, systems, languages, and applications*, pages 187–204, 2003.

[16] P. A. Kulkarni. JIT compilation policy for modern machines. In *Proceedings of the ACM international conference on Object oriented programming systems languages and applications*, pages 773–788, 2011.

[17] P. A. Kulkarni, D. B. Whalley, and G. S. Tyson. Evaluating heuristic optimization phase order search algorithms. In *CGO '07: Proceedings of the International Symposium on Code Generation and Optimization*, pages 157–169, 2007.

[18] P. A. Kulkarni, M. R. Jantz, and D. B. Whalley. Improving both the performance benefits and speed of optimization phase sequence searches. In *Proceedings of the ACM SIGPLAN/SIGBED 2010 conference on Languages, compilers, and tools for embedded systems*, LCTES '10, pages 95–104, 2010. ISBN 978-1-60558-953-4.

[19] S. Kulkarni and J. Cavazos. Mitigating the compiler optimization phase-ordering problem using machine learning. In *Proceedings of the ACM international conference on Object oriented programming systems languages and applications*, OOPSLA '12, pages 147–162. ACM, 2012.

[20] H. Lee, D. von Dincklage, A. Diwan, and J. E. B. Moss. Understanding the behavior of compiler optimizations. *Software Practice & Experience*, 36(8):835–844, July 2006.

[21] M. Paleczny, C. Vick, and C. Click. The Java hotspottm server compiler. In *Proceedings of the Symposium on JavaTM Virtual Machine Research and Technology Symposium*, pages 1–12, Berkeley, CA, USA, 2001. USENIX.

[22] Z. Pan and R. Eigenmann. PEAK: a fast and effective performance tuning system via compiler optimization orchestration. *ACM Trans. Program. Lang. Syst.*, 30:17:1–17:43, May 2008.

[23] R. Sanchez, J. Amaral, D. Szafron, M. Pirvu, and M. Stoodley. Using machines to learn method-specific compilation strategies. In *Code Generation and Optimization*, pages 257 –266, April 2011.

[24] SPEC98. Specjvm98 benchmarks. http://www.spec.org/jvm98/, 1998.

[25] S. Triantafyllis, M. Vachharajani, N. Vachharajani and D. I. August. Compiler optimization-space exploration. In *Proceedings of the International Symposium on Code Generation and Optimization*, pages 204–215. IEEE, 2003.

A Modular Approach to On-Stack Replacement in LLVM

Nurudeen Lameed   Laurie Hendren

Sable Research Group
School of Computer Science
McGill University, Montréal, Québec, Canada
{nlamee,hendren}@cs.mcgill.ca
http://www.sable.mcgill.ca/mclab

Abstract

On-stack replacement (OSR) is a technique that allows a virtual machine to interrupt running code during the execution of a function/method, to re-optimize the function on-the-fly using an optimizing JIT compiler, and then to resume the interrupted function at the point and state at which it was interrupted. OSR is particularly useful for programs with potentially long-running loops, as it allows dynamic optimization of those loops as soon as they become hot.

This paper presents a modular approach to implementing OSR for the LLVM compiler infrastructure. This is an important step forward because LLVM is gaining popular support, and adding the OSR capability allows compiler developers to develop new dynamic techniques. In particular, it will enable more sophisticated LLVM-based JIT compiler approaches. Indeed, other compiler/VM developers can use our approach because it is a clean modular addition to the standard LLVM distribution. Further, our approach is defined completely at the LLVM-IR level and thus does not require any modifications to the target code generation.

The OSR implementation can be used by different compilers to support a variety of dynamic optimizations. As a demonstration of our OSR approach, we have used it to support dynamic inlining in McVM. McVM is a virtual machine for MATLAB which uses a LLVM-based JIT compiler. MATLAB is a popular dynamic language for scientific and engineering applications that typically manipulate large matrices and often contain long-running loops, and is thus an ideal target for dynamic JIT compilation and OSRs. Using our McVM example, we demonstrate reasonable overheads for our benchmark set, and performance improvements when using it to perform dynamic inlining.

Categories and Subject Descriptors   D.3.4 [*Processors*]: Compilers

General Terms   Experimentation, Languages, Performance

Keywords   On-Stack Replacement, LLVM, MATLAB, JIT Compiler Optimization

1. Introduction

Virtual machines (VMs) with Just-in-Time (JIT) compilers have become common place for a wide variety of languages. Such systems have an advantage over static compilers in that compilation decisions can be made on-the-fly and they can adapt to the characteristics of the running program. On-stack replacement (OSR) is one approach that has been used to enable on-the-fly optimization of functions/methods [10, 12, 18, 21]. A key benefit of OSR is that it can be used to interrupt a long-running function/method (without waiting for the function to complete), and then restart an optimized version of the function at the program point and state at which it was interrupted.

LLVM is an open compiler infrastructure that can be used to build JIT compilers for VMs [1, 14]. It supports a well-defined code representation known as the LLVM IR, as well as supporting a large number of optimizations and code generators. LLVM has been used in production systems, as well as in many research projects. For instance, MacRuby is an LLVM-based implementation of Ruby on Mac OS X core technologies[1]; Rubinius[2] is another implementation of Ruby based on LLVM JIT. Unladen-swallow is a fast LLVM implementation of Python[3]. VMKit[4] is an LLVM-based project that works to ease the development of new language VMs, and which has three different VMs currently developed (Java, .Net, and a prototype R implementation). A common theme of these diverse projects is that they could benefit from further on-the-fly optimizations, but unfortunately LLVM does not support OSR-based optimizations. Indeed, we agree with the developers of VMKit who believe that using OSR would enable them to speculate and develop runtime optimizations that can improve the performance of their VMs[5]. Thus, given the value of and need for OSR and the wide-spread adoption of LLVM in both industry and academia, our paper aims to fill this important void and provide an approach and modular implementation of OSR for LLVM.

Implementing OSR in a non-Java VM and general-purpose compiler toolkits such as LLVM requires novel approaches. Some of the challenges to implementing OSR in LLVM include:

(1) At what point should the program be interrupted and how should such points be expressed within the existing design of LLVM, without changing the LLVM IR?

(2) The static single-assignment (SSA) nature of the LLVM IR requires correct updates of control flow graphs (CFGs) of LLVM

---

[1] http://macruby.org/

[2] http://rubini.us/

[3] http://code.google.com/p/unladen-swallow/

[4] Previously http://vmkit.llvm.org/ and now http://vmkit2.gforge.inria.fr/

[5] Private communication with the authors, October 2012.

code, thus program transformations to handle OSR-related control flow must be done carefully and fit into the structure imposed by LLVM.

(3) LLVM generates a fixed address for each function; how then should the code of a new version of the running function be made accessible at the old address without recompiling the callers of the function? This was actually a particularly challenging issue to solve.

(4) The OSR implementation must provide a clean integration with LLVM's capabilities for function inlining.

(5) As there are many users of LLVM, the OSR implementation should not require modifications to the existing LLVM installations. Ideally the OSR implementation could just be added to an LLVM installation without requiring any recompilation of the installation.

We addressed these and other challenges by developing a modular approach to implementing OSR that fits naturally in the LLVM compiler infrastructure.

To illustrate a typical use of our OSR implementation, we have used the implementation to support a selective dynamic inlining optimization in a MATLAB VM. MATLAB [15] is a popular platform for programming scientific applications [17]. It is a dynamic language designed for manipulation of matrices and vectors, which are common in scientific applications [9]. The dynamic features of the language, such as dynamic typing and loading, contribute to its appeal but also prevent efficient compilation. MATLAB programs often have potentially long-running loops, and because its optimization can benefit greatly from on-the-fly information such as types and array shapes, we believe that it is an ideal language for OSR-based optimizations. Thus, we wanted to experiment with this idea in McVM/McJIT [7, 16], an open source VM and JIT for MATLAB, which is built upon LLVM.

The main contributions of this paper are:

Modular OSR in LLVM: We have designed and implemented OSR for LLVM. Our approach provides a clean API for JIT compiler writers using LLVM and clean implementation of that API, which integrates seamlessly with the standard LLVM distribution and that should be useful for a wide variety of applications of OSR.

Integrating OSR with inlining in LLVM: We show how we handle the case where the LLVM inliner inlines a function that contains OSR points.

Using OSR in McJIT for selective dynamic inlining: In order to demonstrate the effectiveness of our OSR module, we have implemented an OSR-based dynamic inliner that will inline function calls within dynamically hot loop bodies. This has been completely implemented in McVM/McJIT.

Experimental measurements of overheads/benefits: We have performed a variety of measurements on a set of 16 MATLAB benchmarks. We have measured the overheads of OSRs and selective dynamic inlining. This shows that the overheads are usually acceptable and that dynamic inlining can result in performance improvements.

The rest of the paper is organized as follows. In Section 2, we classify OSR techniques according to their runtime transition capabilities. In Section 3, we outline the application programming interface (API) and demonstrate the usage our OSR module, from a JIT compiler writer's point of view. In Section 4, we describe the implementation of our API and the integration of inlining. In Section 5, we present a case study of using the OSR support to implement a selective and dynamic inlining of function calls in long-running loops in the McVM JIT compiler for MATLAB. Section 6 reviews some related work upon which we are building. We conclude the paper and highlight some future work in Section 7.

2. OSR Classification

The term OSR is used in the literature [3, 10, 12, 18, 21] to describe a variety of similar, but different, techniques for enabling an on-the-fly transition from one version of running code to another semantically equivalent version. To see how these existing techniques relate to each other, and to our proposed OSR implementation, we propose a classification of OSR transitions, as illustrated in Figure 1.

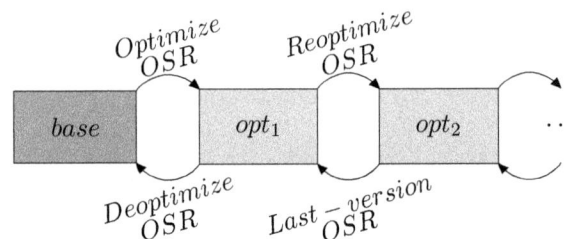

Figure 1. OSR classification.

In most systems with OSR support, the execution of the running code often begins with interpretation or the execution of the code compiled by a non-optimizing base-line compiler. We refer to this version of the running code as the *base* version. This is shown in the darker shaded block of Figure 1.

We call an OSR transition from the *base* version to more optimized code (such as opt_1 in Figure 1) an *Optimize OSR*. The OSR support in the Java HotSpot server compiler [18] uses this kind of transition.

Some virtual machines allow an OSR transition from optimized code such as opt_1 in Figure 1 to unoptimized code (the *base* version). We call this a *Deoptimize OSR* transition. This was the original OSR transition pioneered by Hölzle et al [12] to allow online debugging of optimized code in the SELF [6] virtual machine.

Systems such as the Jikes RVM [3], V8 VM[6], and JavaScript-Core[7] support both *Optimize OSR* and *Deoptimize OSR* transitions. Once a system has deoptimized back to the base code, it can potentially trigger another *Optimize OSR*, perhaps at a higher-level of optimization.

We call a transition from optimized code such as opt_1 to more optimized code such as opt_2 in Figure 1 a *Reoptimize OSR*. Further, we call an OSR transition from more optimized code (e.g., opt_2) to the last version of less optimized code (e.g., opt_1) a *Last-version OSR*.

The OSR technique presented in this paper supports both OSR transitions to a more optimized version and deoptimizations to the last version. Thus, if one starts with the base code, our OSR machinery can be used to perform an *Optimize OSR* transition. From that state, our OSR machinery can be used either as a *Deoptimize OSR* transition to return to the base code (which is the last version of the code), or as a *Reoptimize OSR* to transition to an even more optimized version. Our OSR implementation always caches the last version of the code, so it can also be used to support a *Last-version OSR* to transition from a higher-level of optimization to the previous level.

We now present the API of our OSR implementation[8].

---

[6] https://developers.google.com/v8/

[7] http://trac.webkit.org/wiki/JavaScriptCore/

[8] Available at http://www.sable.mcgill.ca/mclab/mcosr/

3. The OSR API

The key objective of this work was to build a modular system with a clean interface that is easy to use for VM and JIT compiler writers. In this section, we present the API of our OSR module and how JIT compiler developers who are already building JITs/VMs with LLVM can use our module to add OSR functionality to their existing JITs. We provide some concrete examples, based on our McJIT implementation of OSR-based dynamic inlining.

Figure 2(a) represents the structure of a typical JIT developed using LLVM. *LLVM CodeGen* is the front-end that produces LLVM IR for the JIT. The JIT compiler may perform transformations on the IR via the *LLVM Optimizer*. This is typically a collection of transformation and optimization passes that are run on the LLVM IR. The output (i.e., the transformed LLVM IR) from the optimizer is passed to the target code generator, *Target CodeGen*, that produces the appropriate machine code for the code in LLVM IR.

In Figure 2(b), we show a JIT (such as that shown in Figure 2(a)) that has been retrofitted with OSR support components (the shaded components). We describe the functions of *Inserter* and *OSR Pass* shown in Figure 2(b) shortly. In Section 4, we present the implementation of these components and how they interact with the JIT to provide OSR support to the JIT.

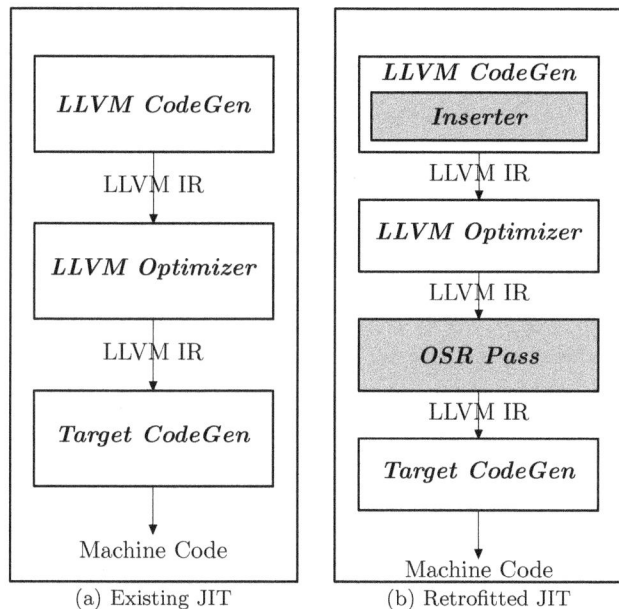

Figure 2. Retrofitting an existing JIT with OSR support.

3.1 Adding the OSR Point Inserter

To support OSR, a JIT compiler must be able to mark the program points (henceforth called OSR points) where a running program may trigger an OSR. A developer can add this capability to an existing JIT by modifying the compiler to call the *genOSRSignal* function, provided by our API, to insert an OSR point at the beginning of a loop during the LLVM code generation of the loop. The LLVM IR is in SSA form. As will be shown later, an OSR point instruction must be inserted into its own basic block, which must be preceded by the loop header block containing all the ϕ nodes. This ensures that if OSR occurs at runtime, the continuation block can be efficiently determined.

In addition to marking the spot of an OSR point, the JIT compiler writer will want to indicate what transformation should occur if that OSR point triggers at runtime. Thus, the *genOSRSignal* function requires an argument which is a pointer to a *code transformer*

function - i.e. the function that will perform the required transformation at runtime when an OSR is triggered. A JIT developer that desires different transformations at different OSR points can simply define multiple code transformers, and then insert OSR points with the desired transformation for each point. A valid transformer is a function pointer of the type *Transformer* that takes two arguments as shown below.

```
typedef unsigned int OSRLabel;
typedef bool
(*Transformer) (llvm::Function*, OSRLabel);
```

The first argument is a pointer to the function to be transformed. The second argument is an unsigned integer representing the label of the OSR point that triggered the current OSR event. The code of the transformer is executed if the executing function triggers an OSR event at a corresponding label. A user may specify a *null* transformer if no transformation is required. As an example of a transformation, our OSR-based dynamic inliner (Section 5.1) uses the transformer shown in Figure 3. It inlines all call sites annotated with label *osrPt*.

```
1  bool  inlineAnnotatedCallSites (llvm::Function *F,
2                                   osr::OSRLabel osrPt) {
3      ...
4      llvm::McJITInliner  inliner (FIM, osrPt, TD);
5      inliner.addFunction ( inlineVersion );
6      inliner.inlineFunctions  ();
7      ...
8  }
```

Figure 3. A code transformer.

To illustrate with a concrete example of inserting OSR points, our OSR-based dynamic inlining implementation uses the code snippet shown in Figure 4 to insert conditional OSR points after generating the loop header block containing only ϕ nodes. In the code snippet (lines 6 – 12), a new basic block *osr* is created and the call to *genOSRSignal* inserts an OSR point into the block. The rest of the code inserts a conditional branch instruction into *target* and completes the generation of the LLVM IR for the loop.

```
1   ...
2   // get the loop header block  --- the target
3   llvm::BasicBlock* target = builder.GetInsertBlock ();
4   llvm::Function* F = target −>getParent();
5   // create the osr instruction  block
6   llvm::BasicBlock* osrBB =
7       llvm::BasicBlock::Create(F−>getContext(), "osr", F);
8   // now create an osr pt and register a transformer
9   llvm:: Instruction * marker =
10      osr::Osr::genOSRSignal(osrBB,
11                inlineAnnotatedCallSites ,
12                loopInitializationBB );
13  ...
14  // create the osr condition  instruction
15  llvm:: Value *osrCond = builder.CreateICmpUGT(counter,
16          getThreshold ( context ), "ocond");
17  builder.CreateCondBr (osrCond, osrBB, fallThru );
18  ...
```

Figure 4. Sample code for inserting an OSR point.

3.2 Adding the OSR Transformation Pass

After modifying the JIT with the capability to insert OSR points, the next step is to add the creation and running of the OSR transformation pass. When the OSR pass is run on a function with OSR points, the pass automatically instruments the function by adding the OSR machinery code at all the OSR points (note that the JIT-compiler developer only has to invoke the OSR pass, the pass itself is provided by our OSR module).

The OSR pass is derived from the LLVM function pass. Figure 5 shows a simplified interface of the pass. An LLVM front-end, that is, an LLVM code generator, can use the following code snippet to create and run the OSR pass on a function F after the original LLVM optimizer in Figure 2(b) finishes.

```
llvm::FunctionPass* OIP = osr::createOSRInfoPass();
OIP->runOnFunction(*F);
```

The OSR pass can also be added to an LLVM function pass manager.

```
namespace osr {
  class OSRInfoPass : public llvm::FunctionPass {
  public:
    OSRInfoPass();
    virtual bool runOnFunction(llvm::Function& F);
    virtual const char* getPassName() const
    { return "OSR Info Collection Pass"; } ...
  };
  llvm::FunctionPass* createOSRInfoPass();
}
```

Figure 5. The OSR Pass interface.

3.3 Initialization and Finalization

To configure the OSR subsystem during the JIT's start-up time, the JIT developer must add a call to the method *Osr::init*. This method initializes the data structures and registers the functions used later by the OSR subsystem. The JIT developer must also add a call to the method **void** Osr:releaseMemory() to de-allocate the memory allocated by the OSR system. The code snippet in Figure 6 show how an existing JIT can initialize and release the memory used by the OSR subsystem. As shown in line 4, the arguments to Osr::init are: a JIT execution engine and the module. The execution engine and the module are used to register the functions used by the system.

```
1  int main(int argc, const char** argv) {
2    ...
3    // initialize  the OSR data structures  ...
4    Osr:: init (EE, module);
5
6    ...  // JIT's Code
7
8    // free up the memory used for OSR ...
9    Osr::releaseMemory();
10   ...
11   return 0;
12 }
```

Figure 6. Initialization and Finalization in the JIT's *main* function.

4. Implementation

In the previous section, we outlined our API which provides a simple and modular approach to adding OSR support to LLVM-based JIT compilers. In this section, we present our implementation of the API. Our implementation assumes that the application is single-threaded. We first discuss the main challenges that influenced our implementation decisions, and our solution to those challenges.

4.1 Implementation Challenges

Our first challenge was how to mark OSR points. Ideally, we needed an instruction to represent an OSR point in a function.

However, adding a new instruction to LLVM is a non-trivial process and requires rebuilding the entire LLVM system. It will also require users of our OSR module to recompile their existing LLVM installations. Hence, we decided to use the existing call instruction to mark an OSR point. This also gives us some flexibility as the signature of the called function can change without the need to rebuild any LLVM library.

A related challenge was to identify at which program points OSR instructions should be allowed. We decided that the beginning of loop bodies were ideal points because we could ensure that the control flow and phi-nodes in the IR could be correctly patched in a way that does not disrupt other optimization phases in LLVM.

The next issue that we considered was portability. We decided to implement at the LLVM IR, rather than at a lower level, for portability. This is similar to the approach used in Jikes research VM [10], which uses byte-code, rather than machine code to represent the transformed code. This approach also fits well with the extensible LLVM pass manager framework.

A very LLVM-specific challenge was to ensure that the code of the new version is accessible at the old address without recompiling all the callers of the function. Finding a solution to this was really a key point in getting an efficient and local solution.

Finally, when performing an OSR, we need to save the current state (i.e., the set of live values) of an executing function and restore the same state later. Thus, the challenge is how to restore values while at the same time keeping the SSA-form CFG of the function consistent.

We now explain our approach which addresses all these challenges. In particular, we describe the implementation of *Inserter* and *OSR Pass* shown in Figure 2(b).

4.2 OSR Point

In Section 3.1, we explained how a developer can add the capability to insert OSR points to an existing JIT. Here we describe the representation of OSR points.

We represent an OSR point with a call to a native function named *@__osrSignal*. It has the following signature.

```
declare void @__osrSignal(i8*, i64)
```

The first formal parameter is a pointer to some memory location. A corresponding argument is a pointer to the function containing the call instruction. This is used to simplify the integration of inlining; we discuss this in detail in Section 4.5. The second formal parameter is an unsigned integer. A function may have multiple OSR points; the integer uniquely identifies an OSR point.

The OSR module maintains a table named OSR function table (*oft*). The table maps a function in LLVM IR onto a set of OSR-point entries. The set can grow or shrink dynamically as new OSR points are added (e.g., after a dynamic inlining) and old OSR points removed (e.g., after an OSR). An entry e in the set is an ordered pair.

$$e = (osr\_call\_inst, code\_transformer)$$

The first member of the pair — *osr_call_inst* — is the call instruction that marks the position of an OSR point in a basic block. The second is the *code_transformer* (Section 3.1).

4.3 The OSR Pass

The OSR pass in Figure 2(b) is a key component of our OSR implementation. As shown in Figure 5, the OSR transformation pass is derived from the LLVM *FunctionPass* type. Like all LLVM function passes, the OSR pass runs on a function via its *runOnFunction* (Figure 5) method.

The pass first inspects a function's *oft* entry to determine whether the function has at least one OSR point. It returns immediately if the function has no OSR points. Otherwise, it instruments the function

146

at each OSR point. Figure 7 shows a simplified CFG of a loop with no OSR points. The basic block labelled *LH1* is the loop header. *LB* contains the code for the body of the loop; and the loop exits at *LE*.

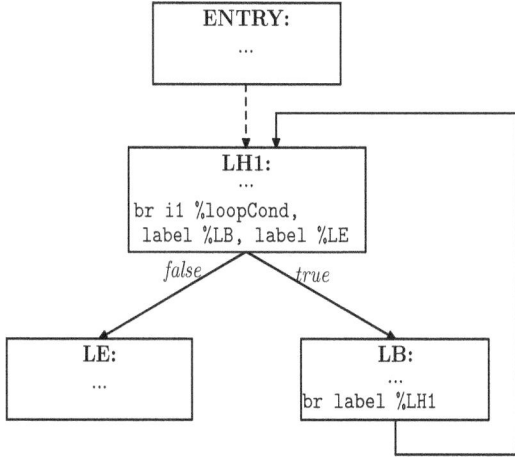

Figure 7. A CFG of a loop with no OSR points.

Figure 8 shows a simplified CFG for the loop in Figure 7 with an OSR point. This represents typical code an LLVM front-end will generate with OSR enabled. Insertion of OSR points is performed by *Inserter* shown in Figure 2(b). The loop header block (now *LH0* in the Figure 8) terminates with a conditional branch instruction that evaluates the Boolean flag *%osrCond* and branches to either the basic block labelled *OSR* or to *LH1*. *LH1* contains the loop termination condition instruction. *LB* contains the code for the body of the loop; the loop exits at *LE*.

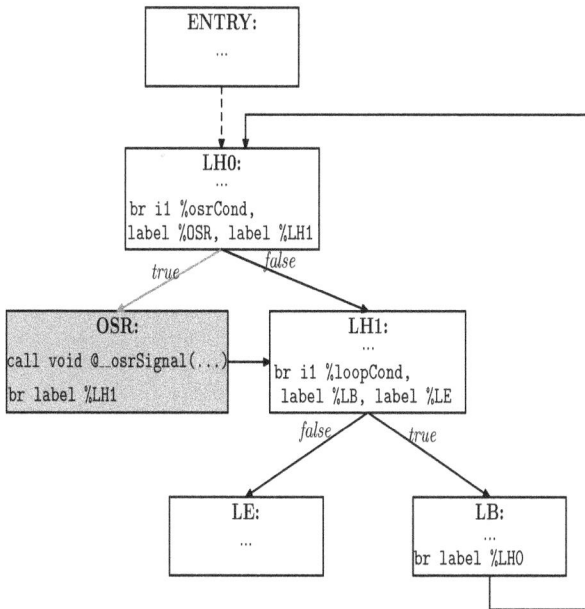

Figure 8. The CFG of the loop in Figure 7 after inserting an OSR point.

The OSR compilation pass performs a liveness analysis on the SSA-form CFG to determine the set of live variables at a loop header such as *LH0* in Figure 8. It creates, using the LLVM cloning support, a copy of the function named the *control version*. As we explain later in this section, this is used to support the transition

from one version of the function to another at runtime. It also creates a descriptor [10, 12] for the function. The descriptor contains useful information for reconstructing the state of a function during an OSR event. In our approach, a descriptor is composed of:

- a pointer to the current version of the function;
- a pointer to the control version of the function;
- a map of variables from the original version of the function onto those in the control version; and
- the sets of the live variables collected at all OSR points.

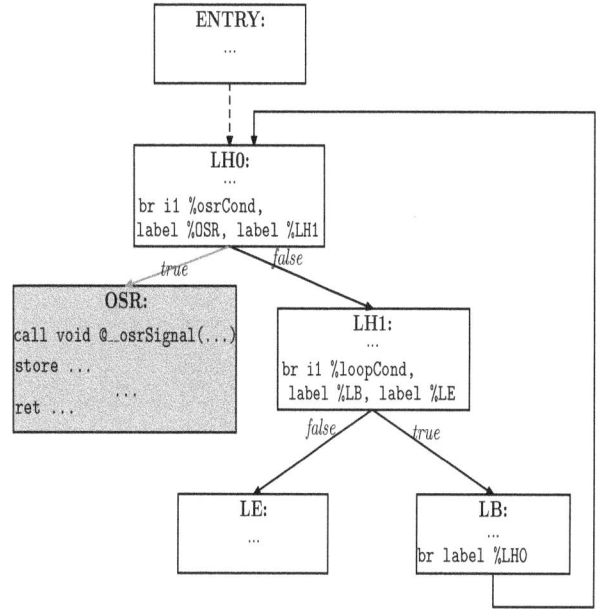

Figure 9. The transformed CFG of the loop in Figure 8 after running the OSR Pass.

After running the OSR pass on the loop shown in Figure 8, the CFG will be transformed into that shown in Figure 9. Notice that in the transformed CFG, the OSR block now contains the code to save the runtime values of the live variables and terminates with a return statement. We now describe in detail the kinds of instrumentation added to an OSR block.

4.3.1 Saving Live Values

To ensure that an executing function remains in a consistent state after a transition from the running version to a new version, we must save the current state of the executing function. This means that we need to determine the live variables at all OSR points where an OSR transition may be triggered. Dead variables are not useful.

As highlighted in Section 3, we require that the header of a loop with an OSR point always terminates with a conditional branch instruction of the form:

```
br i1 %et, label %osr, label %cont
```

This instruction tests whether the function should perform OSR. If the test succeeds (i.e., *%et* is set to `true`), the succeeding block beginning at label *%osr* will be executed and OSR transition will begin. However, if the test fails, execution will continue at the continuation block, *%cont*. This is the normal execution path.

In *%osr* block, we generate instructions for saving the runtime value of each live variable computed by the liveness analysis. The code snippet in Figure 10 shows a typical *osr* block in a simplified form.

```
1  osr:
2      call void @__osrSignal(f, i64 1)
3      store double %7, double* @live
4      store double %8, double* @live1
5      ...
6      store i32 1, i32* @osr_flag
7      call void @__recompile(f, i32 1)
8      call void @f(...)
9      call void @__recompileOpt(f)
10     ret void
```

Figure 10. OSR instrumentation.

The call to @__osrSignal(f, i64 1) in line 2 marks the beginning of the block. Following this call is a sequence of `store` instructions. Each instruction in the sequence saves the runtime value of a live variable into a global variable @live*. The last `store` instruction stores the value 1 into @osr_flag. If @osr_flag is non-zero at runtime, then the executing function is performing an OSR transition. We explain the functions of the instructions in lines 7 – 10 later.

The saved variables are mapped onto the variables in the control version. This is a key step as it allows us to correctly restore the state of the executing function during an OSR.

4.4 Restoration of State and Recompilation

The protocol used to signify that a function is transitioning from the executing version to a new version, typically, a more optimized version[9], is to set a global flag. The flag is reset after the transition.

At runtime, the running function executes the code to save its current state. It then calls the compiler to recompile itself and, if a code *transformer* is present, the function is transformed before recompilation. The compiler retrieves the descriptor of the function and updates the running version using the *control* version as illustrated in Figure 11.

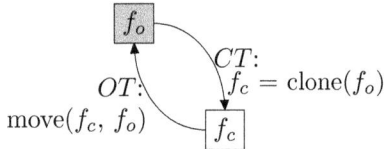

Figure 11. State management cycle.

Let f_o denote the original version of the LLVM IR of the running function, and f_c denote the control version that was generated by cloning the original version. We denote the set of all the live variables of f_o at the program point p_o with $V_o(p_o)$. Similarly, $V_c(p_c)$ denotes the state of the control version at the matching program point p_c. Because f_c is a copy of f_o, it follows that

$$V_o(p_o) \equiv V_c(p_c).$$

Figure 11 illustrates the state management cycle of the running function. The function starts with version f_o. At compilation time[10] (shown as event CT in Figure 11), we clone f_o to obtain f_c. We then compile f_o. At runtime, when an OSR (event OT in Figure 11) is triggered by the running function, we first remove the instructions in f_o and then *move* the code (LLVM IR) of f_c into f_o, transform/optimize as indicated by the OSR transform, and then recompile f_o and execute the machine code of f_o.

---

[9] It may also transition from an optimized version to a less optimized version depending on the application.

[10] This includes the original compilation and all subsequent recompilations due to OSR.

This technique ensures that the machine code of the running function is always accessible at the same address. Hence, there is no need to recompile its callers: the machine code of the transformed f_o is immediately available to them at the old entry point of the running function.

To locate the continuation program point p_o ($p_o \equiv p_c$), the compiler recovers the OSR entry of the current OSR identifier; using the variable mappings in the descriptor, finds the instruction that corresponds to the current OSR point. From this, it determines the basic block of the instruction. And because the basic block of an OSR point instruction has one and only one predecessor, the compiler determines the required target, p_o.

4.4.1 Restoration of State

To restore the state of the executing function, we create a new basic block named *prolog* and generate instructions to load all the saved values in this block; we then create another basic block that merges a new variable defined in the *prolog* with that entering the loop via the loop's entry edge. We ensure that a loop header has only two predecessors and because LLVM IR is in SSA form, the new block consists of ϕ nodes with two incoming edges: one from the initial loop's entry edge and the other from *prolog*. The ϕ nodes defined in the merger block are used to update the users of an instruction that corresponds to a saved live variable in the previous version of the function.

Figure 12 shows a typical CFG of a running function before inserting the code for recovering the state of the function. The basic block *LH1* defines a ϕ node for an induction variable ($\%i$ in Figure 12) of a loop in the function. The body of the loop, *LB*, contains a `add` instruction that increments the value of $\%i$ by 1.

Assuming that we are recovering the value of $\%i$ from the global variable @live_i, Figure 13 shows the CFG after inserting the blocks for restoring the runtime value of $\%i$. In this figure, *prolog* contains the instruction that will load the runtime value of $\%i$ from the global variable @live_i into $\%_i$; similarly, the basic block *prolog.exit* contains a ϕ instruction ($\%_m_i$) that merges $\%_i$ from *prolog* and the value 1 from *ENTRY*. This variable (i.e., $\%_m_i$) replaces the incoming value (1) from *ENTRY* in the definition of $\%i$ in the loop header (*LH1*) as shown in Figure 13. Notice that the incoming block *ENTRY* has been replaced with *prolog.exit* (*PE*) in the definition of $\%i$ in *LH1*.

Fixing the CFG to keep the SSA form consistent is non-trivial. A simple replacement of a variable with a new variable does not work. Only variables dominated by the definitions in the merger block need to be replaced. New ϕ nodes might be needed at some nodes with multiple incoming edges (i.e., only those that are in the dominance frontier of the merger block). Fortunately, the LLVM framework provides an SSA Updater that can be used to update the SSA-form CFG. We exploited the SSA Updater to fix the CFG.

To complete the state restoration process, we must fix the control flow to ensure that the function continues at the correct program point. For this, we insert a new entry block named *prolog.entry* that loads @osr_flag and tests the loaded value for zero to determine, during execution, whether the function is completing an osr transition or its being called following a recent completion of an OSR. The content of the new entry block is shown in the following code snippet.

```
1  prolog.entry :
2      %osrPt = load i32* @osr_flag
3      %cond = icmp eq i32 %osrPt, 0
4      br i1 %cond, label %entry, label %prolog
```

If $\%osrPt$ is non-zero, the test succeeds and the function is completing an OSR; it will branch to $\%prolog$. In $\%prolog$, all the live values will be restored and control will pass to the target block: the loop header where execution will continue. However, if $\%osrPt$

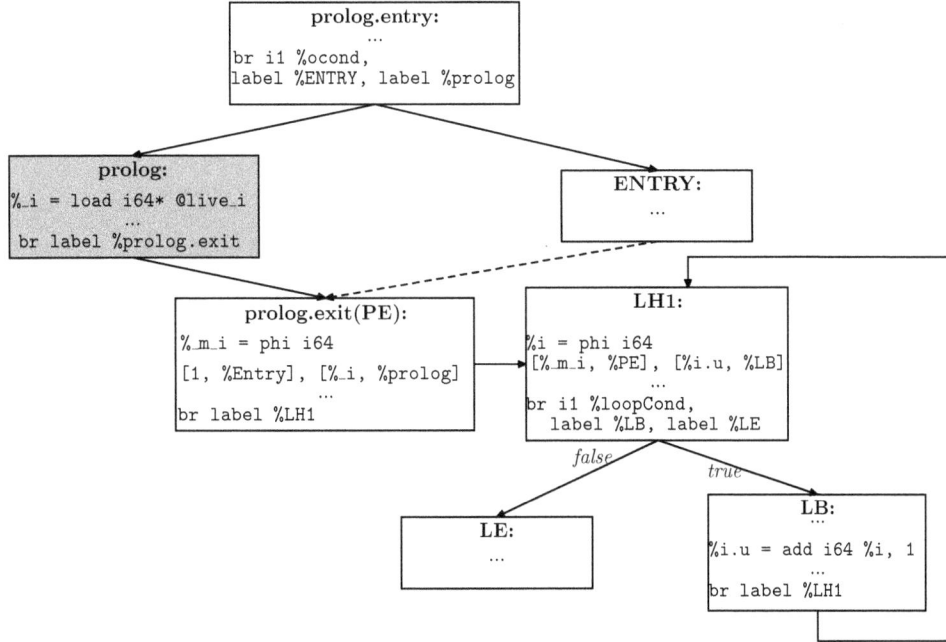

Figure 13. The CFG of the loop represented by Figure 12 after inserting the state recovery blocks.

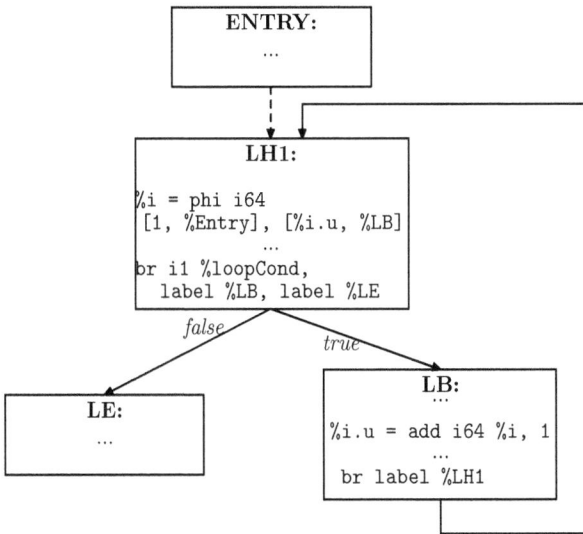

Figure 12. A CFG of a loop of a running function before inserting the blocks for state recovery.

is zero, the function is not currently making a transition: it is being called anew. It will branch to the original entry basic block, where its execution will continue.

As shown in Figure 13, the basic block *prolog.entry* terminates with a conditional branch instruction. The new version of the running function will begin its execution from *prolog.entry*. After executing the block, it will continue at either *prolog* or *ENTRY* (the original entry block of the function) depending on the runtime value of *%cond*.

4.4.2 Recompilation

We now return to the instructions in lines 7 – 10 of Figure 10. The instruction in line 7 calls the compiler to perform OSR and recompile f using the code transformer attached to OSR point 1. After that, function f will call itself (as shown in line 8), but this will execute the machine code generated for its new version. This works because the LLVM recompilation subsystem replaces the instruction at the entry point of function f with a jump to the entry point of the new version. During this call, the function completes OSR and resumes execution. The original call will eventually return to the caller any return value returned by the recursive call.

Normally after an OSR, subsequent calls (if any) of f executes the code in the *prolog.entry*, which tests whether or not the function is currently performing an OSR. However, this test succeeds only during an OSR transition; in other words, the execution of the code in *prolog.entry* after an OSR has been completed is redundant. To optimize away the *prolog.entry*, we again call the compiler (line 9 in Figure 10) but this time, the compiler only removes the *prolog.entry* and consequently, other dead blocks, and recompile f. In Section 5.2, we compare the performance of our benchmarks when the *prolog.entry* is eliminated with the performance of the same benchmarks when the *prolog.entry* is not eliminated.

4.5 Inlining Support

Earlier, we discussed the implementation of OSR points and how the OSR transformation pass handles OSR points. However, we did not specify how we handled OSR points inserted into a function from an inlined call site. A seamless integration of inlining optimization poses further challenges. When an OSR event is triggered at runtime, the runtime system must retrieve the code transformer attached to the OSR point from the *oft* entry of the running function. How then does the system know the original function that defined an inlined OSR point? Here we explain how our approach handles inlining.

Remember that an OSR point instruction is a call to a function. The first argument is a pointer to the enclosing function. Therefore, when an OSR point is inlined from another function, the first argument to the inlined OSR point (i.e., a call instruction) is a function pointer to the inlined function. From this, we can recover the *transformer* associated with this point by inspecting *oft* using this pointer. We can then modify these OSR points by changing the first argument into a pointer to the current function and assign a new ID to each inlined OSR point. We must also update the *oft* entry of the caller to reflect these changes.

We distinguish two inlining strategies: static and dynamic. In static inlining, a call site is expanded before executing the *caller*. This expansion may introduce a new OSR point from the *callee* into the caller and invalidates all the state information collected for the existing OSR points. We regenerate this information after any inlining process.

Dynamic inlining concerns inlining of call sites in a running function during the execution of the function after observing, for some time, its runtime behaviour. Typically, we profile a program to determine *hot* call sites and inline those subject to some heuristics. We used OSR support to implement dynamic inlining of call sites in long-running loops. We discuss this implementation next.

5. Case Study: Dynamic Inlining

In this section, we present an example application of our OSR approach to support selective dynamic inlining in McJIT. We selected this as our first application of OSR because inlining impacts OSR since it must properly deal with OSR points in the inlined functions. Moreover, inlining can increase the opportunity for loop vectorization and provide larger scopes for subsequent optimizations.

5.1 The McJIT dynamic inliner

In our approach to dynamic inlining, we first modified McJIT to identify potential inlining candidates. In our case, a call is considered an inlining candidate if the body of the called function is less than 20 basic blocks, or it is less than 50 basic blocks and it has an interpreter environment associated with the body. McJIT generates LLVM IR for each function in a program. The LLVM IR generated by McJIT may contain calls to the interpreter for special cases and for those cases the symbol environment set-up code facilitates the interaction with the interpreter. In our case, inlining can reduce the interpreter environment overheads.

We then modified McJIT so that loops which contain potential inlining candidates are instrumented with with a hotness counter and a conditional which contains an OSR point (where the OSR point is associated with a new McJIT inlining transformer). When an OSR triggers (i.e. the hotness counter reaches a threshold), the McJIT inlining transformation will inline all potential inlining candidates associated with that OSR point.

There are many strategies for determining which loops should be given an OSR point, and a JIT developer can define any strategy that is suitable for his/her situation. For McJIT, we defined two such general strategies, as follows:

CLOSEST Strategy: The LLVM front-end is expected to insert OSR points only in the loop that is closest to the region that is being considered for optimization. For example, to implement a dynamic inlining optimization using this strategy, an OSR point is inserted at the beginning of the closest loop enclosing an interesting call site. This strategy is useful for triggering an OSR as early as possible, i.e., as soon as that closest enclosing loop becomes hot.

OUTER Strategy: The LLVM front-end is expected to insert an OSR point at the beginning of the body of the outer-most loop of a loop nest containing the region of interest. This approach is particularly useful for triggering many optimizations in a loop nest with a single OSR event. In the case of dynamic inlining, one OSR will trigger inlining of all inlining candidates within the loop nest. The potential drawback of this strategy is that the OSR will not trigger until the outermost loop becomes hot, thus potentially delaying an optimization.

In Figure 14, we illustrate the difference between the two strategies using an hypothetical loop nest. We use a call site to represent an interesting region for optimization.

A loop is represented with a box. The box labelled L_0 denotes the outer-most loop of the loop nest. The nest contains four loops and has a depth of 3. Loops L_1 and L_3 are at the same nesting level. And L_2 is nested inside L_1. The loop nest has three call sites: C_0 in loop L_0, C_2 in loop L_2, and C_3 in loop L_3. Figure 14(a) shows the loop nest with no OSR points.

With the outer-most-loops strategy, an OSR point will be inserted only at the beginning of the outer-most loop, L_0 as shown in Figure 14(b). However, if the strategy is closest-enclosing loops, the front-end will insert an OSR point at the beginning of loops L_0, L_2, and L_3 as shown in Figure 14(c). Although C_2 is inside L_1, no OSR points are inserted into L_1 because L_1 is not the closest-enclosing loop of C_2.

As shown in the figure, the outer-most-loops strategy causes only one OSR point to be inserted into the entire loop nest, while the closest-enclosing-loops strategy causes three OSR points to be inserted. Thus, depending on the optimization performed during an OSR event, the choice of strategy can make a difference in performance.

In our VM, a user specifies an OSR strategy from the command line when invoking the VM, like the following example.

```
./mcvm -jit_enable true -jit_osr_enable true
    -jit_osr_strategy outer.
```

This command starts McVM with OSR enabled with *outer* strategy. In our JIT, the default strategy is *outer*.

When the OSR triggers it calls the McJIT inliner transformation. Our McJIT inliner calls the LLVM basic-inliner library to do the actual inlining. However, the McJIT inliner must also do some extra work because it must inline the correct version of *callee* function body. The key point is that if the *callee* has an OSR point, it must not inline the version of the callee which has already been instrumented with the code to store values of the live variables at this OSR point. If this version is inlined into the *caller* — the function that is performing OSR— the instrumentation becomes invalid as the code does not correctly save the state of the caller at that inlined OSR point. We resolved this problem by recovering the *control* version of the called function (*callee*) and modifying the call site. We change the function called by the call instruction to the control version of the callee. For instance, if the inlined call site is **call void** @f(...), and the control version of f is f', then the call site will be changed to **call void** @f'(...). Note that the control version has an identical OSR point but is not instrumented to save the runtime values of live variables at that program point. For consistency, the function descriptor of the function is updated after inlining as outlined earlier.

5.2 Experimental Evaluation

We used our McJIT dynamic inliner to study the overheads of OSR and the potential performance benefit of inlining. We used a collection of MATLAB benchmarks from a previous MATLAB research project and other sources [9, 19, 20], Table 1 gives a short description of each benchmark. All the benchmarks have one or more loops, the table also lists the total number of loops and max loop depth for each benchmark.

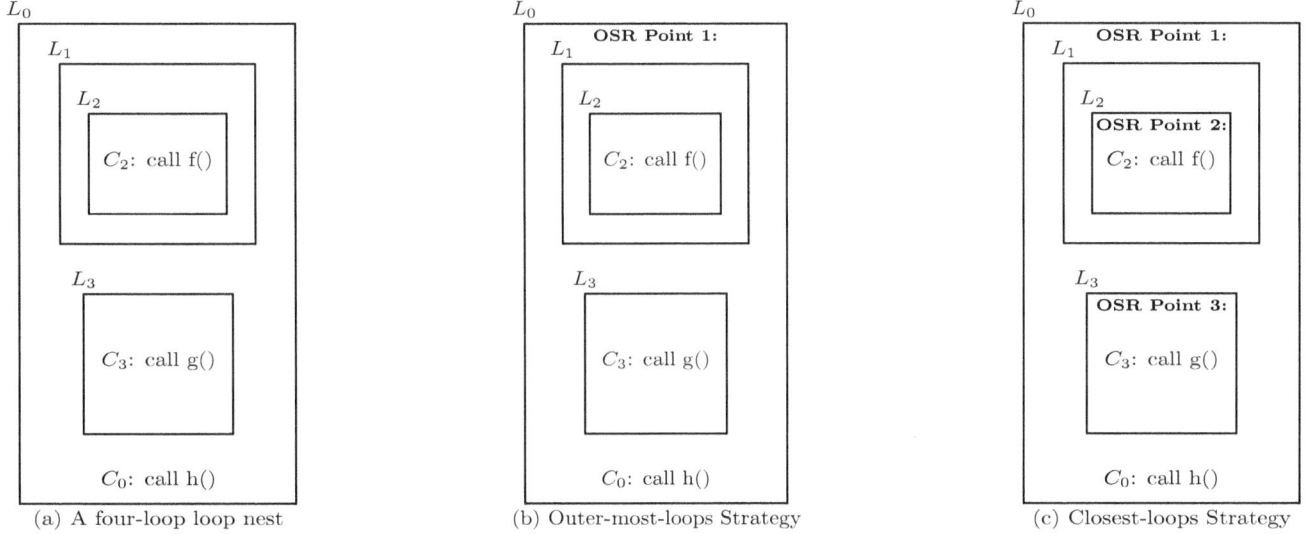

L_0	L_0	L_0
(a) A four-loop loop nest	(b) Outer-most-loops Strategy	(c) Closest-loops Strategy

Figure 14. A loop nest showing the placement of OSR points using the closest or outer-most strategy.

BM	Description	# Loops	Max Depth
adpt	adaptive quadrature using Simpsons rule	4	2
capr	capacitance of a transmission line using finite difference and and Gauss-Seidel iteration.	10	2
clos	transitive closure of a directed graph	4	2
crni	Crank-Nicholson solution to the one dimensional heat equation	7	2
dich	Dirichlet solution to Laplaces equation	6	3
diff	Youngs two-slit diffraction experiment	13	4
edit	computes the edit distance of two strings	7	2
fdtd	3D FDTD of a hexahedral cavity with conducting walls	1	1
fft	fast fourier transform	6	3
fiff	finite-difference solution to the wave equation	13	4
mbrt	Mandelbrot set	3	2
nb1d	N-body problem coded using 1d arrays for the displacement vectors	6	2
nfrc	computes a Newton fractal in the complex plane -2..2,-2i..2i	3	2
nnet	neural network learning AND/OR/XOR functions	11	3
schr	solves 2-D Schroedinger equation	1	1
sim	Minimizes a function with simulated annealing	2	2

Table 1. The benchmarks.

The configuration of the computer used for the experimental work is:

Processor: Intel(R) Core(TM) i7-3930K CPU @ 3.20GHz
RAM: 16 GB;
Cache Memory: L1 32KB, L2 256KB, L3 12MB;
Operating System: Ubuntu 12.04 x86-64;
LLVM: version 3.0; and McJit: version 1.0.

Our main objectives were:

• To measure the overhead of OSR events on the benchmarks over the outer-most and closest-loop strategies. The overhead includes the cost of instrumentation and performing OSR transitions. We return to this in Section 5.2.1.

• To measure the impact of selective inlining on the benchmarks. We discuss this in detail in Section 5.2.2.

We show the results of our experiments in Table 2(a) and Table 2(b). For these experiments, we collected the execution times (shown as **t(s)** in the tables) measured in seconds, for 7 runs of each benchmark. To increase the reliability of our data, we discarded the highest and the lowest values and computed the average of the remaining 5 values. To measure the variation in the execution times, we computed the standard deviation (STD) (shown as **std**) of the 5 values for each benchmark under 3 different categories. All the results shown in both tables were collected using the outer-most-loops strategy, with the default LLVM code-generation optimization level.

The column labelled **Normal** gives the average execution times and the corresponding STDs of the benchmarks ran with OSR disabled, while the column labelled **With OSR** gives similar data when OSR was enabled. Column **With OSR** in Table 2(b) shows

BM	Normal(N) t(s)	std	With OSR(O) t(s)	std	#OSR I	T	Ratio O/N
adpt	17.94	0.06	17.84	0.08	1	1	0.99
capr	11.61	0.01	11.63	0.02	2	2	1.00
clos	16.96	0.01	16.96	0.01	0	0	1.00
crni	7.20	0.04	7.40	0.04	1	1	1.03
dich	13.92	0.01	13.92	0.00	0	0	1.00
diff	12.73	0.07	12.80	0.09	0	0	1.01
edit	6.58	0.03	6.66	0.09	1	0	1.01
fdtd	12.14	0.03	12.16	0.05	0	0	1.00
fft	13.95	0.05	14.05	0.03	1	1	1.01
fiff	8.02	0.01	8.05	0.01	1	1	1.00
mbrt	9.05	0.11	9.22	0.11	1	1	1.02
nb1d	3.44	0.02	3.47	0.01	0	0	1.01
nfrc	9.68	0.05	10.00	0.04	2	2	1.03
nnet	5.41	0.02	5.59	0.03	2	1	1.03
schr	11.40	0.01	11.42	0.03	0	0	1.00
sim	15.26	0.03	15.92	0.07	1	1	1.04
GM							1.01

(a) OSR overhead.

BM	Normal(N) t(s)	std	With OSR(O) t(s)	std	#OSR I	T	FI	CA	Ratio O/N
adpt	17.94	0.06	17.85	0.06	1	1	1	F	0.99
capr	11.61	0.01	11.69	0.02	2	2	2	T	1.01
clos	16.96	0.01	17.18	0.22	0	0	0	F	1.01
crni	7.2	0.04	6.73	0.24	1	1	1	T	**0.93**
dich	13.92	0.01	13.94	0.01	0	0	0	F	1.00
diff	12.73	0.07	12.74	0.04	0	0	0	F	1.00
edit	6.58	0.03	6.66	0.07	1	0	0	F	1.01
fdtd	12.14	0.03	12.13	0.03	0	0	0	F	1.00
fft	13.95	0.05	13.91	0.02	1	1	2	F	1.00
fiff	8.02	0.01	8.26	0.03	1	1	1	F	1.03
mbrt	9.05	0.11	9.06	0.03	1	1	1	F	1.00
nb1d	3.44	0.02	3.47	0.01	0	0	0	F	1.01
nfrc	9.68	0.05	4.26	0.02	2	2	5	T	**0.44**
nnet	5.41	0.02	5.71	0.03	2	1	1	F	1.05
schr	11.4	0.01	11.45	0.05	0	0	0	F	1.00
sim	15.26	0.03	14.72	0.09	1	1	1	F	**0.96**
GM									0.95

(b) Dynamic inlining using OSR.

Table 2. Experimental results (lower execution ratio is better).

the results obtained when dynamic inlining plus some optimizations enabled by inlining were on.

The number of OSR points instrumented at JIT compilation time is shown under **I** of the column labelled **#OSR**; while the number of OSR events triggered at runtime is shown under the column labelled **T** of **#OSR**. The execution ratio for a benchmark is shown as the ratio of the average execution time when OSR was enabled to the average execution time when OSR was disabled (this is the default case). Columns **O/N** of Table 2(a) and **O/N** of Table 2(b) show, respectively, the ratio for each benchmark when OSR only was enabled and when OSR and inlining were enabled. The last row of Table 2(a) and Table 2(b) shows the average execution ratio (the geometric mean (GM)) over all the benchmarks. In Table 2(b), we show the number of functions inlined under **FI**. The column labelled **CA** indicates whether at least one function in the benchmark is called again after it has completed an OSR event.

The STDs of our data sets range from 0.00 to 0.24, showing that the execution times are quite reliable. We now discuss the results of our experiments in detail.

5.2.1 Cost of Code Instrumentation and OSR

Because our approach is based on code instrumentation, we wanted to measure the overhead of code instrumentation and triggering OSRs. This will allow us to assess the performance and develop an effective instrumentation strategy.

Column **O/N** of Table 2(a) shows that the overheads range from about 0 to 4%; this is also the range for the closest-enclosing-loops strategy, suggesting that the overheads under the two strategies are close. Out of the 16 benchmarks, 10 have at least one OSR point; and 8 of these 10 benchmarks triggered one or more OSR events. We have not shown the table of the results for the closest-enclosing loops because out of the 8 benchmarks that triggered an OSR event, the outer-most and the closest-enclosing loops are different only in 3 benchmarks: *mbrt*, *nfrc*, and *sim*. The execution ratios for these benchmarks under the closest-enclosing-loops strategy are: 1.00 for *mbrt*, 1.02 for *nfrc*, and 1.04 for *sim*. The *mbrt* and *nfrc* benchmarks have lower execution ratios under the closest-enclosing-loops strategy. It is not entirely clear whether the closest-enclosing-loops strategy is more effective than the outer-most-loops strategy; although, with these results, it appears that using the closest-loops strategy results in lower overheads. The choice between these two will depend largely on the kinds of the optimizing transformations expected at OSR points. We return to this discussion in Section 5.2.2, where we examine the effectiveness of our dynamic inlining optimization.

We investigated the space performance and found that, depending on the strategy, the three benchmarks (*mbrt*, *nfrc* and *sim*) compiled up to 3% more instructions under the closest-enclosing-loops strategy. This is hardly surprising; the OSR overhead depends on the number of OSR points instrumented and the number of OSR points triggered at runtime. The size of the instrumentation code added at an OSR point in a function depends on the size of the live variables of the function at that point, and this varies depending on the position of the OSR point in a loop nest. The outer-most loop is likely to have the smallest set of live variables.

Although the overhead peaked at 4%, the average overhead over all the benchmarks (shown as GM in Table 2(a)) is 1%. Thus, we conclude that on average, the overhead is reasonable and practical for computation-intensive applications. As we continue to develop effective optimizations for MATLAB programs, we will work on techniques to use OSR points in locations where subsequent optimizations are likely to offset this cost and therefore increase performance.

5.2.2 Effectiveness of Selective Inlining With OSR

Our objective here is to show that our approach can be used to support dynamic optimization. So, we measured the execution times of the benchmarks when dynamic inlining is enabled. When an OSR is triggered, we inline call sites in the corresponding loop nest. Column **With OSR** of Table 2(b) shows the results of this experiment.

The results show significant improvements for *crni*, *nfrc* and *sim*. This shows that our dynamic inlining is particularly effective for this class of programs. Further investigation revealed that these benchmarks inlined multiple small functions and several of these functions fall back to the McVM's interpreter to compute some complicated expressions. McJIT's interactions with the interpreter is facilitated by setting up a symbol environment for binding variables at runtime. Our dynamic inlining enables optimization that eliminates the environment set-up instructions in the inlined code. This is the main cause of performance improvement in *nfrc* and *sim*, and is impossible to do without inlining.

Only the *fiff* and *nnet* show a real decrease in performance when using the outer-most-loop strategy with inlining. We found that the function inlined by *nnet* contains some expensive cell array operations, which our optimizer is currently unable to handle. The benchmark also triggered OSR event once, but performed three OSR instrumentation phases: two at the compilation time and one re-instrumentation during the only OSR event.

We wanted to assess the impact of recompilation to optimize the *prolog.entry* block added during an OSR event; so we turned off recompilation after OSR and re-collected the execution times for the benchmarks. Out of the 9 benchmarks that performed inlining, only 3 benchmarks contain at least a further call to a function that completed an OSR. These are the rows with the value "T" against the column labelled **CA** in Table 2(b). The results for these benchmarks under the no-recompilation after OSR is: 1.01 for *capr*, 0.95 for *crni*, and 0.45 for *nfrc*. These results suggest that the recompilation to remove the *prolog.entry* contributes to the increase in performance for *capr* and *nfrc*. The basic block has the potential to disrupt LLVM optimizations and removing it might lead to better performance. The recompilation after OSR does not result in a slowdown for the other benchmarks.

In Section 5.2.1, we mentioned that the kinds of the optimizing transformations can guide the choice of strategy that lead to better performance. Considering the 3 benchmarks with a loop nest where the outer-most and closest-enclosing loops are different, that is, *mbrt*, *nfrc* and *sim*, we found that the outer-most-loop strategy outperforms the closest-enclosing-loop strategy. In particular, the *sim* benchmark results in about 5% performance degradation. These results support our claim.

We recorded the average performance improvement over all the benchmarks (shown as GM in Table 2(b)) of 5%. We conclude that our OSR approach is effective, in that efficiently supports this optimization, and that it works smoothly with inlining. To see further benefits of OSR for MATLAB, we shall develop more sophisticated optimizations that leverage the on-the-fly dynamic type and shape information that is very beneficial for generating better code.

6. Related Work

Hölzle et al [12] used an OSR technique to dynamically de-optimize running optimized code to debug the executing program. OSR techniques have been in used in several implementations of the Java programming language, including Jikes research VM [3, 10] and HotSpot [18] to support adaptive recompilation of running programs. A more general-purpose approach to OSR for the Jikes VM was suggested by Soman and Krintz [21] which decouples OSR from the program code. Our approach is more similar to the original Jikes approach in that we also implement OSR points via explicit instrumentation and OSR points in the code. However, we have designed our OSR points and OSR triggering mechanism to fit naturally into the SSA-form LLVM IR and tool set. Moreover, the LLVM IR is entirely different from Java byte-code and presents new challenges to OSR implementation at the IR level (Section 4). Our approach is also general-purpose in the sense that the OSR can potentially trigger any optimization or de-optimization that can be expressed as an LLVM transform.

Recently, Süsskraut et al [23] developed a tool in LLVM for making a transition from a slow version of a running function to a fast version. Like Süsskraut et al, our system is based on LLVM. However, there are significant differences in the approaches. While their system creates two versions of the same function statically, and transitions from one version to another at runtime, our proposed solution instruments and recompiles code dynamically at runtime. This is more suitable for an adaptive JIT. Secondly, the approach used by Süsskraut et al stores the values of local variables in a specially allocated area that is always accessible when an old stack frame is destroyed and a new stack frame is created for the executing function. This requires a special memory management facility beyond that provided by LLVM. In contrast to their approach, our approach does not require a special allocation because the stack frame is not destroyed until OSR transition is completed. The recursive call of the executing function essentially extends the old stack frame. We only have to copy the old addresses and scalar values from the old stack frame onto the new stack frame. Finally, another notable difference between our approach and that taken by Süsskraut et al is that their approach requires instrumenting the caller to support OSR in a called function. This may result in high instrumentation overhead. In our approach, we do not instrument a caller to support OSR in a callee.

Inlining is an important compiler optimization. It has been used successfully in many production compilers, especially compilers for object-oriented programming languages. Several techniques for effective inlining were introduced in the several implementations of SELF [6, 13]. SELF-93 [13] uses heuristics to determine the root method for recompilation by traversing the call stack. It then in-lines the traversed call stack into the root method. The HotSpot Server VM [18] uses a similar inlining strategy.

Online profile-directed inlining has been explored in many VMs [2, 4, 5, 8, 11, 22]. The Jikes research VM [3] considers the effect of inlining in its cost-benefit model for recompilation by raising the expected benefit of recompiling a method with a frequently executed call site. Suganuma et al report that for inlining decisions for non-tiny methods, heuristics based solely on online profile data outperforms those based on offline, static data [22]. Online profile-directed inlining in a MATLAB compiler has not been reported in the literature. We expect that by using online profiling information to identify hot call sites and guide inlining decisions, inlining of the most critical call sites will boost performance.

7. Conclusions and Future Work

In this paper, we have introduced a modular approach to implementing OSR for LLVM-based JIT compilers, and demonstrated the approach by implementing selective dynamic inlining for MATLAB. Our approach should be very easy for others to adopt because it is based on the LLVM and is implemented as an LLVM pass. Furthermore, we found a solution which does not require any special data structures for storing stack frame values, nor any instrumentation in the callers of functions containing OSR points. It also does not introduce any changes to LLVM which would require rebuilding the LLVM system. Finally, our approach also provides a solution for the case where a function body containing OSR points is inlined, in a way that maintains the OSR points and adapts them to the inlined context.

We used our OSR strategy in the McJIT implementation, and using this implementation, we demonstrated the feasibility of the approach by measuring the overheads of the OSR instrumentation for two OSR placement strategies: outer-most loops and closest-enclosing loops. On our benchmark set, we found overheads of 0 to 4%. Further, we used the OSR machinery to implement dynamic incremental function inlining. On our benchmarks, we found some performance improvements and slight degradations, with several benchmarks showing good performance improvements.

Our ultimate goal is to use OSR to handle recompilation of key loops, taking advantage of type knowledge to apply more sophisticated loop optimizations, including parallelizing optimizations which can leverage GPU and multicores. Thus, as McJIT and MATLAB-specific optimizations develop, we plan to use OSR to enable such optimizations. In addition to our own future uses of our OSR implementation, we also hope that other groups will also use our OSR approach in LLVM-based JITs for other languages, and we look forward to seeing their results.

Acknowledgments

This work was supported in part by NSERC and FQRNT. We thank all the anonymous reviewers for their helpful comments and suggestions on this version, and previous versions, of this paper. We particularly would like to thank the VEE reviewer who suggested that we include a categorization for the kinds of OSR transitions.

References

[1] LLVM. http://www.llvm.org/.

[2] A. Adl-Tabatabai, J. Bharadwaj, D. Chen, A. Ghuloum, V. Menon, B. Murphy, M. Serrano, and T. Shpeisman. StarJIT: A Dynamic Compiler for Managed Runtime Environments. *Intel Technology Journal*, 7(1):19–31, Feb 2003.

[3] B. Alpern, S. Augart, S. M. Blackburn, M. Butrico, A. Cocchi, P. Cheng, J. Dolby, S. Fink, D. Grove, M. Hind, K. S. McKinley, M. Mergen, J. E. B. Moss, T. Ngo, and V. Sarkar. The Jikes Research Virtual Machine Project: Building an Open-Source Research Community. *IBM Syst. J.*, 44(2):399–417, 2005.

[4] M. Arnold, S. Fink, D. Grove, M. Hind, and P. F. Sweeney. Adaptive Optimization in the Jalapeño JVM. In *Proceedings of the 15th ACM SIGPLAN Conference on Object-Oriented Programming, Systems, Languages, and Applications*, OOPSLA '00, pages 47–65, New York, USA, 2000. ACM.

[5] M. Arnold, M. Hind, and B. G. Ryder. Online Feedback-Directed Optimization of Java. In *Proceedings of the 17th ACM SIGPLAN Conference on Object-Oriented Programming, Systems, Languages, and Applications*, OOPSLA '02, pages 111–129, New York, USA, 2002. ACM.

[6] C. Chambers and D. Ungar. Making Pure Object-Oriented Languages Practical. In *Conference Proceedings on Object-Oriented Programming Systems, Languages, and Applications*, OOPSLA '91, pages 1–15, New York, USA, 1991. ACM.

[7] M. Chevalier-Boisvert, L. Hendren, and C. Verbrugge. Optimizing MATLAB through Just-In-Time Specialization. In *International Conference on Compiler Construction*, pages 46–65, March 2010.

[8] M. Cierniak, G.-Y. Lueh, and J. M. Stichnoth. Practicing JUDO: Java Under Dynamic Optimizations. In *Proceedings of the ACM SIGPLAN 2000 Conference on Programming Language Design and Implementation*, PLDI '00, pages 13–26, New York, USA, 2000. ACM.

[9] Cleve Moler. *Numerical Computing with MATLAB*. SIAM, 2004.

[10] S. J. Fink and F. Qian. Design, Implementation and Evaluation of Adaptive Recompilation with On-stack Replacement. In *Proceedings of the International Symposium on Code Generation and Optimization: Feedback-Directed and Runtime Optimization*, CGO '03, pages 241–252, Washington, DC, USA, 2003. IEEE Computer Society.

[11] K. Hazelwood and D. Grove. Adaptive Online Context-Sensitive Inlining. In *Proceedings of the International Symposium on Code Generation and Optimization: Feedback-Directed and Runtime Optimization*, CGO '03, pages 253–264, Washington, DC, USA, 2003. IEEE Computer Society.

[12] U. Hölzle, C. Chambers, and D. Ungar. Debugging Optimized Code with Dynamic Deoptimization. In *Proceedings of the ACM SIGPLAN 1992 Conference on Programming Language Design and Implementation*, PLDI '92, pages 32–43, New York, NY, USA, 1992. ACM.

[13] U. Hölzle and D. Ungar. A Third-Generation SELF Implementation: Reconciling Responsiveness with Performance. In *Proceedings of the Ninth Annual Conference on Object-Oriented Programming Systems, Language, and Applications*, OOPSLA '94, pages 229–243, New York, NY, USA, 1994. ACM.

[14] C. Lattner and V. Adve. LLVM: A Compilation Framework for Lifelong Program Analysis & Transformation. In *CGO '04: Proceedings of the International Symposium on Code Generation and Optimization*, pages 75–86, Washington, DC, USA, 2004. IEEE Computer Society.

[15] MathWorks. *MATLAB Programming Fundamentals*. The MathWorks, Inc., 2009.

[16] McLAB. The McVM Virtual Machine and its JIT Compiler, 2012. http://www.sable.mcgill.ca/mclab/mcvm_mcjit.html.

[17] C. Moler. The Growth of MATLAB™ and The MathWorks over Two Decades, 2006. http://www.mathworks.com/company/newsletters/news_notes/clevescorner/jan06.pdf.

[18] M. Paleczny, C. Vick, and C. Click. The Java HotSpot Server Compiler. In *Proceedings of the 2001 Symposium on JavaTM Virtual Machine Research and Technology Symposium - Volume 1*, JVM'01, pages 1–12, Berkeley, CA, USA, 2001. USENIX Association.

[19] Press, H. William and Teukolsky, A. Saul and Vetterling, T. William and Flannery, P. Brian. *Numerical Recipes : the Art of Scientific Computing*. Cambridge University Press, 1986.

[20] L. D. Rose, K. Gallivan, E. Gallopoulos, B. A. Marsolf, and D. A. Padua. FALCON: A MATLAB Interactive Restructuring Compiler. In *LCPC '95: Proceedings of the 8th International Workshop on Languages and Compilers for Parallel Computing*, pages 269–288, London, UK, 1996. Springer-Verlag.

[21] S. Soman and C. Krintz. Efficient and General On-Stack Replacement for Aggressive Program Specialization. In *Software Engineering Research and Practice*, pages 925–932, 2006.

[22] T. Suganuma, T. Yasue, and T. Nakatani. An Empirical Study of Method In-lining for a Java Just-In-Time Compiler. In *Proceedings of the 2nd Java Virtual Machine Research and Technology Symposium*, pages 91–104, Berkeley, CA, USA, 2002. USENIX Association.

[23] M. Süsskraut, T. Knauth, S. Weigert, U. Schiffel, M. Meinhold, and C. Fetzer. Prospect: A Compiler Framework for Speculative Parallelization. In *Proceedings of the 8th Annual IEEE/ACM International Symposium on Code Generation and Optimization*, pages 131–140, New York, USA, 2010. ACM.

A Framework for Application Guidance
in Virtual Memory Systems

Michael R. Jantz

University of Kansas

mjantz@ittc.ku.edu

Carl Strickland

Arizona State University

cdstrick@asu.edu

Karthik Kumar

Intel Corporation

karthik.kumar@intel.com

Martin Dimitrov

Intel Corporation

martin.p.dimitrov@intel.com

Kshitij A. Doshi

Intel Corporation

kshitij.a.doshi@intel.com

Abstract

This paper proposes a collaborative approach in which applications can provide guidance to the operating system regarding allocation and recycling of physical memory. The operating system incorporates this guidance to decide which physical page should be used to back a particular virtual page. The key intuition behind this approach is that application software, as a generator of memory accesses, is best equipped to inform the operating system about the relative access rates and overlapping patterns of usage of its own address space. It is also capable of steering its own algorithms in order to keep its dynamic memory footprint under check when there is a need to reduce power or to contain the spillover effects from bursts in demand. Application software, working cooperatively with the operating system, can therefore help the latter schedule memory more effectively and efficiently than when the operating system is forced to act alone without such guidance. It is particularly difficult to achieve power efficiency without application guidance since power expended in memory is a function not merely of the intensity with which memory is accessed in time but also how many physical ranks are affected by an application's memory usage.

Our framework introduces an abstraction called "colors" for the application to communicate its intent to the operating system. We modify the operating system to receive this communication in an efficient way, and to organize physical memory pages into intermediate level grouping structures called "trays" which capture the physically independent access channels and self-refresh domains, so that it can apply this guidance without entangling the application in lower level details of power or bandwidth management. This paper describes how we re-architect the memory management of a recent Linux kernel to realize a three way collaboration between hardware, supervisory software, and application tasks.

VEE'13, March 16–17, 2013, Houston, Texas, USA.
Copyright © 2013 ACM 978-1-4503-1266-0/13/03 . . . $15.00

Categories and Subject Descriptors D.4 [*Software*]: Operating Systems; D.4.2 [*Operating Systems*]: Storage Management—Allocation / deallocation strategies

General Terms Design, Performance

Keywords Memory virtualization, Memory management, Resource allocation, Power, Performance, Containerization

1. Introduction

Recent trends in computer systems include an increased focus on power and energy consumption and the need to support multi-tenant use cases in which physical resources need to be multiplexed efficiently without causing performance interference. When multiplexing CPU, network, and storage facilities among multiple tasks a system level scheduling policy can perform fine-grained reassignments of the resources on a continuing basis to take into account task deadlines, shifting throughput demands, load-balancing needs and supply constraints. Many recent works address how best to allocate CPU time, and storage and network throughputs to meet competing service quality objectives [24, 28], and to reduce CPU power during periods of low demand [1].

By comparison, it is very challenging to obtain precise control over distribution of memory capacity, bandwidth, or power, when virtualizing and multiplexing system memory. That is because these effects intimately depend upon how an operating system binds virtual addresses to physical addresses. An operating system uses heuristics that reclaim either the oldest, or the least recently touched, or a least frequently used physical pages in order to fill demands. Over time, after repeated allocations and reclaims, there is little guarantee that a collection of intensely accessed physical pages would remain confined to a small number of memory modules (or DIMMs). Even if an application reduces its dynamic memory footprint, its memory accesses can remain spread out across sufficiently many memory ranks to keep the ranks from saving much power. The layout of each application's hot pages affects not just which memory modules can transition to lower power states during intervals of low activity, but also how much one program's activity in memory interferes with the responsiveness that other programs experience. Thus a more discriminating approach than is available in current systems for multiplexing of physical memory is highly desirable.

This paper proposes a collaborative approach in which applications can provide guidance to the operating system in allocation and recycling of physical memory. This guidance helps the operating system take into account several factors when choosing which physical page should be used to back a particular virtual page. Thus, for example, an application whose high-intensity accesses are concentrated among a small fraction of its total address space can achieve power-efficient performance by guiding the operating system to co-locate the active pages among a small fraction of DRAM banks. Recent studies show that memory consumes up to 40% of total system power in enterprise servers [22] making memory power a dominant factor in overall power consumption. Conversely, an application that is very intensive in its memory accesses may prefer that pages in its virtual address span are distributed as widely as possible among independent memory channels; and it can guide the operating system accordingly.

In order to provide these hints without entangling applications into lower level memory management details, we introduce the concept of coloring. Application software or middleware uses a number of colors to signal to the operating system a collection of hints. The operating system takes these hints into account during physical page allocation. Colors are applied against application selected ranges of virtual address space; a color is simply a concise way for an application to indicate to the operating system that some common behavior or intention spans those pages, even if the pages are not virtually contiguous. Colors can be applied at any time and can be changed as well, and the OS makes the best effort possible to take them into account when performing memory allocation, recycling, or page migration decisions. In addition to specializing placement, colors can also be used to signify memory priority or cache grouping, so that an OS can optionally support color-based displacement in order to implement software-guided affinitization of memory to tasks. This is particularly useful in consolidated systems where memory provisioning is important for ensuring performance quality-of-service (QoS) guarantees.

Once an application colors various portions of its range with a few distinct colors, it tells the operating system what attributes (or combinations of attributes) it wants to associate with those colors. Depending upon how sophisticated an operating system implementation is, or what degrees of freedom are available to it in a given hardware configuration, the operating system tunes its allocation, displacement, migration, and power management decisions to take advantage of the information. At the same time, system properties and statistics that are necessary for the application to control its own behavior flow back from the OS, creating a closed feed-back loop between the application and host. That applications can guide the OS at a fine grained level in allocation and placement of pages is also an essential element of adapting applications to systems in which all memory is not homogeneous: for example, NVDIMMs, slower but higher capacity DIMMs, and secondary memory controllers may be used in an enterprise system to provide varying capabilities and performance. Mobile platforms represent another potential application as system-on-chip (SoC) designs are beginning to incorporate independently powered memory banks. The approach proposed in this paper takes a critical first step in meeting the need for a fine-grained, power-aware, flexible provisioning of memory.

The physical arrangement of memory modules, and that of the channels connecting them to processors, together with the power control domains are all opaque to applications in our approach. In line with what has come to be expected from modern computer systems, our approach virtualizes memory and presents the illusion to every task that it has at its disposal a large array of memory locations. By hiding the lower level physical details from applications we preserve the benefits of modularity – applications do not need to become hardware aware in order to deliver memory management guidance to the operating system. Comparatively minor changes to the operating system bring about the necessary three way collabora-

tion between hardware, supervisory software, and application tasks. We re-architect the memory management of a recent Linux kernel in order to achieve this objective. The OS reads the memory hardware configuration and constructs a software representation (called "trays") of all the power manageable memory units. We used Linux kernel version 2.6.32 as a vehicle upon which to implement trays. We modified the kernel's page management routines to perform allocation and recycling over trays. We created application programming interfaces (APIs) and a suite of tools by which applications can monitor memory resources in order to implement coloring and associating intents with colors.

Our framework is the first to provide a system-level implementation of flexible, application-guided memory management. It supports such usage scenarios as prioritization of memory capacity and memory bandwidth, and saving power by transitioning more memory ranks into self-refresh states. It is easy to admit new scenarios such as application guided read-ahead or page prefill on a subset of ranges, differential placement of pages between fast and slow memory, and aggressive recycling of pages that applications can flag as transient. The major contributions of this work are:

- We describe in detail the design and implementation of our framework, which we believe is the first to provide for three way collaboration between hardware, supervisory software, and application tasks.

- We show how our framework can be used to achieve various objectives, including power savings, capacity provisioning, performance optimization, etc.

The next section places the contributions of this work in the context of related work and is followed by a description of relevant background information. We then describe the detailed design of our framework and present several experiments to showcase and evaluate potential use cases of application-guided memory management. We finally discuss potential future work before concluding the paper.

2. Related Work

Researchers and engineers have proposed various power management schemes for memory systems. Bi et. al. [4] suggest predicting memory reference patterns to allow ranks to transition into low power states. Delaluz et. al. [8] track memory bank usage in the operating system and selectively turn banks on and off at context switch points to manage DRAM energy consumption. Along these same lines, *memory compaction* has recently been integrated into the Linux kernel [7]. This technique, which reduces external fragmentation, is also used for power management because it allows memory scattered across banks to be compacted into fewer banks, in a way that is transparent to the application. Fan et. al. [10] employ petrinets to model and evaluate memory controller policies for manipulating multiple power states. Lin et. al. [23] construct an adaptive thread grouping and scheduling framework which assigns groups of threads to exclusive DRAM channels and ranks in order to jointly manage memory performance, power, and thermal characteristics. While these techniques employ additional hardware and system-level analysis to improve memory power management, our framework achieves similar objectives by facilitating collaboration between the application and host system.

Other works have explored integrating information at the application-level with the OS and hardware to aid resource management. Some projects, such as Exokernel [9] and Dune [3], attempt to give applications direct access to physical resources. In contrast to these works, our framework does not expose any physical structures or privileged instructions directly to applications. More similar to this work are approaches that enable applications to share additional information about their memory usage with lower levels of memory management. Prior system calls, such as *madvise* and *vadvise*, and various NUMA interfaces [20] have allowed applications to provide hints to the memory management system. Some API's (such as Android's ashmem [12] and Oracle's Transcendent Memory [25]) allow the application or guest OS to allocate memory that may be freed by the host at any time (for instance, to reduce memory pressure). Banga, et. al. [2] propose a model and API that allows applications to communicate their resource requirements to the OS through the use of resource containers. Brown and Mowry [6] integrate a modified SUIF compiler, which inserts *release* and *prefetch* hints using an extra analysis pass, with a runtime layer and simple OS support to improve response time of interactive applications in the presence of memory-intensive applications. While these works evince some of the benefits of increased collaboration between applications and the OS, the coloring API provided by our framework enables a much broader spectrum of hints to be overlapped and provides a concise and powerful way to say multiple things about a given range of pages.

Also related is the concept of cache coloring [19], where the operating system groups pages of physical memory (as the same *color*) if they map to the same location in a physically indexed cache. Despite their similar names, coloring in our framework is different than coloring in these systems. Cache coloring aims to reduce cache conflicts by exploiting spatial or temporal locality when mapping virtual pages to physical pages of different colors, while colors in our framework primarily serve to facilitate communication between the application and system-level memory management.

Finally, prior work has also explored virtual memory techniques for energy efficiency. Lebeck et. al. [21] propose several policies for making page allocation power aware. Zhou et. al. [29] track the page miss ratio curve, i.e. page miss rate vs. memory size curve, as a performance-directed metric to determine the dynamic memory demands of applications. Petrov et. al. [26] propose virtual page tag reduction for low-power translation look-aside buffers (TLBs). Huang et. al. [18] propose the concept of power-aware virtual memory, which uses the power management features in RAMBUS memory devices to put individual modules into low power modes dynamically under software control. All of these works highlight the importance and advantages of power-awareness in the virtual memory system – and explore the potential energy savings. In contrast to this work, however, these systems do not provide any sort of closed-loop feedback between application software and lower level memory management, and thus, are vulnerable to learning inefficiencies as well as inefficiencies resulting from the OS and application software working at cross purposes.

3. Background

In order to understand the design and intuition of our framework, we first describe how current memory technologies are designed and viewed from each layer of the vertical execution stack, from the hardware up to the application.

Modern server systems employ a Non-Uniform Memory Access (NUMA) architecture which divides memory into separate regions (*nodes*) for each processor or set of processors. Within each NUMA node, memory is spatially organized into *channels*. Each channel employs its own memory controller and contains one or more DIMMs, which, in turn, each contain two or more *ranks*. Ranks comprise the actual memory storage and typically range from 2GB to 8GB in capacity. The memory hardware performs aggressive power management to transition from high power to low power states when either all or some portion of the memory is not active. Ranks are the smallest *power manageable unit*, which implies that transitioning between power states is performed at the

rank level. Thus, different memory allocation strategies must consider an important power-performance tradeoff: distributing memory evenly across the ranks improves bandwidth which leads to better performance, while minimizing the number of active ranks consume less power.

The BIOS is responsible for reading the memory hardware configuration and converting it into physical address ranges used in the operating system. The BIOS provides several *physical address interleaving* configurations, which control how the addresses are actually distributed among the underlying memory hardware units. Different physical address interleaving configurations can have significant power-performance implications. For example, systems tuned for performance might configure the BIOS to fully interleave physical addresses so that consecutive addresses are distributed across all the available ranks.

On boot, the operating system reads the physical address range for each NUMA node from the BIOS and creates data structures to represent and manage physical memory. *Nodes* correspond to the physical NUMA nodes in the hardware. Each node is divided into a number of blocks called *zones* which represent distinct physical address ranges. Different zone types are suitable for different types of usage (e.g. the lowest 16MB of physical memory, which certain devices require, is placed in the *DMA* zone). Next, the operating system creates physical page frames (or simply, *pages*) from the address range covered by each zone. Each page typically addresses 4KB of space. The kernel's physical memory management (allocation and recycling) operates on these pages, which are stored and kept track of on various lists in each zone. For example, a set of lists of pages in each zone called the *free lists* describes all of the physical memory available for allocation.

Finally, the operating system provides each process with its own virtual address space for managing memory at the application level. Virtual memory relieves applications of the need to worry about the size and availability of physical memory resources. Despite these benefits, virtualization adds a layer of abstraction between the application and operating system which makes it impossible for the lower-level memory management routines to derive the purpose of a particular memory allocation. Furthermore, even at the operating system level, many of the details of the underlying memory hardware necessary for managing memory at the rank level have been abstracted away as well. Thus, excessive virtualization makes it extremely difficult to design solutions for applications which require more fine-grained controls over memory resource usage.

4. Application-Guided Memory Management

This section describes the design and implementation of our framework. Enabling applications to guide management of memory hardware resources requires two major components:

1. An interface for communicating to the operating system information about how applications intend to use memory resources (usage patterns), and

2. An operating system with the ability to keep track of which memory hardware units (DIMMs, ranks) host which physical pages, and to use this detail in tailoring memory allocation to usage patterns

We address the first component in the next subsection, which describes our *memory coloring* framework for providing hints to the operating system about how applications intend to use memory resources. Next, we describe the architectural modifications we made to the system-level memory management software to enable management of individual memory hardware units.

4.1 Expressing Application Intent through Colors

A color is an abstraction which allows the application to communicate to the OS hints about how it is going to use memory resources. Colors are sufficiently general as to allow the application to provide different types of performance or power related usage hints. In using colors, application software can be entirely agnostic about how virtual addresses map to physical addresses and how those physical addresses are distributed among memory modules. By coloring any N different virtual pages with the same color, an application communicates to the OS that those N virtual pages are alike in some significant respect, and by associating one or more attributes with that color, the application invites the OS to apply any discretion it may have in selecting the physical page frames for those N virtual pages. As one rather extreme but trivial example, suppose that the application writer uses one color for N virtual pages and then binds with that color a guidance to "use no more than 1 physical page frame" for that color. The OS, if it so chooses, can satisfy a demand fault against any of those N page addresses simply by recycling one physical page frame by reclaiming it from one mapping and using it for another. Or, more practically, the OS may simply interpret such a guidance to allocate normally but then track any page frames so allocated, and reclaim aggressively so that those particular page frames are unlikely to remain mapped for long. A scan-resistant buffer-pool manager at the application level may benefit from this kind of guidance to the operating system.

More generally, an application can use colors to divide its virtual pages into groups. Each color can be used to convey one or more characteristics that the pages with that color share. Contiguous virtual pages may or may not have the same color. In this way an application provides a usage map to the OS, and the OS consults this usage map in selecting an appropriate physical memory scheduling strategy for those virtual pages. An application that uses no colors and therefore provides no guidance is treated normally– that is, the OS applies some default strategy. And even when an application provides extensive guidance through coloring, depending on the particular version of the operating system, the machine configuration (such as how much memory and how finely interleaved it is), and other prevailing run time conditions in the machine, the OS may veer little or a lot from a default strategy. The specializations that an OS may support need not be confined just to selection of physical pages to be allocated or removed from the application's resident set, and they may include such other options as whether or not to fault-ahead or to perform read-aheads or flushing writes; whether or not to undertake migration of active pages from one set of memory banks to another in order to squeeze the active footprint into fewest physical memory modules. In this way, an OS can achieve performance, power, I/O, or capacity efficiencies based on guidance that application tier furnishes through coloring.

Using colors to specify intents instead of specifying intents directly (through a system call such as madvise) is motivated by three considerations- (a) efficiency through conciseness – an application can create the desired mosaic of colors and share it with the OS, instead of having to specify it a chunk at a time, and (b) the ability to give hints that say something horizontal across a collection of pages with the same color, such as, "it is desirable to perform physical page re-circulation among this group of virtual addresses", or, "it is desirable to co-locate the physical pages that happen to bind to this set of virtual addresses", etc., and (c) modularity – the capabilities supported by a particular version of an OS or a particular choice of hardware and system configuration may not support the full generality of hints that another version or configuration can support. An application developer or deployer, or some software tool, can bind colors to the menu of hints at load time or run time. This flexibility also means that even at run time, colors can be altered on the basis of feedback from the

OS or guidance from a performance or power tuning assistant. In our prototype implementation, colors are bound to hints by a combination of configuration files and library software. A custom system call actually applies colors to virtual address ranges.

Let us illustrate the use of colors and hints with a simple example. Suppose we have an application that has one or more address space extents in which memory references are expected to be relatively infrequent (or uniformly distributed, with low aggregate probability of reference). The application uses a color, say *blue* to color these extents. At the same time, suppose the application has a particular small collection of pages in which it hosts some frequently accessed data structures, and the application colors this collection *red*. The coloring intent is to allow the operating system to manage these sets of pages more efficiently – perhaps it can do so by co-locating the *blue* pages on separately power-managed units from those where *red* pages are located, or, co-locating *red* pages separately on their own power-managed units, or both. A possible second intent is to let the operating system page the *blue* ranges more aggressively, while allowing pages in the *red* ranges an extended residency time. By locating *blue* and *red* pages among a compact group of memory ranks, an operating system can increase the likelihood that memory ranks holding the *blue* pages can transition more quickly into self-refresh, and that the activity in *red* pages does not spill over into those ranks. (Other possible tuning options may be desirable as well – for example, allowing a higher clock frequency for one set of memory ranks and reducing clock frequency on others, if that is supported by the particular OS-hardware mix). Since many usage scenarios can be identified to the operating system, we define "intents" and specify them using configuration files. A configuration file with intents labeled *MEM-INTENSITY* and *MEM-CAPACITY* can capture two intentions: (a) that red pages are hot and blue pages are cold, and (b) that about 5% of application's dynamic resident set size (RSS) should fall into red pages, while, even though there are many blue pages, their low probability of access is indicated by their 3% share of the RSS.

1. Alignment to one of a set of standard intents:
   ```
   INTENT MEM-INTENSITY
   ```

2. Further specification for containing total spread:
   ```
   INTENT MEM-CAPACITY
   ```

3. Mapping to a set of colors:
   ```
   MEM-INTENSITY RED  0 //hot pages
   MEM-CAPACITY  RED  5 //hint- 5% of RSS
   MEM-INTENSITY BLUE 1 //cold pages
   MEM-CAPACITY  BLUE 3 //hint- 3% of RSS
   ```

Next let us give an overview of the approach we have taken in implementing a prototype memory management system for receiving and acting upon such guidance. In our implementation, we have organized memory into power-management domains that are closely related to the underlying hardware. We call these management units *trays*, and we map colors to trays and tray based memory allocation and reclaim policies, as described in the following section.

4.2 Memory Containerization with Trays

We introduce a new abstraction called "trays" to organize and facilitate memory management in our framework. A *tray* is a software structure which contains sets of pages that reside on the same power-manageable memory unit. Each zone contains a set of trays and all the lists used to manage pages on the zone are replaced with corresponding lists in each tray. Figure 1 shows how our custom

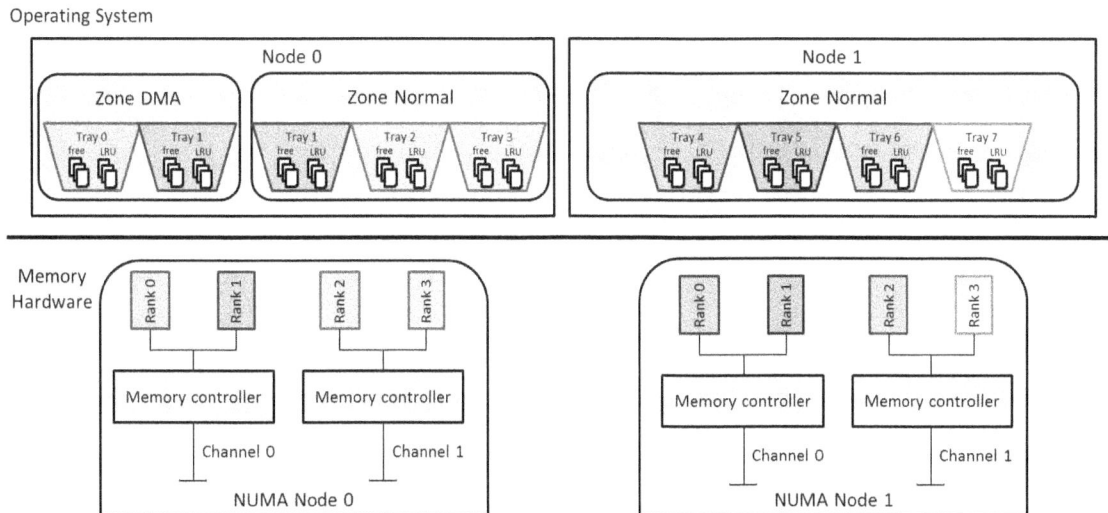

Figure 1. Physical memory representation in the Linux kernel with trays as it relates to the system's memory hardware.

kernel organizes its representation of physical memory with trays in relation to the actual memory hardware.[1]

We have used Linux kernel version 2.6.32 as the baseline upon which to implement trays. The kernel's page management routines, which operate on lists of pages at the zone level were modified quite easily no operate over the same lists, but at a subsidiary level of trays. That is, zones are subdivided into trays, and page allocation, scanning, recycling are all performed at the tray level. While most of these changes are straightforward, the breadth of routines that require modification make the size of our patch substantial. (On last accounting, our kernel patch included modifications to approximately 1,800 lines of code over 34 files). This approach has the advantage that trays are defined as objects with attributes on each zone, which we find easier to reason about and maintain than another approach we considered: implicitly defining a "tray dimension" on each of the memory manager's lists of pages. Finally, this design requires less additional space overhead compared to other approaches. In contrast to the memory region approach proposed by A. Garg [13], which duplicates the entire zone structure for each memory hardware unit, the only structures we duplicate are pointers to list heads for each list of pages in each tray.

Assigning pages to the appropriate tray requires a mapping from the physical addresses served up by the BIOS to the individual memory hardware units. The ACPI 5.0 specification defines a memory power state table (MPST) which exposes this mapping in the operating system [14]. Unfortunately, at the time of this writing, ACPI 5.0 has only been recently released, and we are not able to obtain a system conforming to this specification. Therefore, as a temporary measure, in our prototype implementation we construct the mapping manually from a knowledge of the size and configuration of memory hardware in our experimental system. Specifically, we know that each memory hardware unit stores the same amount of physical memory (2GB, in our case). We can also configure the BIOS to serve up physical addresses sequentially (as opposed to interleaving addresses across memory hardware units). Now, we can compute physical address boundaries for each tray in our system *statically* using the size of our memory hardware units. Finally, at runtime, we simply map each page into the appropriate tray via the page's physical address. Note that, while, in our system, this

mapping is simple enough that it does not require any additional per-page storage, a more complex mapping might require storage of tray information on each page after computing it once during initialization. Our immediate future work will be to rebase the implementation on an ACPI 5.0 compliant kernel that has the MPST information available to the Linux kernel at the point of handoff from BIOS.

5. Experimental Setup

This work presents several experiments to showcase and evaluate our framework's capabilities. In this section, we describe our experimental platform as well as the tools and methodology we use to conduct our experiments, including how we measure power and performance.

5.1 Platform

All of the experiments in this paper were run on an Intel 2600CP server system with two Intel Xeon E5-2680 sockets (codename "Sandy Bridge"). Each socket has 8 2.7GHz cores with hyperthreading enabled and 16 GB of DDR3 memory (for a total of 32 threads and 32 GB of memory). Memory is organized into four channels per socket and each channel contains exactly one DIMM (with two 2 GB ranks each). We install 64-bit SUSE Linux Enterprise Server 11 SP 1 and select a recent Linux kernel (version 2.6.32.59) as our default operating system. The source code of this Linux kernel (available at `kernel.org`) provides the basis of our framework's kernel modifications.

5.2 The HotSpot Java Virtual Machine

Several of our experiments use Sun/Oracle's HotSpot Java Virtual Machine (build 1.6.0_24) [16]. The latest development code for the HotSpot VM is available through Sun's OpenJDK initiative. The HotSpot VM provides a large selection of command-line options, such as various JIT compilation schemes and different garbage collection algorithms, as well as many configurable parameters to tune the VM for a particular machine or application. For all of our experiments with HotSpot, we select the default configuration for server-class machines [15]. We conduct our HotSpot VM experiments over benchmarks selected from two suites of applications: SPECjvm2008 [17] and DaCapo-9.12-bach [5]. Each suite employs a *harness* program to load and iterate the benchmark applications

---

[1] The page interleaving shown in Figure 1 is for pictorial simplicity and is not a restriction.

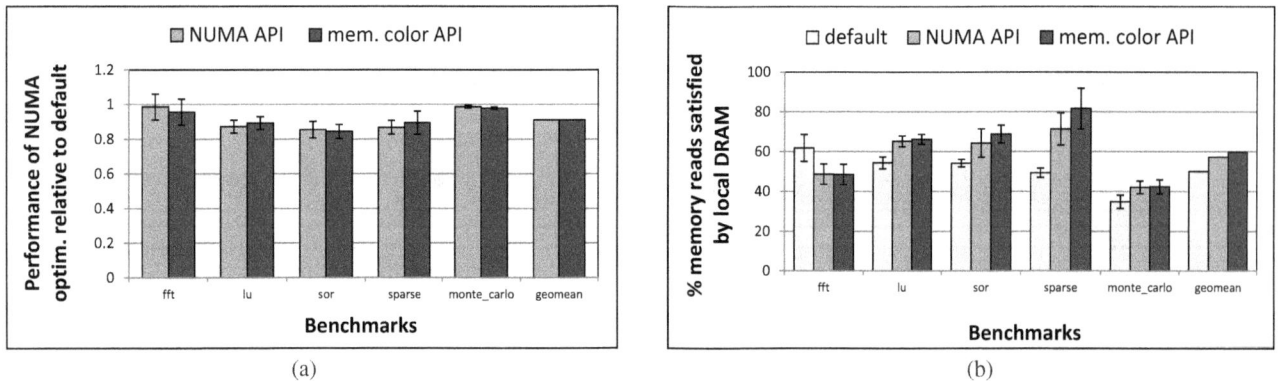

Figure 2. Comparison of implementing the HotSpot NUMA optimization with the default NUMA API vs. our memory coloring framework (a) shows the performance of each implementation relative to the default HotSpot performance. (b) shows the % of NUMA-local memory reads with each configuration.

multiple times in the same run. The SPECjvm2008 harness continuously iterates several benchmark operations for each run, starting a new operation as soon as a previous operation completes. Each run includes a warmup period of two minutes (which is not counted towards the run score) and an iteration period of at least four minutes. The score for each run is the average time it takes to complete one operation during the iteration period. Similarly, the DaCapo harness executes each benchmark operation a specified number of iterations per run. For these applications, we execute the benchmark a total of 31 iterations per run and take the median runtime of the final 30 iterations as the score for each run. For all of our experiments, we report the average score of ten runs as the final score for the benchmark. We discuss the particular applications we use as well as further details about the HotSpot VM relevant to each experiment in the subsequent experimental sections.

5.3 Application Tools for Monitoring Resources

We designed several tools based on custom files in the /proc filesystem to provide applications with memory resource usage information. These tools provide an "on-demand" view of the system's memory configuration as well as an estimate of the total and available memory for each memory hardware unit (rank). Additionally, we have written tools to map specific regions of a process' virtual address space to the memory units backing these regions. These tools are essential for applications which require feedback from the OS to control their own memory usage.

5.4 DRAM Power Measurement

In addition to basic timing for performance measurements, many of our experiments read various activity counters (registers) to measure the impact of our framework with additional metrics, such as power consumption. We estimate DRAM power consumption with Intel's *power governor* library. The power governor framework employs sampling of energy status counters as the basis of its power model. The accuracy of the model, which is based on proprietary formulae, varies based on the DRAM components used. For our experiments, we run a separate instance of a power governor based-tool during each run to compute a DRAM power estimate (in Watts) every 100ms. We report the mean average of these estimates as the average DRAM power consumption over the entire run.

6. Emulating the NUMA API

Modern server systems represent and manage memory resources at the level of individual NUMA nodes. These systems typically provide a library and/or set of tools for applications to control

how their memory usage is allocated across NUMA nodes. In contrast, our framework enables the operating system to manage resources at the more fine-grained level of individual hardware units. While our system provides more precise control, it is also powerful enough to emulate the functionality of tools designed specifically for managing memory at the level of NUMA node. In this section, we demonstrate that our framework effectively emulates the NUMA API by implementing a NUMA optimization in the HotSpot JVM with our framework.

6.1 Exploiting HotSpot's Memory Manager to improve NUMA Locality

The HotSpot JVM employs *garbage collection* (GC) to automatically manage the application's memory resources. The HotSpot memory manager allocates space for the application heap during initialization. As the application runs, objects created by the application are stored in this space. Periodically, when the space becomes full or reaches a preset capacity threshold, the VM runs a collection algorithm to free up space occupied by objects that are no longer reachable. The HotSpot garbage collector is *generational*, meaning that HotSpot divides the heap into two different areas according to the age of the data. Newly created objects are placed in an area called the *eden space*, which is part of the younger generation. Objects that survive some number of young generation collections are eventually promoted, or tenured, to the old generation.

On NUMA systems, this generational organization of memory can be exploited to improve DRAM access locality. The critical observation is thus: *newer objects are more likely to be accessed by the thread that created them.* Therefore, binding new objects to the same NUMA node as the thread that created them should reduce the proportion of memory accesses on remote NUMA nodes, and consequently, improve performance. In order to implement this optimization, HotSpot employs the NUMA API distributed with Linux. During initialization, HotSpot divides the eden space into separate virtual memory areas and informs the OS to back each area with physical memory on a particular NUMA node via the numa_tonode_memory library call. As the application runs, HotSpot keeps track of which areas are bound to which NUMA node and ensures that allocations from each thread are created in the appropriate area.

To implement the NUMA optimization in our framework, we create separate *node affinitization* colors for each NUMA node in the system. Next, we simply replace each call to numa_tonode_memory in HotSpot with a call to color each eden space area with the appropriate node affinitization color. The OS interprets this color as a hint to bind allocation for the colored pages to the set of trays corresponding to memory hardware units on a particular NUMA node. In this way, the node affinitization colors emulate the behavior of the `numa_tonode_memory` library call.

6.2 Experimental Results

We conduct a series of experiments to verify that our framework effectively implements the NUMA optimization in HotSpot. For these experiments, we select the SciMark 2.0 subset of the SPECjvm2008 benchmarks with the large input size. This benchmark set includes five computational kernels common in scientific and engineering calculations and is designed to address the performance of the memory subsystem with out-of-cache problem sizes [17]. We found that enabling the HotSpot NUMA optimization significantly affects the performance of several of these benchmarks, making them good candidates for these experiments. We use the methodology described in Section 5.2 to measure each benchmark's performance. We also employ activity counters to measure the ratio of memory accesses satisfied by NUMA-local vs. NUMA-remote DRAM during each run.

Figure 2(a) shows the performance of each implementation of the NUMA optimization relative to the default configuration's performance of each benchmark. In Figure 2(a), lower bars imply better performance (e.g., the *lu* benchmark runs about 15% faster with the NUMA optimization enabled compared to the default HotSpot configuration). Also, for each result, we plot 95% confidence intervals using the methods described by Georges et. al. [11], and the rightmost bar displays the average (geometric mean) of all the benchmarks. It can be observed that the NUMA optimization improves performance for three of the five SciMark benchmarks, yielding about a 9% average improvement. More importantly, the performance results for each implementation of the NUMA optimization are very similar across all the benchmarks, with the differences between each implementation always within the margin of error. On average, the two implementations perform exactly the same. Similarly, Figure 2(b) plots the percentage of total memory accesses satisfied by NUMA-local memory for each configuration. As expected, the optimization increases the proportion of memory accesses satisfied by local DRAM for most of the benchmarks. Interestingly, the percentage of local memory accesses for one benchmark (*fft*) actually reduces with the optimization enabled. However, in terms of emulating the NUMA API, while these results show slightly more variation between the two implementations, the differences, again, are always within the margin of error. Thus, our framework provides an effective implementation of the NUMA optimization in HotSpot. Furthermore, this experiment shows that our design is flexible enough to supersede tools which exert control over memory at the level of NUMA nodes.

7. Memory Priority for Applications

Our framework provides the architectural infrastructure to enable applications to guide memory management policies for all or a portion of their own memory resources. In this section, we present a "first-of-its-kind" tool which utilizes this infrastructure to enable memory prioritization for applications. Our tool, called *memnice*, allows applications to prioritize their access to memory resources by requesting alternate management policies for low priority memory. Later, we showcase an example of using *memnice* to prioritize the memory usage of a Linux kernel compile.

7.1 *memnice*

Operating systems have long had the ability to prioritize access to the CPU for important threads and applications. In Unix systems, processes set their own priority relative to other processes via the

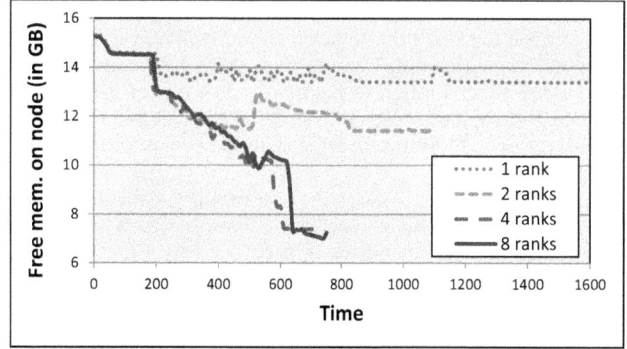

Figure 3. Free memory available during kernel compilations with different memory priorities

nice system call, and the process scheduler uses each process' nice value to prioritize access to the CPU. Prioritizing access to memory resources is much more difficult due to the varying time and space requirements for memory resources and the layers of abstraction between the application and memory hardware. Our framework facilitates solutions for each of these issues enabling us to create the first-ever tool for prioritizing access to memory resources: *memnice*.

In our initial implementation, *memnice* accomplishes memory prioritization by limiting the fraction of physical memory against which allocations can happen[2]. Consider a scenario in which several low-priority applications and one high-priority application compete over the same pool of memory. If left alone, the low-priority applications can expand their memory footprint contending with memory allocations of a higher-priority application, and forcing premature reclaims against a higher-priority application's pages.

In order to ensure the high-priority application runs smoothly, we can restrict the low-priority applications from using certain portions of memory using *memnice*. To implement this scheme in our framework, we enable applications to color portions of their address spaces to reflect the urgency with which pages must be stolen from elsewhere to meet demand fills. In the operating system, we restrict low-priority allocations to only search for free pages from an allowed set of trays. In this way, the low-priority applications are constrained to a smaller fraction of the system's memory, and the high-priority application can call upon larger fractions of system's memory during demand fills.

7.2 Using *memnice* with Kernel Compilation

We showcase our implementation by running several Linux kernel compilations with different memory priority settings. Kernel compilation, unless restricted, can allocate and keep a large number of pages busy, as it proceeds through reading, creating, and writing, a lot of files, including temporary files, from each of a number of threads that run in parallel. For each experiment, we use the *memnice* utility, which is implemented as a simple command-line wrapper, to set the memory priority for the entire address space of the compilation process. We also configured our framework so that children of the root compilation process would inherit its memory priority and apply it to their own address spaces. We run all of our compilations on one node of the system described in Section 5.1.

---

[2] We chose a simple way to force prioritization. In a more refined implementation we would use colors to signal to the operating system that it should force a colored set to do color-local recycling subject to a minimum length of time for which pages are kept mapped before being recycled, to prevent thrashing

For each compilation, we employ four different memory priority configuration to restrict the compilation to a different set of memory resources in each run. These configurations restrict the compilation to use either 1 tray, 2 tray, 4 tray, or all 8 tray of memory on the node. Finally, during each run, we sampled (at a rate of once per second) the `proc` filesystem to estimate the amount of free memory available on the node.

Each line in Figure 3 shows the free memory available on the node during kernel compilations with differing memory priorities. As we can see, each compilation proceeds at first using the same amount of memory resources. However, at around the 200th sample, the compilation restricted to use memory from only 1 tray is constrained from growing its memory footprint any larger than 2GB (recall that our system contains 2GB trays). Similarly, the compilation restricted to two trays stops growing after its footprint reaches about 4GB. The compilations restricted to 4 and 8 trays proceed in pretty much the same way for the entire run, presumably because kernel compilation does not require more than 8GB of memory. Finally, as expected, compilations restricted to use fewer memory resources take much longer to complete. Thus, *memnice* properly constrains the set of memory resources available for each application and is an effective tool for providing efficient, on-demand prioritization of memory resources.

8. Reducing DRAM Power Consumption

Memory power management in current systems occurs under the aegis of a hardware memory controller which transitions memory ranks into low power states (such as "self-refresh") during periods of low activity. To amplify its effectiveness, it is desirable that pages that are very lightly accessed are not mixed up with pages that are accessed often within the same memory ranks. In this section, we show how our framework can bring about periods of low activity more consciously at a memory rank level, instead of relying on such an effect resulting from just happenstance.

For all the experiments in this section, we use a utility that we call *memory scrambler* to simulate memory state on a long-running system. As its name suggests, the"memory scrambler" is designed to keep trays from being wholly free or wholly allocated – it allocates chunks of memory until it exhausts memory, then frees the chunks in random order until a desired amount of memory is freed up (holding down some memory), effectively occupying portions of memory randomly across the physical address space. We perform the experiments described in this section using 16GB of memory from one socket of the server. Before each experiment, we run the scrambler, configured such that it holds down 4GB of memory after it finishes execution.

8.1 Potential of Containerized Memory Management to Reduce DRAM Power Consumption

The default Linux kernel views memory as a large contiguous array of physical pages, sometimes divided into NUMA nodes. That this array is actually a collection of independent power-managed ranks at the hardware level is abstracted away at the point that the kernel takes control of managing the page cache. Over time, as pages become allocated and reclaimed for one purpose after another, it is nearly impossible to keep pages that are infrequently accessed from getting mixed up with pages that are frequently accessed in the same memory banks. Thus, even if only a small fraction of pages are actively accessed, the likelihood remains high that they are scattered widely across all ranks in the system.

The use of *trays* in our customization of the default kernel makes it possible to reduce this dispersion. Trays complement coloring– the application guides the kernel so that virtual pages that are frequently accessed can be mapped to physical pages from one set of trays, while those that are not, can be mapped to physical

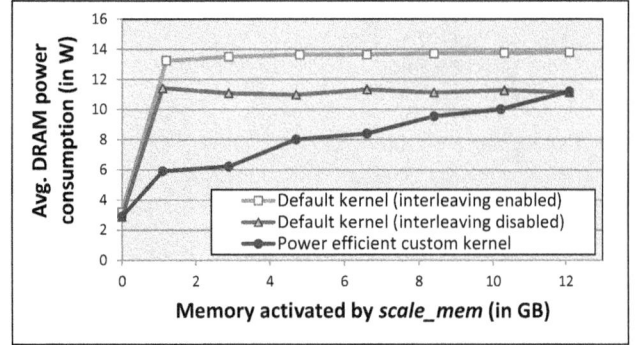

Figure 4. Relationship between memory utilization and power consumption on three different configurations

pages from the remaining trays. If performance demand is such that very high degree of interleaving is requested by an application, the operating system may need to spread out page allocation among more trays; but if that is not necessary then the operating system can keep page allocation biased against such a spread-out. In order to demonstrate the power-saving potential of our framework, we designed a "power-efficient" memory management configuration. We opt, when allocating a page, to choose a tray that has furnished another page for similar use. In this way we reduce the number of additional memory ranks that need to stay powered up.

To keep the first experiment simple, we have used a simplified workload. In this workload, we don't need application coloring because the workload simply allocates increasing amounts of memory in stages, so that in each stage it just allocates enough additional memory to fit in exactly one power-manageable unit. This unit is 2GB, in our case. In each stage, the workload continuously reads and writes the space it has allocated, together with all of the space it allocated in previous stages, for a period of 100 seconds. During each stage, we use power governor (Section 5.4) to measure the average DRAM power consumption.

We compare our custom kernel running the staged workload to the default kernel with two configurations: one with physical addresses interleaved across the memory hardware units (the default in systems tuned for performance) and another with physical addresses served up sequentially by the BIOS. Recall that our custom kernel requires that physical addresses are served up sequentially in order to correctly map trays onto power-manageable units.

Figure 4 shows the average DRAM power consumption during each stage for each system configuration. Thus, during stages when only a fraction of the total system memory is active, our custom kernel consumes much less power than the default kernel. Specifically, during the first stage, the custom kernel consumes about 55% less DRAM power than the default kernel with physical address interleaving enabled and 48% less than the default kernel with interleaving disabled. This is because, with no other processes actively allocating resources, the containerized kernel is able to satisfy the early stage allocations one memory unit at a time. The default kernel, however, has no way to represent power-manageable memory units and will activate memory on every hardware unit during the first stage. As the workload activates more memory, the custom kernel activates more memory hardware units to accommodate the additional resources and eventually consumes as much DRAM power as the default kernel (with interleaving disabled).

In sum, these experiments show that our framework is able to perform memory management over power-manageable units and that this approach has the potential to significantly reduce DRAM power consumption.

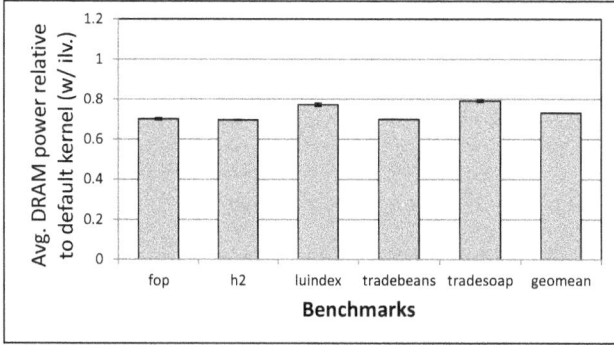 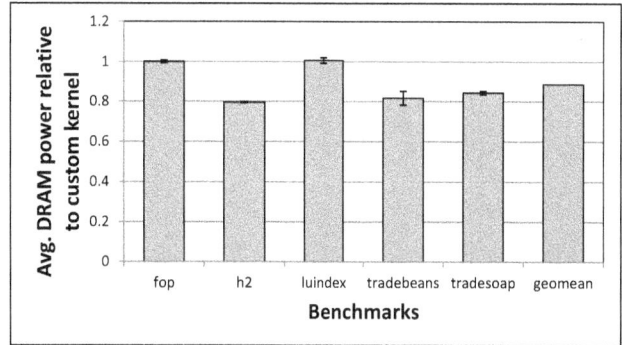

(a)   (b)

Figure 5. Local allocation and recycling reduces DRAM power consumption. (a) shows DRAM power relative to the default kernel (with interleaving enabled) and (b) shows the results relative to the custom kernel without local allocation and recycling.

8.2 Localized Allocation and Recycling to Reduce DRAM Power Consumption

In this section, we show that basic capabilities of our framework can be used to reduce DRAM power consumption over a set of benchmark applications. We create colors to enable applications to restrict their memory allocation and recycling to a population of pages that become allocated to each color (i.e., the OS performs color-local recycling). By restricting allocations of a given color to a subset of memory ranks, the operating system can translate color-confinement into confinement of the active memory footprints to the corresponding groups of ranks. We then measure the impact on power and performance from such confinements.

For these experiments, we selected five Java benchmarks from the DaCapo-9.12-bach benchmark suite for their varying memory usage characteristics. The *h2*, *tradebeans*, and *tradesoap* applications execute thousands of transactions over an in-memory database and require relatively large memory footprints with non-uniform access patterns. In contrast, *fop*, which converts files to PDF format, and *luindex*, which indexes documents using the lucene library, require smaller footprints with more uniform access patterns.

We employ an experimental setup similar to the setup we use in the previous section. All experiments are run on one node of our server system and we again employ the memory scrambling tool to occupy random portions of the physical address space during each run. Each benchmark is run within the HotSpot JVM and we record performance and DRAM power measurements as described in Section 5. Each of the selected benchmarks requires no more than 4GB of total memory resources and we run the benchmarks one at a time. Thus, for each experimental run, we color the entire virtual address space of each benchmark to bind all memory allocation and recycling to a single 4GB DIMM.

Figure 5(a) shows the ratio of DRAM power consumed for each benchmark, between when it is run with local allocation and recycling and when it is run on the default kernel. As the figure shows, the local allocation and recycling consumes significantly less DRAM power than the default kernel configuration; indeed, DRAM power reduces by no less than 20% for each benchmark and the average savings are about 27%. It turns out, however, there are overlapping factors contributing to these power savings. The default configuration interleaves physical addresses across memory hardware units, which typically consumes more power than the alternative of non-interleaved addresses employed by our custom kernel configuration. Additionally, the custom kernel's tray based allocation may help by itself if the application's overall footprint is small enough. In order to isolate the effect of color-based allocation

and recycling, we compare the average DRAM power consumed with and without color guidance with our custom kernel configuration (Figure 5(b)). We find that the database benchmarks are able to reduce power consumption based on color guidance, while the benchmarks with smaller memory footprints do not improve. This is because, without local allocation and recycling enabled, the database benchmarks scatter memory accesses across many power-manageable units, while the memory footprints of *fop* and *luindex* are small enough to require only one or two power-manageable units. Finally, it also appears that the potential reduction in memory bandwidth from localizing allocation and recycling to a single DIMM has very little impact on the performance of these benchmarks. We find that there is virtually no difference in performance between any of the configurations, including when compared to the default Linux kernel.

8.3 Exploiting Generational Garbage Collection

While it is useful to apply coarse-grained coloring over an application's entire virtual address space, let us use this section to describe the potential from using finer-grained control over portions of an application's address space, by evaluating in reality a proposal that has been previously explored through simulation.

The technique we evaluate in this section was first proposed and simulated by Velasco et. al. [27] as a way to reduce DRAM power consumption in systems which employ generational garbage collection. Section 6.1 contained a description of the HotSpot garbage collector. The optimization [27] exploits the observation that during young generation collection, only objects within the young generation are accessed. Thus, if objects in the tenured generation reside on an isolated set of power-manageable units (i.e. no other type of memory resides on them), then these units will power down during young generation collection. It is important to note that this optimization also relies on the assumption that the system "stops the world" (i.e. does not allow application threads to run) during garbage collection to ensure that application threads do not access the tenured generation objects during young generation collection.

In order to implement this optimization in our framework, we arrange to house the tenured generation in a different set of power managed memory units than that allocated to the remainder, by modifying the HotSpot VM to color the tenured generation. When the operating system attempts to allocate resources for a virtual address colored as the tenured generation, it only searches for free memory from a subset of trays that it has earmarked for that color.

We ran the *derby* benchmark from the SPECjvm2008 benchmark suite for evaluation. *derby* is a database benchmark which spends a fair portion of its runtime doing garbage collection. We

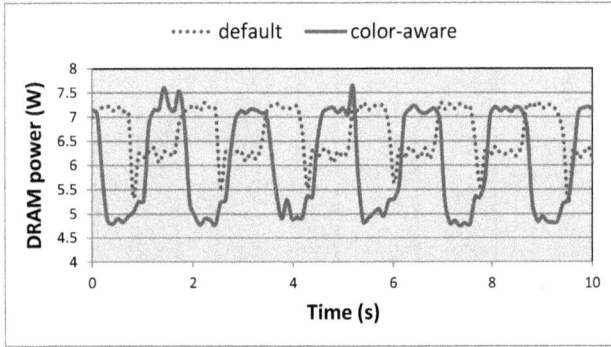

Figure 6. Raw power governor samples with and without "tenured generation optimization" applied

use the same machine and memory scrambler configuration that we use in the previous subsections and we measure performance and DRAM power consumption as described in Section 5.

Figure 6 plots the raw samples collected by the power governor tool during a portion of an experimental run with and without the optimization applied. Each dip corresponds to a separate invocation of the garbage collector. As we can see, the optimized configuration consumes slightly less power during garbage collection. Overall, the optimization reduces DRAM power by almost 9% and does not affect performance on our custom kernel. Thus, isolating the tenured generation memory in HotSpot on its own set of power-manageable units has a small but measurable impact on DRAM power consumption.

9. Future Work

Our current implementation of trays uses memory topology information that we provide to the operating system during its boot-up. This is a temporary measure; an immediate next task is to build upon MPST information that would be available in a Linux kernel that implements ACPI 5.0. Simultaneously we will implement color awareness in selected open source database, web server, and J2EE software packages, so that we can exercise complex, multi-tier workloads at the realistic scale of server systems with memory outlays reaching into hundreds of gigabytes. In these systems, memory power can reach nearly half of the total machine power draw, and therefore they provide an opportunity to explore dramatic power and energy savings from application-engaged containment of memory activities.

The experiments we reported in this paper were on a small scale, in a system with just 16 or 32 gigabytes of memory as our first phase intent was to demonstrate the concept of application influenced virtualization of memory. In the next phase of this work, in addition to exploring the saving of power on a non-trivial scale of a terabyte data or web application services, we plan to explore memory management algorithms that permit applications to maximize performance by biasing placement of high value data so that pages in which performance critical data resides are distributed widely across memory channels. Another element of optimization we plan to explore is application guided read-ahead and/or fault-ahead for those virtual ranges of applications in which there is reason to expect sequential access patterns. We also plan to implement a greater variety of page recycling policies in order to take advantage of color hints from applications; for instance, we would like to create the possibility that trays implement such algorithm options as (a) minimum residency time– where a page is not reclaimed unless it has been mapped for a certain threshold duration, (b) capacity allocation – where, physical pages allocated to different color groups are

recycled on an accelerated basis as needed in order to keep the time-averaged allocation in line with application guided capacities, (c) reserve capacities – in which a certain minimum number of pages are set aside in order to provide a reserve buffer capacity for certain critical usages, etc. We envision that as we bring our studies to large scale software such as a complex database, we will inevitably find new usage cases in which applications can guide the operating system with greater nuance about how certain pages should be treated differently from others. Finally, one avenue of considerable new work that remains is the development of tools for instrumentation, analysis, and control, so that we can facilitate the generation and application of memory usage guidance between application software and operating system.

10. Conclusion

This paper presents a framework for application-guided memory management. We create abstractions called colors and trays to enable three-way collaboration between the application tasks, operating system software, and hardware. Using a re-architected Linux kernel, and detailed measurements of performance, power, and memory usage, we demonstrate several use cases for our framework, including emulation of NUMA APIs, enabling memory priority for applications, and power-efficiency for important applications. Hence, by providing an empirical evaluation that demonstrates the value of application-guided memory management, we have shown that our framework is a critical first step in meeting the need for a fine-grained, power-aware, flexible provisioning of memory.

Acknowledgments

We thank the reviewers, and especially Harvey Tuch, whose thoughtful comments and suggestions significantly improved this paper. We also thank Prasad Kulkarni at the University of Kansas who provided valuable feedback during the review process.

References

[1] V. Anagnostopoulou, M. Dimitrov, and K. A. Doshi. Sla-guided energy savings for enterprise servers. In *IEEE International Symposium on Performance Analysis of Systems and Software*, pages 120–121, 2012.

[2] G. Banga, P. Druschel, and J. C. Mogul. Resource containers: a new facility for resource management in server systems. In *Proceedings of the third symposium on Operating systems design and implementation*, OSDI '99, pages 45–58. USENIX Association, 1999.

[3] A. Belay, A. Bittau, A. Mashtizadeh, D. Terei, D. Mazières, and C. Kozyrakis. Dune: safe user-level access to privileged cpu features. In *Proceedings of the 10th USENIX conference on Operating Systems Design and Implementation*, OSDI'12, pages 335–348. USENIX Association, 2012.

[4] M. Bi, R. Duan, and C. Gniady. Delay-Hiding energy management mechanisms for DRAM. In *International Symposium on High Performance Computer Architecture*, pages 1–10, 2010.

[5] S. M. Blackburn, R. Garner, C. Hoffmann, A. M. Khang, K. S. McKinley, R. Bentzur, A. Diwan, D. Feinberg, D. Frampton, S. Z. Guyer, M. Hirzel, A. Hosking, M. Jump, H. Lee, J. E. B. Moss, A. Phansalkar, D. Stefanović, T. VanDrunen, D. von Dincklage, and B. Wiedermann. The DaCapo Benchmarks: Java Benchmarking Development and Analysis. In *ACM SIGPLAN conference on Object-oriented programming systems, languages, and applications*, pages 169–190, 2006.

[6] A. D. Brown and T. C. Mowry. Taming the memory hogs: using compiler-inserted releases to manage physical memory intelligently. In *Proceedings of the 4th conference on Symposium on Operating System Design & Implementation - Volume 4*, OSDI'00. USENIX Association, 2000.

[7] J. Corbet. Memory Compaction, Jan. 2010. URL http://lwn.net/Articles/368869/.

[8] V. Delaluz, A. Sivasubramaniam, M. Kandemir, N. Vijaykrishnan, and M. Irwin. Scheduler-based dram energy management. In *Design Automation Conference*, pages 697–702, 2002.

[9] D. R. Engler, M. F. Kaashoek, and J. O'Toole, Jr. Exokernel: an operating system architecture for application-level resource management. *SIGOPS Oper. Syst. Rev.*, 29(5):251–266, Dec. 1995.

[10] X. Fan, C. Ellis, and A. Lebeck. Modeling of dram power control policies using deterministic and stochastic petri nets. In *Power-Aware Computer Systems*, pages 37–41, 2003.

[11] A. Georges, D. Buytaert, and L. Eeckhout. Statistically Rigorous Java Performance Evaluation. In *ACM SIGPLAN conference on Object-oriented programming systems and applications*, pages 57–76, 2007.

[12] A. Gonzalez. Android Linux Kernel Additions, 2010. URL http://www.lindusembedded.com/blog/2010/12/07/android-linux-kernel-additions/.

[13] http://lwn.net/Articles/445045/. Ankita Garg: Linux VM Infrastructure to support Memory Power Management, 2011.

[14] http://www.acpi.info/spec.htm. Advanced Configuration and Power Interface Specification, 2011.

[15] http://www.oracle.com/technetwork/java/javase/memorymanagement-whitepaper 150215.pdf. Memory Management in the Java HotSpot Virtual Machine, April 2006.

[16] http://www.oracle.com/technetwork/java/whitepaper 135217.html. Oracle HotSpot JVM, 2012.

[17] http://www.spec.org/jvm2008/. SPECjvm2008, 2008.

[18] H. Huang, P. Pillai, and K. Shin. Design and Implementation of Power-aware Virtual Memory. In *USENIX Annual Technical Conference*, 2003.

[19] R. E. Kessler and M. D. Hill. Page placement algorithms for large real-indexed caches. *ACM Trans. Comput. Syst.*, 10(4):338–359, Nov. 1992.

[20] A. Kleen. A numa api for linux. *SUSE Labs white paper*, August 2004.

[21] A. R. Lebeck, X. Fan, H. Zeng, and C. Ellis. Power aware page allocation. *ACM SIGOPS Operating Systems Review*, 34(5):105–116, 2000.

[22] C. Lefurgy, K. Rajamani, F. Rawson, W. Felter, M. Kistler, and T. W. Keller. Energy management for commercial servers. *Computer*, 36 (12):39–48, Dec. 2003.

[23] C.-H. Lin, C.-L. Yang, and K.-J. King. Ppt: joint performance/power/thermal management of dram memory for multi-core systems. In *ACM/IEEE International Symposium on Low Power Electronics and Design*, pages 93–98, 2009.

[24] L. Lu, P. Varman, and K. Doshi. Decomposing workload bursts for efficient storage resource management. *IEEE Transactions on Parallel and Distributed Systems*, 22(5):860 –873, may 2011.

[25] D. Magenheimer, C. Mason, D. McCracken, and K. Hackel. Transcendent memory and linux. In *Ottawa Linux Symposium*, pages 191–200, 2009.

[26] P. Petrov and A. Orailoglu. Virtual page tag reduction for low-power tlbs. In *IEEE International Conference on Computer Design*, pages 371–374, 2003.

[27] J. M. Velasco, D. Atienza, and K. Olcoz. Memory power optimization of java-based embedded systems exploiting garbage collection information. *Journal of Systems Architecture - Embedded Systems Design*, 58(2):61–72, 2012.

[28] H. Wang, K. Doshi, and P. Varman. Nested qos: Adaptive burst decomposition for slo guarantees in virtualized servers. *Intel Technology Journal*, June, 16:2 2012.

[29] P. Zhou, V. Pandey, J. Sundaresan, A. Raghuraman, Y. Zhou, and S. Kumar. Dynamic tracking of page miss ratio curve for memory management. In *Proceedings of the 11th international conference on Architectural support for programming languages and operating systems*, ASPLOS XI, pages 177–188. ACM, 2004.

Towards Verifiable Resource Accounting for Outsourced Computation

Chen Chen

CyLab, Carnegie Mellon University
Pittsburgh, PA, USA

Petros Maniatis

Intel Labs, ISTC-SC
Berkeley, CA, USA

Adrian Perrig

CyLab, Carnegie Mellon University
Pittsburgh, PA, USA

Amit Vasudevan

CyLab, Carnegie Mellon University
Pittsburgh, PA, USA

Vyas Sekar

Stony Brook University
Stony Brook, NY, USA

Abstract

Outsourced computation services should ideally only charge customers for the resources used by their applications. Unfortunately, no verifiable basis for service providers and customers to reconcile resource accounting exists today. This leads to undesirable outcomes for both providers and consumers—providers cannot prove to customers that they really devoted the resources charged, and customers cannot verify that their invoice maps to their actual usage. As a result, many practical and theoretical attacks exist, aimed at charging customers for resources that their applications did not consume. Moreover, providers cannot charge consumers precisely, which causes them to bear the cost of unaccounted resources or pass these costs inefficiently to their customers.

We introduce ALIBI, a first step toward a vision for *verifiable resource accounting*. ALIBI places a minimal, trusted reference monitor underneath the service provider's software platform. This monitor observes resource allocation to customers' guest virtual machines and reports those observations to customers, for verifiable reconciliation. In this paper, we show that ALIBI efficiently and verifiably tracks guests' memory use and CPU-cycle consumption.

Categories and Subject Descriptors   D.4.6 [*Security and Protection*]: Access controls; K.6.4 [*System Management*]: Management audit; K.6.5 [*Security and Protection*]: Unauthorized access

General Terms   Measurement, Reliability, Security, Verification

Keywords   Cloud computing, Accounting, Metering, Resource auditing

1. Introduction

The computing-as-a-service model – enterprises and businesses outsourcing their applications and services to cloud-based deployments – is here to stay. A key driver behind the adoption of cloud services is the promise of reduced operating and capital expenses, and the ability to achieve elastic scaling without having to maintain a dedicated (and overprovisioned) compute infrastructure. Surveys indicate that 61% of IT executives and CIOs rated the "pay only for what you use" as a very important perceived benefit of the cloud model and more than 80% of respondents rated competitive pricing and performance assurances/Service-Level Agreements (SLAs) as important benefits [3].

Despite this confirmation that resource usage and billing are top concerns for IT managers, the verifiability of usage claims or services provided has so far received limited attention from industry and academia [34, 39]. Anecdotal evidence suggests that customers perceive a disconnect between their workloads and charges [1, 4, 12, 29]. At the same time, providers suffer too as they are unable to accurately justify resource costs. For example, providers today do not account for memory bandwidth, internal network resources, power/cooling costs, or I/O stress [22, 30, 46]. This accounting inaccuracy and uncertainty creates economic inefficiency, as providers lose revenue from undercharging or customers lose confidence from overcharging. While trust in cloud providers may be a viable model for some, others may prefer "trust but verify" given providers' incentive to overcharge. Such guaranteed resource accounting is especially important to thwart demonstrated attacks on cloud accounting [27, 42, 50].

Our overarching vision is to develop a basis for *verifiable resource accounting* to assure customers of the absence of billing inflation, thereby forestalling billing disputes. Furthermore, the enhanced transparency of precise resource accounting helps cloud users optimize their utilization.

Unfortunately, existing trustworthy computing mechanisms provide limited forms of assurance such as launch integrity [40] or input-output equivalence [18], but do not address resource accounting guarantees. An alternative is to develop "clean-slate" solutions such as a new resource-accounting OS or hypervisor [25]; however, these are not viable given the existing legacy of deployed cloud infrastructure.

The challenge here is to achieve verifiable resource accounting with *low overhead* and *minimal changes* to existing deployment models. To this end, we propose an architecture that leverages recent advances in *nested virtualization* [9, 48]. Specifically, we envision a thin lightweight hypervisor atop which today's legacy hypervisors and guest operating systems can run with minor or no modification. Thus, this approach lends itself to an immediately

VEE'13,   March 16–17, 2013, Houston, Texas, USA.
Copyright © 2013 ACM 978-1-4503-1266-0/13/03...$15.00

deployable alternative for current provider and customer side infrastructures.

The properties of verifiable resource accounting, however, do not directly map to the applications targeted by nested virtualization (e.g., defending against hypervisor-level rootkits or addressing compatibility issues with public clouds). Thus, we need to identify and extend the appropriate resource allocation "chokepoints" to provide the necessary hooks, while guaranteeing that customer jobs run untampered.

As a proof-of-concept implementation, we demonstrate verifiable resource accounting by extending the Turtles nested virtualization framework [9], in which we build a minimal trusted *Observer*, observing, accounting for, and reporting resource use. As a starting point, we show this for the two most commonly accounted resources, CPU and memory, which are directly observable by lower virtualization layers, thanks to existing virtualization support in hardware.

Our prototype, ALIBI, is limited and is intended as a proof of concept of verifiable accounting. It demonstrates that: (i) verifiable accounting is possible and efficient in the existing cloud-computing usage model; (ii) nested virtualization is an effective mechanism to provide trustworthy resource accounting; and (iii) a number of documented accounting attacks can be thus thwarted. Our evaluation of the salient points of our system shows that resource accounting and verifiability add little overhead to that of nested virtualization, which is already efficient for CPU-bound workloads. While there is non-trivial overhead for I/O bound workloads, recent and future advances in virtualizing or simplifying interrupts [17], as well as hardware support for nested virtualization [37] make the approach promising.

While ALIBI already represents a significant advance over the status quo in resolving the uncertainty in resource accounting, we acknowledge that this is only a first step. Beyond the aforementioned performance limitations of nested virtualization for I/O-intensive workloads, we need to address several other issues to fully realize our vision for verifiable accounting. As future work, we plan to extend our framework to handle other charged resources, such as I/O requests or provider-specific API requests (e.g., Amazon S3), which are most often not directly observable by the low layers of virtualization. While we expect non-trivial challenges in addressing these issues, the initial success demonstrated here, the experiences we gained in the process, and emerging processor roadmaps give us reasons to be optimistic in our quest.

2. Motivation

In this section, we survey the landscape of outsourced computation, identify shortcomings in how resources are invoiced, and derive the desirable properties for addressing those shortcomings.

2.1 The Lifecycle of Outsourced Computation

The typical outsourced-computation pattern we study in this work is *Infrastructure as a Service* (IaaS), exemplified by Amazon's Elastic Compute Cloud (EC2)[1], Rackspace[2], and Azure[3] among others. IaaS offers customers a virtual-hardware infrastructure to run their applications.

A new customer starts by creating an account on the platform, and exchanging private/public key-pairs, to be able to authenticate and encrypt future communication channels. After account establishment, a customer can upload a virtual-machine image to platform-local storage, which contains a virtual boot disk with an OS, needed applications, and data. The platform operator may require mild customization of that image to improve performance or compatibility, e.g., installing customized device drivers or BIOS. The customer then launches an *instance*, by booting that customized image in a platform guest VM, and either directly logs into that instance to manage it, or lets it serve requests from remote clients (e.g., HTTP requests). While her instance is running, the customer may use additional hosting features, such as local storage (e.g., Amazon's Elastic Block Store (EBS)[4]). Later on, the customer terminates that instance.

The platform provider charges the customer either for provisioned services or according to usage. For example, EC2 charges a customer for the total time her instance is in a running state (length of time between launch and termination, even if the virtual CPU is idle in between). Additionally, EC2 charges the customer per distinct I/O request sent by her instance to a mounted EBS volume[5]. The former is an instance of a provisioned service, charged whether it is used or not, while the latter is an instance of a pay-per-use service. Although platform operators provide some SLAs (e.g., Amazon offers a minimum-availability guarantee[6], and a credit process when that guarantee is violated during a pay cycle), most provisioned services (e.g., a provisioned-IOPS EBS volume, which has a provisioned bandwidth of up to 1000 I/O operations per second) are not accompanied by precise SLAs. Except for small differences, other providers, such as Microsoft's Windows Azure service, operate in a similar fashion for their IaaS products.

To summarize, the lifecycle of a customer's VM on a provider's platform has the following steps: (i) Image installation; (ii) Image customization; (iii) Instance launch of an installed image; (iv) Execution accounting of resource use by the instance; (v) Instance termination; and (vi) Customer invoicing based on instance-usage accounting.

2.2 Challenges with Unverified Resource Use

We now identify how lack of verifiability can cause accounting inaccuracy and deception in the context of the outsourced-computation lifecycle.

Image Installation The transfer of a new VM image from the customer to the platform incurs network costs, and the storage of an installed image incurs storage costs. If the installation channel lacks integrity guarantees, external attackers may cause extraneous storage and network charges. In fact, the management interfaces of both EC2 and Eucalyptus, an open-source cloud-management platform, were found vulnerable to such abuse, making this a realistic threat. Somorovsky et al. [42] used variants of XML signature-wrapping attacks [28] to hijack the command stream between a legitimate customer and the provider. In this fashion, an attacker may replace the image installed by a customer and cause subsequent launches to bring up the wrong image.

In a similar fashion, the provider is currently unconstrained from performing image installation; e.g., by discarding the image supplied by the customer and replacing it with another. This is a special case of outsourced-storage integrity and retrievability [41].

Image Customization Before execution, a customer's image may be modified for the hosting platform. For example, the provider may install its proprietary drivers or BIOS into the image. This may constitute a legitimate reason why the image that runs in the cloud is different from the customer-supplied image. Furthermore, the provider may wish to conceal proprietary information about its platform and its customizations.

---

[1] aws.amazon.com/ec2/

[2] www.rackspace.com

[3] www.windowsazure.com

[4] aws.amazon.com/ebs/

[5] aws.amazon.com/ec2/pricing/

[6] aws.amazon.com/ec2-sla/

Instance Launch A launch event (i.e., when an image is launched within a VM instance) is significant for accounting purposes – this is the time when actual charges start accruing for on-demand pricing schemes. Unfortunately, nothing stops a greedy provider from spuriously starting an instance and there is no defense against external attackers who abuse the control interfaces [42] to start an instance on behalf of an unsuspecting customer.

Execution Accounting There is little a customer can do to ensure that, after launch, her instance continues to run the intended image; e.g., the platform or an external attacker can suspend the instance, replace its image with another, and resume it. Practical attacks have been demonstrated against the prevalent (sampling-based) scheduling and accounting where malicious customers can run their own tasks but cause charges to be attributed to other customers. One such attack, described by Zhou et al. [50], allows instances that share a physical CPU to suspend themselves right before a scheduler tick is issued. As a result, the victim customer's instance that is subsequently scheduled gets charged for being active during the scheduler tick.

On the other hand, platform providers, even when promising dedicated resources, can inflate charges. For example, larger EC2 instances (e.g., a "Medium" instance) are assigned – and charged – dedicated CPUs and memory while the instance is running. But a customer may wonder if the CPU she is paying for is really dedicated; can a provider *overbook* (or, more bluntly put, *double-charge*) by "dedicating" the same physical CPU to multiple instances?

Liu and Ding have identified ways in which a platform provider can subvert the integrity of resource metering [27]. Even assuming limited attack capabilities – in their case, an attacker who can only change privileged software but not system software or the customer's image – a malicious provider can inflate resource use by arbitrarily prolonging responses to the customer instance's system requests. Such requests include the setup period between instance launch and control transfer to the customer's image; the handling of system calls, hypercalls, exceptions, and I/O requests; the issuance of extraneous interrupts; and the implementation of platform features in local or remote libraries.

Instance Termination Termination is the end point of the CPU-charging period for instances and, consequently, it is another critical event for proper accounting. Premature termination of an instance (e.g., against the customer's intentions) may indicate the replacement of the image in a running instance with another arbitrary one. Also, delayed termination past the point dictated by the customer or her management scripts may be an avenue for deceptively inflating usage charges.

Invoicing The invoice generated by the provider and submitted to the customer for payment is intended as a summarized record of the customer's use of the provider's resources. The challenge with verifiable accounting is to ensure that this record is consistent with the actual usage incurred by the customer's VMs. For example, an external attacker, especially one with unchecked access to the management interface, may pass her own use of the platform as incurred by a different customer. Conversely, the platform operator may generate inflated invoices, since customers cannot witness the usage of their own instances, to associate the invoice with the actual expenditure.

3. Desired Properties

The implication of the above weaknesses is that the customer who receives an invoice at the end of a billing cycle cannot distinguish between charges for her legitimate VM image, or some attacker-installed VM image running on her behalf, or charges arbitrarily

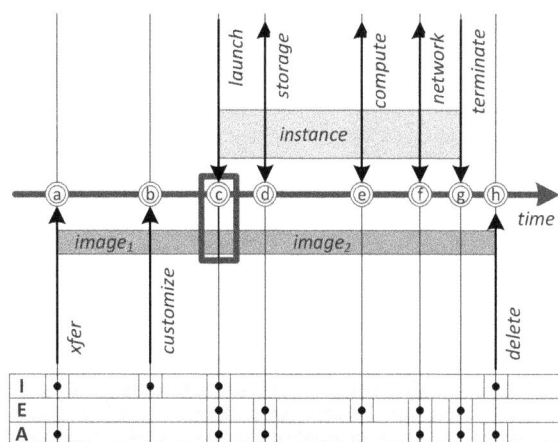

Figure 1. The System Model: There are three types of integrity properties Image (I), Execution (E), and Accounting (A). The figure shows a timeline during the lifecycle of an outsourced computation task and how different events relate to the integrity properties we require for verifiable accounting.

and undeservedly assessed by a deceitful provider. Building on the attack scenarios described above, we identify three properties: Image Integrity (*what* is executing), Execution Integrity (*how* it is executing), and Accounting Integrity (*how much* provider charges customer). To achieve *verifiability*, a customer needs assurance that the provider cannot violate the integrity properties undetected and, conversely, a correct provider needs assurance to avoid slander for purported integrity violations.

To formulate these properties, we consider the system model illustrated in Figure 1. The customer-provider interface includes operations to transfer new images (*xfer*), to *customize* images before launch, and to *delete* images from storage, to stop incurring storage costs. Instances can be *launch*ed using a previously-installed image, and *terminate*d later on. While an instance is running, it undergoes state changes, including requests for *storage*, *network*, and *compute*. Some of these operations are relevant to images (I), some to execution (E), and some are chargeable events relevant to accounting (A), as shown at the bottom of the figure.

Image Integrity Informally, the OS, programs, and data making up the customer's *image* must have the contents intended by the customer at the time of each instance launch. In other words, the sequence of management operations – image installation, image customization, and instance launch given an image – have the same effect on instance launches (i.e., cause the same image to boot upon instance launch) as they would have if the customer were executing these operations on a trusted exclusive platform.

Note that this property can be maintained while the provider modifies customer images without explicit customer authorization (e.g., by moving them from block device to block device, compressing them, deduplicating them, copying them, etc.). The requirement is that upon a customer-initiated launch, the launched image is as the customer intended via her explicit operations.

Execution Integrity Similarly, changes to the *state* of an image while it is executing in an instance are "correct" if the sequence of actions (instruction execution, requests received externally, non-deterministic interrupts) taken by an image instance between launch and termination have the same effects on the instance state (its local storage while it is running), and external interfaces (e.g., responses sent to remote requests) as it would have, if that

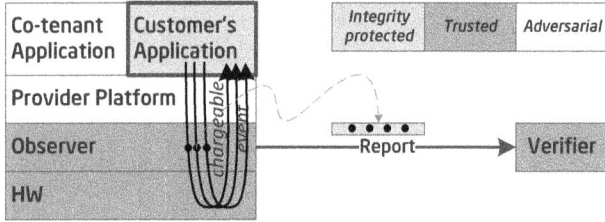

Figure 2. The conceptual architecture of ALIBI. We envision a lightweight trusted Observer that runs below the cloud provider's platform software. This trusted layer generates an attested report or witness of the execution of the guest VM to the customer.

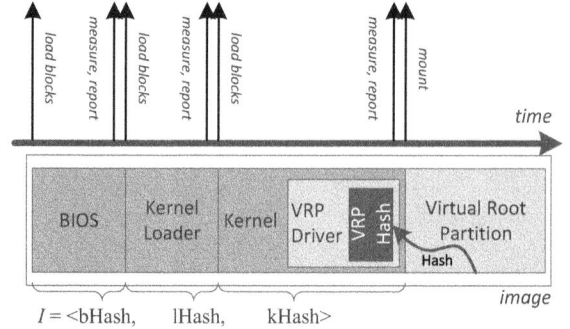

Figure 3. Instance Attestation: Timeline of instance launch showing the different hashes of the BIOS, kernel loader, and kernel being computed in sequence.

same image were executing under the same sequence of actions on a trusted, correct, exclusive platform.

Since all external devices are under the control of the platform, execution integrity cannot prevent network packets or disk blocks from being malicious, or triggering non-control data vulnerabilities [10]. Integrity here assumes a correct CPU and memory system. This property does not restrict platform operations from suspending an instance, migrating it, or otherwise manipulating it, as long as those manipulations do not alter the behavior of the instance.

Accounting Integrity This property ensures that the customer is only charged for *chargeable* events, such as CPU-cycle utilization, while an instance is running. In other words, the provider cannot charge the customer for spurious events (e.g., for having used a CPU cycle while another instance was using it). Similarly, the property ensures that the customer cannot incur unaccounted chargeable events.

A charging model (i.e., a specification of what events should be charged how much), maps a sequence of image and execution actions to an invoice. Accounting integrity then ensures that the provider invoices the customer as if the customer had run her sequence of actions on a trusted, exclusive platform, and applied the charging model on the resulting action sequence[7].

Verifiable resource accounting requires us to satisfy *all three properties*. With accounting integrity alone, the customer may know that the right events were measured in the invoice (i.e., she was not charged for fictitious cycles), but she cannot know if those events corresponded to her jobs. For that, it is essential to ensure the *correct* execution of the *right* image (execution and image integrity, respectively). Similarly, image integrity alone is meaningless; the provider may charge for arbitrary, spurious events that have nothing to do with the customer's image and precluding that scenario requires accounting integrity. Image integrity, even with accounting integrity, is insufficient, since the provider may inject arbitrary code charges for correct events issued by an instance launched with the correct image, albeit for an incorrect execution.

4. ALIBI Design

The conceptual architecture of our system, ALIBI, is shown in Figure 2. At a high level, ALIBI uses nested virtualization to place a trusted Observer at the highest privilege level underneath the provider's platform software and all customer instances. The Observer collects all chargeable events incurred by a customer instance, and offers them to the customer, as a *trustworthy witness* of the provider's invoice at the end of a billing cycle. At the same

time, the Observer protects the execution of the customer instance against tampering by other instances or by the provider itself, while ensuring that the provider does not miss customer actions that it should be charging for.

We consider two case studies of resource accounting:

CPU Usage The customer agreed to be charged while her application is executing on the provider's CPUs, but not when it is suspended.

Memory Utilization The customer agreed to be charged for the amount of physical memory her applications use, e.g., as the number of pages integrated over allocated time.

In the next sections we explain in order how ALIBI guarantees the three integrity properties from Section 3. Image integrity is protected via *attested instance launch* (Section 4.1). Execution integrity is protected via *guest-platform isolation* (Section 4.2). Accounting integrity is protected via *trustworthy attribution* (Section 4.3). Trust in the operation of the Observer itself is established via *authenticated boot* (Section 4.4). We revisit the lifecycle of an outsourced computation in Section 5, arguing that the weaknesses we identified earlier (Section 2.2) are removed by ALIBI.

Viewed in a general systems context, ALIBI builds on the well-known concepts of reference monitors and virtualization. Our contribution lies in the careful extension of these ideas to meet the particular integrity requirements of verifiable resource accounting.

4.1 Image Integrity via Attested Instance Launch

Image integrity requires that the Observer verify the customer's image when it is first loaded into an instance by the provider platform. If an image were loaded directly and entirely into a sufficient number of memory pages, then the Observer could measure those pages – i.e., hash them in a canonical order with a cryptographic hash function – and compare them to a hash submitted by the customer during image installation.

Unfortunately, VM images are almost never entirely in memory. Although the kernel remains pinned in (guest) memory, user-space processes are placed into guest virtual memory on demand, in the somewhat unpredictable order of process launch, via the init process or the shell. Furthermore, memory-page contents may be swapped out by the instance OS to reuse guest physical memory, or even by the platform provider, to reuse host physical memory, when managing multiple concurrent instances on the same physical hardware (e.g., via ballooning or transcendent memory).

To address this problem, ALIBI uses a hybrid software attestation approach. As in prior systems that bring up an attested kernel (e.g., SecVisor [40]), the customer's BIOS, kernel boot loader,

---

[7] Charging functions may not be independent from other concurrent users of the platform (e.g., some resources may have congestion pricing, as for example Amazon does with EC2's spot instances). We narrow our scope here to simpler, independent-charge models.

and kernel are measured and launched one after the other. All remaining data are loaded from the installed image by mounting it in an integrity-protected fashion, either at the file system level, or the storage block device level; protection is done in a traditional chained-hash mechanism (e.g., SFS-RO [16] and dm-verity [2]), and the root hash is hard-coded in the device driver, which is itself statically compiled into the attested kernel. Figure 3 illustrates the image structure.

These properties are guaranteed as follows. The Observer is told explicitly about the $\mathcal{I} = \langle \text{bHash}, \text{lHash}, \text{kHash} \rangle$ triple, containing the cryptographic hash of the BIOS, the kernel loader, and the kernel, respectively, when a new customer image is installed in the platform. Each successive stage of the instance boot process registers itself with the Observer (via a hypercall), reporting what customer image it belongs to (a customer-configured ID), what stage it is (BIOS, loader, kernel), and what guest physical memory pages it occupies; the Observer hashes those memory pages, matches the hash against the corresponding component of $\mathcal{I}$ for that image ID, and records the memory range as part of the instance for the given image.

Once the instance kernel is registered and loaded, it mounts its root partition using the integrity-protected filesystem driver. Recall that the root hash for the file system is embedded in the kernel (as part of the statically compiled device driver), so kHash protects the root partition as well.

At the end of this process, the Observer knows the memory pages occupied by the static and dynamic portions of the customer instance, and that their contents are consistent with the customer's registered image.

4.2 Execution Integrity via Guest-Platform Isolation

ALIBI provides execution integrity by protecting three assets of the running customer instance: its state in memory, its state in storage, and its control flow.

Memory: Given a current allocation of physical memory pages $\mathcal{M}$ to an instance i, the Observer enforces the invariant that memory in $\mathcal{M}$ can only be written while i is executing.

ALIBI enforces this invariant via the Memory Management Unit (MMU), and in particular the Extended Page Tables (EPTs) on Intel processors. An EPT maps guest physical pages to host physical pages, and associates write/execute permissions with each such mapped page, much like traditional page tables. When a guest attempts to access a guest physical page that has not as yet been mapped to a host physical page in the EPT, an EPT violation trap gives control to the hypervisor, which performs the mapping, and resumes the guest. In our case, the Observer write- and execute-protects all pages in $\mathcal{M}$ by modifying the platform software's EPT, while i is not executing. When the platform software attempts to pass control to the customer instance, the instance's EPT will be installed, which automatically unprotects pages in $\mathcal{M}$. When the instance loses control, e.g., because of a hypercall or an interrupt, the Observer automatically re-protects $\mathcal{M}$ by installing the platform software's EPT again.

When an instance is first launched via the mechanism described in Section 4.1, the Observer only associates with the instance the memory pages holding content that has been measured and matched against the image integrity digest $\mathcal{I}$. To capture further modifications of $\mathcal{M}$, the Observer also write-protects the memory-management structures of the platform software. This ensures that the Observer interposes (via EPT violation traps) on all modifications of memory allocations by the platform to its guests. The Observer applies the protection described above to $\mathcal{M}$ as that changes over time, since changes are always essentially effected by the Observer first.

One subtle issue here is that the platform software may have legitimate reasons to modify the contents of a guest's page unbeknownst to that guest, e.g., when migrating the guest to another physical machine, or swapping guest-physical pages out or back in again. While the above protections ensure that the Observer prevents the platform from manipulating guest pages when they are in memory, it does not prevent the pages from being arbitrarily modified when they are swapped out and then swapped back in. This requires an additional, but straightforward, protection. Specifically, when the provider platform needs to unmap a guest physical page (e.g., to swap it to disk), the Observer intercepts this request as above (since all modifications to the guest's EPT by the platform result in a protection trap down to the Observer). At this time, it computes a cryptographic hash of the contents, and records the hash for the guest page address. If the platform later maps another physical page to the same guest page, the Observer once again interposes on this call to check that the contents have not been modified, by checking if the hash matches the recorded value. Manifests of such page hashes can be transmitted to remote Observers during migration. Our prototype does not yet implement this protection.

Note that platform software may write-share memory pages with an instance (and instances may also share pages with each other). We require the guest to explicitly mark some of its pages as authorized for sharing with the platform, and exclude them from the protection described above. For read-shared pages, as might happen, for example, with the Kernel Samepage Merging (KSM) mechanism in Linux-KVM, our protections still apply with appropriate manipulation of the relevant EPTs when the platform attempts to map the same page to multiple guests.

Storage: Instances typically have at their disposal some local storage (EC2 calls it "instance storage") for their lifetime. ALIBI protects that storage by mounting it via an integrity-protected filesystem (a read-write variant of dm-verity [2]), in a manner similar to how the root partition is mounted. Although the mutability of this storage makes integrity protection somewhat more expensive for a naïve implementation, systems such as CloudVisor [48] have demonstrated acceptable performance for even stronger protection of this form (adding confidentiality).

Control Flow: To protect the control flow of instances, ALIBI protects the stacks of a guest (both user-space and kernel-space) as part of protecting the allocated memory pages to an instance. As a result, the call stacks of processes in the instance cannot be directly altered by the platform or other instances.

While an instance is not running, platform software has control of the guest-CPU state, including the stack-pointer and instruction-pointer registers (RSP and RIP), which also affect control flow when the instance resumes, as well as general-purpose registers, which may indirectly affect control flow upon resumption, and model-specific registers, which may affect the general operation of an instance (e.g., disable memory paging). ALIBI uses memory protections on the data structures holding guest state in the platform software, after an instance is launched; when platform software attempts to modify such state, the Observer validates the modification before allowing it to affect guest operation.

In general, ALIBI limits the options of in-flight modifications of guest state available to the platform. In particular, it only allows changes to RSP and RIP that are consistent with handling of guest-mode exceptions (e.g., emulated I/O requests) that, typically, amount to advancing the RIP register to the next instruction following the one that caused an exception. ALIBI also explicitly records general-purpose registers holding return data from a hypercall, and allows the platform software to modify those registers.

Finally, the control flow of an instance may be affected by the initial instruction executed when the instance is launched (in the

BIOS segment of the image). ALIBI only allows a newly launched instance to be started at a given, fixed initial entry point (typically, the entry point into the BIOS). Subsequent stages in the bootstrap process are protected as described above.

4.3 Accounting Integrity via Bracketing

Accounting integrity relies on three fundamental components, all of which must be verifiable to both parties' satisfaction: (a) chargeable-event detection, (b) chargeable-event attribution, and (c) chargeable-event reporting. Event detection (Section 4.3.1) must ensure that only real events are captured (which precludes spurious charges), and no real events are missed (which precludes service theft). Event attribution (Section 4.3.2) must verifiably associate a detected event with a customer to charge. Finally, event reporting (Section 4.3.3) must protect the collected information at rest on the provider's infrastructure, and in transit to customers.

4.3.1 Event Detection

In this work, we focus on chargeable events that are directly observable by the Observer. For example, given the protections required for image and execution integrity (Sections 4.1 and 4.2), the Observer sees every transfer of control (and, therefore, of the CPU) between the platform software and customer instances. Similarly, the Observer sees every memory allocation and deallocation by the platform software to customer instances. We defer to future work those chargeable events that are not necessarily observable by the Observer, such as I/O requests, especially for directly-assigned devices.

Such direct detection is effective for both instantaneous charging events (e.g., requests for growing a guest's memory footprint) and time-based charging events (e.g., duration of CPU possession by a customer instance). For time-based events, the Observer collects instantaneous events denoting the beginning and end of possession of a chargeable device, from which the duration can then be computed easily (e.g., using clock time, a cycle counter, or other monotonically increasing hardware performance counters).

4.3.2 Event Attribution

Verifiable attribution implies that the provider cannot charge customers for chargeable events willy-nilly, but is bound to charge the customer whose image incurred the event.

ALIBI builds its verifiable attribution machinery on CPU ownership. Because of the attested instance launch mechanism (Section 4.1), the Observer can associate definitively a set of memory pages with a given installed image. Consequently, the Observer can attribute ownership of the CPU to a given image when the CPU enters the pages associated to that image. This means that ALIBI can attribute events that acquire or relinquish ownership of other resources to the appropriate customer image that currently holds the CPU.

4.3.3 Event Reporting

Verifiable reporting implies that the provider cannot report incorrect chargeable-event measurements to the customers, but must report accurate values.

The ALIBI Observer collects event measurements (e.g., CPU possession and guest memory footprint) during the entire lifetime of the customer image execution. The Observer then packages these measurements along with the attestation triplet for a customer image (from Section 4.1) in a signed report that also includes the platform software state (see Section 4.4 below). Finally the Observer ships the signed report to the related customer along with an invoice.

4.4 Trust via Authenticated Boot

Fundamental to any security property that can be ascertained external to a platform manifesting the property of interest is a *root of trust*. ALIBI relies on a Trusted Platform Module (TPM) [5] on the provider platform for this purpose.

At a high-level, the TPM can be thought of as possessing a public-private key-pair, with the property that the private key is only handled within a secure environment inside the TPM. The TPM also contains Platform Configuration Registers (PCRs) that can be used to record the state of software executing on the platform. The PCRs are append-only, so previous records cannot be eliminated without a reboot.

Initially ALIBI is started via a dynamic root of trust mechanism on the provider platform. This can be done for example, by using a trusted boot-loader such as `tboot` [7] or `oslo` [24]. The authenticated boot mechanism ensures that integrity measurements are taken of all loaded code modules. These measurements are extended into one or more PCRs, so that a history of all modules loaded is maintained and cannot be rolled back.

With accumulated measurements from authenticated boot, the root of trust for reporting (or commonly called an attestation) becomes useful. ALIBI uses the TPM to generate an attestation, which is essentially a signature computed with the TPM's private key over some of the relevant PCRs. Given the TPM's corresponding public key, an external verifier can check that the signature is valid and conclude that the PCR values in the attestation represent the software state of the platform (i.e., a correctly loaded ALIBI hypervisor). Note that numerous solutions exist to obtain the TPM's authentic public key [31]. One straightforward approach is to obtain a public-key certificate from the provider which binds the public key to the provider identity.

5. Lifecycle of a Verifiably Accounted Job

As discussed previously, the design of ALIBI makes one practical assumption about the nature of IaaS deployments. In order to assure the customer that the Observer itself was running, we assume that a hardware root of trust, i.e., a TPM chip, is present on the platform and provisioned with appropriate cryptographic material by the manufacturer; this assumption is reasonable given the increasing availability of server-grade hardware platforms equipped with trusted-execution features[8] and the emergence of high-assurance cloud-service solutions such as that by Enomaly[9]. We now review the lifecycle of an outsourced job with ALIBI and highlight how ALIBI addresses the accounting vulnerabilities from Section 2.2.

Image Installation When a customer installs a new VM image, she provides a random nonce, along with the integrity triple $\mathcal{I}$, and only presumes the installation successful upon receiving a receipt containing the triple, the nonce, and a signature on the two from the Observer. Even though the customer may not be directly contacting the Observer, but may instead be using the platform API or web interface, a receipt from the Observer indicates the latter has identified a particular VM image as protected. The nonce protects the installation channel from replay attacks, and the signature protects the communication between the customer and the Observer from the intervening platform software.

Image Customization Customization may result in changes to the customer's image, but is transparent to ALIBI. When a customer is

---

[8] http://www.intel.com/content/www/us/en/architecture-and-technology/trusted-execution-technology/trusted-execution-technology-server-platforms-matrix.html

[9] http://www.enomaly.com/High-Assurance-E.484.0.html

done modifying an image, she must reinstall it, as described above, possibly uninstalling the original version of the image.

The explicit re-installation of a customized image prevents surreptitious image modifications before launch, which would be otherwise open to the platform and external attackers hijacking the control interface.

Note here that in this work, we assume the "easier" version of customization, where the platform provider may recommend certain stock device drivers (e.g., paravirtualized Xen device drivers) that must be installed and the customer explicitly and manually installs those drivers to its image before launching. As such, we assume that the stock device drivers are as trusted by the customer as the rest of her image software. We leave for future work the "harder" version of customization, where image modifications are not trusted (e.g., may come in binary form from the provider), which may require more complex solutions, perhaps akin to OSck [20], adapted to the outsourced domain.

Instance Launch Launch for a particular installed image works as described in Section 4.1. The attested instance-launch mechanism ensures that instances are launched legitimately only with full visibility to the Observer, only from images that have been explicitly installed by the customer. What is more, this mechanism ensures that the launch-point state of an instance is consistent with the image, and cannot be modified undetected by the platform.

Execution Accounting During instance execution, integrity is guaranteed through the state and control-flow protections described in Section 4.2. Consequently, surreptitious modifications of system libraries or the internal functionality of an instance [27] are not possible.

The Observer accounts for CPU and memory as described in Section 4.3, and has full visibility of related chargeable events. Although the platform can delay the execution of operations in platform software on behalf of the customer (e.g., the handling of hypercalls issued by the instance), this happens outside the CPU-control of the instance, does not constitute a chargeable event, and is therefore immaterial to the customer's invoice. Note, however, that in a model that charges customers for system costs, this might be more complex to handle, as we describe in Section 8.

Similarly, scheduling tricks [50] have no effect, since charging is done via explicit counting of events, rather than the bias-prone sampling. This also means that the platform cannot charge two customers for the "same CPU cycle" since the CPU instruction pointer can only be in one memory location at a time, and the Observer keeps track of the memory footprint of an instance via its EPT.

Instance Termination When an instance terminates, a running period ends and the platform explicitly deregisters an image from the Observer, thereby removing the physical pages it had previously allocated to that image from the Observer's protection. No (execution-related) chargeable events are collected for that image beyond instance termination.

Invoicing When invoicing the customer, the platform also presents a witness report (Section 4.3.3) consisting of Observer-signed event traces supporting that invoice. Those traces are periodically passed to the platform as the Observer collects them, to minimize the storage requirements for the Observer, but the platform must accumulate and supply those traces to the customer along with an invoice.

The witness report is associated with the precise image that was launched and protected during runtime by the Observer. As a result, an invoice for charges substantiated with a witness generated by an image that the customer did not install can easily be detected as fraudulent.

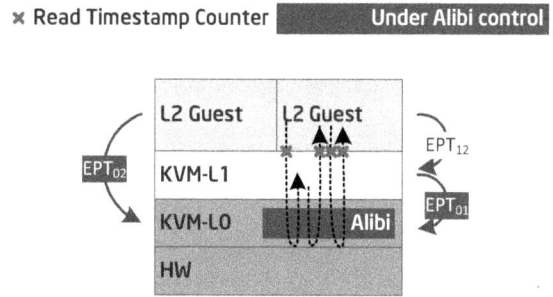

Figure 4. ALIBI Implementation: We currently leverage the nested virtualization support provided via the Turtles project in KVM. ALIBI is a lightweight extension to this nested virtualization codebase. While our current prototype runs KVM as the L_1 hypervisor, this is purely for convenience and does not represent a fundamental constraint.

6. Implementation

In this section, we describe the pieces of the ALIBI prototype we have implemented, and demonstrate the salient aspects of the design from Section 4.

As shown in Figure 4, we have implemented ALIBI on the open-source Linux-KVM hypervisor codebase. Our prototype is based on the Linux-KVM kernel, version 3.5.0, with support for efficient nesting provided by the Turtles developers as separate patches, as yet unincorporated into the mainline kernel. For the purposes of our prototype, we assume that the platform already uses KVM as its virtualization software, and that customer guests run the Linux OS. We implement the ALIBI Observer using another layer of KVM virtualization, below the purported provider's KVM software platform.

We chose KVM because of its advanced and efficient support for nested virtualization [9] on top of modern CPUs' hardware-virtualization features[10]. Although this support is not part of our contribution, we review it in Section 6.1, since it forms the basis for ALIBI's implementation. Then we describe how we implement the particular kind of isolation that is essential for ALIBI's integrity, in Section 6.2. We delve into the implementation details for providing accounting for the two types of resources in Section 6.3. In describing our implementation, we describe specifics pertaining to the Intel platform we use for prototyping; analogous support exists on AMD platforms as well.

6.1 Background: Nested Virtualization with KVM

The basic tools offered by hardware support for virtualization are CPU-state and physical-memory virtualization. Intel-architecture processors virtualize CPU state by providing a data structure in physical memory, called the Virtual Machine Control Structure (VMCS) in Intel's processors, where the host's state is held while a guest is executing, and where the guest's state is held while the host is executing. The VMCS also holds configuration information about what the guest is allowed to do (e.g., which privileged instructions it may invoke without trapping to the host, etc.).

Physical memory is virtualized via an extra layer of page tables, which are called Extended Page Tables (EPT) for Intel's processors; the EPT maps guest physical addresses (GPA) to host physical

---

[10] On a pragmatic, but slightly non-technical note, we chose KVM because the Turtles code is publicly available. The mechanisms we envision can also be incrementally added to other nested virtualization platforms such as CloudVisor [48]. Unfortunately, the CloudVisor authors could not yet provide us with the source code when we requested it.

addresses (HPA), and can contain read/write/execute protections for mapped pages separate of those in the regular OS-managed page table maintained by the guest. If the CPU attempts to access a GPA in violation of the EPT, the CPU traps from guest to host mode with an `EPT_VIOLATION` exception.

With nested virtualization, these two virtualization mechanisms must themselves be virtualized. In the absence of explicit hardware support for such nested virtualization, host software such as KVM must do this virtualization of the VMCS and EPT in software[11]. Especially since the hardware knows nothing about nesting, only the "bottom-most," Level-0 (L_0) hypervisor (running the ALIBI Observer) uses a native EPT and a native VMCS. The "middle," Level-1 (L_1) hypervisor (the platform's KVM layer in our case) is just a guest of L_0, and so is the nested, Level-2 (L_2) guest holding customer images. This means that the L_0 KVM must maintain a separate VMCS and EPT for its L_1 guest ($VMCS_{01}$ and EPT_{01}), and for its L_2 guest ($VMCS_{02}$ and EPT_{02}). The platform software, L_1, also thinks it is maintaining a VMCS and an EPT for its guest ($VMCS_{12}$ and EPT_{12}).

Nested-virtualization support in KVM allows L_0 to know how L_1 maintains $VMCS_{12}$ and EPT_{12}, and compose them with its own $VMCS_{01}$ and EPT_{01}, to produce appropriate $VMCS_{02}$ and EPT_{02}; doing this efficiently saves unnecessary and costly control transfers across L_0, L_1, and L_2. For VMCSes this is straightforward; L_0 updates its own $VMCS_{02}$ structures according to $VMCS_{12}$ when L_1 issues (and traps on) a `VMWRITE` instruction, and when L_0 passes control to L_2. For EPTs, when L_0 first starts L_2, it marks EPT_{02} empty. Each time that L_2 accesses a nested guest physical address (NGPA) that is not yet mapped in EPT_{02}, an `EPT_VIOLATION` exception occurs, trapping back to L_0, which handles the exception via the `nested_tdp_page_fault` function in KVM; this walks EPT_{12}, trying to find a GPA for the unmapped NGPA; if it finds none, it passes on the job to L_1, by injecting it with the `EPT_VIOLATION` fault; if L_0 does find a mapping in EPT_{12}, it write-protects that mapping (by changing the permissions of the EPT_{01} entry pointing to the page holding the appropriate entry of EPT_{12}), it then adds the mapping to its EPT_{02}, and resumes the L_2 guest.

The write protection of L_1's EPT serves the purpose of monitoring remappings of customer-guest memory by the platform software: if L_1 attempts to modify that mapping in its EPT_{12} – e.g., because it is swapping out a guest physical page – since the memory holding its EPT is write-protected by L_0, an `EPT_VIOLATION` will occur, allowing L_0 to update its EPT_{02} to match the modified mapping by L_1.

6.2 Protected Execution

To offer execution integrity, the Observer at L_0 must protect the contents of the guest (L_2) physical memory, which L_1 maps to L_2, from L_1 itself. L_0 detects allocations by L_1: L_1 marks those allocations in its EPT_{12}, which L_0 monitors, so L_0 is alerted every time such EPT_{12} modifications occur (see Section 6.1). At that time, L_0 write-protects newly allocated pages for as long as L_1 is running. When L_2 starts running, L_0 unprotects those pages, until L_2 exits. Our current prototype does not yet implement vetting of platform-initiated VMCS changes.

6.3 Accounting Case Studies

In addition to the mechanisms ensuring the integrity properties of ALIBI, the prototype addresses the particular case studies we consider as described below.

---

[11] Several variants exist, but we present here the one we have used, as first described in Turtles [9].

CPU cycles: To measure the CPU cycles used, the Observer takes measurements of the `IA32_TIME_STAMP_COUNTER` model-specific register at each bracketing event: entry into and exit from the instance. The Observer already receives traps for these events with the nested virtualization implementation as described previously in Section 6.1.

To protect the accounting integrity of the timestamp counter, our prototype had to ensure that the register cannot be modified by guests. We do this by enabling an appropriate control field in the related VMCSes ($VMCS_{01}$ for the platform and $VMCS_{02}$ for the customer instance) that causes a trap when the `WRMSR` instruction is executed with the TSC register as an argument. The Observer turns such `WRMSR` instructions into no-ops.

We also take care when the TSC register is set to be virtualized by the platform (this means that the register is auto-loaded from a previously stored value in the VMCS upon entry, and auto-stored back into the VMCS upon exit from that guest). When such virtualization occurs, we measure the advancement of the counter from the virtual value.

Memory: The invariant we maintain for memory accounting is that a customer is charged for a physical page only while that page is accessible to its instance. For the page to be accessible, the EPT_{02} must map it, and the platform (L_1) must have allocated it to the instance.

We record the assignment of ownership of a page to a guest in the Observer when the relevant entry in EPT_{02} is synchronized with EPT_{01} and EPT_{12}. This occurs when a L_2 guest first accesses an assigned page, causing an EPT violation, and L_0 first synchronizes its EPT_{02} entry; and when the L_1 platform modifies a page mapping in EPT_{12}, which causes a protection trap back to L_0. In the latter case, the KVM shadowing logic is used, which marks the relevant entry in EPT_{02} as unsynchronized. Later, when an invalidation occurs (e.g., through the `INVEPT` instruction), L_0 resynchronizes the EPT_{02} entry, unassigning the old page and assigning to the guest the new one (this happens in the `ept_sync_page` function in KVM).

We record the relinquishment of ownership of a page by a guest (i) when a page mapping is modified by L_1 (as described in the previous paragraph), and (ii) when L_1 unmaps a page from a guest, e.g., due to swapping. Then an EPT violation trap to L_0 occurs, and L_0 records the relinquishment.

7. Evaluation

We now present the evaluation of our prototype implementation and analysis of nested virtualization overheads with macro benchmarks that represent real-life CPU/memory and I/O-bound workloads.

Our setup consisted of an HP ML110 machine booted with a single Intel Xeon E31220 3.10GHz core with 8GB of memory. The host OS was Ubuntu 12.04 with a kernel that is based on the KVM git branch "next"[12] with nested virtualization patches[13] added. For both L_1 and L_2 guests we used an Ubuntu 9.04 (Jaunty) guest with the default kernel versions (2.6.18-10). L_1 was configured with 3GB of memory and L_2 was configured with 2GB of memory. For the I/O experiments we used the integrated e1000e 1Gb/s NIC connected via a Netgear gigabit router to an e1000e NIC on another machine.

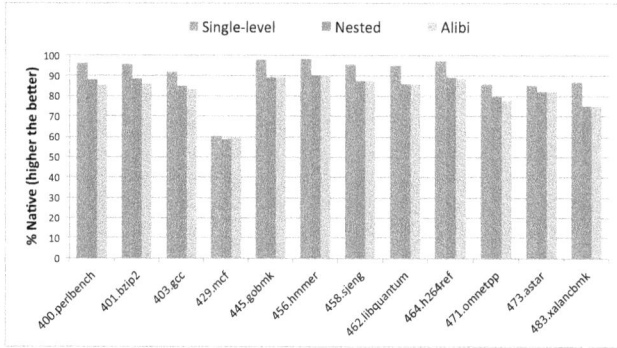

Figure 5. SPEC CINT2006 results. We see that for most of the CPU intensive benchmarks ALIBI adds little overhead over that of nested virtualization.

7.1 Compute/Memory-bound Workloads

SPEC CINT2006 is an industry-standard benchmark designed to measure the performance of the CPU and memory subsystem. We executed CINT2006 in four setups: host (without virtualization), single-level guest, nested guest, and nested guest with ALIBI accounting. We used KVM as both L_0 and L_1 hypervisor with multi-dimensional (EPT) paging. The results are depicted in Figure 5.

We compared the impact of running the workloads in a nested guest (with and without accounting) with running the same workload in a single-level guest, i.e., the overhead added by the additional level of virtualization and accounting. As seen a single-level virtualization imposes, on an average, a 9.5% slowdown when compared to a non-virtualized system. Nested virtualization imposes an additional 6.8% slowdown on average. The primary source of nested virtualization overhead is guest exits due to interrupts and privileged instructions [9] which we expect will diminish with newer hardware [17]. Note that ALIBI's integrity and accounting mechanisms impose a negligibly small overhead ($\approx 0.5\%$) in addition to that imposed by nested virtualization.

We note that this additional overhead imposed by nested virtualization/ALIBI is already quite low given that cloud consumers are willing to pay the cost of single-level virtualization for other benefits such as reduced infrastructure and management costs. We envision verifiable accounting as an *opt-in* service where consumers can choose if they want the additional assurances about accounting; jobs whose owners wish to run without such assurances can be placed by the provider on machines without ALIBI, and the provider can dynamically start machines with or without ALIBI based on demand for the service. Thus, we speculate a <6% overhead is a small cost that customers may be willing to incur given that it eliminates the (potentially unbounded) uncertainty in accounting that exists today. Given that providers also have an economic and management incentive to motivate adoption of verified accounting, we expect that providers will *subsidize* such services. For example, it is not unreasonable to expect that cloud vendors may offer a 3–6% discount to offset the potential overhead for customers running over ALIBI.

7.2 I/O Intensive Workloads

To examine the performance of a nested guest in the case of I/O intensive workloads we used netperf, a TCP streaming applica-

---

[12] Commit hash ade38c311a0ad8c32e902fe1d0ae74d0d44bc71e

[13] The nested virtualization support in KVM is still not mainstream and currently only exists as a patch-set at http://comments.gmane.org/gmane.comp.emulators.kvm.devel/95395

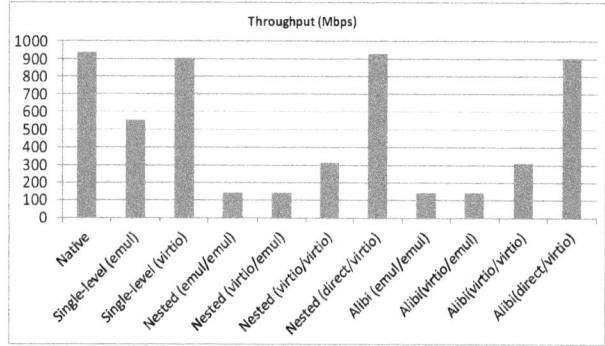

Figure 6. Performance of netperf in combinations of I/O virtualization methods between L_0/L_1 and L_1/L_2. emul, virtio and direct refer to device emulation, para-virtualization and direct device assignment, respectively.

tion that attempts to maximize the amount of data sent over a single TCP connection. We measured the performance on the sender side, with the default settings of netperf (16,384 byte messages).

There are three commonly used approaches to provide I/O services to a guest virtual machine: (i) the hypervisor *emulates* a known device and the guest uses an unmodified driver to interact with it [43]; (ii) a *para-virtual driver* is installed in the guest [36]; or (iii) the hypervisor performs *direct device assignment* where a real device is assigned to the guest which then controls the device directly [17].

These three basic I/O approaches for a single-level guest imply nine possible combinations in the two-level nested guest case. Of the nine potential combinations we evaluate the following interesting cases of virtualization method between L_0/L_1 and L_1/L_2: (a) L_0/L_1 and L_1/L_2 with emulation; (b) L_0/L_1 with para-virtualization and L_1/L_2 with emulation; (c) L_0/L_1 and L_1/L_2 with para-virtualization; and (d) L_0/L_1 with direct device assignment and L_1/L_2 with virtio. Figure 6 shows the results for running the netperf TCP stream test on the host, in a single-level guest, and in a nested guest (with and without accounting) using the I/O virtualization combinations described above. We used KVM's default emulated NIC (RTL-8139) and virtio [36] for a para-virtual NIC. All tests used a single CPU core.

On the native system (without virtualization), netperf easily achieved line rate (939 Mb/s). Emulation gives a much lower throughput: On a single-level guest we get 60% of the line rate. On the nested guest the throughput is much lower (15% of the line rate) and the overhead is dominated by the cost of device emulation between L_1 and L_2. Each L_2 exit is trapped by L_0 and forwarded to L_1. For each L_2 exit, L_1 then executes multiple privileged instructions, incurring multiple exits back to L_0. In this way the overhead for each L_2 exit is multiplied.

The para-virtual virtio NIC performs better than emulation since it reduces the number of exits. Using virtio for both L_0/L_1 and L_1/L_2 gives 44% of the line rate, better but still considerably below native performance.

Using direct device assignment between L_0 and L_1 and virtio between L_1 and L_2 enables the L_2 guest to achieve near native performance. However, the measured performance is still suboptimal because 70% of the CPU is used for running a workload that takes 48% on the native system. Unfortunately on current x86 architecture, interrupts cannot be directly assigned to guests, so both the interrupt itself and its End-Of-Interrupt (EOI) signaling cause exits. The more interrupts the device generates, the more exits, and therefore the higher the virtualization overhead – which is amplified in the nested case.

The ALIBI CPU and memory accounting overhead in all nested combinations add very little overhead (less than 1%) than what is already imposed by nested virtualization.

Although I/O-bound workload overheads are non-trivial with nested virtualization, we expect recent and future advances in virtualizing or simplifying interrupts [17], as well as (anticipated) hardware support for nested virtualization [37] to reduce this overhead significantly.

8. Discussion

TCB size: We acknowledge that in our current implementation, ALIBI does not meet our goal of having a minimal trusted base. Since ALIBI relies on the nested virtualization support in KVM, it has to invariably include the KVM codebase and the Linux kernel itself in its TCB. This is an artifact of our current prototype and our pragmatic choice in choosing KVM because of the readily available codebase and nested virtualization support. The actual protection mechanisms that ALIBI adds are negligible (few hundred lines of code) over the basic nested virtualization support. We believe that this can be added to more lightweight nested virtualization solutions including CloudVisor [48] and XMHF [45].

Stochastic correctness: It is possible to provide a weaker form of accounting integrity without explicitly providing image and execution integrity. This might make sense under a weaker threat model where the customer is running on a benign, bug-free platform. In this case, "good faith" usage observations might give loose assurances to customers by external randomized auditing mechanisms. For example, the customer can create a known workload with a pre-specified billing footprint and synthetically inject it into the cloud to see if there are obvious discrepancies. In our threat model, the platform may inflate costs or may have bugs exploitable by others. In this case, this form of "stochastic accounting integrity" without execution and image integrity is less applicable as it tells the customer nothing about what code actually incurred the charges.

Multi-core support: Our current prototype implementation supports a single processor core. We chose to support only a single core primarily for ease of debugging. There is no fundamental limitation either in the Linux-KVM codebase or in the ALIBI architecture that precludes support for multi-core platforms. For example, Linux-KVM nested virtualization already maintains multiple VM-CS/VCPU/EPT structures for SMP support. Our existing prototype can be reinforced with SMP support by simply converting the existing global data structures for CPU and memory accounting and memory protection logic to be VCPU-relative. We also note that some of the current best practices in public clouds make support for multi-core much easier. Although we have yet to implement such support, we are cautiously optimistic.

Resources expended by providers: Our design does not currently account for external costs that a provider or ALIBI incurs on behalf of a specific customer: e.g., cycles for servicing hypercalls, or due to cache/memory contention. These costs can be ameliorated by better job placement, so the platform should be in part responsible. Another alternative is that these costs may be amortized into the billing mechanism if the provider can have an estimate of the overhead it incurs as a function of the offered load. We are also considering more systematic causality-based tracking to attribute system/Alibi costs to the proper job, to enable different charging models.

Physical attacks: The root of trust in ALIBI lies with the TPM chip on the provider's infrastructure. If the provider can physically tamper with properties of the TPM chip, she can tamper with the integrity of the Observer without being detected by customers, which can, in turn, turn a blind observing eye to provider tampering with the verifiable-accounting properties of ALIBI. Although extremely difficult, attacks against TPM properties have been demonstrated – for example, via *cold-boot attacks* [19] that recover from memory TPM encryption or signing keys, or more sophisticated hardware-probing attacks. Such attacks are in the purview of a sophisticated platform today, but will reduce in feasibility as trusted-execution functionality moves deeper into the hardware platform. For example, an MMU that directly encrypts memory never puts secret data such as keys on DRAM and, therefore, eliminates cold-boot or bus eavesdropping attacks. Today's TPM chips, although not tamper-resistant, are tamper-evident: physical attack against them renders them visibly altered. Periodic physical inspection by an external compliance agency, akin to a Privacy CA, might be a plausible interim solution. What is more, CPU manufacturers hint that trusted execution without an external TPM chip might be coming in their future products [47]; physically attacking CPUs is significantly harder than attacking motherboard-soldered chips.

9. Related Work

We discuss related work in different aspects of cloud computing and trusted computing and place these in the context of our work for enabling verifiable resource accounting.

Nested virtualization: While the idea of nested virtualization has been around since the early days of virtualization, it is only recently that we see practical implementations. The two works closest to ALIBI in this respect are Turtles [9] and CloudVisor [48]. ALIBI builds on and extends the memory protection techniques that these approaches develop. The key difference, however, is in the applications and threats that these systems target. Turtles is focused on being able to run any hypervisor in the cloud and other security properties (e.g., to protect against hypervisor-level rootkits). CloudVisor, on the other hand, is designed to prevent a malicious platform operator from inferring private information residing in a guest VM's memory. These systems differ in one key aspect: CloudVisor does not attempt to provide a full-fledged hypervisor for multi-level nested virtualization that Turtles can provide. In this respect, ALIBI is arguably closer to CloudVisor in that we only need one more level of virtualization and do not need multi-level nesting. At the same time, however, some of the mechanisms in CloudVisor (e.g., encrypting pages) are likely an overkill for ALIBI, since we only care about integrity and not confidentiality. CloudVisor further assumes that the cloud provider has no incentive to be malicious or misconfigured, which is not true in the accounting scenarios we tackle. Consequently, it does not provide any correctness of the accounting and execution integrity properties. That said, the ALIBI extensions can be easily added to the CloudVisor implementation as well if the sources are made available.

Attacks in the cloud: The multiplexed and untrusted nature of cloud environments leads to attacks by co-resident tenants and by the providers themselves. These include side channel attacks to expose confidential information or identify co-resident tenants [35, 49]. More directly related, there are practically demonstrated attacks against today's cloud accounting including attacks against management interfaces [28, 42] and current resource management mechanisms [44, 50]. Liu and Ding discuss a taxonomy of potential attacks [27]. Our goal is to protect against these specific types of accounting vulnerabilities and at the same time allow cloud providers to be able to justify the resource consumption.

Cloud accountability: Cloud customers may want to ensure that the provider faithfully runs their application software and respects input-output equivalence [18]; that has not tampered or lost their data [8, 23]; and respects certain performance SLAs [32]. These target other types of accountability; our work focuses specifically on trustworthy resource accounting.

Cloud monitoring and benchmarking: Recent work from Li et al. compares the costs of running applications under different popular providers [26]. Other work makes the case for a unified set of benchmarks to evaluate cloud providers [11, 21]. Several efforts have identified challenges in scalably monitoring resource consumption in cloud and virtualized environments [6, 14, 33]. While such tools are also motivated by resource monitoring, they do not focus on verifiability of the measurements.

Integrity: There is rich literature on protecting control flow integrity [15]. Such work guarantees that a program follows valid execution paths allowed by the control flow graph. While this guarantee is necessary for accounting correctness, it is not sufficient. For example, without the protections we enable, the provider could arbitrarily inflate the resource footprint by forcing the program to take valid but unnecessary code paths. Image integrity is related to the recent work on Root of Trust for Installation [38] but in the cloud context.

Rearchitecting OS and hypervisors: As we discussed earlier, one could envision clean-slate solutions where the operating system and the hypervisor are rearchitected to support resource accounting as a first-class primitive and also minimize the threat surface. This includes recent work revisiting the design and implementation of isolation kernels [25] and other work on microkernel-like hypervisors [13]. By leveraging nested virtualization, our work explores a different point in the design space and incurs a small overhead in favor of immediate deployability.

10. Conclusions and Future Work

As computation is rapidly turning into a "utility," the need for trustworthy metering of usage is ever more imminent. The *multiplexed* and *untrusted* nature of cloud computing makes the problem of accounting not only more relevant but also significantly more challenging compared to traditional utilities (e.g., water, power, ISPs). For example, providers may have incentives to be malicious to increase their revenues; other co-resident or remote customers may try to steal resources for their own benefit; and customers have obvious incentives to dispute usage. What is fundamentally lacking today is a basis for verifiable resource accounting leading to severe sources of uncertainty and inefficiency for all entities involved in the cloud ecosystem.

As a first step to bridge this gap, we present the design and implementation of ALIBI. Our design reflects a conscious choice to enable cloud customers and providers to benefit from ALIBI with minimal changes. To this end, we envision a novel, and perhaps viable, use-case for nested virtualization. We demonstrate practical protection schemes against a range of existing accounting vulnerabilities. Our implementation adds negligible overhead over the cost of nested virtualization; we expect that future hardware and software optimizations will further drive these overheads down, in the same way that the adoption of cloud computing spurred innovation in traditional virtualization technologies.

We acknowledge the need to address a range of additional concerns to realize the full vision of verifiable accounting. This includes the need for better formalisms to reason about accounting equivalence, accounting for I/O resources, carefully attributing provider-incurred cost (e.g., cost of hypercalls, cost of power/cooling), among other factors. While we fully expect to run into sig-

nificant "brick walls" in addressing these issues, the initial success shown here, the experiences we gained in the process, and emerging processor roadmaps give us reasons to be optimistic in our quest.

Acknowledgments

We thank our shepherd, Gernot Heiser, for his help while preparing the final version of this paper, as well as the anonymous reviewers for their detailed comments. Rekha Bachwani, Yanlin Li, John Manferdelli, and David Wagner have provided valuable ideas and feedback. Nadav Har'El helpfully answered our questions about the pending Turtles nested-virtualization optimizations in the mainline Linux-KVM codebase. This work was funded in part by the Intel Science and Technology Center for Secure Computing.

References

[1] Cloud storage providers need sharper billing metrics. http://www.networkworld.com/news/2011/061711-cloud-storage-providers-need-sharper.html?page=2.

[2] dm-verity: device-mapper block integrity checking target. http://code.google.com/p/cryptsetup/wiki/DMVerity. Retrieved 2/2013.

[3] IT Cloud Services User Survey: Top Benefits and Challenges. http://blogs.idc.com/ie/?p=210.

[4] Service billing is hard. http://perspectives.mvdirona.com/2009/02/16/ServiceBillingIsHard.aspx.

[5] TPM Main Specification Level 2 Version 1.2, Revision 103 (Trusted Computing Group). http://www.trustedcomputinggroup.org/resources/tpm_main_specification/.

[6] VMWare vCenter Chargeback. http://www.vmware.com/products/vcenter-chargeback/overview.html.

[7] The Trusted Boot Project (tboot). http://tboot.sourceforge.net/, Sept. 2007.

[8] G. Ateniese, R. Burns, R. Curtmola, J. Herring, L. Kissner, Z. Peterson, and D. Song. Provable Data Possession at Untrusted Stores. In *ACM CCS*, 2007.

[9] M. Ben-Yehuda, M. D. Day, Z. Dubitzky, M. Factor, N. Har'El, A. Gordon, A. Liguori, O. Wasserman, and B.-A. Yassour. The Turtles Project: Design and Implementation of Nested Virtualization. In *OSDI*, 2010.

[10] S. Chen, J. Xu, E. C. Sezer, P. Gauriar, and R. K. Iyer. Non-Control-Data Attacks are Realistic Threats. In *USENIX Security*, 2005.

[11] Y. Chen, A. Ganapathi, R. Griffith, and R. Katz. The Case for Evaluating MapReduce Performance Using Workload Suites. In *Proc. MASCOTS*, 2011.

[12] R. Cohen. Navigating the Fog - Billing, Metering and Measuring the Cloud. Cloud computing journal http://cloudcomputing.syscon.com/node/858723.

[13] P. Colp, M. Nanavati, J. Zhu, W. Aiello, G. Coker, T. Deegan, P. Loscocco, and A. Warfield. Breaking Up is Hard to Do: Security and Functionality in a Commodity Hypervisor. In *SOSP*, 2011.

[14] J. Du, N. Sherawat, and W. Zwaenepoel. Performance Profiling in a Virtualized Environment. In *Proc. HotCloud*, 2010.

[15] U. Erlingsson, M. Abadi, M. Vrable, M. Budiu, and G. C. Necula. XFI: Software Guards for System Address Spaces. In *OSDI*, 2006.

[16] K. Fu, M. F. Kaashoek, and D. Mazières. Fast and Secure Distributed Read-only File System. *ACM TOCS*, 20(1), 2002.

[17] A. Gordon, N. Amit, N. Har'El, M. Ben-Yehuda, A. Landau, A. Schuster, and D. Tsafrir. ELI: Bare-Metal Performance for I/O Virtualization. In *ASPLOS*, 2012.

[18] A. Haeberlen, P. Aditya, R. Rodrigues, and P. Druschel. Accountable Virtual Machines. In *OSDI*, 2010.

[19] J. A. Halderman, S. D. Schoen, N. Heninger, W. Clarkson, W. Paul, J. A. Calandrino, A. J. Feldman, J. Appelbaum, and E. W. Felten. Lest

We Remember: Cold Boot Attacks on Encryption Keys. In *USENIX Security*, 2008.

[20] O. S. Hofmann, A. M. Dunn, S. Kim, I. Roy, and E. Witchel. Ensuring Operating System Kernel Integrity with OSck. In *ASPLOS*, 2011.

[21] S. Huang, J. Huang, J. Dai, T. Xie, and B. Huang. The HiBench benchmark suite: Characterization of the MapReduce-based data analysis. In *Proc. ICDE Workshops*, 2010.

[22] R. Iyer, R. Illikkal, L. Zhao, D. Newell, and J. Moses. Virtual Platform Architectures for Resource Metering in Datacenters. In *SIGMETRICS*, 2009.

[23] A. Juels and B. S. Kaliski. PORs: Proofs of retrievability for large files. In *ACM CCS*, 2007.

[24] B. Kauer. OSLO: Improving the Security of Trusted Computing. In *USENIX Security*, 2007.

[25] A. Kvalnes, D. Johansen, R. van Renesse, F. B. Schneider, and S. V. Valvag. Design Principles for Isolation Kernels. Technical Report 2011-70, Computer Science Department, University of Tromsø, 2011.

[26] A. Li, X. Yang, S. Kandula, and M. Zhang. CloudCmp: Comparing Public Cloud Providers. In *IMC*, 2010.

[27] M. Liu and X. Ding. On Trustworthiness of CPU Usage Metering and Accounting. In *ICDCS-SPCC*, 2010.

[28] M. McIntosh and P. Austel. XML signature Element Wrapping Attacks and Countermeasures. In *ACM SWS*, 2005.

[29] A. Mihoob, C. Molina-Jimenez, and S. Shrivastava. A Case for Consumer-centric Resource Accounting Models. In *Proc. International Conference on Cloud Computing*, 2010.

[30] J. C. Mogul. Operating systems should support business change. In *HotOS*, 2005.

[31] B. Parno. Bootstrapping Trust in a "Trusted" Platform. In *HotSec*, 2008.

[32] R. A. Popa, J. R. Lorch, D. Molnar, H. J. Wang, and L. Zhuang. Enabling Security in Cloud Storage SLAs with CloudProof. In *Proc. USENIX ATC*, 2011.

[33] G. Ren, E. Tune, T. Moseley, Y. Shi, S. Rus, and R. Hundt. Google-Wide Profiling: A Continuous Profiling Infrastructure for Data Centers. *IEEE Micro*, 2010.

[34] K. Ren, C. Wang, and Q. Wang. Security Challenges for the Public Cloud. *IEEE Internet Computing*, 16(1), 2012.

[35] T. Ristenpart, E. Tromer, H. Shacham, and S. Savage. Hey, You, Get off of my cloud: Exploring Information Leakage in Third-Party Compute Clouds. In *ACM CCS*, 2009.

[36] R. Russell. virtio: Towards a De-Facto Standard for Virtual I/O Devices. *ACM SIGOPS OSR*, 42(5), 2008.

[37] R. Sahita. Intel Virtualization Technology Extensions for High Performance Protection Domains. https://intel.activeevents.com/sf12/scheduler/catalog.do, Sept. 2012. Intel Developer Forum 2012, Session ID FUTS003.

[38] J. Schiffman, T. Moyer, T. Jaeger, and P. McDaniel. Network-Based Root of Trust for Installation. *IEEE Security and Privacy*, 9(1), 2011.

[39] V. Sekar and P. Maniatis. Verifiable Resource Accounting for Cloud Computing Services. In *ACM CCSW*, 2011.

[40] A. Seshadri, M. Luk, N. Qu, and A. Perrig. SecVisor: A Tiny Hypervisor to Provide Lifetime Kernel Code Integrity for Commodity OSes. In *SOSP*, 2007.

[41] M. A. Shah, M. Baker, J. C. Mogul, and R. Swaminathan. Auditing to Keep Online Storage Services Honest. In *HotOS*, 2007.

[42] J. Somorovsky, M. Heiderich, M. Jensen, J. Schwenk, N. Gruschka, and L. Lo Iacono. All Your Clouds are Belong to us – Security Analysis of Cloud Management Interfaces. In *ACM CCSW*, 2011.

[43] J. Sugerman, G. Venkitachalam, and B.-H. Lim. Virtualizing I/O Devices on VMware Workstation's Hosted Virtual Machine Monitor. In *USENIX ATC*, 2001.

[44] V. Varadarajan, B. Farley, T. Ristenpart, and M. M. Swift. Resource-Freeing Attacks: Improve Your Cloud Performance (at Your Neighbor's Expense). In *ACM CCS*, 2012.

[45] A. Vasudevan, S. Chaki, L. Jia, J. McCune, J. Newsome, and A. Datta. Design, Implementation and Verification of an eXtensible and Modular Hypervisor Framework. In *IEEE S&P*, 2013.

[46] M. Wachs, L. Xu, A. Kanevsky, and G. R. Ganger. Exertion-based Billing for Cloud Storage Access. In *HotCloud*, 2011.

[47] A. Wolfe. Intel CTO Envisions On-Chip Data Centers. http://www.informationweek.com/news/global-cio/interviews/showArticle.jhtml?articleID=221900325, Nov. 2009.

[48] F. Zhang, J. Chen, H. Chen, and B. Zang. CloudVisor: Retrofitting Protection of Virtual Machines in Multi-tenant Cloud with Nested Virtualization. In *SOSP*, 2011.

[49] Y. Zhang, A. Juels, M. K. Reiter, and T. Ristenpart. Cross-VM Side Channels and Their Use to Extract Private Keys. In *ACM CCS*, 2012.

[50] F. Zhou, M. Goel, P. Desnoyers, and R. Sundaram. Scheduler Vulnerabilities and Coordinated Attacks in Cloud Computing. In *IEEE NCA*, 2011.

Leveraging Phase Change Memory to Achieve Efficient Virtual Machine Execution

Ruijin Zhou

Intelligent Design of Efficient Architectures Laboratory
University of Florida
zhourj@ufl.edu

Tao Li

Intelligent Design of Efficient Architectures Laboratory
University of Florida
taoli@ece.ufl.edu

Abstract

Virtualization technology is being widely adopted by servers and data centers in the cloud computing era to improve resource utilization and energy efficiency. Nevertheless, the heterogeneous memory demands from multiple virtual machines (VM) make it more challenging to design efficient memory systems. Even worse, mission critical VM management activities (e.g. checkpointing) could incur significant runtime overhead due to intensive IO operations. In this paper, we propose to leverage the adaptable and non-volatile features of the emerging phase change memory (PCM) to achieve efficient virtual machine execution. Towards this end, we exploit VM-aware PCM management mechanisms, which 1) smartly tune SLC/MLC page allocation within a single VM and across different VMs and 2) keep critical checkpointing pages in PCM to reduce I/O traffic. Experimental results show that our single VM design (IntraVM) improves performance by 10% and 20% compared to pure SLC- and MLC- based systems. Further incorporating VM-aware resource management schemes (IntraVM+InterVM) increases system performance by 15%. In addition, our design saves 46% of checkpoint/restore duration and reduces 50% of overall IO penalty to the system.

Categories and Subject Descriptors   D.4.8 [Operating Systems]: Performance; C.4 [Computer System Organization]: Performance of Systems

General Terms   Management, Performance, Design

Keywords   Virtualization, Phase Change Memory, Checkpointing, Memory Management

1. Introduction

Virtualization [1] improves server utilization by allowing a physical machine to host multiple virtual machines (VMs). Among all the shared hardware resources, memory largely affects the performance of VMs. It is more challenging to design efficient memory subsystems for the virtualized platforms since the VMs have various memory demands and the applications running within each VM further manifest heterogeneous working sets. Therefore, it is both desirable and crucial to have a memory system that is adaptable to different memory requirements of VMs and applications. Moreover, the design of intelligent memory systems could benefit critical VM management activities. For instance, checkpointing is widely used for system backup, fault tolerance and disaster recovery in virtualized servers and data centers. Nevertheless, it is regarded as one of the most expensive VM operations since significant IO operations are involved to transfer the entire VM memory image back to the disk. If the main memory is non-volatile, the checkpoint/restore duration and IO penalty on the system can be reduced by substituting unnecessary IO transactions with memory-to-memory operations.

Recent advances in emerging memory technologies provide new opportunities to build efficient and intelligent memory systems for virtual machine execution. In this work, we explore the opportunity of leveraging phase change memory (PCM) [2] to achieve this goal. PCM is one of the most promising technologies for future memory system design due to its superior scalability, non-volatility and capability of storing multiple bits per cell (i.e. Multi Level Cell or MLC). Recent work [2, 3, 5, 7] incorporates PCM management schemes at hardware memory controller level and the software is only invoked to ensure the correct execution. It is our belief that the virtual machine monitor (VMM), which has full knowledge of system runtime characteristics, should play a more active role in improving the efficiency of PCM systems.

Adhering to this philosophy, we explored holistic, VM-aware PCM-based memory system design that can intelligently manage memory resources via the cooperation between VMM and hardware. Our proposed design includes three layers of management, namely, hardware (physical page frame), memory page and VM. At the bottom layer, hardware interacts with physical memory and exposes the PCM device features to the VMM. The memory page management layer considers not only the tradeoff between latency and capacity within single VM but also the heterogeneous memory demands across multiple VMs. Our scheme dynamically identifies the optimal SLC (one bit per cell)/MLC page ratio for both single and multiple VMs. The top layer, VM-level management, targets the optimization of performance critical VM activities (e.g. checkpoint/restore). Our scheme exploits lazy restore mechanism [5] and PCM non-volatility to retain all SLC pages of that checkpoint within the main memory and only writes back MLC pages of the checkpoint to disk. Doing so not only reduces the checkpoint/restore time but also the IO penalty to other normal running VMs. Experimental results show that our single VM design (*IntraVM*) enhances the system performance by 10% and 20% respectively compared to the SLC- and MLC- based design. This improvement is comparable to hardware-based solution. Further incorporating VM-aware optimizations (*IntraVM+InterVM*) increases performance by 15%. In terms of checkpoint/restore, our proposed design not only achieves 46% less checkpoint/restore time but also reduces 50% overall IO penalty to the system.

The rest of this paper is organized as follows: Section 2 provides background and motivation. Section 3 describes our design in detail. Sections 4 and 5 present our simulation framework and experimental results. Section 6 discusses related work and Section 7 concludes the paper.

2. Background and Motivation

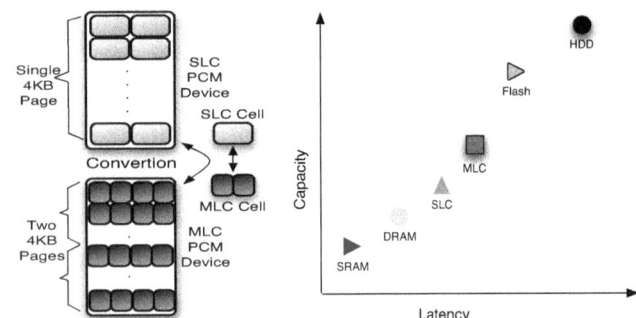

Figure 1. The Conversion between SLC/MLC Pages

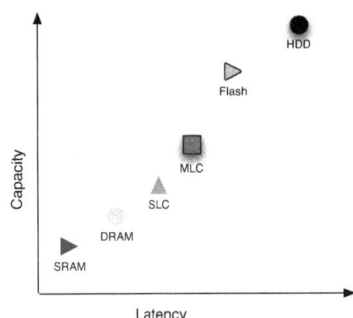

Figure 2. The Trade-off between Capacity and Latency on SLC, MLC and other material (Figure not to scale)

2.1. Phase Change Memory and Hardware-based Hybrid PCM Design

Phase change memory (PCM) is a promising technology to build future memory systems due to its high scalability and non-volatile nature [2, 6]. A PCM device that stores one-bit per cell is denoted as a single-level cell (SLC) while the one that can represent multiple bits per cell is called a multi-level cell (MLC). Note that in this paper, a MLC is assumed to contain 2 bits per cell. A PCM cell can be programmed to be either a SLC (1 bit per cell) or a MLC (2 bits per cell). The high density of MLC comes at the price of high latency. From the software perspective, a single 4KB page mapped to SLC devices can be converted to two 4KB (total 8KB) pages when the PCM devices are configured as MLC and vice versa, as illustrated in Figure 1. Therefore, the PCM device doubles its effective capacity when converted from SLC to MLC.

Prior studies [7, 8] proposed hardware-based hybrid PCM systems that can achieve the benefit of both SLC and MLC. Existing design largely focuses on the hardware level and the software is only used to ensure the correctness. As a result, the management of SLC and MLC devices is limited to the memory controller.

2.2. Xen and Virtual Machine Monitor

Xen is one of the most popular virtual machine monitors (VMM) that allow multiple virtual machines to run on top of a single server [1, 9]. Since there are several virtual machines competing for memory resources, Xen needs to balance the memory allocation across different VMs. After a VM boots up and runs, most memory requests are directly handled by the hardware without involving the VMM. However, machine to physical page tables, which contain page allocation information for all guest VMs, are considered as privileged data and can only be accessed by the VMM. In addition, the VMM validates critical operations such as installing a new page table or updating a page table entry [1, 9, 10]. This allows the VMM to have comprehensive knowledge of memory requests from all guest VMs.

VMs may run a wide range of workloads, leading to quite different demands on memory resource. Therefore, balancing memory utilization across VMs can improve the overall system performance. To achieve this, [11] proposed the balloon technology to resize VM memory capacity. As a kernel space driver, the balloon driver provides the OS an illusion that it requests more memory to run. In fact, the VMM reclaims the allocated memory to the balloon driver and the available memory for that VM is reduced. To balance the memory requirement across different VMs, the VMM pages out the memory of one VM's balloon driver to provide free memory for another VM by shrinking its balloon driver.

Checkpoint/restore [14] is a crucial event in the virtualized environment to support system backup, fault tolerance and disaster recovery for servers and data centers [26]. Checkpointing a running VM involves creating a snapshot of its memory, IO device states, network connections, and the contents of its virtual CPU registers. After a checkpoint is created, the VMM writes it back to the permanent storage (i.e. hard disk). When a VM is restored from that checkpoint, the VMM performs disk IOs to reload it back to memory and CPU registers. Performance degradation is unavoidable due to bursty, high-volume disk IO operations. Therefore, how to reduce IO traffic becomes an important issue for checkpoint/restore.

2.3. Motivation

Conventional DRAM systems with fixed capacity cannot adapt with varying memory demands during the different execution phases of workloads, which could result in low performance due to increased page faults. A hardware-based hybrid PCM system with adaptable memory capacity [7] is proposed to address this issue. Based on the physical addresses issued to the memory controller, the ratio of SLC and MLC pages are determined. In order to guarantee the correctness, balloon technology is used to adjust the available memory that is visible to the OS. Nevertheless, the hardware memory controller is not aware of system-wide runtime and resource utilization characteristics (e.g. memory demands across different VMs, domain switch, VM specific activities), which hinders the hardware approach from fully exploiting the benefits of hybrid PCM systems in virtualized execution environment. To achieve better coordination between hardware and software, we propose to incorporate virtual machine monitor, which has the ability to control both hardware and software behavior, into PCM management schemes.

Within a single VM, there is a tradeoff between memory access speed and capacity. As can be seen in Figure 2, although SLC pages have fast access speed, the effective capacity of SLC-based memory is smaller, which can potentially lead to more page faults, triggering expensive IO requests. On the other hand, the capacity of MLC-based memory is larger whereas accessing pages in MLC mode is slower. If the ratio between SLC and MLC pages for single VM can be tuned according to the memory demand, the performance can be improved by not only having the least number of page faults but also achieving the maximal benefit from the lower latency provided by the SLC devices.

Across different VMs, there is conflict between maximum memory supplies and variable memory demands. The maximum available memory capacity is prescribed when a VM is created. However, during execution, memory demands will vary, which makes the maximum memory supplies unbalanced. In an extreme case, the idle VMs may occupy a large fraction of faster memory pages (SLC) while other busy VMs are suffering from slower pages (MLC or HDD), which will degrade overall performance.

Furthermore, checkpoint/restore, as a frequent VM behavior, triggers significant amount of IO requests to transport all the memory pages to disk. These bursty IO requests not only determine the performance of checkpoint/restore but also affect the IO performance of normal running VMs. Due to the non-volatile feature of PCM, there is no need to swap the entire VM memory to disk. If the VM checkpoint pages can be appropriately distributed between MLC and HDD, the amount of disk data transfer will be significantly reduced, which will further result in faster checkpoint/restore time and lower IO performance degradation for normal running VMs.

Different VMs require different memory capacities to keep the same page miss ratio. As shown in Figure 3, VM_2 which exhibits poor memory locality and needs more memory capacity, is categorized as capacity sensitive VM while VM_3, which manifests good memory locality and requires less memory capacity, is attributed to latency sensitive VM. To achieve better performance, it is critical to identify the optimal page distribution ratio among SLC, MLC, and HDD. As shown in Figure 4, for latency sensitive VMs, we need to allocate more SLC pages so they can benefit from fast access. For capacity sensitive VMs, we prefer to assign more MLC pages so that the number of page faults can decrease. For checkpointed VMs, part of its memory pages can remain in memory as MLC mode.

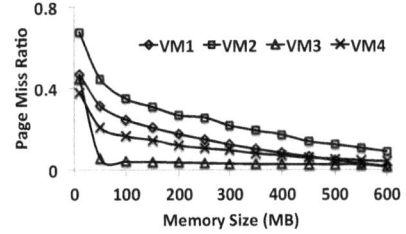

Figure 3. The Miss Ratio Curves on four Different VMs When Increasing Memory Size

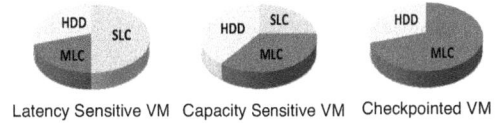

Figure 4. The Desirable Memory Distribution for Different Types of VMs

3. PCM System Design and Optimization for Effective Virtual Machine Execution

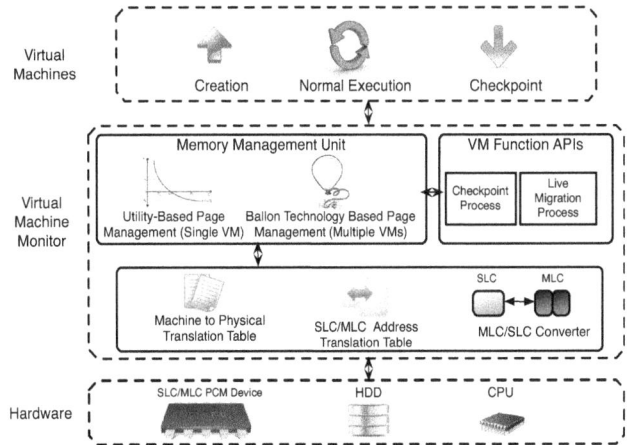

Figure 5. An Overview of the Proposed Cooperative and Cross-layer PCM System for Effective Virtual Machine Execution

In this paper, we explore PCM system design and optimization for platforms that use virtualization technologies. Unlike the existing approaches, our design exposes the emerging PCM device features to the VMM. Meanwhile, it employs the cooperative intra-/inter-VM memory resource allocation mechanisms to dynamically allocate/balance SLC/MLC PCM pages that manifest different characteristics within and across VMs, resulting in more desirable trade-off between memory capacity and access latency. Moreover, we propose VMM management techniques that leverage the PCM technologies to facilitate key operations such as VM creation, checkpoint/restore and live migration. Figure 5 provides an overview of the proposed cooperative and cross-layer PCM system for efficient virtual machine execution.

3.1. VMM Support for Hybrid PCM Page Frame Tuning

At the hardware level, we use PCM that consists of MLC devices. Those devices can operate in either MLC or SLC modes, which differ in both storage capacity and access latency. We implemented three new functions in VMM to interact with the underlying PCM hardware. Among those, *Switch_page_type* is invoked to switch the operating mode of a physical page between MLC and SLC; *MLC_alloc ()* is responsible for allocating MLC pages; and *SLC_alloc ()* is used for SLC page allocation. Based on the information provided, the memory controller reconfigures the MLC/SLC devices.

Note that the above dynamic page tuning requires that the VMM track physical memory pages in each type. To this end, we extend one bit in machine to physical translation table (in VMM) to indicate whether a page is in SLC or MLC mode. Since only free memory pages can be adapted on-the-fly, two page lists, namely *free_MLC_list* and *free_SLC_list*, which track the available MLC and SLC pages, are added to our design. Initially, all the free PCM pages are added to the *free_MLC_list*. At runtime, the following events will trigger MLC/SLC page tuning: (1) switching a PCM page to a different mode, and (2) requesting PCM pages in a specific mode. For (1), the MLC/SLC PCM manager, which is the software module that converts the SLC/MLC pages through memory controller, will first check the target free list to determine whether there are available pages. If so, it performs a page copying from the source to the destination and reclaims the source page by putting it back into the corresponding free list. If not, the MLC/SLC PCM manager will identify a page in the source free list and convert it to the target page type. It then performs page copying and frees up the unused page to the corresponding free list. For (2), the MLC/SLC PCM manager iteratively invokes operation (1) until it collects sufficient free pages. In both cases, if there are no sufficient free pages, the MLC/SLC PCM manager will discard the request and inform the VMM.

Due to dynamic tuning, the physical address will inevitably be shifted. In order to correctly locate the physical page frame, the SLC/MLC address translation table is implemented to maintain the addresses for both SLC and MLC pages. In addition, as shown in Figure 1, one SLC page can only be converted to two contiguous MLC pages and vice versa. Therefore, the SLC/MLC address translation table can also be used to easily locate the contiguous pages for conversion.

3.2. PCM Page Management in Virtualized Platform

3.2.1. Virtual Memory Management

Our page management consists of two parts: information collector and load balancer. To make the information collector aware of page accesses, we customize the method proposed in [28, 29], which traps memory accesses as minor page faults by giving the pages of interest a higher access privilege. Here, we define two types of minor page faults: SLC minor page fault and MLC minor page fault. The information collector uses both types of minor page faults to gather memory locality statistics by customizing the LRU

and Stack Algorithm in [16]. However, only MLC minor page faults will trigger the load balancer to tune the number of SLC pages, MLC pages and the size of balloon driver for each VM. Sampling mechanism [29] is also used to lower the cost of memory tracking. As a result, our tracking and management scheme are disabled periodically and the memory pages remain in their current type during those periods. Figure 6 shows the flow of PCM page management.

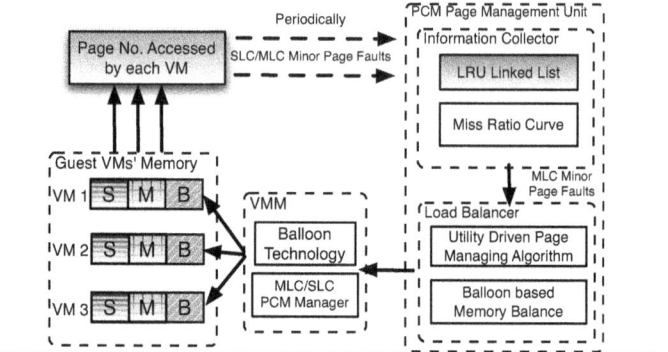

Figure 6. The Flow of PCM Page Management (S: SLC Mode; M: MLC Mode; B: Pages in Balloon Driver)

In order to form an LRU histogram for virtual memory page usage, we implemented a counter array to track the access frequency for all the pages. If a page is accessed, the corresponding counter will be incremented by 1. Based on the LRU histogram, the miss ratio can be computed as:

$$MR(m) = 1 - \frac{\sum_{i=1}^{m} Hit[i]}{\sum_{i=1}^{n} Hit[i] + Hit[\infty]} \quad (1)$$

where m is the number of pages provided; n is the total number of available pages; *Hit[i]* is the number of times that page i is hit; *Hit[∞]* is the number of accesses which results in a miss even if all n pages are allocated [3]. Using equation (1), the load balancer can compute the miss ratio curve for each VM, as shown in Figure 3.

Due to temporal locality in memory access, it is desirable to give the most recently used page faster access time (SLC mode). As shown in Figure 7, we implemented two LRU linked lists: i.e. *SLC list* and *MLC list* to manage the virtual memory pages. Note that the lengths of those lists are limited by the maximum physical memory size of SLC and MLC pages allocated by the VMM. When a page in the MLC mode is accessed (①), it will first locate another free MLC page (②). Then, they will be put together and converted to one SLC page (③) and inserted at the end of *SLC list* (④). In case that the *SLC list* reaches the maximum physical SLC memory size and there are more pages coming into the *SLC list*, the page at the head of *SLC list* will be de-queued (⑤) and the page will be converted to MLC mode (⑥). At the same time, a free MLC page will be released and inserted at the head of MLC list (⑦). When the *MLC list* reaches the maximum physical MLC memory size and there are more pages to be evicted from the *SLC list*, pages at the head of *MLC list* will be evicted from memory and swapped to disk (⑧).

In order to further lower the cost, upon the SLC minor page faults, we only increment the counter associated with that page.

For each MLC minor page fault, our scheme increments the corresponding counter, updates the list and invokes the load balancer to tune the SLC/MLC pages.

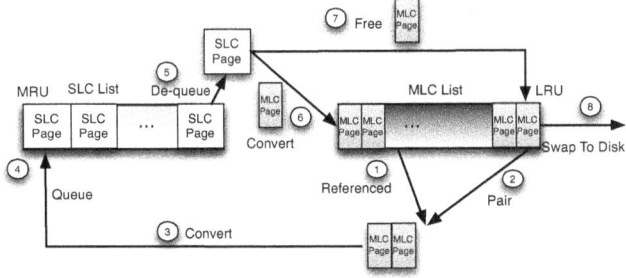

Figure 7. Virtual Memory Page Management

3.2.2. Intra-VM Utility Driven PCM Page Allocation

We apply the utility function based methods [3, 4] to determine two values in miss ratio curve: m_1 for the SLC size and m_2 for the total memory size, which indicate how many SLC and MLC pages should be allocated respectively to achieve the optimal efficiency.

Note that whenever a VM increases one unit of page in SLC, it needs to trade in two units of page residing in MLC, as illustrated in Figure 1. Therefore, when m_1 (SLC) is increased by 1, m_2 (SLC+MLC) will decrease by 1. The additional low-latency SLC pages brought by increasing m_1 will cause the reduction of total PCM capacity (decreasing m_2), which will further lead to increase in page faults. To determine m_1 and m_2, we define the utility functions as

$$\Delta MR(m) = \frac{MR(m+\Delta m) - MR(m)}{\Delta m} \qquad (2)$$

$$U_{m_1} = -\Delta MR(m_1) \times \frac{latency\ of\ MLC}{latency\ of\ SLC} \qquad (3)$$

$$U_{m2} = -\Delta MR(m_2) \times \frac{latency\ of\ HDD}{latency\ of\ MLC} \qquad (4)$$

$$U_{slc} = U_{m_1} + U_{m_2} \quad (increase\ m_1; reduce\ m_2) \qquad (5)$$

$$U_{mlc} = U_{m_1} + U_{m_2} \quad (reduce\ m_1; increase\ m_2) \qquad (6)$$

In the above equations, $\Delta MR(m)$ indicates the difference in miss ratio if the page supply is changed by Δm. U_{m_1} defines the utility of changing m_1. If point m_1 in miss ratio curve shifts right (increase), $-\Delta MR(m_1)$ will become positive, which suggests the benefit of moving some pages from MLC to SLC. The latency ratio between SLC and MLC is used to weight the change, i.e. $-\Delta MR(m_1)$. Following the same philosophy, U_{m_2} defines the utility of changing pages from HDD to MLC. Recall that when we vary the number of SLC or MLC pages, both m_1 and m_2 will change. Therefore, U_{slc} defines the utility of morphing two MLC pages into one SLC page, while U_{mlc} illustrates the utility of changing one SLC page into two MLC pages. Upon MLC minor page fault, the load balancer will compute U_{slc} and U_{mlc} to determine the ratio of SLC/MLC pages within one VM. If U_{slc} is greater than 0, it is worth increasing one unit of SLC by reducing two units of MLC. If U_{mlc} is greater than 0, it is worth to morph one SLC page into two MLC pages. If both U_{slc} and U_{mlc} are negative, the load balancer will maintain current allocation between SLC and MLC pages,

indicating the desirable tradeoff between memory access latency and the number of page faults.

Note that in our design, the abovementioned techniques are integrated into the MMU in the hypervisor. Unlike the hardware-based method [7] that manages PCM systems in the form of circuit level columns and rows, our schemes work at page granularity, which makes it easier to interact with the software layer. Besides, we abstract the utilities of both SLC and MLC for each individual VM. Doing so opens up the possibility to further exploit PCM features in virtualized environments.

3.2.3. Inter-VM PCM Resource Adaptation

In highly utilized virtual servers, asymmetric memory resource allocation is common: some VMs run memory intensive jobs with less available memory space while other VMs are idle with plenty of unused memory pages. Therefore, only tuning SLC/MLC pages within each VM cannot achieve the optimal memory efficiency. This motivates us to further extend our intra-VM page balancer to support better memory utilization across VMs.

Recall that VM balloon technology makes it possible to resize memory for individual VM by changing the size of balloon within guest VMs. Our technique leverages this balloon feature to reallocate memory resources across different VMs. We refer the VM that demands more memory as a caller VM and the VM from which the memory is being deprived as a victim VM. In case a VM runs out of PCM SLC/MLC pages but still benefits from providing more pages (as indicated by the utility function), it will become a caller VM. Upon a request, the VMM will check other VMs for available pages based on their utility functions (U_{mlc} or U_{slc}). Since a VM can benefit from increasing the number of a given type of PCM page if the corresponding utility value is positive, only the one with the lowest negative utility value will be selected as victim VM. Doing so will solve the asymmetrical memory distribution problem. Note that VM priority can also be incorporated into our proposed utility function to solve the issue when there are multiple callers. In the case of over-commitment (i.e., the total number of requested memory pages exceeds the memory capacity when all the pages are in MLC mode), there will be no victim VM in the system. Our scheme will select the VM with lower priority and swap their MLC pages to disk. In this study, all the VMs are assumed to have the same priority for simplicity and arbitration is done in a round robin fashion.

The runtime overhead of our proposed scheme includes maintenance overhead for the minor page faults and the page table. Compared with real page faults, which invoke disk IO access, these maintenance activities only invoke memory or memory-to-memory operations, which are less expensive. In addition, during most of the execution period, applications only access their working set pages (in SLC mode). On a SLC minor page fault, our scheme only sets the hit counters, which takes O(1) time. Therefore, most of the time, the load balancer is not triggered and the overhead is low. Coupling with sampling mechanism [29] further lowers the overhead in real systems.

3.3. Benefits for VM Dedicated Behaviors

VM dedicated behaviors include VM creation, shutdown, normal execution, checkpoint/restore, and live migration. VM creation and shutdown can be treated as a normal running VM, which can directly benefit from our technique. VM checkpoint/restore, which is the basis for VM live migration, can also take advantage of the PCM non-volatile feature. Instead of dumping the entire memory to disk, part of the checkpointed memory can stay in memory to reduce IO traffic.

Based on the non-volatility of PCM and the *IntraVM+InterVM* schemes, we redesign the checkpoint/restore routine. In the checkpoint routine as shown in Figure 8, once the checkpoint command is issued, a preparation signal is sent to checkpoint VM to inform the guest OS (①). Meanwhile, VMM collects page allocation information from the information collector (in section 3.2.1) (②) and classifies the pages into 4 categories: Working Set pages (SLC page), Page Table Pages, Non Working Set Pages (MLC Pages) and Pages with VM State (vCPU, Device) (③). Working Set Pages, Page Table Pages and VM State Pages will be transferred to MLC pages and marked as checkpoint pages; Non Working Set pages will be dumped to disk (④). A *checkpoint_page_list* is implemented to track those checkpoint pages in memory (⑤). The freed pages will be put back into the *free_SLC_list* and *free_MLC_list*.

In the restore routine as shown in Figure 9, the VMM first reads in the *checkpoint_page_list* and locates the checkpoint pages (①). And then, VM state information is used to create an empty VM while Page Table Pages and Working Set Pages will be transferred to SLC page (②③). At this point, we leverage the lazy restore concept [5] to resume the VM in advance. Since the VM is running with its minimal requirement (VM state, Page Table Pages and Working Set Pages), it is possible that Non Working Set Pages will be accessed and cause page fault during the execution. To solve this issue, whenever there is a page fault, the fetch on demand process [26] will be invoked to request an SLC page from the *free_SLC_list* and bring the pages from disk to memory (④). At the same time, the Information Collector and Load Balancer will be invoked to perform PCM page management as discussed in Section 3.2.

Note that there are two caveats when keeping checkpoint pages in MLC pages: 1) When active VMs are greedy for memory capacities, memory pages for the checkpointed VM will be dumped to disk and later restored using traditional schemes. 2) The availability of checkpoints can be maintained by adopting architectures similar to RAMCloud [30], which are designed to share the memory system among several servers (i.e., as SAN for disk). In that case, VM live migration will work just as the checkpoint/restore scheme and the disk IO is replaced by the network IO operations. Since the network IO operations are more expensive than disk IO operations, the benefit for VM live migration is expected to be more significant than that for checkpoint/restore.

Compared with traditional checkpoint/restore schemes, our approach significantly reduces the amount of IO requests by saving

some memory pages in PCM. The benefits include 1) improving the checkpoint/restore time by keeping the critical data in memory, and 2) reducing the IO penalty for other running VMs by reducing the amount of data written to disk. Furthermore, when using our approach, the checkpoint/restore latency is no longer proportional to the memory size but depends on the ratio of SLC/MLC pages (determined by the size of working set).

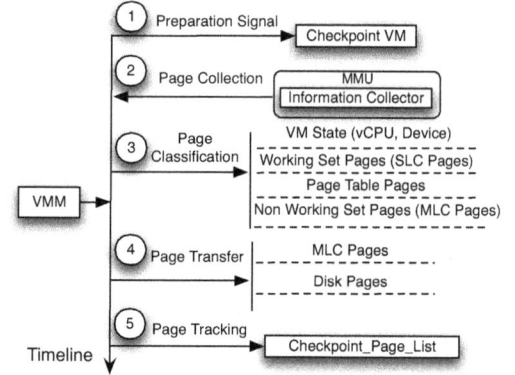

Figure 8. The Save Stage of Checkpointing

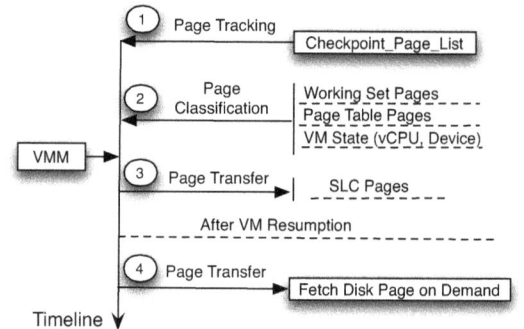

Figure 9. The Restore Stage of Checkpointing

The implementation overheads for our PCM system design are summarized as: 0.2% of memory space for SLC, MLC Page lists and 0.1% for the counter array. 95% of total minor page faults are SLC minor page fault, which only takes 1us to set the counter. Only 5% of total minor page faults are MLC minor page fault, which takes 1ms, on average, to update the linked list and trigger the load balancer.

4. Experimental Setup

4.1. Simulated Hardware Platform

We evaluate the efficiency of our design using Simics full-system simulator [17] with g-cache timing model and further integrate it with DRAMSim2 memory subsystem simulator [18]. Since Simics does not simulate paging functionality, we implemented a new simulator module [19] to model the behavior and timing cost for paging. We further extend it with our proposed PCM page management scheme and the associated overheads are counted in our modeling. The sampling interval is determined via empirical approach. DRAM is simulated as cache on top of PCM. We express PCM device and circuit characteristics using conventional DDR timing parameters. This allows characterizing PCM in the context of more familiar DRAM parameters [20]. Table 1 lists the configuration of simulated machine and the average access latency on SLC, MLC and HDD, which are consistent with recent published work [7][20][21][22].

Table 1. The Configuration of Simulated Machine

Processor	4-OOO-core, 2GHz
Private L1 Cache	16K I-cache and 16K D-cache, 64-byte lines, 4-way set associative
Private L2 Cache	1MB, 64-byte lines, 4-way set associative
DRAM cache	4MB, write-back, 50 cycle access time (25ns)
Main Memory Size	600MB for page management experiments; 2~16GB for checkpoint experiments
PCM SLC Page	Reads: 250 cycles (125ns); Writes: 700 cycles (350ns)
PCM MLC Page	Reads: 500 cycles (250ns); Writes: 1700 cycles (850ns)
Page Conversion	SLC to MLC: 1950 cycles; MLC to SLC: 1200 cycles
Hard Disk Drive	1500K cycles access time
Memory to Memory Copy	1200~2000 cycles access time

4.2. Virtualization Layer

We port Xen 4.1.0 [9] together with Debian Linux 2.6.26 kernel with PAE support into Simics. In order to track VM behaviors such as memory update, domain switches and checkpoint, we also instrument the Xen hypervisor and Memory Management Unit (MMU) in Linux kernel with the HAPs and Magic Instructions, which are APIs provided by Simics for communication between software and simulated machines. Shadow page table is enabled and magic instructions are instrumented into minor page fault interrupt service routine so that all the minor page faults will be passed to Simics. In order to track the behavior of checkpoint, we insert magic instructions into xc_domain_save.c and xc_domain_restore.c, which are the source codes for VM checkpointing. By doing this, the simulated machine is aware of all VM behaviors. On booting, Xen starts up a control domain called dom0, from which we create several guest VMs (domU) and launch our workloads.

4.3. Workloads

To emulate various memory access patterns in virtualized data center servers, we use a mix of SPEC 2006 and PARSEC benchmarks in our simulations. We boot up a maximum of 6 domains in Xen and mix multiple benchmarks to emulate the following virtualization scenarios: one VM runs one benchmark, one VM runs multiple benchmarks, multiple VMs run one benchmark each, and multiple VMs run multiple benchmarks each. Table 2 summarizes the simulated workload execution scenarios. To measure the performance of VM checkpoint operations, we run SPEC 2006 and PARSEC workloads (as summarized in Table 3) in each VM.

Table 2. A Summary of Simulated Workload Execution Scenarios

Category	Benchmark Name	Description
\multicolumn{3}{c}{Heterogeneous Workloads}		
VM itself	boot-i-dom	Boot up i VMs
SPEC	gcc-i-dom	Run i copies of gcc in i VMs
	lbm-i-dom	Run i copies of lbm in i VMs
	povtray-i-dom	Run i copies of povtray in i VMs
	milc-i-dom	Run i copies of milc in i VMs
	mcf-i-dom	Run i copies of mcf in i VMs
	cacu-i-dom	Run i copies of cactusADMI in i VMs
	GemsFDTD-i-dom	Run i copies of GemsFDTD in i VMs
	bzip-i-dom	Run i copies of bzip in i VMs
Mix SPEC	GL-i-dom	Run i copies of gcc and lbm in i VMs
	GLP-i-dom	Run i copies of gcc, lbm and povtray in i VMs
	GLMP-i-dom	Run i copies of gcc, lbm, milc and povtray in i VMs
	GC-i-dom	Run i copies of GemsFDTD and cactusADM in i VMs
	MLMB-i-dom	Run i copies of mcf, lbm, milc and bzip in i VMs
	BGC-i-dom	Run i copies of bzip, GemsFDTD, CactusADM in i VMs
	MLMGB-i-dom	Run i copies of mcf,lbm,milc, GemsFDTD,bzip in i VMs
PARSEC	black-i-dom	Run i copies of blacksholes in i VMs
	Swaptions-i-dom	Run i copies of swaptions in i VMs
	freqmin-i-dom	Run i copies of freqmin in i VMs
	x264-i-dom	Run i copies of x264 in i VMs
	BSFX-i-dom	Run i copies of blacksholes, swaptions,freqmin,x264 in i VMs
Mix SPEC and PARSEC	black-x264-i-dom	Run i copies of blacksholes and x264 in i VMs
	MSXM-i-dom	Run i copies of mcf,swaptions,x264 and milc in i Ms
	black-x264	Run blacksholes and x264 in seperate VMs
	mcf-milc	Run mcf and milc in seperate VMs
	freqmin-Gems	Run freqmin and GemsFDTD in seperate VMs
	milc-swim	Run milc and swim in seperate VMs

* i ranges from 1 to 6 indicating the number of active VMs

Table 3. A Summary of Simulated Checkpointing Scenarios

		Description
\multicolumn{3}{c}{Checkpoint Scenarios}		
SPEC	mcf	Run mcf in VM before checkpoint happens
	povtray	Run povtray in VM before checkpoint happens
	G-L-M-P	Run gcc-lbm-povtray-milc in VM before checkpoint happens
	B-G-C	Run CacusADM, GemsFDTD bzip in VM before checkpoint happens
	milc	Run milc in VM before checkpoint happens
	M-L-M-B-G	Run mcf,lbm,milc, bzip, GemsFDTD in VM before checkpoint happens
	Gems	Run GemsFDTD in VM before checkpoint happens
	GC	Run CacusADM, GemsFDTD in VM before checkpoint happens
	Cacu	Run CacusADM in VM before checkpoint happens
Mix SPEC and PARSEC	M-S-X-M	Run mcf, swap, x264 and milc in VM before checkpoint happens
	black-x264	Run mcf in VM before checkpoint happens
	B-X-S-F	Run blacksholes, x264, swaptions and freqmin in VM before checkpoint happens
PARSEC	x264	Run x264 in VM before checkpoint happens
	freqmin	Run freqmin in VM before checkpoint happens
	blacksholes	Run blacksholes in VM before checkpoint happens
	swaptions	Run swaptions in VM before checkpoint happens

5. Evaluation Results

In this section, we begin by characterizing the performance of phase change memory system on virtualized platforms and existing hardware-based hybrid PCM system. Then, we evaluate the performance of pure MLC-based (*pure-MLC*), pure SLC-based (*pure-SLC*), and hybrid SLC/MLC with Intra-VM management (*IntraVM*) systems under symmetric memory allocation. We further incorporate VM-aware dynamic memory balancing with Intra-VM management (*IntraVM+InterVM*) and compare it with *IntraVM* under asymmetric memory allocation scenarios. In the end, we evaluate the efficiency of our checkpoint schemes in terms of data transfer time and the IO performance penalty on other running VMs.

5.1. Characterizing Hardware-based PCM Design

We first analyze the impact on memory latency when increasing the capacity of phase change memory system by morphing SLC pages into MLC pages. Figure 10 (a) shows that the number of page faults reduces by 30% on average as more SLC pages are replaced by MLC pages. On the other hand, MLC pages increase the memory latency by 3.5X as well, as shown in Figure 10 (b). The optimal operation point, on which the system gains the most benefit from SLC pages while suffering the least page fault penalty, is the lowest point for each line in Figure 10 (c). Figure 10 (c) shows that the execution time decreases as we increase memory capacity at the initial stage. As the system exhausts the benefit of reducing page faults, it suffers significantly from the high latency MLC pages. As can be seen in Figures 10, some of the benchmarks (e.g. *povtray-1-dom*) are affected dramatically by memory capacity (up to 90% page fault reduction) while some benchmarks (e.g. *milc-1-dom*) are not (less than 5% page fault reduction). Therefore, the optimal operating point varies across different workloads. It is critical for the system to identify the corresponding optimal operating point on the fly.

Note that existing hardware-based hybrid PCM design [7] uses memory controllers to tune the ratio of SLC/MLC cells in circuit level. We evaluate the performance of such design in virtualized execution scenarios and the results are shown in Figure 11. As can be seen, the hardware-only approach can reduce total execution time by 10% compared to pure-SLC system and 18% compared to pure-MLC system.

5.2. IntraVM PCM Page Allocation Scheme

In this section, we only turn on the *IntraVM* function and compare it with *pure-MLC*, *pure-SLC* and hardware-based hybrid PCM schemes. The total execution time for those designs is shown in Figure 12.

We observe that *pure-MLC* system is about 1.47X slower than *pure-SLC* system while it reduces 11% page faults. The penalty of page faults is much more expensive than the memory access time, as indicated in Table 1. The performance of *pure-SLC* and *pure-MLC* systems varies across different benchmarks. As can be observed in Figure 12, by enabling *IntraVM* scheme, page faults penalty is reduced by 8%, which results in 10% improvement in

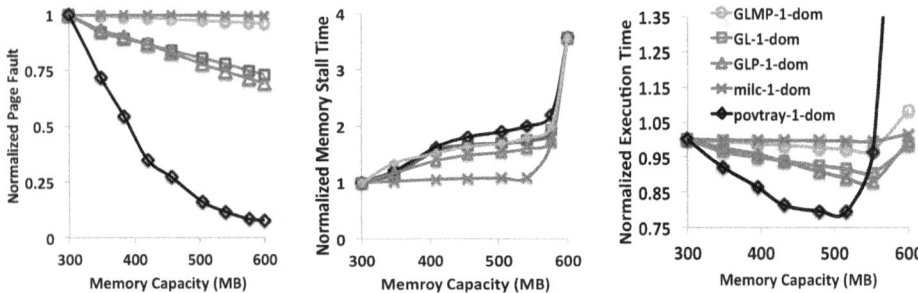

total execution time compared with *pure-SLC* based system. On the other hand, compared with *pure-MLC* based system, the *IntraVM* scheme improves 43% in memory stall time, which leads to 20% improvement in total execution time. Although designed at the software layer, the *IntraVM* scheme yields equally well performance compared to hardware-based hybrid PCM system. This is because 1) both designs seek the optimal ratio of SLC/MLC in the case of single VM; 2) hardware-based solution is triggered much more frequently than *IntraVM*, which makes accumulated overhead equivalent to our design.

Furthermore, our IntraVM design can be improved by incorporating advanced page replacement algorithms. Theoretically, Belady's optimal algorithm [27] can achieve the best performance by leveraging future page access information. Nevertheless, LRU algorithm is a more practical method, which yields relatively good estimation. We use Belady's optimal algorithm as the theoretical upper bound of our design, which is shown as *IntraVM Upper Limit* line in Figure 12. As can be seen, by deploying the Belady's optimal algorithm, total execution time of *IntraVM* design can be further reduced by around 25%.

By further analyzing the results in Figure 12, we found that: 1) the major component of execution time for latency sensitive VMs (e.g. *povtray-1-dom*, *GemsFDTD-1-dom*) is memory latency so that the impact of improving memory stall time overwhelms page fault penalty; 2) page fault penalty dominates the capacity sensitive VMs (e.g. *lbm-1-dom*, *MSXM-1-dom*) so that performance is improved by reducing the number of page faults. Figure 13 presents the page distribution of both latency and capacity sensitive VMs. On latency sensitive VMs (e.g. *povtray-1-dom*), the *IntraVM* scheme dynamically assigns more SLC pages to improve the memory stall time. In contrast, *IntraVM* scheme assigns more high capacity MLC pages (around 94% of total memory pages) to reduce the page faults on capacity sensitive VMs (e.g. *mcf-1-dom*). It is also observed that capacity sensitive VMs consume 1.4X memory pages compared with latency sensitive VMs. Although the dominant part of execution time for different types of VMs varies, our *IntraVM* scheme successfully adapts itself across different types of VMs and shows better performance across all the cases.

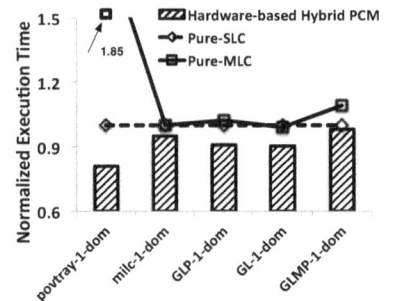

Figure 10. The Effect on (a) Page Faults, (b) Memory Latency, (c) Overall Execution Time when Memory Capacity Increases for Single VM (Normalized to Pure SLC System)

Figure 11. The Total Execution Time for Hardware-based Hybrid PCM (Normalized to Pure SLC System)

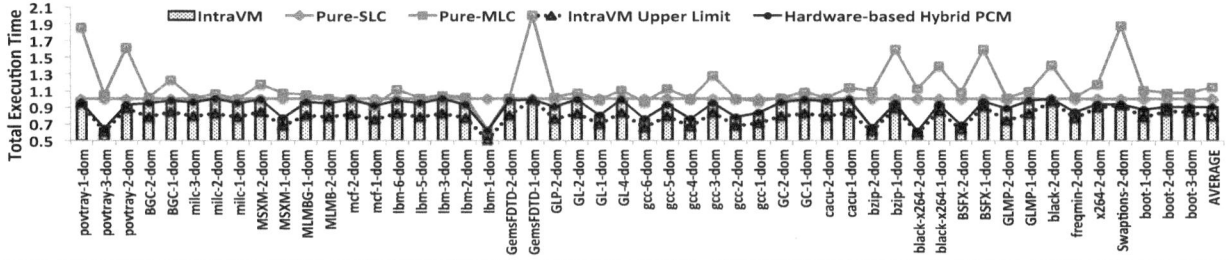

Figure 12. The Total Execution Time for *IntraVM* Scheme (Normalized to Pure SLC System)

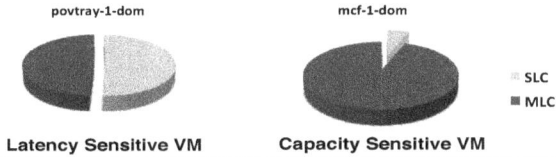

Figure 13. Page Distribution for Different Types of Workloads

5.3. IntraVM+InterVM PCM Page Allocation Scheme

Although not exhibiting huge advantages over hardware-based hybrid PCM system, the *IntraVM* scheme shifts the PCM memory management to software level, which opens the possibility to leverage the full system information (e.g. different memory demands from different VMs) and system behaviors (e.g. memory reallocation among different VMs).

To fully leverage the full system information and resources, we further incorporate VM-aware management and enable both *InterVM* and *IntraVM* schemes in our system (*IntraVM+InterVM*). We select workloads with at least two VMs running and create asymmetric memory allocation by 1) running the same benchmarks in different VMs with different memory supplies, 2) running different benchmarks in different VMs with the same memory supply for each VM.

Figure 14 shows page miss ratio of two VMs running different benchmarks (e.g. *mcf-milc*). As can be seen, when *IntraVM* scheme is enabled, the optimal SLC/MLC ratio within one VM is located and shown as dashed line. However, in this case, U_{SLC} for *milc*-VM is negative while U_{MLC} for *mcf*-VM is positive. With *IntraVM+InterVM* scheme, *mcf*-VM borrows SLC pages from *milc*-VM and converts them into MLC pages as shown in Figure 15. By doing this, the number of page faults for *mcf*-VM is reduced due to extended MLC pages. Meanwhile, the number of page faults for *milc*-VM will not increase because it still has enough SLC pages to keep low page miss ratio. Upon this situation, the overall page faults will be reduced, which results in significant performance improvement (20% better than *IntraVM* scheme).

Besides, we found that capacity intensive VM (e.g. *mcf*-VM) tends to grab MLC pages from other VMs while latency sensitive VM (e.g. *milc*-VM) has intention to borrow SLC pages from other VMs.

On the other hand, Figure 16 shows two VMs have different memory supplies but execute the same workloads (e.g. *BGC-2-dom*). With *IntraVM* scheme, the VM with smaller available memory size (VM$_1$) will have to suffer from higher page faults than the VM with larger memory size (VM$_2$). In this case, the U_{mlc} for VM$_1$ is positive while U_{mlc} for VM$_2$ is negative. With *IntraVM+InterVM* scheme, VM$_1$ borrows MLC pages from VM$_2$ as shown in Figure 17. By doing so, the memory difference between two VMs becomes smaller and the overall page faults for entire system are reduced by around 25%, which leads to 40% performance improvement in total execution time. In addition, we found that MLC pages have higher possibility to be shifted between VMs than SLC pages in the situation that VMs have different memory supplies at the beginning.

In Figure 18, we classify our benchmarks into 3 groups. In Group 1, we run same workloads in different VMs with different memory supplies. As can be seen, the total execution time is improved by around 32% on average. In Group 2, we run the same workloads in VMs with same memory configuration but start them at a different time. Only 4% of improvement can be achieved in this situation because there are no idle pages to be tuned among VMs. In Group 3, we run different workloads inside different VMs with same memory configuration. At this situation, 10% of performance improvement can be achieved by enabling *IntraVM+InterVM* scheme. Averaging all the benchmarks, our scheme can yield a 15% performance improvement compared to the hardware-based method [7]. Furthermore, we found that the larger the difference between memory supply and memory demands is, the better our schemes will perform.

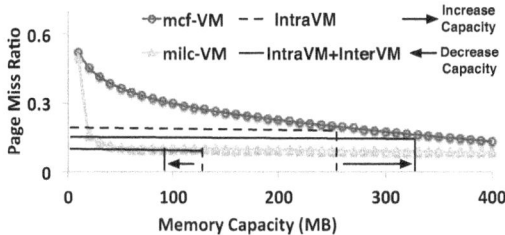

Figure 14. Page Miss Ratio for *mcf-milc* Workload

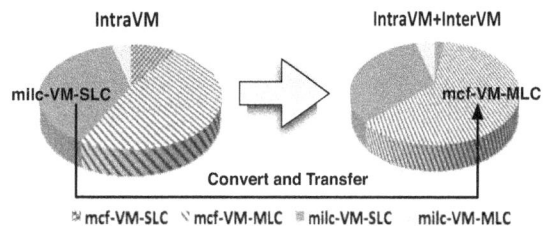

Figure 15. Page Distribution for (a) *IntraVM*, (b) *IntraVM+InterVM*

187

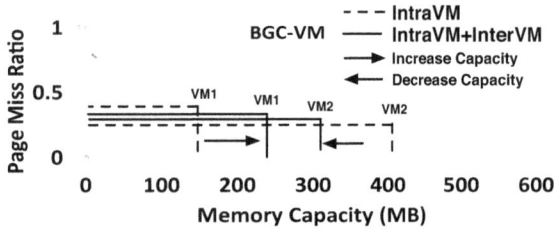

Figure 16. Page Miss Ratio for *BGC-2-doms* Workload

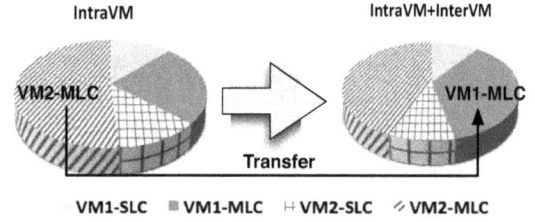

Figure 17. Page Distribution for (a) *IntraVM*, (b) *IntraVM+InterVM*

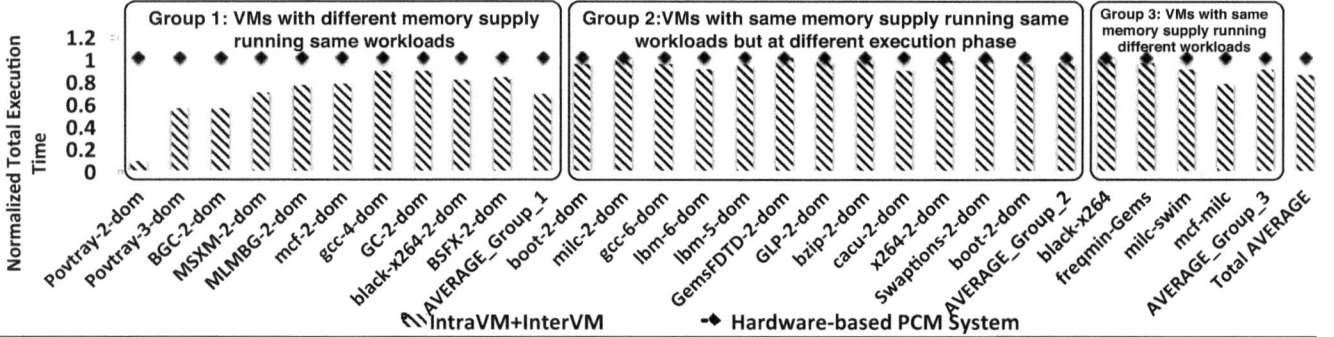

Figure 18. The Total Execution Time for *IntraVM+InterVM* System (Normalized to *Hardware-based PCM* System)

5.4. Checkpoint/Restore Efficiency

This section evaluates two major impacts of checkpointing on virtualized system: 1) the time it takes to checkpoint and restore a VM and 2) the IO penalty for other normal running VMs upon checkpointing.

To evaluate the effect of reducing checkpoint/restore time, we retrieve the memory allocation information just before a checkpoint (save stage) is made. We observe that, on average, only 46% of memory pages are in MLC mode (as shown in Figure 19), which means only 46% of memory pages need to be dumped to the disk. In Figure 20, by replacing expensive IO operations with much cheaper memory-to-memory copy operations (as shown in Table 1), our approach achieves around 46% improvement in data transfer time compared with contemporary DRAM-based method [5]. Further analysis shows that the improvement varies from 40% to 75% across different workloads and the results are highly related to the size of the working set (pages in SLC mode) before checkpointing. As can be seen in Figure 19, the memory distribution before checkpointing varies across different workloads. Some of the workloads exhibit large working sets (about 70% pages in SLC mode), while some of them have small working sets (about 30% pages in SLC mode). Workloads, which have larger working sets, gain larger improvement in data transfer time (see Figures 20 and 21). If the entire VM memory is in SLC mode before checkpointing happens, only memory-to-memory copy operations are triggered since we only consolidate the SLC pages to MLC pages. The average data transfer time is only 0.03% of traditional methods. On the other hand, if the entire VM memory is in MLC mode before checkpointing occurs, the data

transfer time will be close to that of conventional DRAM-based methods (shown as dark black line in Figure 20) since our scheme opt to dump all the pages in MLC mode to disk. Although both of aforementioned scenarios rarely occur in our experiments, they provide the upper and lower boundaries of our approach.

To further evaluate the side effect of checkpoint/restore on other running VMs, we measure the IOPS of one VM while the other one is being checkpointed. Note that the longer the checkpoint/restore is, the longer the running VM will suffer from low IO bandwidth. We use *IO Penalty*Time* to indicate the total IO penalty the running VM will suffer. As can be seen from Figure 21, as the memory size increases, the overall IO penalty for the running VM increases. However, the overall IO penalty for our proposed PCM system is (22%) lower than the DRAM-based system because our PCM with *IntraVM+InterVM* scheme takes less time to checkpoint/restore. Further comparing (a) and (b), we found that the improvement of our scheme is more significant in latency sensitive VMs (34%) than capacity sensitive VMs (13%) because there is less MLC pages to be dumped to disk in latency sensitive VMs. Figure 22 shows IO penalty for running VM when the number of checkpointing VMs increases. As can be seen, a PCM system equipped with *IntraVM+InterVM* scheme also has (50%) lower IO penalty than a DRAM-based system because the overall IO traffic generated by checkpointing or restoring is less in our schemes than the traditional DRAM-based schemes. As compared in Figure 22 (a) and (b), Latency Sensitive VM can benefit more from our scheme than Capacity Sensitive VM due to higher percentage of SLC pages. Besides, the improvement increases as the number of VM increases.

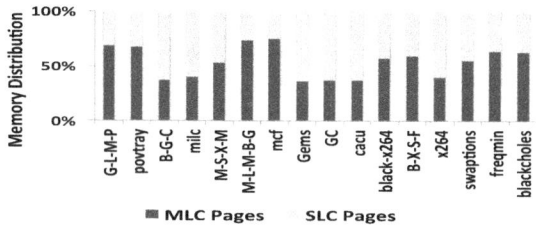

Figure 19. Memory Page Distributions Before Checkpoint

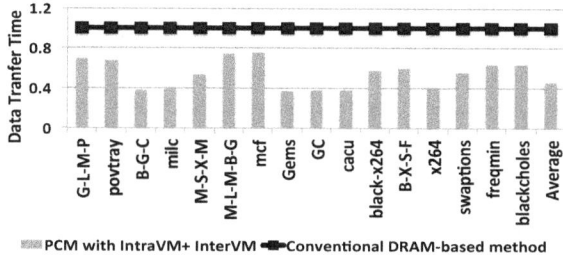

Figure 20. Percentage of Reduction on Data Transfer Time in both Save and Restore Stages

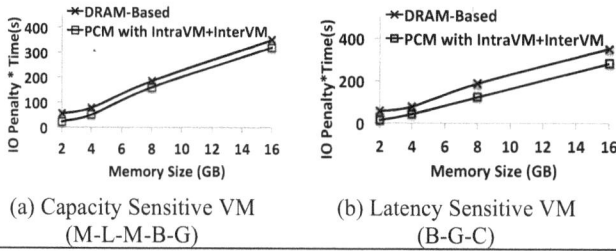

(a) Capacity Sensitive VM (M-L-M-B-G)

(b) Latency Sensitive VM (B-G-C)

Figure 21. The Overall IO Penalty for Running VM as the Memory Size of Checkpointing VM Increases

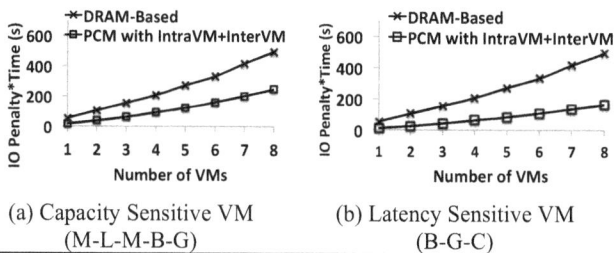

(a) Capacity Sensitive VM (M-L-M-B-G)

(b) Latency Sensitive VM (B-G-C)

Figure 22. The Overall IO Penalty for Running VM as the Number of Checkpointing VM Increases

6. Related Work

[7] proposed Morphable Memory Systems (MMS), which trades off latency with capacity in a SLC/MLC PCM memory system using hardware based approach. To achieve this, MMS uses a memory monitoring hardware to collect the physical addresses issued to the memory controller and further estimates the size of SLC. Our work differs from [7] in that we use cooperative and

cross-layer software/hardware approach and our PCM page management unit makes decisions based on the full-system execution characteristics. Instead of just using OS balloon technology to guarantee the correctness upon memory change, our design further extend the functionality of VM balloon technology to gain performance improvement. We evaluate the efficiency of applying SLC/MLC PCM memory design on virtualized platforms and shows that our design yields 15% performance improvement compared to [7]. Furthermore, the non-volatile feature of PCM is not considered in [7]. [12] proposed to dynamically monitor the memory usage of each virtual machine, predicts its memory needs, and periodically reallocates the memory. Our work differs from [12] in that we propose VMM support for SLC/MLC PCM system and our page management considers both SLC and MLC PCM. [29] proposed a low cost working set tracking scheme, which can vary the sampling period based on the working set size. This work can be incorporated in our sampling scheme to further lower the cost of memory tracking. [5] proposed a method to perform fast VM restore based on working set estimation. Their method only loads the active working set back in memory and starts restore using a lazy scheme. Nevertheless, [5] is based on DRAM while we take both SLC and MLC PCM into consideration. There are other ways, such as page hashing [24] and copy on write [25], to improve checkpointing performance. These methods are orthogonal to our approach and can be combined with our proposal. [31] proposed to use 3D PCM to store checkpoint in MPP system. Our work differs from [31] in that we analyze the working set pages for each virtual machine and make checkpoints based on the detailed page distribution from our PCM page management scheme.

7. Conclusion

Virtualization improves resource utilization at the price of lowering the performance and efficiency of the memory subsystem. The non-volatile and resizable features make PCM a desirable candidate for designing adaptive and intelligent memory systems on virtualized platforms. The goal of this work is to better incorporate PCM technology into virtualized environments. To achieve this goal, we propose 1) hypervisor-level, collaborative management of non-volatile memory and storage (SLC/MLC PCM memory and hard disk), 2) a VM-aware SLC/MLC page balancer, 3) SLC/MLC page tuning in cooperation with VM ballooning to improve the performance of critical VM operations, and 4) leveraging the non-volatile property of PCM to reduce IO requests. Our experimental results show that the proposed techniques can improve the overall performance by 10% compared with *pure-SLC* systems and 20% compared with *pure-MLC* systems. Introducing advanced page replacement algorithm to *IntraVM* design can yield 25% performance improvement. By incorporating VM-aware optimization, the overall performance can be further improved by 15%. In terms of checkpointing, our design achieves 46% less checkpoint/restore time and reduces around 50% of overall IO penalty to the system.

Acknowledgements

This work is supported in part by NSF grants 1117261, 0937869, 0916384, 0845721(CAREER), 0834288, 0811611, 0720476, by SRC grants 2008-HJ-1798, 2007-RJ-1651G, by Microsoft Research Trustworthy Computing, Safe and Scalable Multi-core Computing Awards, by NASA/Florida Space Grant Consortium FSREGP Award 16296041-Y4, and by three IBM Faculty Awards.

References

[1] P. Barham et al., Xen and the Art of Virtualization, SOSP 2003.

[2] G. Burr et al., Phase Change Memory Technology, IBM T.J. Watson Research Center, Yorktown Heights, NY 10598.

[3] P. Zhou et al., Dynamic Tracking of Page Miss Ratio Curve for Memory Management, ASPLOS 2004.

[4] M. Qureshi et al., Utility-based Cache Partitioning: A Low-Overhead, High-Performance, Runtime Mechanism to Partition Shared Caches, MICRO 2006.

[5] I. Zhang et al., Fast Restore of Checkpointed Memory using Working Set Estimation, VEE 2011.

[6] Benjamin Lee et al., Phase Change Technology and the Future of Main Memory, Micro, IEEE 2010.

[7] M. Qureshi et al, Morphable Memory System: A Robust Architecture for Exploiting Multi-Level Phase Change Memories, ISCA 2010.

[8] X. Dong et al, AdaMS: Adaptive MLC/SLC Phase-Change Memory Design for File Storage; ASP-DAC, 2011.

[9] Xen wiki http://wiki.xensource.com/xenwiki/Xen4.0

[10] A. Krapf, et al., Virtual Memory and MMU Concepts

[11] C. Waldspurger, Memory Resource Management in VMware ESX Server, SIGOPS Oper. Syst. 2002.

[12] W. Zhao, et al., Dynamic Memory Balancing for Virtual Machines;,VEE 2009.

[13] D. Gupta et al., Difference Engine: Harnessing Memory Redundancy in Virtual Machines, OSDI 2008.

[14] G. Vall'ee et al., Checkpoint/Restart of Virtual Machines Based on Xen, HAPCW 2006.

[15] P. Lu et al., Virtual Machine Memory Access Tracing with Hypervisor Exclusive Cache, USENIX ATC, 2007.

[16] R. Mattson, et al., Evaluation Techniques for Storage Hierarchies, IBM Systems Journal, 1970.

[17] Simics full system simulator www.virtutech.com/

[18] DRAMSim2: http://www.ece.umd.edu/dramsim/

[19] S. Chhabra, et al., i-NVMM: A Secure Non-Volatile Main Memory System with Incremental Encryption, ISCA 2011.

[20] Benjamin Lee et al, Architecting Phase Change Memory as a Scalable DRAM Alternative, ISCA 2009.

[21] P. Zhou et al., A Durable and Energy Efficient Main Memory Using Phase Change Memory Technology, ISCA 2009.

[22] M. Qureshi et al., Scalable High Performance Main Memory System Using Phase-Change Memory Technology, ISCA 2009.

[23] G. Tesauro et al., Utility-Function-Driven Resource Allocation in Autonomic Systems, IBM Watson Research, ICAC 2005.

[24] S. Albers et al., Page Migration with Limited Local Memory Capacity, Workshop on WADS 1995.

[25] J. Smith et al., Effects of Copy-on-Write Memory Management on the Response Time, Computing Systems, 1988.

[26] E. Park et al., Fast and Space-Efficient Virtual Machine Checkpointing, VEE 2011.

[27] A. Aho et al., Principles of Optimal Page Replacement, Journal of the ACM (JACM) 1971.

[28] V. Application, Intel 64 and IA-32 Architecture Software Developer's Manual, 2006.

[29] W. Zhao et al., Low Cost Working Set Size Tracking, USENIX ATC 2011.

[30] J. Ousterhout, et al. The Case for RAMClouds: Scalable High-Performance Storage Entirely in DRAM, SIGOPS 2009.

[31] X. Dong, et al, Leveraging 3D PCRAM Technologies to Reduce Checkpoint Overhead for Future Exascale Systems, SC 2009.

Preemptable Ticket Spinlocks: Improving Consolidated Performance in the Cloud

Jiannan Ouyang

Department of Computer Science
University of Pittsburgh
Pittsburgh, PA 15260
ouyang@cs.pitt.edu

John R. Lange

Department of Computer Science
University of Pittsburgh
Pittsburgh, PA 15260
jacklange@cs.pitt.edu

Abstract

When executing inside a virtual machine environment, OS level synchronization primitives are faced with significant challenges due to the scheduling behavior of the underlying virtual machine monitor. Operations that are ensured to last only a short amount of time on real hardware, are capable of taking considerably longer when running virtualized. This change in assumptions has significant impact when an OS is executing inside a critical region that is protected by a spinlock. The interaction between OS level spinlocks and VMM scheduling is known as the *Lock Holder Preemption* problem and has a significant impact on overall VM performance. However, with the use of ticket locks instead of generic spinlocks, virtual environments must also contend with waiters being preempted before they are able to acquire the lock. This has the effect of blocking access to a lock, even if the lock itself is available. We identify this scenario as the *Lock Waiter Preemption* problem. In order to solve both problems we introduce Preemptable Ticket spinlocks, a new locking primitive that is designed to enable a VM to always make forward progress by relaxing the ordering guarantees offered by ticket locks. We show that the use of Preemptable Ticket spinlocks improves VM performance by $5.32X$ on average, when running on a non paravirtual VMM, and by $7.91X$ when running on a VMM that supports a paravirtual locking interface, when executing a set of microbenchmarks as well as a realistic e-commerce benchmark.

Categories and Subject Descriptors D.4.1 [*Process Management*]: Mutual exclusion

Keywords Virtual Machines; Lock Holder Preemption; Paravirtualization

1. Introduction

Synchronization has long been recognized as a source of bottlenecks in SMP and multicore operating systems. With the increased use of virtualization, multi-core CPUs, and consolidated Infrastructure as a Service (IaaS) clouds this issue has become more significant due to the *Lock Holder Preemption* problem [15]. Lock

VEE'13, March 16–17, 2013, Houston, Texas, USA.

holder preemption occurs whenever a virtual machine's (VM's) virtual CPU (vCPU) is scheduled off of a physical CPU while a lock is held inside the VM's context. The result is that when the VM's other vCPUs are attempting to acquire the lock they must wait until the vCPU holding the lock is scheduled back in by the VMM so it can release the lock. As kernel level synchronization is most often accomplished using spinlocks, the time spent waiting on a lock is wasted in a busy loop. While numerous attempts have been made to address this problem, the solutions have targeted only generic spinlock behaviors and not more advanced locking primitives such as ticket spinlocks (spinlocks that ensure consistent ordering of acquisitions). As a result of the introduction of ticket spinlocks virtual machine synchronization now must contend not only with Lock Holder Preemption but also *Lock Waiter Preemption*.

Ticket spinlocks [9] are a form of spinlock that enforces ordering among lock acquisitions. Whenever a thread of execution attempts to acquire a ticket spinlock it either (1) acquires the lock immediately, or (2) is granted a ticket which determines the order among all outstanding lock requests. The introduction of ticket spinlocks was meant to ensure fairness and prevent starvation among competing threads by preventing any single thread from obtaining a lock before another thread that requested it first. In this manner each thread must wait to acquire a lock until after it has been held by every other thread that previously tried to acquire it. This ensures that a given thread is never preempted by another thread while trying to acquire the same lock, and thus guarantees that well behaved threads will all acquire the lock in a timely manner.

While ticket spinlocks have been shown to provide advantages to performance and consistency for native OS environments, they pose a new challenge for virtualized environments. This is due to the fact that when running inside a VM, the use of a ticket spinlock can result in multiple threads waiting to acquire a spinlock that is currently available. This problem exists whenever a VMM preempts a waiter that has not yet acquired the lock. In this case even if the lock is released, no other thread is allowed to acquire it until the next waiter is allowed to run, resulting in a scenario where there is contention over an idle resource. We denote this situation as the *Lock Waiter Preemption* problem.

Lock holder preemption has traditionally been addressed using a combination of configuration, software and hardware techniques. Initial workarounds to the lock holder preemption problem required that every vCPU belonging to a given VM be gang scheduled in order to avoid this problem altogether [16]. While this eliminates the lock holder preemption problem, it does so in a way that dramatically reduces the amount of possible consolidation and increases the amount of cross VM interference. As a result of these drawbacks, several attempts have been made to address the lock holder preemption problem on a per vCPU level in order to move away from the gang scheduling model. These approaches focus on detecting when a given vCPU is stuck spinning on a busy lock, so that the VMM can adjust its scheduling decisions based on the lock dependency. The detection techniques vary, but can be roughly classified by where they are implemented: inside the VMM (relying on hardware virtualization features such as Pause Loop Exiting), or inside both VMM and guest OS (paravirtual). Unfortunately, while these approaches have been effective in addressing the *lock holder preemption* problem they are unable to handle the *lock waiter preemption* problem.

We propose to address the problem of lock waiter preemption through the introduction of a new spinlock primitive called Preemptable Ticket spinlocks. Preemptable Ticket spinlocks improve the performance of traditional ticket spinlocks by allowing preemption of a waiter that has been detected to be unresponsive. Unresponsiveness is determined via a linearly increasing timeout that allows earlier waiters a window of opportunity in which they can acquire a lock before the lock is offered to later waiters. Preemptable Ticket spinlocks provide performance benefits when running either with or without VMM support (a specialized paravirtual interface), however VMM support does provide overall superior performance.

Preemptable Ticket spinlocks are based on the observation that forward progress is preferable to fairness in the face of contention. In the case where lock waiter preemption is preventing a guest from acquiring a lock, then a thread waiting on the lock should be able to preempt the next thread in line if that thread is incapable of acquiring the lock in a reasonable amount of time. While Preemptable Ticket spinlocks do allow preemption, which technically breaks the ordering guarantees of standard ticket locks, it does so in a way that minimizes the loss of fairness by always granting priority to earlier lock waiters. Priority is granted via a time based window which gradually increases the number of ticket values capable of acquiring the lock. The choice of a time based window is based on the observation that VMM level preemption typically results in large periods of unresponsiveness, while other causes of unresponsiveness typically result in periods orders of magnitude smaller. This means that a timeout based detection approach can be implemented with high accuracy and relatively low overhead. The use of timeouts also allows the implementation of linearly expanding exclusivity windows, which ensure that if an earlier ticket holder is able to acquire a lock it will do so before a later ticket holder is offered the chance. In this way early ticket holders are only preempted if they are inactive for a long period of time, almost always as the result of the vCPU being preempted by the VMM.

In this paper we make the following contributions:

- Identify the lock waiter preemption problem and quantify its effects on VM performance

- Propose Preemptable Ticket spinlocks as an alternative spinlock primitive to address the lock waiter preemption problem

- Describe the implementation of Preemptable Ticket spinlocks inside the Linux kernel and KVM VMM

- Evaluate the performance of Preemptable Ticket spinlocks over a set of micro and macro level benchmarks

The rest of the paper is organized as follows. Section 2 briefly reviews previous works. In section 3 we present some background of the problem. Then in section 4 we introduce our solution, the Preemptable Ticket spinlock and discuss its implementation issues in section 5. We evaluate our proposed solution in section 6, and discuss possible future optimization in 7. Finally, we conclude in section 8.

2. Related Work

Due to the impact virtual machine scheduling has on synchronization performance, significant research efforts have sought to optimize the interaction between the guest OS and VMM. In general the existing approaches have fallen into the following categories.

Preemption Aware Scheduling Initially, VMM architectures dealt with guest locking problems by requiring that every VM be executed using co-scheduling [11]. This approach was adopted by the virtual machine scheduler in VMware ESX [16]. Advances on this approach were explored by [18, 19], that proposed an adaptive co-scheduling scheme, that allowed the VMM scheduler to dynamically alternate between co-scheduling and asynchronous scheduling of a VM's set of vCPUs. The choice of scheduling approaches is based on the detection of long lived lock contention in the guest OS. Finally, in [14] the authors proposed a "balancing scheduler" scheme that associates a VM's individual vCPUs with dedicated physical CPUs, but does not require that the vCPUs be co-scheduled. These solutions add host side scheduling constraints, and are complementary to Preemptable Ticket spinlock.

Paravirtual Locks Paravirtual approaches to solve the lock holder preemption problem was first explored in [15], where the authors adopted a lock avoidance approach in which the guest OS provided scheduler hints to the underlying VMM. These hints demarcated non-preemptable regions of guest execution that corresponded to critical sections in which a non-blocking lock was held. [6] proposed another paravirtual lock approach (later adopted by Xen and KVM [12]), that uses a loop counter to detect "unusually long" wait times for a spinlock. When the time spent waiting for a lock reaches a given threshold, the VMM is notified via a hypercall that a vCPU is currently blocked by a held lock. The VMM then halts the waiting vCPU until the lock is detected to be available. These solutions are capable of delivering good performance, however, paravirtual approaches require guest kernel modifications, leading to compatibility and standardization issues. Moreover, these approaches are also designed to handle generic spinlocks, and so do not take into account the behavior of ticket spinlocks and the resulting problem caused by lock waiter preemption.

Hardware enabled Pause-Loop Exiting Hardware based solutions to the lock holder preemption problem were introduced in [17]. In this work authors proposed an approach that relied on a spin detection buffer (SDB) that served to detect vCPUs spinning on a preempted lock. Similar hardware feature has already been adopted by both Intel's (Pause-Loop Exiting) and AMD's (Pause Filter) virtualization extensions. With these features enabled, hardware is able to detect spinning vCPUs by generating VM exits as a result of executing certain number of pause instructions during the the spinlocks' busy wait loops. Unfortunately, even with these features in place, it remains difficult for a VMM to accurately detect a preempted lock holder due to the lack of information resulting from the semantic gap [5].

Preemptable Adaptive Locks Alternative spinlock behaviors have been proposed in [7] that allow adaptive preemption of queue-based locks. This approach has been implemented as adding time publishing heuristic into queue based lock such as MCS lock [10], which requires each thread periodically records its current timestamp to a shared memory location. The preemptive feature of these locks allows a thread to be removed from the queue after a certain period of time. These locks are meant to gracefully fail in the face of preemption, allowing a thread to specify a timeout value that determines how long it is willing to wait to acquire a given lock. However publishing timestamp is too expensive to implement in kernel spinlock, and a lock that may fail do not directly attempt to solve either the lock holder or waiter preemption problem. Instead they provide a mechanism by which the programmer can react to preemption when it occurs, thus placing a greater burden on OS developers.

3. VM based OS synchronization

Among the challenges that virtualization poses to OS designers is fact that the underlying virtual hardware can be arbitrarily scheduled by the underlying VMM. This has serious consequences for timing sensitive operations in the guest OS that requires and assumes exclusive access to the underlying hardware as well as atomic execute. These regions are generally protected by disabling interrupts and acquiring a spinlock, based on the assumption that the operations will be short in duration and so won't result in long delays for other contending threads. Unfortunately, due to the semantic gap [5], a VMM is incapable of taking into consideration current lock state when it is scheduling the CPU amongst various vCPUs. The result is that occasionally a VM that is holding a lock for what should be a short period of time is scheduled out by the underlying VMM, resulting in an orders of magnitude increase in the duration of a critical region.

Lock Holder Preemption The scheduling out of a vCPU currently holding a lock is referred to as the Lock Holder Preemption problem. These situations often result in serious performance degradation, especially if the lock being held is one that is frequently acquired by other vCPUs in the system. In this case, each vCPU attempting to acquire the lock will enter into a busy wait loop and stall the entire vCPU until the VMM reschedules the lock holder for execution. While OS developers have introduced new synchronization primitives [8] that avoid some of these pitfalls, spinlocks remain as one of the primary synchronization primitives in modern operating systems. Previous work [6] has shown that up to 7.6% of guest execution time can be attributed to stalls due to lock holder preemption in generic spinlocks. And this problem get more severe under queue-based locks, up to 99.3% of guest execution time can be wasted on spinning.

Solving the lock holder preemption problem has been the focus of a number of different approaches looking to optimize performance for multicore VMs. While these approaches have focused on different techniques for actually handling a preempted lock holder, they have all relied on heuristic based detection of lock contention. In particular, they have focused their efforts on detecting when a thread begins to spin on a lock that is currently held by a preempted vCPU. The use of heuristics is necessary to avoid significant performance overheads introduced by more accurate sampling or monitoring approaches. Once a spinning vCPU has been detected it is up to the VMM to either schedule out the spinning vCPU or schedule in the vCPU currently holding the lock.

Ticket Spinlocks Ticket spinlocks are a relatively recent modification to the global spinlock architecture found in Linux. Introduced in kernel version 2.6.25, ticket spinlocks are designed to improve lock fairness and prevent starvation. Each ticket spinlock includes a "head" as well as a "tail" field indicating the current number of threads waiting for the lock. The lock is always granted to the next waiter in the queue, thus guaranteeing that locks are dispatched in FIFO order and no thread will ever experience starvation.

Lock Waiter Preemption Restricting lock acquisitions to a FIFO schedule expands the lock holder preemption problem by creating an environment where anyone with an earlier position in a lock's queue is effectively holding the lock as far as threads later in the queue are concerned. Thus, when executing inside a virtual machine environment, if a vCPU currently holding a ticket is preempted, all subsequent ticket holders must wait for the preempted

vCPU to be rescheduled. This can result in execution being blocked by lock contention even when the lock in question is available. We call this problem Lock Waiter Preemption.

To determine the severity of the lock waiter preemption problem, we instrumented the Linux ticket lock implementation to profile VM preemptions during lock operations. Lock preemption was identified by detecting inordinately long wait times for a given lock, where long wait times were conservatively chosen to be 2048 iterations of the inner loop of a busy waiting spinlock. On our machine, 2048 iterations corresponded to roughly $1\mu s$, an amount of time that exceeds the time a thread would spend holding a lock according to statistics [6]. Next we separated the lock waiter preemption scenarios from the set of detected preemptions, by checking whether the stalled lock was in fact available. To make this determination we modified the existing spinlock structure to include a `holder_id` variable that served as an indicator of lock availability. The value of `holder_id` was set to the thread id of a given lock holder on acquisition and cleared when the lock was released.

Table 1 includes the results of our analysis after running the hackbench [1] and ebizzy [2] benchmarks with 1 and 2 VMs. While the amount of detected preemption was low, previous work [6] has shown that even with a low rate of preemption, significant performance degradation can occur. Furthermore, as more VMs are deployed on the system, it is expected that preemption will increase. Column 2 shows the number of preemptions that occurred in the midst of lock operations during the benchmark's execution. Interestingly, as the number of VMs increased the number of preemptions declined, we surmise that this is due to decreasing VM performance due to the overcommitment of resources. Column 3 shows the number of preemptions in which lock acquisitions were delayed because of either lock holder or lock waiter preemption. While these delays were infrequent when compared to the total number of lock acquisitions in column 2, it should be noted that even a limited degree of preemption can cause significant performance degradation. Furthermore, while the total number of preemptions declined when additional VMs were added, the number of preemptions resulting in stalled lock acquisitions actually increased. More critically, the stalled lock operations were predominantly due to a preempted lock waiter and *not* a preempted lock holder. The degree of the issue is shown more clearly in column 4, which provides the percentage of stalled lock acquisitions resulting from a preempted lock waiter. As can be seen, even when a physical machine is overcommitted by a factor of only 2, lock waiter preemption becomes the dominant source of synchronization overhead.

	N	$N_h + N_w$	N_w	$\frac{N_w}{N_h + N_w}$
hackbench x1	$1.11E8$	1089	452	41.5%
hackbench x2	$9.65E7$	44342	39221	88.5%
ebizzy x1	$2.86E8$	294	166	56.5%
ebizzy x2	$9.56E5$	1017	980	96.4%

Table 1. An analysis of the Lock Waiter Preemption Problem in the Linux Kernel. N is the number of lock acquisitions, while N_h and N_w represent the number of lock holder and lock waiter preemptions, respectively. $N_w/(N_h + N_w)$ shows the percentage of preemptions due to the lock waiter preemption problem.

4. Preemptable Ticket Spinlocks

In order to address the Lock Waiter Preemption problem, we introduce Preemptable Ticket spinlocks. Preemptable Ticket spinlocks are a hybrid spinlock architecture that combines the features of both ticket and generic spinlocks in order to preserve the fairness of ticket spinlocks while avoiding the Lock Waiter Preemption problem.

4.1 Approach

The intuition behind Preemptable Ticket spinlocks is that making forward progress is more important than ensuring fairness. Preemptable Ticket spinlocks leverage the advantages of both generic spinlocks and ticket locks in order to ensure fairness in the absence of preemption while also supporting out of order lock acquisition when the waiters in the queue are preempted. In these situations performance of a given lock waiter is degraded primarily by the VMM scheduler and not by the violation of the ordering of lock acquisitions. That is, a lock waiter can be preempted without perceptively adding to the waiter's execution time.

The primary goal of Preemptable Ticket spinlocks is to add adaptive preemptibility to ticket locks, while retaining the ordering guarantees as much as possible. This is done via the use of a *proportional timeout threshold* that determines the ability of a thread to acquire a lock based on that thread's position among the set of threads currently waiting on the lock. In Preemptable Ticket spinlocks, a thread can acquire a lock out-of-order *if* it has been waiting longer than its *timeout threshold*. We denote such a thread as a *timed out* waiter. The *timeout threshold* is calculated from a standard timeout period τ that is multiplied with the thread's current lock queue position index n as shown in the following equation,

$$timeout\_threshold = n \times \tau \qquad (1)$$

in which τ is a constant parameter of Preemptable Ticket spinlock.

To calculate the position index value n, two variables are maintained for each lock, (1) num_request indicates the total number of lock requests of a lock, and (2) num_grant indicates the total number of lock requests that have been granted. In addition, each thread has a local variable named ticket, which represents the queue position of the request. num_request and num_grant are maintained by each thread in a distributed fashion for each lock. When acquiring a lock, the current num_request value is stored into the thread's local ticket variable, and then atomically incremented by 1. Conversely, when releasing a lock, num_grant is atomically incremented by 1.

The location of a thread in a given lock's queue is denoted as the position index value n, and is calculated based on a thread's ticket value as well as the current value of num_grant,

$$n = ticket - num\_grant \qquad (2)$$

This position value indicates the number of waiters for a given lock before the current thread. Because ticket stores the number of outstanding lock requests at the request time, and num_grant contains the number of lock requests that have been granted, we can determine the number of pending requests before current thread (and thus the thread's queue position) as (ticket - num_grant). Note that it is possible for a thread to have a negative position in the queue (ticket < num_grant). This can result whenever a lock has been preemptively acquired and the preempted core is then rescheduled at a later point in time. In this case a negative position indicates that later threads have violated the lock order, in which case the preempted thread should attempt to acquire the lock immediately.

With the described behavior, Preemptable Ticket spinlocks are able to preserve lock ordering in the absence of VM preemption, while also adapting to increased physical resource contention by allowing limited ordering violations. Figure 1 provides an illustrative example of the functionality of Preemptable Ticket spinlocks. The timeout threshold is indicated by the number above each node, and is set proportionally based on the node's position in the queue. In the initial stage (a), four nodes are waiting while $N1$ is hold-

ing the lock. At this point the vCPU hosting $N2$ is preempted by VMM. In the following stage (b), $N1$ releases the lock, causing the timeout threshold to be updated for each node. At this point the lock is available but no node can acquire it because the next waiter in the queue $N2$ is currently preempted. This is the lock waiter preemption problem. In stage (c) node $N3$ reaches the timeout threshold and acquires the lock out-of-order before $N2$. Finally at stage (d), $N3$ releases the lock, causing $N4$ to update it's timeout threshold. At this point, $N4$ has still not reached the timeout threshold, so $N2$ is able to immediately acquire the lock without contention.

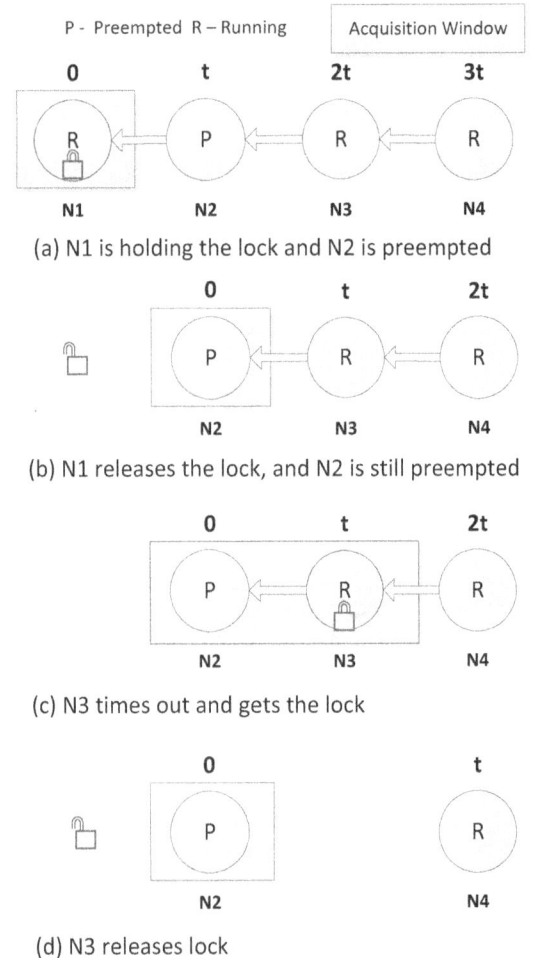

Figure 1. Preemptable Ticket Spinlock Illustration. R indicates a running vCPU, P means a vCPU is preempted. Nodes in acquisition window are timed out nodes and are able to acquire the lock in random order. On top of each node is its timeout threshold, and below is its node ID.

4.2 Preemption Adaptivity

Preemptable Ticket spinlocks are a hybrid lock algorithm that combines the benefits of generic spinlocks and ticket locks by relaxing the ordering guarantees provided by ticket locks. The underlying feature of Preemptable Ticket spinlocks is a timeout threshold that controls when a given waiter can acquire the lock in a random order. The timeout threshold is derived from a tunable constant denoted as τ, combined with a waiter's queue position index n. The behavior of a Preemptable Ticket spinlock can be tuned to match the behavior of either a generic spinlock, a ticket lock, or a combination of the two depending on the value assigned to τ. The following equation shows the behavior of Preemptable Ticket spinlock for different values of τ.

$$lock = \begin{cases} spinlock & \tau = 0 \\ preemtable \quad ticket \quad spinlock & 0 < \tau < \infty \\ ticket \quad lock & \tau = \infty \end{cases}$$

A τ value of 0 results in an immediate timeout that mimics the behavior of a generic spinlock, while setting $\tau = \infty$ will prevent a timeout from ever occurring and so generate the strict ordering behavior of a standard ticket lock. Preemptable Ticket spinlocks are thus able to tune their behavior by trading off between aggressiveness and fairness depending on the state of the system and the behavior of the underlying VMM scheduler.

A well chosen τ value can provide both good performance and fairness. Fairness is ensured when τ is large enough that lock waiters will not time out prematurely. Performance is ensured when τ is small enough that a lock waiter is able to promptly detect when an earlier waiter is preempted. According to previous work [6], the lock holding time and preemption time in fact differ by orders of magnitude. Typically lock holding time is less than $1\mu s$ while the time between a vCPU's preemption and rescheduling is at least $1ms$. Thus we choose a value of τ that is slightly larger than typical lock holding time, $\sim 2\mu s$ for our implementation.

4.3 Fairness

Locking *fairness* relates to the variance in wait times that threads experience while trying to acquire a lock. A truly fair lock implementation should result in a variance near 0, that is every thread waits the same amount of time to acquire a lock. The standard technique for achieving fairness is to ensure that locks are granted in the same order in which the requests were made, FIFO ordering. With generic spinlocks all waiters have an equal chance of acquiring a lock, regardless of when the waiter first requested it. This makes generic spinlocks an "unfair" locking implementation. Ticket spinlocks implement strict ordering that enforced via the use of tickets assigned consecutively to new lock requests. An earlier waiter with smaller ticket value always get the lock before a waiter that requested the lock at a later point in time.

In contrast to these locking behaviors, Preemptable Ticket spinlocks ensure that,

- For all waiters yet to reach their timeout threshold, strict ordering is preserved

- Waiters that have reached their timeout threshold have priority over those who have not

- All waiters that have reached their timeout threshold have equal priority among themselves

The first point holds because the timeout threshold is proportional to a waiter's queue position. Earlier waiters have smaller thresholds, and thus they time out earlier than those who are later in the queue. The second point holds because according to equation 2, the position index of a non-timed-out waiter is larger or equal than the number of timed out waiters. Thus all non-timed-out waiters have timeout thresholds no less than $x \times \tau$, where x is the number of waiters who have passed their timeout threshold. With a proper value of τ the threshold is long enough for every timed out waiter to complete their critical sections in the absence of preemption. In other words, every thread that has reached its timeout threshold will have time to acquire and release the lock *before* the next waiter

times out. This ensures that priority is given to a preempted waiter immediately after it is rescheduled, and furthermore all non-timed-out waiters will wait until every thread that has timed out has acquired the lock. Thus while ordering is violated, the violations are minimized to those vCPUs that have been preempted by the VMM.

Based on the description above, it is straight forward to show that the number of ordering violations experienced by a given lock is bounded by the number of vCPUs assigned to a VM. Furthermore, the probability that a preempted waiter is unable to immediately acquire the lock after rescheduling is given by $P(x) = x/R$, where x is the number of lock acquisitions that have occurred since a lock waiter was preempted, and R is the number of outstanding waiters that have been preempted. Thus for a simple case, where a set of waiters are preempted and rescheduled simultaneously, we can derive the cumulative density function shown in figure 2. From this we can see that the probability that a preempted waiter has acquired the lock increases linearly based on the number of waiters that were simultaneously preempted by the VMM. The number of ordering violations is limited by the number of lock waiters preempted by the VMM at any given point at time, and in the worst case is bounded to the number of active vCPUs assigned to the VM. While more dynamic scheduling cases will alter the shape of the CDF, they will not change the worst case bounds.

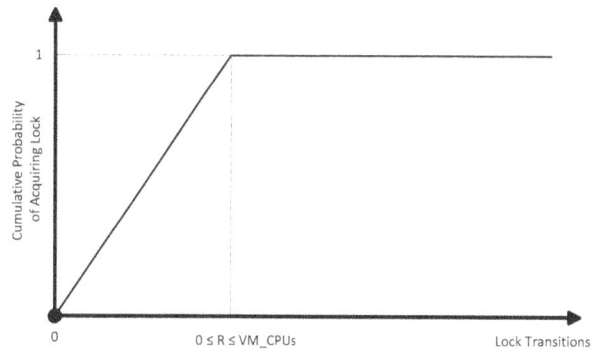

Figure 2. Cumulative Density Function showing the probability of having acquired a lock after being rescheduled following a preemption. The horizontal axis represents the number of lock acquisitions necessary before the preempted waiter is able to acquire the lock. R is the number of preempted waiters currently contending for the lock. VM_CPUS is the number of vCPUs assigned to the VM.

Note that the above discussion only holds for a lock waiter preemption case in which the time spent holding a lock is less than the base timeout value τ. While our approach is effective in addressing the lock waiter preemption problem, it is important to note that it does not address lock holder preemption. In the case of lock holder preemption, all lock waiters will time out due to the fact that preemption time is considerably larger than the timeout threshold. Lock holder preemption represents the worst case in regards to fairness, in that every waiter in the queue will reach its timeout threshold and compete equally for the lock. In this case our approach will degenerate to a generic spinlock behavior. However this behavior will still be bounded by the number of vCPUs. Furthermore, we believe that the case of lock holder preemption will be relatively low based on our earlier results in Table 1.

4.4 Host Independence

Unlike previous solutions [6, 12–15, 17–19], Preemptable Ticket spinlocks work in the absence of any VMM side support, which makes it a solution where host side modifications such as paravirtualization are not feasible. Preemptable Ticket spinlocks can be implemented entirely inside a guest OS and are capable of detecting lock waiter preemption adaptively based on a single timeout directly measurable by the guest. However, while Preemptable Ticket spinlocks are capable of operating independently without VMM support, it is possible to further improve their performance by combining them with existing lock holder preemption solutions. This is important because while Preemptable Ticket spinlocks address lock waiter preemption they actually increase the likelihood of lock holder preemption due to the fact that they allow the lock to be acquired more often. We have investigated the integration of Preemptable Ticket spinlocks with existing solutions to the lock holder preemption problem, and provide results of this integration in our evaluation.

5. Implementing Preemptable Ticket Spinlocks in Linux/KVM

In order to evaluate the efficacy of Preemptable Ticket spinlocks, we have implemented them inside version 3.5.0 of the Linux kernel. Our implementation acts as a drop in replacement for the standard ticket spinlock implementation currently supported by the kernel. The implementation consisted of only ~60 lines of C and assembly code, and consists of a modified spinlock datatype as well as modifications to the lock, unlock, islocked and trylock operations. The implementation resides entirely in the guest kernel and does not require any additional VMM side support in order to function correctly. While Preemptable Ticket spinlocks are capable of functioning fully on top of any virtualization environment, they are also able to benefit from extended paravirtual operations, which we will discuss later.

5.1 Preemptable Ticket

Figures 3 shows the implementation of *lock* and *unlock* operations. As part of our modifications we added code to maintain the timeout threshold, while also changing the semantics of some of the existing data fields. The existing kernel spinlock data structure contains variables to track the head and tail of a queue in order to implement the proper ticket semantics. These fields are equivalent to the num_request and num_grant fields we discussed in section 4.1. In order to detect a preempted lock waiter we have added another field named lock which indicates the availability of the lock.

In the lock function, we declare a local struct inc which acts as a local copy of the head and tail values, timeout which is used as the timeout threshold, and current_head which is another local copy of head used to detect changes to the value of head. At line 7 the code atomically updates inc in order to increase the value of head. At this point inc.tail is regarded as the "ticket" of the current thread. Line 10-11 shows the fast path, which handles the case of an uncontended lock acquisition.

Lines 13-27 implement the core of the proportional timeout functionality. The timeout threshold is initialized in line 14, and updated in line 23 whenever head's value changes. This ensures that the timeout threshold is always proportional to the number of pending lock requests that arrived previously, according to equation 2. A timed out thread will break out of the loop at line 27. A thread should also break out of the loop when it's ticket is equal to the current head, meaning that it is due to acquire the lock based on the ticket ordering. Besides, a thread breaks out of the loop if it's ticket is less than the current value of head, which can result

from a preemption followed by a rescheduling as discussed in Section 4.1. Finally, line 29–35 implement a generic spinlock which is invoked by every thread that is allowed past the wait loop.

```
1  #define TIMEOUT_UNIT (1<<14)
2  void __ticket_spin_lock(arch_spinlock_t *lock)
3  {
4    register struct __raw_tickets inc={.tail=1};
5    unsigned int timeout = 0;
6    __ticket_t current_head;
7    inc = xadd(&lock->tickets,inc);
8
9    // fast path
10   if (likely(inc.head == inc.tail))
11     goto spin;
12
13   // wait in queue
14   timeout = TIMEOUT_UNIT
15     * (inc.tail - inc.head);
16   do {
17     current_head =
18         ACCESS_ONCE(lock->tickets.head);
19     if (inc.tail <= current_head) {
20       goto spin;
21     } else if (inc.head != current_head) {
22       inc.head = current_head;
23       timeout =  TIMEOUT_UNIT
24           * (inc.tail - inc.head);
25     }
26     cpu_relax();
27   } while (timeout--);
28
29 spin:
30   for (;;) {
31     if (xchg(&lock->lock, 1) == 0)
32       goto out;
33     cpu_relax();
34   }
35 out: barrier();
36 }
37
38 void __ticket_spin_unlock(arch_spinlock_t *
       lock) {
39   __add(&lock->tickets.head, 1,
         UNLOCK_LOCK_PREFIX);
40   xchg(&lock->lock, 0);
41 }
```

Figure 3. Kernel Implementation: lock and unlock

The unlock operation is relatively simple, and is implemented by combining the unlock operations of both ticket and generic spinlocks. The operation atomically increments head by 1 and clears the lock value.

While the lock and unlock operations provide the necessary functionality for basic locking, the Linux kernel also requires additional locking semantics for certain cases. In particular Linux makes consistent use of other spinlock primitives such as islocked and trylock. In order to fully support Preemptable Ticket spinlocks through the kernel, we had to modify these operations as well. Figure 4 shows the implementation of these primitives. At line 3 our code modifications return true if it detects the presence of earlier waiters for the lock or if the lock is currently not available. The trylock operation attempts to acquire a given lock, but immediately returns 0 if the lock is not available. In order to support Preemptable Ticket spinlocks we modified the implementation at lines 18-19, where we added an atomic check to determine whether the lock is free and if there are no earlier waiters. Other than these mini-

```
1   int __ticket_spin_is_locked(arch_spinlock_t *
        lock) {
2     struct __raw_tickets tmp = ACCESS_ONCE(lock
        ->tickets);
3     return (tmp.tail != tmp.head) || (
        ACCESS_ONCE(lock->lock)==1);
4   }
5
6   int __ticket_spin_trylock(
7               arch_spinlock_t *lock) {
8     arch_spinlock_t old, new;
9     *(u64 *)&old = ACCESS_ONCE(*(u64 *)lock);
10    if (old.tickets.head != old.tickets.tail)
11      return 0;
12    if (ACCESS_ONCE(lock->lock) == 1)
13      return 0;
14    new.head_tail = old.head_tail +
15          (1 << TICKET_SHIFT);
16    new.lock = 1;
17    /* cmpxchg is a full barrier */
18    if (cmpxchg((u64 *)lock, *(u64 *)&old,
19          *(u64 *)&new) == *(u64 *)&old) {
20      return 1;
21    } else return 0;
22  }
```

Figure 4. Kernel Implementation: islocked and trylock

mal changes, the existing implementations were left as originally written.

5.2 Paravirtual Preemptable Ticket Spinlock

In addition to the fully encapsulated Preemptable Ticket spinlock implementation, we also implemented a paravirtual version based on a paravirtual ticket lock patch submitted to the Linux Kernel Mailing List (LKML) [12] on May 2, 2012. It includes both guest and host side modifications, which we adopted and extended to support Preemptable Ticket spinlocks.

The paravirtual interface includes the ability to capture `halt` instructions from the guest vCPU. These instructions are emulated by switching the halting vCPU to a sleep state until a special hypercall is received to wake it up. This interface allows a guest OS to notify the VMM when it is appropriate to place a vCPU into a sleep state and when to wake it up via a hypercall invocation. The purpose of this interface is to allow a guest to place a lock waiter vCPU into sleep state on the host since it is unable to make forward progress due to a preempted lock holder.

In the original implementation, the `halt` instruction is executed whenever a thread reaches a timeout threshold (2048 iterations of a spinlock by default). As soon as the lock is released, the next waiter is woken up using a hypercall. This approach essentially converts a busy wait lock into a blocking lock, and prevents a spinning vCPU from wasting a significant amount of time spinning on an unavailable lock.

Our paravirtual Preemptable Ticket spinlock implementation also executes `halt` after spinning on the `lock` variable longer than a threshold (2048 iterations in this paper). However, when releasing the lock, a wakeup hypercall is sent for every sleeping vCPU instead of only the next thread in the queue. Because Preemptable Ticket spinlocks allow out-of-order lock acquisition, an in-order wake up can actually cause a deadlock scenario when `ticket < num_grant`.

While we have implemented a paravirtual version of Preemptable Ticket spinlock, it is important to note that they are designed to function correctly with either full system or paravirtual VMM ar-

chitectures. As we will show, Preemptable Ticket spinlocks provide performance benefits when used with either environment. The rationale for a non-paravirtual locking implementation is that while paravirtual interfaces do provide benefits to performance and information sharing, they are not always portable and can introduce compatibility issues across different VMMs as well as different versions of the same VMM. Preemptable Ticket spinlocks are capable of functioning on top of any unmodified or paravirtual VMM architecture.

6. Evaluation

In this section, we empirically evaluate how *ticket locks*, paravirtual ticket locks (*pv-lock*), and paravirtual preemptable ticket locks (*pv-preemptable-lock*) improve application performance when running in a VM on either a full system or paravirtual VMM architecture. Our evaluation uses a combination of microbenchmarks as well as a real world workload based on the Dell DVD Store [4] benchmark.

6.1 Experimental Setup

Each experiment was run on a single Dell Optiplex with an 8 core 2.6 GHz Intel Core i7 CPU, 8 GB of RAM, and a 1 Gbit NIC. The experiments were all executed inside an 8 core VM image configured to use 1GB RAM. A Fedora 17 environment was used for both the host and guests, and was configured to use a modified version of the Linux kernel based on version 3.5.0. In order to conduct a fair evaluation, we implemented *pv-lock* and *pv-preemptable-lock* in otherwise identical configurations of the 3.5.0 kernel, we also include results that compare the various spinlock implementations against the stock kernel implementation.

For the evaluation we selected benchmarks that focus on CPU intensive, memory intensive and I/O intensive workloads. These benchmarks include three microbenchmarks (ebizzy, hackbench, and kernbench) as well as a real world web application benchmark (the Dell DVD store).

Ebizzy [2] is designed to generate a workload that resembles a common web application server. It is highly threaded, has a large in-memory working set size, and allocates and deallocates memory frequently. We execute ebizzy 5 times using 16 threads for each run, and performance is measured as the sustained throughput (records/second).

Hackbench [1] is a multi-threaded program that exercises Unix-socket (or pipe) performance. We execute hackbench 5 times using 4 threads with 10,000 loops. Performance is measured based on the completion time (seconds).

Kernbench [3] executes parallel kernel compilations using a variable degree of parallelization of the compilation process. Kernbench was executed 3 times and configured to use 8 compilation processes in order to saturate the vCPUs of an 8 core VM. Performance was measured based on the completion time (seconds).

Dell DVD Stores [4] is an open source simulation of an online e-commerce site. The benchmark interfaces an Apache website with a MySQL database running in the same VM. For our evaluation we configured a single client machine to emulate 32 independent clients each issuing search requests for 3 minutes following 1 minute warmup period. Performance is determined based on the transaction throughput (operations per minute) observed by the client.

In order to evaluate lock performance under realistic cloud scenarios we overcommitted the physical resources to a set of VMs all running the same benchmark. To simplify our evaluation we recorded the performance of a single VM randomly selected from the set.

In addition to evaluating different guest locking implementations, we also evaluated each guest lock implementation when running on both a paravirtual and full system VMM environment.

These results are meant to demonstrate the portability of the approaches, and determine how well they will perform in both optimized and non-optimized environments.

6.2 Microbenchmarks

Figure 5 shows the experimental results of the three microbenchmarks for each locking implementation. As expected, performance degrades as the number of competing VMs increases, however the degree of degradation depends on the choice of locking behavior. As cloud providers seek to maximize utilization by increasing consolidation as much as possible, the ability to sustain performance in the face of competing workloads becomes critical. As time spent waiting for a lock is wasted from the point of view of the resource provider, we try to measure the degree to which the different locking approaches can minimize the overheads due to lock contention.

Figures 5(a) shows results of each locking approach on *hackbench*, which mainly exercises the IPC subsystem. While each locking implementation has comparable performance in the single VM case, those designed to handle preemption are significantly better when executing in an overcommitted environment. In the two VM case, the speedups of *preemptable-lock*, *pv-lock* and *pv-preemptable-lock* are $3.89X$, $4.80X$ and $4.97X$ respectively, indicating that (1) Preemptable Ticket spinlocks significantly improve lock performance under overcommitted configurations without any host side support, (2) host side paravirtual interfaces improve lock performance further, (3) *pv-preemptable-lock* performs even better than *pv-lock* because it addresses both lock holder and waiter preemption. This trend is more obvious in the three VM case, where the speedups of *preemptable-lock*, *pv-lock* and *pv-preemptable-lock* are $9.63X$, $13.68X$ and $15.35X$ respectively. Note that less than 6% of Preemptable Ticket spinlock overhead can be observed in one VM case. This is due to the overhead of code added into ticket lock, which slows down the code path slightly. In less severe overcommitted configurations, where the preemption rate is low, the overhead becomes observable. However, with greater overcommitting of resources the overhead swamped by the overall performance improvement.

Figure 5(b) depicts the performance and speedup of each lock algorithm when executing *kernbench*. The results show that each of the four lock algorithms provides comparable performance when only one VM is executing, and lock preemption is rare. When the number of VMs increases, all three lock implementations yield significantly better performance compared to the generic *ticket lock*. Similar to *hackbench*, the same patterns are observed in the two VM case. In these scenarios the speedups of *preemptable-lock*, *pv-lock* and *pv-preemptable-lock* are $2.37X$, $2.47X$, $3.12X$. The result again confirms our hypothesis that Preemptable Ticket spinlocks improve performance even without paravirtual interfaces, and also yield better performance than *pv-lock* on a host with a paravirtual locking interface because it uniquely identifies and adapts to instances of lock waiter preemption. It is interesting that when configured with three VMs, all three preemption optimized lock algorithms exhibit almost the same performance, around $7.3X$ speedup. A possible reason for this is that kernbench is an I/O intensive workload, and with three parallel instances running the host I/O capacity becomes the bottleneck. In such a scenario, locking performance cannot improve performance past what the hardware I/O system is capable of.

In figure 5(c) we scale up to five VMs running *ebizzy* to compare lock algorithms with high preemption rates. Results show that while comparable performance is achieved under the single VM case, the high preemption rate (three VMs or more) results in the Preemptable Ticket spinlocks outperforming the others. Moreover, *preemptable-lock* achieves the best speedup in the 3 VM case even without host side paravirtual support. This may due to the fact that *preemptable-lock* does not have context switching overheads caused by the paravirtual interfaces entering and exiting the VMM. It also should be noted that *pv-lock* has superior performance when executing with 2 VMs. However, as the number of VMs increases on the same hardware *pv-preemptable-lock* begins to achieve better performance, as a result of the greater levels of contention. Intuitively this is because *pv-lock* is able to perform well when the preemption rate is low, however it's performance degrades as the level of resource contention increases resulting in a greater number of preemptions.

In summary, the lock waiter preemption problem is a situation best handled inside a guest OS without the need of VMM support. Because of this Preemptable Ticket spinlocks are specifically designed for both full system and paravirtual virtual environments. This allows our approach to adapt to guest behavior, and does not require communication with the VMM. This property becomes more significant as more VMs share the host and preemption becomes much more frequent. Our results show that when executing on a non-paravirtual VMM, *preemptable-lock* is able to improve guest performance significantly compared to *ticket-lock* when the host is overcommitted.

Paravirtual lock interfaces enable the guest to notify the VMM whenever it should transition a vCPU into and out of a sleep state due to a long waiting lock. This approach essentially converts a busy waiting lock in the guest into a sleep and wake up lock in the host. The benefit arises from the fact that the duration of preemption for a vCPU is on the order of milliseconds, which is $1000X$ longer than normal lock waiting time. With paravirtualization we are able to reduce this wait time at the cost of additional context switches and sleep-wakeup overhead. Our results show that *pv-lock* and *pv-preemptable-lock* are able to outperform *ticket-lock* significantly and yield better performance than *preemptable-lock* in most overcommitted cases.

While paravirtualization is able to deliver substantial improvements for performance, our *pv-preemptable-lock* is still able to outperform the *pv-lock* implementation. This is due to the fact that *pv-preemptable-lock* is able to address the problem from two directions. First when there is a preempted lock waiter, we do not require traps into the VMM that trigger sleep and/or wakeup operations. Instead, the ticket queue is reordered entirely inside the guest OS. The lock which is only available to the preempted lock waiter in *pv-lock* is available to other waiters in *pv-preemptable-lock* after a given timeout period. This allows the *pv-preemptable-lock* implementation to avoid unnecessary overheads due to the exit and entry costs required for a paravirtual interface. Second, for the case of preempted lock holders *pv-preemptable-lock* is able to improve system performance by leveraging the paravirtual lock interfaces. In other words, paravirtual locking is required to solve the lock holder preemption problem, whereas Preemptable Ticket spinlocks are required to address the lock waiter preemption problem. Obtaining the optimized performance requires utilizing a combination of both approaches.

6.3 Real World Workload benchmark

Finally, we evaluated the performance of different lock implementations when running a real world web application benchmark. The Dell DVD Store is a three tier benchmark, where tier 1 is a php web store application, tier 2 is an apache web server, and tier 3 is a MySQL database server. For these tests we ran the three tiers along with a client program sending login and search requests inside of a single VM environment. The experiments were conducted with up to 4 VMs executing the benchmark in parallel on the same physical host in order to show the performance of the different locking approaches under varying real world load scenarios.

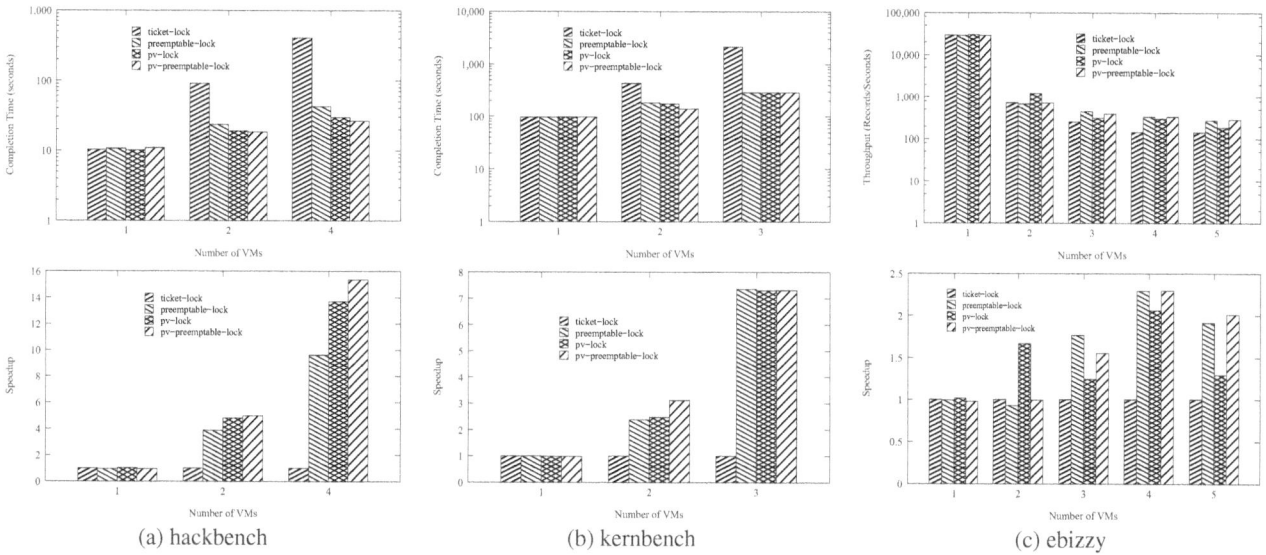

(a) hackbench	(b) kernbench	(c) ebizzy

Figure 5. Microbenchmarks Performance. *ticket-lock* and *preemptable-lock* show non-paravirtual performance results for a ticket lock and Preemptable Ticket spinlock kernel respectively. *pv-lock* and *pv-preemptable-lock* show performance results for paravirtual ticket locks and paravirtual Preemptable Ticket spinlocks

Figure 6 depicts the performance of each lock implementation when running on both a paravirtual and non-paravirtual VMM. Again, all lock algorithms show comparable performance under low overcommitted cases (one or two VMs), however, as the number of VMs increases, the results begin to mirror what was seen with the other benchmarks. Three of the preemption optimized algorithms outperformed *ticket-lock* significantly, which indicates the severity of performance degradation caused by preemption under overcommitted cases. While *preemptable-lock* yields obvious performance boosts without host side support, the two paravirtual solutions improved performance further. Moreover, *pv-preemptable-lock* is even better than *pv-lock* because it's unique ability to address lock waiter preemption. *pv-lock* yields best speedup in case of 2 VMs, but it has largest performance degradation in 1 VM case, and is outperformed by *pv-preemptable-lock* as number of VMs goes up.

7. Discussion and Future Works

By calculating the average speedup across all cases, we get that Preemptable Ticket spinlock can improve VM performance on average by $5.32X$ compared to the existing ticket lock architecture when running on a full system VMM. On a VMM that supports a paravirtual locking interface, Preemptable Ticket spinlocks can achieve $7.91X$ speedup over ticket locks on average, and a $1.08X$ speedup compared to pv-lock. The results show that Preemptable Ticket spinlocks effectively address the lock waiter preemption problem and can do so without any VMM modification. However when coupled with a paravirtual locking interface, Preemptable Ticket spinlocks can improve VM performance further compared to previous approach.

Though Preemptable Ticket spinlocks have demonstrated the ability to adapt to preemption on a overcommitted host, there are still further opportunities to fully optimize the lock behavior. In particular, further performance gains might be achieved through the integration of Preemptable Ticket spinlocks with other VMM scheduling algorithms. For instance, Complete Fair Scheduling (CFS), as used by KVM, tries to give equal shares of the CPU to each vCPU. Preemptable Ticket spinlocks could be used to pro-

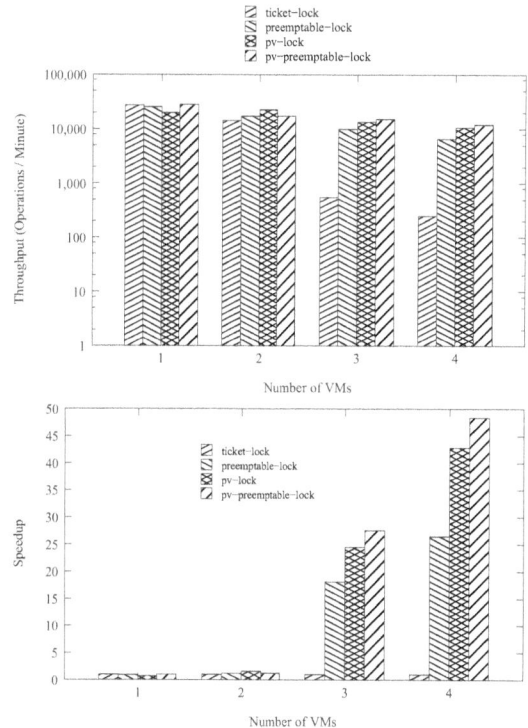

Figure 6. Dell DVD Store Performance

vide inputs for other scheduling algorithms, such as co-scheduling and balanced scheduling, that can utilize dependency information about the currently running vCPUs. While we expect that a combined approach would improve overall performance, it is important to note that a combined approach is not required to achieve performance benefits when deploying our approach on other VMM architectures.

8. Conclusions

In this paper we have introduced Preemptable Ticket spinlocks as a new locking primitive targeting virtual machine environments that addresses lock waiter preemption. In particular, Preemptable Ticket spinlocks are able to avoid performance overheads that result from both lock holder and lock waiter preemption. While existing solutions are designed to only address lock holder preemption, Preemptable Ticket spinlocks are the first to fully address both preemption issues. Preemptable Ticket spinlocks are capable of addressing lock waiter preemption independently from the underlying VMM architecture, but when combined with a paravirtual lock interface it can handle lock holder preemption as well. With Preemptable Ticket spinlocks we are able to show that VM performance can be improved on average by $5.32X$, when running on a non paravirtual VMM, and by $7.91X$ when running on a VMM that supports a paravirtual locking interface.

Acknowledgments

We would like to thank Wencan Luo for insightful feedbacks and Raghavendra K. T. for discussions on the *pv-lock* patch. We would like to also thank the anonymous reviewers for helpful comments on the paper.

References

[1] Hackbench, 2008. http://people.redhat.com/mingo/cfs-scheduler/tools/hackbench.c/.

[2] Ebizzy 0.30, 2009. http://sourceforge.net/projects/ebizzy/.

[3] Kernbench 0.50, 2009. http://freecode.com/projects/kernbench.

[4] Dell dvd store database test suite 2.1, December 2010. http://linux.dell.com/dvdstore/.

[5] CHEN, P. M., AND NOBLE, B. D. When virtual is better than real. In *The 8th Workshop on Hot Topics in Operating Systems (HotOS-VIII)* (2001).

[6] FRIEBEL, T. How to deal with lock-holder preemption. Presented at the Xen Summit North America, July 2008.

[7] HE, B., SCHERER, W., AND SCOTT, M. Preemption adaptivity in time-published queue-based spin locks. In *High Performance Comput-*
ing HiPC 2005, D. Bader, M. Parashar, V. Sridhar, and V. Prasanna, Eds., vol. 3769 of *Lecture Notes in Computer Science*. Springer Berlin / Heidelberg, 2005, pp. 7–18.

[8] MCKENNEY, P., AND SLINGWINE, J. Read-copy update: Using execution history to solve concurrency problems. In *Parallel and Distributed Computing and Systems* (1998), pp. 509–518.

[9] MELLOR-CRUMMEY, J., AND SCOTT, M. Algorithms for scalable synchronization on shared-memory multiprocessors. *ACM Transactions on Computer Systems (TOCS) 9*, 1 (1991), 21–65.

[10] MELLOR-CRUMMEY, J., AND SCOTT, M. Synchronization without contention. *ACM SIGPLAN Notices 26*, 4 (1991), 269–278.

[11] OUSTERHOUT, J. Scheduling techniques for concurrent systems. In *Proceedings of the 3rd International Conference on Distributed Computing Systems* (1982), pp. 22–30.

[12] RAGHAVENDRA, K., AND FITZHARDINGE, J. Paravirtualized ticket spinlocks, May 2012.

[13] RIEL, R. V. Directed yield for pause loop exiting, 2011.

[14] SUKWONG, O., AND KIM, H. S. Is co-scheduling too expensive for smp vms? In *Proceedings of the sixth conference on Computer systems* (New York, NY, USA, 2011), EuroSys '11, ACM, pp. 257–272.

[15] UHLIG, V., LEVASSEUR, J., SKOGLUND, E., AND DANNOWSKI, U. Towards scalable multiprocessor virtual machines. In *Proceedings of the 3rd conference on Virtual Machine Research And Technology Symposium - Volume 3* (Berkeley, CA, USA, 2004), VM'04, USENIX Association, pp. 4–4.

[16] VMWARE, I. Vmware(r) vsphere(tm): The cpu scheduler in vmware esx(r) 4.1, 2010.

[17] WELLS, P. M., CHAKRABORTY, K., AND SOHI, G. S. Hardware support for spin management in overcommitted virtual machines. In *Proceedings of the 15th international conference on Parallel architectures and compilation techniques* (New York, NY, USA, 2006), PACT '06, ACM, pp. 124–133.

[18] WENG, C., LIU, Q., YU, L., AND LI, M. Dynamic adaptive scheduling for virtual machines. In *Proceedings of the 20th international symposium on High performance distributed computing* (New York, NY, USA, 2011), HPDC '11, ACM, pp. 239–250.

[19] ZHANG, L., CHEN, Y., DONG, Y., AND LIU, C. Lock-visor: An efficient transitory co-scheduling for mp guest. In *Proceedings of the 41st International Conference on Parallel Processing* (Pittsburgh, PA, USA, 2012), pp. 88–97.

Author Index